John Harper's Field

*The Scots-Irish Wars
and
Settlements of Colonial New England,
the New York Borderlands,
and the Ohio Frontier*

J. L. Miller

Heritage Books
2025

HERITAGE BOOKS
AN IMPRINT OF HERITAGE BOOKS, INC.

Books, CDs, and more—Worldwide

For our listing of thousands of titles see our website
at
www.HeritageBooks.com

Published 2025 by
HERITAGE BOOKS, INC.
Publishing Division
5810 Ruatan Street
Berwyn Heights, MD 20740

Copyright © 2025 John L. Miller

Cover art: The image at the top is *Adventures of Col. Harper*, John R. Chaplin, *The Illustrated American Advertiser Vol. 5, The Historical Picture Gallery or Scenes and Incidents in American History*, (Boston: D. Bigalow & Co. 1856) 447. The lower image of *Middle Fort/Fort Defiance* is by R. L. Adams from a sketch by R. A. Grider.

All rights reserved. No part of this book may be reproduced or transmitted in any form or by any means, electronic or mechanical, including photocopying, recording or by any information storage and retrieval system without written permission from the author, except for the inclusion of brief quotations in a review.

International Standard Book Number
Paperbound: 978-0-7884-5098-3

Contents

Introduction....1

Chapter 1: *New England*.... 3

Chapter 2: *Property Line*.... 28

Chapter 3: *Border War*.... 53

Chapter 4: *Haudenosaunee*....78

Chapter 5: *Johnstown*.... 99

Chapter 6: *Resettlement*....121

Chapter 7: *Empire*....149

Chapter 8: *Ohio*....175

Acknowledgments.... 208

Sources.... 209

Illustration Credits.... 238

Bibliography.... 241

Index.... 250

Introduction

Like many who were drawn into researching the history of the people and the region in which they grew up, my journey started with my own family genealogy. The births, marriages, and deaths of one's ancestors catalogue their lives but tell very little about them or the times in which they lived. Most of our forebears led relatively mundane lives, not all that different from our own, but occasionally a generation comes along that finds itself thrust into a world of great social upheaval. Seldom has a group of people found themselves in an extended and turbulent period of unrest as did the Scots-Irish families who came to North America during the First Great Irish Immigration of the 1720s.

Nearly a hundred years after the arrival of the first European settlers to the shores of Great Britain's North American colonies, the first wave of Scots-Irish immigrants began arriving en masse. Although they came from Northern Ireland, the Ulster Scots were from *Bonnie Auld Scotland* with Caledonian blood as thick as the heather that covered their ancestral heathlands. New England's coastal villages were populated at the time with second and third generation colonialists whose English predecessors had come to the colonies seeking asylum from religious persecution. The invasion of these newcomers, who had come seeking their own refuge from oppression, was not a welcome sight for the citizenry and magistrates of the Massachusetts Bay Colony. The 'Irish', as they were mistakenly characterized, were shunned and driven from the coastal villages to the frontier's outer margins. They were treated as if they were unworthy of equal status to that of a proper colonial Englishman. Many were in fact poor crofters and laymen who had to submit to a three-to-five-year term of indentured servitude to pay for their ocean passage. Some of the Scots-Irish families, however, were led by men of means, education, and breeding equivalent to that of their New England detractors. One such family would prove their mettle by helping to transform the colonies into an independent nation while carving out a piece of the new republic's territory for themselves.

Sixty years before the American Revolution, a father brought his family to America with the same expectations and dreams every immigrant wishes for his children. Few families, then and now, could ever match the accomplishments James Harper's progeny achieved in their first three American generations. Through several wars fought on different frontier fronts, the Harpers fought against French grenadiers, British regulars, German Hessians, and Iroquois and Abenaki warriors. From Maine and Massachusetts to Connecticut and on to New York, they helped tame one frontier after another. Their military careers would serve as a means to an end to help them reach their ultimate goal of owning land, and lots of it.

John Harper Sr was barely in his teens when he crossed the North Atlantic with his family and settled on Maine's Kennebec frontier at the height of the Anglo/Abenaki Wars. He mustered into a militia company and impressed his superiors with his ability to excel at frontier soldiering. His willingness to learn from his company's Mohawk scouts accustomed him to their culture, language, and way of waging war. This was to be the attitude he would instill in his four sons who would use it to help him realize his dreams of landownership. The period between the French and Indian War and the Revolution was a time of incredible opportunities for those who dared to risk it all for a patch of land in a wilderness fraught with danger and privation. The Harpers would not be content with just a few paternal acres on a riverfront homestead lot, setting their sights instead on building an empire of thousands of acres. Incredibly, they did indeed succeed in doing just that.

John Harper Jr was a remarkable young frontiersman who adapted to Native American culture and taught himself to speak their native tongue fluently. He honed his skills and became a charismatic orator who could negotiate at an Indian council fire as well as influence a governor's decisions and garner a king's favor. The enormous tract of Iroquois lands he was able to convince the Oneida chieftains into signing over to him and his family was an astonishing achievement for a second generation Scots-Irish immigrant. His military career was equally impressive. Through courage and determination, he rose from captain of a company of rangers and Indian scouts to colonel of a regiment of militia in the Revolution's brutal New York border war. His early military adventures enhanced his reputation to hero status. Poems were penned in his honor. As the war dragged on, however, Col. Harper's career would suffer from want of support from his superiors and compatriots who did not understand his tolerance for the native peoples. In time, the Indians too would come to harbor their own misgivings towards him.

At war's end, John Harper and his three brothers had fought not just for Independence, but for the land they had already secured and the Iroquois lands that lay waiting for them in the west. The post-Revolution years were a time of great social transformation and displacement of both whites and Indigenous populations. The Harper's relentless pursuit of western lands knew no restraint when it came to coercing Indian chieftains into signing deeds over to them. Those who had fought and sacrificed so much to liberate their hard-won homeland from the British and their Iroquois allies felt entitled to their share of the spoils. We can appreciate the Harpers and men like them for their tremendous sacrifices and contributions to the birth of our republic while at the same time being disquieted by their lack of integrity when dealing with the vanquished Iroquois. The times and circumstances incentivized otherwise good and honorable men into committing whatever duplicitous methods were necessary to get while the getting was good. You might conclude after reading the following chapters, as I did writing them, that the Harpers were heroic and praiseworthy men who all too often yielded to their untethered avarice to get whatever they wanted.

The checkered career of the youngest Harper brother, Alexander, suggests his personal motto might have been Virgil's *'Fortune Favors the Bold'*. Courageous to a fault, he all too often took risks that not only endangered himself but all of those who trusted and followed him. Not satisfied with his family's patented New York lands, and wanting to best his older brother's accomplishments, Alexander set out to claim his own frontier empire. His last adventure was to lead his family of third generation Harpers on a harrowing expedition to a new frontier in the unsettled forests of the Great Northwest Territory. His sons would miraculously survive their father's untimely death and final folly and live to carry on their grandfather's dreams of empire in Ohio.

Chronicling the trials and trails of the Harper family's three generational migration through New England to New York and on to Ohio, from the 1720s to the War of 1812, is the subject of this book. I've attempted to embody this one remarkable family's wars, political intrigues, and transgressions as a reflection of America's frontier zeitgeist and turbulent transformation from colony to country. The contributions of the members of this family of Scots-Irish immigrants to the success of the American Revolution and colonization of the western frontiers were profoundly significant. Viewed through the bright light and retrospective gaze of history, however, some of their achievements might seem tainted by their dearth of ethical concerns. The suffering and tragedies experienced by them and so many of their kinsmen who lived through those momentous times is worthy of our commemoration, if only to remind us of how indebted to them we truly are.

'...To the land vaguely realized westward,
But still unstoried, artless, unenhanced,
Such as she was, such as she would become.'
From *'The Gift Outright'*
By Robert Frost

1
New England
1718-1763
'To avoid oppression and cruel bondage'

In the first week of September 1718, a ship from Northern Ireland's port city of Londonderry arrived and dropped anchor within rowing distance of Boston's Long Wharf at the foot of King Street (today's State Street). Rejoicing at the sight of land, the twenty or so families of the *MacCullum* began to gather their belongings and ready themselves to disembark onto dry land. They had just spent the last three months in the cold, overcrowded hull of their 45-ton vessel and were filled with excitement to finally feel *terra firma* beneath their feet and to take in the sights and smells of a busy city. Having narrowly survived their dangerous and unusually long voyage, the weary immigrants were ready to hit the ground running and start a new life in a promising new land. But those ashore were not at all keen to welcome the newcomers. As one Boston clergyman described it, the newcomers were greeted '*…by a volley of sticks, stones and other offensive weapons…*'. Incredible as it may seem, the few who dared walk down Long Wharf that balmy afternoon were soon forced to return to the stench of their ship's hull. Shipmaster James Law's passengers spoke the same language and worshiped the same God as their stone-throwing reception party, but were not in their view, the right kind of Christians.

The people of Boston and the Massachusetts Bay Colony were the great-grandchildren of John Winthrop's reformed protestants who had arrived in the New World ninety-years before. Being descendants of the original Puritan immigrants, they saw themselves as the guardians of Winthrop's 'Shining City on a Hill', and protectors of their protestant heritage. Boston, in 1718 was the crown jewel of British colonial America's seaport cities. With nearly 12,000 residents it far exceeded both New York and Philadelphia in both population and commerce. Life was good for the average Boston resident who shared heritage and ethnicity with his fellow New Englanders. The Scots-Irish Presbyterians who walked down Long Wharf that day were not the nefarious miscreants their New England brethren took them for. Many were in fact well-bred, educated men of wealth and status. They were also the proud descendants of the Scottish Lowlanders who had been subjected to the same civil and religious persecution as their English forebears. Although Scottish in both blood and heritage, the Ulster Scots were recognized only as 'Irish' by their New England antagonists, which in itself was meant to be an insult to the great-grandsons of the Scottish Lowlanders who had been enticed to settle in northeast Ireland in the early seventeenth-century. [1]

Northern Ireland

England's Ulster Plantation scheme of the 1600s was an ill-conceived attempt to purge the contentious Irish Catholic clansmen from Northern Ireland and replace them with a more congenial people. By granting confiscated Irish lands to members of the Scottish gentry and encouraging them to establish working plantations, the English hoped to attract more desirable tenant crofters and recolonize the island with protestants, deemed to be more suitable. Incentivized by offers of reasonable rents and opportunities for advancement, thousands of Scottish families abandoned their lowland homesteads and crossed over the North Channel to the plantations of northeastern Ireland in the early 1600s. For the most part, the Presbyterian Scots-Irish remained exclusive to their own people, seldom mixing with the native

Catholic population whose resentment towards them only strengthened the Scots-Irish resolve to stick together. Many of the earliest Ulster Scots moved to plantations between the Rivers Foyle and Bann, in the northern Londonderry County towns of Dunboe (Articlave), NewtownLimavady, Ballykelly and Eglinton (Muff). They also made their homes in the Bann Valley villages of Macosquin, Coleraine, Ballymoney, Aghadowey, Garvagh and Killrea. Northern Tyrone County's Foyle River Valley became home to many more Ulster Scots in towns like Ballymagarry, Leckpatrick, Donagheady and Ardstraw. Still others chose to settle on the fertile plantations of Donegal County to the west and Antrim County to the east. Londonderry on Lough Foyle and Coleraine near the mouth of the Bann River were Northern Ireland's major seaports. Life on the plantations was a tenuous existence for the Presbyterian usurpers who kept coming and displacing the contentious Irish crofters. Throughout the seventeenth-century, Irish-Catholics were progressively forced to relinquish more of their lands and by 1703, less than 15% of Northern Ireland's soil remained in the hands of the native Irish who constituted 90% of the island's population. The world however was beginning to shift and the events that would eventually change the course of European history and life on Northern Ireland's plantations, were already in motion.

During England's 'Glorious Revolution' of the late 1680s, the Catholic King James II, King of England, Scotland, and Ireland was deposed in a bloodless rebellion that brought James's daughter Mary II and her husband William III to the throne. The overthrow was the spark that ignited Europe's Nine Years' War (1688-1697), which pitted England and most of Europe against France. Attempting to regain his throne, James II fled to France where he gained the support of Louis XIV before returning to Ireland and

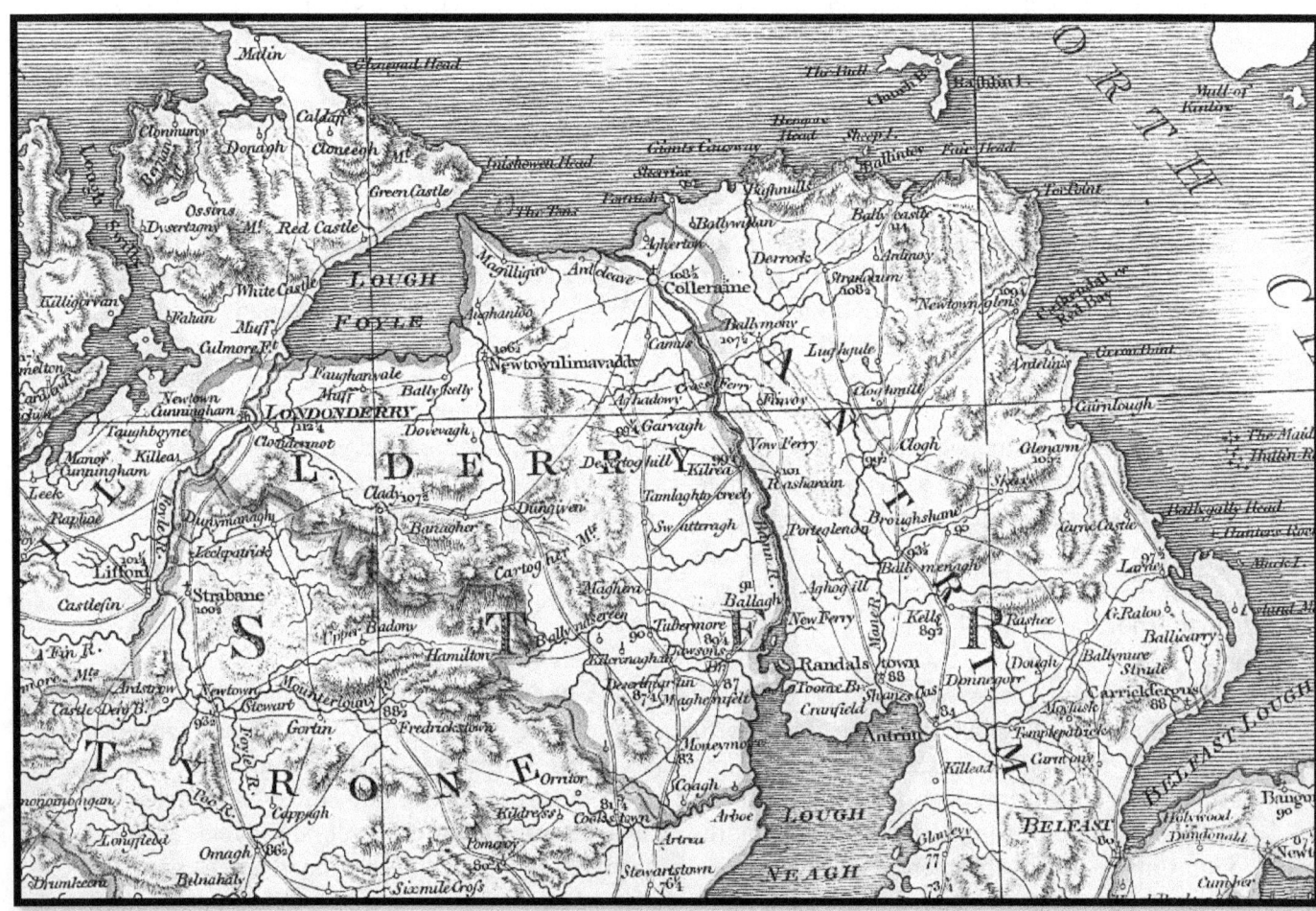

The Villages and Cities of Northern Ireland's Ulster Counties of Derry, Antrim and Tyrone [2]

taking control of his Irish Jacobite army. Ireland's Catholics remained loyal to their Catholic king and revolted against their Ulster neighbors who supported the protestants, William and Mary. The Scots-Irish Presbyterians of Londonderry and Tyrone Counties fought in King William's militia army that was successful in defeating the Jacobites in what became known as the Williamite War (1688-1691). Obviously, the war did little to improve relations between the Ulster protestants and their Papist neighbors and ironically did little to gain the gratitude and favor of the English monarchy for whom they had fought and died.

Although protestant, the Presbyterians were considered nonconformists in the eyes of the reform protestants and were no better than the Catholics against whom they had just fought. Upon William's death in 1702, the Ulster Scots' troubles intensified with the ascension of Queen Anne to the English throne. Through a series of repressive acts that culminated with the Sacramental Test Act of 1704, all those who refused to submit to the Church of England's Eucharist were prohibited from holding any public office, university position or high military ranking. Ministers were expelled from their pulpits and marriages performed by them were nullified, making the children of these marriages illegitimate. The hardships of the Nine Years' War and the economic repercussions that followed, were amplified by Queen Anne's oppressive civil and religious Test Acts. Multiple years of drought and famine coupled with the doubling or even trebling of rents, tested the resolve of Northern Ireland's stalwart Scots-Irish. The grandsons of the original Scots-Irish plantation immigrants were faced with an intolerable situation that prompted many of them to embark upon yet another migratory adventure.

Between 1714 and 1720, the first wave of Northern Ireland's Ulster Scots began boarding ships bound for New England and a fresh start in North America. Five ships, each with twenty to twenty-five families, left Londonderry and Coleraine in 1714. This first wave was followed by another dozen ships over the next three years. By 1718, the pace and number of ships loaded with Ulster families arriving at Boston began to alarm the residents and magistrates of the Massachusetts Bay Colony. Fifteen ships arrived that year with nearly 2,000 new immigrants that added to the previous four year's 1,500 Scots-Irish immigrants. During the late summer months of 1718, the residents of Boston were overwhelmed to see so many ships anchored in their bay. [3]

Massachusetts

Many of the passengers arriving in 1718 were on ships chartered by congregations of Presbyterian parishes with their ministers providing leadership and spiritual guidance. In some instances, a minister would pay the fares for several of his parishioners who were then obliged to settle their debt to the church by submitting to a period of indentured servitude. One of the earliest ships to arrive in Boston that year, the *William and Mary*, carried a cargo of Presbyterian families from the Bann River Valley with the minister of Macosquin, Rev. William Boyd, aboard. Reverend Boyd was bringing with him a petition signed by over three hundred men and nine ministers from Northern Ireland's Londonderry and Antrim Counties. The petition was a request for Massachusetts' Governor Samuel Shute to grant the Irish immigrants a tract of land on which they might settle. Boston's magistrate had no intention of granting any lands within the proximity of their tidy Christian community to the Irish hordes or anyone else who might embark upon their shores. But the Ulster Scots continued to come despite their rude welcoming and uncertain futures.

In the first week of August, a little over a week after the arrival of the *William and Mary*, Brigantine *Robert* laid anchor in Boston's Harbor. Aboard the *Robert*, another twenty plus families of Ulster Scots from Londonderry County were accompanied by their clergyman, Rev. James McGregor of Aghadowey. In his last sermon to his congregation before leaving the Bann River Valley, Rev. McGregor expressed his reasons for leaving Northern Ireland, '*...to avoid oppression and cruel bondage, to shun persecution and designed ruin, and to withdraw from the communion of idolators...*'. Shortly after their arrival, the crew and passengers of the *Robert* were warned to leave Boston and seek haven elsewhere. After spending a good part of that summer and early fall languishing in Boston Harbor, shipmaster James Ferguson decided to weigh anchor and set a course north towards Casco Bay on the southern coast of today's Maine. He found refuge for his ship and tired passengers on the south end of the bay at Porpooduc (Portland). Arriving too late in the season to establish adequate accommodations on land, the families of the *Robert* spent a miserable winter huddled together aboard their ship that became ice-bound just offshore. When the spring thaw finally freed the ship, Capt. Ferguson sailed south to the mouth of the Merrimack River and sailed thirty miles up the river to the small Ulster settlement of Dracut, near today's Lowell, Massachusetts. Some of Rev. McGregor's congregation trekked another fifteen miles north into New Hampshire and joined another Ulster settlement at a place they called Nutfield which was soon after renamed Londonderry in honor of their Irish homeland. [4]

Arriving a few weeks after the *Robert* and the *William and Mary*, shipmaster James Law's *MacCullum* finally reached Boston. His ship had been chartered by a group of Ulster Scots whose intent was to make harbor at New London on the southeastern coast of Connecticut at the mouth of the Thames River. Their ocean crossing, however, had been so exceedingly long and harrowing that the captain prudently decided to anchor at the first port of call he came upon. The 120 souls aboard the ship were led by Rev. James Woodside of the Presbyterian Church of Garvagh. Reverend Woodside was accompanied by many of his Bann Valley congregation who were joined by other Ulster families from Coleraine, NewtownLimavady, Eglinton and Ballykelly. Some of the parishioners who boarded the *MacCullum* during the last week of May 1718, were members of the Scots-Irish Montgomery, Hamilton, Harper, and McFarland families. Thirty years before, many of the older patriarchs of these families had fought alongside protestant King William during the Williamite War. Queen Anne's postwar policies and decrees that drove them from their adopted homeland were followed by their unpleasant reception and expulsion from Boston by their protestant brethren. The hapless passengers of the *MacCullum* were hard-pressed to either head back around the cape towards their original destination on the Connecticut coastline or find another closer port along the northern shore of the Atlantic. Fortunately, they chanced upon a man who was looking for prospective buyers for land he was promoting in the upper Casco Bay's Kennebec River region. [5]

Eight of the wealthiest Boston merchants, known as The Great Proprietors, had recently formed a joint stock company and purchased a large tract of land around the Kennebec and Androscoggin River's Merrymeeting Bay. By the summer of 1715, Massachusetts's General Court validated their title which cleared the way for the surveying and subdividing of the patent into homestead lots. The Pejepscot Land Company found an energetic and persuasive agent to promote the settlement of their lands and encourage the recent immigrant surge of Ulster Scots to take property lots on their patent. Robert Temple Esq. had been an officer in the English army and an heir to a considerable fortune that presumably included shares in the Pejepscot Company. Temple's grandfather Sir Thomas Temple had briefly been 1st Baronet and Lord Protector of the Acadia/Nova Scotia Territory from 1653 to '58, during the time of Cromwell's protectorate. The disputed Acadian Territory of today's Nova Scotia, New Brunswick and eastern Maine, east of the Kennebec River, was constantly in turmoil as to whether France or England was the rightful owner. When France finally gained control following the 2nd Anglo-Dutch War and the Treaty of Breda in 1667, Sir Thomas Temple's proprietary governorship ended. Dying unmarried and without issue seven years later, Sir Thomas's estate and landholdings were left to his brother Purbeck Temple. Upon his death, Purbeck passed along part of his estate to his son Thomas, Robert Temple's father. Part of that inheritance included land on a few of the islands in Boston Harbor, including Deare Island and Noodle's Island which was eventually connected to the mainland and converted into Logan International Airport. [6]

Approached by Robert Temple with the prospects of affordable lands on the northern fringe Massachusetts, the patriarchs of the *MacCullum's* families abandoned their plans to settle on Connecticut's Thames River. Within days of their unpleasant reception in Boston, shipmaster Law's crew

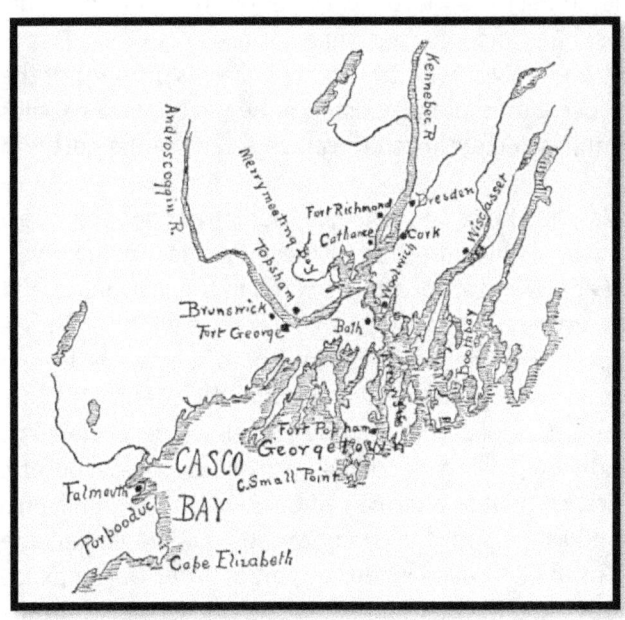
Early Settlements of Casco Bay [7]

raised anchor and sailed back out into the Atlantic, setting a course north by northeast for Casco Bay's Pejepscot lands. At 12 pence an acre and lenient terms as to the span of time they were allowed before they were required to pay off their debt, the Ulster Scots were anxious to get to the frontier and establish themselves on one of the patent's 100-acre homestead lots. A dozen or so settlements were scattered throughout the coves, estuaries and islands of the lower Kennebec and Androscoggin Rivers. Maquoit, Harpswell, New Meadows, Phippsburg, Georgetown, Bath, Woolwick and Arrowick were all within a few miles of each other and a short distance from the inland villages around Merrymeeting Bay and the two rivers that feed into it. Cathance, Cork, and Dresden along the Kennebec and Brunswick and Topsham along the Androscoggin attracted a number of settlers. Other groups established themselves on the south end of Casco Bay between Cape Elizabeth and the mouth of Falmouth River, where the unfortunate families of the *Robert* spent the long, desperate winter of 1718. Temple chartered five more ships throughout 1718 and '19, transporting hundreds more immigrants from Northern Ireland to the Pejepscot Patent settlements. [8]

When the MacCullum reached Casco Bay in early September 1718, four months after leaving Ireland, the Province of Massachusetts was amidst a brief pause in a series of wars that had continually threatened the colonization of New England's frontier settlements. Massachusetts was encouraging settlement of their vulnerable frontier outposts and used the immigrant newcomers as a convenient buffer to shield them against their northern enemies. For a few years at least, Robert Temple's Ulster refugees were able to establish a semblance of civility and normal family life on their frontier homesteads. Village settlements with grist mills and sawmills were filling up with ambitious entrepreneurs whose husbandry and cattle raising skills thrived alongside fishing and lumbering interests. Trading with the local Indians for furs and pelts was a lucrative business for those willing to take the risks involved. The personal interests of some of the less honest fur traders all too often superseded the interests of their communities. Unscrupulous traders invariably undermined the delicate tensions between the whites and Indians by cheating the Indigenous traders and pandering to their weakness for rum. The two peoples of the Kennebec frontier who coexisted within a tenuous peace were sitting on a powder keg of pent-up hostility that needed but a small spark to ignite yet another war.

Several decades before Temple's settlers reached The Kennebec, the first two of what would be four Anglo/Abenaki Wars were fought throughout New England's frontier. King Philip's War (1675-1678) and King William's War (1688-1697) temporarily resolved hostilities between the earliest northern colonialists and their Native American adversaries. These first two wars had primarily been regional conflicts between the Massachusetts, Plymouth, Rhode Island and Connecticut colonies and the local Algonquin tribes of southeastern New England's Wampanoag Confederation. Most of the fighting in King Philip's War was in the southern theaters of Connecticut and Massachusetts. King William's War between New England militias and the Wabanaki Confederation was concentrated in the north. Casco Bay's settlements were nearly all annihilated, with close to four hundred of their residents killed. At the end of these two bloody conflicts and the signing of the first and second Treaties of Casco Bay in 1678 and 1703, the surviving Kennebec settlers were forced to acquiesce to terms dictated by the victorious Algonquins.

Although allowed to return to their burned-out settlements, the survivors were required to pay an annual tribute to their Abenaki stewards and to cease all hostilities and injurious behavior towards them. This of course was a hard pill for the vanquished to swallow and only served to heighten the resentment of the few settlers who dared to return. The peace and cooperation that had existed between the two peoples before the wars would never again be possible and within a decade another war would revisit the northern frontier settlements. [9]

King Philip's War, or the 1st Anglo/Abenaki War, had been an exclusive colonial war between New England settlers and the native peoples of the region. King William's War, or the 2nd Anglo/Abenaki War, was part of a much broader conflict. Europe's Nine Years' War was fought in Ireland as the Williamite War and in North America as King William's War. In North America it was fought to determine whether France or England would reign supreme over the continent, while in Ireland it was fought to secure the throne for King William and Queen Mary. Europe's world order was dramatically altered by the conflict that did relatively nothing to change things in the New World. Casco Bay's Kennebec River would remain the border between New France's Acadian Territory and New England's colonial provinces. Massachusetts northern frontier would continue to be exposed to French militias and their Abenaki allies. King William's War did as little for the Ulster Scots in Northern Ireland as it did for the conditions in what would become for many of them their future homeland. At the end of the 2nd Anglo/Abenaki War, another fragile peace lasted but a few years before war again descended upon the frontier homesteaders of Casco Bay.

Throughout the late seventeenth and early eighteenth century, wars in Europe and America came fast and furious. Europe's War of Spanish Succession (1701-1714) followed almost immediately in the wake of Europe's Nine Years' War. Known in North America as Queen Anne's War, or the 3rd Anglo/Abenaki War, it was to be another inconclusive conflict for the residents of Casco Bay's frontier settlements. The Peace of Utrecht that settled the War of Spanish Succession, did not fully resolve the question as to the sovereignty of the territory between the Kennebec and St. Lawrence rivers. It conceded France's Acadian Nova Scotia Territory to England but maintained France's control of New Brunswick and upper Maine. The Kennebec River would be the boundary between New France and New England. It did, however, clear the way for negotiations in the northeastern frontier. The Treaty of Portsmouth, signed in July 1713, established another temporary secession of hostilities and a tentative peace between the Wabanaki Confederation and Massachusetts' frontier militia forces. This treaty required the Indians to submit their obedience to Queen Anne and pray for Her Majesty's mercy and pardons for their past transgressions. The five major nations of the Algonquin peoples who had fought for their Great French Father throughout the 2nd and 3rd Anglo/Abenaki Wars, were now expected to subjugate themselves to the English queen they had fought against.

The Portsmouth Treaty that Massachusetts negotiators coerced the Wabanaki chieftains into signing, was laced with deception and duplicitous promises that were never meant to be kept. The agreement left the Jesuit missionaries with the unenviable task of explaining to their Abenaki followers why the French king had forsaken them and opened their lands to encroaching English settlers. The treaty left the Indians feeling betrayed and abandoned, but their resentment towards the English settlers who were flooding back into the Kennebec region, posed a far greater threat to them than any European alliances. Having been wooed by France's Jesuit missionaries into accepting Catholicism as their adopted religion, the Abenaki warriors remained loyal to their Catholic priests. The tsunami of Ulster Scots that began descending upon the Kennebec region in 1718, added to the insults of the Treaty of Portsmouth and heightened the ire of the Abenaki peoples who watched as the newcomers violated nearly every term of the agreement. The proprietors of the Pejepscot Patent wasted little time capitalizing on the Portsmouth Treaty and took advantage of the uneasy peace that followed the 3rd Anglo/Abenaki War. [10]

4th Anglo/Abenaki War

On the first of August 1721, two hundred Abenaki warriors and their Jesuit priest, Father Sebastian Rale, met with the leaders of the Kennebec settlements of Georgetown and Arrowick and offered them a simple ultimatum, leave the Kennebec or they would burn every village and kill every settler. Within a few weeks, the General Court of Massachusetts ordered a regiment of three hundred militiamen to be amassed in the eastern sector. They also called for Father Rale to be turned over to them, dead or alive. Having built a church in the Abenaki village of Norridgewock, sixty miles up the Kennebec from the Merrymeeting Bay settlements, Father Rale managed to retain his influence over the Indians even after the humiliation of the Portsmouth Treaty. He encouraged the Abenaki to fight on for their own sovereignty. Deemed to be the principal instigator of Indian unrest, he was of course villainized by the New Englanders who put a hefty price on his head. The nervous peace that hung over the Ulster Scots' settlements ever since their arrival at Casco Bay, was about to take a decisive turn for the worse. [11]

After having crossed the North Atlantic in 1718 and being shunned by the Bostonians, the families of the *MacCullum* were some of the first to recolonize the Casco Bay settlements following the 3rd Anglo/Abenaki War. A group of them settled near each other in two of Merrymeeting Bay's villages where they would form a bond of familial comradery. The families of Robert Hamilton, William Montgomery, James McFarland, James Harper, and James Miller all settled together on the Androscoggin River in Brunswick and Topsham. Robert and Agnes Lecky Hamilton and their two oldest sons Patrick and Robert Jr settled on three adjoining lots on the southside of the river in Brunswick, an earlier settlement that had been abandoned during the previous Indian troubles. The people of Brunswick had built an impressive stone fort, Fort George, where a small garrison of militiamen kept a constant guard over the settlements. The Harpers, McFarlands and Millers took lots on the northside of the Androscoggin in Topsham, just across from Brunswick. James and wife Janet Lewis Harper and their two sons William-19 and Joseph-18 settled on three of Topsham's adjoining riverfront lots, while their daughter Anne and her husband James Miller took a fourth adjoining lot. Two of James and Janet's younger children were also there with them on their Androscoggin homestead, Sarah-16, and John-13. Moses Harper, a cousin of James, settled within a few lots of the rest of the Harpers. James McFarland and his family also settled on a homestead lot near the Harpers, while William and Mary Aken Montgomery and their five children joined one of Robert Temple's nearby settlements on the lower Kennebec River. Many of the older patriarchs of these Scots-Irish families who crossed the Atlantic on the *MacCullum*, had fought together in Ireland's Williamite War. Now, many of their sons would soon be fighting together in another war on Massachusetts' northern frontier. [12]

When the call went out for volunteers to join Massachusetts' eastern sector militia regiment in 1721, James Harper and his three sons, along with cousin Moses, joined Capt. John Giles's Brunswick militia company with about thirty other Androscoggin men. Most of the regiment's volunteers were descendants of the original English families who had settled and resettled in the Kennebec region long before the Ulster Scots arrival. Deemed untrustworthy of high office or civic position, the 'Irish' volunteers were relegated to the lower ranks while all the militia officers were of English descent. The discrimination that had been spat upon them on Boston's Long Wharf was equally as egregious as it was now on the frontier. The Scots-Irish privates and sentries were often subjected to humiliating abuses at the hands of their superior English officers. Remarkably, for an 'Irish' man, James Harper gained the respect of his English superiors and was entrusted with his company's commissary duties as its clerk, a position that denoted a high level of competency and business proclivity. At forty-six, James may have been past his prime to perform soldiering duties but his three sons, William, Joseph, and John, were all too willing to join the fight and prove their grit.

In December, four months after Father Rale's Arrowick visit and ultimatum, Col. Thomas Westbrook was ordered to deploy an expedition to the Abenaki village of Norridgewock with the expressed purpose of capturing or killing Father Rale. Sixteen-year-old Pvt. John Harper, the youngest of the Harper brothers, had gained the attention of Col. Westbrook who detailed him and nine other privates in Capt. Giles's company for duty on his Norridgewock Expedition. Col. Westbrook's expedition was ultimately unsuccessful, having been detected by Indian scouts as they made their way up the Kennebec River. Having alerted the village that was all but deserted by the time the militiamen reached it, they were unable to find and capture their Jesuit quarry. The first raid on Norridgewock accomplished very little other than further enraging the Indians who in the spring began launching their own retaliatory raids on the civilian settlements around Merrymeeting Bay. [13]

The Abenaki's explosive rage came to a head in June 1722 when they attacked Fort George and burnt the village of Brunswick to the ground. About forty families were living in Brunswick at the time and another thirty-five were living just across the Androscoggin in Topsham. Most of the residents of Casco Bay's outer settlements were motivated to leave their homesteads by the disturbing sacking of Brunswick. The ones who stayed were primarily young men who filled the ranks of the local militia companies. Within a month of the raid on Brunswick, James Harper and his wife Janet, along with their daughters Sarah and Anne, left their Topsham homesteads and boarded one of the ships about to set sail for Boston. Along with Anne's husband James Miller and their cousin Moses, the Harpers boarded shipmaster Thomas Sanders' vessel and arrived back in Boston on the 12th of August. All three of the Harper brothers, however, chose to remain on the northern frontier and continue to fight alongside their fellow comrades-in-arms. [14]

The 4th Anglo/Abenaki War, which was more often referred to as Father Rale's War, began in earnest following the attack on Brunswick. Massachusetts called for a thousand more troops to be called up. Robert Temple was commissioned captain of a Kennebec militia company and having been familiar with the Harper brothers, recruited a couple of them into his ranks. Young soldiers were incentivized to join the militia by a monthly salary of £2 and a promise of one hundred acres at war's end. They were further motivated by an award of £15 for every male Indian's scalp and £8 for every man, woman, or child captive they brought in. As appalling as bounties might have seemed, this was an appealing proposal for many of the ambitious young men who had come to the frontier with limited resources.

Soldiers on the Kennebec front would either be posted to a company garrisoned in one of the half-dozen forts scattered throughout the frontier or assigned to one of the many scouting parties ranging through the forests between the Kennebec and Penobscot rivers. The Abenaki Wars were fought with frontier guerrilla-style tactics and pitted a native population fighting for their ancestral homeland against a New England army of conscripted militia soldiers. No smartly uniformed European armies ever formed up into battle lines and fired volley after volley at each other's lines on a field of battle. Skirmishes between roving bands of Abenaki warriors and militiamen were fought in relatively close quarters and often hand-to-hand. Homesteads were frequently ambushed with their occupants either slaughtered or taken hostage by the Indians. These transgressions were regularly returned in kind by the New Englanders. In September of 1722, two and a half months after the raid on Fort George and Brunswick, another large force of Indians fell upon the settlements of Arrowick and Georgetown at the mouth of the Kennebec River. Capt. Temple's militiamen effectively repelled the attack and saved nearly all of the settlers, but the Indians did succeed in killing most of the village's cattle and livestock while torching a couple dozen of their homesteads. [15]

Numerous militia expeditions were deployed against the Abenaki villages along the Kennebec and Penobscot rivers throughout 1723 and into '24. Militia incursions into the interior frontier were for the most part ineffective, as most of the heavy fighting was concentrated on defending the villages and forts along the rugged Maine coastline. After another bloody year of inconclusive warfare, another campaign to take Norridgewock and capture Father Rale was launched in August of 1724. Four companies of fifty men left Fort Richmond on the lower Kennebec in seventeen whale boats and headed up the river towards the Indian village. This time the militiamen caught the Indians and Father Rale by surprise and came down hard on the unsuspecting village. In the carnage that followed, Father Rale was slaughtered along with thirty or more of the Abenaki's most noted warriors. Many of the village's women and children were mercilessly massacred alongside their husbands and fathers. All the village's houses, many of which were reported to be spacious and well furnished, were reduced to ashes along with Father Rale's impressive chapel. The incident demoralized the Catholic Abenaki peoples and succeeded in turning the tide of the war in favor of the New Englanders. The second raid on Norridgewock might also have demoralized some of the Ulster militiamen who were growing weary of all the slaughter and mayhem. The Scots-Irish had not been exposed to the Indians for as long as their New England counterparts whose hatred for them might have seemed unreasonably excessive to the recent immigrants. Having witnessed nearly four years of war and too many of his kinsmen killed, Pvt. John Harper's second visit to Norridgewock and the massacre he took part in may have prompted him into leaving the military and returning to his family in Boston. [16]

Death of Father Sébastien Râle of the Society of Jesus

A few months after the raid on Norridgewock and the death of Father Rale, the tribal leaders of the Wabanaki Confederation began talks with the governor and magistrates of Massachusetts. The Casco Bay frontier finally began to quiet down throughout the winter of 1724/'25 and by that summer all hostilities had ceased. The treaty that was finally signed in December ended the war in the Kennebec sector and soon after another agreement ended the war in Nova Scotia. The troops of Capt. Giles and Capt. Temple's Casco Bay companies had been slowly standing down throughout the year and many of them had been discharged shortly after the Norridgewock raid. The Ulster families who had spent four years on the Kennebec frontier before returning to Boston following the attack on Brunswick, were anxious to see their young men return to them in their lower Massachusetts settlements. The returning veterans of the 4th Abenaki War were disheartened to discover that their Scots-Irish families had been greeted in 1722 with the same contempt they had received in 1718. Their second arrival on Boston's Long Wharf had the added insult of them being treated as traitors for having abandoned their frontier settlements. All their Casco Bay homestead lots were confiscated without recompence for any payments or improvements they had made on their properties. They were again, unceremoniously warned to leave Boston.

After being cast out of Boston for a second time, many of these returning Casco Bay families headed for the scattered settlements of Massachusetts' western frontier. Some rejoined their Ulster relatives in Rev. MacGregor's Merrimac River settlement of Dracut, while others headed for New Hampshire's Ulster settlements of Londonderry and Derry. Several groups of families chose to stay closer to Boston, settling in outlying villages like Concord, Sudbury, Framingham, and Hopkinton. A few hardy souls chose to head further west to the outer margins of Worcester County where they settled in Rutland, Oakham, Brookfield and Leicester. When they settled in a village already populated with New Englanders, the Presbyterian Scots were looked upon as lower-class people and their neighborhoods were sneeringly referred to as 'Irish Rows'. The Harper, Montgomery, McFarland, Hendry, and Hamilton families had for generations formed strong bonds of comradery with each other through their shared hardships in Scotland and Northern Ireland. Their friendships and marriages would bind them together for generations to come. Robert Hamilton and his son Patrick, after being driven from their Brunswick homestead on the

Androscoggin, joined William Montgomery and his family in the Massachusetts settlement of Hopkinton, twenty-five-miles southwest of Boston. Some of the McFarlands and Harpers resettled in the Middlesex County communities of Concord and Sudbury after returning from the north. Remarkably, a few of these returning families managed to settle within sight of Boston and went on to prosper amongst their Anglo neighbors who continued to show nothing but disdain for them. [17]

Noodle's Island

James and Janet Harper were able to stay in the Boston area following their return from Topsham. Noodle's Island had always been a sanctuary for nonconformists and mavericks who stuck a thorn in the backside of Boston's puritan elites. It was a perfect place for a family of determined Ulster Scots to plant their flag and thumb their noses at those who had treated them so unjustly. Having been persuaded by Robert Temple to sail for Casco Bay with the others aboard the *MacCullum*, James Harper's sons had developed an alliance with the man who became an influential contributor to their future prosperity. Their association with Capt. Temple while serving with him in the Kennebec militia seems to have continued following the war. Retaining financial interest in the Island his grandfather Sir Thomas Temple once owned, Capt. Temple built a handsome mansion on Noodle's Island and managed a large farm on which he raised livestock and harvested hay for export to the mainland and ports abroad. Although himself an Englishman of wealth and hereditary gentility, he may not have been blinded by the prejudicial biases that so many of his Boston contemporaries held towards the Presbyterian Ulstermen. Having impressed Capt. Temple with his accounting skills and business savvy while keeping books for Capt. Giles's militia company, James Harper appears to have been invited by the captain to settle on his Island and join one of his family's business enterprises. Perhaps having been a tenant farmer back on one of Northern Ireland's large Ulster plantations before coming to New England, James may have felt comfortable assuming the same position on Noodle's Island. Through his affiliation with one of Boston's wealthier landowners, James knew the Noodle's Island opportunity offered him and his sons their best chance of establishing a foothold in the new world before launching their own future enterprises. [18]

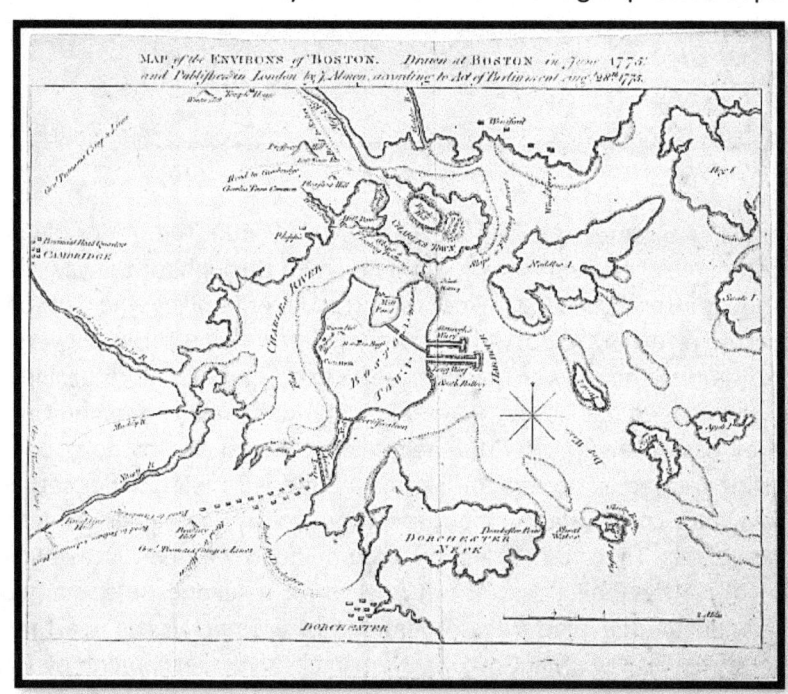
Old Boston Town, Showing the Long Wharf and Noodle's Island

In late 1724, Pvt. John Harper, now nineteen, rejoined his family on Noodle's Island. His return from the war and joyous reunion with his family was unfortunately marred by the recent death of his forty-three-year-old mother, Janet Lewis Harper. Her death was more than likely due to one of the many plagues of smallpox that took so many during these times. John's older sister Sarah was still living with their father James, as she was yet unmarried and obliged to take care of her ageing father. Sister Anne and husband James Miller had returned to Boston after leaving Cosco Bay and settled close to the family's patriarch on Noodle's Island. Having married Anne while still in Northern Ireland before coming to America with the rest of her family, James Miller had brought his younger brother John with him to New England. Returning from the Kennebec settlements in January, before the summer raid on Brunswick, John Miller apparently settled in one of the Ulster villages around Worcester. While little is known about James or his brother John's fate, one account suggests that Anne Harper Miller lived a long and happy life, dying in Boston in the 1790s while in her nineties. [19]

John Harper's two older brothers, William and Joseph, had already left Noodle's Island by the time he returned from the war. They had both married and set off to start their own lives and families in the Ulster settlements of west central Massachusetts and northern Connecticut. Unlike their younger brother, William and Joseph had not served through the entire Anglo/Abenaki War. The oldest of the Harper brothers, William, served for about six months in Capt. Giles's militia company. He had been on sentinel duty at Fort George when the fort was attacked, and the village of Brunswick was destroyed in July of 1722. Less inclined or equipped to handle the rigorous life of a frontier soldier, he was discharged from the army in early '23 and soon after left the front to rejoin his family on Noodle's Island. Shortly after William returned, he married Rachel Robinson and moved from Boston Harbor to nearby Concord, where the couple remained for nearly twenty years before moving further west to another small frontier village in central Massachusetts.

In 1742, William and Rachel Harper and their son George and daughter Jean's husband Alexander McFarland purchased lots in Worcester County's recently plotted settlement of Rutland's West Wing, which was later renamed Oakham. The Harpers and McFarlands were three of the first ten proprietors and founders of the small community of Scots-Irish Presbyterians. William and Rachel's daughter Sarah and her husband James Henderson settled in nearby Rutland; a community of non-conformist Ulster families who had settled there some time after arriving on the brigantine *Robert* with Rev. McGregor's Aghadowey congregation. After their harrowing winter icebound aboard Capt. Ferguson's ship, several of these stalwart families left their compatriots and the Merrimac River settlements of Dracut and Nutfield for the wilds of New England's interior. Some of the descendants of Oakham and Rutland's Henderson, McFarland, and Harper families eventually resettled in New York's Washington County townships of Salem and Hebron. [20]

John Harper's older brother Joseph had also left Noodle's Island by the time of his return from the war. Having only served a year in the Abenaki War with his brothers, Joseph set off to start his own family shortly after returning from the north. At nineteen he married an older woman he had met while aboard the *MacCullum* on their long journey across the North Atlantic in 1718. The Harpers had shared their ship's cold hull with twenty other Ulster families for three long months. One of these families was led by a recently widowed mother with nine children, ages 7-29. William and Margaret Milne Thompson came from Argyllshire, Scotland to northeastern Ireland in 1716, just as the Ulster Scots were beginning their mass exodus to America. William unfortunately died at Coleraine soon after their arrival, leaving his fifty-year-old wife Margaret and their seven sons and two daughters to fend for themselves. With her older son's help, Margaret continued her quest to fulfil her late husband's vision to see his family start a new life in a promising new land.

The Thompson's oldest daughter Miriam was twenty-eight and still unmarried, a fact that would have qualified her as an old maid in the times in which she lived. Being ten years younger than Miriam, Joseph Harper nonetheless became enamored with Miriam during their voyage to the new world. But as their paths would alter, Joseph and his family headed north to Casco Bay after being exiled from Boston, while the Thompsons headed west to the Connecticut River settlements north of Hartford. After returning from his tour of duty on the Kennebec frontier and having never forgotten the woman he had confided in while on the open Atlantic, Joseph set a course west in search of the Thompson family. Finding Miriam still unwed and with her family in the Irish Rows of East Windsor's Scantic Parish, Joseph and Miriam were finally reunited in marriage. Due perhaps in part to Miriam's advanced age, she and Joseph would have but four children together, a relatively small family for the times. Most of Miriam's siblings married and multiplied prolifically, engendering many generations of Thompsons throughout the Hartford and Tolland County communities of East Windsor, Enfield, and Ellington. Descendants of Margaret Milne Thompson, who died in 1752 at the age of eighty-seven, erected an impressive memorial arch in Ellington Cemetery over the headstone of their family's courageous American matriarch. [21]

A couple of other strong bonds of friendship and romance gained momentum as the young passengers aboard the *MacCullum* whiled away the hours on the open sea. William and Mary Akens Montgomery's children were all about the same age as the Harper children with whom they shared the privations of their long ocean voyage. William and Mary's son John Montgomery was fifteen when the family finally reached New England and headed north to Maine's troubled frontier. John and his sixteen-year-old brother James fought alongside the Harper brothers and remained in the Kennebec militias with young John Harper until the end of the Abenaki War. Their parents returned to Boston with their three sisters following the attack on Brunswick and settled briefly in the Irish Rows of Massachusetts' Worcester settlements. The Montgomerys soon joined a community of expatriated Scots-Irish families in the village of Hopkinton, twenty-five miles southwest of Boston. In 1724, William Montgomery, Robert Hamilton, and Robert's son Patrick joined twelve other Ulstermen to form the First Congregational Church of Hopkinton. Robert and Agnes Hamilton's two sons Patrick and Armour were both married in the Hopkinton church to two of the Montgomery daughters, Anne and Agnes, respectively. Another marriage was performed in the church between William and Mary's son James Montgomery and Mary Hendry, the daughter of another family of Scots-Irish immigrants with strong ties to the Harper family.

The Harpers were reputed to have come from Scotland's Dunbartonshire on the Clyde River before migrating across the North Channel to a north Ireland plantation in the Row Valley's Ballykelly and NewtownLimavady area, near to the Montgomerys of Aghadowey. Many of the families who came from the central lowlands of Scotland to Northern Ireland in the early 1600s shared the same threads of commonality that bound people together in those early times; religion, class, ancestry, and common enemies. These same strands would eventually stretch clear across the Atlantic and bind these same families together again in the untamed wilderness of New England, New York, and Ohio. [22]

After returning from the war and spending a few years with his family in Hopkinton, John Montgomery visited his old friend and militia comrade John Harper on Noodle's Island and asked his sister Sarah to marry him. While crossing the Atlantic together at the age of fifteen, Sarah and John apparently formed a fondness for each other that culminated in marriage in December 1727. Shortly thereafter, John Montgomery and his new bride returned to the Kennebec frontier, perhaps to the dismay of both of their families. Following the 4th Anglo/Abenaki War, the Kennebec frontier experienced one of its intermittent periods of relative peace between the white settlers and Abenaki natives. But this peace, like all the others, would prove to be short-lived. John and Sarah may have been induced to return and resettle on the stormy coast of Maine by yet another promoter of a large tract of recently patented lands.

Against the consent of the Governor of Massachusetts and the Great Proprietors, England clumsily attempted to establish another provincial colony adjacent to the Massachusetts Bay Colony's Pejepscot Patent. In 1729, Col. David Dunbar was sent to survey and colonize the Pemaquid Patent, between Sheepscot and Muscongus Bays. Dunbar's intention was to attract another mass movement of Scots-Irish settlers to the new British Colony that was dubbed Georgia. After laying out three settlements, Walpole, Harrington, and Townsend, in the vicinity of today's Bristol and Boothbay, Dunbar persuaded some of the Ulstermen who had left the Kennebec settlements into returning to Maine's Lobster Coast. England's attempt to establish a new colony on the Pemaquid Patent was short lived and by 1732 Massachusetts had regained control over the patent and the proposed colony. Sending their own proprietor, Col. Samuel Waldo, they reestablished the territory as the Waldo Patent and revoked all of Dunbar's homestead deeds. The unfortunate settlers were forced to either renegotiate their deeds with their new landlord or abandon their homesteads and all their improvements. John and Sarah Montgomery renegotiated with their new proprietors and remained on their Walpole Patent homestead along the banks of the

Damariscotta River. Unfortunately, John died in 1743 at the age of forty, leaving his widow Sarah and their young children alone in an unforgiving wilderness. Sarah soon abandoned her frontier abode and returned to her family on Noodle's Island. She died five years later at the age of forty-eight. A hard, short life was the fate of many who braved the frontier wilderness to bring civilization to the New World. [23]

John Harper turned twenty shortly after returning from the Kennebec frontier to rejoin his family on Noodle's Island. With the death of his mother Janet and the absence of his two older brothers, John may have felt obliged to stay and help his fifty-year-old father James. A year after his sister Sarah married his friend John Montgomery, John paid a visit to Hopkinton and asked his friend's sister Abigail for her hand in marriage. After having known each other since their ocean voyage together when they were both thirteen, John and Abigail Montgomery were now both twenty-four and more than ready to start a new life together. In November 1728, John returned with his new bride to Noodle's Island where they would start their family and continue to live with John's father James for another thirteen years. During their years on Noodle's Island, the Harpers would be blessed with the first six of what would eventually be ten children.

John appears to have done quite well for himself on the East Boston Island, especially for an 'Irishman' who had been banished from Boston for his family's nonconformist views. It is not clear, however, if John or any of his family had any strong convictions in any form of Christian orthodoxy other than a traditional compliance to their Presbyterian heritage. Their association with East Boston's Robert Temple Esq. opened more doors and afforded more opportunities than were availed to the Ulster families in the Irish Rows of Massachusetts' outer settlements. Through the lucrative triangle trading network between England, New England, and the Dutch West Indies, Temple and his associates were well positioned on Noodle's Island to benefit from commercial trafficking. Throughout the latter 1720s and into the '30s, John Harper and his father James thrived financially and socially, becoming respected members of their East Boston community. In 1739, two years after the founding of the first Irish organization in America, John became a member of Boston's Charitable Irish Society that provided temporary loans and helped find work for struggling Irish immigrants. The charitable society also organized the first observance of St. Patrick's Day in America and promoted the recognition of Boston's Irish population. Social status and financial security were John's primary focus during this period of his life. Being hardened by war and embittered by oppression, his keen Scottish intellect began to formulate a grand scheme that he hoped would propel him and his sons to wealth and prestige. With land lying idle in the west and just waiting for ambitious speculators to take advantage of it, John began a plan to tailor his son's educations to accommodate the various skills required to carry out their father's grand dreams of empire. [24]

Connecticut River

In 1741, after thirteen years on Noodle's Island, John and Abigail Harper took their first step towards fulfilling John's grand plan. James Harper was now sixty-five and well past his prime, and as no record of his death seems to have been preserved, his sons' decision to leave Boston may in fact have been precipitated by the old man's death. At thirty-six, being the patriarch of his branch of the Harper family, John initiated his westward vision. Land speculation, however, was not yet the primary motivation for leaving East Boston and resettling in the Connecticut River's seaport village of Middletown.

By the mid-eighteenth century, Middletown had become the largest and busiest maritime trading port between Boston and New York City. Being twenty-five miles up the Connecticut River, Middletown might have seemed an unlikely place for a New England seaport. But a shifting sandbar at the mouth of the river made it impractical to build the necessary wharfs and piers at Old Saybrook. The tidal river was fully navigable by seafaring vessels as far up as the Enfield Falls and Windsor Locks, just five miles from the Massachusetts border. Middletown was suitably positioned for the exportation of the interior's timber, livestock, and grain to ports abroad. These vital commodities could be rafted down the river to Middletown wharfs where they could be loaded onto ships bound for England, France, and the Caribbean. These same ships would bring back Europe's finer amenities and the Dutch West Indies rum, molasses, and sugar. The other triangular trading route that was established between New England, West Africa, and the Caribbean, provided New England merchants with another lucrative trading commodity. The Harpers were never known to have traded in, or ever owned, slaves. Judging from their own mistreatment at the hands of the Anglican New Englanders, it is fair to assume they would have had nothing to do with the oppressive dark trade.

John Harper's years on Noodle's Island with his father James and the Temple family, taught him the basics of the highly competitive shipping and international trade business. With his older brother Joseph and Joseph's Thompson in-laws just twenty miles up the Connecticut River from Middletown in East Windsor, John had a familial link to the inland commodities of the upper river's farms and forests. Teaming up with his Thompson relatives, John appears to have gone into the business of lumber and grain exportation. Just as his father had done on Noodle's Island with Robert Temple, John would now do with another established family of New England merchants and traders at Middletown. The Pelton family was just the kind of family a Scots-Irish outsider would need to impress in order to muscle his way into the predominantly English network of businessmen and merchants. John Benson Pelton was a successful Middletown shipping and shipbuilding entrepreneur who seems to have taken a liking to John Harper. While strengthening his ties with the Pelton family and their shipping interests, John's son John Jr developed a friendship with Mr. Pelton's son Nathan who eventually married one of the Thompson girls and became young John's brother-in-law. [25]

Aside from building wealth and status within old New England society, the education of John and Abigail's children was a principal consideration. The Harpers arrived in Middletown in 1741 with five of their first six children after having lost their two-year-old daughter Margaret a few years before leaving Noodle's Island. Their oldest son William was twelve when they came to the Connecticut River with his younger sibling, James-10, Mary-8, John Jr-7 and a second one-year-old daughter named Margaret. The Harpers would add three more to their brood while living in Middletown, Joseph was born a year after their arrival in 1742, Alexander in '44 and Abigail in '45. John and Abigail spent about five years in Middletown before moving up the river in 1747 to East Windsor where they were engaged in a lumber milling operation with their Thompson family relatives. Their tenth and final child Miriam was born in East Windsor in '49. John Harper was less interested in providing a higher academic education for his five sons than he was in developing the necessary skills each would need to contribute to his grand scheme. The education of his three eldest sons, William, James and John, were designed to fulfill specific aspects of his plans.

While John continued to amass a small fortune in shipping and exporting lumber and grain, his grand scheme to acquire land in the Indian territory to the west began to take shape. During his years on the Kennebec frontier, he had learned much about Native American culture, language, and habits. He had developed a respect for the warrior culture of his Algonquin Abenaki enemies and an admiration for the Iroquois Mohawk he had fought alongside. Learning how important it was to show the proper respect to the Indians, he also knew the value of understanding their ethos, and ceremonial rituals. John would tutor his sons with everything he had learned during his time on the Kennebec frontier. The ability to successfully negotiate with the Indians was a skill at least one of his three oldest sons would need to know. Convincing chiefs and sachems to sign their totems on deeds to a large tract of their ancestral homelands was not the only talent his sons would need for his scheme to succeed. Working with self-interested land commissioners, surveyors and the king's colonial representatives was a complicated and all too often duplicitous affair. The subtleties of bribery, coercion and legitimized larceny were tactics best acquired through a practical education in frontier politics and backwoods lawyering. [26]

Born in 1729, William Harper was the oldest of the Harper brothers and the son his father would groom to be the legal and political component of his grand scheme. It is uncertain just how much accredited academic training William received while acquiring his familiarity with the law, but somewhere along the way he learned enough about the profession to convince others of his abilities. Access to law books and tutorial influence was often enough to inspire an intelligent young student to acquire the necessary knowledge and judicial temperament for a career in frontier law. Frontier lawyers and the basic methods they practiced was, in most situations, enough to get them by in the rural communities of colonial America during the eighteenth century. William would never learn to write a proper legal brief, or even a proper letter for that matter, but that was not at all uncommon for frontier lawyers during the times in which Esquire Harper plied his trade. Despite never having earned a law degree he would manage to become a successful lawyer, associate judge, state legislator, and political insider. Without his contributions to his father's plan, the Harper's dreams of empire would never gotten off the ground. [27]

John Harper Jr was born in May 1734, the same year as the legendary frontiersman Daniel Boone with whom he was to share many parallel frontier adventures. They would both lead pioneer settlers into unsettled territories while learning to navigate the complexities of Indian culture to acquire the lands they both sought. John would play the pivotal role in his father's scheme to purchase Indian lands in west central New York. His education would be directed towards the practical aspects of communicating with the Indians and understanding the nuances of their culture. Young John spent his formative years with his family on the Connecticut River at Middletown and East Windsor before setting out on an incredible journey into the western frontier. He developed into a charismatic young man with an imposing nature and a persuasive ability to get from others what he wanted. His early schooling focused on neither law nor politics, as his older brother William's had. He was instead steered towards developing the linguistic and oratorical skills needed to parley around an Indian ceremonial council fire.

John Jr was fortunate in his youth to have lived within a day's ride of a school specializing in teaching gifted young Mohawk and Oneida boys in the ways of the white man. Rev. Eleazer Wheelock established a small school in Lebanon, Connecticut where he taught English, agriculture, and scripture to a select group of talented young Indian boys he hoped to turn into model citizens and proselytizers of the gospel. Some, he hoped, might return to their people as Christian missionaries and convert them into Protestant Christians. Rev. Wheelock's Moors Indian Charity School began accepting a few students in the mid-1750s and continued to school both white and Native American children throughout the '60s. John Harper Sr was very likely a financial contributor to Wheelock's school, a school he would have found convenient for the purpose of exposing his son John to the language and customs of the Iroquois peoples. His bright young son would indeed attend the school and learn to master the native tongue of the Oneida and Mohawk peoples. John would also meet and befriend several of the school's brightest Indian pupils, including a talented young Mohawk boy whose English name was Joseph Brant. While young Daniel Boone was trapping and hunting amongst the Shawnee, Lenape, Chickasaw and Cherokee of the Ohio and Kentucky Territories, young John Harper was learning the ways of New York's Mohawk and Oneida nations. [28]

New York Frontier

The greater portion of New England's Indian lands had been seized, partitioned, and colonized by the mid-1700s, but territories to the west were still beckoning to ambitious speculators and prospective homesteaders. New York's Dutch land barons and patent proprietors along the Hudson River had long since colonized their extensive manors with lease-holding tenants as far north as Albany and west along the Mohawk River to Schenectady. Throughout the first half of the eighteenth-century, smaller patents along the southside of the Mohawk from Schenectady to German Flatts were being granted to investors and speculators with friends in high places. In 1738, New York's Lt. Governor George Clarke acquired an

8,000-acre patent on the upper Susquehanna's Cherry Valley Creek, east of Otsego Lake and fifteen-miles south of the Mohawk. Gentlemen of prestige and position relied upon land agents and trustees to whom they could delegate the messy business of supervising their properties and recruiting settlers to their homestead lots.

The King's Royal Decree limited property ownership by anyone person to 2,000 acres. Accordingly, Lt. Gov. Clarke assigned four proprietary agents to comply with the regulation before quietly dismissing three of them after feigning compliance. Clarke then turned over management of his patent to a Scotsman who had come to New York looking for adventure and opportunity. An active land speculator, John Lindsley apparently had the wherewithal to convince the governor he could manage his patent and attract settlers to its ninety-three homestead lots. For his part in the arrangement, Lindsley was awarded two of the patent's premier 100-acre homestead lots and given the honor of having the patent named in his honor. The settlement that gradually grew around his homestead lots in the center of the patent became known as Lindsley's Bush. By the summer of 1739, Lindsley had only been able to attract seven other inexperienced pioneer families to Lindsley Patent. Were it not for the benevolence of a few local Indians these novice homesteaders may not have even made it through their first winter on the patent. By that spring, most of the settlement's homesteaders abandoned their properties, including Lindsley himself who returned to New York City with his family. The management of the patent then fell to another agent who would prove to be of stouter stuff. [29]

A graduate of Dublin's Trinity College, Rev. Samuel Dunlop came to the New World with the resolve to tame the ungodly wilderness and bring the word of the gospels to the Indigenous population. Having acquainted himself with the Ulster Presbyterian congregation of Londonderry, New Hampshire, Rev. Dunlop convinced a few of the settlement's Scots-Irish families to follow him to the very edge of Christendom. James Campbell, David Ramsey, and Patrick Davidson were persuaded to leave their Londonderry kinsmen in 1741 and embark with their families upon a difficult journey through the wilds to Lindsley's Bush. Joining the few remaining families in the settlement, the tiny community gradually began attracting other Ulster families to the beautiful valley of the cherry blossoms. Growing steadily over the next decade, Lindsley's Bush was renamed Cherry Valley and prospered peacefully with only an occasional hostile incident with the local Mohawk Indians.

New York's western frontier between the two upper branches of the Delaware and the Susquehanna River was still firmly in the grip of the six nations of the Iroquois Confederation. Life in the few white settlements scattered throughout the frontier was a dangerous and often deadly endeavor for the intrepid homesteaders who dared to settle there. Nevertheless, by the early '50s, restless New Englanders were looking westward for opportunities on the patented lands of the upper Mohawk River Valley and its frontier settlements to the south. The Harpers were one such family ready to make the bold move and begin their next phase of the family patriarch's grand scheme.

John and Abigail Harper were both fifty when they brought their nine children, ages 5 to 25, to Cherry Valley in 1754. The Harpers initially settled on Lindsley Patent's lot #35, a 100-acre lot west of the village near the present-day intersection of Irish Hollow Rd. and County Rd. #54. John, however, would not be satisfied with just one homestead lot and was already maneuvering to throw his hat into the arena of empire building. Within a few years of coming to Cherry Valley he managed to acquire his own 500-acre patent, adjacent to and south of Lindsley Patent. Beaver Dam Patent extended down both sides of Cherry Valley Creek to the present-day crossroads hamlet of Roseboom at the junction of routes #166 and #165. Still within four miles of the village of Cherry Valley, the Harpers proceeded to build and operate one of the first sawmills in the area. Besides their sawmill operation, the Harpers also engaged in the lucrative business of trading with the local Indians for furs and pelts. Their arrival in '54 was at the forefront of an influx of settlers that would increase the population of the Cherry Valley settlement from about a dozen families to over forty by 1765. Within a few years of their arrival, the little frontier village would welcome another gristmill, a blacksmith shop, and a small mercantile business. Rev. Dunlop was instrumental in establishing one of the first frontier grammar schools west of Schenectady. Besides teaching the white children of Cherry Valley, grammar, arithmetic, and history, he took in a few of the local Indian children and tutored to them alongside the white children. Several students from the Mohawk River villages of Canajoharie and German Flatts were also sent to him for a rudimentary education.

After Rev. Dunlop took over management of the Lindsley Patent and brought the first Londonderry families to the Mohawk River frontier, he had one last bit of business to address back in Ireland. Having established his homestead on the patent, he traveled back down to New York City and sailed off to fulfill a promise he had made to a bonny young lass back in Northern Ireland. After seven long years apart, Rev. Dunlop found his sweetheart still waiting for him in the Bann River Valley parish of Kilraught, four miles east of the Antrim County village of Ballymoney. Rev. Dunlop and Elizabeth Gault were married within days of the reverend's return and immediately began packing their bags for a honeymoon voyage back across the North Atlantic to the New World. Elizabeth's parents were as delighted to see the determined preacher as was their daughter. As the newlyweds began preparations to return to the colonies, William and Elizabeth Dickson Gault and their young son William Jr began making their own preparations for the long ocean voyage. Mother Gault's brother and sister-in-law, William and Elizabeth Campbell Dickson also joined the Dunlop expedition and journeyed with them to the far-off valley on New York's western frontier.

Arriving in New York Harbor and disembarking on an East River wharf, Rev. Dunlop's party boarded a river sloop and sailed up the Hudson to Albany where they began their overland journey to Cherry Valley. The road from Albany to the little village of Schenectady was a decent thoroughfare for wagon traffic if the weather was agreeable and the ruts and mud were not too deep. But by 1742, the road that continued up the Mohawk to Canajoharie was little more than an old Indian trail with a few Dutch homesteads scattered along the way. Fort Johnson, half-way between Schenectady and Canajoharie, was in its initial stages of being built but might still have offered the weary travelers a brief respite from their travel. William Johnson's trading post was one of the last places they could stock up on some of the provisions they would need to see them through their first winter on the frontier. After reaching the homestead of the Schrembling brothers at what would become the village of Canajoharie, the little caravan of pioneers set out on a twenty-mile trek south along Canajoharie Creek into the Brimstone Hills. Upon passing Tekaharwah Falls and cresting the notch at the head of Cherry Valley Creek, the sight and smell of chimney smoke rising from the cabins of their Ulster relatives must have been a glorious sight. Reaching the small settlement, the Dunlops, Gaults, and Dicksons were overwhelmed with emotion as they reunited with the families who had left

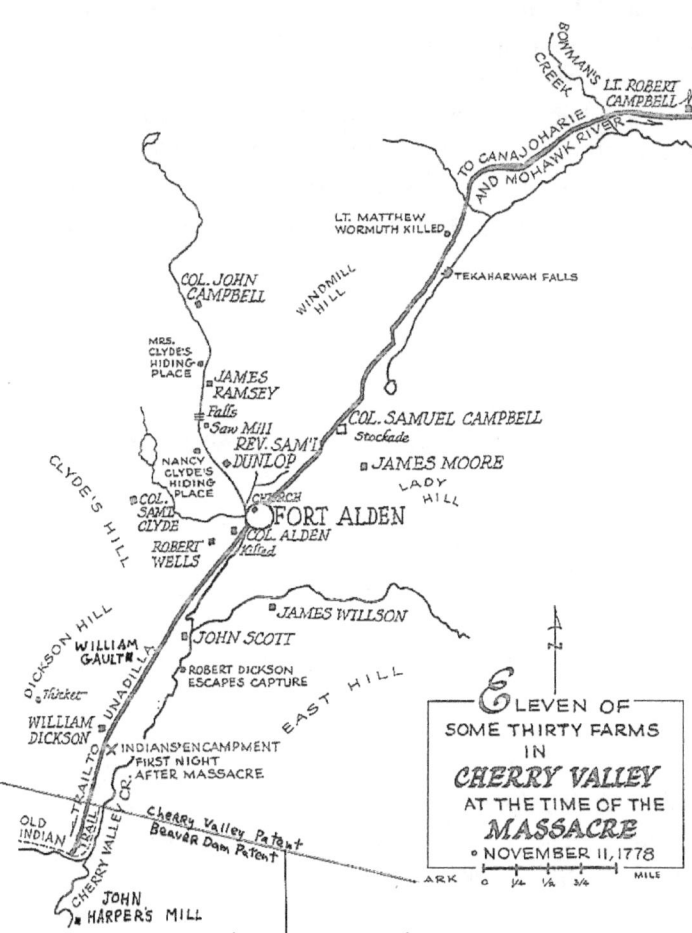

Northern Ireland twenty years earlier on one of Robert Temple's ships. The Campbells, Ramseys, and Davidsons would have welcomed their kinsmen into their humble abodes and offered them shelter until they could begin clearing their own forest openings and building their cabins. Together, their hard work and ingenuity would yield one of the earliest and most substantial settlements in New York's frontier border region. Tragically, however, the settlement of Cherry Valley was doomed to become infamous for the atrocities that would one day be visited upon its citizenry. [30]

William Gault Jr had just turned four when he crossed the Atlantic with his parents and made his way through the wilderness with them to Cherry Valley in '42. The Gault and Dickson cousins settled near each other along the old Indian trail that ran through their settlement connecting Canajoharie to the Susquehanna's Oneida villages of Unadilla and Onaquaga. Their adjacent homesteads were on the south end of Lindsley Patent, between Dickson Hill and East Hill, just over the line from the Harper's Beaver Dam Patent. William was sixteen when the Harper family joined his little settlement in '54 and set up their mill site homestead about a mile south of the Gaults and Dicksons. Having come of age next door to John and Abigail's daughter Margaret, who was about the same age, it was natural for Margaret Harper and William Gault to eventually marry and share a life together. The couple would lead a happy and fruitful life for twenty-five years, raising six of their eight children before the calamity that would shatter their lives descended upon their homestead. The Gaults, like all of Cherry Valley's settlers, would live to regret their decision to stay in their frontier village through the early years of New York's bloody border war. [31]

Margaret Harper Gault's older sister Mary was twenty-one when she came to Cherry Valley with her family and met thirty-one-year-old James Moore and his brother John. Like many of Cherry Valley's families, the Moore brothers had come to the settlement from Londonderry after emigrating with their family from Northern Ireland to New Hampshire in 1720. They originally hailed from the Bann River's Ballynacreemore Parish, just west of Ballymoney and the Gault family's Kilraught Parish. Mary Harper and James Moore were married in 1758 and soon started a family on James' Lady Hill homestead next to the Campbell family. James was a robust fellow who operated the village blacksmith shop while providing for his growing family of three daughters and two sons. James and his older brother John Moore were both actively involved in their community's civil affairs. John was said to have been crippled, which would have been a severe detriment for anyone living on the frontier. He would spend more of his time in Schenectady and Albany where he became a leading proponent of the Whig party in opposition to the Crown and New York's growing loyalist sentiments. [32]

French and Indian War

John Harper Sr's three oldest sons were 25, 23 and 19 when the family arrived in Cherry Valley in the spring of '54. It was a bold move to have come to the Mohawk River frontier when New York was teetering on the brink of yet another war between the European imperialist powers. Europe's Seven Years' War that expanded into North America as the French and Indian War (1754-1763), was yet another attempt to resolve the territorial sovereignty of the disputed lands between the British American colonies and France's Canadian and western territories. England's Royal army and their American militias were allied with most of central New York's Iroquois Confederation while the French were joined by their old northern allies the Wabanaki Confederation. The Lake Champlain/Lake George corridor and the Mohawk River Valley would play major roles in the strategic maneuvering of both armies.

Within a year of their arrival on the Mohawk frontier, the three oldest Harper brothers were thrust into the fray of battle against some of the same enemies their father John faced in Maine's Kennebec wilderness thirty years before. Unlike their father's war that was fought between frontier militias and Indian warriors, this war would be fought by seasoned regiments of European regulars trained in the art of large-scale battlefield formations and lengthy sieges. One of the first major battles of the French and Indian War would be fought on the southern shore of Lake George, seventy-five miles northeast of Cherry Valley and the Harper's Beaver Dam Patent. New York's British colonial forces were led by a handsome young Irishman who had come to the Mohawk River frontier about the same time John Lindsley came in 1739 with his first group of Cherry Valley settlers.

Twenty-three-year-old William Johnson was sent to the Mohawk River wilderness to manage a 6,000-acre patent his uncle Sir Peter Warren acquired on the south side of the Mohawk between Schenectady and Schoharie Creek. The astute young Irishman realized early-on that his uncle's land was on the wrong side of the river to intercept the Indian's trafficking their goods to market via the trails on the north side of the river. He soon established himself on the north side and built an impressive trading post he named Mount Johnson. Before long, he became one of the most successful traders of Indian pelts and furs in the region. Unlike most white traders who went out of their way to cheat the Indians, Johnson gained the trust and respect of his Iroquois counterparts by dealing fairly with them. Adapting to their culture, he became comfortable enough with their customs and rituals to occasionally dress in native garb and share in their ceremonial feasts and festivities. Within five years of arriving on the frontier, he was adopted by the Mohawks who made him an honorary sachem and gave him the Iroquois name, Warraghiyagey. With the trust and influence he gained amongst the Iroquois Indians, particularly the dominant Mohawks, his usefulness to the Crown became indispensable. As rumors of war began circulating through the northern colonies, William was commissioned colonel of a regiment of New York levies and militiamen. Col. Johnson was given the responsibility of convincing the Iroquois chiefs and their warriors to support the British king and his colonial subjects. [33]

Sir William Johnson

The French and Indian War began with the defeat of the British Army near Fort Duquesne, today's Pittsburgh, and the death of the commander-in-chief of the British forces in America, Major General Edward Braddock. Stunned by the loss of their general and nearly half of his 2,000 troops, England pinned their hopes on two other expeditions designed to confront the French forces in New York State. Connecticut's Governor William Shirley was to lead an army up the Mohawk River and over to Lake Ontario's Fort Oswego before continuing across the lake to take Fort Niagara at the mouth of the Niagara River. Colonel Johnson was tasked with leading a regiment of 1,500 provincial New Yorkers and two hundred Mohawk warriors north to Lake Champlain's Crown Point to take Fort St. Frédéric from the French.

Many of Johnson's provincial troops were recruited from the settlements along the Mohawk and throughout the frontier settlements, some of whom were presumably Cherry Valley boys. John Harper's knowledge and experience with frontier Indian warfare and his familiarity with the French and their Abenaki allies, made him a valuable asset for Col. Johnson's Crown Point expedition. At fifty, his services would undoubtedly have been in an advisory role as an aide-de-camp to the colonel. The three oldest Harper brothers were of military age and would have been aching to prove their valor on a field of battle, just as their father had done all those years ago. A friend and Cherry Creek neighbor of James and Mary Moore, Samuel Campbell, was a commissioned ensign in Col. Johnson's regiment and would have encouraged the Harper brothers to join him on the Crown Point expedition. Throughout most of the war the brothers would have spent much of their time in a company of Cherry Valley volunteers led by Capt. Robert McKean. Capt. McKean's rangers were part of a regiment of eight hundred militiamen raised for the defense of the Mohawk frontier settlements. [34]

On route to Crown Point, Col. Johnson halted his advance at Fort Edward, a post on the Hudson River fifteen miles south of Lake George. Leaving a detachment at the fort, Col. Johnson led the bulk of his forces to the south end of Lake George where he established an encampment and waited for intelligence to recommend the right time to advance north to Fort St. Frédéric. Gen. Baron de Dieskau did not wait for Johnson's approach, however. In a bold move the French general took the initiative by deploying two hundred French grenadiers, six hundred Canadian militiamen, and seven hundred Abenaki and Caughnawaga Mohawk warriors down Lake Champlain to South Bay, today's Whitehall. From there he planned to take the garrison at Fort Edward before circling around Johnson's rear flank and surprising his forces on Lake George. But after marching south along Wood Creek and finding the fort's five hundred troops too formidable to attack, Gen. Dieskau began a cautious march north in search of Johnson's army.

On the morning of Sept. 8th, 1755, Col. Johnson sent a scouting party on the road leading south towards Fort Edward to reconnoiter and verify rumors that a French army was approaching from that direction. Learning of Johnson's advancing scout, Gen. Dieskau set up an ambush in a narrow ravine three miles south of Lake George. Johnson's men unwittingly walked directly into the trap and were torn to pieces by Dieskau's Indians attacking from both sides of the road while his grenadiers advanced on their vanguard. The terrible massacre that ensued that morning became known as 'The Bloody Morning Scout'. The French grenadiers and their warriors chased the few surviving militiamen back to Johnson's main encampment where his army and their cannons were waiting behind barricades of overturned wagons, boats, and logs. The British artillery that rained grapeshot down upon the advancing French troops was said to have '...*cut streets, roads and alleys through the perfectly formed lines of French grenadiers...*'. The French eventually withdrew from their field formations while the Indians ran about gathering scalps and torturing their wounded captives. Both commanders were wounded in the bloody foray that concluded with what can only be called a stalemate. While Col. Johnson's expedition to take Fort St. Frédéric was halted and Dieskau's army was forced to return to Canada, neither side could fairly call the battle a victory. Johnson's men did, however, drive the enemy from the field and hold on to both of their positions at Lake George and Fort Edward. This would give the cunning Irishman all the credence he would need to spin the draw to his advantage and promote his reputation as a successful military commander. A grateful King George II awarded the hero of The Battle of Lake George with an English baronetcy and gave him the prestigious title of Superintendent of Indian Affairs in the Northern Department. [35]

Fighting alongside the Harper brothers at the Battle of Lake George was the promising young twelve-year-old Mohawk boy whose English name was Joseph Brant. During the chaos of battle the young warrior was presumably kept under the watchful eye of his guardian and patron, Col. Johnson. Sir William had taken Joseph's older half-sister Molly as his Indian consort and at the age of forty-three married his twenty-one-year-old Mohawk maiden. Throughout their fifteen years together they would have eight children together. Although referred to in his will as '...*my prudent and faithful housekeeper...*', Molly Brant would be Sir William's constant companion and wife throughout his later years. Molly's half-brother Thayendanegea was seven years younger than his half-sister, but even as an adolescent he impressed his powerful new brother-in-law. Taking the boy under his wing, Sir William saw to it that he received an excellent education and European culturalization. He was sent to Reverend Wheelock's Indian Charity School in Connecticut and Sir William personally tutored him on the niceties of social refinement and the subtleties of politics and business. Always remaining true to his Mohawk roots, Joseph became a man of two worlds that were on a collision course with one another. As a grown man, he would be portrayed by his peers as '...*a noble and affable man with a courteous deportment and benevolent disposition...*'. But to those who came to fear and loath him he was '*The Monster Brant*', brutal murderer of women, children and all who stood against him. To John Harper Jr, who would fight with him and against him on many fields of battle, Joseph Brant was neither murderer nor savage. The two young warriors would come to call each other friends and remain so until their deaths. [36]

Over the next three years, following Col. Johnson's contested victory at Lake George, the French and Indian War went poorly for the British and their colonial countrymen. The loss of Fort Oswego in the summer of 1756 was followed by the siege of Fort William Henry the following summer. Sir William had ordered the construction of a formidable fort near the site of his makeshift encampment on Lake George. In August '57, the fort was forced to surrender to an overwhelming force of 8,000 French Grenadiers, Canadian provincials, and Abenaki warriors. The terms of the surrender of Fort William Henry called for the British to lay down their arms and march out of the fort towards Fort Edward under a guard of grenadiers. The French had pledged to protect the unarmed troops from the Indians. The grenadiers, however, could not restrain the young warriors who were hellbent on extracting their bounty of battle spoils. The massacre of the vanquished British and colonial troops as they made their way down to Fort Edward was romanticized in James Fenimore Cooper's *The Last of the Mohicans* and in Michael Mann's 1992 film featuring Daniel Day-Lewis.

The summer campaign of 1758, that followed the loss of their northern forts, began in July with another devastating and costly defeat for the British and colonialists at the Battle of Fort Carillon, at Ticonderoga. With a numerically superior force, the British commander tried to take the French fortification through a series of frontal attacks without the benefit of artillery. His haste and incompetence cost the British 2,500 soldiers killed or wounded before they finally withdrew from the field. As that summer wore on, the tide began to turn in favor of the British with victories at Forts Duquesne, Frontenac and Louisbourg. Britain's good fortunes continued throughout 1759 with victories at Crown Point, Niagara, and Quebec, and the recapturing of Fort Ticonderoga. [37]

Throughout the French and Indian War, the settlements along the Mohawk River and the outlying settlements scattered throughout the frontier were constantly under the threat of attack. Roving bands of French troops and Indian warriors kept the residents of the border region in a constant state of high alert. Cherry Valley's vulnerable position on the frontier outskirts prompted the citizenry to build a small stockade and garrison it with a company of local militiamen. On a cold November morning in 1757, the residents of Cherry Valley awoke to the disturbing news of an attack and brutal massacre at German Flatts, just fifteen miles northwest of their village. The day before, three hundred French troops and Abenaki warriors killed over forty of the settlement's inhabitants, burned all sixty of their homesteads and took 150 prisoners with them back to Quebec. All three of the oldest Harper brothers would have been sent out on patrols with Capt. McKean's Cherry Valley militia to hunt down the French marauders and their Indian accomplices. Cherry Valley's residents managed to avoid the fate of German Flatts' by maintaining a constant vigilance and retaining their small militia garrison. Their village survived relatively unscathed throughout the war, but twenty years later the atrocities of German Flatts would be revisited upon them in the next war.

All the Harpers survived the war, save one. On March 22nd, 1760, while Field Marshal Jeffery Amherst and Col. Johnson were constructing a fleet of small ships at Fort Oswego for their final assault on Montreal, John and Abigail Harper's second son James died of smallpox. He would not live to see the surrender of the French army at Montreal in September or the end of the French and Indian War. Twenty-nine-year-old James Harper would be one of the first interments in the Cherry Valley Cemetery, although his weathered headstone has long since given him up to obscurity. James would not be there for his family when his father's dreams of empire were finally realized eight years later. [38]

Repercussions

Immediately following the French and Indian War another conflict erupted in the Great Lake's Northwest Territory. Resentment over the relentless intrusion of settlers flooding into their ancestral homeland enraged the young Indian warriors of the region. The Ottawa, Huron, Shawnee, Wyandot, Mingos, Kickapoo, Miami, and Lenape, all united with the western Iroquois nations to take up arms against the white interlopers. Pontiac's Rebellion was even more dangerous for the frontier settlers than the previous French War. The isolated homesteaders had to keep a constant vigil against small bands of renegade war parties hunting for scalps and plunder. While most of the bloodiest carnage was on the Ohio frontier, settlements from the Hudson to the Ohio River feared the unpredictable and sudden violence that could rain down upon their communities at any moment.

Through those hard years on the border frontier, the Harpers used their talents to impress the men whose favor they would need to carry-out their grand design. The French War afforded them the opportunity to acquaint themselves with New York's military and political elites, as well as the eastern Iroquois chieftains of the Mohawk and Oneida nations. During the unrest that followed the war, John Harper Jr was often called upon by military commanders and Christian missionaries to accompany them as an interpreter on their expeditions into Indian territory. His time in Rev. Wheelock's Charity School exposed him to the Iroquois dialects and customs of their warrior culture. In November 1764, he traveled to the Oneida village of Onaquaga on the Susquehanna, near today's village of Windsor, with another alumni of Rev. Wheelock's school, Samuel Kirkland. After introducing Kirkland to the village's leading chiefs and spiritual leaders, Gwedethes Agwirongdongwas and Isaac Dakayenensere, John acted as Kirkland's interpreter. Isaac and 'Good Peter', as he was known to the whites, welcomed the white missionaries into their village at a time when tensions between whites and Indians were running high and many of the village's young warriors were off fighting in Pontiac's Rebellion. It was a dangerous time for whites to be moving about in Indian territory and any whites doing so needed a good reason for being there.

Gwedethes Agwirongdongwas, Good Peter

Thirty-year-old John Harper was known to the Onaquaga sachems and had gained enough of their trust by '64 to come and go among their people without being suspected of treachery or mischief. His friendship with Sir William's young protégé, Joseph Brant, helped to reassure the Oneidas to trust in Kirkland and his interpreter. In the summer following his visit to Onaquaga, John traveled to Canajoharie to celebrate his friend Joseph's marriage to Isaac Dakayenensere's beautiful young daughter Nieggen Aoghyatonghsera, or Peggy as she was known to the whites. The trust John had garnered with the Onaquaga sachems would reap enormous dividends three years later when Isaac, Good Peter and three other Oneida chieftains signed a deed to a huge tract of land to the Harpers and their associates. [39]

While Amherst and Col. Johnson were preparing to deploy their fleet down the St. Lawrence to Montreal, and James Harper lay in his freshly dug Cherry Valley grave, William Harper and Margaret Williams of Albany were married on April 13th, 1760. William and Margaret's first child was named after William's recently deceased brother James. A daughter would soon follow and was named after her mother. While spending much of his time mingling with the state's political leaders and land commissioners, William was preparing himself for a career in the judiciary and New York's provincial legislature. He and wife Margaret would spend most of their time living in Schenectady, hobnobbing with local politicians, and traveling to Kingston and New York City to schmooze state officials. Consumed with working in politics and winning the favor of the provincial governors, chief surveyor generals and dubious land commissioners, William also needed to impress the all-powerful Superintendent of Indian Affairs. Without Sir William's support, nothing in the business of appropriating Indian deeds and patent grants could be accomplished. The tricky business of influencing New York's powerful elites and their acolytes was paramount to any parlaying with the Indians for their totems on deeds. While William cajoled influential politicians into facilitating his family's grand scheme, his younger brother John was busy plying the trust he had earned with the Indians toward those ends. [40]

In 1763, John Harper Jr made his way back to his family's old neighborhood on the Connecticut River where he paid a visit to his uncle Joseph and aunt Miriam Thompson Harper in East Windsor. The Harper and Thompson clan would have all turned out to welcome their relative back in the fold and would have been interested in listening to his stories of the battles and campaigns he and his brothers had just taken part in. Aunt Miriam's brother James Thompson and wife Janet would have joined the family reunion with their two young daughters, Miriam and Ruth. Now twenty-one, Miriam would have been just twelve when her Harper cousins left for Cherry Valley in '54. The young lady was now anxious to greet and reacquaint herself with the handsome young man she had known and adored while still just a young girl. John too, had not forgotten about his aunt's young niece and may have been waiting all along for her to mature and grow into womanhood. After getting to know each other all over again, twenty-nine-year-old John Harper and Miriam Thompson were married in the Thompson house in a double wedding ceremony with Miriam's sister Ruth and John's old Middletown friend, Nathan Pelton. Shortly after the ceremony, John and Miriam set out for the backwoods of New York's border region and the Harper family's Beaver Dam Patent. The couple's first child, Archibald, was born a year later and throughout their fifteen years together they would be blessed with six more children. [41]

The Harper family remained on their 500-acre Beaver Dam Patent and Cherry Valley throughout the French and Indian War and Pontiac's Rebellion. The decade of peace and prosperity that followed allowed them to redirect their focus from military concerns to their unrelenting quest for Indian lands and patent grants. The family would suffer another agonizing setback in 1767 when the family matriarch, fifty-eight-year-old Abigail Montgomery Harper, contracted tuberculosis and suffered for months before dying on a cold Sunday morning in late December. Her suffering finally at end, she was buried in the Cherry Valley Cemetery alongside her son James, who like herself, would not live to see her family's dreams of empire come to fruition. [42]

(1676 - 1740)   (1682 - 1725)
James Harper + Janet Lewis

(1698 – 1740)   (?)
1 William Harper + Rachel Robinson
- 1 George Harper + ?
  - 2 Jean Harper + Alexander McFarland
    - 3 Sarah Harper + James Henderson

(1699 - ?)   (?)
2 Anne Harper + James Miller

(1700 – 1791)   (1689 – 1772)
3 Joseph Harper + Miriam Thompson - (William Thompson + Mary Milne)
- 1 James Harper + Sarah Burroughs
  - 2 Joseph Harper + Isabella McKnight

(1701 – 1749)   (1703 – 1743)
4 Sarah Harper + John Montgomery - (William Montgomery + Mary Aken)

(1705 – 1786)   (1709 -1767)
5 John Harper Sr + Abigail Montgomery - (William Montgomery + Mary Aken)

   (1729 – 1816)   (?)
  1 William Harper Esq + Margaret Williams
  - 1 James Harper + ?
    - 2 Margaret Harper + ?

   (1731 – 1760)
  2 James Harper +

   (1733 -1798)   (1725 -1787)
  3 Mary Harper + James Moore
  - 1 Jane Moore + John Powell
    - 2 Abigail Moore + David Cully
      - 3 Mary Moore + Matthew Cully
        - 4 John Moore + Elizabeth Craft
          - 5 James Moore + ?

   (1734 -1811)   (1742 – 1778)   (1745 – 1825)
  4 Col. John Harper Jr + ¹ Miriam Thompson + ² Isabella McKnight Harper
  - 1 Archibald Harper + Sarah Douglas
    - 2 Margaret Harper + Roswell Hotchkiss
      - 3 James Harper + Sarah Montgomery
        - 4 Mary Harper + ?
          - 5 Rebecca Harper + Thomas Montgomery
            - 6 John I. Harper + Amanda Rudd
              - 7 Ruth Harper + Thomas Dunbar
                - 8 Abigail Harper + Daniel Clark – (Isabella McKnight Harper)
                  - 9 Polly Harper + James Ells – (Isabella McKnight Harper)

      (1738 – 1787)   (1738 – 1785)

5 Margaret Harper + William Gault
  1 John Gault + Irene Luce
    2 William Gault + ?
      3 Miriam Gault + John Church
        4 James Gault + Agnus King
          5 Joseph Gault + Esther Dart
            6 Matthew Gault + Sally Griggs
              7 Alexander Gault + ?
                8 Abigail Gault + ?

      (1742 – 1805)   (1745 - ?)

6 Maj. Joseph Harper + Catherine Douglas
  1 Joseph Harper + ?
    2 John Harper + ?
      3 Margaret Harper + ?
        4 Agnus Harper + ?
          5 Mary Harper + ?
            6 Alexander Harper + ?
              7 Montgomery Harper + [1] Sabrine Rice + [2] Angelina Parshall Alger
                8 Joshua Harper + Permelia Luce

      (1743 – 1798)   (1749 – 1833)

7 Lt. Col. Alexander Harper + Elizabeth Bartholomew
  1 Margaret Harper + Aaron Wheeler
    2 John A. Harper + [1] Lorain Minor + [2] Cynthia Harmon
      3 James A. Harper + Sarah Minor
        4 William A. Harper + Sarah Robertson
          5 Elizabeth Harper + Abraham Tappan
            6 Mary Harper + Adna Cowles
              7 Alexander A. Harper + Electra Martin
                8 Robert A. Harper + Polly Hendry

      (1745 – 1786)   (? – 1820)

8 Abigail Harper + Maj. William McFarland
  1 Eunice McFarland + John Tedle

      (1749 – 1813)   (? – 1820)

9 Miriam Harper + Maj. William McFarland
  1 Benjamin Hartwell + Polly Lamont   (Adopted)
    2 Parthenia Mingus + James Hamilton (Adopted)

2
Property Line
1764-1777
'A small tract of vacant and unappropriated land in the county of Ulster'

At the close of the French and Indian War in 1763, the British Empire had a vast and troubled new land to integrate into their North American colonies. Their newly acquired French territories expanded their American territory from the Atlantic to the Mississippi and from the St. Lawrence to Spain's Florida colony. European proprietorship of the continent's western territories had been resolved, but the struggle between its Native American inhabitants and the Anglo usurpers was far from settled. British colonial land speculators, investors and settlers felt they had a right to the territory they had just fought to secure for England and were anxious to begin capitalizing on their hard-earned spoils. The Iroquois of west central New York and their brethren in the Great Lake's Northwest Territory were of a different opinion as to who should be entitled to France's former *Pays d'en Haut*. The Indian nations of the region, who had fought alongside the French armies, had been abandoned by their French fathers and were infuriated by their broken promises. They were not, however, interested in aligning themselves with yet another European power whose promises were every bit as suspect.

Strapped by enormous war debts incurred during the greater European Seven Years' War and America's French and Indian War, King George III was in no hurry to encourage settlement in England's newfound territory or invoke another costly frontier war with the Indians. They could ill afford to manage or govern a new frontier colony. To soothe tensions between the settlers anxious to colonize the western lands and the Indians of western New York and beyond, England imposed a territorial property line to discourage settlers from venturing into Indian territory. The Proclamation Line of 1763 was a unilaterally proclaimed boundary that ran along the Appalachian Mountain ridge between the watersheds of the Atlantic rivers and the St. Lawrence and Mississippi rivers. It was an ill-conceived and unenforceable barrier that failed miserably at pacifying the Indians or stemming the tide of land-hungry settlers streaming into their western lands. It actually had the reverse effect it was intended for. By preventing speculators from obtaining validation from the Crown for any deeds they might wrangle from the Indians, determined settlers were left with no alternative but to squat on any piece of land they found desirable and felt they could defend. Without clear titles to any of the frontier lands, squatters could take their chances with the local Indians and base the ownership of their homesteads on the improvements they made to them. It was shaky legal grounds, but the Crown was a long way from the backwoods of the western frontier. England's Proclamation Line did little to resolve the Indian versus settler problems and ultimately only served to advance the angst and hostility both sides felt for the other. [1]

Most white settlers felt nothing but contempt for their Indigenous frontier neighbors and England's postwar policy towards the Indians did nothing to dissuade those sentiments. Many of the commanders of British forces in the western theater were ignorant of Indian culture and not well versed in the delicate diplomacy required to negotiate with their chiefs and sachems. Gift-giving and ceremonial protocol, if not properly handled, could easily insult the Indians and lead to no good. Considered their just reward for sharing their ancestral homeland with the whites, gifts had long been an expected recompense for their generosity and neglecting that tradition was viewed as highly disrespectful. Disregard for the custom of proper gift-giving was enough to offend and provoke the Indians into taking up the warclub. Having been the recipients of France's tobacco, flour, rum and gunpowder for many years, the western nations had grown accustomed to the staples and fineries of their European benefactors. Anglo arrogance and a stubborn unwillingness to observe the customs and traditions of the defeated French allies would cost the British and their colonial subjects dearly.

Following the French and Indian War, the western Iroquois and the western nations of the *Pays d'en Haut* initiated another brutal war against British Colonial America. Local frontier militias and the King's Royal Regiments were again called out to fight the Indians throughout western New York, Pennsylvania, and the Ohio frontier. Led by the Ottawa chieftain Pontiac, his warriors were believed to have driven over 4,000 homesteaders from their western settlements and killed another 1,000-1,500 militiamen and settlers before Pontiac's Rebellion was finally put down. With the acknowledgement of his king and the trust he had garnered with the Iroquois, Sir William Johnson was called upon to negotiate peace with the western nations. A treaty council was held at Oswego's Fort Ontario in the summer of 1766 between the British and Pontiac's followers. Three-and-a-half years after the Treaty of Paris ended the French and Indian War, Sir William, Pontiac, and representatives of the western nations signed the Treaty of Fort Ontario. The treaty brought about a tenuous resolution to hostilities with promises of limited incursions into the land west of the Proclamation Line. It also laid the groundwork for the establishment of a more permanent and agreeable property line between the native population and the land-hungry whites. [2]

Sir William and Pontiac at Fort Ontario

In late August 1768, small groups of Indians from all over the western territories began arriving and setting up camps in the fields around Fort Stanwix at the head of the Mohawk River, in today's city of Rome, NY. The chiefs and warriors of Pontiac's Ohio nations and New York's Iroquois Confederation were again called back to yet another council fire with the ubiquitous Sir William Johnson. The 3,000 Indians that were soon encamped around the old fort were hosted by British delegations from the provincial colonies of New York, New Jersey, Pennsylvania, Virginia, and the Carolinas. The colonial delegations were led by the two Superintendents of Indian Affairs from the northern and southern departments, Sir William Johnson and South Carolina's John Stuart. Authorized and financed by England's Board of Trade, the Fort Stanwix treaty conference was intended to establish a mutually agreed upon property line that would replace the old irrelevant Proclamation Line of '63, thus hopefully resolving the dispute over white and Indian sovereignty. The conference itself would require an enormous effort just to entertain and pacify the multitude of Indians who were expecting to be wined and dined for what would turn out to be a two-and-a-half-month-long festival of ceremonies and celebrations.

Sir William was a man who knew how to throw a party and was not about to be as foolish as his British contemporaries had been during the aftermath of the French and Indian War that led to Pontiac's Rebellion. Twenty boatloads of gifts were brought up the Mohawk to enhance the tons of pork, rum, tobacco, and flour meant to keep his guests happy and in a receptive mood for negotiating and compromising. With Johnson's understanding of Indigenous culture and ceremonial protocol, the Board of Trade felt confident in his ability to negotiate a beneficial property line for the Crown. Sir William was of course motivated by a strong desire to please the board and win the favor the king who had the power to validate Indian deeds and grant patents on deeds he already possessed. Outside his official duties, William Johnson was just as ambitious as any other land speculator of his age, anxious to gain more access to the western lands his treaty might open up.

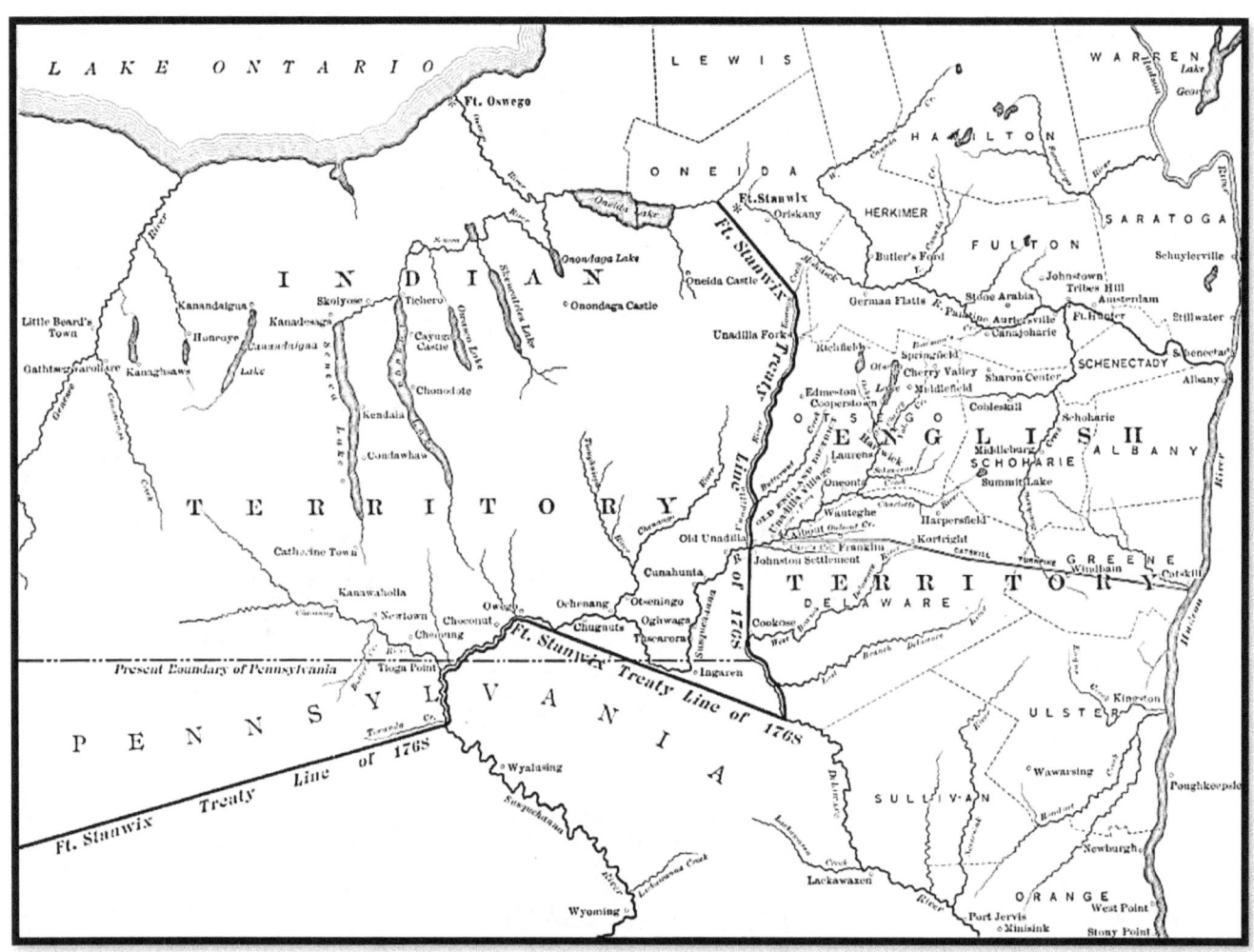

Fort Stanwix Property Line of 1768

On November 5th, 1768, the six chiefs of the Iroquois Confederation's Mohawk, Oneida, Onondaga, Tuscarora, Cayuga, and Seneca nations signed their totems on the Fort Stanwix Treaty. The English paid an unprecedented amount of cash, gifts, and provisions totaling over £13,000 for an agreement they believed would permanently establish a line of demarcation between colonial settlers and the Indian nations of the western frontier. The new Property Line of '68 was to run from a point on Wood Creek about eight miles west of Fort Stanwix along a southwesterly course all the way to the confluence of the Ohio and Tennessee Rivers near Paducah, Kentucky. The portion of the line that ran through New York from Wood Creek, ran along a SSE survey line to the forks of the upper east and west branches of the Tianaderha or Unadilla River. It then continued down the Unadilla River to its confluence with the Susquehanna River at the old Oneida village of Unadilla and today's village of Sidney. From here it continued along another survey line due south to the West Branch of the Delaware River's old Indian village of Coke-ose and today's village of Deposit. It then continued down the West Branch past Shehawken at the confluence of the two branches of the upper Delaware to a bend in the river about six miles below today's village of Hancock. From here another survey line ran WNW back to the Susquehanna and the old Indian village of Owego from whence the line followed the Susquehanna down past its junction with the Chemung River to Towanda in today's Bradford County, Pennsylvania. The property line then took a decidedly southwesterly course towards the Allegheny and Ohio Rivers before continuing down the Ohio to the Tennessee River, just shy of the Mississippi. The portion of the property line between

Unadilla Forks and the bend in the river below Hancock still serves today as the western boundary lines of New York's Otsego and Delaware Counties.

By all appearances, the six nations of the Iroquois Confederation did quite well for themselves at the Fort Stanwix Treaty Conference. They were successful in negotiating a line that retained most of their western territories and set the limit for white colonization to their eastern most Oneida and Mohawk territories that had already begun accommodating white settlers. The western nations who had fought alongside Pontiac in the Ohio and Illinois territory, were not as successful as their eastern brethren who had dominated much of the negotiations. The agreement the western nations petitioned for with the superintendent of the southern district was for the new property line to have run south from the Ohio River along the Kanawha River to the Appalachian Ridge, thus retaining Kentucky and Tennessee as Indian territory. New York's Mohawk and Oneida delegation seemed to have leveraged the lands of their Cherokee, Shawnee, Delaware, and Mingo brothers to their own advantage, thus saving most of their territory at the latter's expense. The Iroquois did concede one valuable piece of land between the Hudson and St. Lawrence waterways known as the Oneida Carry or Deowainsta. The eight-mile portage between Fort Stanwix at the head of the Mohawk and Oneida Lake's Wood Creek had long been controlled by the Oneida Nation who profited mightily from the fur trading traffic that flowed between Lake Ontario and Albany. By either charging or extorting traders who wished to carry their merchandise over their portage, the Oneida had made a healthy profit throughout the years. The sacrifice of this valuable piece of real estate may have enabled them to preserve more of their eastern territory. [3]

Patents

By 1768, the outlying settlements scattered along the southern frontier of the Mohawk River Valley and down through the Schoharie Valley were as far into the Indian's territory as most white settlers were willing to go. Richfield, Springfield, Andrustown, Cherry Valley, Sharon Springs, and Cobleskill were flanked by the Dutch Dorfs along Schoharie Creek. A few substantial settlements on the East Branch of the Delaware from Paghatakan at today's Delaware County village of Margaretville/Arkville to Pawpachton near today's Downsville, completed an arch that encircled the border region between them and the new property line. Before the Fort Stanwix Conference, the process of procuring deeds from the Iroquois for their eastern lands had quietly been going on for a while. Groups of investors and speculators were busy courting chieftains and sachems in anticipation of a permanent border line resolution that would sanction the lands east of the line for purchase.

With treaty in hand, Sir William Johnson returned to his Johnson Hall estate and began lobbying the king and his provincial land commissioners for patent grants on several of his earlier clandestine land purchases. Other prospective proprietors were busy doing the same. Some of the Indian lands had been purchased shortly before the conference while others were deeded shortly after, and a few had even been purchased while the treaty conference was still ongoing. In the three years following the Treaty of Fort Stanwix, between late '68 and '71, sixty land patents totaling hundreds of thousands of acres were granted, over forty of which were in today's Delaware, Otsego, Schoharie and Greene Counties. Two-thirds of what would become Otsego County and half of what would eventually become Delaware County received patent grants during this period. [4]

Seventeen years before the new property line was established, Sir William added to his already immense property holdings by securing a deed from the Oneida chieftains for a seventy-five-mile-long, by two-mile-wide, tract of land containing about 100,000 acres. Johnson's original 1751 purchase ran from the head of the creek known to the Indians as Adaquatangie, and today as Charlotte Creek, down to its junction with the Susquehanna at Oneonta and on down the Susquehanna to the Pennsylvania State line. It contained all the coveted riverfront flats along both sides of the creek and river, one mile from each bank. The Property Line of '68, negotiated by Johnson himself, ceded all the Susquehanna west of the

Unadilla to the Pennsylvania State line back to the Iroquois who were undoubtedly pleased to reclaim nearly half of his original acreage.

The Indians had long claimed that Johnson never fully compensated them for the purchase, which was unusual considering Sir William's reputation for always having dealt fairly with his Native American counterparts. His arrangement with the Oneidas for their Susquehanna lands may have been contingent upon the Crown's confirmation of his deed, which had not been forthcoming. Sir William had already stretched his patronage by having been granted a tract of 90,000 acres on the northside of the Mohawk known as the Royal or Kingsland Grant, and another 50,000 acres in the Kingsborough Patent northeast of Johnstown. The king's reluctance to confirm another large tract of land to Sir William was meant to keep him from extending his holdings too far into the Indian lands of the western frontier and encouraging settlement there on. [5]

When Sir William's Susquehanna River Patent was finally confirmed by the Crown in May of 1770, a year-and-a-half after ratification of the treaty line, his remaining 54,000 acres of the original 100,000-acre purchase was again reduced by half. The Crown had not been totally satisfied with Johnson's treaty agreement, claiming he had been too generous with New York's Iroquois at the expense of the western nations by extending the southwestern property line down the Ohio River all the way to the Tennessee River. Alexander Wallace, a wealthy New York City merchant and favorite of the Crown, was awarded the 28,000-acre Wallace Patent that extended along the Susquehanna from its confluence with Charlotte Creek to the new property line, or Oneonta to Sidney. Johnson was awarded the remaining 26,000-acre Charlotte Creek Patent that ran up the creek from Oneonta to its headwaters near Schoharie County's Summit Lake. Sir William had other irons in the fire and following the treaty's ratification he received several other grants for another 75,000 acres in portions of another eight patents. Such was the duplicitous nature of land acquisitions during the colonial period of empire building and western expansion.

By the time of his untimely death in 1774, just a year before the outbreak of the Revolution, Sir William owned nearly a quarter of a million acres of central New York's former Iroquois lands. Unfortunately for Sir William's children and their families, they would have precious little time to enjoy the lavish lifestyle at Johnson Hall and collect the rents from their many tenants on their vast inherited land holdings. When the Revolution finally reached the Mohawk Valley in '77, the Johnsons and their neighbors had already joined the mass exodus of New York's loyalists to Upper Canada. The eloquent manor house Sir William had built at Johnstown and the entirety of the Johnson family's 225,000-acre land holdings were seized by the Committee of Sequestration and gradually resold to American investors and speculators following the war. [6]

The northern department's superintendent of Indian affair's exploitation of his official position for his own personal benefit, paled in comparison to a fellow Irish expatriate whom Sir William had engaged as his deputy agent of Indian affairs in the western sectors. Like Johnson, George Croghan had come to the colonies as an adventurous young man and quickly adapted himself to the people and the culture of the western Indigenous nations. A charismatic and impressive orator, he established himself as a trusted and successful Indian fur trader and a resourceful emissary for the Crown's interests. Even before Sir William deputized him as an Indian agent in 1756, the clever Irishman had amassed huge tracts of Indian lands in western Pennsylvania and throughout the Ohio Territory.

Following the French and Indian War and throughout the late 1760s, Deputy Agent Croghan and his son-in-law, British Major Augustine Prévost Jr, petitioned the king's New York Provincial Governor for licenses to purchase Indian lands from the Onaquaga Oneida chieftains. Croghan was particularly interested in a 40,000-acre tract of land west of Otsego Lake. He was eventually successful in purchasing the tract and was granted a patent to it in late 1769, a year after the property line was established. His patented lands that included all the present-day Otsego County Townships of Otsego, Burlington, New Lisbon and eastern Exeter, mysteriously grew to over 100,000 acres when finally surveyed in '74. By then,

Croghan had acquired nearly a quarter-million acres throughout today's Otsego County. The ambitious Indian agent and land speculator proved to be a man who could never turn down a deal, even though it meant stretching his resources beyond their means. He was eventually forced to sell off all but his Otsego Patent to satisfy his many creditors and mortgages. He tried to attract homesteaders to establish a settlement on the south end of Otsego Lake around his own estate he dubbed 'Croghan's Forest', thus creating a tenant empire. The world, however, had change since the early days of Sir Wiliam's empire building and by the time of Croghan's death in 1782, he had fallen into insolvency and lost all his holdings. The war and his other failed land ventures in the Ohio Territory added to his mounting financial problems which eventually left him landless and virtually penniless. [7]

Croghan's son-in-law, British Major Augustine Prévost Jr, was just as ambitious as his father-in-law when it came to purchasing Indian lands. His father, British Major General Augustine Prévost of the 60th Regt. of Foot had fought for the king in both the French and Indian War and the American Revolution. During the intermission between the two wars, he had applied for a license to negotiate with the Indians for their lands. In the summer of 1767, the same day Croghan applied for his license that netted his Otsego Patent, Prévost and a group of associates applied for a license to negotiate for a 260,000-acre tract of land between the Susquehanna and the West Branch of the Delaware River. Unfortunately, another group of speculators led by an ambitious family of Ulster-Scots had their eyes on the same plot of land and were one step ahead of the major general and his friends. Three months before Prévost's license application was submitted, John Harper Sr and his four sons presented New York's provincial governor with a certificate from Sir William Johnson authorizing his approval for a license application that would allow the Harpers to negotiate with the Oneidas for the same parcel of land.

Harper Purchase

On August 4th, John Harper Jr and his brother William attended a meeting at Johnson Hall with Sir William and four Oneida chief from Onaquaga. Isaac Dakayenensere and Good Peter Agwirongdongwas were among the chiefs who had come to Sir William's home to seek his advice as to a fair price for the lands they had agreed to sell to the Harpers. The Harpers were offering $1,500 while the chieftains were holding out for £1000, an equivalent of about $2,000. Sir William suggested the Harpers pay $1,800 or an equivalent of £720 in York currency, the latter of which was accepted and agreed upon by both parties. Prévost's estimate of the track's acreage was far more in line with the actual acreage. The Harpers had grossly misrepresented it as being just 100,000 acres. None of the tract had actually been surveyed yet, and as was often the case, acreage was subject to interpretation by whoever's best interest it served. On June 14th, 1768, ten months after the Johnson Hall meeting and a few months before the first Iroquois representatives began arriving at Fort Stanwix for the property line conference, the Harpers and six other investors met again at Sir William's estate for a deed signing ceremony overseen by New York's Provincial Governor, Sir Henry Moore. The Harpers and their associates paid a portion of the £720 York currency they had agreed to, securing the deed to the huge tract of land between the Susquehanna and the West Branch that had curiously grown to match Prévost's 260,000-acre estimate. Augustine Prévost was not to be denied his piece of the pie, however, as he was now and had always been among the other associates in the Harper venture. [8]

John Harper Sr's son John had befriended many of the Oneida leaders whose land it was the Harpers were interested in purchasing. Taking full advantage of the trust he had garnered among the tribal chieftains, he was able to convince them to sign over their ancestral homeland to his family and the white settlers who were sure to follow. His good friends, Isaac and Good Peter, were two of the Oneida chieftains who signed the deed their friend John assured them was to their best advantage. The Harper purchase that commenced at the head of the West Branch of the Delaware was bordered on the southeast by the Great Hardenburgh Patent, the northwest by Johnson and Wallace's patent and on the west side by a proposed patent that would run between the property line and the Canniskutty survey line that ran between the mouth of Walton's Bobs Brook and the mouth of Ouleout Creek.

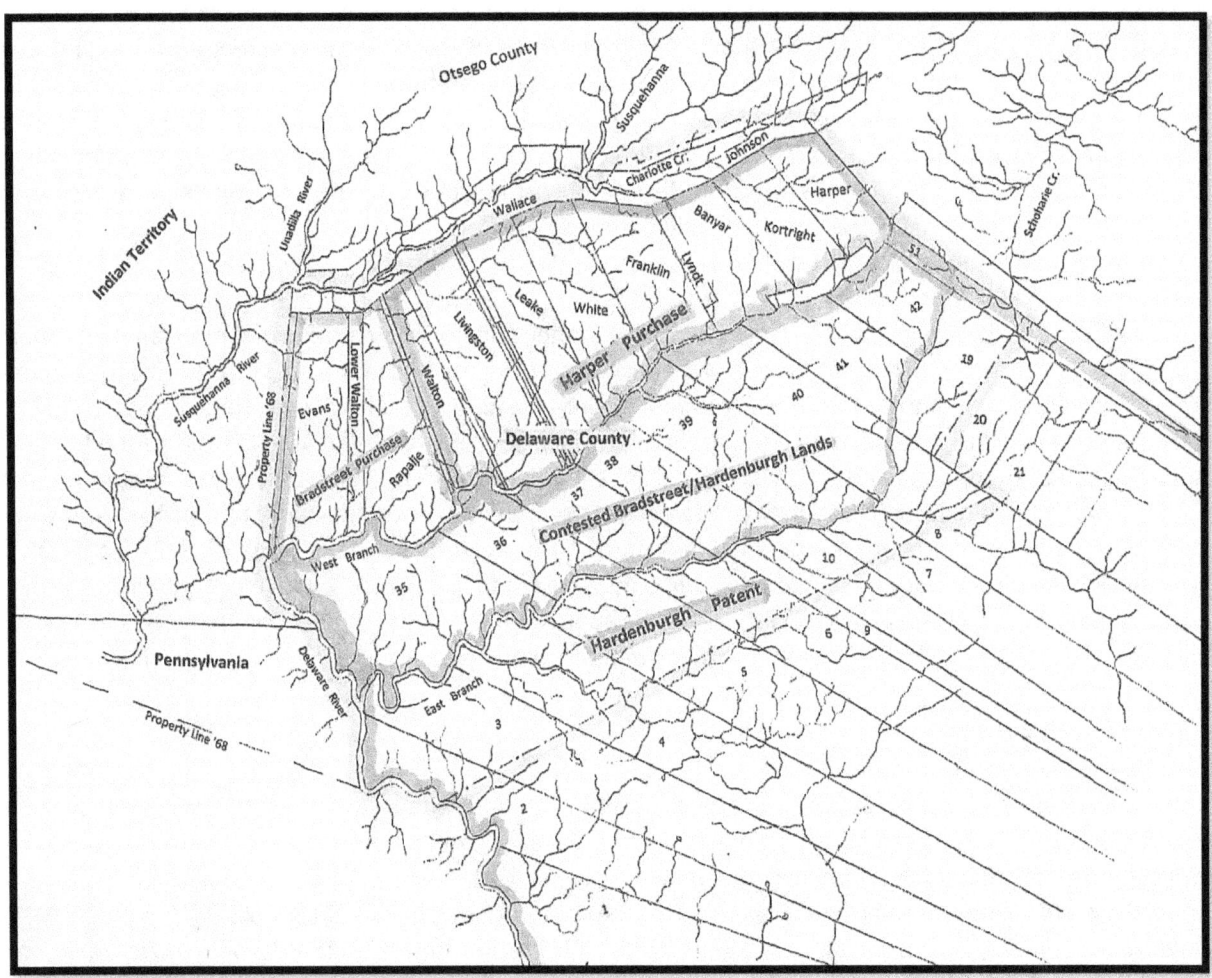

Patents and Land Purchases within New York's Present-Day County of Delaware

On December 8th, 1769, a year after purchasing their deed, John Sr and the four Harper brothers were awarded a patent by their '...*Sovereign Lord George the Third, King of England France & Ireland...*' for 22,000 acres on the far-northeast end of the purchase. The names of seventeen other phantom grantees, who were friends and relatives of the Harpers, were included on the letter of patent to comply with the archaic English rule that allowed for only 1,000 acres to be granted to any one person at a time. Within a few years of securing their patent, the Harpers had surveyed the patent into 220, 100-acre homestead lots which they began advertising for sale or lease. In the spring of '71, all the Harper families, except the Gaults and Moores of Cherry Valley, began clearing and building their homesteads on a few of the lots in the center of their patent. [9]

While the Harpers were surveying their patent into homestead lots, the remainder of their purchase was being surveyed into seven other substantial patents and a half-dozen smaller patents. Between February and June 1770, letters of patent were expeditiously granted by the Crown to groups of wealthy investors and speculators. Many of these grantees had served with distinction throughout the French and Indian War in the King's Royal American Regiments. Lawrence Kortright had made his fortunes privateering during the French and Indian War and was awarded for his service to the king with a 22,000-acre patent next to the Harper Patent. A Pennsylvania businessman and politician, Thomas Wharton, acquired a 30,000-acre patent along with six other investors that included the governor of New Jersey,

Benjamin Franklin's son William Franklin. New York City merchants William Walton and Henry White wrangled their way into patents for 20,000 and 38,000-acre patents respectively. Alexander McKee, John G. Leake, and the ever-scheming Augustine Prévost also managed to acquire large patent grants in the Harper purchase. A half-dozen other British officers were granted patents for smaller tracts of land throughout the Harper purchase.

Most of these patent proprietors immediately began capitalizing on their investments by sending out their own teams of surveyors to run out property lines and subdivide their patents into homestead lots. Within a year-and-a-half of the Fort Stanwix Treaty agreement, much of the land between the Susquehanna and the West Branch of the Delaware was open for settlement. With the exception of the Harpers, none of these frontier profiteers would ever live on, or even lay eyes on their lands. Most of them would remain faithful to the king and eventually forfeit their patents and deeds to the Committee of Sequestration following the Revolution. In the years prior to the war, few homesteaders were anxious to settle any closer to the property line and the Indian territory than the Kortright and Harper Patents on the northeastern end of the Harper purchase. [10]

Hardenburgh Patent and Bradstreet Purchase

In 1706, six decades before the Fort Stanwix Treaty Conference, '... *a small tract of vacant and unappropriated land in the county of Ulster...*', was purchased by Johannis Hardenburgh from the Esopus chieftain Nanisnos for £60. Two years later, the purchase and deed were granted, ratified, and confirmed by Queen Anne and New York's Provincial Governor Edward Cornbury to Hardenburgh and six others. Amazingly, the '*small tract*' ultimately wound up containing around a million-and-a-half acres that included all of today's Sullivan County, the western two-thirds of Ulster County, the southeastern half of Delaware County and nearly all of the Catskill Mountains. The incongruities between Indian deeds and the claims declared in patent petitions by white entrepreneurs was a common and accepted reality of land acquisitions in the eighteenth century. The duplicitous Hardenburgh Patent, would languish in uncertainty and inactivity for the next forty years, owing in part to the inaccessible terrain of the Catskills and the question as to the validity of the original Indian deed.

In 1746, burdened by the vagueness of the property's boundaries and the insistence of the Lenape chieftains that just one signature of a chieftain was not enough to validate an Indian deed, the patent proprietors arranged for another council with the Indians to secure a proper deed for their tract. The Lenape chieftains were also firm in their position that they were still the only rightful owners of the lands between the two branches of the upper Delaware. They insisted that the original 1706 deed signed by the Esopus chieftain did not include their lands, thus defining the East Branch of the Delaware as the Hardenburgh Patent's northwestern boundary. By '46, Johannis Hardenburgh was the only original grantee still invested in the patent. Robert Livingston and the Verplanck family had begun buying up much of the patent rights from the other original grantees. The Livingston families would eventually become proprietors of the majority of the entire Hardenburgh Patent.

Through a series of negotiations and another £149 19s, Hardenburgh and Livingston acquired a second deed from eighteen Lenape and Oneida chieftains for what they claimed was all the lands between the Delawares. They interpreted their second deed as extending their property rights to the West Branch of the Delaware which they presumed to be the main branch of the river, therein laying the grounds for the rub that followed. Assuming that Queen Anne's original 1708 Royal Grant had included all the lands to the West Branch, Hardenburgh and Livingston neglected to petition King George II for a new grant on their second deed of 1746. This minor detail and the question that arose twenty years later as to just which branch of the Delaware truly was the main branch of the river, opened the door for a controversial litigation that would hold the Hardenburgh Patent in limbo for years. [11]

One week before the Fort Stanwix Treaty was signed in late October '68, a huge tract of nearly 350,000 acres of land was signed over by the Oneida chieftains of Onaquaga to an ambitious colonel in the king's army. Many of the attendees of the two-and-a-half-month-long conference were interested in more than just establishing a property line to satisfy their king and his Board of Trade. Col. John Bradstreet had served his king well in both the French and Indian War and Pontiac's Rebellion but his unauthorized attempt to bring about a peaceful resolution to Pontiac's War got him into trouble with his superiors. Accused of having been too easy on the Indians and acquiescing too readily to their demands, he appears to have made more friends among the Native Americans than he did his own British commanders. Throughout the two wars, Bradstreet had served as the army's deputy quartermaster general in Albany where he made many friends among the state's bureaucrats and land commissioners. Bradstreet appears to have used his lucrative Albany appointment as a vehicle to promote his own unsatiable appetite for Indian lands.

Col. John Bradstreet

With the help of George Croghan, John Butler and the promise of a £1,400 payment, Col. Bradstreet managed to convince the Oneida chieftains to sign over all the lands between the Canniskutty line and the proposed property line, as well as all the lands between the East and West Branches of the Delaware River. His new deed described his property lines as starting on the West Branch of the Delaware at the mouth of Canniskutty Creek from whence it followed a survey line NNW to the confluence of Oweritowit, Ouleout Creek, and the Susquehanna. The boundary line then ran down the Susquehanna to the proposed property line at the mouth of the Tianaderha or Unadilla River, then south down along the purposed property line to the West Branch at the Cookhouse, Deposit. From the Cookhouse, instead of returning up the West Branch to its point of origin at the Canniskutty, it took a controversial course by proceeding down the Delaware to Shehawken, Hancock, at the mouth of the Pawpachton or East Branch. The deed then extended his property line up along the East Branch to its source near Grand Gorge, then over to the head of the West Branch near Stamford and down the West Branch to its point of origin at the mouth of the Canniskutty.

Bradstreet and the Oneida chieftains were challenging the validity of the Hardenburgh Patent's northwestern boundary claim. Bradstreet's justification for his audacious attempt to claim all the land between the East and West Branches was based on the simple notion that Johannis Hardenburgh's 1708 and subsequent '46 deed had misrepresented the West Branch of the Delaware as the main branch of the river. His argument was that the river designated in their deeds as the patent's northwest boundary was the East Branch of the Delaware and not the West Branch as the Hardenburgh proprietors claimed. Bradstreet may in fact have had a valid point and the Hardenburgh proprietors may have tipped their hand by recognizing their first deed might only have been for the lands up to the East Branch. Going to the trouble of securing a second deed, the Hardenburgh people's self-admission as to their original deed's failure to clarify their northwest boundary, left a gaping fissure for a legal challenge. Further seizing on the fact that the Hardenburgh proprietors had failed to seek or obtain King George II's confirmation of their second deed, Bradstreet felt confident he could challenge their claim to the land between the rivers. His argument hinged on the definition as to which branch of the Delaware was the 'Main Branch' and which branch its tributary. [12]

After three long years of litigation, New York's provincial magistrates finally pronounced Lake Utsayantha as the 'Head of the Delaware', thereby justifying the Hardenburgh proprietors claim that the West Branch had always been the northwest boundary of their patent. After losing his case against the Hardenburgh proprietors, Col. Bradstreet relinquished his bid for the lands between the two upper

Delawares and died three years later in 1774. Proprietorship of the 85,000 acres between the Canniskutty line and the property line of '68 remained unresolved at his death. The war that broke out a year later and the fact that George Croghan had neglected to transfer all of John Bradstreet's payments to the Oneidas, further complicated efforts by his heirs to secure any part of his original deed. Another round of litigation would have to wait until after the war.

Finally, in early 1786, the colonel's three daughters, son Samuel, and son-in-law Charles J. Evans paid £2,600 for a patent of 55,000 acres of the colonel's original deeded lands between the Susquehanna and the West Branch of the Delaware. Although a far cry from the 350,000 acres their father had claimed as his rightfully deeded property, Colonel Bradstreet's children were fortunate to have recovered what little portion of it they did. Throughout the fifteen years it took to secure this smaller portion of the colonel's original deed, another petition for 30,000 acres of the colonel's land was submitted and granted to John Rapalje and associates. Albany's unscrupulous Land Commissioner Goldsborough Banyar and the State Surveyor General William Cockburn had contrived to facilitate another duplicitous land transaction. Many of the provincial and later state public officers were unsalaried positions, with recompence for their services acquired through the collection of exorbitant fees on license applications, grant petitions and letters of patents. Bribery and extortion could certainly be employed to make the shrewdest of these land commissioners comply with the wishes of an ambitious group of investors. [13]

Pre-War Border Settlement

With all the difficulties facing the proprietors of the Hardenburgh Patent, pressure was mounting to colonize the land and attract settlers to their Great Lots. A requirement imposed on most of the king's patent grants was for the patentees to have settled a specific number of homesteaders on their lands by a certain period of time, usually three to five years. But like so many of the king's property decrees and regulations, few proprietors paid much attention to this one or ever lost their patent due to noncompliance with it. Most of the Great Lots of the Hardenburgh Patent had gone decades without so much as a single homesteader turning a single stone on one of their homestead lots. The proprietors of the patent's fifty Great Lots were disadvantaged by the legal encumbrances that hung over the patent like a dark cloud. They could not transfer clear titles to prospective buyers when they themselves were not in possession of clear titles to their properties in the ever-contested patent. The rugged terrain and the provisional land/lease contracts landlords were reduced to offering to prospective buyers/tenants discouraged many from venturing into the unforgiving Catskills. With all the uncertain legitimacy surrounding the Hardenburgh Patent, there were still a few who could not resist the call of the wild and the promise of a better life on the western frontier.

Emboldened by the end of the French and Indian War, a group of impatient pioneers began eying the *'vacant and unappropriated lands'* of Ulster County's western frontier. Encouraged by Robert Livingston, who offered four men lucrative terms on a modest tract of land on the far northwest end of his Great Lot #7, a caravan of interrelated families from the Hudson River's frontier settlements of Marbletown and Hurley set out for the Delaware's East Branch in the spring of 1763. Six months before the Proclamation Line of '63 was declared, four Dutch families loaded their belongings into ox-drawn carts and headed up Esopus Creek along the old Indian trail through the Great Shandaken. From the ancient Esopus village of Kawiensinck, the little caravan found its way over Pine Hill and down along the Bush Kill into the valley of the Pawpachton. At the conflux of the Bush Kill and the East Branch, an abandoned Lenape village offered the advantages of a partially cleared riverfront flats with open pastures and a few apple orchards. The former Lenape and Esopus inhabitants of Paghatakan had long been acquainted with the Hudson River Dutch fur traders and long-hunters with whom they had interacted and developed congenial relationship. A few families of affable Indians still lingered around Paghatakan and down along the Pawpachton's riverfront flats to Papachton, near today's Downsville. These indigenous holdouts were a mix of old Esopus, Lenape and Tuscarora families who posed little threat to the new settlers. A few of the older Dutch gentlemen were known from time to time to have shared a jug of hard-cider with an old Esopus warrior named Teunis, who told them tall tales of conquest and adventure in the days before Pa'Ka-Ta'Kan knew of the white man. With time and more white settlers, Teunis finally retired to a quiet mountain enclave where he spent the final years of his life on the shores of a small lake that came to bear his name. [14]

The first four pioneer families to penetrate the Catskills were led by two brothers from an old family of exiled Huguenots from the West Flanders or Belgium region of France's Dept. du Nord. Petrus and Hermanus Dumond's great-grandfather, Wallerand Du Mont, had come to New Amsterdam in 1657 as a cadet in the Dutch West Indies Company while New York was still under Dutch rule. The little Niew Nederland's outpost of Wiltwyck had been the center of trade and commerce between the Dutch fur traders and the Esopus Indians for fifty years by the time Du Mont arrived there in the early '60s. Wallerand served as a member of the Military Council and fought through the 2nd Esopus War. His military accomplishments and subsequent success as a Kingston merchant secured his position as a magistrate of the growing Hudson River community. It also propelled his family's ascension into the hierarchy of New York's old Dutch political elites. Wallerand Du Mont's grandson, and Petrus and Hermanus Dumond's father, Igenas, had married Catherine Schuyler, a member of one of New York's prominent Dutch families and daughter of Albany's Mayor David Schuyler.

Petrus and Maria Dumond were both thirty-five when they brought their seven children, ages 1-11, to Paghatakan in 1763. Petrus' younger brother Hermanus had only been married to his wife Janneke (Ginny) Brink for a few years before coming to the valley of the East Branch with their infant daughter. Petrus' wife Maria's brother Johannis Van Waggenen had just married his second wife Helena Kittle a year before bringing her and their young daughter along on the expedition into the Catskill frontier. The Van Waggenen's also brought along Johannis' two daughters by his first wife Elizabeth Burhans and their fourteen-year-old son Simeon Van Waggenen. The fourth family, who came to the Pawpachton settlement with the Marbletown and Hurley families, was another close relative of the Van Waggenens and Dumonds. Peter Hendricks had just recently married Jeremias Kittle's widow Eva Merkle Kittle of Marbletown and joined the Catskill expedition with her and her two sons, twenty-year-old Jeremias and nine-year-old Frederick Kittle. [15]

The first couple of years on the Paghatakan settlement were difficult ones for the four Dutch patriarchs and their families. Were it not for the help and generosity of the few lingering Lenape families, they might not have made it through their first couple of winters on the frontier. Most Hudson River families were reluctant to venture any further into the Catskills than the few scattered settlements along Esopus Creek in the Great Shandaken. Following the Fort Stanwix Treaty of '68, another seven or eight families gradually began filtering into the valley of the Delaware's East Branch, many of whom were relatives of the first four families. By 1771, Peter Burgher and his brother-in-law Albertus Sluyter, Johannis Deyo and wife Geertje Van Waggenen, Peter Hynpagh, James Merkle, John Barrows, and William Yaple were all living in the settlement. Johannis Van Wagenen's son Simeon had established his own homestead near the Dumonds, while Frederick Kittle had taken over his stepfather Peter Hendricks's farm following the old man's death around 1770. By 1778, when the turmoil of war finally reached their quiet river valley, forty families were known to have been living along the East Branch from Paghatakan to Papachton and on down to the confluence of the Beaver Kill near today's village of East Branch. [16]

With Bradstreet's Purchase in limbo and the disputed Hardenburgh Patent lands between the two upper Delawares tied up in litigation, most of the borderland's pre-Revolutionary War settlements were either in the two Susquehanna River patents or the Harper and Kortright Patents north of the West Branch. The Wallace and Johnson Patents had the advantage of communication with the Mohawk's frontier settlements via the Susquehanna River and Cherry Valley Creek. The Harper and Kortright settlers were bound to civilization by the old Indian trails that led to the Dutch settlements along Schoharie Creek.

While the Harpers and Lawrence Kortright were trying to attract homesteaders to their patents, Sir William Johnson was busy finding buyers and tenants for his Charlotte Creek Patent and his patented lands north of the Mohawk River. On a business trip to New York City in 1772, he had a fortuitous encounter with a successful Scottish importer and distributor of whiskey and rum.

Archibald MacDonell was the son of John MacDonell of Leek, an influential chieftain of Glengarry, Scotland's powerful Clan Donald. Sir William was keenly aware of the young man's familial ties and the advantages a link with his clansmen might benefit his interests. Scottish Highlanders and their families had been gradually coming to America since before the French and Indian War, with many of them settling on Sir William's Mohawk River properties and fighting with him at Lake George, Niagara and throughout New York's frontier. With another war on the horizon threatening to make New York's frontier another major front in the conflict, Sir William was extremely interested in attracting more loyalist Highlander tenants to his patented lands. The proposal he suggested to Archibald MacDonell was communicated back to his father and uncles in Scotland who jumped at the chance to come to America and defend their king's sovereignty. Within a year, fifty MacDonell Highlanders from Glengarry, Glenmorison, Urquhart and Strathglass were sailing for New York with their families aboard the British frigate *Pearl*. John MacDonell of Leek and his two brothers, Allan MacDonell of Cullachie and Alexander MacDonell of Aberchlder, led the expedition that included their brother-in-law Ranald MacDonell of Ardnabie and their cousin 'Spanish John' MacDonell of Scotus. [17]

Two weeks after landing in New York on October 18th, 1773, the *Pearl's* fifty Scottish families arrived at Albany where they were joined by another twenty Highlander families who agreed to Sir William's terms on his patented lands along the Mohawk and Susquehanna Rivers. Most of these Highlanders chose to take-up lots on Sir William's Royal and Kingsborough Patents on the north side of the Mohawk. At least fifteen of the *Pearl's* families elected to settle on Johnson's Adageghteinge or Charlotte Creek Patent, twenty miles south of Cherry Valley and just six miles northwest of the Harper family's settlement. Spanish John MacDonell of Scotus purchased several patent lots, totaling 491 acres, along both sides of Charlotte Creek at the mouth of Middle Brook and around today's township of Davenport's Butts Corner, Hoseaville, Fergusonville and Simpsonville. The MacDonell clansmen who settled on Charlotte Creek's 'Scottish Bush' with Spanish John, would when the time came, fight with him and serve under him in his company in Col. Sir John Johnson's Royal Regiment of New York loyalists.

Sir William had already settled two wealthy families of German immigrants on two sizable tracts of land on his Charlotte Creek Patent. In 1760, Christopher Servos and his brother Peter emigrated from the German Rhineland Palatinate of Koblenz and settled on a 150-acre lot of Sir William's property between his Fort Johnson and Johnstown estates on the north side of the Mohawk River. There is speculation that Christopher's wife Clara was sister to Sir William's first wife Catherine Weisenberg. A week after securing his Charlotte Creek Patent in 1770, Sir William offered Christopher Servos £200 and 1,500 acres on his new frontier patent in exchange for his Mohawk River property and all its improvements. Fifty-year-old Christopher took Johnson up on his offer and moved with his wife and eleven children to the frontier property near the present-day village of South Worcester. Within a few years, Christopher and his five sons had established two fine farms, a potash house, and a grist mill on their property.

In 1770, Sir William sold another large tract of land on his Charlotte Creek Patent. Johan and Dorothy Bartholomew and their twelve sons and five daughters established their own settlement on a 1,000-acre tract next to the Servos family. The Servos and Bartholomew settlements were just a few miles up the creek from the Highlander's Scottish Bush. 'Bartholomew's Settlement' and the Servos settlement were both between South Worcester and Summit Township's Charlotteville. The Bartholomeus were exiled Huguenots from the German-speaking lands of France's Alsace district who first settled in Germantown, PA around 1760 before coming to Charlotte Creek in '70. Described as 'Upper Leather' by many of their frontier neighbors who thought of them as aristocratic, the Bartholomeus would have also been considered to be what New Englanders and the Scots-Irish referred to as 'High Dutch', a reference meant to denote their German lineage. The old Hudson River Dutch settlers who came before the 1660s, while the Dutch still controlled Niew Nederland, were given the moniker 'Low Dutch' in reference to their origins in the lowland countries of the Netherlands. Relations between the Celtic frontiersmen and their Teutonic contemporaries were often contentious. As the war approached the border region and the Charlotte Creek settlements, the MacDonell clan prepared to defend their king's sovereignty while Johan Bartholomew and all twelve of his sons declared their ardent support for Congress. Christopher Servos made the fateful decision to remain on his frontier homestead while maintaining a steadfast attachment to the king, a risky and often fatal strategy. [18]

Johnson's Charlotte Creek Patent bordered Lawrence Kortright's 22,000-acre patent and the Harper family's 22,000-acre patent. In the years just prior to the Revolution, both Kortright and the Harpers were as actively engaged in encouraging settlers to take-up homestead lots on their patents as Sir William was. While Sir William preferred settling his patent with homesteaders friendly to the Crown and his political preferences, the Harpers tended to favor homesteaders who conformed to their own political views. Kortright seems to have had little interest in the politics of his prospective buyers, being that he was far removed from the frontier and preoccupied with his fleet of merchant ships and his New York City mercantile businesses. A considerable number of Johnson's Scottish Highlanders were drawn to Kortright Patent's terrain and its proximity to MacDonell's Charlotte Creek settlement. The two predominantly loyalist patents on the Harper's immediate north and western flanks, posed more of a threat to them than another Tory enclave on their southeastern flank. While most of the Paghatakan settlers on the East Branch were hurling verbal abuse at the few rebel families in their midst, a smaller community of budding loyalists on the West Branch was beginning to rattle their sabers just across the river from the Harper Patent. [19]

Although contested by Bradstreet, Hardenburgh Patent's Great Lot #42 that laid just across the West Branch from the Harper and Kortright Patents was still claimed by Robert R. Livingston, the patriarch of the Livingston family who owned a third of the entire Hardenburgh Patent by the early 1770s. Lying between the upper East and West Branches of the Delaware, in what would become the upper half of Delaware County's Stamford township and a lesser portion of the township of Roxbury, Great Lot #42 had been surveyed into 300 homestead lots varying in size from 100 to 150 acres each. Two miles south of today's village of Stamford in the charming little valley of Town Brook, a group of investors from Connecticut's Stamford area purchased a one-square-mile section of Livingston's Great Lot. Their section, which would eventually come to be called the Town Plot or New Stamford, was laid out into sixty-four, 10-acre lots within a grid of streets enclosing all four sides of each interior lot. With the slow steady flow of prewar settlers buying or leasing homestead lots on the frontier patents, New Stamford attracted a few of the Highlander clansmen who had journeyed to America on the *Pearl*.

Another clan of Highlanders from the Strathspey region of northern Scotland were also attracted to the New Stamford lots. A group of families totaling 224 passengers left the Port of Greenock aboard the *George* in May 1774. A full quarter of the *George's* passengers were of the Grant family and another quarter were allied families of the Grant Clan. Dr. James Stewart, who appears to have been one of their leading members, settled in New Stamford along with many of his Grant family relatives and kinsmen. He and his oldest sons were enthusiastic supporters of the Crown, as were most of the Grants who settled with him on Town Brook and along the West Branch's southside flats. When the time came to take up arms and declare alliances, Dr. Stewart led twenty-four Scots and twenty-six Dutch volunteers to Oswego where they enlisted in Sir John Johnson's Royal Regiment of New York loyalists. Most of these recruits came from New Stamford and the upper Schoharie Creek settlements around today's Gilboa and Prattsville area. The few rebel families who lived in the New Stamford area before the war would all be forced from their homesteads when the war finally reached their doorstep in '77. The families of John More and Samuel Ferris left before being routed from their homesteads by the Indians and Tories, but

David Brown and Daniel Bennet's families would be escorted from their homesteads at the end of a bayonet or spear. [20]

Besides the Harper family's rebel homesteaders and the few New Stamford rebel families, there were a few other rebel settlements and homesteaders scattered down along the Susquehanna to the Indian property line. A brazen and determined Presbyterian clergyman attempted to start a settlement on the very edge of Christendom, just feet from the Indian property line of '68. In 1772, Reverend William Johnston's family and a few other families settled on four narrow lots in Alexander Wallace's Susquehanna River Patent. Johnston Settlement would eventually become known as Delaware County's Sidney Plains and later just Sidney. Rev. Johnston's four southside riverfront lots totaled 572 acres and were separated from the Indian territory by just one other narrow lot, 150 yards in width. Having practiced his profession in Massachusetts' Scots-Irish community of Worcester and New Hampshire's Windham, Rev. Johnston was no stranger to the frontier or the type of men who called it home. He might have been thinking his settlement could serve well as a missionary location and a frontier trading post where whites and Indians could exchange ideas and goods under the watchful eye of his Christian guidance. Unfortunately, after just five years on the frontier, the Johnstons and a few of their neighbors were driven from their property by the very people the good reverend hoped to convert and profit from. Not all of Johnston Settlement's pioneers chose to abandon their homesteads at the start of New York's border war. A few of the settlements families and their patriarchs remained a brief time before finally heading off for the British loyalist regiments at Fort Niagara. These families were joined by a few other Tory families who had settled along the Unadilla River and Butternuts Creek, between today's Otsego County townships of Unadilla and Edmeston. [21]

There were those on the frontier who chose the solitude of a secluded frontier homestead over the collective advantages of a frontier settlement. Between the Indian property line and the source of the Susquehanna River at Otsego Lake, a half-dozen pioneers opened a riverfront clearing and built their homesteads far from civilization and noisy neighbors. A couple of Scottish families had tried to establish a settlement at the mouth of the Ouleout, but they appear to have succumbed to the privations of frontier life and disappeared mysteriously from the pages of history. Daniel Ogden and his family were more fortunate than the Ouleout settlers in that they managed to establish a reasonably productive homestead at the mouth of Otsdawa Creek, near today's village of Otego. Joachim Van Volkenburgh and his Mohawk wife Maria Berry of Magus Land, settled further up the Susquehanna on one of Arendt Bradt's riverfront patents at the mouth of Schenevus Creek near today's hamlet of Colliersville.

While the Susquehanna and the East Branch of the Delaware were slowly attracting settlers to their river flats, the West Branch of the Delaware remained uninhabited by whites or even Native Americans prior to the Revolution. The Lenape and Oneida peoples who lived in the surrounding territory were wary of the West Branch, claiming it was home to angry and unruly spirits. A small and impoverished group of Indians had tried to live on the river at a place called the Coke-ose that was later anglicized to the Cookhouse, being today's village of Deposit. The local Indians who avoided the West Branch, utilized it only in the summer months for hunting when other valleys were hunted out. By the time the Revolution reached the upper Delaware River Valleys, few white settlers had ventured any further into the West Branch's foreboding valley than New Stamford and the Kortright and Harper Patents at the headwaters of the river.

A few brazen millwrights did try to settle a little further down the West Branch where they planned to ride out the war on their millsite homesteads. Hugh Rose settled on a millsite at the mouth of today's Rose Brook where he managed to successfully keep a hospitable tavern for Whigs and Tories all throughout the war. Isaac Sawyer and St. Leger Cowley also settled on the river between today's Hobart and Bloomville before the war, but unlike Rose, were unsuccessful in riding out the war on their millsite homesteads. They would both suffer mightily for attempting to remain on the frontier too long. By the winter of 1777/'78, the sounds of the woodcutter's axe and the clinking of cow bells had fallen silent. Only the occasional serenade of a pack of howling wolves or the screech of a lonely owl might be heard echoing throughout the abandoned forests of the Susquehanna and Delaware River Valleys. [22]

Harpersfield

In the spring of 1771, John Harper Sr settled on the family's patent along with five of his eight children and their families. The men immediately began the arduous task of surveying the patent into its 220 homestead lots. Within a year or two of their arrival, another fifteen to twenty families had taken up their own lots throughout the patent. John's wife and mother to all the Harper children had died at the age of fifty-eight on their Beaver Dam/Cherry Valley homestead, three years before the family moved to Harpersfield. Abigail Montgomery Harper would unfortunately not live to see her husband's dream of empire come to fruition or her sons rise to the status of British colonial landed gentry. The sixty-five-year-old widower and family patriarch was now ready to turn over supervision of his family's holdings and business to his two oldest sons John Jr and William and his two younger sons Joseph and Alexander. John and Abigail's two oldest daughters, Mary and Margaret, would not accompany the family to their frontier patent. They remained instead on their Cherry Valley homesteads with their families and husbands James Moore and William Gault. The two younger Harper daughters did, however, join the family on their upper Delaware River settlement. Abigail and Miriam came to the family's patent with Abigail's husband William McFarland. Twenty-one-year-old Miriam lived with her sister and brother-in-law and their six-year-old daughter Eunice. John Harper Jr and wife Miriam built a small log cabin on lot #108, in the center of the patent, where today a small monument commemorates the site of their first crude home. John and Miriam brought their first five children with them to their family's settlement, Archibald-7, Margaret-5, James-4, Mary-2, and newborn Abigail. Joseph and Alexander's families took the two adjoining homestead lots, #133 and #82, on either side of John and Miriam's Center Brook lot. These three lots in the center of the Harper Patent were known simply as 'The Centre', which later became the Delaware County village of Harpersfield. [23]

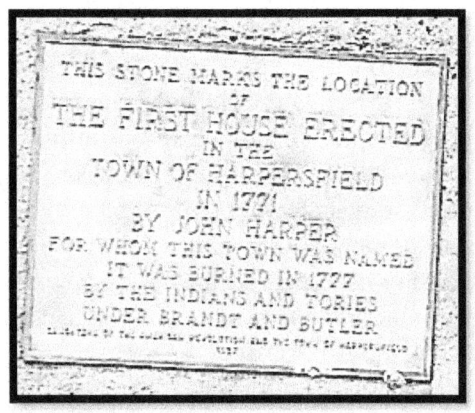

The two younger Harper brothers, Joseph and Alexander, were just approaching their teenage years when their family moved to New York's Cherry Valley in 1754. Joseph had just turned thirteen while his younger brother Alexander was but eleven. Having grown to maturity on their family's Beaver Dam millsite homestead, the two brothers were well versed in frontier life by the time they and their families moved on to their upper Delaware River patent in '71. Joseph and Catherine Douglas Harper had been married for eight years when they arrived at their family's patent with their three children, Joseph-4, John-3, and Margaret-1. Little is known as to how Catherine and Joseph became acquainted and eventually married. Catherine's parents, James and Elizabeth Douglas, were known to have resided in Ulster County's Montgomery township prior to the Revolution and her brother James served in the Ulster County militia during the war. Following the war, Catherine's parents brought their family to their son-in-law's patent and settled on homestead lot #160 near Odell Lake, a mile south of The Centre. [24]

Alexander and Elizabeth Bartholomew Harper were married the same year the Harpers moved from their Beaver Dam homestead to Harpersfield. The 'Upper Leather' family of Johan and Dorothy Bartholomew had only been on their Charlotte Creek acreage for a little over a year when Alexander met and quickly married their twenty-one-year-old daughter Elizabeth. Bartholomew Settlement was just six miles from The Centre, and being one of the few families in the area whose politics aligned with the Harpers, the two families might have welcomed such a union. Alexander and Elizabeth were however an odd couple, and their marriage may have raised more than a few eyebrows among their Scots-Irish neighbors. Ethnicity and social class all too often engendered deep passions of bigotry and racism between the various European nationalities of eighteenth-century colonial America. As they had been in north Ireland and throughout the first two or three generations in America, the Scots-Irish were seldom found mingling or marrying outside their own Scottish clans. Charlotte Creek's German Servos and Bartholomew families were certainly not kinsmen to the Harpers or any of their patent's homesteaders, nor were they of the same socioeconomic class. The thread that bound the Harpers and Bartholomeus together was woven in part by their mutual respect for each other's wealth and land, and their growing disdain for their British Monarch. The two rebel families would spend the war years together in the Schoharie Valley forts after being driven from their settlements at the onset of the border war. [25]

John and Abigail Harper's two youngest children, daughters Abigail and Miriam, were just nine and six when their parents brought them to Cherry Valley in 1754 and by the mid-60s, both were coming of age. In '65, first-cousins-once-removed, Abigail Harper and William McFarland were married by Rev. Samuel Dunlop in Cherry Valley's First Presbyterian Church, the first English speaking church west of the Hudson. William's grandfather James McFarland came to New England aboard the *MacCullum* in 1718 with Abigail's grandfather James Harper and her thirteen-year-old father to be, John Harper Sr. After being expelled from Boston and settling in Maine's Androscoggin and Kennebec River settlements with the Harpers, Hamiltons and Montgomerys, the McFarlands fought alongside their Ulster kinsmen throughout the Anglo/Abenaki War.

Returning to Massachusetts following the war, James McFarland settled in the Irish Rows of Massachusetts' Concord settlement near John Harper's brother William. James McFarland's son Alexander was born in 1718, either onboard or just after the *MacCullum* dropped anchor in Casco Bay. After growing up in Concord and reaching maturity he married William Harper's daughter Jane around 1740. In '42, Alexander and Jane Harper McFarland joined Jane's father William and brother George Harper and purchased lots in Massachusetts' Worcester County settlement of Oakham, then referred to as Rutland's West Wing. Alexander and Jane's son William McFarland was born in Oakham around 1745 and after growing up with his Harper cousins, headed west to New York's frontier settlement of Cherry Valley. In Cherry Valley, he met his mother Jane's uncle John Harper Sr and her two cousins, Abigail and Miriam Harper. William McFarland and Abigail Harper were married in 1765, and upon moving to the Harper family's patent in '71, took homestead lot #61 a mile up Center Brook from Abigail's father and brothers at The Centre. The young couple came with what may have been their only child, Eunice, or at least their only child to reach maturity as no other biological children were attributed to the couple.

Abigail Harper McFarland's younger sister Miriam would have been twenty-one and still single when she moved with her family to their frontier patent in 1771. It appears she lived with her sister and husband William through her early years. She would in fact finally marry at the age of thirty-six to a man she knew all too well, as she had been living with him for the past fifteen years. Miriam Harper and William McFarland were married shortly after the death of Miriam's sister Abigail in 1786. A marriage to the sibling of a deceased spouse was not thought of as anything unusual or unnatural in eighteenth-century frontier communities, nor was marriage between first or second cousins as frowned upon as it might be in later generations. Curiously, William sired but one child with Abigail and none with Miriam, an indication that might suggest a concern for the possibility of genetic complications. William and Miriam did eventually adopt and raise three young orphans after the war. [26]

As the patents and settlements of the upper Delaware and Susquehanna River region began filling up with energetic new homestead families, the Harpers were one of the few patent proprietors who actually lived on their property. Most speculators and investors were only interested in the land's potential profits that leases and sales brought in. The value of their patented properties increased expeditiously by the collective improvements of the first settlers, which encouraged others to follow and buy more lots from the absentee proprietors. Leases and sales were purposely offered on favorable terms for the earliest purchasers who were afforded the added advantage of selecting the most coveted riverfront flats.

Harper Patent's riverfront lots were not as adaptable for agricultural purposes as were many of the other patents. A third of Harpersfield's river front exposure was actually included within an old 6,000-acre patent that had been granted to Arendt Bradt and a group of Dutch investors back in 1740. Lawrence Kortright's adjacent patent had no access to the West Branch of the Delaware, as it too was blocked by the Bradt Patent. The upper river was in fact little more than a small winding stream with marshland meadows on both sides from Stamford to Hobart. The majority of the Harper Patent's 220, 100-acre lots were laid out in rectangular plots to accommodate small farms, but the patent's riverfront lots were purposely plotted into long narrow strips; a mile or more in length and a little over two hundred yards wide. The Harper's riverfront lots seem to have been intended to inspire a village settlement with a gridwork of streets and cross streets, much like New Stamford's Town Brook Plot. The Harper's plan for a mountain metropolis might have stood a better chance of success had the river been large enough to accommodate the industry that would one day fuel the region's economic engine: logging, and the rafting of timber to the shipyards of Philadelphia. [27]

The Harpers petitioned for their 22,000-acre patent on the far northeast end of their Oneida land purchase, for one simple reason, it was closer to civilization than the rest of the 260,000-acre purchase. It is hard to imagine today that the little hamlet of Harpersfield or The Centre, where the Harper family settled in '71, was a crossroads hub on one of the first major thoroughfares into west central New York. The network of old Indian trails that morphed into the early roads that connected the Schoharie Valley with the upper Delaware and Susquehanna Valleys, crested atop the watershed between the three major rivers of New York's frontier border region. The trails that split off into Harpersfield intersected with trails to Charlotte Creek, the Delaware's upper East and West Branches and the old Potawa trail that led to Catskill on the Hudson. One can follow the old Indian trails that became the Susquehanna/Catskill Turnpike by taking State Highway #23 west from the village of Catskill to Cairo, then county highway #142 to Durham and on to county road #20 through West Durham, Manorkill, Conesville, and West Conesville to Gilboa. Then take South Gilboa Road back to State Highway # 23 to Stamford and Harpersfield. At West Harpersfield, one of the old trails continued along route #23 to Charlotte Creek and the village of Davenport, while another split off towards the Susquehanna and the Oneida village of Unadilla. The highland trail shadowed route #33 to Kortright's Doonan Corners and Turnpike Rd. to West Meredith, then along highway #14 on through Treadwell to highway #357 through Franklin and passed the East Sidney Dam to Nathaniel Wattle's Ferry (Unadilla) on the Susquehanna. [28]

It was reasonable at the time for the Harpers to assume their settlement at The Centre would stand to benefit from the travelers and commerce that flowed along the trails intersecting on their patent. Other routes, however, would gradually offer more direct and easier access from the Hudson River to New York's interior frontier settlements. In time, the old Indian trail up Esopus Creek and over Pine Hill would be improved and incorporated into the Esopus/Jericho Turnpike from Kingston to Bainbridge on the Susquehanna. But in 1771, and throughout the five years leading up to the American Revolution, Harpersfield maintained its strategic position on the western frontier's border region. During those tough times, the Harper's lifeline to civilization and the much-needed staples they could not grow or kill for themselves was by way of the old Indian trail over Blenheim Hill to Mill Creek and on down to the Dutch settlements in the Schoharie Valley. Flour, salt, sugar, and the indispensable libations so essential for life on the frontier, were all carried into the bush on the backs of men and horses.

While the Harpers and their patent's neighbors struggled to survive by helping each other through those first few hungry winters on the frontier, the MacDonells on Charlotte Creek, and the Dutch settlers of Paghatakan were all doing the same. The early homesteaders, who depended upon each other's generosity and support to weather the hardships of pioneer life, were about to find some of their neighbors, friends and even some of their own family members turning away from them. While many of the frontier settlements of the upper Delaware and Susquehanna River region were being settled by families friendly to the Crown, the Harpers and most of their patent's homesteaders found themselves increasingly uncomfortable with their frontier neighbors. The years between the arrival of the Harpers and their neighbors and the start of the Revolution's New York Border War in '77, were not easy ones for the rebel families. They faced the usual privations of frontier life while dealing with the increasing hostility and intimidation from their frontier loyalist neighbors. The Harper's and their patent's denizens were not about to be swayed from their steadfast solidarity with Congress and the rebellion.

Alliances

On April 19th, 1775, the opening volleys of the American Revolution filled the crisp morning air around Concord Bridge with the cries of wounded and dying New Englanders and British Regulars. As news of the skirmish reached the Harpers and their neighbors on the New York frontier, another long, brutal winter was finally loosening its grip. Every available hand was out preparing the fields for spring planting. Few were surprised by the news they all knew was coming, and fewer still were unsettled as to which side they would support when the time came. That time, however, would not come to the patented lands of the western Catskills for another two years. Through the first year of the war, Washington's army laid siege to Boston and the British fleet anchored in Boston Harbor, while General Richard Montgomery led a Continental army up the Hudson and through the Lake Champlain corridor to Montreal and on to Quebec. Washington's siege succeeded in driving the British fleet out of Boston to Nova Scotia, while Montgomery's campaign met with utter disaster and the young general's death at Quebec on New Year's Eve 1775.

During the spring and summer of '76, a relief corps of Continental and militia soldiers was sent north to rescue Montgomery's failed expedition, while Washington's army lay in wait on Manhattan Island for the anticipated British invasion of New York City. The second Canadian expedition met with a similar fate as the first and Washington's army suffered a crushing defeat at the Battle of Long Island which very nearly cost him his army and the war. While the British settled into their garrisons in New York City, Staten Island and western Long Island, their Canadian forces took control of the St. Lawrence River and Lake Ontario from Quebec to Fort Niagara. New York's frontier settlements along the Mohawk River and throughout Tryon County's border region found themselves between an empire and a hard place.

Throughout 1775 and '76, New York's frontier borderlands remained out of the way of any major theaters of the war. There was, however, another war of conscience being fought for the hearts and minds of the frontier's young men. loyalist leaders and rebel insurgents were both trying to persuade their friends, neighbors, and associates into joining them and fighting for their respective causes. The chieftains and sachems of the Iroquois nations were being aggressively courted and enticed into picking a side in the fight that was to come. By the summer of '76, Sir William Johnson had been dead for two years and his son Sir John Johnson had been given his father's baronet title and taken over his empire and tenant fiefdom. After being arrested and paroled by the Tryon County Committee of Safety in January, Sir John fled to Canada in May with 170 of his tenants and loyalist followers, thus abandoning all his father's property and leaving control of the Mohawk Valley to the rebels.

Sir John was made brigadier general of the First Brigade of the King's Royal Regiment of New York Loyalists, known more commonly as Johnson's Royal Greens. Gen. Johnson appointed his associate and former Johnstown neighbor, John Butler, major of an irregular unit of Tory soldiers and Indian warriors assigned to terrorize the border region's rebel settlements. Major Butler's rangers were led by two extremely capable captains, the major's son Captain Walter Butler and the ubiquitous Captain Joseph Brant. The methods employed by the two captains and their fellow compatriots was a guerrilla-style of warfare aimed at destroying the homesteads and crops of the backwoods settlements. Captains Butler and Brant would become two of the most vilified and despised loyalist leaders on the rebel frontier, blamed for every atrocity committed upon the border region's population, whether justifiable or not. [29]

Following the exodus of Sir John and his Johnstown loyalists, the commanders of the Northern Department's Continental Army began refurbishing forts and blockhouses from Schenectady to the headwaters of the Mohawk. Renamed Fort Schuyler in honor of Major General Philip Schuyler, old Fort Stanwix on the border region's western most flank had fallen into disrepair after the French and Indian War. By the summer of '77, the old fort had been brought back to its former glory and garrisoned with a regiment of Continental Levies and Tryon County militiamen. Between Fort Schuyler at Rome and Fort Hunter at the mouth of Schoharie Creek, a line of garrisoned forts was established down along the Mohawk. German Flatts' Forts Herkimer and Dayton, Canajoharie, and Stone Arabia's Forts Plain and Paris, and Old Fort Johnson were supported by a dozen or more palisaded stone houses and blockhouses. The citizenry of the river settlements could take some comfort in knowing they had a safe harbor to run to should they be informed in time of an approaching war party. But the frontier settlements south of the Mohawk and throughout the frontier borderlands were left dangerously exposed to Butler and Brant's rangers who could attack at will from their Susquehanna strongholds. [30]

Twenty miles down the Susquehanna from the property line, just above Broome County's present-day village of Windsor, the ancient Oneida village of Onaquaga stretched along both sides of the river and on a large island. By the time the Revolution reached the upper Susquehanna, the once predominantly Oneida village had become an intermingled community of Oneida, Onondaga, Tuscarora, and Lenape peoples living in an impressive collection of well-built log homes, barns, and a church with an active Christian Missionary. By 1777, Onaquaga had become the eastern headquarters and commissary for Capt. Brant's warriors and Tories. In January, while the cold winds and deep snowdrifts enveloped the Susquehanna Valley, hundreds of young Iroquois warriors from the western nations began gathering at Onaquaga. It might be noted here that Onaquaga was just one of the village's fifty different spellings referenced in Gov. Clinton's Public Papers, while Paghatakan had just fourteen different spellings.

With Capt. Brant away gathering more western recruits, John Harper Jr was ordered to pay a visit to Onaquaga. The Scots-Irish frontiersman had recently been appointed captain of a small company of scouts and rangers assigned to reconnoiter the frontier and protect the border region's vulnerable settlements. Capt. Harper's assignment was to proceed to the Indian village and find out if the Iroquois intended to join the king and take up arms against the rebels, or whether they could be convinced into remaining neutral in the fight to come. New York's Provincial Congress and Committee of Safety, *'…recommended to General Schuyler, Mr. John Harper, of the County of Tryon, as the proper person to be employed in that service, the said John Harper being, as this committee are well informed, very intimately acquainted at Onaquaga Castle, and warmly attached to the American cause…'*. Accompanied by a company of militia to the property line, Capt. Harper left the company at Johnston Settlement and continued down the river in a harsh February gale with just two of his scouts, one white, one Indian.

Being well versed in the ceremonial customs and parlance, Capt. Harper brought along a young fatted ox and plenty of rum to the Onaquaga Indian council fire. he was one of only a few white men other than Sir William Johnson who was entitled to a voice at a council fire of the Six Nations of the Iroquois Confederation. Authorized by Congress to offer a gift of one hundred weight of gunpowder, he read a letter promising to pay any moneys owed to the Indian by unscrupulous land speculators and to evict those who had settled on their lands illegally. After offering the proverbial fatted calf as a ceremonial feast, Capt. Harper adorned himself in Indian attire and painted his face before plying his oratorical skills and deliberating his case for neutrality. After a night of festive feasting and voluminous drinking, he left the council fire with the impression he had swayed the chiefs and sachems to remain neutral and stay out of the fight to come. But as the cunning Iroquois could often be, they again played the ends against the middle while keeping their true purport to themselves. This was a skill they had honed over centuries of parleying with the Dutch, French, English, and now the Americans. A few weeks after the Onaquaga parley,

Capt. Brant returned to the village and began rallying the seven hundred warriors who had gathered there, into taking up arms against the rebels in support of the British king. [31]

As if by their very nature, the Harper men seemed utterly incapable of staying out of their own way at times throughout their military and civilian careers. Upon Capt. Harper's return from Onaquaga and having reported the council fire as having been successful in securing the Indian's declaration of neutrality, Harper curiously undid any feelings of goodwill he might have secured amongst the Onaquaga elders. After a mysterious encounter with a lone and friendly Indian on a forest trail, the captain reported later that the Indian, who was well known to him, failed to recognize his old friend and was tricked by him into telling him the whereabouts of a small hunting party of his fellow Indians. Hurrying back to Harpersfield, Capt. Harper gathered several of his rangers who allegedly helped him capture the band of Indians on the Susquehanna at the mouth of Schenevus Creek, near today's Colliersville. One account of this incident suggests as many as nineteen Indians were carried off towards Albany and slaughtered along the way before being buried in a mass grave on Harper Patent's lot #22 on the west side of Zufys or Titus Lake. Another account places this godless acre on the patent's lot #56, a mile-and-a-half north of The Centre. Either way, the incident seems like a duplicitous and foolish course of action by a military officer who had just gained a major concession of neutrality from a potential enemy. A more prudent man might have excused a dozen weary warriors sleeping around a lonely campfire so soon after having convinced their elders to stay out of the fight to come. But perhaps our protagonist was a pragmatic man who suspected all along their declaration of neutrality was insincere. There would be plenty more transgressions and broken promises to look back upon after the war and wonder as to how so many men could have found so many ways to justify their crimes. [32]

As the fighting season of '77 began to unfold, settlers throughout the border region began to realize the war was finally about to descend upon them. New York's frontier denizens from the Mohawk to the upper Susquehanna and Delaware Rivers and throughout old Ulster County's frontier to the Indian property line were about to be drawn into the fight that would end later that year on the bloody fields of Freeman's Farm and Bemis Heights. Throughout that spring and summer, British commanders at Quebec and New York City were busy finalizing plans to mobilize their forces in preparation for their next campaign to take control of the Hudson and sever New England off from the rest of the colonies. If successful, their three-pronged offensive with Albany as its terminus, would effectively give England control of the Hudson/Lake Champlain corridor from New York City to Quebec, and the Mohawk River corridor from Lake Ontario to the Hudson.

With British General John Burgoyne slowly assembling his troops at Quebec for an invasion of New York through the Lake Champlain corridor, General Sir William Howe was preparing an armada of British warships to sail up the Hudson for a triumphant rendezvous with Burgoyne at Albany. A third prong of England's strategy was to deploy a flanking campaign down the Mohawk corridor from Lake Ontario's Fort Oswego to Albany. Brevet Brigadier General Barrymore 'Barry' St. Leger would lead the Mohawk River expedition. As summer wore on and the American commanders became aware of the impending invasions, an aggressive campaign was launched to counter Britain's three campaigns. Men and resources were sent north to slow down Burgoyne's advance through New York's northern forests, while Washington cleverly distracted Gen. Howe through a series of feigning actions and maneuvers meant to divert his New York forces to other theaters. While the northern department focused on Burgoyne's advance towards Albany, little attention was given to St. Leger's western campaign or the forts and settlements along his Mohawk River route. Fort Schuyler was, however, reinforced with a full regiment of continentals and Tryon County militia with orders to hold New York's western corridor at all costs. Fortunately for the frontier residents and militias, the British struggled to initiate and coordinate their ambitious campaigns, giving the Americans plenty of time to mobilize an effective resistance. [33]

While New York prepared for battle, Capt. Brant's Onaquaga warriors waited anxiously for their chance to prove their mettle and address the grievances that had been accumulating between them and the intrusive white settlers for years. Throughout the spring of '77, over a thousand warriors gathered on the Susquehanna. With mouths to feed and restless warriors to preoccupy, Brant began sending out small raiding parties to pillage for livestock and provisions throughout the frontier settlements. On the 2nd of June, a prelude to war finally arrived on New York's frontier border region. With 80 to 100 warriors, Capt. Brant crossed over the property line and into Rev. William Johnston's settlement across from the confluence of the Susquehanna and Unadilla Rivers. By that time, four or five other families had joined the Johnstons and their relatives in their settlement while at least another twenty were living up along the Susquehanna between the property line and the Charlotte Creek settlements. Having been warned of Brant's approach and realizing the potential for bloodshed that such an encounter might bring, Rev. Johnston sent a rider up the river to the militia outpost at Cherry Valley. The commanding officer quickly responded by sending a sergeant and forty of his militiamen back with the rider to Johnston Settlement.

Unfazed by the presents of the small militia force, Brant's warriors demanded and took whatever provisions they wanted, even stripping the clothes lines of any apparel that caught their fancy. Refraining from any overt acts of violence, Brant delivered a warning and an ultimatum that left little doubt as to who's side the Indians would fight for and just what the frontier settlements could expect from them in the months and years ahead. Given the choice between joining his army and fighting for the Crown or staying on their homesteads and suffering the consequences, the Johnstons and their neighbors were given two days to decide whether to stay, leave, or join the Indians. A few of the families chose to side with the Indians and their king. Included among them were the Dingmans and the Woodcocks. John Carr attempted to stay on his millsite homestead a couple of miles up the river at the mouth of the creek that still bears his name. Rev. Johnston and wife Nancy, along with their two sons, Witter and Hugh, and four daughters, loaded their wagons and headed up the Susquehanna for Cherry Valley. Before departing they buried what tools, implements and household furnishings they could not carry with them in hopes that one day they would return and reclaim their settlement. 34

Capt. Joseph Brant

The Johnstons and their neighbors were luckier than most, as this would be the last time a white settlement was given the courtesy of a warning before being visited by Brant and Butler's soldiers. Throughout the summer of '77, as Indian raids intensified and rumors of war grew harder and harder to ignore, settlers on Harper's Patent and the surrounding patents began readying themselves for the inevitable. After torching Johnston Settlement's abandoned homesteads, Capt. Brant's raiding parties continue to harass and drive out the few lingering settlers up along the Susquehanna. The small group of impoverished Scottish families around the mouth of Ouleout Creek were presumed to have taken up with the Indians. Daniel Ogden and Henry Scrambling abandoned their homesteads near Otsdawa Creek and joined Schenevus Creek's Joachim Van Volkenburgh in joining Capt. Harper's ranger company. Four months after Capt. Harper's Onaquaga council fire and three weeks after the destruction of Johnston Settlement, another attempt was made to try and sway the Indians from the path they were about to embark upon.

Brigadier General Nicholas Herkimer of the Tryon County Militia was called upon to hold another peace conference with Capt. Brant and his warriors. A messenger was sent to Onaquaga with a summons for Brant to meet with the general and his militia at Rev. Johnston's burnt-out settlement at the property line. On the 20th of June, Gen. Herkimer and a regiment of 380 soldiers arrived at the settlement and waited for Brant to answer their invitation. After eight days of waiting, Brant finally appeared on the Susquehanna flats with around 140 of his warriors. The cagy Mohawk leader implied to Herkimer that he had another five hundred warriors camped nearby should the General and his men start any trouble.

Herkimer's regiment included a few volunteers who had personal reasons for joining his expedition. Rev. Johnston and his son Witter were of course there, as were a couple of the settlers who had just been driven from their Susquehanna homesteads. Daniel Ogden and his former neighbor's worst fears were sadly realized as they passed by their burnt-out homesteads before arriving on Sidney Plains to find the Johnston's homes similarly deposed. Having been played by the Iroquois sachems at Onaquaga in February, Capt. Harper was again called upon to participate in one last-ditch effort to persuade the Iroquois to stay out of the fight to come. [35]

Initially cordial, Herkimer's summit gradually digressed into a tense exchange of vociferous accusations of past transgressions by the loudest and most belligerent on either side. Both Brant and Herkimer struggled to hold their young hot-headed subordinates in line, as tempers flared, and old personal grievances fueled heated exchanges between the brashest of the antagonists. Cooler heads on both sides did all within their power to divert a bloody skirmish from breaking out. By day's end, no one's mind was changed, as both sides reiterated their alliances and dug their heels deeper into their own convictions. As the opposing parties retired to their respective camps following a second day of futile talks and stalemate, divine intervention dispelled any possibility of violence. A sudden and ferocious thunderstorm descended upon the valley, sending both sides scurrying for cover and wetting their gunpowder. Within six weeks of the Johnston Settlement summit, the insults and threats hurled at the conference would be answered and the blood both sides lusted for would flow like water into a small, wooded creek on the banks of the Mohawk River.

Oriskany

In the aftermath of Herkimer's contentious conference, a tenuous calm before the storm fell over an anxious frontier. England's campaign to bring the Americans to their knees by severing New England off from the rest of the colonies was well under way. With Burgoyne slowly advancing down the Lake Champlain corridor towards Saratoga, General Barry St. Leger arrived at Fort Oswego and began mobilizing his Mohawk River invasion. After remaining a few weeks on the Susquehanna following his conference with Herkimer, Capt. Brant appeared at Oswego in late July with about three hundred of his Iroquois warriors. Five hundred more Seneca and Cayuga warriors were on their way. St. Leger's army consisted of two hundred British Grenadiers from the King's 34th and 8th Regiments, 250 New York Loyalists, one hundred Hessian Jagers, and about forty artillerymen. Another one hundred or more Canadian militiamen swelled St. Leger's army to over 1,500. Lt. Col. Sir John Johnson and Major John Butler took command of the New York loyalists and Indians, with their field command being led by Capt. Brant and the major's son Capt. Walter Butler.

On the 26th of July, with his expedition's troops and provisions loaded on a flotilla of bateaux, St. Leger began his journey up Oswego River and on across Oneida Lake to Wood Creek and the Oneida Carry. St. Leger brought along two six-pound artillery pieces, two three-pounders and four small cohorns, or mortars, accompanied by the necessary wagonloads of ammunition and accoutrements. Setting out ahead of the main force, Capt. Brant led an advance guard of 230 warriors and arrived at Fort Schuyler a day before St. Leger's troops reached the fort on the 2nd of August. Immediately upon his arrival, St. Leger sent out a flag to propose a parley in hopes of persuading Col. Peter Gansevoort to surrender the fort and all his 550 New York soldiers and 150 Massachusetts troops. As expected, Col. Gansevoort coolly refused the British general's offer of capitulation, prompting St. Leger to surround the fort and settle in for a siege and bombardment he hoped might change the rebel colonel's mind. [36]

After a few days of bombardment that did relatively minor damage to the fort and Col. Gansevoort's resolve, St. Leger learned of a rapidly advancing column of militiamen marching up the Mohawk towards the fort and his position. For several days, Gen. Herkimer had been calling upon the men of Tryon County to rise and join his militia brigade assembling at his German Flatts estate in preparation for the relief of Fort Schuyler. The call was enthusiastically answered by the young men along the Mohawk from Canajoharie to German Flatts and throughout the backwoods settlements from Andrustown to Cherry Valley. Within a few days, Herkimer had assembled over eight hundred militiamen and fifty Oneida warriors at Fort Dayton on the Mohawk at today's village of Herkimer. Col. Ebenezer Cox's 1st Tryon County Regt., Col. Jacob Klock's 2nd Regt., Col. Frederick Visscher's 3rd Regt. and Col. Peter Bellinger's 4th Tryon Regt. comprised the core of Herkimer's brigade that set out for Fort Schuyler on the morning of August 4th.

Herkimer's long column of young inexperienced recruits and fifteen wagon loads of provisions and equipment stretched for a mile-and-a-half. A few of his relief column's commanders had been with him at Johnston Settlement, Col. Cox and Klock being two of the loudest belligerents who had taunted for blood that day. After an eight-mile march up the northside of the Mohawk, Herkimer's column prepared to encamp for the night at Sterling Creek, twenty miles east of Fort Schuyler. The general had planned on halting there for a day to allow for more volunteers from Schenectady and Albany to catch-up with his brigade before marching on to confront St. Leger's superior forces. Regrettably, the same officers who had teased for violence in June, were now pressing the general with the same bellicose taunts to hurry forward without hesitation. Against his better judgment, Gen. Herkimer reluctantly obliged his impatient colonels and resumed his march early the next morning.

Moving forward along a narrow woodland road, Herkimer forded his column of men and wagons across to the southside of the river and marched on to within four miles of Fort Schuyler before bedding his troops down for a second night. They had reached the Oneida village of Oriska, today's Oriskany, where they were warmly received by the Oneida war chief, Yan Yerry, who agreed to join Herkimer's expedition with fifty to sixty of his best Oneida warriors. Gen. Herkimer sent a runner out to Fort Schuyler with a message for Col. Gansevoort informing him of his approach and plans for a coordinated assault on St. Leger's forces. The plan called for Gansevoort's troops to sally out from the fort while his troops arrived and attacked the enemy from the rear. But again, while his tired troops slept, Herkimer had to endure a second evening of accusations from Colonels Cox, Klock and Visscher who accused him of cowardice hesitation and even treasonous motives for dithering away precious time. The three colonels succeeded in intimidating the beleaguered general into acquiescing to their demands again and hurry on towards the enemy without waiting for Col. Gansevoort's reply.

Informed of Herkimer's advance, Gen. St. Leger sent out a reception party to greet the Dutch commander and his Tryon County militiamen. Col. Johnson, Major Butler, and Capt. Brant were dispatched with a detachment of five hundred loyalist rangers, German Hessians, and Iroquois warriors. An ambush position was set up a few miles down the Mohawk from Fort Schuyler on a forested hummock flanked by two marshy ravines. At ten o'clock on the morning of the 6th of August 1777, Brant's warriors came down hard on Herkimer's caravan while it was stretched out on the hill with the advance guard approaching the forward ravine and the rearguard with the teamster's wagons still crossing the rear ravine. Many of Brant's warriors had been with him at Johnston Settlement where the indignant slander from the pugnacious Col. Cox nearly turned the conference into a skirmish. These same warriors were now thrilled to recognize the colonel riding at the head of his regiment. Col. Ebenezer Cox and a few of the other officers who had precipitated the hasty advance toward the enemy were shot down in the first thunderous volley of gunfire. Col. Bellinger, who had been one of the few officers to side with Gen. Herkimer in the intense argument the night before, was wounded and carried off by the Indians to suffer a slow and torturous death.

The first devastating volleys of musket fire on the militia's exposed lines, so surprised the Tryon County boys they had all they could do just to keep their wits about them. While running around frantically seeking cover behind trees and brush, officers scrambled to establish order within their ranks while fighting off furious warriors rushing upon them with tomahawks and warclubs. Within minutes, Gen. Herkimer was down, his leg shattered by a bullet that passed through his horse killing the mare and immobilizing the general. Bleeding profusely and stubbornly refusing to be taken from the field, he ordered his men to prop him up against a tree where he calmly lit his pipe and proceeded to direct his panicking troops to form up around the crest of the hill. The fighting being so up close and fierce, men firing their rifles from behind trees were often run up upon and killed before they could reload or retreat. Adjusting to the Indians tactics, officers directed their men to fight behind trees in tandem with the first man firing only after the other had reloaded and was again ready to fire. Hand-to-hand combat became so vicious, men were often unsure of who was before them and who was behind them. Combatants on opposing sides might have recognized familiar faces peering out from behind the trees and through the clouds of black-powder smoke. Just months before, some had been neighbors, acquaintances and even friends, hoisting a pint at their local taverns or communing together at their churches.

After forty-five minutes of mano-a-mano combat, militia officers began forming their men into small defensive groups that could hold off their attackers from all sides. Col. Johnson's loyalist rangers and Hessian Jagers were ordered to fix bayonets and charge into the mass of humanity on the hill. Some of Johnson's rangers were the highly effective Scottish Highlanders who had been enticed to come to America by his father Sir William Johnson a few years before the war. These Highlander warriors must have been a fearsome sight as they came charging through the forest with their claymores ablaze and their pipers piping an odious-pibroch. Remarkably, Herkimer's militia slowly regained enough order and composure to raise an effective defense against the onslaught of Indians and rangers. Sensing their stiffening resistance, Col. Johnson hurriedly rode back to St. Leger's camp to request additional troops to finish off the Tryon County boys. As he did so, a thunderous deluge of rain descended over the battle scene, bringing the carnage to a temporary halt, albeit just for an hour. The heavy rain dampened the fire locks and cartridges in the rifles of those who could still stand and fight. The dying who lay on the ground crying out for their mothers and water, may have sensed a moment of absolution from the cool heavenly rain as it washed away their blood and tears.

As the rain began to let up, riflemen reset their primers and replaced their soggy cartridges as the fighting resumed with a renewed vigor. Returning with a fresh company of loyalist troops led by Capt. Donald MacDonell, Col. Johnson's men stormed over the defensive breastworks the rebels had managed to throw up during the lull. Just when all seemed lost, an Indian runner arrived with news that a detachment of Col. Gansevoort's troops had sallied out of Fort Schuyler and were looting Johnson's empty loyalist and Indian encampments. After six hours of vicious fighting, Col. Johnson rallied his troops and marched back towards the fort to defend against the rebel marauders pillaging their supplies and munitions. But before they could make it back, Col. Marinus Willett and his 200-man detachment had already sacked their camps and were back in the fort with several wagonloads of much-needed provisions and arms.

Just 150 of Herkimer's 850-man militia brigade were still fit for duty when the enemy finally withdrew from the field. Four hundred of his men, along with one hundred of the enemy, lay dead or dying amongst the tangled bramble and mass of mangled humanity on that unholy patch of earth. Many of the militiamen had suffered mercilessly agonizing deaths at the hands of their captors and their scalping knives. General Herkimer survived the battle and was carried back to his home on the Mohawk. His shattered leg, which was initially non-life threatening, became infected and following a botched surgery to amputate the putrefied limb, he died at the age of forty-nine with the death knell tolling from every steeple in the valley. Too many of Tryon County's best young militia officers and soldiers were gone too soon. The Battle of Oriskany would be the Revolution's bloodiest, in terms of fatalities, of the entire war. At Saratoga's Freeman's Farm and Bemis Heights two months later, the Continental army would suffer just ninety casualties and another 250 wounded.

Four days after the annihilation of Herkimer's brigade, while St. Leger's artillery continued their relentless bombardment of Fort Schuyler, Col. Gansevoort initiated a daring attempt to try to relieve his besieged fort. The ever-resourceful Marinus Willett and one of his trusted lieutenants were sent on another dangerous mission outside the walls of the fort. Slipping away under cover of darkness, the two men laced their way through enemy lines and began a thirty-mile marathon down the Mohawk towards German Flatts. Ever on the alert for Indians and Tories who might be lingering about in the forests, the two relentless runners finally arrived safely at Fort Dayton. Here, Col. Willett learned first-hand from the convalescing survivors of Herkimer's expedition the full extent of their devastating defeat. Realizing the Mohawk River militias were in no shape to rejoin another relief column; Willett secured a horse and rode on towards Albany where he hoped to influence the deployment of another formidable relief column. Reaching Albany, he found the village teaming with militias and Levies from all over New York and New England gathering to join Gen. Gates' army for the defense against Burgoyne's oncoming forces. Willett also learned of a detachment from Col. Van Cortlandt's 2nd and Col. Livingston's 4th Dutchess County Regiments had already been forming into a brigade in preparation to march for the relief of Fort Schuyler. At the head of the 900-man brigade, Major General Benedict Arnold welcomed the intelligence Col. Willett brought with him concerning the fort's condition and the enemy's strength. Arnold was briefed on the horrific losses at Oriskany and the reduced state of the Tryon County militias he had been counting on to join his forces.

Marching up the Mohawk towards Fort Schuyler, Gen. Arnold and Col. Willett arrived at Fort Dayton on the evening of the 17th and were saddened to learn of Gen. Herkimer's death the day before. Gen. Arnold planned to halt at Fort Dayton long enough for more troops to catch up and join his brigade before advancing any further towards the siege. Another coordinated attack with Col. Gansevoort's troops was being planned, this time without the adverse influence of colonels Cox and Klock. Learning of Arnold's approach and having been led to believe his forces were much larger than they actually were, Gen. St. Leger took pause and weighed his options. Many of his Iroquois warriors had grown distraught over their heavy losses at Oriskany and further lamented the loss of their provisions and booty to Col. Willett's surprise sortie. Some had already begun drifting off into the forests and returning to their villages. Around 2 o'clock on the afternoon of August 22nd, with his supplies running low and Arnold's brigade marching ever closer, St. Leger made a hasty decision to raise the siege and head back posthaste for Fort Oswego. Believing the erroneous reports of Arnold's brigade being over 3,000 strong, the British abandoned their camps in such a hurried confusion they left much of their baggage and armaments behind.

Arnold and Willett's brigade, which had grown to 1,200 troops, did not arrive at the fort until two days after the British retreat. Finding the enemy long-gone, Arnold and Gansevoort's men rejoiced in jubilant celebration, toasting to the fort's liberation and to the Mohawk River still being firmly in American control. But having marched over the battleground where Herkimer's brave lads had laid for the past eighteen days, many of Arnold's men were still in shock at what they had seen. One of his soldiers wrote in his journal, '… *we had to march over the ground where Herkimer's battle was fought, and as the dead had not been buried, and the weather warm, they were much swollen and of a purple color which represented the fragility of man in a very figurative sense, we must have marched over and vary near about four hundred dead bodies…*'. General Arnold and his men, however, had little time to mourn their comrade's fate or savor their victory with the brave defenders of Fort Schuyler. No sooner had they arrived, most of Arnold's men were turned about and marched back down the Mohawk to rejoin Gen. Gate's army amassing at Stillwater in preparation for the big battle to come. [37]

'Brave Herkimer our General is dead,
And Col. Cox is Slain;
And many more and valiant men,
We ne'er shall see again'

3

Border War
1777-1778
'these bullets shall whistle through your hearts'

Having advanced his 8,500 troops down the Lake Champlain corridor through June and July 1777, General John Burgoyne's army was now struggling to make its way south from Skenesborough to Fort Edward on route to Albany. Burgoyne's advance was being relentlessly impeded by rebel militias blocking the roadways with fallen trees and debris. With Burgoyne bogged down and advancing slowly through the month of August, militiamen from all over New York and Massachusetts were streaming into Gen. Horatio Gates' defensive positions around the upper Hudson River village of Stillwater, twenty miles north of Albany. While Benedict Arnold and Marinus Willett were heading up the Mohawk in route to Fort Schuyler, the British suffered a devastating loss of nearly 1,000 troops taken prisoner at Bennington in mid-August. On his return from Fort Schuyler with his troops, Gen. Arnold collected as many of the Mohawk River militiamen who were still willing to join the fight after their shocking ordeal at Oriskany. With every able-bodied man between the ages of 16 to 60 heading north to Stillwater, settlements along the Mohawk and Schoharie Creek were left unprotected and at the mercy of the valley's lingering loyalist sympathizers. Only a few small companies of rebel militia were left to protect the Schoharie citizenry and their rich farmland. The entire valley and its vital crops were at grave risk of being taken or destroyed by the Tories and Indians. With Gen. St. Leger in full retreat, the northern commanders were now focused on the threat inching towards them from Canada and less concerned with the Mohawk frontier or the Schoharie Creek settlements. The Battle of Saratoga was just weeks away and every available resource was being requisitioned for the fight to come.

Schoharie

The wide Schoharie Valley was first settled in 1713 by families of German refugees sent to America following the devastation of their Rhineland-Palatinate homeland during Queen Anne's War and the War of Spanish Succession. Unwilling to accept the influx of Palatine refugees fleeing into England, Queen Anne and her magistrates devised a plan to send their unwanted guests to the outlying hinterlands of the American Colonies. Many of them were sent to New York's Hudson River Valley where they were forced to work as indentured servants turning pine pitch into the pine tar used to waterproof the ships of Her Majesty's Royal Navy. The enterprise failed to meet the realm's expectations and was neglected along with the poor refugees who were left with few options. A group of desperate Rhineland families resolved to abandon their impoverished encampments along the Hudson and set out into the wilderness for the Schoharie and Upper Mohawk River Valleys. Throughout the 1720s and '30s, they came and settled along Schoharie Creek and the Mohawk River between Canajoharie and German Flatts. Schoharie's broad valley flats and rich alluvial soil made many of these industrious German pioneers, and subsequent generations, successful farmers and proprietors of large tracts of patented lands. Referred to by their Anglo neighbors as the 'Palatine Dutch', Schoharie's Dutch Reformed Lutherans managed to Christianize many of the valley's original Mohawk Indians and maintained a relatively peaceful coexistence with them for nearly seventy years.

As the Revolution began creeping closer and closer to their quiet valley in the summer of '77, Schoharie's young men of fighting age were forced to declare their alliance for king or Congress. The valley's fragile social order was splintered into hostile factions that were teetering on the brink of violence. The greater majority of the valley's Palatine Dutch and their Mohawk friends chose to side with the king's men and were beginning to form up into local loyalist organizations. Two of Schoharie's leading citizens, who had only recently expressed their support for the king, were now ready to openly declare their fidelity and convince their neighbors to join them in resistance to the rebel insurgents. George Mann was the son of a wealthy Schoharie tavern owner and had initially been a captain of a local rebel militia company before secretly conspiring to form his own loyalist company. Adam Crysler had always been a faithful and outspoken supporter of the king, having been a commissioned ensign in the British Army during the French and Indian War. He also has wielded considerable influence over the local population and the valley's two Mohawk leaders, Seth's Henry and David Ogeyonda. Seth's Henry was the son of one of the last Schoharie chieftains and a direct descendant of the first Schoharie Chieftain Karighondonte. The young Mohawk prince would become one of the border war's most effective warriors, feared and despised by frontier settlers and rebel militiamen almost as much as Captain Joseph Brant. [1]

The Vrooman family was one of the richest families in the Schoharie Valley. They owned a large track of flatland between Middleburg and Fultonham known as Vrooman's Flatts and by 1790 owned one out of every five of Schoharie Valley's 160 African slaves. Peter Vrooman was put in command of the 15th Albany County Militia Regiment charged with protecting the Schoharie settlements during the early years of the border war. But by early August 1777, most of Col. Vrooman's Albany and Schoharie militiamen had been sent to join the other Tryon and Albany County regiments gathering at Stillwater. Only a few partial companies of his militia were still in the Schoharie Valley during those tumultuous weeks in August while Fort Schuyler lay besieged, and Burgoyne crept ever closer to Albany. As news of Herkimer's disaster at Oriskany began filtering into the valley, Schoharie's emboldened Tories began preparing to take control of the valley by forcing the local population to submit to the king's sovereignty. After subduing the valley, the Tories planned to join St. Leger after his capture of Fort Schuyler and marching with him as his army descended the Mohawk in route to Albany to join Burgoyne's triumphant army. Along with Capt. Mann's gathering at his father's tavern near the village of Schoharie, Adam Crysler was rallying the local loyalists in the upper valley at his mill near Breakabeen. Capt. Mann and Crysler had for some time been secretly coercing the local farm boys into joining them and fighting for their king. With Albany and Tryon County's Committee of Safety directing the rebel militias to apprehend and arrest all the known Tories throughout the frontier settlements, Schoharie's two loyalist leaders were secretly organizing their supporters in defiance of the rebels and their Committees of Safety. [2]

The Flockey

While St. Leger's expedition was preparing to leave Oswego for Fort Schuyler in late July, Col. Sir John Johnson sent one of his favorite officers on a special mission into the backwoods of Tryon and Albany County. Col. Johnson had known Spanish John MacDonell of Scotus since he and his Highland clansmen arrived in America aboard the *Pearl* in '73 and bought the 500-acre tract of land on his father's Charlotte Creek Patent. Spanish John was the acknowledged leader of the Scottish clansmen who had come to America, in part, to help their patron Sir William Johnson defend the king's sovereignty and put down the colonial rebellion.

In 1740, at the age of twelve, John MacDonell was sent from his ancestral home in the Glengarry Highlands to Italy to study for the priesthood in Rome's prestigious Scots College. Too restless in spirit for the priesthood, the young adventurer soon found himself a cadet in a company of St. James' Irlandia and Hibernia Regiments, fighting for the King of Spain in the Italian campaign of the War of Austrian Succession. The young Scottish cadet fought valiantly at the Battle of Velletri in 1744 and was severely wounded and very nearly left for dead on the field. After recovering from his wounds, he was promoted at the age of sixteen to lieutenant in the Irish army and upon returning to Scotland took a prominent role in the Jacobite Rebellion of '45. His unusual moniker was given to him presumably because of his service to the Spanish King. It also served to differentiate him from the multitude of Scotland's John MacDonells. Spanish John was a proud adherent to the proper eighteenth-century code of conduct for a gentleman and an officer and was highly respected by his peers for his military acumen. He was also a man who would not have agreed with the proposition that '...*all men are created equal...*'. In reference to Jefferson's claim, he stated in his memoirs '... *a holding I have never been able to make head or tail of, as it is clear against the common sense of any man who goes through the world with his eyes open...*'. These were clearly not the words of an adherent to the Age of Enlightenment. Spanish John's credentials and politics earned him the trust and confidence of Col. Johnson who commissioned him captain of a company in his Royal Regiment of New York Loyalists. [3]

Spanish John MacDonell of Scotus

Confident in Spanish John's abilities, Sir John sent the Highlander on a risky mission to help subdue the Schoharie settlements and bring them under the king's domain. At the very least, if unsuccessful in conquering the valley, his Schoharie expedition might serve to draw off one or two rebel companies from St. Leger's advance down the Mohawk should the capture of Fort Schuyler prove successful. Leaving Fort Oswego the day before St. Leger's departure, MacDonell set a course for the Susquehanna through the backwoods of the Onondaga Indian territory south of Oneida Lake. With the help of an Indian guide and his Iroquois warriors he reached the headwaters of the Unadilla River and proceeded by canoe down to the Susquehanna and up Charlotte Creek. After nine days on the trail, the loyalists finally reached their old settlements on Johnson Patent on August 2nd, around the same time St. Leger reached Fort Schuyler. When MacDonell and his fellow Highlanders reached their old Scottish Bush homesteads they were greeted by their wives and children who had remained on Charlotte Creek following their husbands and father's exodus to Canada the year before.

The Servos and Bartholomew families were still living on their properties a few miles up the creek from Scottish Bush. Several of New Stamford, Kortright and Harper Patent settlers also remained on their homesteads while many others had already abandoned their homes for the security of Cherry Valley or Schoharie Valley. Feeling a sense of urgency by MacDonell's sudden reemergence on Charlotte Creek and the growing number of Tory supporters in their midst, the rebel families on Harper Patent were beginning to prepare to evacuate their vulnerable settlement. MacDonell had picked up several more loyalist sympathizers and Indians on his trek through the western forests and upon his arrival began recruiting the few uncommitted or indifferent frontier stragglers. There were several loyalists on nearby Kortright Patent who were more than ready to make a stand and throw in with MacDonell and his Tories. Hanging about for the better part of a week before launching their invasion on Schoharie Valley, MacDonell and his Highlanders spent considerable effort recruiting the frontier's reluctant young men into their little army. If met with stiff resistance to their coercive tactics of persuasion, the Highlanders would resort to a more punitive approach with threats of imprisonment and destruction of the recusant's home and family. But the Harper family and their core of rebel supporters defiantly clung to their homesteads, disregarding the harassment they endured from their Tory neighbors and MacDonell's conscripts. [4]

Throughout the summer of '77, John Harper and his brother William had desperately been trying to convince the State's Council of Safety in Kingston to appropriate more troops and resources for the protection of the frontier settlements. The northern commanders, however, were more focused on the protection of Albany and Schenectady and the rumors of the enemy's Hudson River campaign. After having consistently ignored and underestimated the threat to the frontier settlements throughout the early years of the war, the Harpers were finally able to convince the Kingston committee members to appropriate funding for the formation of two companies of frontier rangers. The Council resolved that Capt. John Harper, and his brother Lt. Alexander Harper of Harpersfield should lead the first company of rangers for the protection of the upper Delaware's West Branch settlements. Capt. Samuel Clyde and Lt. Samuel Campbell of Cherry Valley were commissioned to lead the second company to patrol the settlements throughout the upper Susquehanna region. With only twenty-five volunteer rangers delegated to each outfit, the two companies together barely equaled a single company of a regular militia regiment. Upon returning to Schoharie with his commissions, Capt. Harper and his brother were informed of MacDonell's Tories and Indians lurking about in the woods around their Harpersfield settlement. They immediately set out to assess the situation and assist their families and friends still living on their frontier patent.

    Arriving on the patent just as MacDonell was preparing to invade their settlement, the Harper brothers and their brother-in-law William McFarland gathered their families and a few of their belongings and prepared to set out over Blenheim Hill to Schoharie's Middle Fort. Several of their neighbors had already been taken prisoner, while a few others had agreed to MacDonell's offer of protection and joined his Tory outfit. Miriam and John Harper's four oldest children, Archibald-13, Margaret-11, James-10, and Mary-8 helped their parents with their three younger siblings, Rebecca-4, John-3, and Ruth-1, while the captain prepared to guide them through the forest. Joseph and Catherine Harper's ten and nine-year-old sons, Joseph and John, helped their parents look after their five-year-old sister Agnes, while Alexander and Elizabeth strapped their two young sons, John-3 and James-1, to a horse and set out with the others for Schoharie just ahead of the oncoming Tories and Indians. All but what they could carry on their horses and backs was lost, their cabins torched, and their stores of summer crops confiscated or burnt. The homesteads they had worked so hard to establish and the settlement they had watched grow was lost. It would be another six years before any of them would return to their frontier homes and start the grueling process of reclaiming the forests and recultivating their overgrown fields. [5]

    While MacDonell continued his business of terrorizing the rebel settlers and recruiting frontier loyalists throughout Harpersfield and surrounding settlements, the Harper brothers and their families settled into whatever accommodations the rebel families of Schoharie could provide them with. Other Harperfield refugee families, including the Hendrys, Gaylords, Patchins and Stevens, were joined by Charlotte Creek's Bartholomew brothers and their families. Thomas Hendry's youngest son David was among those who failed to elude the Tory invaders, and rather than comply with their demands to join their ranks was captured, bound, and forced to march alongside his captors. Before leaving Harpersfield, after having spent a week trashing the settlement and pressuring young men to join him, MacDonell received word that Adam Crysler had assembled nearly eighty loyalists at his mill in the upper Schoharie Valley village of Breakabeen. Having managed to recruit another thirty or so volunteers, MacDonell's party finally left the upper Delaware settlements and headed for the valley where he arrived late in the evening of Saturday, the 9th of August. Finding many of the valley's young men eager to join their cause, Spanish John and Crysler were confident their little army would grow efficiently once most of the citizenry came to their senses and rallied to support the Crown. On Sunday morning, while St. Leger was continuing his bombardment of Fort Schuyler and Herkimer's four hundred fallen soldiers lay swollen and purple in their forested ravine, the people of Schoharie awoke to the news that the war had finally descended upon their quiet valley. [6]

    Assembling their men at the Breakabeen mill, MacDonell and Crysler spent that Sunday recruiting more followers and assessing the strength of the local rebel resistance. Fifteen miles down Schoharie Creek, just outside the village of Schoharie at the Mann family's two-story brick tavern, George Mann was gathering his followers and organizing them into a loyalist militia company. Capt. Mann had originally been a captain in Col. Vrooman's Albany militia regiment but by '77 had deserted to the enemy. Ordering all his recruits to take an oath of loyalty to the king, he proceeded to take control of the valley by posting guards on all the roads leading into and out of the valley. Rather than risk retaliation from his Tory followers and the destruction of their family farms and property, a considerable number of the lower valley's farmers submitted to Mann's demands.

Capt. Mann's company of conscripts posed a formidable threat to the valley's small rebel company that was garrisoned in and around Johannas Becker's stone house, at what would become Schoharie's Middle Fort. Capt. Jacob Hager was one of the few remaining rebel officers still with Col. Vrooman and his handful of militiamen during those first few weeks of August. Hager was said to have been a highly effective officer whose aggressive and intimidating nature occasionally got in the way of his political aspirations. Like Capt. Harper, Capt. Hager was a man of action and the kind of man you would want by your side in a fight. Recognizing that Becker's stone house offered one of the best logistic positions and defensive structures in the mid-Schoharie Valley, Col. Vrooman instructed his men to board up the windows and form what breastworks they could throw together around the house. Col. Vrooman and Capt. Hager's meager forces were grossly outnumbered by the loyalists, but the sight of Capt. Harper and his Harpersfield boys riding in ahead of MacDonell's Tories gave the Schoharie rebels a much-needed boost of morale. [7]

Early Monday morning, after hearing reports of MacDonell's increasing numbers, Col. Vrooman recognized the dire situation his small force of militiamen faced. Ordering Capt. Hager to proceed on foot to Albany to request reinforcements for the relief of his men and the valley, the colonel held out little hope a relief column would arrive in time to save them. By mid-afternoon, the Tories had advanced down the valley from Crysler's Breakabeen mill to a farm within two miles of Becker's stone house and Col. Vrooman's nervous militia. From his encampment near Mill Valley Creek, Spanish John sent a flag to Becker's house, demanding Col. Vrooman surrender his garrison. Resigned to defeat, Col. Vrooman was quoted as having said when asked by Capt. Harper what should be done, '...*nothing at all, we be so weak we cannot do anything...*'. Harper was not the kind of man to suffer defeat so willingly. A response to the Highlander's ultimatum was drafted and signed by the defiant captain, but not his superior Col. Vrooman. There would be no capitulation while he and his Scots-Irish kinsmen were still breathing. Harper and Vrooman both knew full well that their men and their precarious little fortress could not hold out for long. They also knew that Capt. Hager's hike to Albany would not bring about a relief column in time to save them. Speed was of the essence and Harper knew reinforcements were the only hope his men had of holding their tenuous position and surviving an attack from MacDonell's superior forces. As the afternoon slowly turned to dusk and Col. Vrooman vacillated on what to do, Capt. Harper took the initiative and called for his small black mare to be saddled and harnessed.

It was already past sunset by the time Capt. Harper mounted his mare and set out down the valley towards the village of Schoharie and the Duanesburg Road to Albany. Realizing that Capt. Mann had posted guards on all the roads, Harper opted not to challenge his sentinels in the darkness and decided to hold up in a Schoharie tavern for the night before continuing his ride to Albany at first light. After a hot meal and a few pints of ale in Johannas Lawyer's public house, the captain retired to his room for a few hours of sleep. Shortly after laying down, he was disturbed by a ruckus and a pounding on his door by an angry group of local Tories demanding he open up and turn himself over to them. Having anticipated the possibility of just such an interruption, the captain unbolted his door and swung it wide open with his two pistols aimed at the lead intruder and asserted '... *death to the first man*

Adventures of Colonel Harper

who should step over its threshold...'. The Tories thought better of their unwelcomed visit and made a hasty retreat from the doorway and back to Mann's Tavern from whence they had come.

At dawn the next morning, after a restless night, Capt. Harper left Lawyers Tavern and rode through the village of Schoharie before crossing the Fox Creek Bridge and stopping at the very tavern from which his recent visitors had launched their nocturnal visit. Capt. Harper's curiously audacious visit to the headquarters of Mann's Tory followers defies all that one might find prudent and wise for anyone's self-preservation. But knowing full well that the Tories intended to impede his passage to Albany, the intrepid captain's bold attempt at intimidation seems to have caught the dumbfounded Tories off guard and momentarily set them back on their heels. Harper's aggressive threats of reprisal on anyone who might dare follow him seem to have had their desired effect and gave him the head start he was hoping for. Galloping off he rode fast and hard, looking back over his shoulder from time to time to see if any of his detractors had failed to heed his warnings. [8]

Capt. Harper's thirty-five-mile ride from Schoharie to Albany took him up Barton Hill Rd. to Quaker Street and the Duanesburg Road to Duanesburg before dropping down towards Albany on the Old State Road and Western Turnpike, today's U.S. Hwy. #20. Presuming to have alternated his pace between a gallop and a canter, his ride would have taken about five to six hours, putting him in Albany around two or three in the afternoon of Tuesday the 12th. Just before reaching Duanesburg, ten miles into his ride, Harper had noticed two horsemen trailing him from a safe distance. Rounding a turn on the forest road he quickly dismounted his horse, unsheathed his saber and set it close by, then cocked his two trusty pistols and made ready to face his assailants. As the two cohorts turned the corner, they suddenly came face-to-face with the same two pistols that had discouraged the captain's Tory visitors the night before. In a thunderous voice and tenor that stopped his pursuers in their tracks he bellowed '... *Stop you villains, face about and be off this instant or these bullets shall whistle through your hearts...*'. Capt. Harper recognized both would-be assassins who instantly abided his command and turned their horses about and sped back down the road from whence they came. Seth's Henry and David Ogeyonda were both well known to the militia captain and all the Schoharie citizenry. Seth's Henry was said to have continued shadowing the captain from a safe distance almost all the way to Albany before returning to Schoharie. [9]

Colonel Harper Confronting the Indians

After galloping into Albany, Capt. Harper immediately inquired as to where he might find the officer in charge. Col. Goose Van Schaick oversaw Albany's garrison at the time and after being briefed as to the Schoharie situation, offered a detachment of his 1st New York Regiment to accompany the captain back to Schoharie. Adamant that a company of foot soldiers would take too long to reach the valley, Harper insisted that a detachment of calvary was Schoharie's only hope. As it happened, a company of Col. Elisha Sheldon's 2nd Continental Regiment of Light Dragoons was in Albany that day in route to join Gen. Gates at Stillwater. Capt. Jean Louis deVernejoux, a French volunteer with an arrogant disposition and propensity for controversy, was ordered to assist Capt. Harper and follow him back to the Schoharie Valley with a detachment of twenty-eight Connecticut Dragoons. deVernejoux's 2nd company of dragoons were known as The Blacks for the black horses they were all required to ride. The Blacks were an impressive and intimidating corps of cavalry, clad in blue regimental uniforms and capped with an ornate French-style steel helmet adorned with a long black horsehair plume. They carried carbines, pistols, and swords, and were trained to fight on horseback or on foot. Evening was already well along by the time the dragoons were finally saddled and ready to ride. With just a half-moon to light their way and Capt. Harper to guide their advance, the dragoons rode off on their midnight ride towards Duanesburg and the Schoharie Valley. [10]

Galloping down Barton Hill early Wednesday morning with the sun to their backs, Capt. Harper and the dragoons headed directly for Capt. Mann's Tory tavern from whence the captain had departed the morning before. The thundering hooves and startling sight of deVernejoux's Light Horse sent shivers of shock and awe down the backs of Mann's Schoharie farm boys. A blast from the company's trumpeter added an extra measure of drama and dread. Harper's first order of business was to arrest Capt. Mann and as many of his Tory followers as he could catch. The turncoat captain's first impulse was to hide himself in a nearby mound of stacked wheat. Unable to corner the fox, the intimidating cavalrymen did manage to capture a few of Mann's recent inductees and convince several of them to denounce their oath to the king in exchange for pardons and paroles. The reluctant ones were rounded up and bound together by a long rope for transport to an appropriate place of detention.

Having eliminated the threat of Mann's Tory cabal, the tired dragoons halted their advance at a nearby tavern where they rested their sweaty mounts and toasted to the success of their Tory rout. As news of their arrival spread through the valley, emboldened Schoharie boys began turning out with their rusty old muskets and flintlock pistols, ready now to join the fight and finally commit to the rebel cause. Around noon, having rested their horses and refreshed themselves with food and drink, Capt. Harper and the dragoons began their march up the valley with their new militia recruits and Tory prisoners. Before reaching Becker's stone house and Col. Vrooman's beleaguered militia, one of their captives, David Ogeyonda, slipped his bindings and made off into the brush. Seth's Henry's partner was chased down and shot by one of the dragoons. Laying wounded and pleading for quarter, a local farm boy delivered the *coup de grâce* with a bullet through the Mohawk's head. This day's first blood would not be its last. [11]

With the mid-day sun reflecting off their shiny steel helmets, the sight of the approaching dragoons roused the militiamen and rangers to fire a few welcoming volleys for their returning captain and deVernejoux's company of Continental Light Horsemen. Col. Vrooman's earlier resignation was replaced by an overwhelming sense of relief and astonishment that Capt. Harper could have returned so quickly with such an impressive corps of cavalry men. Fortunately, MacDonell had not yet advanced on the garrison and was still encamped two miles up the valley from Becker's stone house. Learning of the dragoon's arrival, MacDonell resolved to abandon his position and slowly withdraw back up the valley, regretting his hesitation to take the garrison when he had the opportunity. His reasoning for not attacking the rebel fortification while it was still woefully undermanned suggests he may have been waiting for Capt. Mann and his recruits to join his forces before initiating an attack. Being trained in European warfare and the tactics of mounted engagements, the wily Highlander's retreat may have also been a calculated maneuver to reposition his forces on more advantageous grounds. Finding a suitable rise above a swampy lowland pasture on Adam Crysler's lower farm near today's hamlet of Fultonham, Spanish John positioned his men and waited for the Continental cavalry to approach the boggy flats.

After spending most of the afternoon beefing up their defenses around Becker's stone house, the rebels received word that MacDonell had withdrawn up the valley. Col. Vrooman and his captains decided their best option was to now take the battle to the Tories. They needed to take swift action and attack before the Tories could fully retreat back into the forests where their equestrian advantage would be marginalized. Needing every man and every horse they had; they could ill afford to leave too many troops behind to guard their prisoners. Improvising a solution, they made their captives climb a ladder to the ridge of Becker's two-story house where their only option for escape was to slide down a steep pitched roof before falling twenty more feet to the ground. [12]

As the late afternoon sun slipped behind an ominous looking thunderhead gathering over the western mountain ridge known to the locals as Onistagarawa, the Continental horsemen and Schoharie militia began their advance up the valley towards MacDonell's new position. deVernejoux's twenty-eight dragoons were closely followed by Capt. Harper's mounted rangers and Schoharie's mounted militiamen. Trailing behind the ad-hoc cavalry corps, Col. Vrooman led a company of recently emboldened Schoharie farm boys jogging to keep up with the horsemen. In all, the Schoharie rebels numbered no more than forty horsemen and another two or three dozen foot soldiers. MacDonell and Crysler were said to have had around thirty Charlotte Creek Highlanders, eighty Schoharie Tories and about twenty of Seth Henry's Schoharie Mohawks. Crysler, however, had deployed about thirty-five of his local Tories to his Breakabeen mill to prevent the rebels from encircling them should some of them take the Clauverwie highroad along the eastern ridge. The king's men still held a two-to-one advantage over the rebel militia and cavalry that would have to charge across a soggy lowland marsh known to the local Dutch as *die flâche* and to the local Yorkers as the flockey. MacDonell's high ground above the flockey added a distinct tactical advantage to his superior numerical one. [13]

Riding two-abreast along the old road that hugged the base of Onistagarawa, the Continentals rode through today's Fultonham and crossed over a small millstream into Adam Crysler's low-lying pasture. Immediately spying the Tory position on their right flank, the dragoons swung about and quickly assembled into a cavalry formation with alternately mounted and unmounted troops, while Capt. Harper kept his mounted militia ready in reserve. Capt. deVernejoux was frantically barking out orders and trying to hold his men in an orderly formation when the Tories unleashed their first devastating enfilade on the exposed horsemen. Privates Charles West and Thomas Rose were both mortally wounded in the chaos of the first couple of volleys. Pvt. Edward Basset was shot through the side and in the shoulder while Pvt. Amasa Scott's left hand was mangled by a ball. Lt. David Wirt and his horse were both killed, as were several other horses.

Realizing their position was untenable, deVernejoux ordered his trumpeter, John Conley, to sound the call to mount and charge with sabers drawn. Harper's horsemen joined the dragoons and charged with them up the slope towards MacDonell's position. Within a few chaotic minutes the advantage was turned, and the panic-stricken loyalists broke and ran. Several were trampled by the stampeding Blacks and slashed by the sword wielding horsemen. As the Tories and Indians scrambled up the steep and heavily forested hill behind Crysler's farm, dusk and the unfavorable equestrian terrain brought a halt to the skirmish and a reprieve for the stunned Highlanders and their Schoharie comrades. At about the same time, those ominous thunder clouds that had been gathering all afternoon finally delivered their promise, dampening rifle cartridges and discouraging any further exchange of fire. [14]

Driven from the valley, Spanish John retreated to his Highlander refuge on Charlotte Creek before heading back through the wilderness to Fort Oswego. Arriving about the same time as St. Leger's exhausted troops, the failure of MacDonell's Schoharie campaign paled in comparison to St. Leger's Fort Schuyler debacle. Returning with around forty new recruits for Col. Johnson's Loyalist Regiment, MacDonell was awarded a captain's commission for his service and contribution to the Crown. Crysler too was eventually elevated to captain while the turncoat Capt. Mann was soon captured and imprisoned in an Albany jail for the remainder of the war. Capt. Jean Louis deVernejoux returned to Albany with his dragoons and rejoined Col. Sheldon's Continental Lighthorse on their march to Stillwater. The French captain's victorious cavalry charge at the Battle of the Flockey was soon overshadowed by his arrogant and disparaging treatment of his subordinates. After arriving at Stillwater and suffering what he perceived as an intolerable offense to his pride by being recommissioned to a reduction in rank, his career in the Continental Army came to an abrupt end. Capt. deVernejoux deserted his command and simply vanished. His second company's command was given to his twenty-year-old 1st lieutenant, Thomas Youngs Seymour, who went on to distinguish himself at Saratoga as the 'Beau Sabreur of Saratoga'. Capt. Seymour went on to serve throughout the rest of the war in Col. Sheldon's 2nd Continental Regiment of Light Dragoons. [15]

The Battle of the Flockey awakened Schoharie Valley and the surrounding settlements to the realities of a war that had already been in full swing for over two years. Although relatively insignificant in comparison to other major developments of that summer, it did mark the first time an untested frontier militia played a major part in turning back a Tory invasion. The victory at Saratoga and the defiant stand at Fort Schuyler proved that an upstart American Army of Continental soldiers and untrained militia volunteers could hold off and defeat the most powerful army in the world. The collective sigh of relief that resonated through the frontier settlements following the news of Burgoyne's surrender would unfortunately prove to be all too fleeting. After the return of the Continental regiments to their Connecticut, Hudson Highlands, and northern New Jersey garrisons, the protection of the northern department's frontier once again fell solely upon the shoulders of New York's local militias. Leaders and heroes would be needed to inspire the common man to sacrifice all he loved and cherished for the furtherance of an abstract cause. Capt. John Harper emerged from the Battle of the Flockey as one of those frontier heroes and leaders.

Colonel Harper's Charge
A Ballad of Schoharie
Thomas Dunn English
'...*The whole of the foeman seem stricken with one dread,*
'Tis Colonel John Harper with horsemen a hundred.
We gazed but a moment in rapture and wonder,
Rides Harper like lightning, we fall like the thunder.
To saddle McDonald, your doom has been spoken.
The tigers are on you, the bars have been broken.
Whose horse the swiftest may ride from the foray.
No hope for the footman of savage or Tory...'

Soon after the Battle of the Flockey, Capt. Harper gathered a group of volunteers to accompany him and his rangers on a reconnaissance scout to Harpersfield and Kortright. Finding their homesteads and settlements in ashes and the few remaining settlers hiding in the woods, Harper's men rounded up those friendly to the cause and threatened those who stubbornly held out for the king with imprisonment or worse. Harper and his fellow frontier refugees returned to Schoharie Valley to prepare for the winter that was now closing in upon them. Three forts were being hastily built to garrison the local militia and their families and whatever Continental troops that might eventually be dispatched to the frontier. The village of Schoharie's Reformed Dutch Church was enclosed within a palisade and transformed into what became Schoharie Valley's Lower Fort, or The Old Schoharie Stone Fort. The temporary breastworks that had been thrown up around Johannas Becker's stone house were replaced with a more permanent stockade fortification and became the valley's main militia headquarters. Middle Fort was equipped with barracks and crude huts for the soldiers and their families who would call the fort their home throughout the rest of the border war. The fort was constructed with corner blockhouses and equipped with a few nine-pound cannons. A smaller fortification known as the valley's Upper Fort was erected around Johannas Feck's house near today's Fultonham. All three forts sheltered the valley's residents in times of danger when their homesteads were under attack by the enemy.

Schoharie's three forts reinforced the frontier border region's line of defensive fortifications and blockhouses that stretched from Fort Schuyler on the upper Mohawk to Schenectady and the Hudson River. They connected the northern Mohawk River forts with the southern forts in Old Ulster County's frontier districts of Mamakating, Rochester and Woodstock that protected the rear flank of the Hudson Highlands from Westchester County to Kingston. The garrisoned troops in the Great Shandaken, Lackawack, and Minisink forts along the lower Delaware were tasked with patrolling and protecting the frontier settlements along the Delaware's East Branch and the Catskills' upper Rondout, Neversink and Esopus settlements. [16]

Connecticut and New York militia regiments had been building and fortifying forts along the lower Hudson all through the summer of '77 in anticipation of the third prong of the Albany campaign. In early October, with Burgoyne on the ropes and St. Leger already back in Fort Oswego, the British launched their belated Hudson River campaign. Finally acknowledging the disaster Burgoyne was facing, Gen. William Howe sent Gen. Henry Clinton and his Royal fleet up the river on what was now a diversionary expedition to draw off some of Gates' Continental forces from Saratoga. Five miles up the river from the Tappen Zee, two American forts had been built on the west side of the Hudson below Bear Mountain and directly across from a high protrusion known as Anthony's Nose, just north of Peekskill. The larger of the two, Fort Montgomery, was flanked by Fort Clinton on the south side of Popolopen Creek. Gen. Clinton's flotilla of ships was loaded with 1,100 British Regulars supported by another 1,000 troops marching by foot up the Hudson.

The day before Burgoyne's army was defeated at Bemis Heights on the 7th of October, Clinton's British forces attacked and easily overtook Fort Montgomery and Fort Clinton's six hundred rebel defenders in a brutal bayonet assault. While Gates continued pressuring Burgoyne into surrendering, word of the inevitable surrender prompted Gen. Clinton to withdraw his troops and abandon the two forts they held for less than a week. As a parting gift for New York's recently formed government, the British unleashed one last punitive strike on the rebel insurgents. While Burgoyne prepared to handover his sword, Clinton's redcoats marched through the streets of Kingston setting fire to every house and business, sending the state's committeemen fleeing into the countryside with whatever documents and papers they could carry.

Roosa's Rangers

With the young men of the upper Susquehanna and the Delaware's upper West Branch running off to join Tory companies or rebel militias, those along the Delaware's East Branch were faced with their own tough decisions. Being removed and somewhat insulated from the Mohawk and Hudson River theaters, their quiet valley remained relatively unaffected by the war throughout the summer of 1777. But they too were about to be drawn into the fight that would leave their bountiful valley deserted and their homes in ruins. The Dutch settlers of Paghatakan and Pawpachton were nearly all voicing their support for the king, but as of yet had limited their support of the Tories to just providing them with cattle and provisions when pressed. The settlers of the southeastern border region were Hardenburgh leaseholders, most of whom felt more contempt for their overbearing landlords than for the Crown. Being within Old Ulster County's outlying frontier districts of Woodstock and Rochester, their ties to civilization were with the Hudson's Dutch communities of Kingston, Hurley and Marbletown. Many naïvely hoped that if the rebellion was quickly put down and they remained firmly in support of the king, their land/lease contracts might be terminated and their properties made available for purchase by fee simple. The promise of land was a primary recruiting incentive for both sides during the war and for most frontier homesteaders it meant more to them than Independence or fidelity.

In mid-April, while Albany, Ulster and Tryon County Committees of Safety were sending out patrols to hunt down Tories and bring in loyalist sympathizers, a bold if not foolish plan was hatched by a former captain in Col. Jonathan Hasbrouck's 4th Ulster County Militia Regiment. After being court-martialed and cashiered for insubordination in February, Capt. Jacobus Roosa traded his rebel captain's stripes for a lieutenant's commission in Col. Edmund Fanning's 4th American Regiment of the King's Loyalist Army. Awarding officer commissions to loyalist volunteers came with the requirement that they muster a certain number of recruits into their regiments. Lt. Roosa was under an obligation to bring in his quota of recruits. The turncoat lieutenant devised a plan to entice young Catskill Mountain recruits into joining his Royal Loyalist Regiment in New York City. Rather than slipping off into the backwoods and joining one of the frontier Tory outfits, the thought of parading through the streets of New York in a handsome British uniform was as powerful an incentive as was the fifty acres each of the conscripts was promised. The British offer of fifty acres for every recruit, was inflated by Lt. Roosa to one hundred acres, with another fifty acres for each of their children. His added assurance that the insurrection would be over by harvest time and the thought of going home to their own farms to *'enjoy their bottle and lass'*, quickly quelled any reservations a prospective young recruit might have had. [17]

Having grown up in Marbletown, west of Kingston, Jacobus Roosa was familiar with many of the Dutch families on the Delaware's East Branch and was presumably related to a few of them. With loyalist sentiments running high amongst most of the Paghatakan and Pawpachton settlers, the East Branch was fertile ground for a recruiting foray. The Middagh brothers, John, Jacob, Stephen, and Martin had settled together at the mouth of the Beaver Kill where they cleared a substantial homestead site and built a horse-powered grist mill. Growing up on their father's Marbletown farm, the brothers were well known to Lt. Roosa. Pvt. Jacob Middagh had mustered into a company of Col. Fanning's Loyalist Regiment shortly before Roosa traded his blue captain's uniform for a redcoat lieutenant's. Being acquainted with Pvt. Middagh, Lt. Roosa persuaded the young man with the promise of a promotion in rank, to help him meet his lieutenant commission's quota. The plan called for Middagh to return to the East Branch and recruit as many of the valley's young men as he could, then quietly hike over the mountains to rendezvous with the lieutenant at the Shandaken tavern of Jacob Longyear. On April 23rd, Pvt. Middagh and six or eight of his East Branch recruits met Lt. Roosa and twenty of his followers at Longyear's tavern near the present-day hamlet of Mount Pleasant. Convincing three of Jacob Longyear's five sons and a half dozen of their neighbors to join them, Lt. Roosa and Pvt. Middagh's party set out on their ninety-mile journey to New York City through Ulster and Orange County's rebel-infested backwoods. [18]

Traveling by night down Esopus Creek to the Shokan house of a fellow loyalist, the Roosa party held up for the first day of their journey and waited for another moonless night to continue towards New York City. Recruiting volunteers as they made their way through the backwoods of Marbletown, the little band of defectors found refuge for a second day at the home of another loyalist sympathizer. With their numbers swelling to over thirty, the path forward grew ever more hazardous as they passed by Ulster County's Rondout and Wallkill settlements. Crossing the Shawangunks and fording the Wallkill south of New Paltz, some of the young men began questioning the wisdom of their decision to join the expedition. A few even began peeling off into the forest and heading back to their families in the Catskills. With exaggerated rumors of Roosa's numbers and their threat to the countryside, Ulster militia patrols were sent out to hunt them down and bring them in. Running into a couple of rebel militiamen, several of Roosa's nervous rangers fired on them. They wounded a lieutenant who managed to ride back to Newburgh to inform his regiment of the encounter. Capt. John A. Hardenburgh of Col. Levi Pawling's 3rd Regiment of Ulster Militia, immediately set off with his company to intercept and capture the loyalist conspirators. South of the frontier village of New Britain and five miles southwest of Newburgh, Roosa and Middagh learned that Hardenburgh's rebel militia was closing in on them. Making off for the high ridge of the Schunnemunk Mountains, they hoped to hide out long enough to avoid detection, or if necessary, make a stand. With another thirty-five miles of Orange County's rebel highlands between them and New York City, their chances of joining Col. Fanning's regiment were growing thinner by the mile. [19]

Discovering the loyalist's hiding place, the rebel militia encircled their prey and exchanged a few volleys with them before engaging in a running skirmish. About five of Roosa's Rangers were killed before the militia rounded up the rest and brought them in. On April 30th, one week after leaving Jacob Longyear's tavern on Esopus Creek, Lt. Roosa and Pvt. Middagh and what was left of their little band of recruits stood before a court-martial tribunal at Fort Montgomery. Pleading for mercy and regretting they had ever met Roosa or Middagh, the disheartened young recruits from the East Branch and the Great Shandaken all stood charged with treasonous insurrection against the State of New York. A handful were recommended for clemency while the rest were found guilty and sentenced to hang. Sent to Kingston to await their day on the gallows, the Council of Safety deliberated and devised an alternative option for the young, misguided rangers. With many in, or barely through, their teens, the Catskill Mountain boys were offered commutations of their death sentences if they would denounce their loyalist pledges and enlist in a Continental Regiment. Having been motivated to join the British army by promises of personal gain and less by fidelity to the king, the rangers were quick to accept their pardons and change their stripes. The perpetrators of the plot were offered no such deal and were both unceremoniously hung in Kingston on May 13th, two weeks after their capture.

After being paroled the accidental rebel volunteers were mustered into the Continental Army in an Ulster or Dutchess County regiment or in a local county militia company. Many of them were assigned to Col. Lewis Dubois's 5th New York Regiment stationed along the Hudson River and spent the summer of '77 building parapets around forts Montgomery and Clinton. Some of the Catskill boys who had imagined parading through the streets of New York in a handsome British uniform and returning home to their own 100-acre farms by harvest time, were among the seventy-five killed and 263 captured when the two forts were taken by the British in October. Two of tavern owner Jacob Longyear's five sons, Jacob Jr and Andries were among the defenders of Fort Montgomery when Col. Edmund Fanning's American Regiment stormed the fort with their merciless bayonets. The two brothers were presumed to have been killed by the troops of the loyalist regiment they would have been among, had they not been captured in the Schunnemunks five months earlier. Several of Roosa's Rangers actually did fulfill their dreams of parading through the streets of New York City, albeit under a heavy guard of British Regulars escorting them to the East River's prison hulks and their long agonizing deaths. [20]

The end of the Saratoga, Fort Schuyler and Hudson River campaigns brought an end to the fighting season of 1777. The British had been defeated and driven back up or back down the three waterway corridors they used to invade into the heart of New York's frontier territory. With Schenectady and Albany secured and the settlements along the Mohawk and Schoharie valleys temporarily secure enough to harvest their fall crops, the frontier settled into an eerily quiet winter. Tryon County's outlying settlements had all been abandoned with their former residents either living in a rebel-held fort and settlement or in a British fort on the shores of Lake Ontario. The momentary sense of relief and satisfaction the residents of New York's borderlands felt at the end of that triumphant year, was chastened by the realization that their frontier war was just beginning.

Cobleskill

The fighting season of 1778 marked the beginning of all-out war for the residents of New York's frontier border region. Pledging their fidelity to either king or Congress, the last of the lingering homesteaders headed off towards the eastern settlements or the western wilderness. The frontier between the old Indian property line of '68 and the string of militia forts and settlements along the Mohawk and Schoharie Valleys and throughout Ulster County's frontier was about to suffer some of the most horrific atrocities of the war. Captain Brant had withdrawn to his Susquehanna stronghold at Onaquaga following Oriskany and the Saratoga campaigns and throughout that winter rallied his warriors and welcomed new Tories into his ranks. By May, Brant's army had swelled to nearly four hundred Indians and Tories, all of whom were growing restless for scalps and booty. Brant's first objective was to feed his hungry troops by plundering cattle and crops from the isolated settlements south of the Mohawk River. Springfield at the head of Otsego Lake was targeted, as was nearby Cherry Valley where many of the Susquehanna refugees fled after being forced from their lower settlements. After successfully plundering

Springfield without molesting or killing any of the homesteaders, Brant's warriors feasted on their cattle and hogs before heading east towards their second target.

On the 29th of May, Brant and his men encamped in the woods on Lady Hill, east of the unsuspecting village of Cherry Valley. Observing the stockade that had been built around Samuel Campbell's house at the foot of the hill, Brant viewed what he thought was a formidable company of militia soldiers marching and drilling around the stockade. Reluctant to attack a settlement with such an impressive corps of militia, Brant decided to abort his attack and march on to another village fifteen miles southeast on the Cobus Kill. Unbeknownst to Brant, the soldiers he observed from Lady Hill were the village's young boys, parading and pretending to be real rebel militiamen just like their fathers and older brothers. The young Campbell boys and the sons of James and Mary Harper Moore, John-11 and James-10, and their Gault cousins, John-12, William-11 and James-7, had no inkling of the disaster that might have befallen their village had they not been playing at soldiering that day. [21]

By the summer of '78, about twenty families of Palatine Dutch extraction were living on the fertile Cobus Kill flats, eight miles west of the village of Schoharie. When scouting parties began bringing in reports of Brant's forces in the area, a company of thirty to forty militiamen led by Capt. William Patrick was sent out from Schoharie to bolster Capt. Christian Brown's twenty-man Cobleskill militia. On the 30th, the reinforced militia encountered a small company of Tories and Indians lingering around the house of Committeeman George Warner. A running skirmish ensued with the Schoharie militiamen chasing Brant's decoy party west in the direction of today's Warnerville, south of the current village of Cobleskill. Brant's 350 warriors were waiting in ambush for the grossly outnumbered militiamen. The frantic hand-to-hand Battle of Cobleskill was as much a massacre as it was a battle. Within minutes, Captain Patrick was dead, and half of the militiamen were either dead, captured or wounded. Captain Brown then led the surviving militiamen in a fighting retreat. The resident homesteaders who had fled into the forests at the onset of the battle, watched from a safe distance as their houses, barns and stores were all put to the torch and their livestock driven off or killed.

After gathering up as many cattle and livestock as they could herd off, Brant's warriors drove their bounty up the Cobus Kill and over to Summit Lake before dropping down into Charlotte Creek Valley. Brant's attacks on the peripheral settlements of the border region during the summer of '78, were primarily motivated by the need to feed his hungry men. Another incentive for the attacks was fueled by the seething rage of his Tory soldiers, many of whom had suffered the indignation of having their former homesteads confiscated and their wives and children held in captivity by the rebels. A few weeks after his attack on Cobleskill, Brant led another couple of small raids on the remote settlements north of Otsego Lake. Throughout June and July, Brant's warriors and Tories were relentless in their harassment of frontier homesteaders and their settlements. [22]

One of the foremost bases and supply line depots used by Brant and his warriors during the early summer of '78 was the Charlotte Creek settlement of Christopher Servos and his five sons. The Servos family had long been known to have held their king's interests in higher regard than that of Congress and their rebellious neighbors. Four of fifty-seven-year-old Christopher's five sons were of fighting age and were inclined to agree with their father's loyalist sympathies, at least in the early years of the war. It had been suspected that one or two of his older sons had been among Brant's Tories at Cobleskill and that the Servos family had aided the raiding party on its advance and retreat from the battle. Scouts had been sent out earlier in the war to reconnoiter activities on the Servos compound and had arrested and briefly held Christopher and his two older sons captive before being paroled.

Six weeks after the Battle of Cobleskill, a capable and aggressive commander with frontier experience was finally assigned to the border frontier. Gen. Washington had at last answered the calls from his northern commanders to send more troops and resources to the northern frontier. In late July, several weeks after serving with distinction at the Battle of Monmouth, Lt. Col. William Butler arrived at Schoharie's Middle Fort with about 230 soldiers: a 130-man detachment of the 4th Pennsylvania Regiment and two companies of Daniel Morgan's elite corps of Virginia and Pennsylvania riflemen. Morgan's two rifle companies were led by Captains Gabriel Long and James Parr with Captain Commandant Thomas Posey as their commanding officer. With no relationship to New York's loyalist Butler family, William Butler had been a fur trader in western Pennsylvania and throughout the Ohio territory before the war and was well versed in Indian culture and their style of warfare. His orders were to protect the frontier settlements and punish the loyalist settlers who were suspected of aiding and victualing the enemy.

Reinforcing Col. Vrooman's meager Schoharie militia forces, Col. Butler was eager to take the offensive against the enemy that had been harassing the frontier settlements with impunity. With reports coming in of Brant's continued presence in the upper Susquehanna and Charlotte Creek vicinity, Butler sent out a small scout to assess the enemy's strength and the extent to which they relied upon families like the Servos' for help. Unfamiliar with the terrain, the southern riflemen would have relied on a few of Capt. Harper's rangers to guide them through the forests. One or two of the Bartholomew brothers, who had grown up next to the Servos family on their adjacent Charlotte Creek property, might have been sent out on the scout to brief them on the layout of the Servos homestead and surrounding terrain.

On August 5th, two months after the massacre at Cobleskill, Capt. Gabriel Long led a detachment of Morgan's riflemen and Harper's frontier rangers to the Servos settlement and quietly surrounded it. Two of his best men were sent into the settlement to confront Mr. Servos and convince the German gentleman to give himself and his family up peacefully to the rebel authorities. But the two rebel emissaries, Privates Timothy Murphy and David Ellerson, had their own ideas as to how to eliminate the Servos problem. Murphy took it upon himself to call out the family patriarch and provoke him into an altercation. With his wife by his side, Christopher rebuked the insolent private's demand to surrender and grabbed for a nearby axe while telling the '...*damn rebel...*' to desist and remove himself from his property. Murphy's impulsive response to the challenge was to push Clara Servos aside while telling her '...*Mother, he never will sleep with you again...*', then firing his rifle at point-blank range sending a bullet through the old man's heart. Murphy was alleged to have returned to Middle Fort with the '*upper leather*' gentleman's bloody scalp.

Had Murphy done his due diligence and acted as a proper Continental soldier, Christopher Servos would have been arrested and confined for the duration of the war in an Albany prison. Upon his release, he might have had the resources to claim partial compensation for his confiscated property, just as his grandchildren did long after the war. Two of the Servos brothers, Daniel and Jacob, went on to serve as lieutenants in Major John Butler's Regiment of New York Loyalists while three of their younger brothers, John, Philip and Christian, eventually enlisted in the Continental Army. This gave their children the grounds to apply to Congress for partial reclamation of their family's Charlotte Creek property. Timothy Murphy's murder of Christopher Servos and his propensity for provoking similar incidents might suggest something other than the claim made by every nineteenth-century historian as to him being the greatest hero of the Revolution's New York border war. [23]

Wyoming Valley

After his raids on the upper Susquehanna and Mohawk River settlements and his last visit with the Servos family, Capt. Brant led his warriors and their confiscated cattle back down the river to Onaquaga. Brant intended to hold up for a while to let his men rest and wait for more Tory recruits to join his army. Word came in however, that British Maj. John Butler was at the confluence of the Susquehanna and Chemung rivers assembling a force of loyalists and Indians for a raid on the lower Susquehanna settlements. Brant was ordered to join the major for a war council where it was decided that he and his warriors should remain at Onaquaga, as rumors were circulating of an attack on the Indian stronghold. After their Tioga Point conference, Maj. Butler and his son Capt. Butler marched down the Susquehanna with their regiment of 150 loyalist rangers, a company of Col. John Johnson's Royal Greens, and five hundred Seneca warriors. Schoharie's Adam Crysler was among the loyalist rangers who accompanied Butler's expedition. Part of the British strategy for attacking such an isolated and insignificant outpost was to try to force Washington to divert some of his troops away from northern New Jersey to the western frontier. Most of the Connecticut men who had settled in the disputed Westmoreland Territory and the Wyoming Valley were with Washington in northern New Jersey where they were harassing British garrisons on Staten Island.

With word of Butler's approach, the few remaining Wyoming Valley militiamen and residents ran for protection into one of the valley's scattered fortifications, Forty Fort being the most formidable. With the absence of virtually every man and boy of fighting age the stockade's commander Col. Zebulon Butler, another Butler with no relationship to the loyalist Butlers, had only old men and young boys with which to make an army out of. Col. Butler's makeshift army, as expected, proved woefully inadequate. Maj. John Butler's loyalist rangers and British regulars made quick work of overpowering the valley's eight forts. The inept militia scattered and ran for their lives while unrestrained Seneca warriors unleashed a fury of hellfire on the terrified citizenry and fleeing soldiers. One of the Seneca warriors later said of the attack *'…I took my tomahawk and sword and went amongst the enemy…and cut men down, two and more as I went by…We never left any wounded, but killed them as we went along…'*.

By the end of the day, Maj. Butler's men and their Indian comrades had destroyed all eight forts, torched over a thousand dwellings, and butchered 375 of Wyoming Valley's defenseless citizens. All of the predominantly women, children and old men who fled that day were chased down and scalped before they were mercilessly bludgeoned to death. The Wyoming Massacre was without a doubt one of the worst atrocities of the entire border war. Newspapers printed graphic details and disturbing accounts of the horrific event that justifiably incited a fervor of disgust and calls for retribution. The papers also vilified *'The Monster Brant'*, who was surprised to learn he was presumed to have been responsible for the massacre. Capt. Brant was in fact still in Onaquaga at the time and many miles from the Susquehanna's Wyoming Valley on July 3rd, 1778. The Wyoming Massacre sanctioned the equivalent slaughter of Indian women, children, and old men by rebel militias throughout the rest of the war. [24]

Two weeks after the Wyoming Massacre, Capt. Brant and his warriors were back in the upper Susquehanna's Otsego Lake neighborhoods, hunting for more cattle and scalps. Five miles north of Springfield, a clustering of homesteads in today's Warren Township, known then as Andrustown, were easy prey for the hungry foragers. The scattered homesteaders offered little resistance as the Indians ran unopposed through their remote settlements, torching every home and barn while destroying their wagons and farming implements. Twenty-two men were either killed or taken captive and all the livestock was either driven off or butchered in their pastures. The women and children who survived were left without the benefit of shelter, food, or many of their men and older sons. [25]

Dumond Affair

While Brant's warriors were repeatedly terrorizing the Tryon County settlements, Old Ulster County's frontier settlements were beginning to feel the heat of that first summer of guerrilla warfare. The East Branch of the Delaware was known to the commanders of the Tryon, Albany, and Ulster County militias as a bastion of Tory activities and loyalist support. Aside from the hapless young recruits who had joined Middagh and Roosa the summer before, Brant was known to have been actively recruiting the valley's young men and relying upon the loyalist sympathizers of Paghatakan and Pawpachton for cattle and supplies. Throughout the late summer of 1778, what few rebel sympathizers there were in the valley, began to prepare to abandon their frontier farms. A few of them were contemplating hanging on long enough to harvest one last crop before packing up their belongings and heading east. By late August, most of the Whig homesteaders were being escorted over Pine Hill by militia companies sent out from Fort Shandaken for their relief. Another militia scout from Schoharie's Middle Fort was also sent out to the

East Branch in late August. The Schoharie scout, however, was not intended for the relief of the rebel settlers but was meant to round up any Tory dissidents still lingering in the valley. Unfortunately, an effective line of communication between the Ulster and Tryon County militia commanders had not yet been established, rendering it impossible to coordinate the two scouts that had no knowledge of each other's deployment or movements.

After the Ulster militia had escorted the last group of Paghatakan families over Pine Hill to the safety of Fort Shandaken, two of the family's patriarchs turned around and headed back over the hill to gather their remaining livestock and provisions. On the morning of August 26th, after having loaded their wagons and harnessed their horses, Hermanus Dumond and his companion John Barrows set out for Pine Hill along the Bush Kill east towards Shandaken. Before they had gone far, they were confronted by the advance guard of the Schoharie scouting party. The Schoharie scout was led by a capable young Virginia captain from Morgan's rifle corps who had been assigned to the Schoharie frontier along with Col. William Butler's 4th Pennsylvania detachment. Capt. Thomas Posey had grown up on the Potomac River on a plantation adjacent to George Washington's Mount Vernon estate and was said to have been a favorite of the generals. Capt. Posey was accompanied on the scout by the frontier ranger Lt. Alexander Harper, the youngest of the Harper brothers. The Virginian was new to the northern territory and would have relied on his second-in-command to help guide his scout through the forest and inform him as to the sentiments of the East Branch residents. The Harper's settlement on the West Branch was fewer than twenty miles from the East Branch settlements, and while not at all friendly with his Low Dutch neighbors, Alexander would have certainly been aware of the valley's sympathies. Hermanus Dumond was acknowledged by his Paghatakan neighbors as being one of the leaders of their community and an ardent supporter of the king's loyalist faction. But what was not known to Dumond's neighbors or the Schoharie scout, was that he had been Ulster County's militia commander Col. John Cantine's, '...*chief man for intelligence...*'.

Advancing up Schoharie Creek from Middle Fort and continuing over to the headwaters of the East Branch, Capt. Posey's sixty-man scout arrived at Paghatakan and broke off into two separate parties. Posey led half the men down the East Branch towards Pawpachton while Lt. Harper and his men combed the area around Paghatakan and the Bush Kill. As Harper's men came upon Dumond and Barrows making their way east up the Bush Kill towards Pine Hill, the two East Branchers took the scout to be a Tory scouting party, as they had approached them from the west. Sensing their confusion, Lt. Harper appears to have taken full advantage of their misconception and played along with it to extract a confession of loyalist affiliations from the two men. Harper told the two Dutch homesteaders, who spoke only broken English, they would be taken back to Butler and recruited into his army. Lt. Harper purposely misled them to believe that the Butler he was referring to was British Maj. John Butler and not Schoharie's Col. William Butler. The fact that Dumond and his companion were directing their wagons towards the east and the rebel settlements should have suggested to Lt. Harper, they were indeed Whig sympathizers and not Tories. But the prospect of returning to Middle Fort with two dead Tories, their horses, and their wagons full of provisions proved too tempting a trophy for the ambitious young lieutenant to resist.

Dumond knew all too well that if he were taken back to Niagara and interrogated by British intelligence, his role as a rebel spy would be exposed and he would be hung from the nearest tree. Considering his options while continuing to be misled by Lt. Harper's deception, forty-six-year-old Hermanus made a desperate decision. He and his companion attempted to escape from their captors by fleeing into the woods in hopes of making it back to their families in Shandaken. No match for the younger Schoharie scouts, Dumond was quickly tracked down and shot by one of Harper's Schoharie militiamen. Being nearly twenty years younger, John Barrows succeeded in escaping and making his way back to his family and the Ulster militia at Fort Shandaken. He would later give a full deposition as to the events that transpired between Dumond, himself, and the Schoharie lieutenant.

Having been gut shot through the bowels, Dumond was carried back to Simeon Van Waggenen's Paghatakan tavern and laid out on a table where he suffered even more depredation at the hands of his rebel countrymen. Stripped of his boots, hat, and jacket as he lay dying, Posey and Harper continued in vain to extract a confession of Toryism from their victim to justify their actions. They ultimately had to settle for his attempted escape as proof of his Tory identity and justification for their murder of Col. Cantine's spy. As news of Dumond's demise found its way back through Col. Cantine to Gov. Clinton, Posey and Harper were both brought up on charges of misconduct. Attempting to exonerate himself of any culpability in the affair, Lt. Harper tried to pad his deposition by downplaying his deceitful trickery and manipulation of the two confused Paghatakan rebels. On October 5th, Gov. Clinton wrote a letter to Schoharie's Col. Butler expressing his confidence in Capt. Posey's conduct but questioning that of Lt. Harper's, '... *It is not however, so clear to me that Mr. Harper, judging from his own account, did not make use of deception which might have betrayed a better man than Dumond into imprudent expressions in his situation which if so, is wrong...*'.

Capt. Thomas Posey

The influences of political patronage and familial ties were instrumental in achieving an acquittal of all charges for the captain and his mischievous lieutenant. Ironically, the burden of guilt for the unhappy incident was assigned to Dumond for having attempted his escape. Within a few months of the Dumond affair, Capt. Thomas Posey was promoted by his childhood neighbor and Commander-in-Chief to major of the 7th Virginia Regiment and was eventually promoted to Lt. Colonel. He went on to distinguish himself in the battle of Stony Point, and at Charleston and Yorktown. His post-war political career was as exalted as was his wartime honors, serving terms as a Kentucky state senator, a U.S. senator from Louisiana and a governor of the Indiana Territory. Within a year of the Dumond affair, Lt. Alexander Harper was promoted to captain by his older brother John. Capt. Harper went on to further prove his incompetence as an officer by leading another frontier scout into an ambush and spending the remainder of the war in captivity. [26]

William's Flatts

Two successive raids on the northern and southern perimeters of New York's border region were carried out in September by Capt. Brant and one of his most trusted lieutenants, Ben Shanks. The warrior known to his fellow Delaware Indians as Huycon, was invaluable to Brant. His coercive recruiting of East Branch 'volunteers' and his terrorizing foraging raids throughout Ulster County's Mamakating and Rochester districts earned him a fearsome reputation. He was described as '...*one of the most frightful specimens of humanity that the eye could rest upon...*'. Having spent his youth in the Shawangunk Mountains and Rondout Creek Valley, Ben Shanks was well acquainted with the settlements of the Lackawack, Wawarsing and Honk Hill neighborhoods, north of today's Ellenville.

On the 7th of September 1778, while Brant was preparing to launch another attack on the Mohawk River settlements, Lt. Shanks struck a devastating blow to the Rondout settlements around Fort Lackawack. He had attacked the settlements two months earlier and taken two prisoners, Jacob Osterhout and George Anderson. But Osterhout and Anderson had managed to escape their captors while being marched off to Fort Niagara, killing all their Indian escorts. Enraged, Lt. Shank's second attack on the Lackawack settlements was a retaliatory strike for the killing of his warriors. Knowing that Fort Lackawack was garrisoned with additional troops following his July attack, his September raid was a masterfully executed feign, meant only to draw the fort's soldiers out into the open where they could be led into an ambuscade.

After burning a few homesteads and capturing another couple of settlers, Ben Shanks' thirty-five warriors made a hasty exit up Rondout Creek along the old Sun Trail that led west to the Willowemoc and the East Branch of the Delaware. Reaching Chestnut Creek, about ten miles up the Rondout near the present-day head of the Rondout Reservoir, Shanks' warriors assumed an ambuscade position and waited for the militia posse they knew would be sent out after them. Led by Lt. John Graham, a brash young officer in Capt. Elias Hasbrouck's Ulster County militia company, twenty recently recruited militia volunteers were hastily assembled and rode off to track down the Indians and rescue their compatriots. Late that afternoon, as it was nearing dusk, a lone trooper staggered back into Fort Lackawack with the shocking news that Lt. Graham and nearly all of his inexperienced soldiers had been ambushed and literally cut to pieces on Chestnut Creek. Without delay, another larger and better led response to Lt. Shanks' atrocity was organized and deployed. Capt. Samuel Clark's Independent Company of Ulster County militia was a seasoned corps of fifty-two experienced frontiersmen who knew the lay of the land and the ways of their Indian adversaries. Setting out a day behind their quarry, Capt. Clark's determined frontiersmen hied their way up the forest trail with an urgency fueled by revenge. With a full moon to guide their way, they marched nonstop until they reached the East Branch of the Delaware, two days after the massacre on Chestnut Creek.

After reaching the East Branch, Clarke learned that Lt. Shanks had encamped on William Rose's Flatts, today's village of Downsville's Knox Avenue. Aware that Shanks would have posted guards at the entrance of Downs Brook, Capt. Clark cautiously led his men on a circuitous route to the rear flank of the Indian encampment. Advancing up the river and today's Huntley Hollow, he led his troops over a mountain saddle and into today's upper Gregory/Tiffany Hollow before quietly proceeding down the brook toward the Indian's encampment. Around 5PM on the afternoon of the 9th, Clark's men opened fire on Ben Shanks' warriors, catching them totally by surprise. After a three-hour forest skirmish fought behind trees and boulders, darkness finally descended on the field putting an end to the intense fighting. At daybreak, the militia awoke to find the Indians had slipped off in the night, leaving five or six of their dead behind. Burying the Indians and four or five of his own men, Capt. Clark decided against any further pursuit of the enemy, determining it to be too risky and taking them too deep into Indian territory. They had avenged their brothers and punished Ben Shanks for his massacre of Lt. Graham and his militia volunteers. [27]

German Flatts

Returning from Lackawack and William's Flatts to Onaquaga on the Susquehanna, Lt. Shanks' war party arrived too late to join Capt. Brant's second expedition to the Mohawk River Valley. The valley's settlements that stretched along the river from Schenectady and Caughnawaga to German Flatts were home to some of the descendants of the early Low Dutch settlers of Niew Nederland's Hudson River Valley. During the early eighteen-century the Palatine or High Dutch extended their Schoharie settlements into the upper Mohawk Valley through Canajoharie, Stone Arabia, and Palatine Bridge to West Canada Creek. As they had in the Schoharie Valley, they turned the forested wilderness into a lush farmland with wheat and cornfields patched between pastures of cattle and livestock. Unfortunately for these hard-working homesteaders, their bountiful farms were tempting targets for the Indian foraging parties that depended on their crops and cattle for their own survival. With German Flatts in his crosshairs Capt. Brant led a force of about 150 Seneca, Onondaga, and Cayuga warriors up the Susquehanna to the Unadilla River where another three hundred Tory rangers joined them. One of Maj. John Butler's captains, who had been with him during the Wyoming Massacre two months earlier, led the Tory rangers. Capt. William

Caldwell and Capt. Brant's combined forces were about to revisit some of the same neighborhoods Brant and his warriors devastated earlier that summer.

With rumors circulating of Brant's impending invasion of German Flatts or possibly Cherry Valley, scouts were sent out to gather information on the enemy's movements. Lt. Hans Adam F. Helmer led an eight-man scouting party to the upper Unadilla River where they unexpectedly ran straight into the vanguard of Brant and Caldwell's advancing army. Near the Tory homestead of Percifer Carr, between today's New Berlin and South Edmeston, the startled militiamen engaged in a brief skirmish in which two or three of Lt. Helmer's men were killed. Surviving the fight unscathed, the intrepid lieutenant made his escape and set out on a dead run up Wharton Creek ahead of Brant and Caldwell's 450 troops. After running thirty-five miles through present-day Otsego and Herkimer Counties warning the countryside along his way, Lt. Helmer finally reached the Mohawk settlements. With his clothing torn to tatters and his arms and legs bleeding from the bramble, his cautionary warning convinced the homesteaders of German Flatts to seek refuge behind the palisades of Forts Herkimer and Dayton. Two hundred settlers, who were initially reluctant to believe that such a large force was heading their way, crowded into the two forts just ahead of Brant's warclubs and Caldwell's bayonets.

At 6AM on the morning of Sept. 17th, the morning after Lt. Helmer's marathon run to Fort Herkimer, Brant and Caldwell's Tories attacked the abandoned settlements of German Flatts. Only two or three stubborn homesteaders were killed in the attack as the invaders ran unabated through the settlements. They burned over sixty dwellings and their barns full of the recent harvest and all their farming implements. Eight hundred horses, cattle, sheep, and oxen were herded off to Onaquaga while the warriors slaughtered what livestock they could not take with them. Lt. Helmer was hailed as a hero for averting a far worst catastrophe. Far more deaths and misery would have ensued had he not warned the settlers of the impending attack. Performed

The destruction of German Flatts was the last straw for the frontier commanders charged with protecting the border region's settlements. The devastating losses of homes, livelihoods, and sustenance would need avenging in a dramatic and equally devastating manner. Within days of the German Flatts attack, the commanders of the Northern Department began planning an offensive campaign to punish the Indians and deliver the same wrath upon their Susquehanna settlements and strongholds. The dangerous mission was to be executed by Col. William Butler's Pennsylvania riflemen and Capt. John Harper's frontier rangers. [28]

Onaquaga

On the morning of Oct. 2nd, 1778, two weeks after Brant and Caldwell's raid on German Flatts, Lt. Col. William Butler set out from Schoharie's Middle Fort for the Susquehanna and the Indian strongholds of Unadilla and Onaquaga. He headed a force that included four companies of the 4th Pennsylvania Regiment consisting of 160 troopers and seventy-seven riflemen from Morgan's Virginia Rifle Corps. Another thirty Schoharie militiamen and Tryon County rangers were brought along to help guide and scout ahead of the main force. Butler's men were carrying six days' worth of provisions on their backs while their packhorses carried another five days' worth. The expedition was relying heavily on reconnaissance Butler had received from an intrepid spy who had slipped into the Tory ranks at Unadilla. Pvt. John McKenzie of Capt. James Parr's rifle company somehow managed, at significant risk to himself, to infiltrate and extract information from his unsuspecting comrades as to the strength of their army. McKenzie reported that anywhere from 900 to 1,100 Indians and Tories were in Unadilla and Onaquaga. Capt. Harper and three of his rangers had earlier captured three prisoners near Unadilla who were interrogated into confessing there were about three hundred people at Unadilla and another four hundred at Onaquaga. McKenzie and Harper's reports would have included old men and women, which after taking into account, the estimated number of warriors and Tory fighters was still a formidable force for Butler's 260 men.

Σ The evening before Col. Butler and his men departed Middle Fort, an advance scout was sent out to patrol the roads for any defectors who might attempt to run out ahead of the expedition to warn the enemy. Several of Capt. Harper's rangers and a small detachment of Capt. Parr's company led by Lt. William Stevens were assigned to scout out ahead of the main force. Capt. Harper had advised Col. Butler of Brant's preference for the upper Susquehanna and Charlotte Creek trails as his main route through the frontier and warned of the danger of running into his superior forces on one of those trails. Heeding the warning, Butler wisely chose a less traveled corridor to the Susquehanna's Indian strongholds. The West Branch of the Delaware River was far less frequented by Indians and frontier travelers, primarily because of its many entwined tributaries and difficulties of the terrain. The West Branch was primarily traversed by canoe, a convenience the Schoharie troops were not equipped with. Traveling by foot down the valley and over the watershed to the Susquehanna Valley was no easy task, a fact Butler's men were about to learn the hard way.

Σ Slipping out of Middle Fort with as little fanfare as possible, Butler quietly led his men up Schoharie Creek trying to avoid arousing the countryside of their advance. Upon reaching Henry Mattice's mill at Mill Creek, near today's North Blenheim, Butler's troops rested for the night before departing the valley. In the morning, the troops headed up Mill Creek and over Blenheim Hill to the headwaters of the West Branch at Lake Utsayantha. Hiking on another three or four miles, they rested for the second night at Isaac Sawyer's mill near the present village of Hobart. On the third day out, their progress was hampered by heavy rain and the many swollen streams they had to cross. Trudging fewer than ten miles they stopped for the night at another millsite homestead run by St. Leger Cowley near today's Bloomville. The weather was gradually turning from bad to worse as an early winter wind delivered icy rain that graduated into snow flurries.

Σ From Cowley's mill, the expedition made its way down the river through what would one day become the village of Delhi and on to the flats across from the mouth of the Little Delaware River. At this point, they left the West Branch and headed up Platner Brook towards the watershed between the Delaware and Susquehanna Rivers. Settling down for the fourth night three miles up the brook, the expedition spent the next day crossing over to the Susquehanna by way of East Handsome Brook to Ouleout Creek. At the confluence of the Ouleout and Susquehanna River they spent another night in the old abandoned Scottish settlement of Albout. Col. Butler and his men now knew they were about to enter dangerous territory, too far from any relief column that might be sent out to rescue them should they meet up with a superior force of Brant's warriors.

Σ From the Ouleout, the expedition continued along the southside of the Susquehanna through Rev. Johnston's abandoned settlement before crossing over the old Property Line of '68 and into Indian territory. A short, uneasy night was spent encamped at Tent Creek near the present village of Bainbridge before their march was resumed at around 3AM the next morning. Their seventh day's march did not end until nine that evening after marching eighteen hours and twenty-five miles to a bend in the river just above Onaquaga and the present-day village of Windsor. After a brief pause to check their firearms for dry cartridges and fix bayonets, Col. Butler ordered his men to cross the river and advance upon the Indian village. To their surprise and relief, the village was all but empty except for the dogs and chickens running around in confusion. Brant and his warriors, who had no intelligence of Butler's approaching forces, were on their way down the Delaware to forage for cattle and scalps in the Minisink settlements. The remaining villagers and a few young warriors had been forewarned of the advancing militia and had fled into the forest only hours before their arrival. With Brant to the south and Onaquaga abandoned, Butler's men had free rein to ravage the village while feasting on fresh fruits and vegetables. With their bellies full, they got back to the serious business of destroying every house, barn, and storage bin while slaughtering all the livestock and fowl in the village. The militiamen who sacked Onaquaga that night were amazed at the quality of the Indian village. Its forty houses were built of squared logs with stone fireplaces, shingled roofs, and in some cases glass windows which were a rarity on the frontier. Col. Butler later wrote in his journal, '...*It was the finest Indian town I ever saw...*'.

As dawn broke over the valley, flames from the burning houses and bins of corn and wheat illuminated the early morning sky with a hellish yellow glow. With thick black smoke rising from the village, Butler's men hurried to finish their work before the smoke alerted every Indian and Tory between them and Schoharie. Leaving Onaquaga in ruins, the troops crossed back over the Susquehanna and hurried back up the river to the abandoned Indian village of Cunnahunta, near today's Afton. Here, they finally felt safe enough to rest for a while after forty-eight hours of relentless marching and plundering. They had purposely avoided torching Cunnahunta or the other Indian villages they passed on their way to Onaquaga to avoid alerting the Indians of their approach. Daring not to linger too long at Cunnahunta, they set the village ablaze before continuing up the river torching everything along their way. After destroying the Indian village of Unadilla, across from Johnston's former settlement, they continued their trail of destruction back to Ouleout Creek where they encamped for one last nervous night on the Susquehanna River.

Relieved to be finally leaving the Susquehanna, Col. Butler's men began a slow slog up Ouleout Creek through an intermittent rain that continued all day and throughout their entire journey back to Schoharie's Middle Fort. On the tenth day of the expedition, they only managed to travel about four to five miles before settling in for the night on Handsome Brook, still on the Susquehanna side of the watershed. The next day, believing Brant might have returned to Onaquaga and sent out a war party in pursuit of them, Butler led his men on a forced march back over the mountain and into the valley of the West Branch. The bad weather was not letting up and the eleven days' worth of provisions they brought with them was nearly all gone. Continuing their race back up the West Branch in the chilling rain and fog, their lead scouts mistook Elk Creek above today's Delhi for the river and proceeded to lead the troops up the creek without their proverbial paddle. It was a costly error for the men who were already beaten down by fatigue and hunger. They floundered through the forest for most of the next day before finally finding their way back to the river.

After spending another night at Isaac Sawyer's millsite, it took Butler's men one more day's hike to cross over Blenheim Hill and into the Schoharie Valley. Arriving too late in the day to continue on to the fort, they spent their last night on the trail again hosted by Henry Mattice at North Blenheim. Finally reaching the end of their 200-mile, fourteen day, and fourteen nights journey, they arrived back at Middle Fort in the afternoon of the 16th of October. Their comrades and families were relieved to welcome them back, having all but given up ever seeing them again. Honoring the returning heroes with a *feu de joie* and a well-deserved albeit short furlough, the tired men quickly recuperated from their harrowing ordeal. Col. Butler wrote a dispatch to Gov. Clinton praising his expedition's accomplishments and proclaiming '...*I am well convinced that it has sufficiently secured these frontiers from any further disturbance from the savages at least this winter...*'. It took but a few weeks, however, before a '...*further disturbance from the savages...*' proved his communique embarrassingly shortsighted. [29]

While Col. Butler was still preparing his troops for the Onaquaga expedition, tragedy struck the Harper family. Capt. Harper's attention throughout the summer of '78 had been preoccupied by his wife Miriam's worsening health which by September had begun to rapidly decline. When the Johnsons and their loyalist neighbors left for Canada at the onset of the war, their abandoned estates offered an opportunity for comfortable housing for some of the continental officers and their families. Having been a Tryon County Commissioner of Sequestration along with his brother William, John Harper took advantage of their positions and took possession of one of the Johnson family's confiscated estates. For an annual rent of £15, the Harper family moved into Sir William Johnson's daughter Nancy and husband Daniel Claus' estate between old Fort Johnson and Johnstown. While tending to his duties as captain of his Tryon County ranger company, John would have had precious little time to spend with his dying wife throughout that turbulent summer. On the 25th of September, thirty-six-year-old Miriam Thompson Harper finally died, leaving her busy husband with eight motherless children, ages 2-14.

Taking a brief leave of duty to bury his wife and attend to his children, Capt. Harper's frontier rangers would have had to go with Col. Butler to Onaquaga without him. He had his own expedition to lead back to the Connecticut River where many of his and Miriam's relatives still lived. John's cousin Joseph and wife Isabella McKnight Harper's five children were about the same age as John and Miriam's eight children, seven of whom would spend the remainder of the war with their East Windsor second cousins. Bidding farewell to his children, Capt. Harper promptly returned to the front with his oldest son, fourteen-year-old Archibald. Officers with teenage sons too young for active duty often recruited them to serve as their waiters, taking care of their father's routine tasks. Archibald would have been responsible for grooming and saddling his father's horse, cleaning his guns and uniforms, and performing whatever menial chores were required. The young waiter would see and learn firsthand how an officer behaved and what was expected of the continental soldier that Archibald would soon become. [30]

Cherry Valley

With Indian raids intensifying throughout the summer and fall of 1778, many of Cherry Valley's Scots-Irish settlers defiantly refused to leave their frontier settlement on the headwaters of the upper Susquehanna. James and Mary Harper Moore and their five children, ages 10-19, stubbornly held out on their homestead along with Mary's sister Margaret and husband William Gault and their six children, ages 3-12. The Harpers, Moores, and Gaults had remained in Cherry Valley throughout the French and Indian War and came through it relatively unscathed. Confident they could withstand another war, the Moores and Gaults chose again to remain and endure whatever might come their way. By the summer of '78, Cherry Valley had about three hundred residents living on the scattered homesteads in and around the little village, some of whom had recently relocated there after having been driven from their lower Susquehanna settlements. Rev. William Johnston and his family had joined the little colony after they were driven from their settlement by Brant in '77. While many of the village's men and older boys were off serving in Capt. Robert McKean's militia company in other parts of the frontier, rumors of an impending attack had been circulating all summer. Heeding these threats, a detachment of Col. Ichabod Alden's 7th Massachusetts Regiment was deployed to the village and a palisade fortification was hastily constructed around the village's church and meetinghouse. By November, having not seen anything of the enemy, the residents of Cherry Valley felt confident they would not be attacked that late in the season. They were, unfortunately, sadly mistaken.

Returning to Onaquaga from their Minisink raid, Capt. Brant and his warriors were outraged to find their Susquehanna villages in ashes and their cache of winter provisions destroyed by Col. Butler's Schoharie arsonists. The offence called for retribution and one last raid on a white settlement before winter set in. British Maj. John Butler's son Walter was given his first major command as captain and was on his way to the borderlands with two other captains and three hundred Indians and Tories supported by fifty British regulars. His Seneca and Cayuga warriors were in an ugly mood and aching for a fight when they met up with three hundred more of Brant's angry warriors at Onaquaga. Capt. Brant, however, was not at all enthusiastic about staging another raid so late in the season and so deep into rebel territory. His knowledge of the border region's terrain and the difficulties of traversing it during winter months compelled him to voice his objections to any further raids until spring. Overruled by the brash young captain who was eager for fame and glory, Capt. Butler rejected Brant's objections and ordered the expedition to proceed to Cherry Valley. During the first week of November, Captains Butler, Brant, MacDonell, and Caldwell led their 650 men up the Susquehanna with the intent of unleashing hell's fury on the unsuspecting frontier settlement and Alden's Massachusetts troopers. [31]

In the late morning hours of November 11th, one month after the destruction of Onaquaga and Unadilla, the residents of Cherry Valley were shocked to hear the war cries of Tories and Indian warriors running unopposed through their terrified community. Spanish John MacDonell and Capt. William Caldwell's two hundred Tories and British regulars surrounded Fort Alden and the two hundred Massachusetts troopers within the palisades. Col. Alden and most of his officers had been garrisoned outside the fort in a few nearby village homes and were cut down in the opening minutes of the attack as they desperately tried to make it back into the fort. Without effective leadership, the Massachusetts troopers cowered within the fort and failed to venture out to assist the helpless villagers or confront the enemy. A few of the villagers made it into the fort, but too many of the families whose husbands and brothers were off fighting elsewhere were brutally killed and scalped in their cabins.

One of the village's most prominent members, Robert Wells, was slain along with his wife Mary, daughter Jane, four more of his children, and three of the family's slaves. Rev. Samuel Dunlop, the preacher who had led the Ulster families to Cherry Valley in 1741, was confronted in his doorway by a party of Seneca warriors who mercilessly made him watch as they butchered and dismembered his beloved wife Elizabeth. It was said that Elizabeth's limbs were hung from a nearby apple tree where they were feasted upon by vultures. William Dickson's wife Elizabeth was killed later in the day as she attempted to find food for her young children, having hidden with them on the wooded hillside behind their homestead. The following morning, thirteen-year-old Samuel Dickson ventured out of his hiding place and spied his mother's flowing red hair hanging from a drying pole. A local militiaman who returned to his homestead shortly after the massacre found his dead wife and four of his young children's limbs strewn about the yard in the bloody snow.

Incident in Cherry Valley-Fate of Jane Wells

The Wells family, Elizabeth Dickson, Elizabeth Gault Dunlop and her seventy-eight-year-old father William Gault Sr, were all brutally murdered that day along with thirty other denizens of Cherry Valley, the majority of whom were women and children. Thirty-two houses and thirty-two barns full of that season's harvest were set ablaze along with the village's three mills. The fort and church were about all that remained of the once thriving frontier community. The gruesome nature of the brutal assaults even shocked the British loyalist officers who from thereafter seldom spoke or wrote of the incident. Capt. Walter Butler blamed Capt. Brant for losing control of his Indians while Brant who had argued against the raid, reminded the young captain just who was the commanding officer of the offensive. Spanish John MacDonell, who had been unimpressed by the performance of his Indians and Tories at The Battle of the Flockey, vowed to never again participate in an offensive if the majority of the force were Indians. But the notorious Capt. William Caldwell, who had seen worse at the Wyoming Valley Massacre, was said to have been unfazed by the carnage.

After four hours of mayhem, the sated avengers rounded up the lucky villagers who had been spared and retired for the evening in an encampment on the south end of the settlement near the Dickson farm. Their hostages, nearly all of whom were women and children, were to be taken back to Fort Niagara where they would run the gauntlet should they survive the trip. Some of those who survived all of this would be adopted into Indian families as recompence for the loss of one of their own family members. Others would be used as ransom for imprisoned loyalist families and eventually exchanged. There are numerous narratives of white women, who after being captured and held by the Indians for a while, found that they preferred life with their captors to the life they led before. The Iroquois held women in high esteem and never made a decision that effected the whole tribe without first consulting with the mothers.

Liberated from a society of white men who treated them as chattel with no voice or opinion on matters of importance, some white women chose to remain with their adopted Indian families and their men.

Throughout that first night and into the next day, the Tories and Indians lingered about the Dickson farm before starting their 300-mile journey back to Fort Niagara through an intensifying snowstorm. Just one day into their journey, Capt. Brant convinced the other captains of the futility of trying to keep their captives alive while treading through knee-deep snow and feeding them and themselves with what little provisions they could carry. Most of the hostages were grudgingly released and sent back to what was left of their Cherry Valley settlement. Just two of the hostage families were targeted and retained for their ransom value, being the wives and children of two notable military and political rebel leaders.

In the years leading up to the Revolution, Cherry Valley's Samuel Campbell, Samuel Clyde and John Moore were selected to serve as Canajoharie District's delegates to the Tryon County Committee of Safety. The Committees of Safety were responsible for weeding out loyalist sympathizers from the district and organizing rebel resistance. Furthermore, John Moore had been selected to represent Tryon County as a delegate to the New York Provincial and State Congress from 1775 to '77 and was present when the State Constitution was adopted at Kingston in April 1777. By late 1778, Capt. Campbell and Lt. Clyde had risen from their frontier ranger company ranks to Col. Samuel Campbell and Lt. Col. Samuel Clyde of the 1st Regiment of Tryon County Militia. They had both been with Gen. Herkimer and Col. Cox at Oriskany where Samuel took command of the regiment after Cox was killed. The Moore and Campbell families would have been extremely valuable hostages and bartering chips for Capt. Butler whose mother and four younger siblings were being held by the rebels in Albany. Col. Campbell's wife Jane and the couple's four young children, William-10, Eleanor-8, James-6, and Matthew-3, were held back when most of the other hostages were released. Being the sister of the Harper brothers and the wife of Committeeman John Moores' brother James, Mary Moore and her three daughters, Jane-19, Abigail-16, and Mary-13, would have made equally valuable ransom hostages for the Butlers. [32]

With their homes, barns, and granaries in ashes and all their livestock driven off or killed, the 175 survivors of the massacre huddled together around the last glowing embers of their smoldering cabins. The day after the massacre a detachment from the 2nd Tryon County Regiment of Militia under Col. Jacob Klock was dispatched to Cherry Valley to assess the situation while the enemy was still nearby. According to Mary Moore and Margaret Gault's brother William Harper, who later reported, *'...Col. Klock arrived there the day after, warmed himself and turned about, marching back without affording the distressed inhabitants the least assistance or relief, even to bury the dead or collect the small remains of their cattle or goods...'*. As inexcusable as this sounds, the indifferent militia colonel later explained his decision not to assist the survivors or pursue the enemy on the inclement weather. The village's refugees later asserted that Col. Klock's lack of action had at the very least, been an unconscionable act of misconduct. His actions before the massacre were as egregious as his lack of concern following it. He had been ordered to send a detachment of two hundred militiamen to reinforce Fort Alden's troops and was expected to have arrived there on the 9th, two days before the attack. His reasoning for not reaching the fort before the attack was as vague as his abandonment of the survivors after it.

Ethnic tensions and jealous rivalry between the frontier's Scots-Irish settlers and their Palatine neighbors might better explain Col. Klock's inaction than the stormy weather. Cherry Valley's predominantly Scots-Irish population had never felt any fondness for the residents of the Mohawk River's Palatine Dutch settlers who naturally reciprocated in kind. The Harpers demonstrated their contempt for their Dutch contemporaries on many occasions and Col. Klock's behavior during the Cherry Valley affair only served to deepen their resentment for their Teutonic neighbors. [33]

After burying the bodies of their dead in a mass grave, the Cherry Valley survivors staggered over the hill through a winter storm to Canajoharie with only the clothes on their backs and the few belongings they could carry. The little band of refugees continued down the Mohawk to Schenectady where they hoped to be granted some form of relief from the governor and the recently formed State of New York. But due to a convoluted regulation intended to keep the frontier settlements and their forts supported by local citizens and their militias, the homeless survivors were denied any state assistance. They had abandoned their settlement and the fort that had been built to protect them, thus disqualifying them for any assistance. Brutalized by the enemy and brushed aside by their militia and now the state, the proud Scot-Irish refugees were forced to endure the humiliation of having to rely on the kindness of strangers. Ironically, the Moore and Campbell family members who had been carried off to Fort Niagara by their captors, were better treated by the enemy than their kinsmen were by their own countrymen. [34]

Having completed their long journey along the snowbound trails of west central New York, Mary Moore and her three daughters were mercifully spared the running of the gauntlet. Capt. Harper's friendship with Joseph Brant seems to have influenced the lenient treatment he afforded his sister and nieces. Another surprising development also contributed to the Harper women's milder treatment. Mary's oldest daughter Jane had caught the eye of one of Capt. Butler's Tory officers who was charged with guarding the Harpers and Campbells. The two unlikely admirers formed an implausible relationship with each other. Whether by opportunistic use of beguiling charm and beauty or a genuine attraction, nineteen-year-old Jane was able to turn her captor into captive by rousing the young man's fancy. Indifferent to her family's political views, Jane Moore and Capt. John Powell were married at Fort Niagara within a year of the Cherry Valley Massacre. Awkward as it may have seemed, Jane's mother Mary and her two sisters remained captive for over two years under the watchful eye of Maj. John Butler and Capt. John and Jane Harper Powell.

It was not until early 1781, after countless letters between the Butlers and Gov. Clinton, did the Moore women finally get released and exchanged for the Butler family. Mary and her two daughters, Abigail and Mary, returned to Schenectady for a reunion with father James and the two Moore boys. Jane, however, remained with the exiled Tories in Canada after the war and never again returned to visit her family or the village her husband John helped destroy. But to their credit, John and Jane Powell were said to have done all they could to lessen the suffering of the mothers and children who were captured and held prisoner at Fort Niagara throughout the remainder of the war. [35]

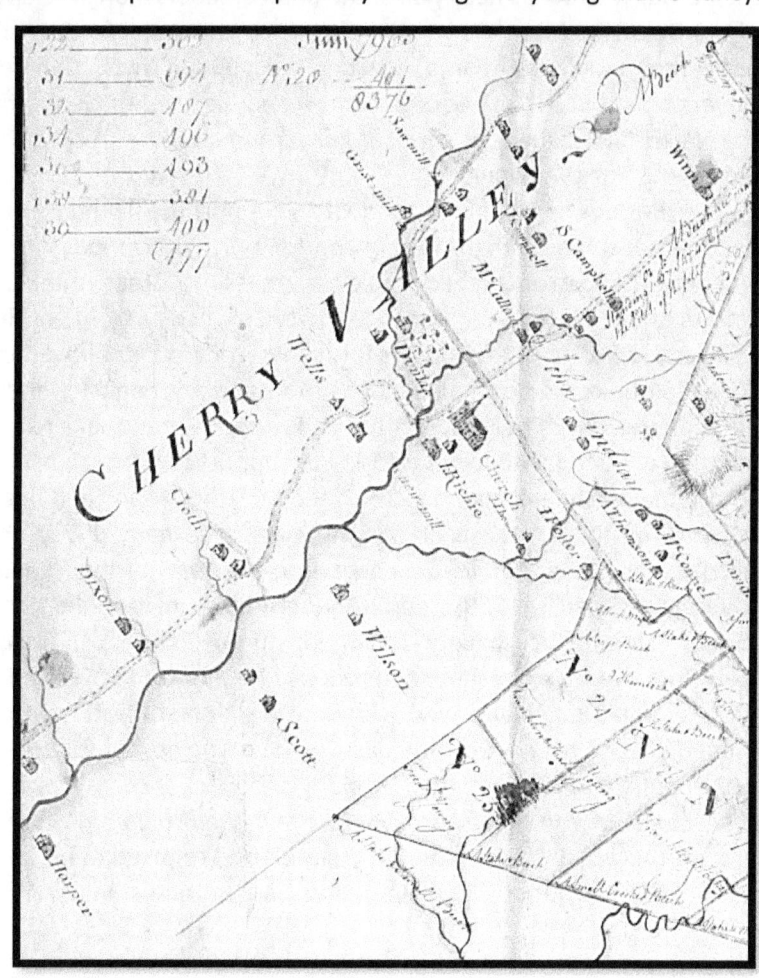

Cherry Valley Section of 'A Map of Two Tracts of Land on the South Side of the Mohawk River, 1772'. [36]

4

Haudenosaunee
1778-1780
'Curse their God and their King, and look upwards'

Following the Cherry Valley massacre in November, New York's border frontier fell into a deceptively quiet repose that lasted until that spring. The winter of 1778/'79 was another one of the Little Ice Age's shockingly cold and snowy winters. Men could not easily move about for long in the frozen landscape that covered the mountain trails of the borderlands. It was not until early April that the first roving bands of marauders returned to the forests looking for plunder. The settlers between the Mohawk River and the lower Delaware's Minisink settlements were again about to be thrust into the brutality of the border war. While nearly all of the homesteaders along the upper Susquehanna and the two branches of the Delaware River had left their homes by now, the few peripheral settlements that still clung to the hope they would be spared, pleaded for support from Congress and the Continental commanders. Governor and Brig. Gen. George Clinton and his brother Gen. James Clinton were growing frustrated by the Northern Department's lack of concern and failure to organize any viable solution to the continuing Indian and Tory invasions.

Besides neglecting to adequately support the frontier forts, General Horatio Gates' attention had become consumed with the idea of another northern campaign to Canada and another attempt to capture Quebec. The loss of Quebec would severely limit Great Britain's control of the St. Lawrence and Lake Ontario and reduce the threat to New York's western frontier. The two previous Canadian campaigns of 1775 and '76 were utter disasters for the Americans, but buoyed by his victory over Burgoyne at Saratoga, Gates felt he could do what Generals Montgomery, Schuyler and Arnold could not. General Washington and Congress were not at all enthusiastic about Gates' plans to launch another risky and costly northern invasion of Canada. Although refusing to support his campaign, Congress recognized they could no longer ignore the Indian and Tory threats to their northern flank and began looking for another solution.

Throughout the winter months and into early 1779, Washington and his advisors worked to finalize plans for a *tour de force* deep into the heart of the Iroquois Territory. Its goal was to punish and severely hamper the British and Iroquois' ability to continue harassing the frontier settlements. On the 25th of February, Washington finally convinced Congress to finance his plans for an assault on western New York's Iroquois territory and proposed Major General John Sullivan as the expedition's commander. The mission's objectives were clarified in a forceful letter from Washington to Gen. Sullivan, '...*The immediate objects are the total destruction of the hostile tribes of the six nations and devastation of their settlements and the capture of as many prisoners of every age and sex as possible... It is essential to ruin their crops now in the ground and prevent them planting more...*'. As far back as Washington's great-grandfather John Washington, the Iroquois had referred to his family as 'Destroyers of Towns' and by the time of the Revolution, Washington had earned the name *Conotocaurious*, 'Devourers of Villages'. [1]

Onondaga

The success of Lt. Col. William Butler's destruction of the Susquehanna villages of Onaquaga, Unadilla and Cunnahunta convinced Washington and most of New York's military commanders of the importance of taking the fight to the Indians. By destroying their village strongholds and supply line depots, Butler's expedition had made it harder for Brant's warriors to conduct their raids while freely coming and going along the Susquehanna's tributary corridors. It had not, however, eliminated the threat or discouraged them from continuing their harassment of the frontier settlements, as the residents of Cherry Valley were the first to realize. As the spring of '79 began opening the trails and frozen waterways of the border region, Brant's men began where they had left off by resuming their forays into their enemy's territory seemingly unaffected by the loss of their Susquehanna villages. Frustrated by Gate's sluggish support of the frontier and sensing the urgency to act now rather than wait for Sullivan's expedition to get under way, Gov. Clinton and his brother James began planning their own preemptive strike on the Indians and their supply lines. Clinton's plan, like Butler's, was meant to deprive the enemy of their village safe-havens and make it harder for them to come and go along their northern invasion corridor along the Mohawk River.

By early April, Sullivan's campaign was nowhere near ready to commence their path of destruction through the Haudenosaunee. Impatient to take the offensive, Gen. James Clinton ordered Col. Goose Van Schaick and his 1st Regiment of Albany County militia to proceed up the Mohawk to Fort Schuyler and relieve Col. Peter Gansevoort's 3rd Albany regiment that had been garrisoned there since the siege in '77. Replacing his brother-in-law's regiment and refreshing the fort's garrison was Van Schaick's stated assignment, but his actual objective was far more aggressive. Shortly after arriving at the fort, Van Schaick began preparing his troops for an expedition into the Onondaga Indian territory in hopes of replicating Butler's successful destruction of the Oneidas' Susquehanna villages. The Van Schaick expedition would target the scattered villages south of Onondaga Lake and down along Onondaga Creek through the Tully Valley. Unlike the Susquehanna villages, the Onondaga villages posed no real threat to the rebels and its residents often lent aid and shelter to rebel scouting parties passing through the area. A few bands of young Onondaga warriors had taken up arms against the Americans, but as a general policy, the Onondaga people tried to maintain neutrality throughout the early years of the war. In a war that was growing evermore punitive and retaliatory, neutrality was becoming a risky stance for anyone to take, be they white or Indian.

With Fort Schuyler abuzz with activity, Col. Van Schaick began quietly mobilizing three companies of his Albany County Regiment and six other companies assigned to join the expedition: one company of Col. Butler's 4th Pennsylvania Regiment that had been with him on the Susquehanna expedition; one company that had been with Col. Alden's 7th Massachusetts Regiment at Cherry Valley; three companies from the 3rd, 4th and 5th New York Regiments; and one company led by Capt. Robert McKean including many of the Cherry Valley militiamen who had lost family members during the massacre. It had been less than six months since many of these men witnessed the unspeakable carnage the Indians inflicted upon their friends, neighbors and loved ones. They were enraged by the butchery inflicted by Brant's warriors and were now more than ready to pay back in kind on any Indian they came across. John Harper's brother-in-law James Moore was an ensign in Capt. McKean's company and may not yet have known if his wife Mary and three daughters were still alive. Ensign Moore and his Cherry Valley militia comrades were ready to do some killing. Capt. Harper and his rangers were not on Van Schaick's Onondaga expedition, as he would have undoubtedly preferred to have nothing to do with an unprovoked attack on a neutral village. He knew the Onondaga people and he knew the damage such an attack would do to the credibility of the rebel militias and the cycle of retribution it would surely fuel.

In the early evening hours of April 18th, Col. Van Schaick and his second in command, the ever-present Lt. Col. Marinus Willett, led 558 men out of Fort Schuyler. The expedition marched a few miles to Wood Creek where they boarded twenty-nine bateaux loaded with eight days of provisions and proceeded down the creek to Oneida Lake. As the flotilla set out across the lake, the night was lit with but a sliver of a new moon. After reaching the southwestern shore near the middle of the lake late in the afternoon of the next day, the army rested for the night. In the morning, the expedition marched southwest into the lands of the Onondaga and encamped for a second night a few miles east of Onondaga Creek and the villages they planned to attack the next morning. Before dawn on the 21st, Van Schaick's soldiers approached the first of a dozen small villages they ransacked throughout most of the day. Unlike Butler's Onaquaga expedition, where the villages they swept through were empty of inhabitants, Van Schaick's soldiers found most of the Onondaga villages full of women, children, and older men. Most of the village's young warriors were out hunting, while the few who were nearby could do little against such an overwhelming force.

With images of Cherry Valley fresh in their minds, even the most stoic rebel militiamen found restraining their primeval impulses beyond their control. Allegations of brutality, mutilations and rape were of course denied by Van Schaick and his officers in their reports. Just a dozen villagers were reported to have been killed and another forty taken prisoner. But having witnessed the atrocities inflicted upon their own women and children, it is more likely than not, more innocent Indian families lost more of their loved ones than what Van Schaick reported. The rebels burned over fifty houses in the half-dozen villages while killing all the cattle and livestock they could find and destroying every granary and stockpile of corn and beans in the villages. The expedition was back at Fort Schuyler by mid-day of the 24th, having traveled over 150 miles in five and a half days without losing a man. Hailed as a great success, the Onondaga campaign succeeded in turning the Onondaga territory into a virtual wasteland. But an even more significant and longer lasting consequence of the raid was to turn a former friendly nation into another enemy, further damaging the trust between whites and Indians. Washington was inspired by the success of the Onondaga campaign and hoped his upcoming expedition might be equally triumphant. He would not be disappointed, as much worse was about to be unleashed upon the Iroquois villages of western New York. [2]

Easton, Schenectady, Fort Pitt

With all that Washington had to contend with during the winter of 1778/'79, New York's troubled border region was never far from mind. While the British were comfortably settled in their New York, Staten Island, and western Long Island quarters, they continued to strategize on how to open up a channel of communication through the Hudson/Lake Champlain corridor to Quebec. Militias throughout the Hudson Highlands of Orange, Ulster and Dutchess counties were in a state of constant readiness for HMS warships sailing up the river at any time. Connecticut's coastline militias from New London to Stamford were guarding against British ships crossing the Sound or companies of dragoons attacking the panhandle communities through Westchester County. From his northcentral New Jersey encampment at Middlebrook, Washington waited and watched as the British began signaling they were preparing for a southern offensive to harass the port cities of South Carolina and Georgia. He suspected their southern campaign was, in part, an attempt to draw off regiments from his Continental Army, thus leaving his northern flank more vulnerable to another Hudson River invasion. He was reluctant to take the bait and remained focused on the northern theater while waiting for the British to play their hand.

During the first few winter months of 1779, Washington was afforded a little time to finalize his plans for an invasion into western New York's Indian territory. He busied himself with learning as much as he could about the strength of the loyalist and Indian forces. He studied maps and interviewed frontier hunters and fur traders as to the location of Iroquois settlements and the terrain into which he was about to send nearly a third of his Continental Army. As preparations got underway following Congress's approval of Washington's Indian solution, the campaign commanders began assembling resources and troops at their respective staging areas of deployment. Congress' directive was '...*to take all measures necessary to protect the settlers and to punish the Indians*...'. The units assigned to the campaign were thought to be more adept at Indian warfare and the rigors of wilderness travel. Four brigades of New York, New Jersey, New Hampshire, and Pennsylvania Regiments, totaling around 4,000 men, were to rendezvous on the Susquehanna River before commencing a scorched-earth march through west central New York's Finger Lakes region. It was a risky project that required enormous amounts of supplies, troops, and equipment at a time when other fronts were under imminent threat of attack from British forces. Coordination of the Sullivan Campaign would be a complicated logistical challenge for the commanders of three separate expeditions that would enter the Iroquois territory from three different directions. [3]

On the 7th of May, Major General John Sullivan arrived on the lower Delaware River at its confluence with the Lehigh River and began organizing his expedition in the small Pennsylvania village of Easton. Gen. Sullivan immediately directed his commissary general and deputy quartermaster general to begin requisitioning supplies and provisions he would need for his long march through the wilderness. Besides the accoutrements of war, tents, blankets, packhorses, wagons, knapsacks, canteens, clothing and boots would be needed along with the necessary rations and foodstuffs. Whiskey and rum were of utmost importance for any soldiering endeavor that hoped to succeed. Commissaries were tasked with moving heaven and earth to secure enough of the precious commodity. Supply shortages and delivery delays were a widespread problem for the Continental Army. Pack meat often arrived rancid, and bread was all too often moldy and unfit for consumption. Sullivan quickly grew frustrated with the lack of cooperation from Pennsylvania officials who were reluctant to fill his requests for supplies. Every state's treasury was stretched thin and the prospect of sending supplies off on an expedition into a faraway territory was not an appealing investment. His 2,500 Continental troops would languish for over six weeks in Easton while his quartermasters and commissaries struggled to buy, bribe, or coerce contractors and civilians out of their wagons, horses, blankets, and whiskey.

Major General John Sullivan

The first sixty-five miles of Sullivan's trek into the wilderness would have to follow an old Indian trail over eastern Pennsylvania's Blue Mountain Ridge and onto the Pocono Plateau of the upper Appalachian Mountain range. The trail would first need to be cleared, leveled and widened into a passable road for the transport of the expedition's train of wagons and artillery pieces from Easton to the Susquehanna River. Through mid-May and into June, while Sullivan wrestled with his supply issues in Easton, fatigue parties were sent out to work the old trail through the Poconos to the Susquehanna's Wyoming Valley, today's Scranton/Wilkes-Barre area. Sullivan's military road into the frontier would only be the first leg of the long, arduous journey into the territory of the Iroquois Nations. His expedition consisted of three brigades, the first of which was commanded by Brig. Gen. William Maxwell and consisted of the 1st, 2nd and 3rd New Jersey Regiments and Col. Oliver Spencer's 5th New Jersey Regiment. The second brigade was led by Brig. Gen. Enoch Poor and was made up of the 1st, 2nd and 3rd New Hampshire Regiments and the late Col. Alden's Massachusetts Regiment that had been at Cherry Valley. Brig. Gen. Edward Hand commanded the third brigade which included the 11th Pennsylvania Regiment and Lt. Col. William Butler's 4th Pennsylvania Regiment that was deployed from Schoharie's Middle Fort after having destroyed the Susquehanna Indian villages the year before. Gen. Hand's third brigade also included a detachment of Daniel Morgan's Riflemen, an independent company of Wyoming Valley volunteers and a regiment of German soldiers.

While Gen. Sullivan's three brigades languished in Easton, a fourth brigade of around 1,800 soldiers was preparing to deploy from the north. Gov. Clinton's brother, Major General James Clinton, was ordered to assemble five New York Regiments of Albany and Tryon County levies and militiamen at Schenectady and prepare them to march. His frontier regiments were as well versed in fighting against the Tories and their Iroquois allies as any outfit in the Continental Army. Gen. Clinton's quartermasters were faced with the same problems Sullivan was having at Easton. New York was also hard-pressed to support such a grand scale expedition. After gathering his troops at Schenectady, Clinton directed his army up the Mohawk River to Canajoharie where his fourth brigade spent the entire month of June bartering for the necessary gear and provisions the expedition would need.

Just like Sullivan's expedition, Clinton's first phase of his journey would involve opening a road over the Brimstone Hills from the Mohawk Valley to the head of the Susquehanna River. The existing roads to Cherry Valley and Springfield needed to be widened and improved to accommodate five hundred wagonloads of equipment and three months' worth of provisions. Two hundred and twenty river bateaux meant to carry the expedition down the Susquehanna would also need to be carried over Clinton's Road from Canajoharie to the head of Otsego Lake. The twenty-mile-long road through the Mohawk highlands required weeks of work to prepare it to handle the excessive amount of traffic. By the first week of July, Clinton's expedition had successfully traversed the mountain road and sailed or marched to the lower end of Otsego Lake, at today's Cooperstown. For the next five weeks, Clinton's expedition would stall at the lake. Clinton's brigade was comprised of Col. William Van Cortlandt's 2nd New York Regiment, Col. Peter Gansevoort and Lt. Col. Marinus Willett's 3rd New York Regiment, Col. Frederick Weisenfeld's 4th New York Regiment and Col. Lewis DuBois's 5th New York Regiment. Two companies of Col. John Lamb's celebrated artillery regiment also accompanied the fourth brigade.

Maj. Gen. James Clinton

Capt. John Harper was not about to be left out of an opportunity to explore more of the western Indian lands he and his family hoped to own one day. His frontier company of experienced rangers and Oneida scouts were a welcome addition to Gen. Clinton's expedition. He would lead his scouts out ahead of the main force as they made their way down the Susquehanna before heading deeper into enemy territory. An added benefit for the strained coffers of the Continental budget was the willingness of Capt. Harper to finance and supply his own troops. Being head of an independent company gave the captain a certain autonomy while affording him the opportunity to impress the very men he would need to further his military career. Gen. Clinton and his brother George were two of the men who could affect the trajectory of his own ambitions and further his family's dream of empire. [4]

With Sullivan and Clinton's expeditions planning to rendezvous before approaching the Iroquois lands from the southeast, a third expedition was preparing to attack the Iroquois settlements from the southwest. Headquartered at Fort Pitt at the confluence of the Allegheny and Monongahela rivers at today's Pittsburgh, Lt. Col. Daniel Brodhead was preparing a 600-man expedition to advance up the Allegheny and into the western Indian territory. Brodhead was given the same mandate as the other two eastern expeditions. The villages of the Mingo and Munsee tribes along the Allegheny were to be destroyed and as many of their occupants of every age and sex killed or taken prisoner. Col. Brodhead's expedition consisted of his own 8th Pennsylvania Regiment, three companies of Lt. Col. Moses Pawling's Maryland and Virginia riflemen and a party of Lenape warriors and scouts. After ascending and completing their work on the Allegheny, the Fort Pitt expedition was to rendezvous with the combined Sullivan/Clinton forces on the Genesee River. If practicable, the grand plan called for Sullivan, Clinton, and Brodhead's combined force of over 5,000 to continue west and lay siege to Fort Niagara on Lake Ontario. The three-pronged campaign would take an incredible amount of luck to achieve all its objectives. With hundreds of wilderness miles between their points of origin, rendezvous, and their objectives, coordinating movement and timing would have been an

Lt. Col. Daniel Brodhead

incredibly difficult task. Their only means of communication was conveyed by runners and riders carrying dispatches along dangerous Indian trails through enemy territory. [5]

West Branch, Minisink, Northumberland

As the fighting season of 1779 got underway with Sullivan, Clinton and Brodhead struggling to get their Indian campaigns up and running, the British Tories and their Indian cohorts began organizing their own summer stratagems. The concentration of Continental troops and resources at their respective base camps left much of the frontier in an even greater state of vulnerability. Through April and May, British commanders at Fort Niagara were interpreting their intelligence and working on a defensive strategy to counter the American advance into Indian territory. Capt. Brant and his restless warriors were not in the mood to sit idly by while the British commanders waited for the Continental Army's next move. Col. Van Schaick's attack on the neutral Onondaga villages in mid-April further enraged the Iroquois warriors who were still reeling from the destruction of their Susquehanna villages. Raiding parties of forty to sixty warriors were again preparing to attack settlements along the upper Mohawk River from German Flatts to Canajoharie, while others were preparing to go hunting further south along the lower Delaware in the Cushetunk and Minisink region from Cochecton to Port Jervis. Smaller parties of a dozen or less Tories and warriors had not stopped scouring the frontier looking to vent their rage on any unsuspecting families foolish enough to still be holding out on their isolated homesteads.

One of these smaller war parties that had remained throughout the winter in the forests surrounding the Schoharie settlements was not about to wait for Capt. Brant's orders or winter to let up. It was led by the notorious Seth's Henry, one of the Schoharie Indians who had followed Capt. Harper on his daring ride to Albany in '77. A month before the Onondaga campaign, Seth's Henry led a small foray into the valley of the Delaware's West Branch for the express purpose of punishing the millwrights who had assisted Col. Butler's Schoharie troops on their march to and from Onaquaga six months earlier. With four or five warriors, Seth's Henry retraced Butler's trail and came upon the mill site homesteads of Isaac Sawyer and St. Ledger Cowley between today's Bloomville and Hobart. The two millwrights were easily overpowered and captured separately before being bound and carried off down the West Branch in canoes bound for Lake Ontario.

After reaching the Cookhouse and crossing over to the Susquehanna, Seth's Henry and his captives made their way towards the Chemung River and the trail that would take them the rest of the way to Fort Niagara. But somewhere along the winding Susquehanna, the intrepid millers managed to slip their binds and kill a few of their captors before running off into the forest. They took off on a frantic run towards the eastern settlements and their West Branch homesteads. Sawyer and Cowley were desperate to get back to their families before Seth's Henry and the remainder of his infuriated warriors reached their homes and took their fury out on their defenseless families. The Indians did indeed reach the millwright's cabins before them, but the Indians were frustrated to find the women and children had wisely abandoned them and gone off to Albany for refuge. Now, further incensed by humiliation, Seth's Henry and his warriors chose another nearby Harpersfield homestead to take their vengeance out on. After slaughtering all but one of the McKee family members and torching their Harpersfield, Odell Lake home, they carried off sixteen-year-old Anne McKee and took her back to Niagara as compensation for having lost their other two captives. The stubborn settler who refused to leave his isolated clearings put himself and his family in great peril. Many more of these private tragedies would play out on countless frontier families before New York's brutal border war finally ended. [6]

While smaller and more personal vendettas continued throughout the frontier, the ever-diligent Joseph Brant sensed an opportunity and took advantage of the preoccupied Continental armies. In late June, while Clinton was transporting his bateaux from Canajoharie to Otsego Lake and Sullivan was digging into his Wyoming Valley encampment after crossing the Poconos, Brant and three hundred of his warriors gathered on the Susquehanna at the ruins of their Onaquaga village. After waiting nearly a month for Clinton to make a move, Brant became impatient and set out with ninety of his best warriors and Tories for the lower Delaware's Minisink settlements while leaving the rest of his troops on the Susquehanna to check Clinton's pending advance. Brant had staged a raid on the Minisink villages the year before, while Col. Butler's Schoharie rebels were laying waste to his defenseless Susquehanna villages in October. He was planning a quick strike on the rebel settlements and a speedy return to Onaquaga before Clinton's forces finally set out down the Susquehanna.

Crossing from the Susquehanna to the Delaware and the Cookhouse (Deposit) Brant quickly led his ninety warriors down the river through Shehawken (Hancock) to the Cushetunk. From here he staged a lightning strike on several of the Minisink settlements along the lower Delaware and the Neversink River's Mamakating and Peenpack settlements. After laying waste to Mahackamack (Port Jervis) and the Basher Kill villages of Huguenot, Cuddebackville, and Godeffroy for a second time in just nine months, Brant's warriors started back up the Delaware to rejoin his main force at Onaquaga. This second raid on the people of the Minisink was met with much stiffer resistance and a more formidable response than Brant's previous visit. Warned of Brant's approach, riders were sent out to Goshen and Warwick, twenty miles east, where Lt. Col. Benjamin Tusten and Col. John Hathorn's militia were garrisoned. A detachment of around 130 militiamen, many of whom were leading citizens of their settlements, were hastily assembled and immediately sent out in pursuit of Brant's retreating war party.

On the morning of July 22nd, while the Indians were herding their plundered cattle across the Delaware near the mouth of the Lackawaxen at Minisink Ford, Tusten and Hathorn's men caught up with them. Unfortunately for the militia colonels, most of their troops were raw recruits with little to no experience with Indian warfare. Alerted to their approach, Brant's frontier fighters quickly outflanked the untried militiamen and surrounded isolated groups of them as they scattered and ran. An intense running skirmish dissolved into an orgy of hand-to-hand combat between terrified young farm boys and the Indians who excelled at such warfare. By late afternoon, Col. Tusten and forty-seven of his men were either already dead or slowly dying. Given no quarter, many of the militiamen were mercilessly killed while trying to surrender. Brant lost just six or seven of his men.

Called a massacre by the people of Goshen, the defeat of a larger force by an inferior one might be more properly characterized as a tactical success, rather than a massacre. But branding Capt. Brant as a butcher was a common theme throughout the war, even at times when he was nowhere near the scene of the crime for which he was accused. Returning to Onaquaga on the 28th, Brant was surprised to learn that Clinton had not yet started his journey down the Susquehanna. Nearly two more weeks would pass before Clinton finally did embark. Sullivan, however, was about to start his march up the Susquehanna after his long delay in the Wyoming Valley. Informed by runners of Sullivan's advance, Brant sent his men from Onaquaga to Chemung, an old Indian village a few miles up the Chemung River from its confluence with the Susquehanna, while he and a few of his best warriors headed up the Susquehanna to the Unadilla River. Silently hiking through the backwoods from the upper Unadilla to the hills above Otsego Lake, Brant watched and assessed Clinton's forces size and readiness. Turning back to rejoin his troops, Brant's little scouting party raided a few homesteads along the way and led off what cattle and horses they could drive back to their hungry brothers-in-arms at Chemung. [7]

While Brant was returning to Onaquaga after the Battle at Minisink Ford, another British assault was underway one hundred miles southwest at the confluence of the Susquehanna and its West Branch. Maj. John Butler had established his forward base at Canadasaga, on the north end of Seneca Lake, where he was planning to launch his Niagara forces to confront Sullivan's impending advance. From Canadasaga, Maj. Butler sent one of his best captains, Spanish John MacDonell, south to the lower Susquehanna with 100 of his Highland rangers and 200 Seneca warriors under the control of their Seneca Chief Hiokatoo. Butler hoped that MacDonell's excursion might draw off some of Sullivan's troops on route up the Susquehanna. But their primary mission was to round up as many cattle as possible and hurry back with their plunder to Butler's hungry troops at Canadasaga. After reaching the West Branch of the Susquehanna near today's Williamsport, MacDonell continued down the river to its confluence with the main branch of the Susquehanna and the rebel settlements of Northumberland, Sunbury and Shamokin.

On the 28th of July, the same day Brant returned to Onaquaga from the Minisink, MacDonell's troops attacked the garrison at Northumberland's Fort Freeland and quickly took the fort following a brief clash with the fort's thirty militiamen. Having been appalled by the carnage at Cherry Valley and the barbarism his Indians inflicted on the helpless citizenry, MacDonell insisted Hiokatoo firmly hold his Seneca warriors in check. Fifty-two women, children and old men were peacefully evacuated from the fort without being molested while the surviving rebel militiamen were taken prisoner and escorted back to Fort Niagara to spend the rest of the war in a Quebec prison. Spanish John had managed to avoid another Cherry Valley, but while his men were collecting their prisoners and plunder a relief column of the local militia arrived and attempted to engage MacDonell's superior force with just seventy-five men. The Highlanders and Seneca warriors had little trouble defending themselves and made quick work of the outnumbered rebels, killing nearly half of them. Three weeks later, Capt. MacDonell's men and plunder arrived back at Canadasaga, just as Maj. Butler was preparing to march his army south to meet Sulivan and Clinton's approaching brigades. [8]

Tioga Point

With his road from Easton to the Susquehanna finally ready for the teamsters' wagons, Gen. Sullivan finally got his expedition underway on the 18th of June. The crude road took the Continental army north along the East Branch of Bushkill Creek and over Wind Gap through the Blue Mountain Range of eastern Pennsylvania's Appalachian Mountains. Continuing north through today's Monroe County, the wagon train struggled on through the Pocono Mountains before crossing Tunkhannock and Tobyhanna Creeks and into the great swamp forests of southern Lackawanna County. Between the Poconos and the Susquehanna lay three forested swamps, one of which was known as the 'Shades of Death' and was loathed by every frontiersman and Native American who had the misfortune of trying to cross it. The journey to the Susquehanna was an excruciatingly difficult ordeal, described by one of Sullivan's officers as '... *nothing but rocks and mountains and great parts of it was as dark after the sundown, when it was noon day...*'. It took a wagon five days to reach the Susquehanna's Wyoming Valley.

The troops of Sullivan's three brigades all arrived within a week of leaving Easton, but it would be nearly six more weeks before all the expedition's wagons reached their encampments on the Susquehanna. Sullivan's patience was running thin as he waited for his wagons to arrive with enough of the necessary provisions he estimated his army would need to sustain them throughout their wilderness journey. A surgeon in one of the regiments described the situation in his journal, '... *The long stay of the army at Wyoming was owing to the infamous conduct of the commissaries and quartermasters employed in furnishing the necessary provisions and stores. And finally, when the army did march, it was so scantily supplied that the success of the expedition is by that means, rendered exceedingly precarious...*'. Another contradictory account suggests the long Wyoming halt was due to Sullivan's overestimation of the provisions his expedition would actually need to sustain itself. He had of course, no way of knowing how bountiful the Iroquois cornfields, orchards and gardens he was sent to destroy would be, or the extent to which his troops could depend on their foraging to sustain them. [9]

By the end of July, about the time Brant was at the Minisink and MacDonell was at Fort Freeland, Gen. Sullivan was finally ready to start marching his three brigades up the Susquehanna. Feeling confident he finally had enough supplies, or at least all the supplies he was likely to get, he ordered his troops to march on the 31st of July after six agonizing weeks of languishing in the Wyoming Valley. His restless troops were understandably relieved to be finally moving. One hundred miles lay ahead of them along the river's Great Warriors Path before they would reach Tioga Point at the confluence of the Chemung River and their rendezvous with Clinton's army descending the Susquehanna from the north. Scouts were sent out in front of the main body while fatigue companies cleared and widened the trail to accommodate the expedition's six-mile-long caravan. The wagons were shadowed by one hundred riverboats full of provisions and 1,200 overburdened packhorses loaded with the rest of their supplies. Seven hundred beef cattle were driven up behind the troops with an auxiliary of camp followers who quite often tagged along on such excursions for a variety of reasons. Women were known to accompany long military campaigns, tending to domestic chores and nursing the ill and injured soldiers.

After eleven grueling days of trudging along the Great Warriors Path, Sullivan's brigades finally began filing into Tioga Point on the 11th of August, three and a half months after assembling at Easton in early May. The Susquehanna's Indian villages they passed along the way had already been destroyed by earlier militia expeditions, in retribution for the Wyoming Massacre the year before. The Moravian Indian village of Wyalusing, which had been the pride of the Christian Munsee Indians, lay in ruin. All eighty of the village's well-built framed houses and their impressive church were reduced to ash, while Lackawannah, Quialtimmock, Tunkhannock and Queen Esther's Town had all met similar fates. The remnants of these once flourishing villages were the first Indian villages most of Sullivan's men had ever seen, but they would certainly not be the last. [10]

As Sullivan's troops began working their way up the Susquehanna and into Iroquois territory, they did so with a renewed faith in the justness of their cause and a feeling of hope they might actually prevail in that cause. News of Gen. 'Mad' Anthony Wayne's stunning victory over the British at Stony Point on the 16th had just reached them, giving a much-needed lift to their morale. Six weeks earlier, while they were still at Easton, 8,000 British regulars had set out from Manhattan by ship and by foot up the Hudson to Kings Landing near Peekskill. The Kings Ferry that ran from Verplanks Point on the east side to Stony Point on the west side was a major river crossing for the Continental army and a significant logistic position for whoever should control it. After reaching Stony Point, the British easily captured the two forts on either side of Kings Ferry with little resistance.

With so many of the northern troops heading off into Indian territory, the Continentals had no other choice but to concede the two forts rather than chance a counter offensive. But while the British were settling into their Stony Point fort, Gen. Wayne staged a daring midnight bayonet assault on the breastworks and forced the British to relinquish the fort they had just captured to the Americans. In yet another turn, realizing that holding the fort would be more trouble than it was worth, Gen. Wayne's troops stripped it of its guns and armaments and abandoned it to the British. Three months later, the British finally concluded that manning and supplying two forts on their northern front while shifting their focus to their southern campaigns would be an untenable situation. 'Mad' Anthony's *coup de main* and Washington's masterful gambit finally convinced the British to end their obsession with controlling the Hudson and cutting off New England from the rest of the colonies. No one was happier with this turn of events than Gov. George Clinton, who could now focus more of his attention and resources on the northern frontier border war. [11]

Gov. Clinton's brother James spent the month of July readying his troops for the long trip down the Susquehanna to Tioga Point. Gen. Clinton needed this time to prepare not only his flotilla of bateaux, but the river itself upon which his men and supplies would travel. The Susquehanna is a formidable river once it collects the contributions from its first three major tributaries, Oak, Cherry Valley and Schenevus Creeks. During the midsummer months after the spring freshet has run its course, the first fifteen miles of the river from Otsego Lake to Charlotte Creek is little more than a slow meandering creek. It was too shallow to accommodate the expedition's river bateaux loaded with 200 lbs. of cargo and three to four passengers. The situation required Clinton's engineers to come up with a solution to the problem. Ingeniously, they directed their troops to build a dam at the lake's outlet, thereby raising the lake's level and creating their own spring freshet upon releasing its pent-up waters. The dam was an engineering success, but it took all of six weeks for the water to rise sufficiently enough to generate its desired effect.

On the morning of August 9th, with his 220 fully loaded boats strung out along the river below the dam, Clinton's men blasted the dam and sent their flotilla racing off down their manufactured river freshet. With most of Clinton's 1,800 troops marching down the river alongside the flotilla, the northern prong of the Sullivan/Clinton campaign finally got underway. [12]

Capt. Harper's company of independent frontier rangers and Oneida warriors set out ahead of Clinton's troops as they started their march down the Susquehanna. Their familiarity with the border region's frontier was put to task as they were assigned the treacherous duty of patrolling for Indian activity out in front of the expedition's advance guard. A few of Harper's men had very personal reasons for volunteering for this dangerous assignment. Having been forced from their Susquehanna homesteads by Brant two years earlier, they were anxious to revisit their homes and see for themselves if there might be anything to go back to after the war. It must have been exceedingly difficult for these men to revisit their once thriving little clearings they had raised their families on. The first two days of the expedition's journey down the winding Susquehanna was slow going and as they approached the mouth of Schenevus Creek, at today's Colliersville, they made their second encampment around the burnt-out homestead of Joachim Van Volkenburgh. A Schoharie native of Palatine Dutch descent, Van Volkenburgh had years ago taken a Mohawk wife and chosen to live among her people. He was one of the very first white men to settle on the border frontier before the war. As an accomplished frontiersman who knew the ways and tongue of his wife's people, he proved to be one of Capt. Harper's most trusted scouts. This, however, would be the last time the old Dutch frontiersman would ever see his riverfront abode, as he would be killed two years later.

From Joachim's homestead, the caravan proceeded down the river past the confluence of Charlotte Creek and encamped a third night at another one of Harper's ranger's riverfront homes at Otsdawa Creek, near today's village of Otego. Lt. Daniel Ogden had been with Van Volkenburgh and Capt. Harper at the contentious Johnston Settlement summit between Joseph Brant and Gen. Herkimer in '77. He too lamented as he passed by the burnt-out ruins of his family's former homestead before encamping with the expedition for a fourth night at the ruins of Johnston's Settlement. Rev. Johnston's son Witter, now a lieutenant in Col. Gansevoort's 3rd N.Y. Regt., spent a haunted night with his regiment on the ruins of his family's once proud frontier settlement. The feelings of anguish these three men must have felt at the sight of their defiled homes would have quickly turned to outrage that fueled their righteous sense of reprisal as they headed towards the homeland of the Haudenosaunee peoples. [13]

Crossing the old Indian Property Line of '68, Clinton's brigade continued down the Susquehanna through the Indian villages destroyed ten months earlier by Col. Butler's 4th Pennsylvania and Schoharie militiamen. Passing through the ruins, some of Clinton's frontier veterans may have been proud of their handywork, while others may have felt a sting of guilt for having destroyed such a superb string of Indian settlements. After passing through the ashes of Cunnahunta, the expedition encamped for two days in what was left of Onaquaga and waited for a regiment of five hundred New York Levies from Ulster County to join their convoy. Hard-pressed for time, Clinton left before Col. Albert Pawling's regiment arrived, assuming he would catch up with them after reaching Onaquaga. But Pawlings had unexpectedly turned his regiment around and returned to Wawarsing without ever reaching the Susquehanna. The loss of Pawling's troops reduced the size of Clinton's brigade and made them far more vulnerable should they encounter an Indian war party before reaching Sullivan at Tioga Point.

From Onaquaga, the Susquehanna flows south into Pennsylvania before rounding the Great Bend and heading back northwest into New York State. Part of Clinton's brigade appears to have diverted from the river at Onaquaga and marched west along Occanum Creek towards the confluence of the Susquehanna and Chenango Rivers. Their path would have shadowed today's New York Interstate #86. In a diary kept by Ensign John Barr of the 4th New York Regiment, he recorded the mileage from Otsego Lake to Tioga Point as being two hundred miles by river and 160 by land. The river from today's Windsor to Binghamton would account for all but ten miles of Barr's mileage discrepancy. After reuniting with the flotilla at the Chenango River in today's Binghamton, Clinton deployed a small detachment of frontier veterans to ascend the Chenango and destroy the few small Indian villages scattered along the river. The main force continued a few miles on down the Susquehanna, destroying the village of Choconut, near today's Endicott/Vestal, before marching westward another fifteen miles towards the Indian village of Ahwaga, today's Owego. A few miles before reaching Ahwaga, the expedition ran headlong into a large body of troops sent out by Sullivan to assist Clinton's caravan on the rest of their journey to Tioga Point.

Rumors of Capt. Brant and a large body of Indians secreted in the area, prompted Sullivan to dispatch Generals Poor and Hand with nine hundred troops up the river to protect and escort Clinton on to Tioga Point. After their long march from the Chenango River, and Poor's and Hand's from Tioga Point, the combined forces paused for a day at Ahwaga while they torched the impressive Indian village and surrounding orchards and cornfields. The 2,700 troops then marched on through the Susquehanna's ancient Indian village of Manckatawangum, between today's Nichols and Barton, and did the same to that unfortunate village. It was near Manckatawangum that some of Clinton's men found the remains of the Indians killed by Sawyer and Cowley as they made their daring escape from their captors earlier that year. After two weeks of paddling down the Susquehanna, Clinton's brigade of bateaux finally arrived at Tioga Point on the 22nd of August, eleven days after Sullivan's arrival. Greeted by Sullivan's troops with a salvo of cannon salutes, a jubilant day of toasting and celebration followed while the commanders huddled together to map out their approach into the lands of the Iroquois Nations. [14]

While Sullivan and Clinton's troops were celebrating at Tioga Point, Lt. Col. Daniel Brodhead's western expedition was already well on its way up the Allegheny River into Iroquois territory. They left Fort Pitt on the 11th of August, the same day Sullivan arrived at Tioga Point and Clinton's bateau men paddled from Van Volkenburghs to Lt. Ogden's burned-out homesteads. Brodhead's men had already destroyed several Mingo and Munsee villages along the Allegheny and the Lenape villages of Buckaloon and Conewago, near Brokenstraw Creek. They continued up the river another thirty-five miles through today's Warren County, Pennsylvania before reaching the Seneca villages of Yoghroonwago on the upper Allegheny in New York's Cattaraugus County. This bountiful cluster of Seneca villages near the current village of Salamanca on today's Allegheny Indian Reservation, had 130 well-built houses and five hundred acres of some of the best cornfields, gardens and orchards many of Brodhead's men had ever seen.

After burning the Yoghroonwago villages and all their crops, Col. Brodhead turned his troops around and headed back towards Fort Pitt after little more than a month on the trail. On the 14th of September, while Sullivan was on the Genesee River destroying the Seneca villages of Gathchegwarohare and Little Beards Town, Brodhead's troops arrived back at Fort Pitt after never having come anywhere near Sullivan's forces. Whether this third prong of the campaign was ever really meant to hook up with the main expedition, is unclear. But with only six hundred men, Brodhead's expedition might only have been a diversionary ploy, meant to draw British and Indian forces away from Sullivan and Clinton's advancing troops. [15]

Haudenosaunee

After four days of preparation for their offensive into Iroquois territory, Clinton and Sullivan's four brigades were finally ready to depart Tioga Point and march up along the Chemung River. The heavy baggage and sick troops were left at Tioga Point with a garrison of 250 soldiers to protect the post they named Fort Sullivan. Hundreds of packhorses and mules were loaded with twenty-seven days' worth of provisions for the 3,500 troops who were about to make a 275-mile round-trip hike through the western wilderness. The Women and sutlers who had tagged along behind the army from Easton and Schenectady were also left at the forward base. Six three-pound brass artillery pieces and two howitzers with three wagonloads and four boatloads of ammunition accompanied the artillerymen. Dozens of wagonloads of axes, hatchets, scythes, and torches were brought along to equip the men for their demolition duties.

Rifle, knapsack, canteen and powder horn were carried by each man as they walked alongside their field officers on horseback. On cold nights they slept eight to a tent, on warmer ones they slept under the stars. Whiskey was brought along in abundant supply; four gallons for field officers and two gallons for the commissioned officers, while rum was allotted in generous portions to the enlisted men. [16]

Capt. Harper was required to sign for his scouts and ranger's provisions, being that they were not part of the regular army and were there of their own volition. It's unclear if the captain was ever reimbursed by Congress for his men's provisions, or if the debt was forgiven for his company's outstanding service to the expedition. Either way, Capt. Harper was not about to miss out on a chance to explore western New York's Indian territory. Always in the forefront of John and his brother's mind was the dream of empire their father had weaned them on. The Harper family's 260,000-acre purchase of the Oneida lands, and their subsequent 22,000-acre patent grant, was largely due to Capt. Harper's uncanny ability to assimilate into the warrior culture of the Iroquois peoples. His inherent appreciation for their way of life was instilled in him early by his father and by his experiences at Rev. Wheelock's Charity School. Ten years before the Revolution and the Sullivan/Clinton Campaign, Sir William Johnson had been the man whose favor one needed to facilitate any land transaction with the Indians. But now, with Sir William long gone, the man to impress was New York's Governor George Clinton, and by impressing his brother Brig. Gen. James Clinton, Harper hoped to do just that. He was not unlike others of his time who seized on every opportunity to rise above their station. Finagling politicians and land commissioners while manipulating sachems and chieftains was one means to that end. The land Capt. Harper was about to tread represented incredible wealth for those cunning and ruthless enough to reap its rewards. But first, the war would need to be won, and its original residents subdued and evicted.

On the 26th of August, Sullivan and Clinton's Continental troops marched out of their Tioga Point encampment and began their path of destruction through the lands of the Six Nations. Marching north along the east side of the Chemung River on the old Seneca trail known as The Forbidden Path, the columns of soldiers and caravan of wagons and boats found the going slow and tedious. The weather was not at all obliging, having rained heavily for days which riled up the river and turned the trail to mud. Late on the afternoon of the third day, after losing a boatload of ammo and baggage in the river and having advanced just twelve miles, they arrived at the old Indian village of Chemung, a few miles upriver from the present hamlet of Chemung. Upon resuming their march the following morning, they discovered a force of 250 British grenadiers and loyalists huddled behind a makeshift breastwork with another 1,000 Seneca and Cayuga warriors positioned around them. Maj. John Butler and Captains Walter Butler and Spanish John MacDonell led the loyalists, while the Indians were under the command of Cornplanter, Sayenqueraghta, Fish Carrier and Capt. Brant. With a superior force nearly three times that of their enemy, Sullivan's four brigades quickly assembled into battle formation on the east side of Baldwin Creek and prepared to attack.

The Battle of Newtown was a short but decisive victory for the Continentals. After encircling and dispersing the British troops, they sent most of their Indians scurrying up the river after firing an artillery barrage over their heads. Preferring to fight face-to-face in close combat, the Indians were reluctant to fight against a battlefield formation, particularly if the enemy had artillery. Sullivan's overwhelming show of force demonstrated to Maj. Butler the futility of facing his expedition again on a field of battle. It also encouraged a great many of the Iroquois to abandon Maj. Butler's army and head back to their villages and families ahead of the impending onslaught. After the battle, Sullivan tarried on the battlefield for a day, burying his three casualties and arranging for his thirty-four wounded soldiers to be carried back to the base at Tioga Point. Sensing the British had neither the men nor the stomach for another confrontation, he sent four of his heavy brass three-pounders back with the wounded. The lighter they could travel, the faster they could do the business they came to do and get back out of the wilderness before winter. [17]

With the Indians on the run and the British in full retreat towards the Genesee River, the Continentals advanced with little resistance save the occasional skirmish with a band of roving warriors. Advancing up the Chemung about five more miles to the beautiful Cayuga village of Kanawaholla at Newtown Creek, in today's Elmira, Sullivan's men destroyed the cornfields and girdled some of the most glorious orchards in all of western New York. After their work was done at Kanawaholla they continued north through Queanettquaga, or Catharine's Town, towards the south end of Seneca Lake where they arrived on the 3rd of September after slashing and burning everything along the way. Many of the officers recorded in their journals that the farmland and crops they destroyed were some of the finest they had ever seen. Their path of destruction then continued up the east side of Seneca Lake, obliterating every orchard, cornfield, beanstalk, and squash patch from Watkins Glen to Geneva. The Seneca villages of Condawhaw and Kendaia were put to the torch. Today, this region flourishes with some of the most renowned vineyards and wineries in the State.

Major John Butler

It was not easy work destroying the Indian village's homes and crops, nor was it an enjoyable job for many of the young men who were tasked with doing so. Most of them knew just how hard it was to open a forest clearing and work the soil into production. Those who questioned the morality of what they were doing had no recourse but to follow their orders and do it quickly. Gen. Clinton's brigade chaplain, Rev. John Gano, listened to the concerns of some of his expedition's soul-sickened arsonists and commented in his memoirs, '... *Some of the young soldiers were under great distress of mind concerning their souls and frequently came to me and conversed with me. I mentioned a text to Gen. Sullivan which frequently occurred to me when I thought of the Indians and the devastation which were made in their country, Isaiah 8:21; They shall walk through them, and be hungry, and curse their God and their King, and look upwards...*'. While this may have soothed some of the distraught soldiers, one point the reverend failed to recognize was that many of the Seneca and Cayuga peoples had been converted to Christianity long ago. The suggestion to '*curse their God*' while looking upwards for redemption from the same God, seems not to have bothered the well-meaning reverend or the few who knew no better. [18]

Reaching the principal Seneca Castle of Kanadaseaga on the north end of Seneca Lake on the 7th, the Continentals spent all the next day destroying crops and torching the village's sixty well-build homes. An entry in one of the officer's journals described the day's work, '... *we destroyed a 150-acre field of the best corn I had ever seen, with some of the stacks [stocks] over 16 feet in height, we destroyed great quantities of beans, potatoes, pumpkins, cucumbers, squash and watermelons...*'. As the troops were destroying Kanadaseaga, Capt. Harper and fifty of his rangers were sent on a separate mission to destroy a small Cayuga village on the Seneca River. Skoi-Yase was about eight miles east of Kanadaseaga and halfway between the outlets of Seneca and Cayuga Lakes. The Seneca County village of Waterloo now sits on the site of the once proud Cayuga village. Harper's volunteer corps was made up of frontiersmen, many of whom had lost their own homesteads to the arsonist's torch. Rev. Gano's biblical quote seems to have fallen on Capt. Harper's and his ranger's and Oneida scout's deaf ears. They didn't have the heart to destroy all of Skoi-Yase or its lush cornfields, orchards and gardens. Two weeks after their raid, while the expedition was returning from the Genesee country on route back to Tioga Point, another detachment was assigned to finish the job Harper's men half-heartedly performed. They had purposely left too much of the village intact, trying to leave something for the poor Cayuga villagers who would now have to face the long winter without food or shelter. [19]

Burning of an Indian Village

Rushing back from Skoi-Yase to join the expedition, Capt. Harper and his rangers caught up with the troops as they were making their way from Kanadaseaga towards the Seneca village of Kannandaguah on the north end of Canandaigua Lake. Many of the smaller and larger villages they slashed their way through had only been abandoned a few hours before their arrival. Packs and blankets were left behind after an apparently hasty departure, while potatoes were found roasting on fires still burning. Leaving the village of Kannandaguah in ruins, the campaign pressed on towards the Genesee River and the prestigious Seneca village of Little Beards Town. After destroying a small village on the north end of Honeoye Lake, Sullivan made the bold decision to leave most of his heavy baggage and packhorses at Honeoye. Capt. John Cummings and a garrison of three hundred men, many of whom were described as sick, lame, or lazy, were left behind to help the main body move lighter and faster. Sullivan planned to make a lightning strike on Little Beards Town before the British could stage a counterattack. Maj. Butler's loyalists and Capt. Brant's warriors, who now numbered far less than they had at Newtown, had been retreating ahead of the Continentals since Newtown and were now committed to making one last stand at the Genesee. A company of the King's Regiment of Light Infantry had been sent out from Fort Niagara to join Butler at Little Beards Town where they hoped to discourage Sullivan from advancing on to Niagara, which was just seventy miles from the Genesee.

Marching past the north ends of lakes Canadice and Hemlock, Sullivan's troops encamped on the night of the 12th a few miles east of the southern end of Conesus Lake, near today's hamlet of Foots Corners. A forward patrol was sent out that night to reconnoiter the trail forward and observe if any of the enemy were lingering about. Two of Morgan's Riflemen, Lt. Thomas Boyd and Sgt. Michael Parker, led twenty-two other scouts down around the south end of Conesus Lake and continued along a trail five miles west to the Seneca village of Gathtsegwarahare on Canaseraga Creek, a mile east of today's Mount Morris. Moving quietly through a moonless night, Lt. Boyd's scout somehow managed to slip past an encampment of three hundred Indians on the west side of Conesus Lake. Reaching the Seneca village around daybreak, they found it nearly empty except for a few old Tuscarora men and dogs.

Two or three of Boyd's scouts were members of Capt. Harper's volunteer corps, including Lt. Gerrett Putnam and the irascible Pvt. Timothy Murphy. Murphy could not help himself from firing on the old harmless men, killing a couple of them. Boyd then had no alternative but to turn his men about and head back towards Sullivan's encampment, knowing Murphy's shots had announced their presence to every Indian and Tory within earshot. Within a few miles they ran into a small party of Seneca warriors, and although warned by his Mohawk scout Lt. Han Yost not to follow them, Lt. Boyd unwisely ignored his advice and ordered his men to chase after them. Realizing too late that Thaosagwat had been right, Boyd's men were lured directly into an ambush and surrounded by the large party of Indians they had passed by the night before. The warriors descended upon their prey like a pack of hungry wolves, quickly killing Han Yost and eleven of his companions in a desperate hand-to-hand skirmish. Only eight of Boyd's scouts managed to escape and make their way back to their comrades now on the march towards them and the Genesee. Boyd and Parker were both captured alive and led off towards Little Beards Town ahead of the advancing Continentals.

After being fired upon by the same Indians who had ambushed Lt. Boyd's scout earlier that morning, Sullivan's army marched on towards the abandoned village of Gathtsegwarahare, reaching it around dusk. Maj. John Butler's forces were now within three miles of the Continentals, just across the

Genesee in Little Beards Town. Recognizing the futility of engaging Sullivan's superior force, Butler hastily evacuated the village and began a rapid withdrawal back towards Fort Niagara for what he anticipated might be a long siege should Sullivan choose to continue his advance. Sullivan, however, had no intention of going any further than the Genesee and Little Beards Town.

On the 14th of September, after sacking Gathtsegwarahare, Sullivan crossed the Genesee and entered Little Beards Town unopposed. His troops were amazed at the size and splendor of the Indian village. With over 120 well-built houses and an equal number of barns and outbuildings, many of the troops were initially hard-pressed to do the dirty work they were sent there to do. But after finding what they would find there, their reservations were abruptly subdued. The mangled and desecrated bodies of Lt. Boyd and Sgt. Parker had been left behind and deliberately displayed by Maj. Butler and his Indians as a parting gift and warning to those who might be so unwise as to follow them. The two officer's bodies were said to have been *'…striped naked and their heads cut off…their eyes punched out…finger and toenails bruised off…their privates nearly cut off and hanging down…and dogs had eaten part of their shoulders away…'.* The unbridled rage of the Seneca warriors, who's homeland now lay in ruin, had been taken out on the two unfortunate officers who were purposely kept alive while they were slowly tortured to death. [20]

With Col. Brodhead's Allegany expedition already back in Fort Pitt by the time Sullivan's troops reached the Genesee River, the general decided to terminate the expedition and head back to Tioga Point. Advancing on to Niagara would have required his troops to march another eighty miles before laying siege to a well-fortified garrison that could be resupplied and reinforced with British Regulars by ships from Montreal and Quebec. Fall was already in the air and the prospect of a 250-mile winter march back to civilization, should a protracted siege fail, was enough to convince Sullivan to end his thus-far successful expedition. He would later be chastised by some for not having finished off Butler's army while he had them on the run and Fort Niagara was within his sights. But most of those who criticized him had never been in that part of the country and knew little about a winter spent in the western wilderness. Having just destroyed one of the largest Seneca villages in all of Haudenosaunee and burnt an estimated 15,000 bushels of corn, Sullivan felt his expedition had done all that was expected of it. It had been thirteen weeks since his troops left Easton and eleven since Clinton's troops started their journey down the Susquehanna from Otsego Lake. Their men were more than ready to head for home. With nights turning colder and dawning with light frost, the need to hasten back to civilization grew ever-more urgent. Their provisions were running low, and their overburdened packhorses and mules were breaking down from fatigue. Great numbers of the poor exhausted animals had to be shot along the way. So many of their bleached skulls, found years later by the Indians, were lined up along The Forbidden Path north of today's Elmira, that the village that eventually sprang up around them became known as Horseheads.

Five days after leaving Little Beards Town in ruin and collecting Capt. Cumming's Honeoye troops and packhorses, the expedition was back at Kanadaseaga on the north end of Seneca Lake. From here, Sullivan split up his brigades and ordered them to march for Tioga Point along both sides of Seneca and Cayuga lakes. Another detachment of around a hundred New York troops led by Col. Gansevoort was sent east through Onondaga territory to Fort Schuyler. Capt. Harper's company would have gone along with Gansevoort on his overland journey to the upper Mohawk River, acting as guides through the Indian territory he and his rangers knew well. Unbeknownst to Gansevoort or Harper, Capt. Brant and a party of Seneca warriors followed their party all the way back to Fort Schuyler. Long after the war, Brant told Col. Gansevoort that he and his warriors were so close behind them that they often roasted their venison on the fires left behind by his troops. Had Harper's volunteers not been with Gansevoort, Brant's warriors may have done more than just roast their breakfasts on their fires. [21]

All of Sullivan and Clinton's Continentals were back at Tioga Point by the first of October, having spent nearly six weeks plundering the lands of the Six Nations. As each of the regiments came staggering into Fort Sullivan, a feu de joie hailed their arrival, and the tired soldiers were treated with a feast of roasted oxen. They toasted with whiskey and grog to the success of the expedition. They had destroyed every house, barn and storage bin in over forty Iroquois villages, smashing or burning all the crops both in the field and in their cribs. They killed all the cattle and livestock they could gather and cut down or girdled thousands of lush grape vines and fruit-laden apple, plum and peach trees. Over 150,000 bushels of corn were estimated to have been destroyed. Some were prouder of their work than others, but all were satisfied they had done their duty to God and country. Anxious to return to the civilization they felt more comfortable with, the men were finally ordered to destroy the barracks and breastworks of Fort Sullivan and begin their descent down the Susquehanna back to Easton. Throughout the whole campaign only forty men had been lost. Aside from Lieutenants Boyd and Parker and their twelve comrades, most of the other fatalities were from illness or fatigue.

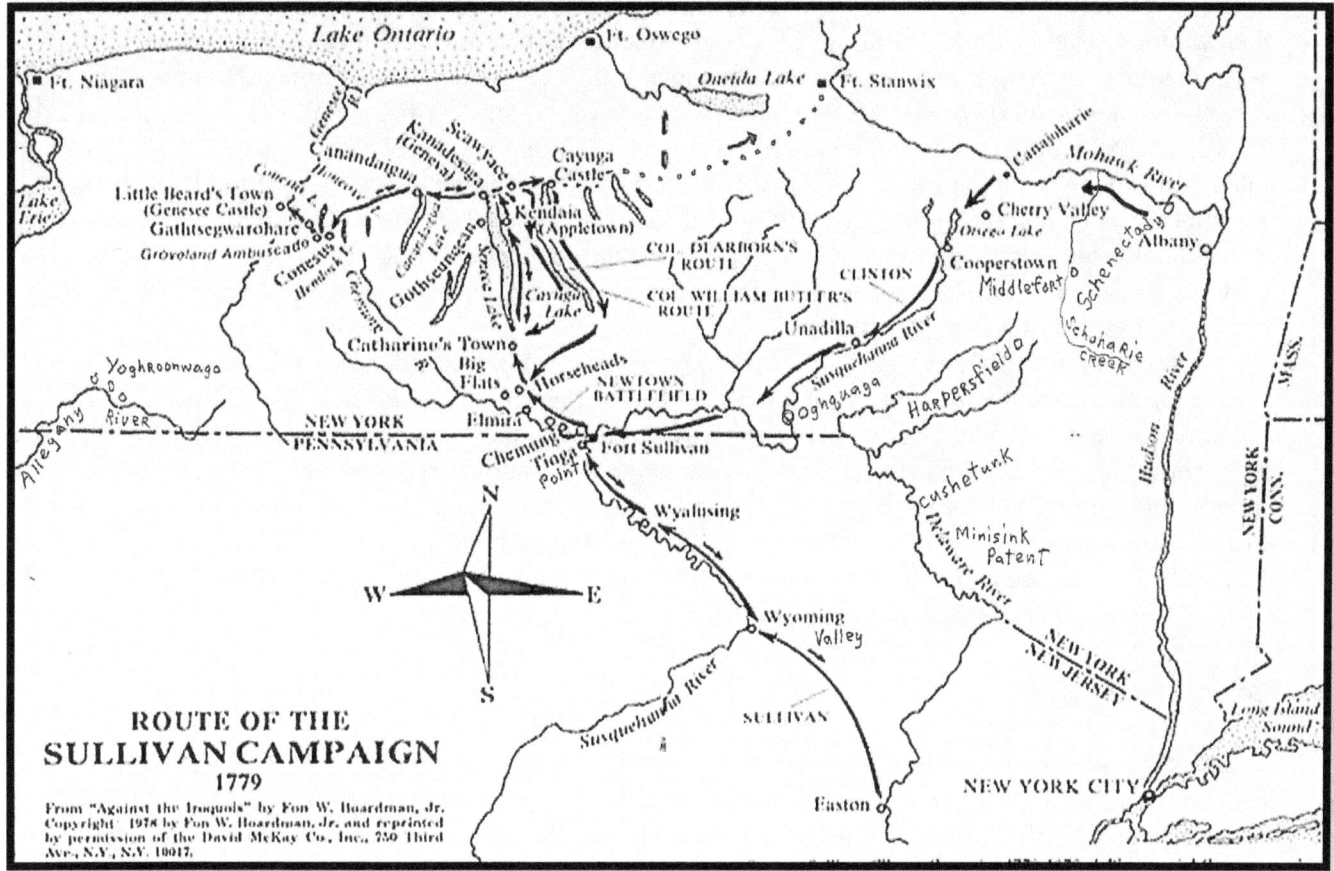

The total devastation of their villages and food supplies was a catastrophic loss for the Iroquois families who were now reduced to the support of their British allies. Disgusted by the cruelty of Sullivan's and Van Schaick's earlier campaign, three hundred Onondaga, Tuscarora, and Oneida warriors who had sided with Congress and fought alongside the rebels, deserted their Continental companies and joined their Iroquois brethren at Fort Niagara. Some of Capt. Harper's scouts may have been among them. The grounds around Fort Niagara were overwhelmed with families of desperate Indians seeking refuge from the winter to come. Four to five thousand Iroquois refugees were said to have setup make-shift huts and lean-tos around the fort and up along the Niagara River as far as Lewiston. The winter of 1779/'80 was reported to have been one of the coldest and snowiest on record. One account stated that the lake-effect snow piled up five to six feet deep and stayed on the ground throughout the entire winter. All the game perished, and in the spring, vast numbers of deer and other animals were found dead as the melting snow exposed their frozen carcasses. Thousands of Indians died of starvation or hypothermia before that terrible winter finally ended.

A surprisingly fortuitous event happened in the spring of 1780 for the peoples of the Onondaga Nation. In late April, the few starving Onondaga families who remained or had returned to their lands south of Onondaga Lakes received an incredible blessing and gift from their Great Creator. The region through which Col. Van Schaick carried out his scorched-earth campaign was visited by the emergence of the seventeen-year Periodical Cicada (Brood VII). Millions of cicadas arise from the ground every seventeen or thirteen years to breed and generate the next generation to continue their unique life cycle. Roasted or fried until browned, a handful of cicadas made a life-saving meal of nutrients for the starving Onondagas and their children. The Onondaga still honour the periodical return of the Ogweñ-yo''da'. Their chorus of incessant chirping reassures their people of their creator's wish for them to survive. [22]

After returning to civilization, Sullivan's three brigades and Clinton's four regiments settled into their winter quarters in northern New Jersey and the Hudson Highlands where they waited for their spring assignments. Capt. Harper's rangers and scouts rejoined their comrades in one of the Schoharie Valley's three militia forts. Rejoicing with their families who had waited for over five months to see their loved ones again, many of Harper's volunteers settled in for the winter in Schoharie's Middle Fort. The stories told by the young returning voyagers were laced with their embellished exploits and shamelessly proud accomplishments, neglecting the horrors they had seen and inflicted. They would also have told of the bountiful and fertile farmland they hiked through during their trek through the Finger Lakes Region. Within a decade of the Sullivan/Clinton Campaign, many of these same young men returned with their families to the lands they had devastated.

Men like John Harper looked upon the western lands and envisioned the potential profits they could reap from another large purchase of Indian lands. Their dreams of empire, their father John Sr. imparted to them, had been put on hold by the war. But the war had not doused their ambitions. Having been shrewdly aware of the importance of influencing and garnering the favor of men like Sir William Johnson before the war, the Harpers intuitively knew the importance of gaining the favor of New York's Gov. Clinton after the war was won. Having volunteered and paid for his ranger's support during Gen. James Clinton's campaign, Capt. Harper's motives were in part inspired by a calculated design to gain the favor of the general and his brother the governor.

Colonel John Harper

Capt. Harper spent the winter in the former estate of loyalist Daniel Claus where he had lived with his family and wife Miriam before her death the year before. John utilized the off-season to lobby for himself and his brother's military promotions. With his recent self-financed participation in the Sullivan Campaign, coupled with his reputation as an effective frontier ranger captain, the hero of Schoharie's Battle of the Flockey was poised for an impressive promotion. General James Clinton was now the commander of the Army of the Northern Department, and through his influence, New York's Council of Appointments recommissioned Capt. Harper to colonel of the 5th Tryon County Regiment of Militia. His younger brother Joseph received a commission for 1st major in his brother's regiment. Harpersfield's Thomas Hendry Sr was appointed 2nd major while the millwright, St Leger Cowley, who had escaped with Isaac Sawyer from Seth's Henry's war party the year before, served as Col. Harper's regimental adjutant. Revolutionary War militia regiments were a loosely organized corps of recruits who signed on for either a three, nine or one-year stint, while always being available on a moment's notice when needed. The regiments were regionally oriented with companies made up of recruits from the same neighborhoods and settlements. Most of the 5th regiment's rank and file was made up of men from the abandoned settlements of Harpersfield, Kortright and the Susquehanna and Charlotte Creek settlements. All of Col. Harper's former company of rangers and scouts joined his militia regiment along with nearly all of Harper Patent's homesteaders and Scots-Irish kinsmen.

The first company of Col. John Harper's Tryon County Regiment was commanded by the youngest Harper brother Alexander, with the Harper's brother-in-law William McFarland as his company's 1st lieutenant. Another brother-in-law of Capt. Alexander Harper, Joseph Bartholomew, served as 1st lieutenant in the regiment's fourth company of Charlotte Creek recruits. Rev. William Johnston's son Witter served as captain of the 5th regiment's sixth company. Another dispossessed Susquehanna refugee, Daniel Ogden, was assigned to serve as 2nd lieutenant in the regiment's third company. 2nd Major Thomas Hendry's sons Thomas Jr. and John Hendry both served as 2nd lieutenants in separate companies. Thomas Hendry and his four sons, Daniel, Thomas, John, and James were some of the first settlers on the Harper family's patent before the war. Nepotism, patronage, and ethnicity were major considerations when appointing officers to lead a frontier militia regiment and its companies.

Two months after Capt. John Harper was promoted to colonel of the 5th Tryon County Militia Regiment on the 3rd of March 1780, he was again commissioned lieutenant colonel of the 2nd Regiment of New York Levies. Having officered his militia regiment with many of the same men he had come to trust as captain of his small outfit of rangers and scouts, Colonel Harper was now in a league that required a whole new level of military prowess. Very few of the colonel's former rangers and militiamen transferred to his new regiment of New York Levies. His brother Alexander retained his rank as captain but was transferred to Col. Peter Vrooman's 15th Albany Regiment of Levies. Brother Joseph was the only officer that followed Col. Harper into his regiment of levies, being reduced however from major to lieutenant. Timothy Murphy, Joachim Van Volkenburgh and Garrett Putman were a few of the former rangers assigned to Col. Harper's new outfit. The colonel's son and former waiter, Archibald, was now sixteen and ready for military service as a private in his father's regiment. Few of Col. Harper's 450 Levies were from the frontier borderlands, most were from the lower Mohawk River settlements or the upper Hudson's Columbia and Albany County communities.

John had been an exceedingly effective frontier commander who had gained a reputation as a fearless fighter and leader of men. His daring and legendary ride to Albany and the cavalry charge that drove MacDonell and his Tories from the Schoharie Valley made him a hero and a local celebrity. But the question was, did he possess enough of the necessary military experience to organize, administrate, and lead an entire regiment of Continental soldiers? Convincing other high-ranking commanders in the Army of the Northern Department might require more than just fearless courage and a resolve to fight. The nuances of military and political diplomacy might prove challenging for a headstrong Scots Irishman with little patience for petty intrigues or self-promoting competitors. Col. Harper's frontier experiences and familiarity with the Native American warrior culture and their ways of waging war, gave him a distinct advantage over many of the other border region commanders who knew little of the enemy they were fighting. But it also exposed him to a certain predisposition held by eighteenth-century gentlemen who were suspicious of those who fraternized with the uncivilized *beasts of the forest.* Even Jefferson himself could not refrain from expressing his disdain for Native Americans when he wrote in the Declaration of Independence, '...*the inhabitants of our frontiers, the merciless Indian savages...*'. John Harper's success as a Revolutionary War colonel would depend as much on his understanding of the enemy beside him, as it would the enemy before him. His triumphs as a frontier captain might be reassuring for the men beneath him but might also invoke the jealousy of those around and above him. [23]

Sugar Boilers

A little over a month after being promoted from lieutenant to captain and transferred to the 15th Albany Regiment, Capt. Alexander Harper proved himself again to be a less than steady commander. A certain stigma had followed him since the dubious affair on the East Branch and the suspicious circumstances surrounding the death of Paghatakan's Hermanus Dumond. Overanxious to distance himself from the debacle and prove his worth as a military leader, Capt. Harper convinced Col. Vrooman to send him on an excursion into enemy territory. In early April he led a small detachment of his militia company from Schoharie's Middle Fort to his family's frontier patent and the abandoned settlement of Harpersfield. The snow was still deep enough to require snowshoes to navigate, but the days had begun to warm up enough for the maple trees to start running with sap. It had also warmed just enough for Capt. Brant and his warriors to resume their raids on the frontier settlements. After the devastating Sullivan Campaign and winter that followed, Iroquois warriors were incensed with a renewed sense of rage to pay back cruelty with cruelty. Nevertheless, the recently appointed captain felt it was early enough in the season to avoid running into any Indian war parties.

On April 7th, 1780, having trudged through the snow from Schoharie to Harpersfield, Capt. Harper and thirteen volunteers from his militia company were back in the old neighborhood where he and some of his men had lived before the onset of war. By midday, Capt. Harper had split up his men into groups of three or four and positioned them on different homestead sites, all within a mile radius of each other. With the spring sap dripping from the maple trees they had tapped while still living on their homesteads, fires were lit and the sap began boiling in kettles they had conveniently left behind. Maj. Thomas Hendry and his two sons, James and Lt. John Hendry, were glad to be back on their old homestead sitting around a warm fire and stirring their sap into sweet maple syrup. Brothers Isaac and Freegift Patchin were similarly engaged on their own old homestead near to the Thorp brothers, Daniel and Ezra. William Lamb and his eleven-year-old son Willy were also hard at work on their old homestead, stoking the fire and tasting the boiling syrup. Capt. Harper's brother-in-law, William Stevens, had unfortunately become too sick to do any sugar boiling and was reduced to lay by the fireplace in one of the abandoned cabins.

With sweet smoke wafting through the forest canopy from the fires beneath the boiling kettles, Capt. Brant and a war party of fourteen Indians and five Tories had little trouble finding and overpowering each of the isolated camps. In a well-coordinated raid, with only five more men than Capt. Harper, the cunning Capt. Brant was able to take the unwitting captain and ten of his sugar boilers into captivity. Three of the sugar boilers were killed in the assaults. Maj. Hendry and his son James were both killed while trying to repel their assailants. William Stevens, who had only recently married Alexander's wife's sister, Hannah Bartholomew, met his demise while lying helplessly ill in his cabin, too sick to put up much of a fight. Stevens had come to Schoharie with Col. William Butler's 4th Pennsylvania Regiment and had distinguished himself as an outstanding scout and trusted soldier on Butler's Onaquaga Campaign. While stationed at Middle Fort he had become acquainted with the Harpers and Miss Bartholomew, and had he survived the sugar boiler excursion, would have certainly become a valued member of the Harper clan. Taking such a small party of troops into a dangerous wilderness where Indians were suspected to be roaming and then separating them into different isolated camps, proved to be a foolish and disastrous exercise. Alexander Harper's impetuous nature had gotten him into trouble before, but this time he had played ducks and drakes with the lives of others and got them and himself into more than just a little trouble.

After releasing one of the sugar boilers to run letters back to Col. Vrooman in Middle Fort, Capt. Brant and his nineteen warriors got ready to escort ten able-bodied militiamen back to Fort Niagara through knee-deep snow and frigid rivers. But incredibly, Brant was still not satisfied with his catch, and his good fortune was still with him. Discovering that a family of settlers was still holding out on their homestead just across the river in New Stamford's town plot, Brant sent a few of his best warriors across the Delaware while he and the rest of his men watched over the sugar boilers. Again, his warriors easily captured the family of sixty-six-year-old David Brown. Leaving Mr. Brown's wife and their five younger children behind, David and his three older sons John, Doctor and Solomon were herded off to join Capt. Harper and his men. Now with nearly as many prisoners as Indians, Brant began their grueling 250-mile trek back to Fort Niagara while marshaling their fourteen prisoners. Old David Brown, however, would be spared the long agonizing hike and dreaded gauntlet that awaited them. After just a day on the trail, he was already falling behind and struggling to keep up with the others. As was the custom for those who could not keep up, he was mercilessly tomahawked, scalped and left for the forest scavengers. [24]

Descending the West Branch in canoes, Brant's party crossed over to the Susquehanna from Cookhouse to Onaquaga and continued their journey down to the ruins of Fort Sullivan at Tioga Point. Here, Brant was reunited with another party of warriors he had sent down to the Minisink to wreak havoc on the lower Delaware and Neversink settlements. Adding five more prisoners to Brant's fourteen, they all started up The Forbidden Path towards the Genesee River and Fort Niagara beyond. Surviving on some of the frozen carcasses of Sullivan's euthanized packhorses, Brant's warriors and nineteen prisoners managed to make it back to Fort Niagara and the gauntlet that awaited the rebels. As they approached the fort, a mob of angry Indians prepared to unleash their fury on the exhausted captives, but Capt. Brant had a plan to save Alexander and his men from the gauntlet.

Six months prior, after returning to Fort Niagara after tailing Gansevoort and Harper back to Fort Schuyler, Capt. Brant spent a cold winter confined in the fort with the Butlers, Johnsons and British troops. While his people suffered horribly outside the fort's walls, Capt. Brant enjoyed the benefits of rank and took advantage of a chance to rest after what had to have been an exhausting year. Cooped up in the overcrowded fort with the other officers and their families, the twice widowed Brant had a few months to spend and enjoy with his third Indian wife Catherine Adonwentishon. After having been captured at Cherry Valley in late 1778, Capt. Harper's sister Mary Moore and his two youngest nieces, Abigail and Mary, had only just recently left the fort for Montreal by the time Alexander and his men arrived there in late April. While his oldest niece Jane stayed behind, Mary and her two other daughters were finally being readied for a prisoner exchange after a year and a half of captivity. During the winter months at Fort Niagara, Brant witnessed Maj. John Butler performing the marriage ceremony between British officer Capt. John Powell and Alexander's niece Jane Moore. Realizing Maj. Butler had the authority to perform and certify marriages, Capt. Brant promptly demanded the major marry him to his Indian wife Catherine. Sanctifying their Indian union, which was not recognized as a formal marriage by whites, afforded the man of two worlds and his new wife the respectability they both deserved.

Although having little respect personally for Alexander, Joseph's friendship with his brother John and the influence of Capt. Powell's new bride, saved Alexander's life and those of his men. Eighteenth-century gentlemen of honor were bound by a code that required a certain degree of courtesy extended to other gentlemen of equal rank and social standing. The angry mob of club-wielding Indians waiting for their chance to deliver a blow on the weary white prisoners was made up of women and young boys. Fortunately for Capt. Harper and the sugar boilers, Capt. Brant and Capt. Powell had devised a plan to spare them from running the gauntlet. Having sent runners out ahead just before reaching the fort, Brant instructed Capt. Powell to contrive a pretext to send many of the fiercest warriors encamped around the fort on a fool's errand. Capt. Powell was also advised to form a detachment of his company into a double line through which the captives could be ushered and kept from the clubs and fists of the women and boys who tried to beat his prisoners. It was a lucky day for the captain and his Harpersfield boys, several of whom may not have survived the torturous ordeal. Their reprieve from running the gauntlet did not, however, save them from the long and despairing incarceration they were all about to endure. Shortly after gaining refuge within the walls of the fort, Capt. Harper and his men were loaded onto transports for delivery to the prison ships in Montreal and eventually to the notorious prison at Chamblee.

Captain Harper's niece Jane and husband Capt. Powell would do what they could to lessen the severity of uncle Alexander's incarceration, short of securing an early release for him or any of his men. They would all spend over two-and-a-half years in British custody before finally being released in late November 1782. Emaciated and barely recognizable by their friends and families, Alexander and his men finally made it home alive, save one. Young Lt. John Hendry succumbed to the wretched conditions of his jail cell and died shortly before the rest of his comrades were set free. With the war winding down by the end of '82, none of the sugar boilers or Capt. Harper served any meaningful duty after their release. Alexander returned to Schoharie's Middle Fort where he learned his wife Elizabeth and their four children, Margaret-10, John-8, James-6 and William-4, had recently left the fort for the relative security of eastern New York's village of Lebanon. Capt. Harper had missed three major British invasions of the Mohawk and Schoharie Valleys. His brothers and even his wife Elizabeth had fought through some tough times and miraculously all had survived. But for an excursion into the forest for a little maple syrup, Alexander would have bravely fought alongside his brothers and taken part in their many battles and triumphs. [25]

Fifty years after the sugar boiler affair, one of Capt. Harper's fellow prisoners, Freegift Patchin, told the story of their capture to Josiah Priest, a man who never let the truth get in the way of a good story. Priest was a prolific writer of sensationalized and excessively biased pseudohistory which purposely blurred the line between fiction and nonfiction to appeal to a larger market of readers. '...*Who will spin a story of that savage war...*'. Priest claimed that Patchin told him that Alexander had fooled Capt. Brant into believing Middle Fort had just been reinforced with three hundred Continentals. The inference was that Harper had saved the fort and dissuaded Brant from attacking and capturing all the men, women, and children inside it, thus retrieving Capt. Harper's reputation. Priest also inflated Brant's numbers by more than double. The likelihood that Capt. Brant would have been planning an attack on a fortification with just twenty, or even fifty warriors was ludicrous; that was just not the way Indians waged war. They were seldom known to have attacked a fort unless they were part of an overwhelming force. Furthermore, Brant now had an impressive cache of prisoners and would have had even fewer warriors to stage an assault, being that many of them would be needed to stay behind to guard the captives. Brant was nobody's fool and would certainly have been wary of anything Alexander Harper might tell him. The suspicious narrative of Patchin's capture has been repeated and embellished by subsequent writers since its alleged telling around 1830. The only Harper to have ever saved Schoharie's Middle Fort was Alexander's older brother Col. John Harper. [26]

1780 was an *annus horribilis* for the American fight for Independence. It was also a hard year for the Harper siblings and their families. It began with Alexander's embarrassing capture at Harpersfield and the continued incarceration of his sister Mary Harper Moore and her two daughters. The third Moore daughter had gone over to the enemy by marrying a British officer, much to the dismay of her ardent Whig family. Before the year was over, Joseph Harper would suffer a debilitating wound that would end his military career and leave him disabled for the remainder of his life. John Harper's rise from captain of a small company of rangers to colonel of a militia regiment and lieutenant colonel of a regiment of Levies, would lead to controversy and a court-martial that would not go well for the colonel or his brother William Harper.

5

Johnstown
1780-1783
Schenectady may now be said to be the limit of our western frontier'

Following Sullivan's successful annihilation of the Iroquois villages and crops, there were some who thought the threat of ongoing Indian raids on New York's border region settlements had been eliminated or at least greatly reduced. These hopes were soon dashed, however, by the return of Capt. Brant and his warriors to Harpersfield and the Minisink in the early spring of 1780. '...*The nest are destroyed, but the birds are still on the wing...*'. Throughout April, after the capture of Capt. Harper's sugar boilers, roving bands of Indians and Tories continued harassing the frontier settlers along the Mohawk from German Flatts to Canajoharie. They even revisited the few hardy souls who had returned to Cherry Valley. Anxious to resume plundering for the cattle they so desperately needed, they also needed to feed the rage and indignation they had suffered at the hands of Sullivan's troops. Their determination had only been sharpened by the destruction of their ancestral homeland. Conversely, the resolve of the frontier militias had waned significantly since the heady days following the surrender of Burgoyne and defeat of St. Leger's army in '77. The fever for Independence and freedom from British tyranny that had once ignited the rebel spirit, had gradually been eroded by the burden of three long years of war. Sullivan's campaign did nothing to alleviate their suffering, and as they were about to learn, it only made things worse for them and their families. Militia regiments were finding it harder and harder to call up recruits as many of the frontier's young men were beginning to question their own alliances. While Tory and Indian raids showed no signs of relenting, British commanders at Niagara, Oswego and Quebec began formulating a new offensive strategy to change the intensity and direction of the border war. [1]

Johnstown Raid

In mid-May, alarming news of Gen. Benjamin Lincoln's surrender of Charlestown and 5,000 of his troops reached the north and the militia regiments in the Mohawk and Schoharie Valleys. The news further added to the fears that already gripped the residents of the Mohawk Valley and the militiamen, whose enthusiasm was at an all-time low. If things were not bad enough, rumors were circulating of another two-pronged British invasion marching towards the region from both the north and west. There were confusing reports of a large British and loyalist army moving towards the upper Mohawk from Oswego and another moving down along Lake Champlain. This was all part of Lt. Col. Sir John Johnson's design to divide and conquer the enemy. Col. Johnson had cleverly baited the rebel commanders by sending out runners down through the frontier with the intention of being captured holding phony correspondence that implied two separate invasions. The ruse worked perfectly, diverting the commanders' attention and confusing their militia's response

Lt. Col. John Johnson

to his unilateral invasion down the Lake Champlain corridor. On May 21st, Col. Johnson arrived on the Mohawk with four hundred of his Royal Regiment of New York Loyalists and about two hundred Seneca, Cayuga, and northern Mohawk warriors.

Besides fooling the Tryon County militia commanders with his feigned western invasion, Sir John further muddled their response by taking an unexpected backwoods route from Lake Champlain's Crown Point to Johnstown. Diverting by land from the lake rather than taking the customary route down the lake to South Bay's Skenesborough (Whitehall) and around Lake George to the Hudson, Johnson appeared unopposed on the south end of Great Sacandaga Lake before quietly seizing his father's confiscated estate at Johnstown. Four years had passed since Sir John laid eyes on his family's Johnson Hall Estate, having been forced by the rebels to evacuate it and flee to Canada in 1776. Many of the loyalists in his regiment had also been forced from their homes and were now anxious to impose their revenge on the rebels who had confiscated their property and imprisoned some of their families.

Col. Johnson's first order of business after taking over Johnson Hall was to retrieve a chest full of papers and family memorabilia his family had buried in the basement before their evacuation. Along with their papers, the Johnsons had also buried all their silver plate and coinage. After clearing the area around Johnson Hall, Sir John ordered his troops to initiate a lightning strike on the village of Caughnawaga. Killing many of the rebel villagers and reducing the village to ash, they continued a path of destruction twelve miles down the northside of the Mohawk through Tribes Hill to old Fort Johnson near today's Amsterdam. The loyalists were directed to burn some of the eloquent estates rebel officers had been using as their headquarters, including Sir John's brother-in-law Daniel Claus' home where Col. Harper and his family had been living. For two terrifying days, the avenging loyalists burned and slashed their way through some of the old neighborhoods they had grown up in and shared with their neighbors who they were now slaughtering. They managed to convince, at the point of a bayonet, about 150 of their old neighbors to join their ranks and declare their allegiance to the Crown. Satisfied his men had inflicted enough damage on the Mohawk settlements, Sir John gathered his silver plate and his new recruits and fell back to Mayfield on the south end of Great Sacandaga Lake. With only marginal militia opposition and no forces sent out to trail his retreat from Johnstown, Sir John felt confident enough to encamp for four days on the lake before heading back to Crown Point and on up to Canada.

The success of the first of two Johnstown attack left the frontier militias stunned by the boldness of Col. Johnson's raid and embarrassed by their lack of response. Col. Harper and his fellow commanders looked utterly inept and incapable of organizing or deploying a militia defense. They had failed to rally enough militiamen to offer any resistance to Johnson's forces. They could hardly be faulted for the confusing intelligence that had contributed to their lack of effectiveness in confronting and engaging Col. Johnson's masterfully executed invasion. Col. Harper had only recently been promoted from captain to colonel of a dispirited and shorthanded militia regiment, some of whom had been sent west to confront the phantom invasion. There would of course be accusations of dereliction of duty from the Northern Department's high command and the citizens who had lost their Caughnawaga, Tribes Hill and Johnstown homes and family members. But to be fair, there was plenty of blame to go around. [2]

Throughout the summer months of 1780, Tryon and Albany County militia commanders struggled to maintain their ranks while pleading for more ammunition, supplies and food for their men and woefully undermanned forts. Fort Schuyler at the head of the Mohawk was usually garrisoned with a full regiment of levies and militiamen, but many of the other frontier forts scattered along the Mohawk were lucky if they could muster even a small company of forty or more troops. Infighting between Tryon and Albany County commanders was precipitated, in part, by the malaise that had infected the morale of their frontier soldiers. The lack of troops and provisions designated for the protection of the frontier, frustrated the border region's soldiers and citizenry whose settlements were being destroyed by Indian and Tory war parties. The failure of New York's border war was being blamed by the frontier citizens and soldiers on the neglect of their Northern Department's high command, who in turn blamed the situation on the incompetence of the frontier commanders and their listless militiamen.

Col. Harper's 5th Regiment, those of whom he could assemble, spent the contentious summer and fall of 1780 at Fort Schuyler, where he seems to have provoked the ire of the newly appointed Deputy Adjutant General of the Northern Department, Col. William Malcolm. A wealthy and well-connected New York City merchant, Col. Malcolm had little knowledge of, or appreciation for, the hardships and sacrifices of the backwoods frontier residents. Looking about for a scapegoat to blame the abysmal condition of the frontier militias, Col. Malcolm fixed his attention on Col. Harper for his lack of effectiveness during Col. Johnson's recent raid. In a series of scathing letters sent from Fort Schuyler to Gov. Clinton throughout September and October, Col. Malcolm expressed his total lack of confidence and contempt for Col. Harper. In one letter he wrote, '... *Some companies of Harper's have mutinied on receiving orders to march and the officers are too abettors, not being willing to leave particular places, and I give it as my opinion that they are not a corps to be trusted in the garrison...*'. Other correspondence from Malcolm to Clinton expose an even greater visceral contempt for the frontier commander, '... *I might as well ask Col. Harper about the day of judgement as about his regiment...I really have no patience to mention the instances of his unofficer like conduct...Harper must go, by all accounts he is not a proper person...Gen. Van Rensselaer will tell you that Harper is a blockhead...I have given Harper a furlough...*'. Col. Malcolm apparently harbored contempt for not only Col. Harper, but for his brother William as well. In early October he sent another letter to Gov. Clinton, '... *There is a large quantity of leather at Johnstown forfeited to the state, Mr. Harper* [William] *the commissioner delivered large quantities to his brother on pretense of it being for the use of his regiment and the people seem to think that there will be but a Flemish* [inadequate] *account of it as well as many other things...*'. Within a few weeks, the wealthy New York merchant would regret some of his harsh berating of the Harpers and grudgingly come to realize their importance to the border war. [3]

Schoharie

While brothers, John and William, were dealing with Col. Malcolm's insults and Alexander was wasting away in a Montreal prison ship, Lt. Joseph Harper was co-commanding the militia in Schoharie's Upper Fort with Capt. Jacob Hager. Built around the house of Johannas Feck, Upper Fort was as undermanned and undergunned as were all three of the Schoharie forts. Throughout the early summer months, Lt. Harper and Capt. Hager commanded a garrison of no more than a dozen or two militia soldiers at any one time. Many of the forts' soldiers spent their days out in the fields guarding farm workers in their cornfields and garden patches. The Schoharie and the Mohawk valleys were eerily quiet after Col. Johnson's Johnstown raid and destruction of Caughnawaga. There were no significant attacks on any of the forts or settlements through June and July. Hoping that Sullivan had taken the fight out of the Indians, Schoharie's homesteaders were disheartened when they heard rumors of the notorious Seth's Henry hiding in the backwoods around their settlements with his band of Indians and Tories. Looking for opportunities to attack secluded homesteads and capturing or killing entire families, the Scourge of Schoharie had already notched his warclub with thirty-five kills and forty prisoners by the summer of 1780. Seth's Henry had lived among the valley's Palatine Dutch before the war and was now hunting the very people he more than likely always resented and despised. The capture and escape of Cowley and Sawyer in '79 and the slaughtering of the McKee family had whetted his appetite for revenge and more blood. He was known to have preferred to travel with small parties of eight to ten Indians and Tories, all of whom shared his psychopathy for killing women and children. [4]

In late July, Seth's Henry and his small band of warriors appeared in the neighborhood surrounding Schoharie's Upper Fort in the settlement known as Vroomans Land. Upon surprising and capturing sixty-five-year-old William Bouck and five of his slaves, the Indians hustled their captives up and over Blenheim Hill and into the valley of the Delaware's West Branch. Feeling confident he had not been trailed, Seth's Henry and his party paused at the Tory homestead of Hugh Rose. Mr. Rose had built a small gristmill a few miles down the river near today's South Kortright at the mouth of the brook that came to bear his name. Unbeknownst to Seth's Henry, Upper Fort's Capt. Hager had dispatched a company of twenty men under the command of Lt. Joseph Harper to track down the marauders and bring back their captives. Joseph and his militiamen caught up with the Indians shortly after they left Rose Brook with the johnnycakes and cornmeal Hugh Rose provisioned them with. Surprised and outnumbered by Harper's men, the Indians fled into the forest without their prisoners before they themselves should be made prisoners. Once again Seth's Henry had lost his prey and once again a Harper brother had foiled his plans, first by Capt. John Harper on his ride to Albany in '77, and now by Lt. Joseph Harper on the West Branch. But the intrepid Schoharie Indian was not to be dissuaded from his business and would be back several more times to terrorize the valley of his Mohawk ancestors and the people he had grown to despise. His hatred for the Harpers was now insatiable. [5]

With other small bands of Indians and Tories continuing their sporadic raids throughout the summer, a major assault on a prominent frontier settlement in the Mohawk valley in early August would send a shockwave of fear through the citizenry of the border region. After feigning an attack on Fort Schuyler, Capt. Brant and about four hundred of his warriors and Tories attacked the Mohawk villages around Canajoharie and nearby Fort Plain. Fortunately, many of the villagers had managed to reach the security of the fort before the Indians arrived. The fort's small garrison of militiamen were occupied with fending off half of Brant's warriors while the other half ran unopposed through the village killing and capturing those who did not make it into the fort. About twenty unfortunate homesteaders were killed and scalped while another fifty-five were taken prisoner, many of whom were children. The militia regiments stationed along the Mohawk were again caught off-guard and too outgunned to offer any support against the onslaught of Indians. The villages and surrounding homesteads were destroyed, fifty houses were said to have been torched along with an equal number of barns, a gristmill, and a church. Three hundred head of cattle and horses were run off, while slabs of flesh were sliced from the sides of pigs and sheep as the poor beasts bleated in agony. A six-mile-long, four-mile-wide swath of civilization from Otsquago Creek to Canajoharie Creek was laid waste, along with all the vast stores of foodstuffs and fields of crops. The impoverished families who survived the onslaught faced a long and desperate winter without food, shelter, or the tools to plant another spring's crops.

Capt. Brant's Indians ravaged Canajoharie district virtually unopposed for two full days before retreating southwest to the head of Butternuts Creek, west of Otsego Lake. Here they rested and feasted on Canajoharie's cattle and cornmeal before dividing up into smaller groups and returning to the Mohawk Valley to continue their reign of terror. Brant and a party of seventy-five warriors and five Tories headed off for Harpersfield where they paused while their scouts assessed the strength and preparedness of Schoharie's three forts. A week after his raid on Canajoharie, Capt. Brant led his troops over the summit and down into the Schoharie Valley before descending upon the hapless citizens of Vroomans Land. It had only been a couple of weeks since Seth's Henry's visit to Vroomans Land and his foiled capture of William Bouck. [6]

While Capt. Hager and most of the Upper Fort's militiamen were out working in their own fields or guarding their neighbors working in theirs, Lt. Harper was left in charge of the fort with fewer than a dozen troops. As Brant's men began assaulting the homesteaders scattered about in their fields, Lt. Harper could do nothing with the few troops he had other than defend the fort and protect the few citizens lucky enough to reach its palisades. A fellow lieutenant, Ephraim Vrooman, had gone out to visit his family that morning and upon hearing the commotion, gathered up his five-month-old daughter Christina in his arms and ran off into a cornfield to hide her from the Indians. He was followed by his wife Christina and their four-year-old daughter Janett and two young sons. While hiding themselves in the cornfield, a cry from one of the frightened children gave notice to a nearby group of Indians and Tories. Unfortunately for the

Vroomans, that little group was led by none other than Seth's Henry who had apparently lingered in the area after losing his Bouck family captives. He had jumped at the chance to join Brant's raiding party, and while still incensed by his humiliation at the hands of Lt. Harper, was hungry for revenge and elated to having come upon a Schoharie family he had known and reviled.

Christina Vrooman and Seth's Henry were well acquainted with each other. They harbored a distinct dislike for each other and had been insulting each other upon their every encounter long before the war. While the enraged warrior was peeling the scalp from poor Christina's head, he sarcastically reminded her of a phrase she had once slighted him with years before '...*Now say, what do these Indian dogs do here...*'. While this horrific scene was playing out, a notorious Tory named Beacraft was scalping off the long golden locks of little Janett after having just bashed out her brains with a rock. Holding his innocently amused baby Christina in his arms, Lt. Vrooman managed to fend off another one of the Indians who was trying to skewer them with his lance. The little child laughed and giggled at what she thought was a game, and after a few more glancing misses with his spear, she defused the assailant's resolve and ended the amusing sporting event. Lt. Vrooman's two sons and daughter Christina were spared Seth's Henry's wrath and were delivered to Brant's men to be carried off with about thirty other prisoners. The Vrooman family tragedy was repeated many more times in the cornfields of Schoharie's Vroomans Land on that sad and terrible day in the summer of 1780.

Seth's Henry and Beacrafts Attack on the Vrooman Family

Had Brant been aware of how few troops were behind the palisades of the Upper Fort, Lt. Harper and his men would surely have been attacked, defeated, and easily killed or captured. As it was, Brant and his warriors were satisfied with their Schoharie raid. They had destroyed twenty homesteads and run off with many fine horses and taken many coveted scalps and their brood of prisoners. Before reaching Harpersfield on their retreat towards the Susquehanna, Brant sent word back to the Upper Fort that he had released about half of his captives. Lt. Harper and a few of his troops were sent out to retrieve the fortunate women, children and old men who were happily spared the agonizing journey to Fort Niagara. Little Christina Vrooman was returned to whatever family she had left in Vroomans Land, while her father and two brothers were carried off to the waiting gauntlet and their indefinite imprisonment. [7]

Middle Fort

After the loss of Charleston in May, news reached the north in mid-August of Gen. Gates disastrous defeat at Camden Station by Cornwallis's inferior force of British Regulars. The Carolinas were about to be lost and the whole southern campaign was turning into a disaster, with defeat after defeat for the struggling Continentals. The British army in New York was aggressively attacking Washington's army in northern New Jersey while launching successive raids on Connecticut's coastal villages, military depots and forts. A clandestine scheme known only to a few British commanders in New York was in the works to retake control of the lower Hudson and possibly open the entire river to British ships. In early August, while the Indians were ravaging the frontier settlements, Maj. Gen. Benedict Arnold took command of the garrison at West Point and began to set into motion plans to turn over the fort to the British and desert to the enemy.

Throughout August and September, Arnold conspired and corresponded with the British commanders in New York through his messenger and spy, Major John André. On September 24th, 1780, a Westchester County militia patrol captured Maj. André with letters exposing the plot to turn over the fort. The failed coup dashed England's hopes of controlling the Hudson and opening a corridor between their southern and northern forces, which would have been disastrous for New York's frontier war. Benedict Arnold never received the £20,000, or *the thirty pieces of silver* he was promised for his part in the plot, but he did receive a brigadier generals' commission in the British Army and went on to serve the Crown for the remainder of the war. The name of the once esteemed Continental general who helped save Fort Schuyler and fought gallantly at Quebec and Saratoga will forever be associated with treachery and treason. [8]

While Maj. André dangled beneath the gallows and Arnold went on the lam, Lt. Col. Sir John Johnson was preparing to deploy another invasion into the Mohawk Valley. Johnson's second campaign was thought to have been part of the overall West Point plot, meant to divert northern Continental forces while Arnold facilitated the fort's defeat. If things had gone as the British hoped, Johnson's expedition might have been part of a broader strategy to take Schenectady and Albany after taking the fort. Col. Johnson probably never knew any of this, and quite likely hadn't yet heard of the foiled plot as he prepared to depart Fort Oswego on the 2nd of October. Sir John and recently promoted Col. John Butler set out from Oswego with about 180 British grenadiers from the 8th and 34th Regiments of Foot, 285 of the King's Royal Regiment of New York Loyalists and another 160 of Col. Butler and his son Capt. Walter Butler's frontier rangers. Capt. Brant brought along another seventy warriors, while another party of two hundred Iroquois warriors from Niagara were expected to join the expedition as it proceeded through the backwoods towards the Schoharie and Mohawk settlements.

Col. Johnson set out from Fort Oswego with his seven hundred troops in a flotilla of bateaux and headed up Oswego River and on to the Seneca River for Onondaga Lake. Stashing their boats on the south end of the lake, Sir John's troops marched on foot through the backcountry to the upper Unadilla River and then proceeded down to the Susquehanna. Their caravan of wagons loaded with munitions and provisions included a light weight 4-inch coehorn mortar and a brass three-pound artillery piece referred to as a grasshopper. After rendezvousing on the Susquehanna with Cornplanter and Sayanqueraghta's band of two hundred Seneca warriors, the invasion force of nine hundred continued up Charlotte Creek to Summit Lake where they encamped for the night after two strenuous weeks on the trail. In the morning, they followed Panther Creek down to the edge of the open valley and encamped one last night before beginning their assault on Schoharie's settlements and forts.

Warned of the impending attack by a ranger scouting party, Schoharie's militias in the valley's three forts opened their gates to the citizenry and prepared to defend themselves with what limited troops and ammunition they had. Sir John's Johnstown raid in May had been a personal vendetta for the colonel, meant in part to punish his former Whig neighbors and tenants of his father's Johnstown fiefdom. This second invasion would be more far-reaching and intrusive in scope. A large part of his force was made up of Senaca and Cayuga warriors whose ancestral homeland had just taken the brunt of Sullivan and Clinton's scorched earth campaign. New York's frontier border war was about to devolve even further into the horror of revenge and retaliation. Sir John's second campaign was designed to terrorize deeper into the frontier settlements and deprive them of their food, shelter, and sense of security. The Schoharie and Mohawk River homesteaders were about to get another dose of the hard realities of a retaliatory war directed primarily at civilians. [9]

In the predawn hours of October 17th, Col. Johnson, Brant, and the Butlers stealthily led their men past the valley's Upper Fort with the intent of surprising and gaining the advantage over the valley's operational command center at Middle Fort. This was fortunate for the Upper Fort's commanders, Capt.

Hager and Lt. Harper, who had fewer than a hundred troops in a fort overcrowded with women and children. Nearly succeeding in slipping past the Upper Fort unnoticed, Johnson's rear guard unwittingly alerted a vigilant sentinel who promptly informed his commanders. Sounding the alarm, three shots from the fort's nine-pounder were fired to warn the lower forts of the enemy's approach. After the enemy had completely passed, Lt. Harper was sent out with a small detachment to trail the British column and harass their rear guard with sporadic volleys of rifle fire. No longer in need of concealing their presence, Col. Johnson gave Capt. Brant the signal to turn his warriors loose on the countryside as his main column continued down the valley towards the other two forts. Seneca and Cayuga warriors reveled at the chance to burn and pillage the defenseless homesteads along their way, just as Sullivan's men had done to their villages the year before.

Crossing over to the east side of Schoharie Creek, Col. Johnson's forces continued marching down the flats towards Middle Fort with smoke from the burning homes and fields signaling their advance. Most of Schoharie's homesteaders had replaced their original log cabins with well-furnished framed houses and timber framed mortise and tenon barns. Their well-kept grounds, pastures and cornfields were the pride of the frontier, and their cattle and horses commanded some of the highest prices in the state. Just seventy years had passed since the Palatine Dutch had fled as penniless refugees from the Old World to the New World in 1710. Three generations had turned the Schoharie's wide flat valley into one of the colony's richest agricultural regions, which made very wealthy families out of many of them. The destruction of this beautiful valley and all its bountiful harvests and valuable livestock would deal a huge blow to its inhabitants and the militia regiments who depended upon it. If Col. Johnson could destroy his enemy's source of food, and take and hold the Schoharie forts, the British would have an imposing frontier stronghold with their own source of food to feed their hungry soldiers.

While Johnson's troops were marching down Schoharie Creek towards Middle Fort, another British expedition of about two hundred New York loyalists was finishing their attack on the settlements around Balls Town (Ballston Spa), fifteen miles north of Schenectady. The Balls Town raiders were operating in conjunction with another British and loyalist force of around seven hundred troops that had just taken Forts Ann and George, west of the Hudson and Lake George. These two expeditions were part of a grander plan to link up with Col. Johnson once he took the Schoharie Valley. But again, coordinating three frontier expeditions would prove extremely difficult to accomplish. Having come through the Lake Champlain corridor, Capt. John Munro and Maj. Christopher Carleton's expeditions had left Montreal four days before Col. Johnson left Oswego. But these two northern expeditions' passage to the New York frontier had been far less difficult than Johnson's and had outpaced his Schoharie expedition. Munro and Carleton were already on their retreat to Montreal with their prisoners and reluctant recruits by the time Johnson and his troops reached Schoharie Valley. Schenectady and Albany could very well have fallen had these three expeditions coordinated successfully. The commanders of the three northern invasions were probably not even aware of the clandestine plot to turn West Point over to the British, but had Arnold succeeded, they might all have been directed to fight their way down the Hudson after having taken three of the frontier's most important strongholds.

In September, having heeded rumors of the impending British invasions, Schoharie's Middle Fort was strengthened with two hundred troops from Col. Morris Grahams 3rd Regiment of New York Levies sent to bolster Col. Peter Vrooman's 150 Albany militiamen garrisoned in the fort. Much larger now than the other two Schoharie forts, the fort's garrison was still too small to hold out for long against an attack by Col. Johnson's superior forces. The hope was to at least hold out long enough for reinforcements to reach them. A couple of glaring deficiencies within the fort made that unlikely, however. The fort had not been adequately supplied with enough munitions or provisions to hold out for long should Johnson's troops settle in for a long siege. Furthermore, Middle Fort was disadvantaged by a commanding officer who apparently lacked the experience or the will to fight. Col. Graham's detachment was commanded by Major Melanchthon L. Woolsey, a flamboyant and innately unqualified twenty-three-year-old staff officer with more experience as a clerk than a field commander. Being well connected to some of New York's wealthiest and most influential families through his marriage to a Livingston and his ties to the Schuyler and Van Rensselaer families, Maj. Woolsey was afforded an opportunity that far exceeded his qualifications. Riding into the valley on a proud Spanish mare, the dashing young officer was given command of Middle Fort over the more qualified and tested officer, Col. Vrooman.

Around 8AM on the morning of the 17th, Col. Johnson's troops reached Middle Fort after having slipped past Upper Fort and marched down the valley through an early fall snow squall. With his Indians continuing their incendiary assignments, Sir John set up his two artillery pieces and commenced bombarding the palisaded fort with little to no counterfire from within. Major Woolsey's riflemen had only been issued three rounds of powder and lead per man. Quickly assessing the forts weakness by its lack of responding fire, Col. Johnson decided to send three officers forward under a white flag to propose terms of surrender. Feeling his situation was desperate and lacking the enterprise to attempt a defense, Major Woolsey gave the order to open the gate and let the emissary in for a parley. Lacking a full understanding of frontier warfare and the odious contempt Indians held for their rebel rivals, Woolsey foolishly prepared to capitulate. While he would more than likely have been paroled and allowed to return to his comfortable Connecticut home, many of the fort's frontiersmen would have faced the horrific consequences of Indian retribution.

Knowing for certain that the Indians and Tories would not allow the frontier rangers to lay down their arms and go peacefully into captivity, one of the fort's militiamen took it upon himself to obstruct Woolsey's attempt to surrender. Private Timothy Murphy knew full well how he would be treated by the enemy should he and his fellow rangers be turned over to them. His exploits were well known to the Indians who would have dealt with him the same as they had with his commanding officers at Gathtsegwarahare, Lt. Boyd and Sgt. Parker. Blatantly ignoring Maj. Woolsey, Pvt. Murphy prevented Col. Johnson's flag from entering the fort by firing upon the envoys and forcing them to return to their lines. Verbally reprimanding his insubordinate private, Woolsey signaled the enemy for a second flag to be sent forward while a group of angry officers and soldiers began gathering around him. Murphy then issued a stern warning to the beleaguered major '...*Sooner than see that flag enter this fort will I send a bullet through your heart...*'. As a second flag approached the fort's gate, Murphy fired on it again as a frustrated and addled Maj. Woolsey stood powerlessly by. Col. Johnson attempted a third flag, but that too was fired upon by Murphy before it reached the gate. Rather than challenge his disobedient private and the rangers who had supported his actions, Maj. Woolsey submissively relinquished command of the fort to his second-in-command and sheepishly retired to the barracks.

With Col. Vrooman now in command of Middle Fort, the levies and militiamen were ordered to maintain a carefully measured fire with their meager ammunition in hopes the enemy might not become aware of their tenuous situation. Sir John had probably learned of Munroe and Carleton's retreat soon after emerging from the forest and entering the Schoharie Valley. With the prospect of being without their support and left to confront the Schenectady militias now returning from Balls Town, Johnson determined the fort might not be worth the trouble as it was soon to be reinforced with more rebels. Continuing his sporadic bombardment long enough for his Indians to complete their destruction of the surrounding homesteads and cornfields, Johnson assembled his troops around two o'clock that afternoon and resumed his march down the valley. At around 4 PM he reached the valley's Lower Fort in the village of Schoharie. Not knowing whether Middle Fort had been taken or not, Lower Fort's commander Lt. Col. Volkert Veeder readied his 150 men for Sir John's approaching nine hundred troops. The fort's Albany County militiamen had recently been reinforced with a few companies of the 5th Continental Regiment of Levies.

Lower Fort was a palisade enclosure built around Schoharie's Old Reformed Dutch Church. The old stone church was situated on a rise that provided a distinct advantage for Veeder's riflemen who exposed the enemy troops to a relentless hail of gunfire. Johnson's artillerymen answered the snipers with a bombardment of the church with their brass three pounder and 4-inch mortar that did minor damage other than sending a few shells through the roof. A hole from one of these three-pound shells can still be seen today in the cornice of The Old Stone Fort Museum that now houses several artifacts from Schoharie's storied past. The assault on the fort lasted but a few hours, as Col. Johnson again tarried just long enough for his Indians to torch the surrounding village, which they did with the proficiency of an army of serial arsonists. Before darkness settled in, Sir John raised his brief siege and marched five miles down the west side of Schoharie Creek before resting his tired troops for the night near today's village of Sloansville. It was reported that his Indians destroyed four mills, seventy-four houses, seventy-seven barns full of summer crops and left countless carcasses of butchered livestock to rot in the fields and pastures. Col. Johnson's Schoharie campaign also destroyed the military career of Melanchthon Woolsey, who left Middle Fort on his proud Spanish mare the next day and promptly retired from active duty. [10]

Stone Arabia

Early in the morning of the 18th, with the Schoharie Valley still smoldering behind them, Col. Johnson's forces moved further down along Schoharie Creek towards Fort Hunter and the Mohawk River. Anxious now to get out ahead of the Schenectady militias, they spiked and buried their coehorn mortar and 4-inch shells that had been slowing down their advance and began a hurried march down the west side of the creek. Two parties of Indians were sent out to destroy the surrounding countryside and expand the expeditions path of destruction. One party of 150 Indians and Tories, led by Capt. Brant, torched and pillaged their way down the east side of the Schoharie, while Seth's Henry took a party of twenty Indians and three Tories west to the frontier settlements around New Dorlach, today's Sharon Springs. Lt. Joseph Harper and his militia troops that had been trailing Sir John's army since they passed Upper Fort the morning before were now joined by another detachment sent out by Col. Vrooman from Middle Fort. Johnson's rearguard of arsonists continued their trail of flames while being harassed by the Schoharie militiamen.

Reaching the Mohawk late that afternoon and determining Fort Hunter too formidable to attack, Col. Johnson halted his march a few miles west of the fort and waited for his Indian patrols to catch up with his main column. Gathering his forces near the present-day hamlet of Auriesville and affording his men a brief rest, Sir John sent three companies of loyalists and half of his Indians across the Mohawk to Caughnawaga with orders to destroy any Whig property his first invasion in May might have missed. He then led his main force up along the south side of the Mohawk towards Canajoharie, setting fire to every settlement and homestead along his way. His troops marched on through the night until they came to a narrowing in the river valley between two prominent ridges, known locally as The Noses. Now just four miles east of Canajoharie, Johnson encamped around midnight and waited for dawn to ford his troops across the river and launch his next attack on the Palatine settlements around Stone Arabia.

News of the British invasions had been reverberating through the countryside for days as militias and Continental commanders scrambled to form an organized resistance. Robert Van Rensselaer had recently been promoted from colonel of the 8th Albany County Militia to brigadier general of the 2nd Battalion of Albany and Tryon County Militia Regiments. The Van Rensselaers were one of the upper Hudson's oldest and wealthiest Dutch families with ties to every political and influential family in the state. Being that Robert was a member of the New York State Assembly, and his sister Catherine was married to the Commander of the Northern Department, General Philip Schuyler, his lofty commission was clearly awarded for reasons other than his limited military experience might warrant. Sir John's invasion would be the first test of his military prowess. Rushing to assemble his forces at Schenectady, Gen. Van Rensselaer's first challenge was to procure enough supplies and munitions to support his troops for an effective expedition against Johnson's invasion. Some of the Albany and Schenectady militiamen had been slow to return from the Balls Town and Fort Ann invasions, while others simply lacked the will to fight. He did manage to finally assemble a formidable regiment of around six hundred militiamen and levies. Van Rensselaer's army began their march up the south side of the Mohawk late in the morning of the 18th, while Johnson's troops were descending Schoharie Creek and nearing the Mohawk River.

While Johnson's tired troops settled into their bedrolls at The Noses, Gen. Van Rensselaer's troops reached Fort Hunter around midnight. They were joined here by the Schoharie militiamen who had been sent out by Col. Vrooman to join Lt. Harper's Upper Fort militiamen who had been trailing the enemy without rest for forty hours. Joseph was pleased to find his older brother William among Van Rensselaer's staff, having volunteered his services as an aide-de-camp to the general. Now just fifteen miles from Johnson's encampment, Van Rensselaer and the Harper brothers pushed forward and continued marching through the night toward the enemy. They came within sight of Johnson's army around 8 o'clock on the morning of the 19th at Sprakers Basin, just as the last of his troops were crossing Keator's Rift to join their loyalist comrades on the north side of the Mohawk.

The commander of Stone Arabia's Fort Paris, which was just four miles northwest of Keator's Rift, was informed of Johnson's river crossing by a dispatch runner sent out by Van Rensselaer. Hesitating to ford the river and attack Johnson's rearguard while they were still within sight, Van Rensselaer halted his advance and made the curious decision to leave his troops on the south side of the Mohawk while he rode eight miles up the river to Fort Plain. Leaving his troops at such a critical hour, when the enemy was just before him and the day was still young, Van Rensselaer would later explain his lack of initiative by citing the fatigued state of his troops. They had in fact just finished a 35-mile hike up the Mohawk from Schenectady in less than twenty-four hours. But then, Johnson's men would have been equally tired, having just hiked over two hundred miles for nearly three weeks. Understandably exhausted from their long march, the general's decision to rest his troops before engaging the enemy may have seemed reasonable at the time but as the events of that morning unfolded, his actions came into question.

After learning of Col. Johnson's approach towards Stone Arabia, Fort Paris' commander Col. John Brown sallied out from the fort around 10:30 with about 250 Massachusetts levies and local militiamen. Col. Brown's intelligence had misled him as to the size of Johnson's army, which he soon discovered was four-times that of his own force. As nine hundred troops bore down on him and his men, the Massachusetts colonel was shot and killed alongside thirty-five of his men. His risky decision to confront the enemy outside his fort was due not only to his poor intelligence, but also to his belief that Van Rensselaer's troops would have crossed the river by then and would have been closing in on Johnson's rearguard. But the general was still dining on pork and madeira at Fort Plain with Col. Lewis DuBois while Col. Brown's survivors were staggering back to Fort Paris ahead of Sir John's oncoming troops. After the Battle of Stone Arabia, Capt. Brant and Cornplanter's Seneca warriors made quick work of scalping the dead and dying before commencing their incendiary mayhem throughout the surrounding countryside.

From across the river, frustrated rebels could only watch as the smoke rose from Stone Arabia's homesteads while they waited for orders to cross the river to aid their comrades. Having been furloughed by Col. Malcolm a month earlier and relieved of his command in Col. DuBois' regiment, John Harper had remained nearby. Having railed about the lieutenant colonel's *'unofficer like conduct'* to Gov. Clinton, a reluctant Col. Malcolm suggested in an amended communique to the governor *'...that he be kept near his regiment while Brant is on the borders...'*. Still a colonel of his militia regiment, Col. Harper was not about to leave the frontier at a time like this. And had he still been with Col. DuBois and the 2nd regiment at Fort Plain, he would certainly not have advised DuBois to dine with Gen. Van Rensselaer while Stone Arabia went up in flames. After being furloughed and hearing of the loyalist's return to the Schoharie and Mohawk frontier, Col. Harper gathered as many of his rangers and scouts as he could find and headed for Canajoharie where he knew Sir John would be heading.

Listening to the battle raging from their position on the southside of the Mohawk, Col. Harper and Cherry Valley's Capt. Robert McKean led a small company of rangers and Indians across the river around 11AM. Coming upon several of Col. Brown's men fleeing the field, Harper and McKean learned of the carnage before them and the desperate situation at Stone Arabia. With only a few men, Col. Harper had no alternative but to recross back over the river and relay his intelligence to his commanding officer and impress upon him the urgency of the situation. Catching up with the main force at Walrath's Ferry, a mile below Fort Plain, Harper was disgusted to find Van Rensselaer and the troops still languishing on the south side of the river. Only a few *'unofficer like'* captains and their men were trying to initiate their own disorganized crossing. Infuriated by what he judged to be an utter lack of resolve and a flagrant dereliction of duty; Col. Harper displayed his *'unofficer like conduct'* and rebuked his superior officer for his lack of leadership and courage. Gen. Van Rensselaer and DuBois finally arrived at the ferry around 2PM and began mobilizing the regiment to ford the river, a process that would take another two hours. By the time the rebel army was finally on the same side of the river as the enemy, Sir John had been slashing and burning his way through the countryside for over six hours. Having crushed Col. Brown's regiment and decimated the farms around Stone Arabia, Sir John's troops had crossed Caroga Creek and were advancing through the forest towards St. Johnsville and George Klock's farm, a few miles up the river from Fort Plain.

Klock's Field

Around 5:30 in the afternoon, Gen. Van Rensselaer's army finally came within sight of Col. Johnson's force. The British Regulars and loyalists were lining up into formation in the riverfront fields surrounding George Klock's stone house, a mile down the Mohawk from today's village of St. Johnsville. Dividing his forces into three columns, Van Rensselaer commanded the center while Col. DuBois' 2nd Regiment of Levies advanced along the right flank and another company of militia took the left flank. Col. Harper, along with his brother Lt. Joseph Harper, and about fifty rangers and Oneida warriors were in advance of the center column where they engaged the enemy in the opening volleys of the battle around 6PM. The Battle of Klock's Field was a short and chaotic affair that lasted less than half an hour. When the first shots pierced the cool October air, the sun had already begun slipping beneath the horizon as thick black smoke from the muskets mingled with the smoke from the burning buildings. In the smoke-filled twilight, the American's right and left flanks became confused and started firing on each other while the British took advantage of the chaos and began a slow measured retreat up the river. An intense exchange of fire continued as the two armies engaged in a short running battle from Klock's fields towards a ferry crossing just above St. Johnsville. But as darkness descended, Van Rensselaer rallied his troops and withdrew back to Fox's mill on Caroga Creek where he encamped for the night, while Sir John's army bivouacked on the river and waited for the moon to rise.

Col. Harper and his brother Joseph had tried to control and redirect the panicked militias during the chaotic twilight crossfire in the opening volleys of the battle. Lt. Harper had been running hard for nearly 72 hours and was now running on the last of his dwindling adrenaline. During the confusion and heat of battle, the thirty-nine-year-old lieutenant was shot in the back, quite possibly by one of his own men. A .69 caliber musket ball from a flintlock Brown Bess shattered his scapula and clavicle, nearly severing his left arm at the shoulder. The arm was ultimately saved but rendered useless, ending his military career and leaving him disabled for the remainder of his life.

While Van Rensselaer and DuBois rested for the night on Caroga Creek, Col. Harper's rangers and Oneida scouts took a forward position near Sir John's camp on the river. Fifty Oneida warriors led by Lt. Col. Louis Cook, a Kahnawake Abenaki known to his people as Akiatonharonkwen, joined Harper and his men on the river. Referred to as Col. Louis by his rebel comrades, Akiatonharonkwen was the highest-ranking Native American in the Continental Army. He was a warrior's warrior who had fought for the British in the French and Indian War and was with Arnold at Quebec and Herkimer at Oriskany during the early years of the Revolution. He served with distinction throughout the war, primarily along the Mohawk River with Col. Willett and Col. Harper. Col. Louis was finally killed during the War of 1812, when he was thought to have been over seventy years old.

As a three-quarter waning gibbous began rising around 9PM, Col. Johnson ordered his men to spike their three-pound grasshopper and abandon their heavily ladened wagons before fording to the south side of the Mohawk at King Hendrick's Ford. Under strict orders from Gen. Van Rensselaer to not attack the enemy without his presence, Col. Harper and Col. Louis were obliged to watch helplessly as the enemy crossed the river and made their escape into the night forest. Had they taken the initiative to disobey their commander, they might have been able to kill or capture a significant number of Sir John's vulnerable troops as they waded chest-deep across the river. Shortly before daybreak, after all the enemy troops had crossed the river and were long gone, Colonels DuBois, Harper, Louis, and Samuel Clyde were finally ordered to set out after the enemy. Marching posthaste through the backwoods of German Flatts, Sir John marched through the night setting a course for Onondaga Lake where his fleet of river bateaux had been left.

Lt. Col. Louis Cook, Akiatonharonkwen

After tracking the enemy fifteen miles up the south side of the Mohawk through German Flatts to Fort Herkimer, the Tryon County rangers continued another three or four miles before realizing they were following the wrong trail. Arriving on the scene in a most ungentlemanly fit of rage, Gen. Van Rensselaer reprimanded his men for losing the trail and abruptly ordered them to return to Fort Herkimer. To the consternation of his officers and Col. Louis who raised his sword and accused him of being a Tory, the inept general gave one last impulsive order. He ordered two of Col. Harper's officers, Capt. Wouter Vrooman and Capt. Joshua Drake to lead a small detachment by way of Fort Schuyler to out flank and outpace the enemy before they could reach their bateaux on Onondaga Lake. Col. Johnson's 900 troops easily intercepted and captured the two captains and about fifty of their men after killing a few in a brief skirmish near the Oneida village of Canowaroghare. The British and loyalists made it back to the lake and their bateaux with their captives and set out for home, arriving back at Fort Oswego on the 27th of October, nearly a month after departing for Schoharie.

Although considered at the time as an American victory for having driven the enemy from the field, Col. Johnson's rout of Col. Brown's troops and the daylong unopposed rampage through Stone Arabia, suggests a contrary view of that claim. Having been implored by Col. Harper and others to cross the Mohawk hours before he finally did, Gen. Van Rensselaer's hesitation cost the rebels an excellent opportunity to defeat and possibly capture the whole of Sir John's expedition. Attributing his hesitation on the fatigued state of his troops while neglecting to consider the fatigued condition of his enemy, who had been on the march for two-and-a-half weeks, raised more than one eyebrow. His dithering inaction would soon be challenged. Col. Johnson's expedition succeeded brilliantly in achieving its ultimate objective of leaving the Schoharie and a large section of the Mohawk valley in shambles. Gov. Clinton estimated that Johnson's troops had destroyed 150,000 bushels of wheat and grain while torching over two hundred dwellings and an equal number of barns. The British campaign had done almost as much damage to the rebel's supply of crops and livestock as Sullivan's Campaign had done to the Six Nations the year before. In a letter written by Gov. Clinton a week after the invasion he stated '...*The immediate country on both sides of the Mohawk from Fort Hunter to Fort Rensselaer* [Fort Plain] *at the upper end of Canajoharie including Stone Arabia are burnt and laid to waste. Schenectady may now be said to be the limit of our western frontier...*'. [11]

Five months after the disaster at Stone Arabia, Col. John Harper and his brother William Harper testified in a hearing as to the comportment of Gen. Robert Van Rensselaer's actions on the 19th of October 1780 at Stone Arabia and Klock's Field. The Harper brothers told the court of inquiry that they had both urged the general before and after the engagement at Klock's Field to hurry on and press the enemy. Crossing the Mohawk six hours ahead of the general and observing him lingering on the southside, Col. Harper testified '...*I came to the north bank of the river and hailed the general, intreating him for God sack to cross, but received no reply...*'. William Harper further testified that he pressed the general to attack the enemy when they were encamped by the river following the Battle at Klock's Field, but the general declined. William added that when he was told by the general '...*he was resolved to call the men off...*' as aide-de-camp he advised they encamp near the enemy on the river but was told by the general '...*he would go to the hills...*'.

Van Rensselaer brought eight supporting witnesses to the inquiry, including the complicit Col. DuBois. All the general's witnesses accordingly supported his conduct before, during and after the affair. Predictably, the court was unanimous in their opinion that his conduct was '...*prudent and spirited and the public clamor raised to his prejudice...are without the least foundation...*'. The man who had called John Harper a *'blockhead'* may have salvaged his reputation among his fraternity of Hudson River aristocrats and land barons but the people of the Mohawk whose protection he was entrusted with, never forgave the general for his dereliction. Nor did they ever suspect Col. Harper of being a blockhead. It was an indisputable fact that the dilatory general spent at least two to three hours dining at Fort Plain with Col. DuBois while his men waited for orders to cross the river and attack the enemy. Had he remembered and taken to heart the wise words of Marcus Aurelius, '...*The impediment to action advances action...*', he might have saved Stone Arabia and Col. Brown and his brave soldiers. [12]

It was estimated that before the war there had been about 10,000 people living in the frontier County of Tryon, between the Indian property line of '68 and the counties of Ulster and Albany. In December 1780, shortly after Johnson's raid, Tryon County attempted to take a census. The informal census found that 1,200 former farms were now abandoned and uncultivated, and 350 of the county's families had fled their frontier homes. Seven hundred buildings were reported as having been destroyed, two hundred citizens killed and 120 taken prisoner. Cherry Valley, Springfield, Harpersfield and now Stone Arabia had no one left to conduct the census of their communities. The people of Stone Arabia would never forgive Col. Van Rensselaer for neglecting to support Col. Brown's troops and allowing the enemy to annihilate their Mohawk River settlements. They never acknowledged the renaming of Fort Plain to Fort Rensselaer, as the name of the current village now attests. In a show of benevolent remorse or simply an attempt to assuage guilt, Van Rensselaer offered the Mohawk sufferers refuge on his sprawling Claverack Manor property, east of the Hudson. It is not clear as to how many, or if any of them accepted his chastened generosity. The Harper brothers certainly never forgave the Dutch aristocrat for his cowardice on that disastrous day on the Mohawk. [13]

The Mohawk Frontier

The winter of 1780/81 was one of discontent for the beleaguered residents of New York's frontier and the militias charged with their protection. With the losses incurred by Johnson's devastation of the Schoharie and Mohawk River settlements, the whole Northern Department was teetering on the edge of ruin. From Schenectady and Schoharie to Fort Schuyler at the head of the Mohawk, families of refugee widows and orphans gathered around forts and blockhouses for protection and begged for what little bread the soldiery could spare. It was estimated that over 350 widows and 2,000 fatherless children were now destitute and at the mercy of the state. The militiamen and levies were themselves hard-pressed to find enough to eat. Most of Fort Schuyler's troops were now barefoot and without proper winter attire. Their commanders tried desperately to requisition blankets and clothing from depleted Continental depots and commissaries. Oneida warriors and their starving families were dependent on their white allies to support them through the winter, just as their western Iroquois brethren were dependent on the British at Fort Niagara for support. The British garrisons at Forts Niagara and Oswego were reliant on their supply line from Montreal and Quebec, who in turn were dependent upon ships from London. Although not without their own supply line problems, the British garrisons spent that long winter in much better comfort than their New York frontier adversaries. [14]

On the 1st of January 1781, New York's regiments of levies and militias were reorganized and reassigned with new commanders. The fledgling 1st and 3rd regiments were combined into the 1st regiment under Col. Goose Van Schaick, while the 2nd, 4th and 5th regiments were reorganized into the 2nd New York regiment with another wealthy Hudson River aristocrat, Col. Philip Van Cortlandt, as commander. Many of New York's most experienced and tested frontier officers were reduced in rank, including Col. Harper who had already been furloughed by Col. Malcolm the summer before. Col. Van Cortlandt's 2nd regiment was ordered to garrison the Mohawk Valley's string of forts from Schenectady to Fort Schuyler. Due to the impending southern campaigns, the 2nd regiment was depleted by several of its companies who were reassigned to Continental regiments on the lower Hudson. Gen. Washington was formulating his southern strategy and preparing his Continental army's counter-offensive against Cornwallis's steadily advancing forces. The Northern Department would again have to do with what it had and defend its frontier territory as best it could. [15]

In the spring of '81, a new commander was put in charge of New York's frontier militias. His presence heartened the disaffected militias and anxious citizenry of the border region. Col. Marinus Willett was no stranger to the Northern Department, having been with Gen. Montgomery during the Quebec campaign of '75 and was Col. Gansevoort's second-in-command during the siege of Fort Schuyler in '77. He had also been with Col. Van Schaick on his Onondaga campaign in '79, and with Gen. James Clinton on his expedition into the Iroquois territory with Sullivan, later that same year. Willett's military career began in 1758, at the age of eighteen, when he enlisted in a colonial militia regiment as a captain and rose through the ranks to lieutenant before the end of the French and Indian War. Joining the Sons of Liberty in the early 1770s, the young rebel agitator brawled in the streets of New York City with loyalist sympathizers and incited young men to support the Whigs and their Provincial Congress. Having distinguished himself throughout the early years of the war, Col. Willett was given command of the consolidated Tryon County militias and Levies in April of '81. Although known to be a hard man to get along with, who took little council from others, his decisions and actions were often successful. Commanding from Fort Plain, Col. Willett did what he could to better conditions in the forts throughout the frontier, while trying to reestablish better discipline and decorum in the army's ranks. His reputation as an effective fighter and leader gave the frontier people a much-needed boost of confidence at a time when the future looked bleaker than it ever had.

Col. Marinus Willett

In the middle of February, the ubiquitous Capt. Brant set out on snowshoes from Fort Niagara with about 150 Indians and fifty of Butler's Tory rangers. Two hundred strong, they headed for the upper Mohawk's Fort Schuyler. Brant's mission was to intercept a desperately needed fifty-sled caravan of precious supplies bound for the snowbound fort. Fortunately for the fort's hungry troops, Brant's expedition wallowed through the deep snow for three weeks before reaching the fort one day too late to intercept the convoy. Disheartened at not having deprived the enemy of their much-needed supplies and missing the opportunity to provide his own troops with food and blankets, Brant needed to assuage his disappointed warriors' frustration. Haunting the forest around Fort Schuyler, his warriors soon came upon a fatigue party of woodcutters a mile outside the fort. Prisoners and scalps usually satisfied an angry party of hungry warriors. After killing one of the guards sent out to protect the cutters, Brant's men captured the sixteen cutters and guards and made a hasty retreat into the forest before the fort's commander could send out a rescue party to save their comrades. Brant's men and their captives were all back at Fort Niagara by the end of March. They had failed miserably in their mission to capture the convoy of supplies, but at least they had something to show for their long trek through the winter snow. Disgruntled by the expedition, Capt. Brant's enthusiasm for initiating more raids that spring waned considerably. In early April, sensing his dissatisfaction, the British commanders at Fort Niagara sent the restless captain and a few of his most trusted warriors west to Fort Detroit on the northwest battlefront.

The exhaustion of six long years of war had taken its toll on the morale and resolve of the frontier militia soldiers. Residents of Schenectady and Albany were growing ever more anxious over the reduced state of the military, as many of them packed up their belongings and headed east to safer ground. Things in the south were not going any better for the Continental Army that was struggling to contain the British advance through Georgia and the Carolinas. Many Americans were beginning to think the war was hopeless and the British were closing in on victory. At the beginning of the war, it was estimated there were around 2,500 Tryon and Albany County militiamen on the frontier at any one time, but by the spring of '81 that number had dwindled to less than eight hundred. A percentage of those losses were of course attributed to men being killed or taken prisoner, but as many as a third were believed to have gone over to the enemy. [16]

Fort Schuyler was experiencing a surge in desertions and an increase in seditious behavior. The fort's lack of adequate supplies and its isolated position on the margins of a hostile frontier was hard on the young soldiers sent there. Some of the militiamen were beginning to hedge their bets and maneuvering to position themselves for the inevitability of once again becoming subjects of the Crown. Attacks on the frontier fort were beginning to come more from within the fort, than from the enemy outside the fort. Two separate and suspicious fires broke out that spring in the fort's barracks, rendering the place difficult to garrison and leaving the commanders of the Northern Department with a tough decision to make. They argued over rebuilding the facilities or abandoning the fort altogether. The latter was ultimately decided upon, and the fort's garrison and guns were transferred in May to Fort Herkimer, thirty miles down the Mohawk at German Flatts. Fort Herkimer and its neighboring Fort Dayton, on the north side of the Mohawk, were now the frontier's new frontline. The rebels had fallen back a third of the way down the river towards Schenectady. While the loss of Fort Schuyler represented a concession by the Americans, it was more of a symbolic defeat than a literal one. The commanders of the Tryon and Albany County militias lamented over the loss publicly, but privately they were relieved to be rid of the now untenable outpost they had fought so hard to defend in 1777. [17]

Currytown and Dorlach

Even though Capt. Brant was now absent from the frontier, small raiding parties of Indians and Tories continued harassing what was left of the few border settlements through the spring and summer of 1781. In late April, another brutal attack was conducted on the few hardy souls who had returned to Cherry Valley after its annihilation in 1778. Cobleskill was also revisited in late August by a party of Indians and Tories who also paid another visit to the Schoharie settlements. At significant risk to themselves and their families, homesteaders cautiously returned to their fields with plows and rifles and tried to quietly prepare their fields for another seasonal harvest. One small settlement south of Canajoharie and west of the Schoharie Valley had been left undisturbed by raiding parties that had by now destroyed nearly all its neighboring settlements. Currytown, in today's township of Root, Montgomery County, was a quiet little farming community less than three miles south of The Noses where Johnson's troops rested the night before their attack on Stone Arabia. With virtually every other backwoods settlement from German Flatts to Springfield and Cherry Valley, and from Cobleskill to Fort Hunter in ruins, Currytown remained curiously undisturbed. It was well known to the rebels and the British that Currytown was home to many Tory sympathizers, a factor that contributed to the settlement being overlooked during Sir John's invasion. Knowing that the rebels might not be so inclined to send out a militia company to defend a Tory stronghold, Currytown became a tempting target for any up-and-coming British officer looking for an easy victory and a promotion in rank.

During the first week of July, Col. Willett began getting intelligence of a large body of Indians and Tories moving towards the settlements of the lower Mohawk River valley, with Schenectady quite possibly its terminal destination. Currytown was just twenty-five miles from Schenectady and with the added support of the local Tories sympathizers, might serve as a forward base for an extended expedition into the very heart of rebel territory. Not yet twenty-one, Lt. Johannas Docksteder was out to make a name for himself. The son of a former Mohawk Valley tavern owner, the young office's over-confidence in his own ability to conduct such an audacious assault might just have been enough to succeed where other more prudent men might fail. With the help of an Indian named Quackyack, the young lieutenant led around seventy-five Iroquois warriors and twenty Tories down through the backwoods south of the Mohawk past Otsego Lake and through Cherry Valley to New Dorlach, a sleepy little settlement known today as Sharon Springs. Encamping near New Dorlach on the night of the 8th of July, Docksteder's raiding party was joined by another small party of Indians and about thirty Tories from Currytown, expanding his force to around 150.

Setting out at the crack of dawn and marching eight miles northeast, his men came down hard on the rebel homesteaders of Currytown around 10AM. Caught totally off guard, the Indians ran unopposed through the defenseless settlement plundering and killing humans and animals while putting to the torch all the rebel homes and leaving the Tory houses undisturbed. The pillaging and chaos continued throughout most of the day until satiated with their plunder, the marauders gathered their cattle and prisoners and headed back for their New Dorlach encampment around 4PM. Having Received reports from his scouts of the Currytown raid and the enemy's encampment at New Dorlach, Col. Willett hurriedly gathered as many militiamen as he could muster and headed off from Fort Plain towards their encampment around midnight. He arrived near the enemy with about 170 soldiers just before sunrise on the morning of the 10th. Positioning his men around Lt. Docksteder's sleepy encampment, Willett prepared to engage the enemy. His men had not had enough time to gather much ammo and were woefully undergunned, accordingly a close quarters battle ensued with bayonets and sabers clashing against warclubs and tomahawks. The ferocious skirmishing lasted about an hour-and-a-half before the enemy was routed from the field and sent into a hasty retreat. The Indians ran off without their previous day's plunder but not before killing their Currytown prisoners. Lt. Docksteder lost about twenty men while Willett had a dozen of his men killed and wounded. One very prominent and respected frontier fighter was among the wounded. Cherry Valley's beloved militia Captain Robert McKean, died of his wounds a day after the battle in which he and his son Samuel were both wounded. The Battle at Dorlach was but a minor affair, with the advantage going to the Americans for having driven the enemy from the field. The little victory, however, was a huge boost to the morale and confidence of the disenchanted militiamen who now had something to be proud of. [18]

In the vacuum left by Brant's absence, Lt. Docksteder continued lingering on the frontier following his New Dorlach defeat and persisted throughout the summer to send out his troops on foraging raids, primarily to feed them. Seth's Henry was also still in the border region. In late July, he and his brother Joseph led another raiding party into their old Schoharie Valley neighborhood. They captured a half-dozen homesteaders that included two members of the Bouck family who had eluded Seth's Henry the year before. In mid-August, Docksteder's troops were joined by a detachment of loyalists led by Capt. William Caldwell, a notoriously reviled British captain who had been involved in the Cherry Valley and Wyoming Valley massacres. Caldwell was accompanied by a party of Indians led by another feared and despised frontier warrior, Capt. Brant's trusted lieutenant Ben Shanks. Rendezvousing on the Susquehanna, Docksteder, Caldwell and Ben Shanks set out with their combined forces totaling around four hundred for Ulster County's Rondout Creek settlements of Warwarsing, Napanoch, Kerhonkson and the Honk. Having successfully executed his raid on Fort Lackawack in 1778 and the ambush of Lt. Graham's posse on Chestnut Creek, Ben Shank's was more than familiar with the Rondout settlements and local militias charged with their protection.

With Ben Shanks as his guide, Lt. Docksteder attacked the Rondout settlements only to find a resilient Ulster militia and their forts in a far better state of readiness than he anticipated. The citizenry was also in a readied state of resistance. His raid on the Rondout settlements would not be as successful as the earlier Brant and Ben Shanks raids of '78 and '79. Col. Albert Pawling of the Ulster militia was able to muster enough troops this time to repel the enemy. Docksteder returned to Fort Niagara with just a few prisoners, scalps and very little plunder to show for his efforts. His defeat at Dorlach and his lackluster assault on the Rondout settlements was dismissed by the British commanders at Niagara as a wasted expenditure of lives and resources. His military career and reputation were ruined. The commanders at Niagara and Oswego were now busy with another project and moving ahead with plans for another major campaign into rebel territory. But events in the south were about to change the direction of the war and render this last British invasion on New York's frontier settlements too little and too late. [19]

Battle of Johnstown

While the Northern Department languished through the summer of '81 with militia and levy commanders struggling to hold their regiments together, Gen. Washington was siphoning off New York companies and regiments for a supposed assault on the British base in New York City. Cornwallis's army had steadily been moving north since their victories at Charleston and Camden and was now in Virginia wreaking havoc along the James River and throughout the southern Chesapeake region. New York's frontier troubles were far less pressing than the southern threat. Washington was preoccupied with coordinating his American troops with the French navy, while second-guessing the enemy's next move. Feigning an advance toward Manhattan and Staten Island, the Continentals diverted their march and headed down through northern New Jersey towards Virginia to engage Cornwallis wherever they might find him. This southern campaign was a desperate gamble that had it failed, would have likely resulted in the American Colonies being reinstated and Washington's head impaled upon a pike. But that of course was not to be. In late September, after encountering and encircling Cornwallis's army on the Yorktown peninsula with the French fleet blocking the mouth of the Chesapeake, Washington settled into the siege and battle that would ultimately lead to the triumphant end of the American Revolution.

On the 16th of October, three days before Cornwallis surrendered at Yorktown and a week before the news reached the north, Major John Ross of the 2nd Battalion of the King's Royal New York Regiments set out from Fort Oswego with a force of around 600 soldiers and headed for the Schoharie and Mohawk Valleys. Ross's command included about 175 New York loyalists, 150 of Capt. Walter Butler's Tory rangers and 150 British Regulars from the 8th, 34th and 84th Grenadier Regiments. Another 130 Iroquois warriors accompanied the expedition. It was an impressive array of professional soldiers and experienced frontier fighters led by a very capable Scottish-born officer. Having received a lieutenant's commission in the 34th Regiment of Foot at the age of eighteen, Lt. Ross rose through the ranks to captain by the end of the French and Indian War. He led Burgoyne's advance guard through New York's northern wilderness in '77 and had been severely wounded at Hubbardton before the British army's capitulation at Saratoga. Col. Sir John Johnson and Col. John Butler had relinquished their field commands for administrative positions, affording the young major an opportunity to lead his own campaign into the rebel's Mohawk Valley. Had the border region not been recently favored with an equally capable and aggressive commander, Maj.

Ross might very well have accomplished all his objectives and driven the rebel front all the way back to Schenectady. [20]

With Fort Schuyler deserted and the upper Mohawk Valley nearly void of troops and inhabitants, Ross's expedition managed to penetrate deep into rebel territory before being detected. After departing Fort Oswego and ascending the Oswego and Oneida rivers to Oneida Lake, Maj. Ross and Capt. Butler left twenty men with their bateaux and directed their troops south up Chittenango Creek. Marching southeast passed Cazenovia Lake to the watershed of the Chenango River, the expedition continued due east through the backwoods to the upper Unadilla River and towards the head of Otsego Lake. They may have followed a course along New York's historic Western Turnpike route #20 before diverting northeast from Dorlach to the Tory friendly settlement of Currytown, where they were finally spotted by a rebel patrol early on the morning of the 24th. Many of the local militiamen were in the Saratoga and Lake George area responding to another phantom force of loyalists rumored to be coming down along Lake Champlain. Upon discovering the invasions actual approach, Col. Marinus Willett began gathering as many troops as he could from the blockhouses and settlements around Fort Plain. Meanwhile, Maj. Ross turned north from Currytown to the river villages of Randall and Stone Ridge and commenced plundering his way down along the south side of the river towards Schoharie Creek and Fort Hunter.

Crossing over Schoharie Creek unopposed around 3AM, Maj. Ross halted his fatigued troops and waited for daybreak. In the morning, he dispatched his Indians and Tories to the settlements of Warrensbush and Florida, in the vicinity of today's South Amsterdam. His arsonists were now within twelve miles of the terrified residents of Schenectady. With smoke from the burning homesteads drifting through the crisp October air, the rebel countryside was now on full alarm. Besides the loss of their homes and livelihoods, the residents of the lower Mohawk lost over two hundred cows, horses, sheep and hogs, a loss they could ill afford. Successfully destroying the settlements along a twenty-mile stretch of the Mohawk, Maj. Ross wisely determined that Schenectady was a bridge too far and better left uncrossed. Had he come to that bridge earlier in the year, before Willett took command of the militia and levies from men like Van Rensselaer, Van Cortlandt, Malcolm and Woolsey, his expedition might have been far more disastrous for the Americans. Resolving to turn back, Ross forded his men across to the north side of the river near old Fort Johnson and led them northwest up the road to Johnstown and Johnson Hall. By 2PM on the afternoon of the 25th, Ross's troops were resting on the lawn of the Johnson family's confiscated estate. Their rest, however, would be brief. [21]

While Maj. Ross's men were still laying waste to everything from Currytown to Warrensburg, Col. Willett had managed to gather about seventy-five local Tryon County militiamen and 325 New York Levies. Before reaching Johnstown in the late afternoon hours of the 25th, Willett's rebels were joined by another 150 frontier rangers and Oneida warriors and around 60 Massachusetts Troopers led by Maj. Aaron Rowley. Ross had lost about fifty of his men to fatigue and desertion since leaving his bateaux on Oneida Lake, eight days earlier. Now in command of about 525 tired troops, his loyalists and grenadiers were about to square-off against Col. Willett's force of around six hundred and their three-pound artillery piece. Without hesitating, or leaving his men to take a dinner break, Col. Willett prepared to lead an attack against Maj. Ross's formations in a field half a mile behind Johnson Hall. The militia and levies were grateful to finally be serving under a commander with the resolve and courage to initiate an offensive and take the momentum from the enemy. Unfortunately, however, Willett's frontal assault buckled under the relentless fire from the British rifles, as his militia soon fled the field in a panicked retreat and headed back towards the village of Johnstown. Fortunately, Col. Willett had sent Maj. Rowley and his Massachusetts troopers on a flanking maneuver around the left flank of the enemy, and they were now dispensing a hot fire on the enemy's rear. Ever present on the frontier, Col. John Harper and over fifty of his rangers along with another fifty of Col. Louis Akiatonharonkwen's warriors had joined Rowley's men and were helping to divert the grenadiers fire with his flanking detachment.

Quickly calming and regrouping his panicked militiamen, Col. Willett rejoined the fight and pressed the enemy between his flanking detachment. Intense skirmishing between disjointed groups of troops and Indians continued throughout the late afternoon, with the advantage shifting back and forth. The rebel's artillery piece was at one point captured by the British but later recaptured by the rebels in the chaos of battle. As dusk slowly turned to darkness, Maj. Ross and Col. Willett were both compelled to begin withdrawing their troops from the field and regroup their scattered forces. Both sides of the Battle of Johnstown could technically declare victory, as night brought an end to the fighting with both sides still on the field. The British however, had no intention of resuming the fight in the morning, nor were they interested in hanging about while the rebel ranks filled with more and more incoming militiamen. [22]

Maj. Ross lost no time after withdrawing from the field and immediately began an all-night retreat up Old Fish House Road, Rt. #29, and on to the Northern Trail, Rt. #10, before heading for the headwaters of Caroga Creek. The remainder of his expedition's 130 Iroquois warriors left the battlefield and hiked back to Fort Niagara and their families. Finding it unsafe to return to Fort Oswego by way of Oneida Lake, from whence they came, Ross and Capt. Butler directed their march towards the southern foothills of the Adirondacks. They set a course for Cape Vincent on the St. Lawrence and the British garrison at Fort Haldimand on Carlton, or Bucks Island. It was a bold and risky decision to take an army through the northern forests with November coming on and their provisions nearly exhausted. But the rebels, who they expected to give chase, would have to deal with the same terrain and hopefully might opt out of the chase. But men like Col. Harper and Col. Willett were not the type to let up once they had their opponent on the ropes. Ross's men were cold and exhausted as they set off into the northern wilderness. From the head of Caroga Creek, Maj. Ross struggled to find and stay on the trail, but his Indian guide was ultimately able to get his troops to upper East Canada Creek which they crossed in the vicinity of today's village of Stratford on the Fulton/Herkimer County Line. From here the journey became increasingly difficult as they struggled through Salisbury's Jerseyfields toward the head of Black Creek at today's Black Creek Reservoir.

Col. Willett had not opted out of the chase, as Ross had hoped, and anticipating their slog through the backcountry would be slow going, he left Johnstown and headed up the Mohawk knowing he had time on his side. He halted at Fort Herkimer for three days while he gathered the heartiest of the frontiersmen and Oneida trackers and provisioned them with five days of rations and clothing suitable for winter. With the Mohawk Valley abuzz with the excitement of victory and the thrill of a fox on the run, Col. Willett had little trouble gathering over five hundred enthusiastic men. He left Fort Herkimer on the morning of the 28th of October and headed up West Canada Creek to intercept the enemy. Col. Harper and Akiatonharonkwen's Oneida warriors had been tracking Ross's retreat and sending out runners to keep Col. Willett informed of the enemy's progress. Heading north along the east side of West Canada Creek through an early winter snowstorm, Willett's forces departed the creek north of Middleville and headed up Hurricane Brook with the intent of intercepting the enemy on Black Creek.

Catching up to within a mile of Ross's troops on Black Creek around 8AM on the morning of the 30th, the rebels continued following their prey down the creek throughout that day. Making for West Canada Creek and the ford near today's Hinkley Reservoir, Maj. Ross hoped to safely get his troops across the river before their pursuers could catch up to them and engage them in a fight they could not win. Capt. Walter Butler commanded the rear guard that was tasked with holding off the rebels until all the troops could get across the river, which they did by 2PM that afternoon. Just as the last of Maj. Ross's troops and their rear guard were finishing their crossing, a pugnacious Capt. Butler and a few of his men defiantly fired across the creek at a group of Akiatonharonkwen's Oneida warriors. In the exchange of fire, a musket ball from one of Col. Louis' warriors grazed the top of Butler's head, laying him out dazed and confused. Multiple reports have come down through the ages as to how twenty-nine-year-old Walter Butler spent his last moments on earth. One romanticized version has Capt. Butler abandoned by his comrades and pleading for his life with the Oneida Indian who shot him. While Butler lay in the snow begging for quarter, the warrior triumphantly told him,'...*me give you Cherry Valley quarter...*', before sinking his tomahawk into his face and removing his bloodied scalp. After stripping him naked and leaving him face down in the snow for the buzzards, the rebels continued pursuing the fleeing grenadiers and loyalists for what was left of the daylight.

Realizing Ross's exhausted troops had another ninety miles of wilderness to tread through before reaching Cape Vincent, Col. Willett decided that further pursuit might not be necessary and might only jeopardize his own men's safety. Turning back down West Canada Creek for the Mohawk, he would later report to Gov. Clinton that he left the enemy *'...to the compassion of a starving wilderness...in a fair way of receiving a punishment better suited to their merit than a musket ball, a tomahawk or captivity...'*. Many of Ross's troops had already ditched their packs and blankets in a desperate attempt to hasten their escape. The rebels captured some of the stragglers who had fallen behind, while those who fell behind after the rebels gave up the chase, soon came to regret having left their packs and blankets behind. Two weeks after crossing West Canada Creek and hiking over the Tug Hill Plateau, Maj. Ross and the remainder of his command finally reached Cape Vincent and Fort Haldimand in mid-November, a month after leaving Fort Oswego. By one account, he returned with just a little over two hundred of his original 475 white soldiers. Having reported that his losses at Johnstown were similar to Col. Willett's reported eighty-five killed, wounded and missing, Ross may have left as many as 150 corpses along the trail from Johnstown to Cape Vincent.

Major John Ross

Maj. John Ross's return from Johnstown and the loss of so many of his British and loyalist troops shocked the commanders at Niagara. But news of Cornwallis's surrender, that had reached them weeks before, had already sent shockwaves through the British high command. The jubilation of the Tryon and Albany County militias and citizenry, whose morale and confidence had suffered so miserably through those final desperate years of the border war, must have been euphoric. Yorktown and the defeat of Maj. Ross's expedition were welcomed news, but the death of the notoriously despised Capt. Walter Butler was celebrated throughout the frontier as fervently as either of those two victories. The young captain's coat, hat and scalp might have brought more at a Schenectady auction than General Cornwallis's sword. Having been admonished for not giving fight to Sir John Johnson during the first Johnstown invasion, Col. Harper might have felt a sense of reparation for his part in the defeat of Ross's army and death of Walter Butler. [23]

Lake Utsayantha

In mid-November, while Maj. Ross and his troops were still struggling through *'a starving wilderness'* towards Fort Haldimand, two of Capt. Brant's trusted lieutenants led sixty-five Indians and Tories on one last foraging raid into the Schoharie Valley. Many claimed that Joseph Brant was on this raid, but the omnipresent captain was still at Fort Detroit at the time and would not return to New York until the summer of 1782. In his stead, others were filling the void and continuing to terrorize the frontier settlements. Lt. Adam Crysler lived in the Schoharie settlements before the war and was well known to his former neighbors. He had been with Capt. MacDonell when Capt. Harper's mounted troops drove their raiding party from the valley at the Battle of the Flockey in '77. He was also with the Indians and Tories at the infamous Cherry Valley and Wyoming massacres in '78. In 1779 he fought at Newtown against Sullivan and Clinton and in '80 was with Col. Johnson on his Schoharie and Mohawk River expedition, fighting in the action at Stone Arabia and Klock's Field. An active and capable soldier, Lt. Crysler had a very personal reason for revisiting his old neighborhood this late in the season. His wife Anna Marie and their five children had been held in captivity by his former rebel neighbors since the beginning of the war. [24]

On the morning of November 13th, after returning to the eastern settlements along the traditional Susquehanna/Charlotte Creek trail, Lt. Crysler and his band of Indians descended Panther Creek and entered the Schoharie Valley. His confiscated Breakabeen mill and farm at Fultonham, where the Battle of the Flocky was fought, would certainly have been on his mind and on his list of retaliatory targets. Surprising the few rebel farmers still holding out in Vroomans Land around Upper Fort, Crysler directed his men up the creek towards Breakabeen where his family was being held. Lt. Crysler shared command of his small band of marauders with an old Schoharie Indian who was well-known and loathed by the residents of the valley. Seth's Henry was not on this expedition to avenge Crysler's grievances or rescue his family, he was only there to collect more scalps and to notch his warclub with more kills, particularly Vrooman family kills. Having captured Lt. Ephraim Vrooman and killing his wife Christina and little daughter Janett the summer before, Seth's Henry was pleased to come upon yet another member of the family he had come to hate. Sixty-year-old Isaac Vrooman, alone and unarmed, provided the avenger with another scalp and another Vrooman family kill.

Being too small a party to linger about for long, Crysler and Seth's Henry's men hurried to abduct the lieutenant's family and rustle up as many head of cattle as they could drive off. A small patrol of militiamen was sent out from Upper Fort to investigate reports of raiders in the valley and upon being informed of the situation, Col. Peter Vrooman immediately gave orders for a detachment to be sent out to give chase and engage with the invaders. Upper Fort's Capt. Jacob Hager and twenty of his frontier rangers were assigned to the task and were joined by a company of about sixty Connecticut troopers commanded by Capt. Aaron Hale. Several of Hager's rangers had been with Col. Harper during the early years of the war while he was still a captain of his small company of frontier rangers and scouts. Joachim Van Volkenburgh, Timothy Murphy and a couple of his brother Alexander's brothers-in-law, Tewalt and Benjamin Bartholomew joined Capt. Hager's company. They and their comrades would have relished the chance to join the company and take part in what might be one of the last chances to engage the enemy who had inflicted so much death and misery on them and their families.

Captain Hager's and Hale's troops set out after Crysler and Seth's Henry after their band had made their way out of the valley with fifty head of cattle and Crysler's wife and children. Heading back towards the Susquehanna, Crysler's party encamped for the night next to Lake Utsayantha at the head of the Delaware's West Branch, near today's village of Stamford. Slowed down by their cattle and civilians, the Schoharie soldiers had little trouble catching up with them. On the morning of the 14th, the Schoharie militiamen surprised the Tories and Indians, and a brief battle ensued. Capt. Hale and his Connecticut boys were inexperienced with Indian warfare and panicked after the first volley, apparently unnerved by the sight and shrieks of the furious looking Indians. A story is told of how Capt. Hager and his contentious Pvt. Murphy confronted the fleeing Capt. Hale and threatened him with a rifle to his chest to turn about and lead his men back into the fray of battle. Timothy Murphy is of course credited with every heroic act of courage that every frontier incident happened to need, whether it was truly him or not. Notwithstanding, in the time it took to rally the Schoharie troops and return to the fight, Crysler and Seth's Henry's warriors had retreated from the field and were making a furtive escape into the dark forest, leaving their cattle behind. The last frontier confrontation of 1781, and one of the last battles of the New York border war, resulted in a quasi-rebel victory for having inadvertently driven the enemy from the field and retrieved the fifty cows they had stolen. Its likely none of the Indians were killed, but the brief skirmish cost the rebel militia one of its best and most respected frontier rangers, the venerated frontiersman Joachim Van Volkenburgh. [25]

The end of the 1781 fighting season brought a welcome end to large-scale battles and campaigns between British and American armies. But it would be another year and a half following the Battle of Johnstown and Cornwallis's surrender before a formal proclamation for the cessation of hostilities was finally declared on April 19th, 1783. The British however, continued to maintain their garrisons in New York City and Long Island before finally evacuating New York on November 25th, 1783. The Continental Army, consequently, could not stand down and disband before then. The frontier militias could not stand down until the summer of '84 when the northern British and Canadian commanders finally resolved to withdraw their troops. They did however retain possession of Forts Niagara and Oswego in protest to America's refusal to return the loyalist's confiscated properties. With the enemy still about and the possibility of peace talks breaking down, the rebel forts along the Mohawk and Schoharie Valleys had to continue to be maintained and garrisoned.

Assured by northern British commanders that no large-scale expeditions would be launched on the frontier while the peace talks were ongoing in Paris, the militias and citizens of Tryon County were shocked to learn in early July 1782 that 450 Indians and 50 New York loyalists were making their way down the Mohawk. Back from the far western fronts of Ohio and Kentucky, Joseph Brant and his Iroquois warriors were not quite ready to give up the fight and resign themselves to defeat. The support promised by the British for their indigenous allies was proving to be woefully insufficient to meet the needs of the starving Iroquois warriors and their families. With their forests nearly depleted of game and their homeland in ruin, Brant was pressured to find food for his desperate people. Finding most of the rebel militia still garrisoned in their Mohawk River forts, Brant's last-ditch raid on the frontier proved harder than he would have liked. Only managing to kill a few unfortunate homesteaders and abscond with a few head of their cattle, many of Brant's warriors became frustrated by the lack of plunder and scalps and turned back for Niagara. With a few more loose ends to attend to, Adam Crysler and Seth's Henry broke off from Brant's main force and set off on one last frontier raid of their own. Hoping to extract one last pound of vengeance before hanging up their rifles, Lt. Crysler's Tories and Indians paid yet another visit to their old neighborhoods looking to settle a few last personal scores. Seven long years of constant bloodshed were nearly over and the last chance to repay old insults was at hand. Sporadic violence and bloodshed continued to plague the frontier throughout those final lawless months of the war. [26]

During those uneasy times, regional conflicts continued to flare up in the frontier theaters of east central New York and the western territories north of the Ohio River. Some of the most horrific atrocities of the entire frontier border wars were inflicted upon individual homesteaders throughout 1782 and '83. Renegade bands of dispossessed Tories who had lost their homesteads to confiscation, roamed the backwoods around their former properties looking to settle old scores with their former rebel neighbors and militia rivals. With the prospects of peace looming on the horizon, retribution was more urgent than ever and the time for reckoning was running thin. The most stalwart of frontier homesteaders who dared return to their settlements during this troubled time, were vulnerable targets for revenge seeking killers who had perfected their trade through seven long years of war.

6

Resettlement
1783-1787
'I Hope so too Madam, for I have seen enough of war'

Although the formal cessation of hostilities was in effect by mid-April 1783, most of the frontier's former settlers did not yet trust the fragile truce enough to return to the ruins of their homesteads and clearings. British regulars were still garrisoned in New York City and Fort Niagara, and the forests were still crawling with bands of renegade Tories and revenge-seeking warriors. The deserted settlements of Andrustown, Richfield Springs, Springfield, Middlefield, Cherry Valley, Kortright, Harpersfield and Johnstons Settlement had all been laid waste by the enemy and nature's relentless reforestation. A year before the Harpers and their patent's prewar settlers returned to Harpersfield, one of the first returning families found their way home and reclaimed their overgrown homestead in the ruins of Cherry Valley.

In the spring of '83, Col. Samuel Campbell boldly defied the border region's few remaining bands of rogue Indians and reestablished his Cherry Valley homestead before few others dared return. Samuel had grown up in Cherry Valley after having been brought there with Rev. Dunlop's first group of Scots-Irish families. As a young man he had served under Sir William Johnson during the French and Indian War and in the early years of the Revolution led a company of rangers with Samuel Clyde. He had also served before the war in Tryon County's Committee of Safety with John Moore. He was later commissioned lieutenant colonel in Col. Ebenezer Cox' 1st Regiment of Tryon County Militia and took command of the regiment after Col. Cox was shot in the opening volleys at The Battle of Oriskany. Samuel Campbell fought bravely throughout the horrific battle in which his brother Robert was killed while fighting at his side.

When Cherry Valley was brutally attacked in late 1778, Colonel Campbell and Lt. Col. Samuel Clyde were both tending to their regimental duties along the Mohawk, too far from their families and homes to be of any help. Col. Campbell's wife Jane and three of their four children, Eleanor-8, James-6 and Matthew-3 were all captured along with their neighbor Mary Harper Moore and her three daughters. Jane Cannon Campbell was an accomplished and respected lady with influential friends in high places. While enroute to Niagara, she was held by the Seneca at Kanadaseago for six months while her three young children were taken from her and adopted into different Seneca families. After learning of her captivity in the Seneca Castle, Col. John Butler demanded she be brought to Fort Niagara where he could see to her wellbeing. Col. Butler's wife Catherine had been friends with Lady Campbell before the war and was now herself being held captive by the rebels in Albany.

Col. Butler and his son Walter were hoping to exchange the Moores and Campbells for Mrs. Butler and her daughter and a few other British officer's wives and children. But it would not be until nearly the end of the war before Jane Campbell and the Moore girls were finally released in late 1782. The Campbell children were retained another year by their Indian families. Spending those early formative years among the Senecas, all three of them learned the ways and language of the Indians and came to love and respect the people who had captured them. Lady Jane and her children were never mistreated by their British or Indian captors. In fact, little Matthew Campbell was revered and treated as a young Indian prince. He was returned at the age of six to his Cherry Valley family in 1783, adorned with the appropriate attire of a young Seneca chief. Matthew and his older brother James both spoke in the dialect of their Indian captors and knew extraordinarily little English when finally reunited with their families. [1]

In late July 1783, a few months after the Campbells return to Cherry Valley, the commander-in-chief of the Continental Army visited the Mohawk forts and the Otsego Lake region. General Washington had long wished to visit the northern frontier and with the cessation of hostilities it was felt safe enough for him to travel into the border region with a small guard. He was being escorted through the frontier by Governor Clinton and a group of Continental and Tryon County militia officers and officials. After touring Lake Champlain's Fort Ticonderoga and Crown Point, the general and his escort headed back down towards the Mohawk River over the Saratoga battlefield before traveling up the river to Canajoharie and Fort Plain. Wishing to view the source of the Susquehanna and the outlet of Otsego Lake from where Gen. James Clinton launched his western expedition in 1779, Gen. Washington and his party headed up Otsquago Creek and over the hill towards the lake through Cherry Valley. It is not known for certain if any of the Harper brothers were among the officers in the entourage, but it does seem reasonable that either William Harper Esq. or Col. Harper would have been among them. William was living in Queen Anne's Chapel Parsonage in '83, less than a mile from Fort Hunter where Washington's party was known to have visited. As a New York State assemblyman, it would have been likely for him to have been invited to meet the general and travel with him through the frontier to his old Cherry Valley home.

Col. Samuel Campbell

Having heard a great deal about the prosperous frontier settlement of Cherry Valley and the horrific massacre that happened there, Gen. Washington felt compelled to visit the village and meet with any of the surviving residents who might have returned. On the afternoon of July 31st, Col. Campbell and his wife Jane were surprised to see a group of soldiers riding up to their homestead. Upon realizing that Washington was among the party, the Campbells warmly welcomed their beloved commander and invited him to dine with them under the shade of an old apple tree next to their humble little log cabin. Lady Campbell prepared as good a meal as she could for her esteemed guests and served them raspberry leaf tea from the family's silver serving set. The general took a particular interest in the two young Campbell boys who spoke as fluently in the native tongue of the Senecas as they did their own father's tongue. Preparing to head for Otsego Lake in the morning after having spent the night with the Campbells, Gov. Clinton commented to Lady Campbell '...*your sons would make good soldiers in time...*', to which she replied '...*I hope their services would never be thus needed...*'. Overhearing their exchange, General Washington was said to have added '...*I hope so too madam, for I have seen enough of war...*'. [2]

Jane Cannon Campbell

Harpersfield

The spring of 1784 broke with a renewed feeling of hope and prosperity for the frontier survivors of the brutal New York border war. Having suffered and sacrificed throughout the dark days of the war, the dispossessed frontier refugees were anxious to return to the patented lands of the border region and begin the arduous work of rebuilding their old homesteads. Those who had settled on the patented lands before the war would soon be joined by a tsunami of new settlers looking for a chance to cultivate their own small patch of land and build a better life for themselves and their children. The proprietors who had secured and surveyed their patents before the war were eager to resume advertising and attracting prospective buyers to their plotted homestead lots. One such resolute family of returning proprietors was more than ready to get back to the business of selling lots and colonizing their patent with new arrivals.

Now nearly eighty, John Harper Sr. was looking forward to returning to Harpersfield with his sons and their families to begin rebuilding their frontier settlement. The Harper family patriarch had been too old to take an active part in the border war but his teenage years on the Kennebec frontier had taught him all he needed to know about frontier life. Having been shunned and spat upon by the welcoming party on Boston's Long Wharf in 1718, he seems to have developed as much respect for the original inhabitants of Colonial America as the more recent ones. From his apprentice years in the Temple family's Noodle's Island businesses, to the years he spent on the Connecticut River honing his marketing and trading skills, his dream of empire had always been his guiding star. After taking the first step toward those goals and moving to New York's fledgling frontier settlement of Cherry Valley in 1754, his dream was finally ready to take flight. His acquisition of the Beaver Dam Patent had served as a pedagogic lesson for his four sons who would outdo their father's wildest expectations. Returning to the family's 22,000-acre patent in the spring of '84, old John Harper had but a year left to enjoy the fruits of his lifelong ambition. With his second wife Rebecca by his side, he died the following April 20th at the age of eighty-one. He must have died satisfied in his sons' many accomplishments and been as proud as any Scots-Irish immigrant father could have ever hoped for. [3]

Returning to their patent at the headwaters of the Delaware's West Branch, the Harpers were joined by some of their prewar patent homesteaders who had just finished fighting with them through seven long years of war. Other veterans joined the Harpersfield returnees while many others began looking further west at the lands of the vanquished Iroquois. The floodgates to the western frontier lands were not open yet, but ambitious speculators and investors were lining up to take advantage of the anticipated deluge of pioneer migrants. The Harpers, like so many others, were intoxicated with land fever and anxious to grab as much of it as they could. There was a sense of entitlement to the land they had fought for and freed from the British and their Native American allies. Opportunists and scoundrels of every stripe were jockeying for position and lining up to take advantage of the defeated and desperate Iroquois peoples. The Harpers were ready to resume their father's dreams of empire that had temporarily been put on hold by the Revolution.

When the Harpers and their patent's homesteaders began returning to their old settlement, a whole new world of local and statewide boundary divisions awaited them. All of New York's counties and district boundaries were about to be redefined along with the western Indian territory. The frontier border region throughout the war had been defined as the whole of Tryon County and the western half of Ulster and Albany counties, with the property line of 1768 as its western border. Within six months of the Paris Peace Treaty signing in September of 1783, Tryon County was renamed Montgomery in honor of the heroic young officer killed during the invasion of Canada, Maj. Gen. Richard Montgomery. While the young nation struggled to form a new government and ratify a Constitution, Gov. Clinton and the State of New York grappled with the problems of legally procuring its western Indian lands and reallocating its counties and townships into more regionally oriented districts. Old Tryon/Montgomery County and the state's western boundary line was tentatively expanded a hundred miles west to Seneca Lake and Massachusetts' unresolved territorial claim to western New York. The Royal Charter of 1620 that gave Massachusetts all the territory between the 40th and 48th latitude from sea to sea, was still a legal encumbrance that had not yet been fully extinguished. Massachusetts and Connecticut long held that their northern and southern boundaries extended all the way to the western sea that turned out to be the Pacific Ocean. It would take multiple Indian treaties and years of wrangling between prospective proprietorships to resolve New York's western lands. And it was to take another 130 years to totally complete the state's reallocation of its now sixty-two counties. The only reminder of the old Indian property line of 1768 that survives to this day is preserved in the western boundary lines of Delaware and Otsego Counties. [4]

During the first five or six years of frontier postwar resettlement the previously patented lands of the old border region were inundated with new settlers. Patent proprietors were eager to accommodate the influx of eastern pioneers making their way through the Catskills to the Susquehanna and Delaware River valleys. Many of the large and smaller patents in the Harper's original Indian land purchase had been confiscated from their original loyalist proprietors. Harper Patent and the adjoining Kortright Patent were two of the few border region properties ready for resettlement following the Revolution. Surveyed into homestead lots and partially settled before the war, these two patents began filling up with new arrivals as soon as the last of the British troops pulled back to Forts Niagara and Oswego in the summer of '84. The Harpers were more than ready to return to their patent and continue attracting settlers to their homestead lots.

Returning to The Centre with their elderly father John Sr, three of the four Harper brothers and their brother-in-law William McFarland began rebuilding their homes and preparing their overgrown clearings for replanting. Col. Harper was returning to the patent with his second wife Isabella McKnight Harper, the widow of his first cousin Joseph Harper of East Windsor. At the cessation of hostilities, John and his son Archibald returned to the Connecticut River to retrieve the other six Harper children John had entrusted to the care of his cousin following the death of his wife Miriam in '78. John learned upon arriving that his favorite cousin Joseph had just recently died. Widowed and left to raise the couple's five children on her own, it seemed only natural for Col. Harper and Isabella to marry and unite their two families of second cousins into one large family. Joseph and Isabella's Connecticut children ranged in age from 4 to 17, with William being the oldest and Joseph-15, John-12, James-7, and little Polly just four. John and Miriam's seven children ranged in age from 8 to 20, Archibald being the oldest with Margaret-18, James-17, Mary-15, Rebecca-11, John-10, and Ruth-8. Within a few years, John and Isabella added to their brood of twelve children two more of their own, Abigail in '85 and Sally in '87. Upon coming of age, three of the East Windsor Harper brothers returned to their childhood friends and relatives on the Connecticut River. Only the oldest son William and youngest daughter Polly Harper stayed with their mother Isabella and stepfather John and their seven cousins. [5]

Capt. Alexander Harper and wife Elizabeth returned to Harpersfield with five of what eventually would be a family of eight children. Being the youngest of the four Harper brothers, Alexander's children were quite a bit younger than most of their Harper cousins. Their oldest child Margaret was not yet twelve but was already a major help to her mother who was nursing her one-month-old sister Elizabeth. Margaret's three young brothers, John-10, James-6, and William-5 were all too young to remember anything about the settlement they and their uncles, aunts and cousins were now returning to. John had been just three and James but a year old when the Harpersfield families were driven from their homes by MacDonell's Tories in '77. William was born in Schoharie's Middle Fort a year and a half after the family's evacuation. Margaret, who was just five at the time, was still able many years later to recount the traumatic ordeal of her early childhood. In an Ohio affidavit attached to her aunt Abigail Bartholomew's 1838 application for a widow's benefit claim to her husband Benjamin's war pension, Margaret Harper Wheeler, then 66, recounted how she and her two little brothers fled with their parents to Schoharie's Middle Fort ahead of the Tories and Indians. She also told of her father Alexander's capture at the hands of Brant's Indians in 1780. She and her siblings were eventually taken to New Lebanon, New York by her mother Elizabeth in '82. Returning to Harpersfield in the spring of '84, Margaret's forty-one-year-old father Alexander had only been freed from his two-and-a-half-year British incarceration for little over a year. Emaciated and weakened, Capt. Harper and his fellow sugar boilers might have only just regained their full strength by that spring.

Lieut. Joseph Harper was returning to the family's patent physically disabled from being shot in the back during the confusion on Klock's Field in 1780. It had been three-and-a-half years since that bullet tore through his shoulder rendering his left arm useless. His grateful nation awarded Joseph with a disability annuity of $96 per annum. Joseph and his wife Catherine's two sons, John-17 and Joseph-16, were depended upon by their father to do their filial responsibilities and perform all the heavy lifting and strenuous work to help rebuild their family's homestead. Joseph's many nephews and nieces would have also lent their poor uncle what help they could. Catherine's three daughters, Margaret-14, Agnes-12 and Mary-10, helped their mother with the domestic chores that could be every bit as exhausting as their brother's work. [6]

In 1765, William McFarland met and married the Harper brother's nineteen-year-old sister Abigail Harper. The McFarland family had come to New England with the Scots-Irish Montgomery, Harper and Thompson families in the early 1720s, during the Great Irish Migration. The McFarlands migrated through New Hampshire and Massachusetts before William came to New York's Cherry Valley during the French and Indian War. During the border war, William fought alongside his Harper brothers-in-law and seems to have formed a lasting bond with Alexander who was closer in age to him than the other Harper brothers. William and Alexander would share many adventures together through the war and into the postwar years. William and Abigail McFarland returned to and resettled on Harper Patent's homestead lot #61, near Abigail's family at The Centre. They were accompanied by their nineteen-year-old daughter Eunice, the only child the couple was ever known to have had. Thirty-five-year-old Miriam Harper, the youngest of the Harper siblings, appears to have lived under the same roof as her older sister and brother-in-law William. As fate would have it, Abigail's unwed spinster sister would be William McFarland's second wife following Abigail's sudden death in 1786, two years after returning to Harpersfield. With William's daughter Eunice now living on Tedle Brook lot #146, with her husband John Tedle, the widower was now alone and faced with what might have been an awkward situation. William did the only gentlemanly thing he could do, which was to marry his sister-in-law Miriam and continue supporting her. William and Miriam Harper McFarland lived together for another twenty-seven years as husband and wife, never having any children of their own. But they did eventually adopt a young boy and take in a young unwed mother and her infant son. [7]

There was one conspicuously absent member of the Harper family who did not return with them to their patent after the war. The oldest of the Harper brothers, William Harper Esq., chose instead to remain closer to the center of political intrigue and the society to which he and his wife Margaret had become accustomed. Having served during the early years of the war as a member of Tryon County's Committee for Safety and a delegate to New York's First Provincial Congress, William preferred to remain closer to Albany and Schenectady where he could better advance his political career. Through the formative years of the state's fledgling government, he served as a Tryon and Montgomery County Representative to the State Assembly from 1781 to 1789.

William and his brother John had spent part of the war years living in the relative comfort of two confiscated loyalist estates. Col. Harper and wife Miriam occupied the estate of Sir William Johnson's daughter Nancy and her husband Daniel Claus, on the north side of the Mohawk near Fort Johnson. William and wife Margaret spent part of the war living just across the river near Fort Hunter in Queen Anne's Chapel Parsonage. At war's end, William seems to have not been enthusiastic about evacuating his well-furnished and elegant home to rejoin his family on their frontier patent. Along with his duties in the state legislature, Esq. Harper was making a decent living representing clients and litigating disputes between individual landowners and patent proprietors in the Fort Hunter area. From his home and office in the parsonage, William continued to help resolve his neighbors' property rights while maneuvering to acquire the parsonage and as much of the acreage around it as he could legally finagle. [8]

Queen Anne's Chapel Parsonage

Queen Anne's Chapel and Parsonage were built in 1712 to accommodate the spiritual needs of her Palatine refugees and to secure safe lodging for the frontier priests sent to Christianize the Mohawk Indians. The Mohawks had graciously allowed the Queen's representatives to use a 300-acre tract of land surrounding the parsonage to serve as a glebe for the support of the church and its priests. In 1740, an ambitious and duplicitous Rev. Henry Barclay convinced the Mohawk to accept five shillings for the entire 300 acres and persuaded their sachems to sign over a deed to him. Within a year he was granted a patent on the property. Upon Barclay's retirement just prior to the Revolution, he donated the property to England's Society for the Propagation of the Gospel in Foreign Parts, an organization designed to promote the Anglican Church in the American Colonies. The Mohawks, however, were displeased with Barclay's donation of the glebe to outsiders and protested the deed they had signed for the land. Therein lay a tricky complication for any legal transfer of proprietorship of the Barclay Patent.

William Harper continued living in the Chapel Parsonage for several years after the war and continued to pursue all legal avenues to secure the house and a portion of the 300-acre Barclay Patent. Forced to concede by the power of the Anglican Church and the state's land commissioners, William was unable to hold on to the parsonage but did manage to secure 104 acres of the original Barclay Patent. By late 1792, he had 32 acres of his patented river flats surveyed and plotted into homestead lots. Not being able to continue living in the parsonage, William finally joined his brothers on the family's frontier patent in the mid-90s and settled on Middle Brook's lot #124. Now sixty-five, William kept his hand in politics and the judiciary as an associate judge for the Court of Common Pleas in the recently formed Otsego County. Queen Anne's Parsonage still stands today on Queen Anne Road just outside of the village of Fort Hunter, three hundred years after it was built. [9]

Harper Patent

The Harpers came back to their patent after the war with a consortium of old and new homesteaders, nearly all of whom were fellow veterans of the Revolution. Some of them were returning to their old Harper Patent homesteads they had abandoned at the start of the border war. Others were from the eastern settlements of New York's Columbia and Dutchess Counties or the war-torn communities of southwestern Connecticut. Many of these families were old colonial New Englanders whose ancestry stretched back to the first puritan immigrants of the Massachusetts Bay Colony. The fortunes they had accumulated through four or five generations of hard work were severely diminished by the turmoil of war and the economic disaster that followed. The western lands and the opportunities they offered, summoned these cash-strapped New Englanders to the patented lands of west central New York. The Harper family and all the other proprietors of the old border region's patented lands were more than happy to accommodate the hopes and expectations of these poor Yankee newcomers. But the returning frontiersmen who had cleared their homesteads before the war and had fought the Tories and Indians to hold on to it felt like they were the rightful owners of the western lands that were now being flooded with the eastern newcomers. The Harper family and their Scots-Irish kinsmen were leery of the new settlers, but at the same time recognized the potential economic boost to their own family fortunes.

One welcomed family with old familial ties to the Harpers came to Harpersfield after the war and took two homestead lots, #39 and #65, near the Harper homesteads at The Centre. Robert Montgomery was a first cousin to the Harper brothers by his father James, who was the older brother of their mother Abigail Montgomery Harper. James Montgomery and his brother John were the two companions of John Harper Sr. who had fought with him in the Kennebec wilderness through the 4th Anglo/Abenaki War. James and Mary Hendry Montgomery's son Robert arrived at his late aunt Abigail's and uncle John's patent with his wife Mary and their eleven children in the late 1780s. The children of Robert and Mary White Montgomery and the children of Robert's cousin Col. John Harper formed a closely-knit bond of kinship with each other, with two sets of Harper/Montgomery second cousins eventually marrying. The great-grandparents of these cousins came to New England together aboard the *MacCullum* in 1718. The two Old World Scots-Irish families had an ancient bond that stretched back for generations through the plantations of Northern Ireland to the upper lowlands of the Scottish Borders. Their intertwined families mingled and migrated together through Massachusetts and Connecticut before claiming their place on the Harpersfield patent. They would continue their migration together to lands far beyond New York's western Catskills. [10]

A couple of the sugar boilers who had been led into captivity by Alexander Harper returned to the scene of the crime and resettled on the same homesteads where they had been captured by Brant in 1780. Two of the younger Hendry brothers, David and William, settled on lots #15 and #16 near where Brant's warriors killed their older brother James and father Thomas. The Hendry's were long time friends of the Harpers and the Scots-Irish frontiersmen whose fathers emigrated together from Northern Ireland to America sixty years earlier. David Hendry had helped the Harpers survey their patent lots back in '71 and like his father and brothers, he too had fought alongside the Harpers through the early years of the war. He was taken prisoner by MacDonell's Tories as they swept through Harpersfield on route to the Schoharie Valley in the summer of '77 but managed to escape in the confusion during the Battle of the Flockey. David would most certainly have been with his father and brothers on that ill-fated sugar boiling expedition had he not contracted smallpox shortly before the debacle. He would spend his life with the Harpers and eventually join them on another western frontier adventure.

Four more of Capt. Harper's POWs returned to Harpersfield a few years after the war and their dreadful incarceration. Brothers Daniel and Ezra Thorp and brothers Isaac and Freegift Patchin had all served together in various Connecticut regiments before being deployed to Schoharie's Middle Fort just days before the sugar boiler expedition. The Patchins and Thorps had grown up together in Norwalk, Connecticut's Wilton Parish. Isaac Patchin came to the frontier and settled prior to the war on Harper Patent's lot #20. In the spring of '87, after an extended convalescence following their two-and-a-half years on a British prison ship, Isaac returned to his overgrown homestead on which he had been captured seven years earlier. His younger brother Freegift followed him back to Harpersfield and took nearby lot #62 on Center Brook next to William McFarland. The Thorp brothers soon joined their old Connecticut friends and settled near them on adjoining homestead lots #42 and #43. [11]

Another one of the sugar boilers returned to his former homestead with Capt. Harper and his fellow surviving members of the expedition. William Lamb did not, however, return with the ten-year-old boy he had taken with him on the doomed expedition. William Lamb's son Willy was one month shy of his eleventh birthday when he was captured along with his father and the rest of the sugar boilers. Fortunately, little Willy Lamb was spared the terrible realities of the prison ships. But Willy's captivity lasted far longer than the others. Joseph Brant had taken pity on the young boy and saw to it that he was placed in custody of his remarkable sister Molly Brant. Adopted into Molly's family as an indentured servant, Willy spent nearly seven years living in Kingston, Ontario with his Mohawk hostess and her family who by all accounts treated him very well. The boy may even have had an opportunity to receive a better education than he would have back on the frontier. But Willy secretly longed for his own family and waited for a chance to escape and rejoin them back on the New York frontier.

Several years after William Lamb reestablished his Harper Patent homestead on lot #84, his eighteen-year-old son Willy made his escape and worked his way back through the wilderness to his astonished family on Center Brook. Given up for dead by a father who cursed the day he chose to bring his young son along with him on Capt. Harper's expedition, his return might have given his dear old, tortured dad a small measure of clemency. It is not known if Willy ever forgave his father or the militia captain who abandoned him to the Indians and stole his youth. He probably never saw a single p of the £3.4 the state allocated to Alexander for the relief of his sugar boilers upon their release in '82. Soon after returning, William Lamb Jr, married one of the Thorp girls and lived out his days to the ripe old age of eighty-five. His obituary said he was haunted in his adult years by the memories of the mistreatment he received at the hands of his Mohawk captors. While that certainly could have been possible, it is more likely the obituary was written by an author with the common bias towards Native Americans that permeated nineteenth century literature and everyday life. [12]

Three of Alexander Harper's brothers-in-law returned to the frontier and reestablished their former properties on the Johnson family's confiscated Charlotte Creek Patent. Benjamin, Theobald (Tewalt) and Joseph Bartholomew were returning after having survived the border war that took three of their brothers, Isaac, Samuel and Theophilus. It had only been a little over four years since another one of Alexander's brothers-in-law and sugar boilers was killed by the Indians as he lay sick and helpless in his lot #57 cabin. William Stevens' widow Hannah Bartholomew Stevens returned to Harpersfield with her second husband Nathaniel Skinner and a six-year-old blind orphan boy they had adopted while living in Schoharie's Middle Fort. Nathaniel and brother-in-law Alexander established one of the first taverns on the old Susquehanna/Catskill Turnpike that ran through the heart of Harpersfield and The Centre. Joshua O'Daniel, despite being blind, was a great comfort to his mother Hannah when she was again widowed in '95 when Nathaniel Skinner died at the age of forty-five. Joshua grew up to be an intelligent and well-respected young man with a keen memory that was often called upon to recount many of the events of the border war and life in the Schoharie forts. Hannah never remarried after the loss of her two husbands and stayed close to her older sister Elizabeth Harper and her Charlotte Creek brothers. When Samuel Wilcox and his wife Sally came to Harpersfield from Dutchess County after the war, they settled on lot #57 and took advantage of William and Hannah Stevens' former cabin that had somehow survived the war intact. It was said that Sally Wilcox scrubbed the split-plank floorboards of the Stevens' cabin for days but could never fully remove the blood stains left by the unfortunate sugar boiler.

The Bartholomew Settlement, six miles north of The Centre and the confiscated property of the loyalist Servos family attracted new homesteaders from Schoharie Valley's Palatine German population. Martin, Peter and John Van Alstyne, Henderick and Bartholomew Hagedorn, Lodowick and Philip Becker and Capt. Lodowick Brickman were all living near the Bartholomeus by 1790. These men had all fought through the war with the Harpers and Bartholomeus while their families sheltered together in Schoharie's three forts. The bonds forged in the Schoharie forts between the High-Dutch and Scots-Irish, defied the norms of New York's prevailing ethnic divisions. Shared privations and a mutual dependency against a common enemy proved stronger than most men's preconceived opinions of each other. The marriage of Alexander Harper to Elizabeth Bartholomew was itself an anomaly that may have troubled some of the frontiersmen and disturbed a few proper eighteenth century gentlemen. But the Harpers never seemed to worry about other people's opinions of them. [13]

Mingling with the returning Harper Patent settlers, the Gaylord family came to Harpersfield after the war and settled on homestead lots #18, #19 and #38, in the same neighborhood as the Hendrys, Thorps and Patchins. Joel, Jedediah and Levi Gaylord came to the frontier with their father Levi Sr and the rest of their Connecticut family. Levi Gaylord Jr had made friends with David Hendry while the two were recuperating from smallpox and working in an army shoe factory on the Connecticut River. All the Gaylord brothers had served throughout the early years of the war as privates and minor officers in Capt. Jehiel Meig's company of Guilford recruits. Their father Levi Sr served as a commissioned ensign in the same company of Col. Andrew Ward's 1st Battalion of Connecticut Troopers. They all fought in the Battles of Long Island, Harlem Heights, and White Plains before spending the rest of the war in various regiments stationed throughout the Hudson Highlands and along the Connecticut coast. Encouraged by Levi Jr's friend David, the Gaylords left Connecticut's war-ravaged coastline for the new frontier and all its promises. Eventually, the Hendrys and Gaylords would move on together to yet another promise on the ever-expanding American frontier. [14]

Another family of Connecticut expatriates came to Harpersfield about the same time as the Patchins, Thorps and Gaylords. Deacon Caleb Gibbs of Litchfield arrived and settled on Harper Patent's adjacent lots #33 and #34 with his wife and five children. One of Caleb's older daughters Candice and her husband Richard Bristol also came with the Gibbs and settled on nearby lot #59. Caleb purchased all three of these lots from his daughter Statira's husband Stephen Judd of Waterbury. Stephen was a highly capable young man who had purchased several lots on Harper Patent. After joining his wife's family in Harpersfield around 1790, Stephen purchased another 2,000 acres in the adjacent Strasburgh Patent that had been one of Col. John Butler's confiscated properties. In '97 the Judds left Harpersfield and moved on to their property, five miles northeast of The Centre. Stephen then petitioned the state to reallocate the western portion of Schoharie County's Blenheim Township into a new township he proposed to name in honor of Thomas Jefferson. Granted his new township, Stephen contributed to the development and growth of the village of Jefferson and financed one of the first institutions of higher learning in the area, Jefferson Academy. He went on to be elected to many of Schoharie County's highest offices and was appointed Lt. Col. of Schoharie's militia in 1807. Two other daughters of Caleb Gibbs, Achsah and Sally, would marry two of Harpersfield's most eligible bachelors, Joel Gaylord, and Isaac Patchin. Upon reaching maturity, the youngest of Caleb's daughters, Phoebe, married James Hendry Jr who had been but nine when his father James and grandfather Thomas were killed by Brant's warriors during the sugar boiler raid. [15]

In the mid-80s, a group of Connecticut Yankees came to Harpersfield and settled together on Harper patent's Middle Brook, two miles north of The Centre. Eden Hamilton, John and Matthew Lindsley, Samuel and John Knapp, Abijah Beard, and Eleazer Starr came from the Danbury area and settled together at what would become known as North Harpersfield. Danbury suffered mightily during the war from a devastating British raid on the village's Continental depot that provided the rebel army with munitions and vital supplies. Gen. William Tryon's British Regulars and Hessian Jägers left the village's homes, barns, businesses, and churches in ashes and tore through the company of local militiamen assigned to protect the depot. Danbury residents and the militiamen who survived the assault, fought alongside Gen. David Wooster's Continentals who skirmished with the redcoat's rearguard as they made their retreat through Ridgefield to Compo Point and their waiting ships. The collateral damages to their village forced many of Danbury's young men to consider other options at war's end. North Harpersfield's veterans were no different than other Connecticut refugees who came to the frontier to start anew and bury the past. [16]

Perhaps having learned of the Harper family's patent through Waterbury's Stephen Judd, Joseph Hotchkiss and his wife Hannah arrived on the patent in the spring of '85 with their five daughters and four sons. The Hotchkiss brothers, Thelus, Ebenezer, Joseph Jr and Roswell, were in their late teens and early twenties when they came to the frontier ready to start their own families on their own homesteads. The Hotchkiss family secured three homestead lots near The Centre, one of which was adjacent to Col. Harper's homestead and was taken by the oldest Hotchkiss brother, twenty-three-year-old Roswell. Within a year of his arrival, Roswell Hotchkiss married the colonel's twenty-year-old daughter Margaret and was soon one of Harpersfield's most industrious citizens. In quick order he established a grist mill, a turning lathe, a nail factory, and a linseed oil distillery, all of which were essential for the development of a frontier settlement. Roswell was also an active member of his community's civic, judicial, and religious organizations, serving at various times as sheriff, supervisor, town clerk, postmaster, judge of common pleas and one of the first trustees of the Presbyterian Congregation of Harpersfield. In 1801, he was chosen as Delaware County's delegate to the State Constitutional Convention. Roswell eventually moved his business enterprise two miles down Center Brook to his father Joseph's lot #181, where before long the little hamlet of West Harpersfield developed around his homestead. In 1790, Roswell Hotchkiss owned one of Harpersfield's two slaves and by 1800 was the only slaveowner left in the entire area, a fact that might not have pleased his father-in-law Col. Harper. [17]

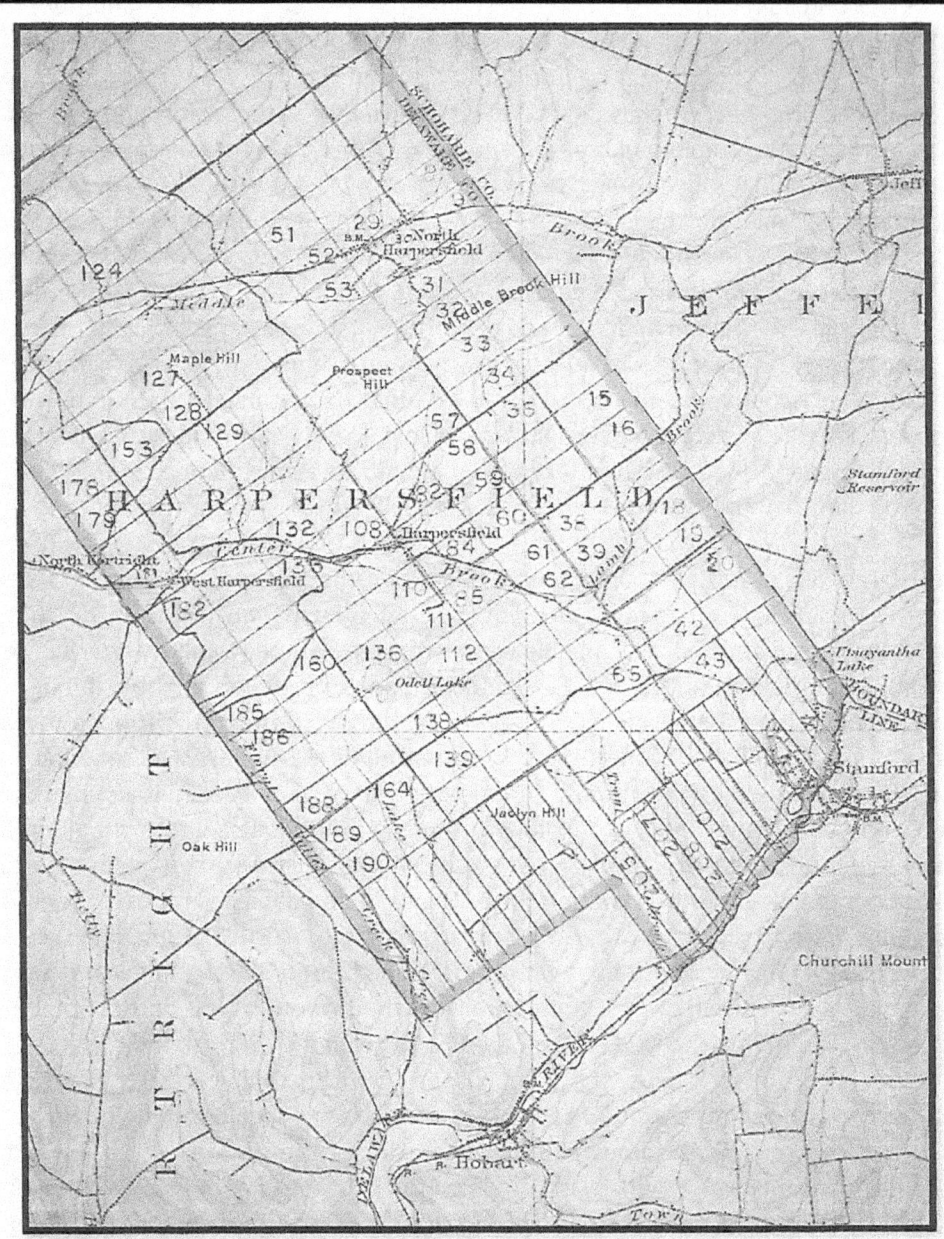

Harper Patent Homestead Lots on USGS 1904 map.

8-Ebenezer Starr: 9-Ezra Nichols: 15,16-William and David Hendry: 18,19- Joel and Jedediah Gaylord: 20-Isaac Patchin: 29-John Lindsley: 30-Eden Hamilton: 31,32-Abijah Baird: 33,34-Caleb Gibbs: 35-Freeman Judd: 38-Joel Gaylord: 39-Robert Montgomery: 42-Ezra Thorp: 43-Daniel Thorp: 51-John Knapp: 52-Samuel Knapp: 53-Matthew Lindsley: 57,58-Samuel Wilcox: 59-Richard Bristol: 60-Aaron Wilcox: 61-William McFarland: 62-Freegift Patchin: 65-John Montgomery: 81-Church Lot: 82-Alexander Harper: 84-William Lamb: 85-Thelus Hotchkiss: 108-Col. John Harper: 110,111,112-Joshua H. Brett: 124-William Harper: 127-John McCullough: 128,129-Benjamin Morse: 132-Roswell Hotchkiss: 133-Col. Harper: 138-Elisha Sheldon: 139-John Wilcox: 152-Thomas Hendry: 153-Jonathan Hubbard: 160-James Douglas: 164-Eliab Wilcox: 173-James Bell: 178-John Hendry: 179-James Brown: 181-Joseph Hotchkiss: 182-Joel Mack: 185-David Hendry: 186-William Bell: 188-William Wardwell: 189-John McClelland: 190-Thomas Porter: 205-David Wilcox: 207, 208-Andrew Rickey: 210-Stephen Churchill:

The West Branch

During the first few years of postwar resettlement, Harper Patent had a distinct advantage over most of the available patented lands. Other patent proprietors had been far less along with their patent surveys and homestead lot plotting when the war broke out and interrupted their progress. Many of the patents between the West Branch of the Delaware and the Susquehanna River were confiscated from their loyalist proprietors and were now being fought over by groups of investors and their lawyers. The original patents of the Harper Family's 260,000-acre Oneida purchase, apart from Kortright and Harper Patent, had gone virtually unsettled before the war. The Susquehanna's Wallace and Johnson patents were the only two other patents in the border region that were known to have had any settlers on them before the war. Around half of the area's prewar settlers never returned to their homesteads and properties, having backed the wrong horse, and lost them to confiscation. Capt. MacDonell and his Charlotte Creek clansmen and all the other frontier loyalists received reparations for about one quarters worth of their property's value from the British Empire they fought and died for. Of all the returning and new settlers to the lands between the Susquehanna and the West Branch, one-half of them were either living on Kortright Patent or Harper Patent after the first five years of postwar resettlement. [19]

The few prewar homesteaders who resettled after the war on the east side of the West Branch across from Kortright and Harper Patents, were returning to their old homesteads on Hardenburgh Patent's Great Lot #42. Many of these Hardenburgh settlers had suffered at the hands of the enemy. Daniel Bennet and his family were one of only a few who returned to their prewar homesteads in old Ulster County's Woodstock District. Early in the war, Daniel and his twelve-year-old son Abijah were captured by the Indians and escorted off to Fort Niagara. Their captivity might have been better than most. Daniel, who was a tailor by trade, was sent to Fort Detroit to make and fit uniforms for British officers. Young Abijah was sent to Montreal where he was conscripted into a British regiment and served throughout the war as a regimental drummer. In November 1782, five-and-a-half years after their capture, the Bennets were finally released about the same time as Capt. Harper and his sugar boilers.

Another returning prewar settler who had been captured and briefly held by the Indians, returned to the frontier and settled on Harper Patent's riverfront lot #217. After his and Isaac Sawyer's escape from Seth's Henry's warriors in '79, St. Leger Cowley served as an adjutant in Col. Harper's 2nd Tryon County Regiment. At wars end, he returned to the West Branch and built another gristmill like the one further down the river where he had entertained Col. Butler's troops during their expedition to Unadilla and Onaquaga in '78. Sawyer never returned to the West Branch after the war. The Cowley family's postwar milling operation near the current village of Stamford was eventually expanded to include a sawmill and carding mill. A few miles down the river, another millwright who had never left his homestead during the war even though he was known to have expressed his preference for the king over Congress, continued living alongside the returning rebel veterans. Hugh Rose managed to do what few had the audacity to try, maintaining a stance of neutrality and surviving on a lonely frontier homestead while entertaining all who came and went, be they Whig, Tory or Indian. It was at his millsite that Capt. Brant held the sugar boilers before setting off with them down the river to Niagara. Mr. Rose continued living on his homestead long after the war and was even elected to serve in several of Stamford Township's public offices. [20]

The earliest returning and new homesteaders to the reclaimed border region, naturally chose to settle on patents that had been surveyed and plotted into lots and made available for lease or purchase. It was also natural for these first pioneers to prefer to live along a waterway transportation route or an overland road that promised trade and traffic. By the late '80s, New Stamford and the Town Plot accounted for nearly half of the population living along the east, or backside, of the Delaware's West Branch from today's Stamford to Hancock. The Hardenburgh Patent's land/lease arrangement understandably stymied growth on the east side and drew people to the west side of the river. The lower West Branch had been settled by virtually no one before the war, not even the Lenape who never established a permanent village in the valley they considered to be home to angry spirits. By 1790, there were still only a few clusters of settlers scattered down along both sides of the river. Although not what anyone might consider a cohesive settlement yet, John and Abel Kidder, Gideon Frisbee, Thomas Farrington and brothers Joseph and William Denio, settled along the river between today's Bloomville and the village of Delhi on the confiscated Franklin Patent, known later as Meredith Patent. The river flat just below today's Delhi and across from the mouth of The Little Delaware had a dozen homesteads on it by the late '80s. William Fraser, Jacob Platner and Bartholomew Yendes were among these first settlers. Fraser and Platner left their names behind to testify to their having once lived there. [21]

A considerable number of West Branch settlers came in the mid-to-late '80s and took up residence on the confiscated loyalist patent of Maj. Gen. Augustine Prévost. Eventually purchased by a group of investors that included Peter V. B. Livingston, Sluman Wattles surveyed the patent into 144 generously proportioned homestead lots that on average contained 250 acres each. About twenty-five veterans and their families, most of whom were from Connecticut's coastal panhandle region, took advantage of these large and modestly priced lots. They settled on the patent's coveted riverfront lots and up along the two brooks that bisect the patent, present-day East, and West Brooks in the township of Walton. The P.V.B. Livingston Patent settlers were joined by about fifteen other Long Island and Connecticut families who settled down along the north side of the river on the adjacent Walton Patent and on the south side of Hardenburgh Patent's Great Lots #36 and #37. [22]

Soon after inheriting his uncle and grandfather's fortunes, William Walton III joined a group of twelve wealthy New York City merchants in founding the city's first Chamber of Commerce. William Walton served as president of the organization through the turbulent years leading up to the American Revolution. He and a few other members of the prestigious chamber used their wealth and influence to secure several large patents in the Harper family's Indian land purchase of 1768. Thomas and Henry White and Lawrence Kortright were both granted their sizable patents in 1770, while Philip Livingston, Elias Desbrosses, John Cruger, and Samuel Verplank were partners in several other large patents. Chamber of Commerce members, Hugh and Alexander Wallace, managed to wrangle half of Sir William Johnson's Susquehanna/Charlotte Creek Patent away from the Superintendent of Indian Affairs. Most of these New York merchants and investors would throw in with the king when the war came and subsequently lose their patented lands to sequestration.

William Walton remained in British occupied New York City throughout the war where he entertained British officers and dignitaries in his Franklin Square Georgian mansion while maintaining an apparent immunity to political partisanship. He was clever and rich enough to maneuver his way through the complexities of political neutrality even though his interests would have been better served had England put down the revolt and returned colonial maritime trade to its proper order. While giving aid and comfort to the British, he also found ways to provide some assistance for the suffering American prisoners held on the British prison ships anchored within sight and smell of his charming estate. This and whatever other devices he might have plied on the Commissioners of Forfeiture, William Walton managed to retain his 20,000-acre patent while undoubtedly holding a stronger affinity for the Crown than for American independence. [23]

The Walton brothers, William, Thomas, and Gerard seem to have had little interest in their remote frontier property between the Susquehanna and the Delaware. When a Long Island doctor came to them with a proposal, they jumped at the chance to have someone else survey and prepare their patent's homestead lots for sale. Reaching an agreement to purchase 1,765 acres of their patent's prime riverfront property, Dr. Platt Townsend made further arrangements with the Waltons to survey the entire patent in exchange for another 1,920 acres. Dr. Townsend was an educated gentleman from a prominent Oyster Bay family who had graduated from Yale before going on to study medicine at Scotland's prestigious Edinburgh University. During the war he had served on the Continental Army's Committee of Examiners interviewing prospective doctors, surgeons, and surgeon's mates to determine who was actually qualified to serve in the army's Medical Corps. Dr. Townsend's western Long Island property had been seized and garrisoned with British troops during their occupation of New York, and like many of Long Island's rebel refugees, he spent the war years just across the sound in Connecticut. Having formed a bond of comradery with four other exiled Long Island families whose estates were left in shambles by the end of the war, Dr. Townsend convinced them to join him on a pioneering expedition into the western Catskills. In the early spring of 1785, Dr. Townsend and his two sons, Isaac and William, forged their way through the wilderness and arrived at Walton Patent accompanied by the families of Joshua Pine, Robert and Gabriel North and the North's cousin William Furman. Dr. Townsend divided his riverfront property into three roughly equal lots of 600 acres each. Keeping the middle lot for himself, he sold the North brothers the eastern riverfront tract while the Pines took the lower tract down the river. [24]

Dr. Platt Townsend

Robert and Gabriel North's family of Newtown, Long Island was thrust into the epicenter of the Revolution when the British invaded New York in the summer of 1776. Benjamin North and his three sons and two sons-in-law were serving in Capt. Abraham Remsen's 3rd Newtown Company in Col. Josiah Smith's Long Island Militia Regiment. On the morning of August 27th, Capt. Remsen and the North boys were positioned with Lt. Col. John Mead's 9th Connecticut Regiment on the American's left flank at Bedford Crossing when all hell broke loose. Outflanked and surprised by a crushing British and Hessian force, the Newtown militia and their Connecticut comrades were driven back to Brooklyn Heights in a chaotic retreat with the rest of Washington's routed army. Gen. Washington's daring amphibious evacuation of his battered troops across the East River saved the Continental army from annihilation and averted a disaster that would have ended the Revolution before it had hardly started. Signing on for the remainder of the war, the North brothers had no idea they would not see their Newtown estate or their sisters and wives for another seven years. [25]

The Pine family had also been driven from their homes when the British invaded New York and Long Island. Prior to the war, Joshua Pine had been in business with James De Lancey, the brother of William Walton's first wife Mary De Lancey. De Lancey and Pine developed a lucrative flour distribution business, with Joshua running flour down the Hudson in his river sloop from his family's grist mills at Fishkill to the De Lancey's merchant ships in New York's East River. The war, however, brought an abrupt end to the Pine/De Lancey partnership, as the two families found themselves on opposite sides of the conflict. The war also forced the Pines to abandon their family's estate between the lower Westchester County's Morrisania and West Farms, in today's Bronx. Joshua and his son Joshua Jr spent the war running supplies and armaments up and down the Hudson for the Continental Army. Joshua's oldest son John and his brother Philip's son Peter became leaders of an elite company of volunteers known as the Westchester Guides. Capt. John Pine and his cousin Peter were entrusted with the dangerous and high-risk assignment of leading officers and troops through a no-mans-land crawling with British light horse, spies, and outlaws. At war's end, Joshua Pine and his three sons, Joshua Jr, Daniel and John, chose not to return to their former New York estate and jumped at the chance to join Dr. Townsend's Catskill expedition. The Pines took the lower one-third portion of Dr. Townsend's riverfront tract that terminated at the Canniskutty Line separating the Harper's Indian land purchase from Col. Bradstreet's purchase, and the Walton Patent from the Rapalje Patent. [26]

Just across the river from the Townsends, Norths and Pine family's Walton Patent properties, Charles Witham Stockton purchased 1,300 acres on the northwest third of sub-division #66 in

Hardenburgh Patent's Great Lot #36. The Stockton family of Burlington and Princeton was one of the wealthiest and most politically influential families of colonial New Jersey. Charles was the first cousin once removed of Richard Stockton, one of the signers of the Declaration of Independence and a member of the Second Continental Congress. Charles and his father Richard W. Stockton were not, however, politically aligned with their cousin Richard and were ardent supporters of the Crown. When the war came, Charles's father secured a captain's commission for himself and an ensign commission for his nineteen-year-old son.

While on a foraging patrol in lower Westchester County, Ensign Stockton was captured by a militia patrol and later exchanged on parole to sit out the remainder of the war. While serving out his parole he was garrisoned in the requisitioned Newtown estate of the North family where he became acquainted with the North brothers' younger sister Elizabeth. At twenty-two, Charles married Elizabeth North the day after her fifteenth birthday. Although the marriage of a British officer to the sister of two officers in the Continental Army may not have initially been a welcomed addition to the North family, a gentleman of Charles Stockton's wealth and stature might have mitigated any objections Robert and Gabriel might have had. In early December 1787, Charles and Elizabeth Stockton arrived on their tract of land across the river from Elizabeth's brothers and Dr. Townsend's homestead. The Stocktons were accompanied by Elizabeth's sister Martha North Smith and her second husband Richard Gosline. The North family's sixty-three-year-old mother Margaret Furman North and a slave girl named Tesse were among the Stockton party that arrived on Charles's riverfront property just as winter was setting in around them. Delaware County's present-day village of Walton was once the farmland pastures of the Townsend, North, and Stockton families. [27]

After the first couple of spring freshets of returning homesteaders to their prewar settlements, more families began threading their way through the mountains to the patented lands of the old border region. In the spring of '86, a young New Jersey adventurist came to the West Branch with an irrepressible spirit of entrepreneurial grit and a dozen young men he had convinced to join him on a grand adventure into the western Catskills. Jesse Dickerson purchased about eight hundred riverfront acres around the mouth of Ganniwissey Creek, today's Trout Creek, from the heirs of Col. John Bradstreet and the two Walton brothers, William and Gerard. Col. Bradstreet's children and son-in-law, Charles John Evans, had just finished surveying the patent they had managed to salvage from their father's original Indian land purchase that had been held up in litigation since before the Revolution. The Waltons had recently secured another smaller patent of 9,000 acres between the Evans Patent and the Rapalje Patent that became known as the Lower Walton Patent.

Jesse Dickerson's dream was to build a city that would serve as the northern terminus for the Delaware River's burgeoning timber industry that would last for another hundred and fifty years. Throughout their first summer on the Delaware frontier, Jesse and his men surveyed and laid out a grid of streets for a village he planned to call Dickerson City. By that fall they had built a few houses, a town hall, a small grist mill, and the sawmill they would use to cut their logs into dimensional lumber for transport down the river in rafts to Philadelphia. Jesse was also planning to run a mercantile business, taking orders from his frontier neighbors and returning from civilization with the finer things of life, rum and snuff for the gentlemen, and tea and linens for the ladies. All was going according to plan until the early hours of October 5th, 1786, when an unseasonably intense thunderstorm unleashed a torrent of rain that did not let up for days. The Great Pumpkin Flood of '86 devastated the early homesteaders along the upper Susquehanna and Delaware rivers. Their crops that had been planted on the low river flats were all swept away by the rising water. Dickerson City's town hall and sawmill, that had been built too close to the river and creek, were also swept away with the pumpkins, squash, corn and beans. Devastated but undaunted, Jesse and his crew went back to work rebuilding their little village only to be thwarted again by Jesse's depleted finances and less than expected income. By the mid-90s, Jesse was forced to surrender his property that was soon after bought by Benjamin Cannon. Mr. Cannon lent his name to the village that replaced Dickerson City, and the reservoir that would eventually inundate both "metropolises". [28]

Another small cluster of settlers converged on the West Branch around the old Lenape village of Coke-ose at the mouth of Oquaga Creek, known then to the whites as the Cookhouse and today as Deposit. Squire Whitaker and his son-in-law Conrad Edick were both seasoned veterans of the frontier border war. Whitaker had been driven from the Wyoming Valley after surviving the horrific massacre by Butler's Tories and Indians in 1778. He fought in Col. John Hathorn's 4th Regiment of Orange County Militia throughout the war and his brothers fought against Brant's warriors in the battle on the banks of the Delaware at Minisink Ford in '79. After first settling at the confluence of the East and West Branches and having his homestead devastated by the Pumpkin Flood, Whitaker moved his family up the West Branch to the Cookhouse. Conrad Edick was a native of German Flatts, who before rising to corporal in Col. Marinus Willett's Tryon County Militia, fought at Stone Arabia and Johnstown. Conrad worked through the summer of '86 with Jesse Dickerson and his crew before moving down the river to Cookhouse where he found the Whitakers and his future bride living in a shanty built against the uprooted stump of a giant hemlock tree.

In the spring of '87, an army veteran and schoolteacher from Goshen came to the frontier and built a lonely cabin on Oquaga Creek, about five miles west of the Whitakers in the present-day Broome County township of Sanford. William MacClure was a well-educated and pious man who spoke three languages and taught mathematics, surveying, and navigation in Connecticut before moving to New York's Orange County and teaching in schools throughout Orange and Dutchess Counties. Hired by the proprietors of the Fisher and Norton Patent to survey their 15,360 acres in the Oneida/Tuscarora Purchase of 1785, MacClure came to the Susquehanna and Delaware wilderness and built his cabin he christened Castle William. Throughout his tenure as surveyor and land agent for several of the area's patent proprietors, travelers heading into the wilds of the western frontier found shelter and a friendly host at Castle William. William also encouraged prospective settlers to take up homestead lots in the area's many patents and his own 6,700-acre patent along the west side of the now obsolete Indian property line. [29]

The East Branch

Twenty miles down the West Branch from the Cookhouse to the old Lenape village at the confluence of the two upper branches of the Delaware, a few stubborn Indians still lingered on Shehawken's river flats after the war. Known to the Delaware Indians as the *wedding of the waters* of the Pawpachton and the Cooquago branches of the Lenape-wihituck, Shehawken is now home to the village of Hancock. An itinerant Baptist preacher named Ezekiel Sampson and his two sons Isaac and Henry, moved onto the Shehawken flats around 1785 and setup a fish-weir on the East Branch. Richard Jones and his son Benjamin also moved onto the Shehawken flats and built a fish-weir on the West Branch side of the confluence. The Joneses were said to have caught great quantities of eel and trout, while the Sampsons reported catching mostly bass and shad in their East Branch snare. Depositions taken from these two men and a few other early settlers were used by the heirs of Col. John Bradstreet to bolster their claim that the East Branch was the main branch of the Delaware and the West Branch its tributary. Allegations were also made that the waters of The Great Pumpkin Flood of '86 were higher on the East Branch than the West Branch, having risen to twenty-one feet and covering the river flats to a depth of eight to ten feet. Being that the lower East Branch is the recipient of the Beaver Kill and Willowemoc Creek waters, it might indeed be the larger of the two branches at the confluence. But above these tributaries, the East Branch clearly appears narrower and shallower than the West Branch. Regardless of the East Branch proponent's claims, the Hardenburgh lawyers were able to sway the courts to their favor and retain their patent's West Branch border. [30]

As late as 1790, very few people were living on the lower East Branch between Hancock and Rock Eddy, today's Downsville. The East Branch's prewar loyalist settlers had all been compelled to settle in Canada after the war. None of the Middagh brothers returned to their homesteads at the mouth of the Beaver Kill, being that Jacob had been hung alongside Jacobus Roosa and the other brothers had run off to join the loyalist rangers. The lower Beaver Kill from the river to its junction with Willowemoc Creek was never an attractive draw for settlers due to the narrowness of the valley and the scarcity of tillable flats. Shortly after the war, Hanse Ousterhout was employed by the proprietors of Hardenburgh's Great Lot #5 to clear and widen the old Sun Trail from the widow Cole's Lackawack tavern to John Shaver's Pawpacton homestead on the East Branch and the now inundated village of Shavertown. In 1778, Capt. Clark's militia company had used the old Sun Trail to track Ben Shanks' war party back to the East Branch and William's Flatts. Widening the old trail to accommodate wagon traffic encouraged several early settlers to take homestead lots along Ousterhout's Road from the upper Neversink River and over Blue Hill into the valley of Willowemoc Creek. The Stewart brothers, Jehiel, William and Luther, established a substantial settlement at the confluence of the Willowemoc and the Beaver Kill that morphed into the villages of Rockland and Roscoe. [31]

Between the tiny hamlet of Shinhopple and the village of Downsville, Russell, Timothy, and Thomas Gregory settled along the East Branch in an area that came to be known accordingly as Gregorytown. The Gregorys came to the frontier in the late '80s from Dutchess County where they had served throughout the war in Col. Luddington's 7th Regiment of Dutchess County Militia. Two returning rebel families who had lived on the same stretch of river during the contentious days before the war, resettled on their former river clearings and what remained of their old homesteads. The fathers of Daniel Bowker and Abraham Sprague were two of the first pioneers to settle on the East Branch below the Dutch settlements of Paghatakan and Pawpachton. Driven from his homestead in 1778, the renowned frontiersman Silas Bowker spent the rest of the war scouting and gathering information on Indian activities on the East Branch for the Ulster County militia commanders.

After his family was driven from the East Branch with the Bowkers and the Pawpachton rebels, Abel Sprague's son Abraham enlisted in Col. Moses Hazen's 2nd Canadian Regiment of Continental levies at the age of thirteen. He fought for over three years skirmishing with British foraging patrols throughout the Hudson Highlands and northern New Jersey. In 1781, Abraham was given a 60-day furlough to recuperate from wounds received during a failed raid on the Staten Island British garrison. Out on furlough, he learned that his father Abel had recently been killed by a party of Indians while scouting along the East Branch. Now sixteen, Abraham returned to the frontier to find and bury his father's mutilated remains. Obsessed with avenging his father's murder, the boy deserted his regiment and spent the remaining years of the war living alone in the Catskill wilderness waging his own war against the people who had killed his poor father, Abel. For many years after the war, the mere mention of his name summoned fear in the hearts of the Indians, and death to those who ventured too close to his riverfront homestead. [32]

A few miles up the river from the Gregorys, Bowkers and Spragues, another group of veterans were gathering around the broad river flats at Rock Eddy. Daniel Wilson and his sons Isaac and Daniel Jr were returning to their prewar clearings and burnt-out cabins on the brook that came to bear their name. Daniel possessed one of the few slaves brought back into the border region following the war. A mile or two up the East Branch, in the vicinity of today's Huntley Hollow, one of the Long Island refugees who came to the frontier in '85 with Dr. Platt Townsend, was settled on a large tract of Hardenburgh Patent land he had somehow managed to secure. The North family's cousin, William Furman, had appropriated a portion of his cousin Elizabeth's husband Charles W. Stockton's Great Lot #36 land acquisition. His 1,300 acres on the southeastern third of sub-division #66 extended from Bear Spring Mountain's summit to the East Branch. Unlike his cousin's wealthy husband, William was unable to hold on to his land and eventually lost most of it before moving on to Bradford County Pennsylvania's Susquehanna River area.

Within earshot of the Furman homestead, in an area referred to before the war as Verplanksburgh and after it Pepacton, a group of returning settlers were taking advantage of the riverfront clearings left behind by the loyalists and Indians before them. A wealthy Albany merchant and fervent supporter of the Crown, John Burch, had purchased 6,000 acres on the northwest side of the river where he had established one of the largest and most successful prewar farming operations on the Delaware frontier. George Bernhardt (Barnhart) and Jacob Kairn had established similarly successful homesteads on the southeastern side of the river in Samuel Verplank's portion of Hardenburgh Patent's Great Lot #6. Joel and Jacob Austin, two notorious Tories, had also forfeited their properties that laid between today's Coles Clove and the Tremper Kill. The overgrown and abandoned clearings were eagerly snatched up by postwar settlers such as John Shaver and his sons Adam and Jacob who established themselves in the area that became known as Shavertown. [33]

Forced from their troubled valley in '78, the Paghatakan and Pawpacton Whig families spent the war years back with their relatives and friends in the old Dutch neighborhoods of Kingston, Marbletown or Hurley. The men of fighting age were mustered into various frontier companies of Ulster and Dutchess County's militia regiments. At war's end, members of the original Dutch families who settled on the river long before the war were anxious to reclaim their family's old properties before the new wave of Yankee migrants flooded onto their river flats. Of the first four family patriarchs who came to Paghatakan in the early 1760s, only Johannas Van Waggenen returned to his former riverfront homestead. Johannas' thirty-five-year-old son Simeon was just fourteen when his father brought him and his family to the frontier in '63 along with Peter Hendrick and his nine-year-old stepson Frederick Kittle. Both of these young men were now ready to establish their own homesteads in the frontier Paghatakan settlement their fathers had struggled so hard to build.

Petrus Dumond's sons John and Igenus returned to their father's hard-earned settlement where his brother Hermanus had spied for the rebels before being killed by Alexander Harper's Schoharie scouting patrol in '78. Petrus never returned to Paghatakan but twelve of his grandchildren would repopulate the East Branch settlement with Dumonds for generations to come. The spy who got away, John Barrows, returned to the scene of the crime where his friend had been murdered and resettled on his old homestead. Albertus Sluyter and his brother-in-law Peter Burgher had come to the Dutch settlement a few years after the Dumonds and the other three original proprietors. Burgher had been killed by the Indians during the evacuation in '78, but his widow Margaret and their two sons returned to their family homestead with the Sluyters following the war. Two other returning prewar settlers, James Phoenix and Benjamin Ackerly, settled near each other in the now inundated hamlet of Arena on the upper end of today's Pepacton Reservoir. Both were experienced millwrights who built the first grist mills for the community that was soon to flourish around them and the other returning Paghatakans. [34]

Ten years before the Paghatakan pioneers crossed over Pine Hill ridge into the valley of the East Branch, a family of German emigrants established a remote homestead and tavern on Esopus Creek in the Great Shandaken district. Between Mount Wittenburg and Mount Tremper, Jacobus Langjahr built a home for his family six miles from his nearest neighbors in Hurley and Marbletown. As early as the mid-1750s, the Bavarian tavern keeper, whose name was anglicized to Longyear, was catering to the occasional fur traders and long hunters heading into the uninhabited Catskills. Twenty years later, Jacobus Roosa chose Longyear's tavern as a safe rendezvous site for his meeting with Jacob Middagh and the East Branch recruits. Longyear's three sons, Christopher, Andries and Jacob Jr, were persuaded to join Roosa's Rangers and set off with them on their treacherous journey through the Hudson Highlands to New York City and Col. Fanning's loyalist regiment. The youngest Longyear brother, nineteen-year-old Christopher, was fortunate to have broken off from the party and returned home before his two older brothers and the rest of the rangers were captured in the Schunnemunks in '77. After pledging his fidelity to Congress and the rebel cause, Christopher served in various Ulster County militia regiments throughout the war and returned to his father's tavern at war's end. Another returning Shandaken veteran, James Merkle, had fought alongside Andries and Jacob Longyear Jr during the Battle of Fort Clinton and Montgomery, but unlike his friends, he had managed to survive that day's brutal carnage. Even more remarkable, he had survived the four years he spent aboard a British prison ship in New York's East River. Other prewar friends of the Longyear's returned to their Great Shandaken neighborhood after the war. Coonradt Misner, Silvester Van Der Mark, Christian Wynner and Cornelius Furlow might have shared more than a one round of ale and old war stories with their childhood friends at the old Bavarian's Esopus Creek tavern. [35]

Cushetunk

The men who resettled down along the Delaware below Shehawken were drawn there by the steep mountain slopes that descended to the river's edge and the enormous virgin timber that covered them. Their primary livelihoods would derive from the log rafts they lashed together and commandeered down the river to the shipyards and lumber merchants of Easton and Philadelphia. The Mamakating district settlements along the Delaware between today's Callicoon and Skinner's Falls were on a stretch of river known to the Lenape as the Cushetunk. During the war, Capt. Brant, Ben Shanks and Lt. Docksteder's Tories and Indians raided the settlements of the lower border region over and over. Further down river, the Minisink Patent and the Peenpack neighborhoods of the lower Neversink River and Basher Kill were likewise attacked many times by these same war parties.

The Cushetunk was settled twenty years before the Revolution by a group of pioneer families from Connecticut. Two separate companies of Connecticut shareholders were formed in the early 1750s with the intent of challenging William Penn's rights to the vast tract of lands between the Delaware and Allegany Rivers, today's Pennsylvania. The Susquehanna Company and the Delaware Company relied on the old New England Charter of 1620 and Connecticut's Royal Charter of 1630 which legitimize their claims to the land between the two rivers. Connecticut's Royal Charter granted the colony all the lands between the 41st and 42nd latitudes from Narragansett Bay to the western sea, which was of yet a mystery as to how absurdly faraway the western sea really was. Working in collusion with the Delaware Company, agents of the Susquehanna Company claimed to have secured deeds from the Indians for all the lands between the Alleghany and a line twenty miles east of the Susquehanna River. That left the Delaware Company to claim all the lands east of the Susquehanna line which included the Delaware River from Hancock to East Stroudsburg.

Both Connecticut company claims were suspect from the start but that did not stop them from encouraging groups of Connecticut families to head west and colonize the territory they appropriately dubbed, Westmoreland. In the summer of 1755, several families from northeastern Connecticut braved the western wilderness and settled in the Delaware River's Cushetunk region. Within five years there were about thirty Connecticut families living in the Cushetunk settlements with even more settled in the Susquehanna's Wyoming Valley. Seen by both the Pennsylvania Quakers and the local Lenape Indians as trespassing interlopers, these early settlers were subjected to relentless attacks and harassment from the time they arrived until the Revolution and for several years thereafter. [36]

Joseph Skinner's family and his four sons, Daniel, Thomas, Moses, and Joseph Jr were one of the first Connecticut families to settle in the Cushetunk. In the fall of '55, within a few months of being killed by the Indians, Joseph bequeathed each of his four sons a one quarter section of his 100-acre lot on the west side of the Delaware. Twenty-two-year-old son Daniel Skinner began buying lots from shareholders of the Delaware Company and was soon one of Cushetunk's biggest landowners. Life for the Skinners and their Cushetunk neighbors would never be easy. Their settlements and homesteads were constantly under siege throughout the French and Indian War and the Revolution, leaving many to abandon their homes for the relative safety of Goshen and the eastern Wallkill settlements. Daniel spent much of the French War serving in the British navy where he learned the value of the tall pines that grew along the Delaware River slopes. Returning to his riverfront property after the war, Daniel began cutting and rafting eighty-foot-long white pine logs, suitable for masts and spars, down the Delaware River to Philadelphia and the shipyards of His Majesty's Royal Navy. He and his fellow boatswain, Josiah Parks, became legendary raftsmen with old Dan Skinner being anointed the Lord High Admiral of the Delaware River. A bottle of fine wine or whiskey was expected from all rafters who piloted their logs down the river past the Admiral's riverfront homestead. Along with the Skinners, the families of Bezaleel Tyler, William Conklin, Nathan Mitchell, Joseph Thomas, David Young, Joseph Ross, and the infamous Indian slayer Tom Quick returned to the Cushetunk after the Revolution and reestablished their burnt-out homesteads along the bloody Delaware. [37]

Not long after turning eighteenth, Josiah Parks returned to his family in Connecticut after having served on a British frigate throughout the Seven Years' War. The young sailor had distinguished himself as a more than capable deckhand and was promoted to boatswain mate. Performing his duties admirably during the Siege of Havana in 1762, he was again promoted to ship's boatswain in charge of the crew and equipment. Josiah came with his parents to the Susquehanna's Wyoming Valley around 1770 where he remained a few years before marrying and moving onto a 150-acre lot on the west side of the Delaware three miles below Shehawken. When the border war's Indian troubles began, he again moved his family a few miles down the Delaware to a more secure position on Equinunk Island in the middle of the river. Here he tried to hold his ground during the first few years of the war but eventually concluded his growing family would be far safer in the eastern settlements.

Returning to Equinunk Island, Josiah Parks was warned by an Indian friend named Old Abram that British Maj. John Butler was on his way to the Wyoming Valley with his Seneca warriors. Running fifty miles through the wilderness from the Delaware to the Susquehanna to warn his family and friends of the impending attack, Josiah was intercepted by a militia patrol who took him for a Tory spy and imprisoned him before he could reach the settlement. After finally being informed of the captured 'Tory', the incensed commander of the Wyoming militia, Col. Zebulon Butler, released the messenger who was known to him to have been a loyal friend of Congress and the Wyoming settlers. Frustrated by his mistreatment, Josiah promptly returned to his homestead on the Delaware before Old Abram's prophecy came to pass and the Wyoming denizens met their ugly fate. He spent the rest of the Revolution scouting with Ulster County militia patrols and seeing to his family's safety. Upon returning with his family to Equinunk Island after the war, Bo'son Parks joined Lord High Admiral Skinner in his logging enterprise and became another Delaware River raftsmen to be celebrated in song and legend. [38]

Otsego

The border region's upper Susquehanna resettlement was in full swing by the late 1780s. Cherry Valley was beginning to welcome new settlers to the once bustling frontier community. Even a few of the original Scots-Irish families who had come with Rev. Dunlop and suffered the atrocities that happened there in '78, returned to their destroyed homes and haunted memories. Samuel and Jane Campbell were joined soon after their early arrival by Samuel's brothers James and John's large families. Samuel's fellow ranger captain and militia colonel, Samuel Clyde, returned to his prewar homestead and was soon after elected sheriff of Montgomery County. Lady Jane Campbell's brother James Cannon and son Andrew also returned with the Campbells and Clydes. William Dickson, whose wife Elizabeth Campbell Dickson lost her life and long red hair to a scalping knife, returned to Cherry Valley and his old homestead next to the Gaults.

William and Margaret Harper Gault never returned to Cherry Valley. Like so many of the frontier's early settlers, William died a broken and disillusioned man. Having fled to Schenectady after the massacre, the Gaults spent the war years in relative poverty, living off the kindness of others and whatever William could borrow or leverage. William died in Schenectady in 1785 at the age of fifty-two and left his oldest son William Gault III the family's original Lindsley Patent lot #51, the same lot on which his father and sister Elizabeth Dunlop had been hacked to pieces in '78. William's wife Margaret, the sister of the Harper brothers, died two years after her husband in Schenectady at the age of fifty-four. William III and his brother John remained in Cherry Valley throughout their lives while siblings James, Joseph, Matthew, Alexander, and Miriam Gault Church traded the hard rocky dirt of the western Catskills for the fertile lands to the west that were just beginning to open for settlement. [39]

While Mary Harper Moore and her two unmarried daughters spent much of the war in Fort Niagara as guests of the King's Royal Army, James Moore and the two Moore boys spent the war living with the rest of Cherry Valley's refugees in Schenectady. James was nearing sixty when the Moores were finally all reunited in '82 and returned to their old homestead near the Campbells, two years later. John and James Jr were now in their mid-teens and more than ready to take on the responsibilities that lay ahead of them and their family. But the Moore children did not seem at all interested in returning to the scene of the crime and living in the community where so many of their childhood friends and relatives had been slaughtered. Shortly after James Sr died in 1787, his daughters Abigail and Mary married two brothers, David, and Matthew Cully Jr. The Moore sisters moved in with their new husbands on their family's homestead, twenty miles down Cherry Valley Creek and the Susquehanna at today's Portlandville, six miles upriver from Oneonta. The two Moore brothers also left their parents' Cherry Valley homestead and went to work for the Cully family before building their own milling operation about five miles up the river at today's village of Milford, then known as Suffrage. Mary Harper Moore spent the waning years of her life living with her son John in Milford before dying in 1798 at the age of sixty-five.

Matthew Cully Sr and his four sons, David, Matthew Jr, John and Thomas, operated a successful grist mill and sawmill business near the upper end of today's Goodyear Lake. Thomas and Mathew Jr had both served in Col. John Harper's 2nd Tryon County Regiment of Levies, Thomas as a commissioned ensign and Matthew as a private. David and Matthew also served part of the time in Albany County's 8th Regiment of Militia. Isaac Collier and his son Peter came to the same area as early as 1783 and settled three miles down the river from the Cully brother's Portlandville mill site homesteads. The Colliers settled around the mouth of Schenevus Creek where the old Indian village of Tiondadon once sat and where the old frontiersman Joachim Van Volkenburgh settled in the early 1760s. The frontier on which Joachim and his Mohawk wife Maria once lived had been radically altered by war and the passage of twenty years, and now the Cullys and Colliers and a whole new breed of men were about to take over a new frontier. [40]

Further up the river from the Cullys, Moores and Colliers, homesteaders were slowly beginning to settle around the two beautiful lakes that give birth to the Susquehanna River. One large patent, south of the Mohawk River's German Flatts and northwest of Canadarago Lakes, had gone virtually unsettled before the Revolution. David Schuyler's 43,000 acres west of the Lake that was originally called Schuyler Lake, would eventually contain all present-day Richfield and the majority of Exeter township. Another large patent, originally owned by the disgraced loyalist George Croghan, contained 100,000 acres and encompassed the whole of today's townships of Otsego, Burlington and New Lisbon. Schuyler and Croghan were both long gone by the time the first settlers felt safe enough to return to the border region and take residence in the gentle rolling hills of today's upper Otsego County. While only a few isolated squatters lived on Schuyler's Patent before the war, the two sons of an excentric English gentleman returned to the patent in 1783 and resettled on what had been their father's 12,000 acres in the center of the patent.

John Tunnicliff purchased his land and settled on Schuyler's patent in the opening years of the French and Indian War, around 1755. A wealthy and well-bred English gentleman and landowner, Tunnicliff had left his native shores for happier hunting grounds after becoming embroiled in a conflict with a neighboring estate owner over his alleged poaching and other related offences. Having settled his homestead in the forests of colonial New York's border region at a dangerous time, the adventurous Englishman soon found it prudent to abandon his property until the British finished their business with the French. Referred to as The Twelve Thousand, Tunnicliff returned to his property in 1770, and with the help of his sons John Jr, William and Joseph, built an estate that included an impressive hunting lodge and sawmill to accommodate his building projects. Hunting and entertaining guests, in the home he called The Oak Lodge near the present-day hamlet of Exeter Corner, Tunnicliff soon found himself imposed upon by yet another inconvenient war. An Englishman and loyalist at heart, he made a bold decision to stay on his property and swear an oath of neutrality before the Albany magistrates. What might seem to have been a dangerous position to put himself and his family into, he did manage to survive the border war, and the many harrowing encounters he had with both rebel militias and Indian war parties. After the war, his two sons, William and John Jr, settled on a 600-acre tract of land purchased by their father in '74 on the north end of Canadarago Lake in the present vicinity of today's village of Richfield Springs. [41]

The other northern Susquehanna patent had laid idle throughout a long series of litigations that followed George Croghan's fiscal demise. Croghan's Patent was so mired in financial trouble and legal complications that the legitimacy of its ownership was in limbo until early 1786. Even when a sheriff's deed to 40,000 acres of the original 100,000 acres was finally secured by two New Jersey Quakers, the validity of the patent's proprietorship was shaky. William Cooper and his partner Andrew Craig purchased half of the shares of the Burlington Company, whose investors held the securities on the debts and arrears incurred by Croghan and his heirs. With the help of their New York attorney, Alexander Hamilton, Cooper and Craig managed to nullify the remaining shareholders' interest in the property and thus take control of the entire stock. The patent, however, would need to be sold at auction to satisfy Croghan's £3,839 arrears and clear the title for a legitimate deed.

On January 13th, 1786, in a smoke-filled Canajoharie tavern, Montgomery County Sheriff Samuel Clyde held what could only be described as an illegal auction of Croghan's Otsego Patent. Col. Clyde was like so many other retired militia commanders who struggled to make ends meet without a pension or any compensation for their service and sacrifice. He was luckier than most, however, in that he had been appointed to a lucrative public position that offered the financially strapped sheriff an opportunity to benefit from any scheme or shady transaction that came his way. For £35, Sheriff Clyde agreed to conspire with Cooper and Craig and hold an irregular auction although an injunction against it had been secured by Croghan's heirs, the Prévost family and their lawyer Aaron Burr.

Judge William Cooper

Going forward with the help of their compliant sheriff and auctioneer, the two Jersey men were able to outmaneuver and outbid Augustine Prévost Jr's representatives. While the auction was temporarily paused for a short lunchbreak and Prévost's people were absent from the tavern, the unscrupulous Jersey men and their compromised sheriff quickly resumed the auction and closed the sale with an uncontested bid from the only bidders in the room. Securing a sheriff's deed for Croghan's Otsego Patent at a much lower price than the £3,839 needed to clear the patent's title, Cooper and Craig paid just £2,700 plus Clyde's fee for all 40,000 acres. Such were the curious indiscretions of more than a few frontier land acquisitions during the early years of New York's empire building. None of this, however, bothered or mattered to the westward-bound pioneers who hungered for their own little piece of the promised land. [42]

As soon as winter eased and pioneers could start traveling through the wilderness, the new proprietors of the Otsego Patent set up an office on the south end of Otsego Lake and began issuing mortgaged deeds to prospective buyers. To secure their own shaky deed and defend against challenges to its legitimacy, Cooper and Craig hurriedly surveyed their 40,000 acres and began writing mortgages on their homestead lots on exceedingly liberal terms and well below market value. Migrants from all over Connecticut, Vermont, Massachusetts, and eastern New York streamed into the rolling hills between Lake

Otsego and Canadarago in today's township of Otsego. Within six weeks of setting up shop, Cooper and Craig issued fifty-four mortgaged deeds to seventy-four settlers described by Cooper as *'the poorest order of men'*. At one dollar per acre and with no down payment, buyers agreed to pay an annual interest of 7% on the principal sum and pay off the full amount of the loan within ten years. This gave Cooper and Craig a healthy return on their original investment, with around £1,000 in annual interest payments and over £14,000 in principal payments over the next ten years. It also gave the poor New England farmer, devastated by war, a chance to start over and build a future for himself and his children.

Cooper encouraged his settlers to buy as much land as they wanted. The average purchaser took out a mortgage on 450 to 500 acres, far more land than most families could work or ever hope to pay off. By contrast, patent proprietors like the Harpers were offering 100-acre homestead lots, while others were offering lots averaging from 150 to 200 acres at most. About half of Cooper's original buyers were in fact small-time speculators who, rather than stay and start a homestead on their property, returned to New England and sold their holdings at a profit. Samuel Tubbs bought around 1,500 acres and sold off all but 400 acres before building a sawmill on his Oaks Creek property with his profits. Another incentive offered by Cooper to promote purchases of larger acreage was to give a free, 35 X 150-foot, village lot to anyone who bought over 250 acres and paid off their mortgage within ten years. Cooper had an aggressive plan to establish more than just the typical rural agrarian settlement. His dreams of empire included a shining city on a lake that would reflect his vision of a frontier metropolis and testify to his own grandiosity. The charming little lakeside village of Cooperstown on the southern end of Otsego Lake, bears witness to the sheer strength of an untethered ambition and a will to succeed at all costs. [43]

Not everyone was thrilled to see so many of Cooper's Yankee settlers coming into the border region. The Harpers and their patent's Scots-Irish settlers were among those who looked upon Cooper and Craig as illicit usurpers, and their *'poorest order of men'* as feckless interlopers. Harpersfield's families and their Cherry Valley kinsmen had suffered horribly throughout the border war defending their homeland from the Tories and Indians. The two pacifist Quakers from New Jersey had never fired a shot during the war, nor had their families suffered through a half-dozen cold winters in an overcrowded frontier fort. They had done nothing in the eyes of the frontiersmen to free the frontier from tyranny and save the patented lands of the border region from British occupation. The schism between the Harpers and William Cooper, and the Scots-Irish frontiersmen and the Yankee newcomers, would soon develop into a broader political divide that would only get wider over the years. While Cooper was amassing his little fiefdom of tenants around Cooper's Town, nearby Cherry Valley was being pushed aside as the old border frontier gave way to a new age of growth and progress.

Down along the Susquehanna, past the Cullys, Moores and Colliers, prewar settlers were returning to what was left of their once thriving little homesteads and settlements. Many of these returning settlers had buried their farming implements and household accoutrements before abandoning their homes at the start of the war. One of their first orders of business was to dig up their old rusty plows, reaping hooks and rakes and begin the grueling work of reclaiming their pasture's seven years' worth of neglect and reforestation. A few of their log cabins may have survived being torched by the enemy, but most would have needed to rebuild their cabins. They would all have been anxious to plant an early crop that might see them through the first long winter on their homestead. Some of the returning frontiersmen who had fought to secure the border lands were occasionally faced with another challenging situation upon their return. The growing encroachment of squatters and trespassers, who were hurrying to take advantage of any vacant clearing, posed an annoying problem for the legitimate property owners and patent proprietors. Erstwhile settlers who had not forgotten the risks they had taken to establish and hold on to their prewar homesteads were not at all happy with having to evict an unwelcomed and often recalcitrant intruder from their land.

Charlotte Creek and Susquehanna Settlements

Tewald, Joseph, and Benjamin Bartholomew returned to Charlotte Creek after the war and reestablished their father Johan's 1,000-acre estate near today's South Worcester. Six miles to the south, their sisters Elizabeth Harper and Hannah Skinner were busy helping their husbands rebuild their homesteads at The Centre. From Bartholomew Settlement to the confluence of Charlotte Creek and the Susquehanna, several Schoharie families who had shared the privations of life in Schoharie's Middle Fort joined the Bartholomeus. Capt. Lodowick Brickman, Henderick and Bartholomew Hagedorn and the Becker brothers Lodowick and Philip, established their own homesteads downstream from the Bartholomeus on the abandoned and confiscated clearings left behind by Spanish John MacDonell and his Tory clansmen. Today's hamlets of Simpsonville and Fergusonville gradually grew around the homesteads of these former Tryon County militiamen and their neighbors. Further downstream at the confluence, the few settlers who had lived there before the war returned to their old homesteads on the river flats at the old Onondaga village of Adaquatingie, where Oneonta now sits. Capt. John Van Der Werker went to work rebuilding the homestead he first cleared there before the war and proceeded to build one of the first gristmills in the area. He and Capt. Brickman had both served as captains in Col. John Harper's 2nd Tryon County Regiment of Levies during the war.

The point of land between Charlotte Creek and the Susquehanna had been known as The Canoe Place for fifty years before Van Der Werker first settled there in '73. In 1723, thirty-three Schoharie families encamped on the site and built a flotilla of canoes before launching an incredible journey down the Susquehanna to southeastern Pennsylvania. Having been denied legitimate titles to their Schoharie lands and threatened with eviction by New York's Governor Hunter, Johann Conrad Weiser Jr led a group of disenchanted Palatine émigrés on a 300-mile journey to the proverbial promised land. Hoping to find Pennsylvania's Quaker colony more amenable to their ways, Weiser took the long backwoods Susquehanna to avoid detection by colonial authorities. Upon reaching Swatara Creek, south of present-day Harrisburg, Weiser's families hiked nearly fifty miles overland to the Tulpehocken Creek Valley near the present-day Berks County city of Reading. The governor of Penn's colony welcomed the industrious Schoharie refugees whose dorfs and villages gradually grew into what became known as the Pennsylvania Dutch settlements. The point of land where Weiser's followers built their canoes and launched their epic exodus, is now home to Oneonta's Fortin Park. [44]

Just down the river from Van Der Werker's homestead at The Canoe Place, a few more prewar settlers returned to their old overgrown clearings between Adaquatingie and Adiga, today's Otego. Henry Scrambling and his brothers George and David returned to their family's old homestead where their father had been killed by the Indians early in the war and George, David and David's wife had been taken prisoner. Two of the Scrambling brother's sisters also came back to the Susquehanna with their husbands John and Andrew Young. One of Col. Harper's most trusted frontier scouts who had served in his ranger company before being commissioned 2nd lieutenant in the Tryon County Regiment of Levies, returned to his old homestead at the mouth of Otsdawa Creek. Lt. Daniel Ogden had last seen his homestead while descending the river with Gen. Clinton as one of John Harper's volunteer rangers on route to Tioga Point in '79. Another one of Col. Harper's lieutenants, 1st Lt. Isaac Quackenboss, also returned to his former Susquehanna homestead near his company's captain, John Van Der Werker. Van Der Werker's 3rd company was officered by 1st Lt. Quackenboss, 2nd Lt. Ogden and Col. Harpers niece's brother-in-law Ensign Thomas Cully. [45]

A mile or two up Otego Creek, a Quaker by the name of John Sleeper returned to the site of his former homestead tavern on his 200-acre lot near today's West Oneonta. Sleeper's adherence to the Quaker principal of nonviolence and conscientious objection to war required him to take the oath of neutrality. But by '78, his nonpartisanship was not enough to secure his family's safety, so he abandoned his frontier homestead and returned with them to their previous home in Burlington, New Jersey.

Returning to their old homestead, the Sleepers were soon joined by another returning settler who had also abandoned his Otego Creek homestead at the onset of the border war. A few more miles up Otego Creek near the present-day village of Laurens, a renowned frontiersman and Indian scout who had gained a fearsome reputation as an effective hunter of indigenous forest dwellers, returned to his former homestead on Adiga Creek. Joseph Mayall served in Col. Harper's regiment of levies and competed with the likes of Timothy Murphy for the most Indian kills and scalps. [46]

Further down the Susquehanna at the old Indian property line of '68, several of Johnston Settlement's refugee families returned to the ruins of their former home in the spring of 1784. After being driven from their settlement by Capt. Brant in '77, Rev. William Johnston and most of the settlement's families found refuge in the homes of some of their former Cherry Valley neighbors and kinsmen. The Presbyterian clergyman who had preached to the Scots-Irish congregations in New Hampshire and Massachusetts before coming with many of them to the Mohawk and Susquehanna frontiers had many friends in Cherry Valley who graciously welcomed him back behind the pulpit. When Gov. Clinton finally sent Col. Alden's Massachusetts' troopers to Cherry Valley to protect the citizenry, Rev. Johnston served as Fort Alden's chaplain while his son Witter was assigned deputy commissioner for the garrison. A year-and-a-half after surviving their first encounter with Brant's warriors, the Johnstons were once again visited by Brant's warriors in November 1778. This time there was no ultimatum or grace period allowed for them to evacuate their homes.

Because of their ties to the fort, Rev. Johnston's two sons, Witter and Hugh, were inside it when the first onslaught of Seneca warriors reached the outskirts of Cherry Valley. Fourteen-year-old Hugh made a daring decision to leave the fort and run to warn his family who were living nearby in the village. Convincing his father to gather the family and flee into the woods, the Johnstons remained concealed until after the threat had passed and the Indians were gone. The Johnstons were fortunate to have survived the horrific massacre that took so many of their friends and neighbors. Having been driven from their first settlement and again from Cherry Valley, Rev. Johnston spent the final years of the war with friends in Schenectady and around Fort Hunter. Shortly after news reached the Mohawk frontier that the Treaty of Paris had been drafted, he gave his last sermon on the virtues of peace at the age of seventy-three. A year later, Witter and his younger brother Hugh returned to their 525-acre settlement on the Susquehanna without their deceased paterfamilias who had led them there twelve years earlier. They returned with their sixty-year-old mother Nancy and two of their sisters, Anne and her husband Peter Sluyter, and Nancy and her husband Stephen Stiles. The quiet little village of Sidney would be their legacy and the village's Pioneer Cemetery their final resting place. [47]

The Old English District

Within four months of the Fort Stanwix Treaty of 1768, John Butler, Staats Long Morris and Clotworthy Upton secured an Indian deed for an 80,000-acre tract of land along the eastside of the Unadilla River and the new Indian property line. Their tract stretched north along the river through the current townships of Unadilla, Butternuts, Morris, Pittsfield and Edmeston. Within a few years their deeded acreage was divided up into a half-dozen patents with a modest number of settlers on them by the early '70s. Many of these earliest homesteaders took the prime riverfront lots up along the eastern banks of the Unadilla as far up as Edmeston while a few more settled along Butternuts Creek between today's Gilbertsville and Morris. The area became known as The Old English District primarily due to its English proprietors and settlers who held fast to their Anglican heritage when the Revolution finally reached the border region.

In the aftermath of the French and Indian War, the British Empire awarded many of its most distinguished army officers and those who had won the favor of the Crown with land in their recently conquered colonial territory. Writs of Mandamus were issued for anywhere from five to thirty thousand acres to dozens of officers who had won the favor of King George III. The prospective proprietors were still obliged to follow legal protocol and secure the appropriate Indian deeds to the land before a legitimate patent could be granted by the provincial land commissioners. Some of these gentlemen hitched their wagons to men like John Butler who knew how to negotiate with the Indians and could represent their interests with surveyors and land commissioners. Before Butler became major and then lieut. colonel of the New York loyalist regiment, he had been one of Sir William Johnson's deputies in the Northern Department of Indian Affairs. Butler was well versed in the complexities of dealing with Iroquois chiefs and New York's shrewd land commissioners. Teaming up with Morris and Upton, Butler plied his many talents to secure the Oneida lands for himself and his wealthy partners.

Clotworthy Upton was an Anglo-Irish courtier and peer who lived on his family's Castle Upton Estate in Northern Ireland's County Antrim. He was Clerk Comptroller for Augusta, Dowager Princess of Wales, and sat in the Irish House of Lords as the 1st Baron Templetown. After Butler helped secure the Indian deed for the 80,000-acre tract of Unadilla lands, the king's agents awarded a 20,000-acre patent to Upton. Butler and Morris were each granted patents for 30,000 acres of the deeded purchase. Upton died shortly after the Revolution never having laid eyes on his Unadilla patent that was confiscated along with Butler's and all the other loyalist's patents, the Morris' patent being one of only a few exceptions. [48]

Staats Long Morris came from an aristocratic family of colonial New York merchants and gentlemen statesmen who served their king well throughout the Seven Years' War. Morris served with distinction as an aide-de-camp to General William Shirley, commander-in-chief of the British/American forces in North America before serving out the final years of the war in India. Returning to America after the war, he dedicated his time and energy to securing as much land as he could in Canada, New York, and East Florida. When the Revolution interrupted his interests, he chose loyalty to England as the surest route to more land, as the king's patronage had thus far served him well. Like many colonial families, the Morris family had its share of disagreement when it came to politics. Staats' brother Lewis Morris sided with the American cause and was delegated to represent New York in the Provincial and Continental Congress. Staats eventually became a member of England's Parliament. While Lewis Morris was scribing his name beneath John Hancock's on the Declaration of Independence, British guns aboard His Majesty's Ships were leveling the Morris family's estate at Morrisania in lower Westchester County, today's South Bronx. As reparation for their losses and appreciation for having been one of the primary financiers of the American Revolution, Staats Morris's Unadilla patent was exempt from confiscation and awarded to Lewis Morris and the American Morris family.

After the war, Lewis Morris's twenty-seven-year-old son Jacob returned to New York City to begin his life in the world of finance and his family's businesses. As a young gentleman, Jacob Morris had entered the Continental Army at the age of nineteen as an aide-de-camp to General Charles Lee and later served on the staff of Generals Arnold, Sullivan, and Greene. Through his conduct and his familial ties, he eventually received an officer's commission of major and continued serving as such throughout the war. Returning to New York, Jacob was elected to the state legislature as a senator and assemblyman but failed to achieve the success his family had expected of him as a businessman and New York socialite. With his father's Unadilla patent waiting to be developed and turned into a profit, the young major saw an opportunity for a fresh start and an opportunity to establish his reputation as a successful frontier land proprietor. The appearance of men like Jacob Morris on the frontier introduced a political shift that threatened those who felt they had just liberated themselves from the ruling class and hierarchy that had held them down for so long. The tilt of young Jacob's head and squint-eyed look in his miniature

Major Jacob Morris

portrait suggests an aristocratic sense of entitlement that would prove antithetical to the border region's frontier veterans.

In June 1787, thirty-one-year-old Jacob Morris wrote a letter to his older brother Lewis in which he recounts his trip up the Hudson to Albany and on to Canajoharie with four wagon loads of provisions and gear. At Canajoharie, the letter tells of his chance encounter with a wagon caravan of surveyors heading for Otsego Lake and down the Susquehanna River to lay out the boundary line between New York and Pennsylvania. This was presumably Simeon De Witt and Gen. James Clinton's surveying party. Reaching the north end of the Lake, Jacob left his wagons and set off down the river to the Cully homestead where he purchased a couple of bateaux from Thomas Cully for eight gallons of rum. Wishing first to assess his land and find a suitable site to settle on, Thomas led the young proprietor overland to his father's patent on the Unadilla's Butternuts Creek. After assessing his property and surrounding countryside, Jacob headed back towards the Susquehanna by a circuitous route up Butternuts Creek and on through today's New Lisbon and Burlington to the Exeter estate of John Tunnicliff near Canadarago Lake. From Tunnicliff's Oak Lodge he traveled down Oak Creek to the Susquehanna and back down to his bateaux at the Cully's Portlandville homestead.

From the Cullys, the adventurous young aristocrat set off down the river with a couple of hired hands in his loaded bateaux. Upon reaching the mouth of the Unadilla River, he and his crew paddled up to Butternuts Creek and up the creek another eight miles to the upper end of his family's frontier patent. Jacob instructed his workers to cut and clear an opening on which to build a makeshift hut for himself and his men before Morris's carpenter, Tobias Houk, and a crew of six slaves, arrived to make better accommodations. By the spring of '89, Jacob's carpenter and slaves had built a small sawmill and a 16' X 24' framed house, one of the first in the area. With his new house ready for occupancy, Jacob sent for his wife Mary and their five young children, ages 1-9, to join him on his 1,000-acre estate. Fifteen years later, he would replace his first house with a grander and more opulent manor house that would become known to the locals as Morris Mansion. The mansion still stands today a few miles south of the village of Morris, at the intersection of State Rd. 51 and Dimock Hollow Rd. [49]

Abijah Gilbert, a well-bred and wealthy Englishman, arrived in Philadelphia in 1785 and met Jacob Morris's father and uncle who promptly sold him, sight unseen, 1,000 acres on the family's frontier patent. Gilbert's property was only two or three miles down the Butternuts from Morris Mansion, between today's village of Morris and Gilbertsville. After spending the winter in Philadelphia, Gilbert traveled to his frontier property in the spring of '86 along the same path Jacob took a year later. Curiously, Major Morris made no mention of Gilbert's passage in his letter to his brother. The omission might have been an attempt to further the boastful claim he made as to having been the first white man to navigate Butternuts Creek, which he must have known was absurd.

Three of the first white settlers of the Unadilla's Old English District had settled further up Butternuts Creek on John Butler's patent as early as 1770. Ironically, none of them were Englishmen but Frenchmen who went by the names of Rénouard, De Villar and Franchot. In 1773, Benjamin Lull and his sons Nathan and Joseph had settled on Butternuts Creek a few miles north of where Morris and Gilbert settled nearly fifteen years later. The Lulls returned to their old prewar clearings at about the same time as the families of Jonathan Moore, Ebenezer Knapp, and Increase Thurston. Most of the twenty or so families who were said to have lived in the Old English District before the war, never returned to their old homesteads. These were the Tory families who were forced to settle along the Niagara River in British occupied Upper Canada. [50]

Three other Writs of Mandamus for 5,000 acres each were awarded to three notable Englishmen who had served their king faithfully throughout the French and Indian War. Dr. Peter Middleton had served as the provincial British army's surgeon general during the Crown Point expedition in 1755 and been with Sir William Johnson at the Battle of Lake George. The Edmeston brothers, Capt. William and Lieut. Robert, both served throughout the war in the King's 48th Regiment of Foot and each had received their 5,000 acres for meritorious conduct. Dr. Middleton's acreage was between the Butler, Morris and Upton patents along a seven-mile stretch of the Unadilla River across from today's South New Berlin. The Edmeston's patents were further up the Unadilla near the forks of the two upper branches. The brothers were the only patent grantees of the Old English District to have lived on their land before the Revolution, albeit briefly. By 1775 they had managed to influence about twenty English families and indentured servants to settle on their frontier patent. Having to spend much of their time away, they employed one of the sergeants from their regiment to oversee their settlements between today's Mount Edmeston and the village of Edmeston on Wharton Creek.

Sergeant Percifer Carr was employed by the Edmestons to function as land agent and caretaker for their patent on the Unadilla River's Indian property line. Carr would soon find himself in the unenviable position of maintaining an isolated homestead on the border between two fighting factions while maintaining a covert alliance to one side over the other. He remained on the border throughout the early years of the war, aiding Brant's warriors on their raiding forays into the eastern settlements. Brant periodically garrisoned his warriors on the Carr farm, and it was there that Lt. Helmer and his rebel scouting party ran into his warriors as they were preparing to launch their raid on German Flatts in 1778. Carr might just as easily have welcomed the rebels to his home had he not been hosting the Indian war party at the time. The ambiguous alliances of those who tried to remain in the border region during the war were often misconstrued by combatants from both sides. In the later years of the war, a roving band of warriors took Carr for a rebel sympathizer and burnt his home to the ground before dragging him and his wife off into captivity. The Carrs spent the final years of the war living with an Indian family before being released and returning to Mount Edmeston in 1783. For all his sacrifice and service to the Edmestons, Percifer was summarily sacked by the heirs of William Edmeston upon the proprietor's death in 1804. Through the final years of their turbulent lives, the tired old frontiersman and his faithful wife were reduced to living off the kindness of their frontier neighbors, some but not all of whom had forgotten their Tory ties. [51]

The resettlement of the Old English District and all of New York's former border region continued at a steady pace throughout the latter half of the 1780s. But as the '90s progressed, settlement of the old frontier began accelerating significantly and the character of the landscape began transforming from wilderness to pastures and villages. New homesteaders heard stories of the bad old days on the frontier but never really comprehended the magnitude of the horrors that had gone on there during the border war. In fact, it was no longer a border region at all and soon would not even be a frontier. Civilization was pushing ever westward, and many of the frontiersmen were anxious to stay one step ahead of it. Men like the Harpers and their Scots-Irish kinsmen, who had liberated the frontier, were now faced with a whole new breed of men who knew nothing of their trials or sacrifices. Men like Jacob Morris and William Cooper were not just interested in colonizing and profiting from their own patents, they were also intent on imposing a political system that would maintain the status-quo of a societal order much like the English model. This of course was not what the Harpers had thought they had fought for, and they were not about to stand idly by while these neophytes transformed their homeland into another colonial-style hegemony. Two ideas as to how to run this new country and fledgling government were about to be tested in the patented lands of New York's former frontier wilderness.

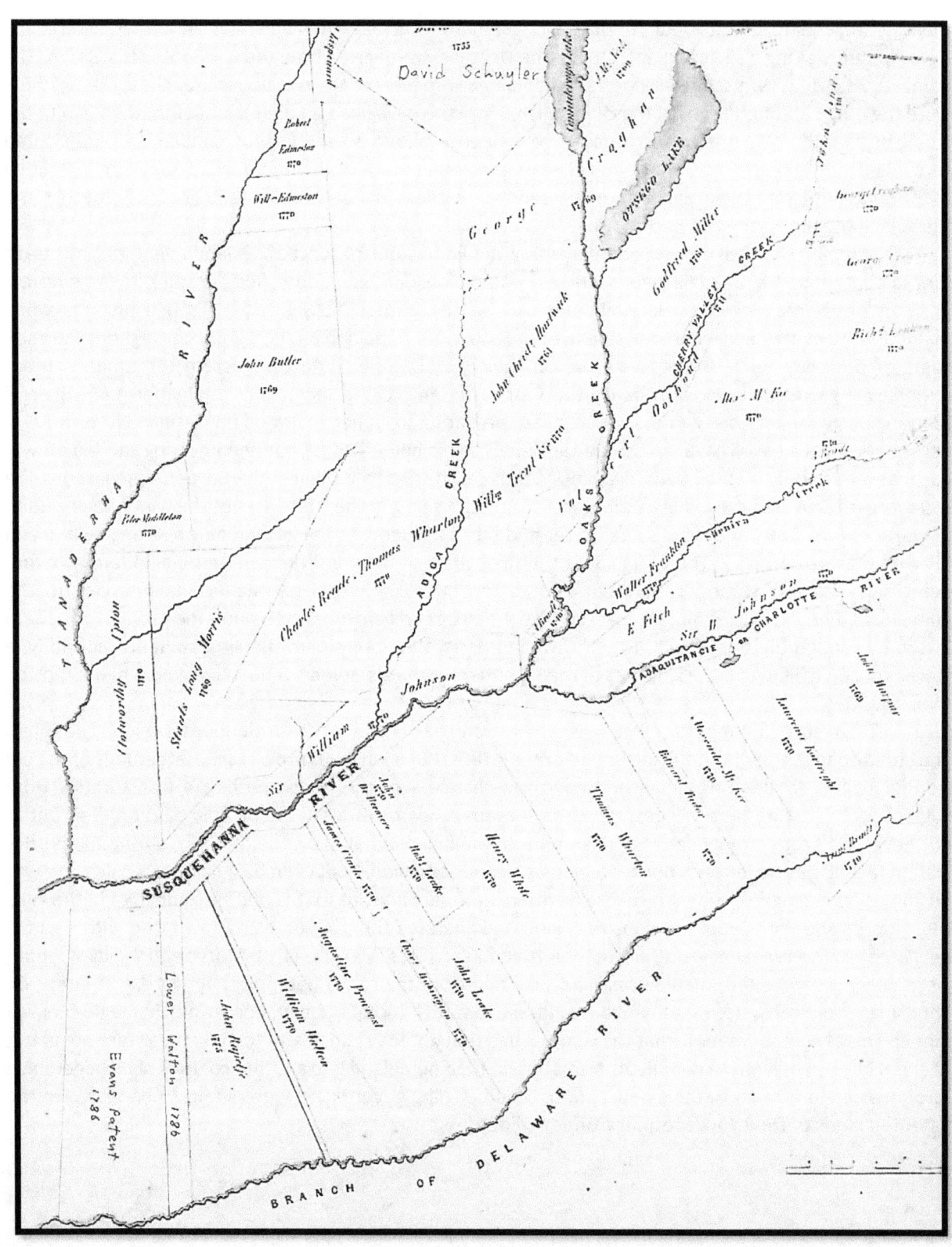

Portion of Simeon De Witt's '1790 Map of the Headwaters of the Rivers Susquehanna & Delaware'. Most of the Patent Proprietors Denoted on the Map were the Original Loyalist Owners who Forfeited their Property to the Committees of Sequestration. 52

7
Empire
1787-1797
"We have no Claim on your land, its just extent will ever remain secure to you"

At the close of the Revolution and New York's border war, the Harpers were ready to return to their Harpersfield patent and reestablish their homesteads at The Centre. Col. Harper was also ready to return to his preoccupation with securing signatures on deeds for more of the Iroquois lands. The old Indian property line of 1768 was now obsolete and the Iroquois lands west of it were now open to those with the ambition, means and skills to negotiate for it. Col. Harper was the type of man who could not stay idle for long or let opportunities slip from his grasp. But since the Harper family's astonishing purchase of 260,000 acres from the Oneidas in '68, the game had changed considerably. No longer was New York a British colony with a superintendent of Indian affairs and a king whose patronage could easily be swayed. Sir William Johnson died in 1774 and with him went the goodwill and favor the Harpers depended upon to further their dream of empire. Col. Harper's carefully groomed friendships with the Oneida and their chieftains had also cooled since his early days as an interpreter and cultural mediator between them and the white missionaries. Although his respect for the Iroquois ethos and hunter-warrior culture had only strengthened during the seven years spent alongside his Oneida scouts, their reciprocal sentiments towards him and their former allies had waned considerably by war's end. Having supported Congress and fought alongside the Americans, the Oneida felt they had earned the right to retain all their territory after the war. Unfortunately, they and the rest of the Iroquois nations were about to learn a hard truth about white people.

From 1783 to '87, the new American republic struggled to fill the vacuum left behind by a Revolution that turned the world on its head. Congress was consumed with the heavy burden of resolving their accrued war debts while dealing with the challenges of convincing thirteen formerly independent colonies to accept the concept of a centralized federal government. Political divisiveness was just beginning to rear its ugly head and in no state were political divisions more prevalent than in New York. The Federalist's determination to create a strong federal government that would oversee individual states faced its most zealous opposition from the state that had suffered more than most during the recent war. The Scots-Irish frontiersmen who had just freed their homeland from British oppression were to be some of the most ardent advocates of Anti-Federalism.

The Harpers and their kinsmen were in league with a governor who had fought with them through a brutal border war while enduring the same petty-mindeness of those who would contest their Irish heritage. Governor George Clinton was a committed Anti-Federalist and a thorn in the side of all who opposed him. The showdown over ratification of the United States Constitution was about to pit Gov. Clinton and New York's frontier representatives against Congress and most of the other states. In July 1788, Assemblyman William Harper, and the Montgomery County delegation to the New York State Ratification Convention in Poughkeepsie, cast their dissenting votes against ratification of the Constitution. They were joined by nearly all of the delegates from Albany, Ulster, and Columbia Counties. Albeit one of the last, New York finally did pass a resolution to ratify the Constitution, but not with the support of the frontier counties. The frontiersmen and their governor were in no hurry to submit or relinquish control of their hard-earned territory to another distant and overbearing sovereignty. Clinton would have preferred for New York to have remained an autonomous, self-governing state and over the next couple of years would do all within his power to try to make it so. The Harpers had lost the support of their prewar patron Sir

William but now had a new benefactor, who like themselves, was set on expanding his realm and taking advantage of a vanquished people. [1]

Fort Schuyler Treaty

Along with all of Congress's headaches, peace with the hostile Iroquois nations was paramount at the conclusion of the Revolutionary War. The Paris Peace Treaty of 1783 failed to even mention the issue of how to deal with the Iroquois from both British and American perspectives. The Mohawk, Seneca, Cayuga, and Onondaga were still technically at war with America, and Congress was anxious to quiet the frontier. In the spring of 1784, preparations for a treaty conference with the four hostile nations began with the authorization of three commissioners from Virginia, Pennsylvania, and Connecticut. The council fire was called, '...*in order to accommodate the Differences which have unhappily arisen between You and Us, in the Course of the late War between Great Britain and America...*'. New York's representation in Congress's treaty conference was conspicuously absent, a slight the governor would cleverly turn to his and the state's advantage.

Governor Clinton and New York's Council of Appointments coordinated their own peace treaty conference by appointing the governor and three commissioners to negotiate with the four hostile nations. Clinton was also anxious to begin negotiations with the two former allied nations, the Oneida and Tuscarora. With an expansionist agenda foremost on his mind, the western lands of the Iroquois beyond the old property line of '68 were now potentially within New York's domain. The race was on to secure as much of the Iroquois territory before Congress, or another state claimed the territory for themselves. Like Connecticut, Massachusetts was stubbornly holding on to their old Royal Colonial Charter that granted them all the lands between their north and south boundary lines, the 42nd and 43rd parallels, all the way to the western sea. New York was of course in the way of the Bay State's ambitions, as were the Iroquois and the private investors competing for their own piece of the prized lands. Clinton feared the indebted federal government could be easily pressured into assisting the New Englanders in their bid for western expansion. He needed to move fast before Congress could assert their authority over the Iroquois lands he felt his state was entitled to. It was of utmost urgency to get to the Iroquois before they could take control of the situation and force the Iroquois to concede their lands to Massachusetts. Procurement and resale of cheap Indian lands to prospective settlers was an attractive way to paydown war debts and secure future sources of revenue for cash-strapped states. [2]

In early April, Governor Clinton sent a message to Joseph Brant and all the principal chieftains of the four hostile nations encamped around Fort Niagara. He proposed they meet with him and the New York Commissioners for a treaty council at Fort Herkimer as soon as they could rally their people and make the journey to German Flatts. A delegation of Oneida and Tuscarora leaders were also invited to attend the council fire. Clinton's objective was to lay the groundwork for peace with Brant's Iroquois while surreptitiously beginning negotiations with the friendly Oneida for their Susquehanna and Chenango River lands. It would be near the end of June before the governor received a response from Brant who insisted the council fire be held thirty miles closer to Niagara at Fort Stanwix, now referred to by the Americans as Fort Schuyler. The ever calculating and cunning Capt. Brant also asserted that a peace treaty between Congress and the four nations be signed and ratified first before any negotiations for land concessions with New York or Massachusetts could proceed. This was not exactly what the governor had in mind, but he remained confident that as soon as Congress came and went, he could resume his clandestine business. Messages were exchanged back and forth throughout the summer and finally in early September the first of over six hundred Iroquois chiefs and warriors began arriving at Fort Schuyler.

Clinton cleverly arranged for his council fire to precede Congress' treaty conference that was scheduled to start in late September. The governor's primary attention was focused on addressing the concerns of the Oneida and Tuscarora delegation who outnumbered the representatives of Brant's four hostile nations by twenty to one. As was customary for any council fire between whites and Indians, Clinton arranged for four bateaux filled with £550 worth of sundry provisions to be delivered to the fort for the ceremonial festivities. Thirty barrels of pork and beef were transported up the Mohawk along with 800 lbs. of tobacco, five hundred gallons of rum and numerous casks of gin, brandy, and madeira. Keeping hungry and thirsty warriors in a festive mood was a time-honored method for avoiding trouble or anything that might threaten the success of a treaty council fire. The governor and his commissioners thought it best not to push too hard for land purchases or concessions at this first council fire, as that would all come later. But as was discovered in the opening palaver of speeches and remarks, an attempt to purchase land from the Oneida had already been quietly initiated by a brazen frontier adventurer and his associates. [3]

New York Governor George Clinton

New York's council fire began on September 4th, 1784, with Governor Clinton addressing the allied nations of the Oneida and Tuscarora by assuring them they had no reason to worry about their lands being taken from them, '...*We have no Claim on your lands; its just extent will ever remain secure to you...*'. Clinton then proposed they first define the boundaries of the Oneida and Tuscarora lands to prevent designing men and intrusive settlers from trying to purchase or settle on their property. The governor and the chiefs were both aware of the meddling speculators maneuvering for tracts of Oneida lands in anticipation of the peace talks and treaty agreements. Clinton assured the Oneidas that any individual, or groups of individuals, who tried to convince them into parting with any of their lands were in violation of the state's constitution and its laws concerning such matters. The Oneida spokesman expressed his thanks to the governor for his proclamation, then continued to inform him that, '... *a certain Man called Thaougweanagen,* [Thaonhwentsawá:kon] *alias Colonel John Harper, has made Proposals to purchase Lands from Us South of the Unadilla. We replied it was contrary to the Minds of our brethren the State of New York, and he replied they knew it and have sent me for the Purpose, & he gave Us Fifty Dollars as an earnest to the Agreement...*'.

In both Kanien'kéha (Mohawk language) and Oneniote'á:ka (Oneida language), Col. Harper's Iroquois name, Thaonhwentsawá:kon, translates literally to *"he is holding the land/earth."* The name seems quite fitting considering the enormous tract of land he purchased from the Onaquaga Oneida in '68 and the circumstances in which he now found himself. Nineteenth century historians purported that Harper was adopted and given his Iroquois name by either the Mohawk or more likely the Oneida people. Sir William had been adopted by the Mohawk and given the name Warraghiyagey, *"he who undertakes great things/does much business."* It seems more likely that Col. Harper was not adopted but awarded an honorary name due to his extensive involvement in land dealings with the Indians. It was a practice of the time for Iroquois nations to simply give non-native men involved in business or political matters with them an onkwehonwehnéha, or honorary name.

Just three months before the Fort Schuyler conference, Col. Harper met with a few Oneida chiefs and their impoverished followers at the Oneida Castle of Kanonwalohale (tkana'alóhale'). The once proud Oneida village was sacked by Brant in 1780 and now lay in ruins with only a few dozen refugee families living there in abject poverty, most of whom were said to have been, '...*drunk and stinking of rum...*'. The colonel was well known and trusted by the Oneida warriors, many of whom had served with him as scouts in his ranger company and had been with him on the Sullivan/Clinton Expedition in '79. Confident in his ability to gain the trust of any Chief he might encounter at Kanonwalohale, he came fully prepared for a council fire negotiation by bringing along the one ineluctable diversion every young warrior craved. Plenty of rum was made available to wash down the roasted ox that guaranteed a festive night of feasting, drinking, ceremonial dancing, and boisterous speeches. The former comrades-in-arms toasted all night long to their old victories and told war stories until dawn when it was discovered that one of the Oneida revelers was dead and *Thaonhwentsawá:kon* was in possession of a deed for 92,000 acres of Oneida lands. The deed was for a prime piece of frontier real estate extending twenty-five miles down the Susquehanna, two miles from the western banks and four miles from the eastern side of the river. It ran from the old Indian property line of '68 to just below the ruins of the old Oneida village of Onaquaga, near today's Windsor. *4*

The Fort Schuyler council fire concluded on amiable terms between New York's commissioners and the Oneida and Tuscarora. Clinton left them with the proclamation, '...*We advise You not to make any Bargain or Agreement for the Sale of any of your Lands, unless those who want to buy do previously obtain and shew You a License from the Government of this State properly authenticated...*'. No actual deals were made for any of their lands, but Clinton had achieved his major goal of convincing the Oneidas that the State of New York and not Congress was who they should deal with for any future land sales. The governor further assured the Oneida that Col. Harper's deed was fraudulent, '...*Brothers ! What this Man has told You is not true. He has done this without our Knowledge and We have not sent him...*'. The governor and his commissioners covered the council fire and left for Albany on the 11th of September. Although they had garnered the trust of the Oneida and Tuscarora, the four hostile nations led by Joseph Brant had refused any substantive concessions to New York and vociferously declared their preference for dealing exclusively with the congressional delegation. *5*

Congress' commissioners arrived at Fort Schuyler on the 3rd of October, three weeks after Clinton and the New York delegation's departure. Having left two of the state's agents behind with six barrels and seventy-six kegs of rum and instructions to keep the Iroquois inebriated, Clinton hoped to frustrate Congress's attempt to convince the Oneida to sell their lands only to them and not to New York. Besides the acquisition of Iroquois lands, Congress had the responsibility of ending the Revolution and signing a peace treaty with the four hostile nations who were still technically at war with America. Other than finding many of the warriors intoxicated, Congress had an unexpected advantage upon their arrival. The spokesman for the four hostile nation's, Joseph Brant, had been called away on other business shortly after New York concluded their convention. The Seneca's Cornplanter and Mohawk's Capt. Aaron Hill assumed Brant's position as lead spokesman and proved to be far less capable of defending their nation's interests than the dynamic Capt. Brant.

The commissioners employed a heavy-handed approach to their negotiations with the four vanquished Iroquois nations and insisted that they alone had the authority to do business with the Iroquois. The two companies of armed militiamen that had accompanied their delegation to Fort Schuyler were posted around the fort as an intimidating reminder that the Iroquois were now a subdued people. One of the indiscreet commissioners reminded them that they were a defeated and reduced people, '...*They are Animals that must be subdued and kept in awe...*'. Pressed into agreeing to the treaty terms, twelve Mohawk, Seneca, Cayuga, Onondaga, Oneida, and Tuscarora chieftains signed the Fort Schuyler peace treaty on October 22nd, 1784, thus effectively ending New York's eight-year-long border war.

The Fort Schuyler treaty had just four simple articles. First, the four hostile nations were to return all the prisoners they had captured and held during the war. Second, the Oneida and Tuscarora were secured in the possession of all the lands on which they were settled. Third, the hostile nations were forced to concede to the United States their vast lands west of Pennsylvania and north of the Ohio River. And fourth, the remaining food and provisions that had been provided for the convention be handed out to the departing Indians, the majority of which was given to the two former allied nations. Upon hearing the details of the treaty concessions, Brant and the western nations were understandably infuriated. The Six Nation's promptly disavowed the treaty, claiming it was unjust and irregular, but Congress would ignore their protestations and continue to insist the treaty was valid and forever binding. [6]

Fort Herkimer Treaty

In the spring of '85, another act was passed by New York's Legislature, '...*to facilitate the Settlement of the Waste and Unappropriated Lands within the State...*'. Preparations were immediately set into motion by Gov. Clinton for a second council fire, this time to be held at German Flatts' Fort Herkimer and only with delegations from the Oneida and Tuscarora Nations. The commissioners of Indian affairs drafted a letter and sent it to the Indians inviting them to a second council fire. The letter bluntly rebuked Col. Harper's illegal purchase of their Susquehanna River lands and declared that his deed had been denounced by the legislature. It also declared that a new law had been passed giving the governor and his commissioners sole authority over Iroquois land purchases and prohibited all others states and individuals from purchasing any of their lands. The pretext for this second council fire was premised on the notion that the governor would protect the Oneida from men like Harper and other unscrupulous individuals and states who might try to swindle them out of their lands. While Clinton, with the help of the legislature, was portraying himself as the great white father and protector of his forest children, the Harper brothers were moving fast to stay one step ahead of events.

Immediately following the first Fort Schuyler treaty conference and before the legislature had time to denounce his deed, Col. Harper had begun an aggressive campaign to authenticate his 92,000-acre Susquehanna River purchase. In late December, two months after Congress and Clinton covered their council fires, Col. Harper submitted a petition to the legislature signed by himself and 150 other associates requesting validation of a title to the Susquehanna lands and pledged its immediate settlement upon confirmation. An addendum was also submitted in support of Harper's petition with the signatures of six allegedly sober Oneida chieftains; Oneyanha (Peter the Quartermaster), Thaghtaghgwesele (Tall William), Aksiaktatye (Capt. Jacob Reed), Cornelius Ogeanyota, William Kayentaronghquah and Cornelius Statshete. The state assembly, in which the colonel's brother William Harper was a member, accepted the petition and initially approved the Susquehanna deed under certain conditions. But by early April, the state senate had rejected the assembly's motion and revoked Harper's deed and petition just days before the commissioners of Indian affairs sent their letter to the Oneida. Their carefully crafted letter that rebuked Harper's deed, ironically put the onus for having dealt with him squarely on their shoulders. The letter went on to tactfully suggest they might make things right by accepting the state's offer to purchase the same piece of property.

On the 23rd of June 1785, the Fort Herkimer council fire was lit and the proceedings between the Oneida and Tuscarora chieftains and Governor Clinton commenced. Col. Harper and his brother William were both in attendance having been invited by the governor. Their presence might have been part of a calculated ploy to demonstrate to the Indians the governor's benevolent intentions to protect them and their lands from men like the Harpers. Admonished at Fort Schuyler for his unscrupulous dealings, one might have thought the colonel would not have chosen to show his face at the council fire. But it has been suggested that Harper's brazen attempt to purchase the Susquehanna lands and continue pressing for his deed's validation was encouraged by Clinton as part of a plan to evaluate the Oneidas disposition and propensity to sell. Col. Harper was very possibly just a shill in Gov. Clinton's broader scheme in which he would swoop in and rescue the Indians from the dastardly villain. [7]

Not mentioning the Harpers by name, Governor Clinton framed his opening speech and strategy by referring to the attempts made, '... *by some White People to purchase Lands from You, South of the Unadilla, whereby much Uneasiness has arisen among You...*'. The calculating governor then offered the Oneida an opportunity to heal the animosity that had arisen between them and some white people by accepting the state's generous offer for their lands. Clinton, however, had his eye on a much larger tract of Oneida land than Harper's 92,000 acres. In a private meeting with one of their leading chief and spokesman, Good Peter Akwirondongwas, Clinton laid out the tract of land he and his commissioners were interested in purchasing, '...*beginning at the Mouth of the Unadilla, following up that Stream 20 Miles; then across to the Chenango River, following that Stream to the Junction of the Susquehanna River, and thence to the Place of Beginning...*'. Although it did not actually specify the southern boundary line of the proposed tract, it was later interpreted to have meant to follow the Susquehanna west from the Chenango River to the mouth of Owego Creek at today's village of Owego. The line would then run along the old property line of '68 southeast to a point on the Delaware River six miles below Hancock, then back up the river along the old property line to the place of beginning at the mouth of the Unadilla River at Sidney. As was all too often the case in land negotiations between whites and Indians, boundary definitions were purposely left vague to accommodate a later interpretation and expansion to the white's advantage. But this time, when the boundary line between New York and Pennsylvania was finally surveyed and ratified in 1787, the southern boundary of Clinton's Oneida/Tuscarora Purchase was reduced to the Pennsylvania state line. [8]

Speaking for the Oneidas after being taken aback by Clinton's enormously enlarged tract, Good Peter politely declined his proposal by proclaiming they could not part with so much of their hunting land. The Oneida chieftain then went on the offensive by reminding the governor of all the Oneida lands east of the old property line that had never been fully paid for. This included the Harper's original 260,000-acre purchase in 1768 and Col. Bradstreet's 85,000 acres. Furthermore, Good Peter went on to inform the governor that Col. Harper had already begun selling lots and encouraging settlement on his refuted Susquehanna property. And again, the Oneida spokesman implied that the incorrigible Thaonhwentsawá:kon had not even paid for his Susquehanna deed by requesting that he point out the person or persons to whom he had given any money to. Up to that point in the talks, the contentious dialog between Clinton and Good Peter had focused primarily on Col. Harper's misgivings and seemed to have come to an impasse. It appeared that nothing would come of the Fort Herkimer council fire.

The night between the fourth and fifth days of the conference marked an abrupt shift in the Oneida's position. The tribal mothers had been consulted and their voices heard. By their tradition, Iroquois chiefs and sachems were required to heed the council of their women on all things pertaining to tribal matters. The abject poverty that blanketed the land of the Haudenosaunee compelled the more pragmatic women of the Oneida Nation to force their men to accept the white man's money and gifts for their lands. On the morning of the 27th, Good Peter was replaced as spokesman for the Oneida by Peter the Quartermaster and Grasshopper, Cornelious Ojistalak. The new spokesmen voiced a more conciliatory tone and indicated they were ready to make a deal. After compromising as to Clinton's proposed northern boundary line from twenty miles up the Unadilla River to just ten, an agreement was struck for a tract of 460,000 acres of Oneida lands that predictably included all of Harper's fraudulent Susquehanna purchase, besting his acreage by five times. The state paid for what was known thereafter as Clinton's Oneida/Tuscarora Purchase, a one-time payment of $11,500 and all the remaining gifts, provisions and rum that had been brought to the council fire. It had not yet been a full year since Clinton's Fort Schuyler promise that their lands, '...*just extent will ever remain secure to you...*'. [9]

Assemblyman William Harper attended the entire Fort Herkimer conference while his brother John left the council fire after the first few days. The colonel had heard enough of the allegations and slights cast upon his reputation by both the governor and the Oneida chieftains. Although publicly reprimanded for his illicit activities, the governor would have been indebted to the man whose pilot expedition to Kanonwalohale had exposed the Oneida's dire situation and their wavering reluctance to sell land to the whites. Favors were sometimes worth more than land. Less than four months after the Oneida/Tuscarora Purchase, John Harper and Matthew Adgate filed an application for a warrant of survey of four townships along the same stretch of the Susquehanna River the colonels disavowed deed had encompassed. Acting as an agent for a prospective patent proprietor could be almost as lucrative as owning a patent. Those practiced in the business of surveying, advertising, and managing settlement of a patent were in short supply and high demand. Investors and speculators who were lining up to purchase large tracts of land would need men like John Harper to manage their property. Knowing the lay of the land as he did and knowing how to entice settlers to frontier homestead lots, Col. Harper would have been a highly sought-after man by the new and inexperienced frontier proprietors. Harper's continued participation in the Oneida lands had been undoubtedly afforded him by the patronage of a grateful governor. [10]

The Oneida/Tuscarora Purchase was surveyed into six sections of 75,000 acres each. Fayette, Greene, and Clinton were eventually combined into the Town of Jericho, while Warren, Chenango and Randolph became the Town of Chenango in what was originally the County of Tioga. Today, the old Town of Jericho comprises Chenango County's Guilford, Bainbridge, Afton, Coventry, most of Oxford, and half of Greene. The old Town of Chenango now includes Broome County's townships of Stanford, Windsor, Colesville, Fenton, Kirkland, and Conklin.

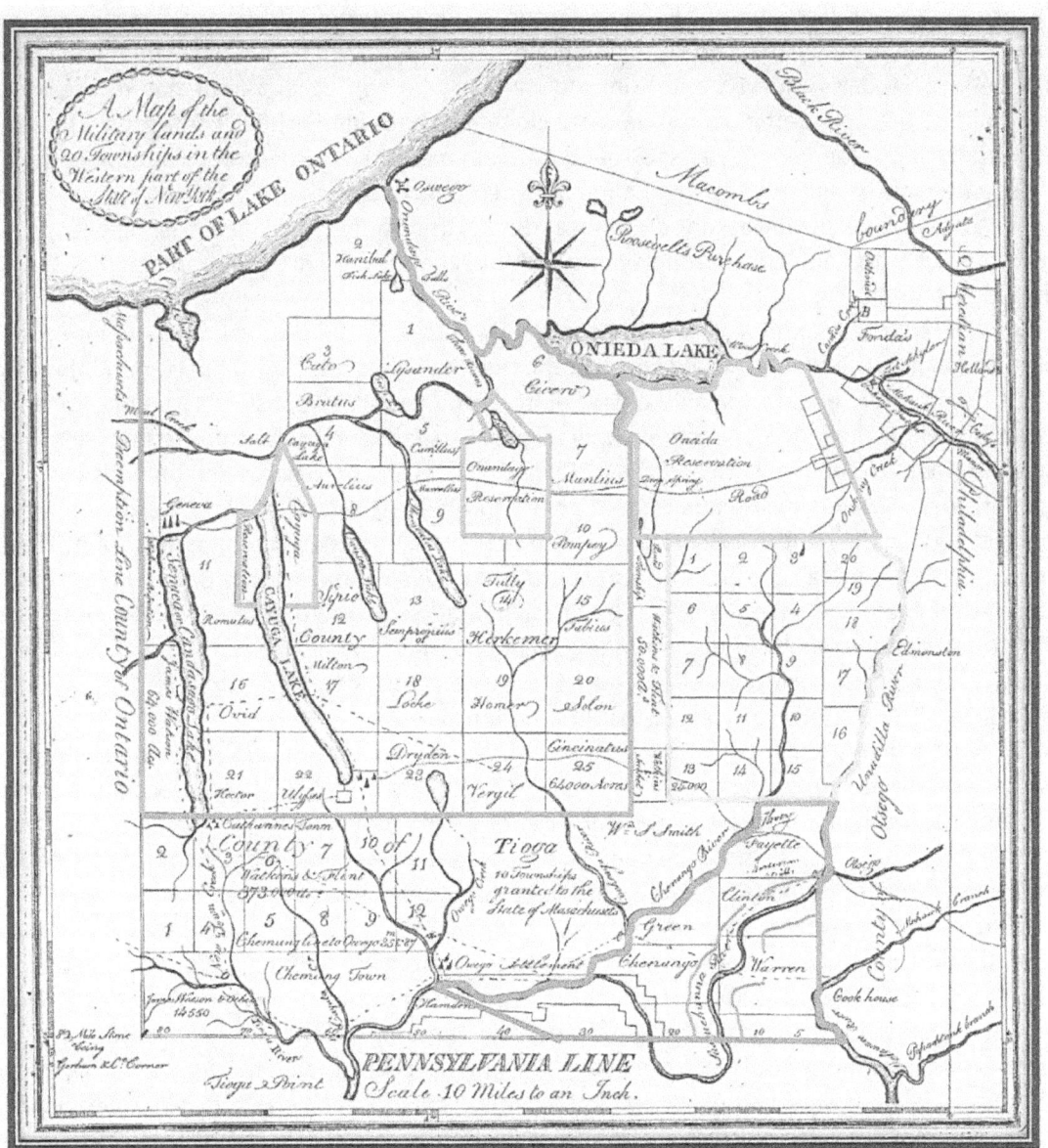

Red - Oneida/Tuscarora Purchase & Harper's Susquehanna land; Yellow - Twenty Townships; Blue - Military Tract; Green - Iroquois Reservations

Massachusetts Preemption Line

Within two years of the Herkimer conference and the Oneida/Tuscarora Purchase, the state of New York had sold nearly 350,000 of their 460,000 acres to private investors and speculators. The land they paid about two-and-a-half cents an acre for was resold for about thirty-six cents an acre. After deducting the purchase price and cost of surveying, the state netted well over $100,000, a fair amount of money for the times. The parcels of most interest to the earliest investors were down along the Susquehanna in the Clinton and Warren townships of what would have been Col. Harpers riverfront property. Many of the smaller investors would buy a square mile section of 640 acres and turn a quick profit by subdividing their acreage into five or six homestead lots. Larger tracts of tens of thousands of acres were bought up by some of the state's leading military and political figures. Included among these large frontier proprietors were the governor's brother James Clinton and the First Chief Justice of the United States Supreme Court and future Governor John Jay. Jacob Morris' uncle Robert Morris of Morrisania and Walter Livingston of the Hardenburgh Patent land baron family were a few of the more notable proprietors of large tracts. Robert Harpur, a well-educated Irish gentleman who rose to prominence in New York City as an educator and politician, bought a large tract of Susquehanna riverfront property between today's Nineveh and Windsor. Harpur, who had no apparent ties to the Scots-Irish Harpers, founded the small settlement of Harpursville that has oftentimes been confused with the Harper family's Harpersfield settlement. It was said that by the summer of 1786, there were but five or six families of white squatters living along the Susquehanna between today's Sidney and Windsor. But as soon as the first proprietors and their agents began surveying and advertising homestead lots on lenient terms, settlers began flooding over the old Indian property line and into the former ancestral homeland of the Oneida and Tuscarora Nations. [12]

New York had a multitude of problems to deal with during the postwar '80s and into the 1790s. Iroquois titles, aggressive groups of land speculators, the Massachusetts' Royal Charter and the emerging federal government were all formidable obstacles to Gov. Clinton's expansionist agenda. In December 1786, an arbitration committee of commissioners from New York and Massachusetts met at Hartford to settle the dispute between the Bay State's Royal Charter claims and New York's presumptive claim to their western territory. The commissioners agreed to establish the Massachusetts Preemption Line, with Massachusetts given the right of soil and purchasing rights to all the Iroquois lands west of it. The survey line ran just west of Seneca Lake and north to south from Lake Ontario's Sodus Bay to milestone #82 on the Pennsylvania State line. In exchange for purchasing rights to all the preemption lands, New York was awarded jurisdiction over the territory, extending its boundaries to Lake Erie and the Niagara River. A few years later, to emphasize their sovereignty over the western territory, New York erected the County of Ontario to include all the territory west of the Preemption Line.

To avoid administering such a complex enterprise, Massachusetts sold their purchasing rights to the land between Seneca Lake and the Genessee River to a group of New England speculators directed by Oliver Phelps and Nathaniel Gorham. The enterprise, however, proved every bit as difficult and complex for Phelps and Gorham. Their corporation quickly fell behind their creditors' demands and they soon found themselves prey to another more aggressive group of investors/speculators. Led by Col. John Livingston, a consortium of wealthy New Yorkers that included five Livingstons, two Schuylers, two Van Rensselaers, seven members of the New York assembly and one state senator, immediately seized on the opportunity to acquire the Seneca lands. The Livingston Company proposed the unique idea of leasing the land from the Iroquois rather than purchasing it outright from them. The concept was more agreeable to the Indians who were suspicious of proposals to purchase their lands with just a onetime payment. The Livingston Leasers aggressively pursued their policy and managed to convince the Seneca to sign on to a long lease for an incredible 999 years on thirteen million acres of their ancestral homeland. They also managed to secure a similar lease with the Oneidas for over five million acres of their land north of Clinton's

Oneida/Tuscarora Purchase. Leasing threatened to undermine Gov. Clinton's ongoing negotiations with the Oneida for the same tract of land.

The prospect of receiving an annual annuity of $2,000 for a thousand years was of course ridiculous and the absurdity of it was soon realized by the Iroquois when the Livingston Company reneged on the agreement by not even producing their first instalment. New York's legislature wasted little time declaring the Livingston leases invalid. To fill that void, Gov. Clinton hurriedly began preparations for another council fire with the four Iroquois nations east of the Preemption Line, the Oneida, Tuscarora, Onondaga, and Cayuga. Clinton would once again portray himself as the great white father and protector of his Iroquois children, saving them from the unscrupulous Livingston Leasers who were just out to rob them of their lands. If Col. Harper had served as Clinton's shill in the Oneida/Tuscarora Purchase, Col. Livingston and his associates would now unwittingly play the same role in the governors next bid for more of the Iroquois lands. [13]

Fort Schuyler Revisited

A second Fort Schuyler council fire was lit in mid-September 1788. By then, Col. Livingston's leasing scheme had unraveled, and Clinton was ready to intensify his efforts to acquire more Oneida lands by fee simple. The governor started the negotiations by reminding the eastern nations of the state's new law that forbid any individuals or other states from purchasing Indian lands in New York. Although initially disappointed by the low turnout, Clinton proceeded to focus all his attention on the Oneida delegation and their lands north of his Oneida/Tuscarora Purchase of '85. Lt. Col. Louis Akiatonharonkwen, the Kahnawá:ke Abenaki warrior who had fought alongside the Harper brothers at Klock's Field, spoke for the Oneidas. Col. Louis was an intelligent and formidable negotiator but no match for the shifty governor who came away from the second Fort Schuyler conference with an incredible concession agreement for an enormous tract of Iroquois lands. In return for a payment of $5,500 worth of cash and goods and a commitment to build the Indians a gristmill and sawmill, the Oneida, Onondaga, and Cayuga Nations agreed to sign over approximately five-and-a-half million acres to Clinton and the State of New York.

New York also agreed to pay an annual annuity of $600 in perpetuity to the Oneidas and reserved a 250,000-acre reservation south of Oneida Lake '...*for your people to live on forever*'. These closing remarks echoed the words spoken by Clinton at the first Fort Schuyler conference when in reference to all their lands he promised them '...*it's just extent will ever remain secure to you...*'. The just extent of their ancestral homeland had shrunk considerably in just four years and today that just extent has shriveled to a mere 18,000 acres. The Onondaga Nation was also granted a reservation of approximately 75,000 acres around and south of Onondaga lake in the vicinity of today's city of Syracuse. Little by Little, the Onondaga sold off their reservation lands and today just 7,500 acres remain, one-tenth its original size. Even the hostile Cayuga were awarded a modest reservation of 64,000 acres around the lower end and outlet of Cayuga Lake. The Cayuga peoples would soon relinquish their reservation and most of them moved further west into Upper Canada. Several lawsuits have been filed by the descendants of the original Iroquois peoples to seek reparation for the just extent of their lands, but their efforts have unfortunately rendered little satisfaction.

New York surveyors began parceling the state's new land into sectioned townships for prospective proprietors. Half a million acres of Oneida lands west of the Unadilla River and directly north of Clinton's Oneida/Tuscarora Purchase of '85 was surveyed into twenty townships of 25,000 acres each. The tract that consists today of the northern half of Chenango County and the southern half of Madison County was then known as Clinton's Twenty Townships. Another million and a half acres of Onondaga and Cayuga lands west of the Twenty Townships were surveyed into twenty-five townships of 64,000 acres each and designated as the Military Tract. These lands were set aside for the bounty lands promised to the state's levies and militiamen for their service during the war. John W. Watkins and Royal W. Flint purchased a tract of 373,000 acres south of the Military Tract and west of the Oneida/Tuscarora Purchase. Another 225,000 acres known as the Tioga Ten Townships, between Owego Creek and the Chenango/Tioughnioga Rivers, were granted to a group of Massachusetts investors. Two million acres north of Oneida Lake and west of the Mohawk River patents were eventually sold to Alexander Macomb while another northern tract of half a million acres was sold to a group headed by members of the Roosevelt family. By 1791, New York had sold or assigned nearly all five-and-a-half million acres and had collected about $1,300,000 from their $5,500 investment. [14]

A few months after the second Fort Schuyler conference and Gov. Clinton's second Iroquois land purchase, the U.S. Constitution was finally ratified in late 1788. Congress and the federal government now had full authority over New York's presumption of authority in all matters related to the purchase and extermination of Indian titles. By then however, Clinton had taken full advantage of a weak Congress and had doubled the size of New York, making it one of the most powerful states in the new republic. He paid down much of his state's war debt by reselling the Iroquois lands and provided the state with a vast source of perpetual revenue from fees and taxes on the western territory. He also kept his promise to his border war militiamen and levies by providing them with the promised bounty lands the state had guaranteed.

George Clinton was enormously popular with the frontier soldiers and settlers who benefited from his wartime leadership and postwar land acquisitions. As a prominent politician and statesman, he continued to be reelected to the governorship of New York until 1796. He would eventually come to within a heartbeat of the Presidency of the United States, serving two different terms as vice-president under Jefferson and Madison. The Harper brothers would continue benefiting from the patronage of the governor they had helped build New York State into the empire state. Clinton would go on to bigger and grander things while the Harpers would return to their preoccupation of acquiring more land.

P.V.B. Livingston Patent

A few months after helping Clinton secure the Oneida/Tuscarora Purchase, Col. Harper filed an affidavit for another warrant of survey. He seems to have been in a hurry and not at all abashed by the thrashing he took at Fort Schuyler and Herkimer. Ever since the early days of the Revolution, a group of associates had had their eyes on a large tract of land between the Susquehanna and the Delaware River. In the spring of 1785, Col. Harper and Lawrence Kortright petitioned the state to hear the claim that had been submitted by them and their associates during the first year of the war. The 35,000-acre tract of land in question had been granted to British Major General Augustine Prévost in 1770 and by '85 had long since been confiscated by the state. The Prévost Patent had sat in a state of legal limbo throughout the war and its proprietorship was now up for grabs.

Gen. Prévost retired from the British army after having defended Charlestown from Gen. Benjamin Lincoln's forces in 1780. Upon returning to England, Augustine Sr left his frontier property to his son, British Major Augustine Prévost Jr. At war's end, Augustine Jr renounced his British army commission and remained in America to pursue his fortunes in his new adopted country. He attempted to hold on to his bequeathed patent through a long series of litigations aimed at overturning the property's confiscation and transferring its ownership to himself. Through his attorney Aaron Burr, who had married the widow of Augustine Jr's uncle James Marcus Prévost, the Prévost Patent litigations dragged on for seven long years. Burr's efforts were ultimately unsuccessful and only succeeded in tying up legal proprietorship of the patent until 1789. Further complicating matters, Augustine Jr was married to George Croghan's daughter Susannah, and as such, was the rightful heir to his father-in-law's estate valued at £140,000. Augustine's attorney also brought suits against William Cooper to rescue all or part of Croghan's Otsego Patent. Both of Burr's lawsuits were finally exhausted and dismissed with prejudice, clearing the way for Harper and Kortright's group of investors to finally assert their claim to the old Prévost Patent. Having waited patiently for longer than they would have liked, Harper, Kortright, Peter Van Brugh Livingston, Robert Adams, Henry

Cuyler, and the ever-present land commissioner Goldsbourgh Banyar, pounced on the opportunity to finally secure title to the elusive Prévost Patent. [15]

On August 8th, 1785, two weeks after the council fire at Fort Herkimer, the governor and the state's land commissioners met in New York City to finally hear Harper and his associates claim to the tract of land in Montgomery County, formerly patented to Augustine Prévost Sr. The following May of '86, pursuant to his warrant of survey, Col. Harper presented Simeon De Witt's survey of the Prévost Patent's 35,078 acres to the board. At the May meeting, Harper also asked the board to prepare letters of patent, or individual deeds to each of the patent lots which were intended to be divided up equally amongst the six petitioners. De Witt's survey was actually performed by one of the petitioners who had already settled on one of the patent's homestead lots. Sluman Wattles would become owner of one-quarter of the patent's 144 homestead lots. As negotiations with the board of land commissioners proceeded and the prospective buyers hustled to line up their creditors and investment partners, a meeting of the grantees was scheduled for the spring of '87 at a New York City coffeehouse.

Cornelius Bradford's widow Catherine had just recently taken proprietorship of her deceased husband's coffeehouse on the corner of Wall and Water streets. Being within sight of the East River's waterfront docks and ships loaded with imported cargo, all types of dealmaking and auctions were conducted in and around Merchants Coffee House. Cases of ale and hogsheads of claret and tobacco were auctioned off in the street, while everything from household furnishings to fine European amenities were sold alongside shackled African slaves and their ill-fated families. On the Ides of March 1787, Col. Harper's associates and a few recently addended grantees met in a second-floor room at Merchant's Coffee House and agreed to divvy up the 144 letters of patent by a lottery draw of ballots. [16]

Merchants Coffee House and East River Slip

During the preceding winter, six new investors had been brought into the Prévost deal by a couple of the original partners assigning their interests over to them. Only three of the original six petitioners were still aboard. Robert Adams had died, and his estate had assigned his shares to three new grantees. Having apparently not been that interested in managing any more frontier property, Lawrence Kortright assigned nearly all his letters of patent to three new investors. Col. Harper appears to have been similarly disposed, preferring to turn a quick profit over the prospects of a more involved investment. Sluman Wattles had become a major player in the Prévost deal by virtue of having been paid for his survey services in property lots, a widespread practice at the time. Wattles aspired to increase his shares even more and become the principal proprietor in what would become the P.V.B. Livingston Patent. Col. Harper seems to have been open to a proposal put forth by Wattles for the colonel to sell and assign all his letters of patent over to him. Being from an affluent family of Connecticut Yankees, Sluman was new to the frontier and perhaps a little too trusting and inexperienced in the ways of the wild west. Dealing with the crafty colonel, who was well-versed in the risky business of frontier land transactions, would not be as straight forward as Wattles might have been used to.

Well in advance of the March 15th meeting at Merchant's Coffee House, Sluman left his wife Mercy and their five children, ages 2-12, on their isolated wilderness homestead and headed for New York City. The Wattles had just moved on to P.V.B. Livingston Patent's lot #67, where West Handsome Brook enters Ouleout Creek at the upper end of today's East Sidney Dam Lake. About two miles southwest of the current village of Franklin on Rt. 357, a small boulder with a bronze plaque embedded in it commemorates the site where Sluman Wattles' homestead once stood. In late November, four months before the March meeting, Sluman made the 200-mile journey down to New York City to negotiate with his creditors and fellow grantees ahead of the meeting. Traveling through the winter cold, he came down with a case of the dreaded smallpox that laid him low for weeks and very nearly cost him his life. He was forced to spend the better part of two months in bed before gradually regaining enough strength to continue his business. When the coffeehouse gathering was finally convened, a weakened but determined Mr. Wattles was awarded thirty-six of the 144 patent lots totaling over 8,800 acres, one-fourth of the entire patent. But the letters of patent would not actually be granted to the grantees for another two years, as Burr and the Prévost's lawsuits were not fully resolved yet. Between the lottery balloting of the lots in '87 and the presentation of the letters of patent in the summer of '89, many of the original grantees had reassigned their shares over to other grantees.

At the 1787 meeting, the land commissioners had given the grantees exactly one month to submit their payments for their allotted letters of patent. Still weak from his bout with smallpox and pressed to get back to his family on the frontier, Mr. Wattles entrusted Col. Harper to transmit his money to the commissioners before the assigned due date. Failure to make his payment on time would technically put Wattles' property in default and subject it to redistribution amongst the other shareholders. Harper of course was fully aware of this and as April 15th came and went, the commissioners had not yet received Wattles' payment. The colonel seems to have intentionally attempted to defraud Sluman out of his rightful interests in the P.V.B. Livingston Patent. Learning of Harper's failure to meet the deadline, Sluman confronted the colonel and accused him of having ruined him by neglecting to deliver his payment on time. Desperate to salvage his money, reputation and property, Wattles appealed to Gov. Clinton and the legislature to make an exception for his delinquent payment. The governor and legislature graciously granted the frantic Mr. Wattles' request and accepted his payment for all his letters of patent. The Treasurer of the State of New York wrote a receipt back-dated April 15th, for £438 11s. 9d. British Stirling, apparently to reflect compliance with the proper due date. Whether Col. Harper purposely intended to cheat Sluman out of his property or not, is unclear, but his negligence certainly suggests he may have had other interests at heart, other than Mr. Wattles. [17]

The Harper family had always held a certain amount of disdain for their New England brethren, having never forgotten how they had been mistreated by them on Boston's Long Wharf in 1718. They also harbored a dislike for Yankee newcomers like Mr. Wattles who had done nothing to liberate New York's frontier border region from the British and their Iroquois allies. A sense of entitlement naturally came to those who had fought and sacrificed so much for the land that was now being bought up by every Johnny-come-lately. Twenty years prior to the granting of the P.V.B. Livingston Patent, Col. Harper and his family purchased 260,000 acres of Oneida lands that included all the said patent and Mr. Wattles' 8,800 acres. The Harpers paid £720 York currency, which was equal to what Sluman was now paying for his thirty-six letters of patent. The Harpers paid less than one cent per acre for the entire Oneida Purchase of '68 or about eight cents an acre for their 22,000-acre portion of the Oneida lands that was awarded them by their grateful king. Mr. Wattles paid one shilling per acre or about twelve cents for his portion of the Oneida lands and the P.V.B. Livingston Patent. [18]

Frontier Census

Settlement of the P.V.B. Livingston Patent was already well under way by the time Sluman Wattles and his fellow grantees received their letters of patent in 1789. Homestead clearings were popping up along the Susquehanna and Delaware River flats and up along a few of their larger tributary creeks. Settlers were also beginning to feel comfortable venturing into the lands west of the old Indian property line of

'68 and into Clinton's recently purchased Iroquois lands. Expansion of the frontier lands and diaspora of the Colonial American population was about to explode into the far reaches of the western territories.

With the Ratification of the U.S. Constitution in 1788, one of the federal government's first official acts was to administer the first decennial census of 1790. The government had two primary purposes for conducting the census and determining the distribution of the country's rapidly dispersing population. First and foremost was the need to determine each state's apportionment to the U.S. House of Representatives. President Washington and Secretary of State Thomas Jefferson were also extremely interested in determining the number of militia age men they would be able to recruit if another war was imminent. The first three of just six census categories were designed to identify the heads of households and all free white males above and below the age of sixteen, the age at which conscription began. The responsibility of conducting the federal census was assigned to each state's federal district court and the U.S. marshal who assigned deputy marshals to assist him. New York's first U.S. marshal was appointed primarily because of his political affiliations and familial patronage. Lt. Col. William Stephen Smith was a well-connected gentleman who had served on General Washington's staff during the final years of the war and by 1790 had married Vice-President John Adams' oldest daughter Abigail.

New York was divided into 155 census districts with assistant deputy marshals directing and tabulating the enumeration of each one of the districts. Due to the immensity of territory in the western frontier districts, more than one census taker was often employed to enumerate them. The old border region county of Tryon was renamed Montgomery County in 1784 and was expanded westward to the Massachusetts Preemption Line in '86. By 1790, Montgomery County was nearly as large as Massachusetts, Vermont and New Hampshire combined. Isolated homesteads scattered throughout the frontier's peripheral settlements were loosely connected to civilization by old Indian trails, crude wagon roads and canoe travel along the rivers and streams. It was no easy task for the deputy marshals to visit and record each family in their district. New York's ten upstate counties were divided into 112 separate census districts. Montgomery County was divided into eleven districts of which seven, Caughnawaga, Palatine, Canajoharie, German Flatts, Mohawk, Herkimertown and Whitestown, extended up along the Mohawk River from Albany County to Lake Ontario. The state's four frontier districts of Chemung, Chenango, Otsego and Harpersfield, along with the southern two-thirds of Canajoharie district, posed a formidable challenge for the census taker charged with enumerating them.

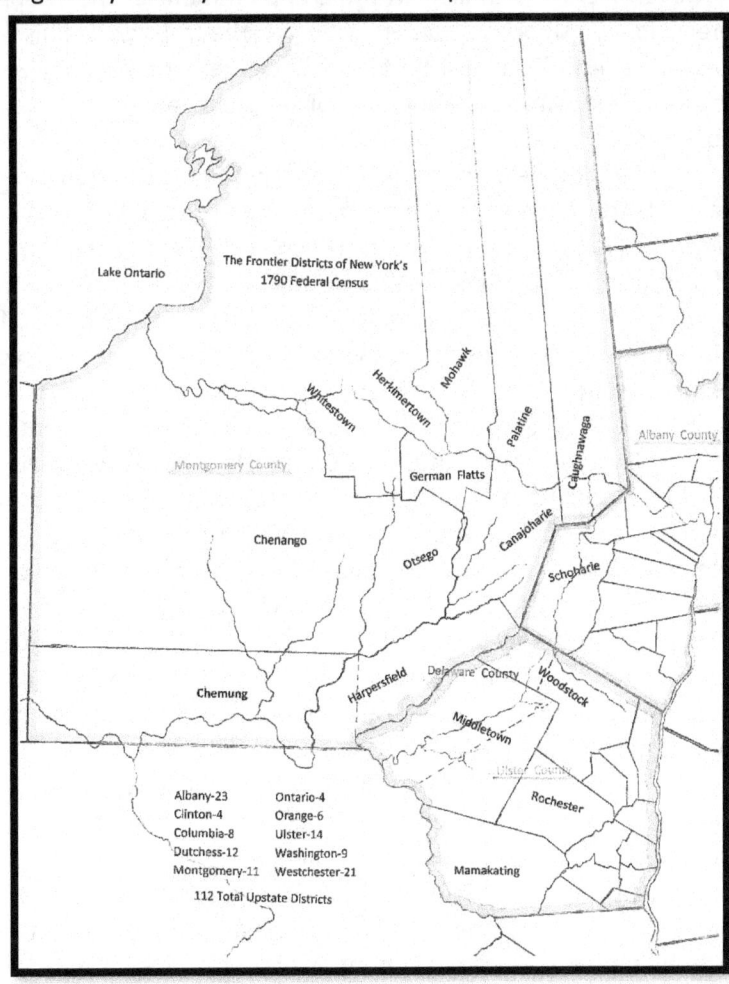

New York's 1790 Frontier Districts

Canajoharie District's Cherry Creek, Sharon Springs and Cobleskill were relatively accessible but the terrain in Montgomery County's Otsego and Harpersfield districts proved more difficult to traverse. The two recently demarcated districts of Chemung and Chenango, both of which extended all the way to the Massachusetts Preemption Line, were even more challenging. Most of Chemung District's families were found living along the Chenango and Susquehanna Rivers in Gov. Clinton's recent Oneida/Tuscarora Purchase of '85. Chenango District was barely canvassed, as the census taker appears to have only visited the few homesteads along the west side of the Unadilla River in one or two of the Twenty Townships. New York's jurisdiction over the lands west of the preemption line had recently been imposed by designating the territory between Seneca Lake and the Genessee River as the new County of Ontario. Only about two hundred families were recorded living in Ontario County's four census districts, most having been encouraged to settle there by Massachusetts or the investment firms that bought the land. [19]

Otsego District

Adherence to the government's predominantly Federalist policies seems to have been an influencing factor in William Smith's choice of deputy marshals. Having served together with Col. Smith as aides to several continental army generals during the war, Maj. Jacob Morris's appointment as Montgomery County's deputy marshal came as no surprise to his frontier neighbors. The Harpers, however, were not thrilled with the appointment of the young Federalist and frontier novice to such a prestigious position. He had only been on the frontier and his Butternuts Creek estate for less than three years. The Anti-Federalist Scots-Irish were beginning to realize their dominance over the land they had recently freed from tyranny was once again falling under the control of a far-off and overreaching government.

Few of New York's eight deputy marshals actually performed the arduous job of circuiting a particular district and enumerating every household therein. Montgomery County's Deputy Marshal Jacob Morris was a rare exception to the rule. Besides being appointed to administer all of Montgomery County's eleven districts and half of Albany County's twenty-three districts, Maj. Morris took it upon himself to perform the enumeration of his own home district. The order of the Otsego District's enumeration shows his Butternuts Creek estate as the first and last stop on his circuitous route through the district. The first recorded entry in his census journal was his carpenter, Tobias Houk, who with his slave Stephen was said to have been living on the Morris Estate while building the house and out-buildings.

Heading down Butternuts Creek, Maj. Morris recorded his neighbor Abijah Gilbert and his family before reaching the Unadilla River and continuing south to the Susquehanna. From William Hannah's tavern near today's village of Unadilla, he continued along a circuit that took him up the Susquehanna to the mouth of Otsdawa Creek and today's village of Otego where he found Lt. Daniel Ogden and the Scramblings families. Recording John Van Der Werks and his family at today's Oneonta, the major continued up the west side of the Susquehanna along the boundary between Otsego and Canajoharie Districts to Isaac Colliers at today's Colliersville. After visiting with the Cully brothers and Col. Harper's nieces at Milford, he pressed on to the source of the Susquehanna where he may have spent a night or two at the Otsego Lakeside home of his friend and fellow Federalist William Cooper.

After recording about sixty to seventy impoverished families on Cooper's Otsego Patent, Morris worked his way on through the district past the south end of Canadarago Lake. Here he came upon the unflappable English gentleman and huntsman, John Tunnicliff, on his 12,000-acre property in the middle of the Schuyler Patent. Tunnicliff was busy rebuilding his estate and hunting lodge that had been destroyed during the war by the rebel militias. Here again, Jacob may have found a gentleman worthy of his time and with whom he could enjoy a brief respite from the banality of most of the other families on his census circuit. Although considered by Morris to be a fellow member of the gentry class, Tunnicliff and the major may not have found much in common when it came to discussing their politics.

Departing from Tunnicliff's Oak Lodge, Jacob headed back towards the Unadilla River through the Old English District and the headwaters of Otego, Otsdawa, Wharton and Butternuts Creek. After another brief respite at John Sleeper's tavern, he recorded the families of Jedediah Peck and Joseph Mayall on Otego Creek, near today's village of Laurens. Descending one creek and ascending the next, he continued through today's townships of New Lisbon, Pittsfield and Edmeston before paying a visit to the impoverished Tory sympathizer, Percifer Carr. Morris showed little sympathy towards the poor old man as he recorded his name while wishing instead, he could have sent him off packing for Canada. On his final approach back to his own estate on Butternuts Creek, Jacob visited the two French gentlemen in his neighborhood that he may have felt were equal to his own level of wealth and gentility, André Rénouard and Louis De Villar. The last recorded entry in the Otsego District register was that of Jacob Morris and his family. The 1790 census indicated there were 1,702 people living on Otsego District's 303 homesteads. It also revealed that eight of those residents were slaves, belonging to just four owners. Five of the eight belonged to Maj. Morris, with the other three belonging to William Cooper, Abijah Gilbert and Tobias Houk. [20]

Harpersfield District

After finishing the Otsego District census, Maj. Morris was responsible for administering over twenty more district censuses, ten in Montgomery County and another dozen in Albany County. It was clear he could never accomplish this without assigning other census takers to these other districts. The neighboring frontier district of Harpersfield included all the territory between the West Branch of the Delaware and the Susquehanna/Charlotte Creek waterways. It was capped on the upper end by Harper Patent and the Pennsylvania State line on the lower end. Morris intentionally chose not to appoint any of the Harpers to serve as enumerators for their Harpersfield District. Colonel Harper and his brothers had by now established a firm political opposition to the Federalist movement to which the assistant deputy was strongly attached. Seizing on the opportunity to trivialize one of the border region's original frontier families and assert his own Federalist authority over the region, Morris fired one of the opening volleys of a political firestorm that was about to consume the old border region and the state.

The man Morris tapped for the Harpersfield census takers job had only recently arrived on the New York frontier and the district to which he would be assigned. Dr. Joshua Howard Brett came from an old Plymouth Bay Colony family with ancestral ties to the Mayflower. He was an excellent and deserving choice for the job. A Yale graduate, he spent most of the Revolution as a surgeon's mate on Capt. John F. William's ship the *Protector*. In the latter years of the war, he served briefly on the Mohawk River in Col. Marinus Willett's regiment as his surgeon. This is when he may have become acquainted with Col. Harper who apparently persuaded him to purchase a few of his patent's homestead lots. Dr. Brett came to Harpersfield in the spring of '88 and settled on one of his three lots near The Centre and the Harper families. The following year he was elected to serve as the town's assessor and shortly thereafter accepted Morris's appointment as census taker. Fulfilling his duties admirably while seeing to his frontier community's medical needs, Dr. Brett was eventually chosen to fill nearly every high office in his town, county, and state government. He also found the time to sire seventeen children with his two wives. [21]

Harpersfield was a challenging district that required its enumerator to navigate a long, circuitous route through a remote wilderness. He would need to trek down along the west side of the West Branch from the Harper settlement to the State line before crossing over to the Susquehanna and back up to Charlotte Creek and Center Brook. Many of the district's settlers were living along the two rivers, but a substantial portion of them lived on the two upper patents on the northern end of the district, Kortright and Harper Patent. Dr. Brett had a daunting mission ahead of him, especially considering his limited experience traversing the border region, as he had only been living there for a little over two years. He would have been enthusiastic, however, to explore the frontier and meet the people he would soon be representing in the state's legislature. While enumerating the pioneer families he visited along the way, the good doctor would have also plied his trade to the sick or injured he might have chanced upon. Although none of the Harpers were officially assigned to the job, it does appear that one of them took it upon himself to join Dr. Brett on his journey around the district. The Harper's were simply not about to be ignored or dismissed by a Federalist outsider who they considered to be an overprivileged frontier interloper. Deputy Marshal Morris would certainly not have been pleased to learn that the Harper brother's brother-in-law, William McFarland, accompanied Dr. Brett through the Harpersfield District.

While Dr. Brett and Lt. McFarland took the trail down the West Branch, another enumerator proceeded to run a series of circuit loops through the heavily populated upper end of the district. From his mill site homestead on the West Branch at today's village of Hobart, Ezra Paine appears to have made several loops recording the Scots-Irish families scattered throughout the hills of Kortright and Harper Patents. The sporadic order of entries in these two patents lends credence to the assumption that whoever did conduct the census in this area, did so in a non-lineal progression. Dr. Brett and McFarland's order of entries unequivocally shows a lineal circuit down the Delaware and back up the Susquehanna, from and back to Harpersfield.

Ezra Paine Esq. and his brother Capt. Edward Paine came to the Harper Patent a couple of years before the 1790 census. The Harper and Paine families had known each other from their early days on the Connecticut River where both families were engaged in mercantile businesses in the Hartford/East Windsor area. The Paine family sent six brothers off to fight the British, three of whom distinguished themselves and rose to high-ranking positions before the Revolution's end. Edward Paine served as a lieutenant in the 5th Company in Col. Comfort Sage's 3rd Battalion of Brig. Gen. James Wadsworth's Brigade, and later as a captain in the 19th Regiment of Connecticut Militia. Ezra served as an ensign and quartermaster under his brother Major Brinton Paine in Col. Roswell Hopkin's 6th Regiment of Dutchess County Militia. After the war, the two brothers migrated west to Harper Patent and at the first Harpersfield town meeting held at Alexander Harper's house in '88, both were elected to prominent positions. Edward was elected as the town's first supervisor and Ezra served as one of the town's path masters and fence viewers. Ezra's experience as a trustworthy quartermaster during the war might have influenced Dr. Brett's decision to suggest he assist him with the Harpersfield census. [22]

The first Monday of August 1790 (August 2nd) was the designated census day from which the state's deputy marshals were given nine months to conduct, conclude and deliver their census results to the state's U.S. marshal and federal district court. The nine-months allotted to perform the census unavoidably contributed to many discrepancies in the final census tally. The fluidity of which settlers were migrating into the western frontier districts made it impossible not to miss some of the families in transit or count others twice. Another frustrating source of inaccuracy was due to the intractable frontiersmen who were suspicious of being put on a list by a suspect government. Escorting Dr. Brett through the furthest reaches of the frontier, William McFarland's presence may have help assure some of the more hesitant Scots-Irish to comply with the census taker's questions. Being unfamiliar with the terrain and its people, the Yankee newcomer would have certainly appreciated McFarland's frontier skills and his familiarity with the reticent frontiersmen.

While Esquire Paine ran his rounds through the upper end of the district, Brett and McFarland made their way down the West Branch crossing over from one patent to the next. They found very few settlers along the river until they came upon Gideon Frisbee in his Elk Creek tavern. Frisbee's Tavern would serve as the area's first judicial courtroom and jury box. Today it houses The Delaware County Historical Association and Museum. After spending a comfortable evening at Frisbee's Tavern, the two enumerators continued their journey through what was to become the village of Delhi and found a group of settlers on the river flats just below the mouth of The Little Delaware River. Riding down through the White, Leake, Babington and P.V.B. Livingston Patents, they came upon the Townsends, Norths and Pines on their Walton Patent properties. Another interesting night might have been spent in the company of Dr. Platt Townsend in what would eventually become the village of Walton. After reaching Dickerson City and continuing to the Cookhouse at today's Deposit, the census takers departed the West Branch of the Delaware and headed up Oquaga Creek towards the Susquehanna to start their return trip back up to Harper Patent. Midway between the two rivers they came upon the secluded cabin known locally as Castle William.

Welcoming the two travelers to his forest abode, William MacClure accommodated his visitors and their horses with food and a brief rest, as he was always known to have done for any weary traveler who passed his way. MacClure was the surveyor who had been hired by several of the large property proprietors in the Oneida/Tuscarora Purchase. Dr. Brett and Lt. McFarland might have enjoyed an entertaining evening with their gracious host, who wrote in his diary on October 2nd, 1790, '... *3 PM. Mr. McFarland and Doctor Britt [Brett] came here & turn'd out their Horses, [I] fed their Horses and [they] want [went] on to 'Quaga [Onaquaga]. They belong to Harpersfield District and are to take all the names of Men, Women & Children being on Order of Congress for that Purpose. I charg'd them nothing for themselves nor Horses...'.* William MacClure's name does not appear in the Harpersfield District census as he told his visitors he had already been enumerated at his home in Orange County before returning to Castle William shortly before their arrival. At least one frontier migrant in transit was not recorded twice on a census tally. [23]

Departing from Castle William, the enumerators reached the Susquehanna near the ruins of the old Oneida village of Onaquaga before heading up the river through the townships of the Oneida/Tuscarora Purchase. Fifty families were recorded along the east side of the river in Warren and Clinton Townships, being today's townships of Windsor, Colesville, Afton and Bainbridge. Gov. Clinton had set aside a generous portion of Clinton Township for the displaced Vermont Sufferers who had lost their property due to the secession of Vermont from New York after the war. Many of these Vermont refugees came from the Connecticut River's Battleboro area where they had served throughout the war in Lt. Col. Timothy Church's Southern Regiment of Cumberland County Militia.

One of the Vermont Sufferers visited by Brett and McFarland, Israel Smith Sr, had been a major in his brother Lt. Col. Seth Smith's Cumberland County Militia Regiment. A few years after the census, Israel's nephew, Jedediah Smith Sr, came and settled near his uncle's Jericho/Bainbridge homestead adjacent to Sidney. In 1799, the legendary hunter, trapper and Rocky Mountain explorer, Jedediah Smith Jr, was born on his father's farm where he lived until his family moved to Ohio around 1810. Another notable Smith, Joseph *'The Glass Looker'*, lived and worked for a while in the Afton/Colesville area before being driven out with his followers who began their epic journey to Utah's Great Salt Lake Plains.

From the old Indian property line, the enumerators soon reached Ouleout Creek where they continued their circuit by crossing back and forth from the river to the creek before following the Ouleout back through the highlands to Kortright and Harper Patents. William returned to his wife Miriam on her family's patent, while Dr. Brett met with Ezra Paine to combine their census tallies. Deputy Marshal Morris may not have known of Paine and McFarland's involvement in the Harpersfield census until all was said and done, having only assigned the responsibility for it to Dr. Brett. Had he known beforehand about the Harper family members' participation, he might have protested Dr. Brett's decision to employ William's assistance. Morris and his fellow Otsego Federalists would never be appreciative of anything the Harpers or any of their kinsmen did. The implementation of the 1790 census exposed the conflicting political sentiments between the leaders of the Otsego and Harpersfield population. Morris and Cooper would lead the Otsego Federalist faction while the Harpers and their Scots-Irish neighbors fervently headed the opposition party.

Harpersfield District's population tally was remarkably similar to that of Otsego District, having just twenty-four more residents on just thirteen more homesteads. There were 1726 residents on 316 homesteads. And like Otsego District, Harpersfield's census revealed seven of its population were slaves, one of which was owned by Col. Harper's son-in-law Roswell Hotchkiss. Almost half of Harpersfield

District's residents were living in either Kortright or Harper Patents, while about half of Otsego District's residents were either living in Cooper's Otsego Patent or in the Old English District. [24]

Before Deputy Marshal Morris submitted all his Montgomery and Albany County district results to the state's U.S. marshal and the federal district court, old Montgomery County was reapportioned into four new counties. On February 16th, 1791, Tioga, Otsego, and Herkimer Counties were partitioned off from the old Tryon/Montgomery County, leaving a drastically reduced Montgomery County. Tioga County was erected from what had been the census district of Chemung and the southwestern section of Harpersfield District west of the old Indian property. Otsego District and the remainder of the Harpersfield District merged with the southern two-thirds of Canajoharie District to form the new county of Otsego. The new county of Herkimer included most of the sparsely populated portions of old Montgomery County's northwestern districts that included Chenango, Whitestown, Herkimertown, Mohawk, most of Palatine and Caughnawaga and the western half of German Flatts. The new Montgomery County was reduced to the southern ends of Palatine and Caughnawaga Districts, the northern third of Canajoharie, and the eastern half of German Flatts.

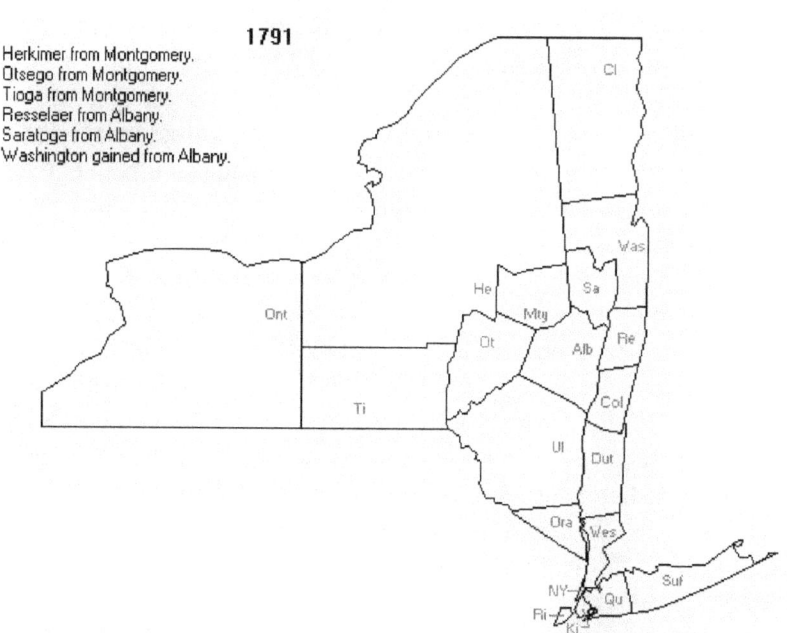

The census totals for all eleven districts of old Montgomery County came to just under 29,000. It is difficult to ascertain a precise count of each of the four new counties but a fair assessment indicates a total count of 15,600 for the new Montgomery County, 6,400 for Herkimer, 4,350 for Otsego and 2,600 for Tioga County. [25]

Election of 1792

The new county of Otsego would soon play a pivotal role in the drama that was about to play out in the political arena. Having narrowly won reelection in 1789, the post-war popularity of New York's first and only governor began to show signs of erosion as the 1792 elections approached. George Clinton had been in state politics for over twenty years, having first been elected to New York's Provincial Assembly in 1768 and later as the state's first governor in '77. While leading his compatriots through the frontier border war as a brigadier general in the state militia, he was elected to serve five consecutive three-year terms as governor. In the years following the Revolution, his purchasing and sales of Iroquois lands doubled the size of New York State and secured its prominence over the other states. The governor's deciding vote in the Council of Appointments that nominated men for civil, judicial, and military commissions was his most powerful tool for staying in power. Gubernatorial patronage was essential for the career of any up-and-coming politician, judge or military officer and the newly erected county of Otsego was awash with potential aspirants.

Otsego County was established with three original townships, Otsego, Cherry Valley and Harpersfield. The new county was about to be intwined in the broader political partisanship that was beginning to define and divide the nation's electorate. The faction that became known as the Federalist party and the frontier faction known originally as the Anti-Federalist party had already butted heads over the ratification of the U. S. Constitution and by 1792 both were solidly entrenched in their political doctrines. The Federalists adhered to the doctrine that only the wealthy and well-educated gentry could be trusted with the responsibility of governing and legislating laws for the benefit of the electorate. A Federalist also believed in a civil hierarchy patterned on the British example of societal order and perceived social status.

The Anti-Federalists, by contrast, favored an egalitarian approach to governance. They believed in the principle that all white men of legal age who owned their own land were entitled to participate in elections and vote for any representative whom they felt reflected their own values, regardless of their station in life. Of New York's 340,000 residents, only white men over the age of twenty-one who owned at least £50 worth of freehold property were eligible to vote in the state elections of '92. But the election for governor, lieutenant governor, and the state's two U.S. senators were further restricted to freehold property owners with at least £100 worth of property. The Democratic-Republican Party, as it came to be called, had a long way to go before reaching a truly democratic government, but they were decidedly further along the way than their Federalist rivals.

The first federal census identified each state's population distribution. Congress was now able to allocate the proper number of delegates from each state to represent them in the U.S. House of Representatives and each state was now able to determine its own allotment of representation in their legislature. It was determined that New York's legislature should consist of twenty-four senators and seventy-three assemblymen to be elected from the state's four electoral districts. Each electoral district was represented by an appropriate number of legislators in accordance with their portion of the electorate. In 1792, New York's western frontier district included the counties of Montgomery, Otsego, Tioga, Herkimer, Ontario, Albany, and the recently erected county of Saratoga. Five senators and twenty assemblymen were allocated to represent the western district. Predictably, the five western district senators included Philip and Peter Schuyler, their brother-in-law Stephen Van Rensselaer, and two other interrelated members of the old Dutch patriarchal families. Of the twenty western district assembly seats, seven were allocated to Albany County, five to Montgomery County, four to Saratoga County and one each to Ontario, Herkimer, Tioga, and Otsego Counties.

Otsego County's first major statewide election was held a year after its founding and pitted the new county's staunchest Federalist against an Anti-Federalist frontiersman. Maj. Jacob Morris and the Harper brother's brother-in-law William McFarland had both used their census jobs to promote their political ambition by familiarizing them with their prospective electorate. By 1792, the Federalists had managed to convince many of the frontier's more recent arrivals to vote their way. Of the 916 votes cast in Otsego County's three townships, nearly all of Otsego and a surprising number of Cherry Valley's postwar settlers cast their votes in favor of Morris. McFarland garnered virtually all of Harpersfield's votes and a few votes from Cherry Valley's original Scots-Irish settlers. But the old frontier had changed, and after receiving 713 votes to McFarland's 203, assemblyman Morris was off to join the other assemblymen and senators in New York's Sixteenth Legislative Session. Otsego County's elections of '92 would not be remembered for its Federalist's resounding victory over the Anti-Federalists, as a far more consequential race would be determined by the new frontier county. [26]

New York's civil, judicial, and military commissions were assigned by a four-member committee of state legislators overseen by the governor. The governor and the four members of the Council of Appointments often invested their patronage in those whose past support they had benefited from or those whose future political support they hoped to gain. The system was designed to establish local governance by assigning municipal offices to the most capable individuals in any given community. It was of course a uniquely corrupt system that led to graft and every form of political corruption imaginable. By the early '90s, William Cooper had managed to apply his political influence to harvest the patronage of Gov. Clinton who appointed him and a few of his Federalist cronies to the new county of Otsego's top public offices. He was also successful in garnering the governor's support to make the village he was building on the south end of Otsego Lake the county seat. This came with an outcry of protest from the two other Otsego County townships, with Harpersfield being the loudest.

Although never having studied the law, William Cooper was appointed first judge of Otsego County. Judge Cooper's friend and fellow Quaker, Richard R. Smith, was given the coveted position of county sheriff. Cooperstown's first editor and journalist, Elihu Phinney, was appointed county treasurer while the ever-aspiring Jacob Morris was given the office of county clerk. All these men were ardent Federalists and for the time being at least, were resolute supporters of Judge Cooper. Trying to give some balance to the judiciary, Gov. Clinton and the Council of Appointments chose several individuals from the outlying communities to serve as associate judges to the courts of common pleas, many of whom were known to have been adherents of the Dem/Rep party. Harpersfield's John M. Brown, census taker Joshua Brett and the oldest Harper brother William were assigned as associate judges under Judge Cooper. Cherry Valley's Ephraim Hudson and Edward Griswold were also awarded associate judgeships with the job of county surrogate going to James Cannon, another Cherry Valley resident. Walton's Dr. Platt Townsend and Burlington's Jedediah Peck were later awarded associate judgeships. [27]

Ten years after the Revolution, the threat of another war with England was very real and an ever-present worry in the minds of the statesmen of that era. In May 1792, Congress passed an act, '... *to provide for the national defense by establishing a uniform militia throughout the United States...*'. Local militia companies were the primary unit of a state's postwar militia army. Led by a captain, lieutenant and ensign, companies were comprised of sixty-four able bodied white men between the ages of eighteen and forty-five. Companies were required to meet twice a year in their respective beats for training day and once a year to rendezvous with their regiment on parade day. A regiment consisted of ten companies of 640 men, with four regiments to a brigade of 2,560 militiamen. Each of New York's four great districts, Western, Eastern, Northern and Southern were to have one brigade led by a major general. The western district was comprised of all old Tryon/Montgomery County which by '92 included Montgomery, Herkimer, Otsego, Tioga and the two new frontier counties of Ontario and Clinton.

Except for Associate Judge William Harper, Otsego County's civil and judiciary positions were denied to all the other Harper brothers and most of their Harpersfield and Cherry Valley kinsmen. Gov. Clinton, however, did not deny them the military positions to which they were more accustomed and better fit for than Cooper's pacifist Quakers. A few months before the elections of 1792, Maj. Gen. Peter Gansevoort's western district militia brigade was strengthened with the 1st Otsego County Militia Regiment. The new regiment was stacked with members of the Harper family and many of their Harpersfield friends and neighbors. Having risen no further than captain during the Revolution, Alexander Harper was given a chance to redeem his rather sketchy wartime exploits by being commissioned lieutenant colonel of the Otsego regiment. Lt. Col. Harper's ever-faithful brother-in-law, William McFarland, was commissioned to serve as his second-in-command as 1st major, with Witter Johnston of Johnston Settlement 2nd major and Harpersfield's doctor, census taker and judge, Joshua Brett, as the regimental surgeon.

Lt. Col. Harper's older brother John was approaching his sixtieth year and undoubtedly past his prime for active military service. Col. Harper had an extraordinarily active and controversial military career during the border war. He had also more recently cast doubts about his character through his activities during the Iroquois land acquisitions and the P.V.B Livingston Patent intrigues. Nevertheless, Gov. Clinton had not forgotten his many contributions to the war effort or his help in securing the Oneida/Tuscarora Purchase. Overlooked by the Council of Appointments for a commission to high office, his family was, however, well rewarded by a grateful governor. Col. Harper's son-in-law, Roswell Hotchkiss, was assigned to Lt. Col. Alexander Harper's staff as his regiment's paymaster. A company of light infantry was formed with the colonel's son James as its lieutenant and his stepson William as the company's ensign. Another Harpersfield company was formed with John M. Brown as captain and one of John's former Tryon County rangers, David Hendry, as the company's lieutenant. One of the sugar boilers who had been led into captivity by Alexander in 1780, Isaac Patchin, was commissioned to ensign in Capt. Brown's and Lt. Hendry's militia company. [28]

Governor Clinton's western district friends were about to become embroiled in a bitter political war that was part of a broader national struggle over the identity of the new republic. Seeking reelection, New York's Anti-Federalist governor was running for his sixth term against the popular and favored Federalist, Chief Justice John Jay. By '92, William Cooper had turned the old Croghan Patent into an impressive collection of frontier settlements rivaling any of the border region's postwar settlements, including Cherry Valley and Harpersfield. Cooper reigned over his Yankee homesteaders with a benevolent but heavy hand, expecting loyalty for his generosity and political guidance. He was an inexperienced frontier developer who saw himself as an up-and-coming gentleman on a par with New York's old and landed gentry. He thrived on the adulation he received from gentlemen like the Schuylers and Van Rensselaers for his Otsego Patent successes and his compliance with their political views. Cooper, however, was an ill-educated and temperamental hothead who would never master the finer aspects of gentlemanly conduct.

With a view to better himself and advance his standings amongst New York's old-school elites, Cooper saw his chance to influence the '92 election by delivering most, if not all, of his Otsego votes for the Federalist candidate. As the first judge of Otsego County and proprietor of a frontier fiefdom of mortgaged farms and indebted villeins, he wielded considerable influence over the new county's electorate. Expecting loyalty from those whose financial security rested firmly in his hands, Cooper set out to persuade his leaseholders to support his choice for the next governor. Cooper's own sense of loyalty was shown to have been purely self-serving, as it had only been a year since Gov. Clinton's patronage had helped him and his Otsego friends secure their prestigious county positions. He was now adamantly opposed to the governor and in full-throttled support of his Federalist opponent.

As the election approached, Judge Cooper used every heavy-handed method he could to influence his county's electorate into voting for Jay and the Federalist candidates. They involved everything from physical bullying to threats of financial ruin and eviction. Exercising the power he held over his indebted homesteaders; he succeeded in coercing nearly all of Otsego's voters into supporting his candidate. His untethered desire to enhance his own political and social aspirations naturally led to making enemies of all those who would not bend to his will. When confronting a known Clinton supporter, Cooper might first try to physically humiliate the dissenting voter and if that had little effect, he could resort to wielding his judicial power with threats of legal suits and fines.

When Col. Harper's nephew James Moore came to Cooperstown to cast his vote for Gov. Clinton, Judge Cooper insisted he cast his vote for John Jay and insinuated, '...*You are a fool, young man, for you cannot know how to vote as well as I can direct you, for I am a man in public office...*'. When the young Scots-Irishman ignored the affront, the judge resorted to threats of imprisonment and demanded Moore pay him a £20 debt he alleged was due to him. Even after the balloting closed, Cooper verbally accosted two prominent Otsego residents for having voted for that, '...*infernal damned rascal Governor Clinton...*'. Happening upon Capt. James Butterfield and Joseph Tunnicliff in Butterfield's White House Tavern, near today's hamlet of Hartwick, the border war veteran and his gentlemen companion were not at all amused by the Quaker's belligerent demeanor. [29]

However offensive or illegal his tactics might have been, the Federalists were delighted with Cooper's zealous campaigning for their candidates. Even before the votes were officially counted, Cooper boasted to his Federalist friends that of the six hundred Otsego votes cast, 585 were for Jay. This was a suspiciously revealing admission from an election official entrusted with overseeing honest balloting. The sheer number of eligible voters from a county with so many indebted homesteaders whose property value was far less than the £100 requirement to vote in a gubernatorial election, cast even more doubt on

Cooper's credibility and his Otsego count. One election observer noted that three out of every four votes cast in Otsego County were by unqualified voters.

Shortly after the polls closed on April 28th, Senator Philip Schuyler sent a letter to William Cooper complimenting him on his efforts, *'...I am certain we should not have had 700 votes from your country...[had you not been]...civil to the young and handsome of the sex...[and]...flattered the old and ugly. And even embraced the toothless and decrepit in order to obtain votes, when will you write a treatise on Electioneering...'.* The condescending reproach of the common man that accompanied the patronizing compliment, epitomized what frontier Republicans hated most about their Federalist antagonists. Approbation from the gentry classes was what Judge Cooper craved more than anything else, but the Schuylers and Van Rensselaers would never think of the ambitious Quaker partisan as anything more than their necessary fool. With the popularity of Chief Justice John Jay on the rise, the Federalists were fully expecting to win the governor's race and many of the legislative races. [30]

After the five days of balloting closed, the sealed ballot boxes were required to be delivered to the secretary of state in Kingston where the canvass committee would count and certify the election. As sheriff, it was Richard R. Smith's responsibility to safely transmit Otsego County's sealed ballot boxes to Kingston. After having delivered the ballot boxes on May 3rd, a technicality arose that would throw the validity of Otsego's ballots into question. Sheriff Smith's commission had expired in mid-February and on April 3rd, he had been elected supervisor of Otsego County. The Council of Appointments commissioned Benjamin Gilbert to succeed Smith as sheriff, but Gilbert was not sworn in until May 11th, eight days after Smith delivered the ballots to Kingston. Having continued to assume the duties of the office of the sheriff during the six weeks prior to Gilbert's taking the oath of office, Smith unwittingly violated the state regulation on ballot box deliveries by not officially being sheriff at the time of the delivery. The delay in Gilbert's ascension to the office of the sheriff was due to the fact that his commission had been held up and not delivered to Cooper's town until after the ballots were delivered. The Federalist candidate for lieutenant governor, Stephen Van Rensselaer, had conspired with Judge Cooper to delay the commission's delivery to Otsego in order to keep the Federalist friendly Sheriff Smith in office through the election and balloting transfer period. Uncertain of Gilbert's political alliances and fearful of his potential mishandling of their ballots, the collaborators assumed that no one would notice or object to interim Sheriff Smith's delivery of the ballot boxes.

There was another glaring miscalculation in the Federalist plot to secure their Otsego County ballot box delivery. There was a state regulation that a county sheriff could not seek or hold any other public office while acting in the capacity of sheriff. Smith's election to Otsego County Supervisor in April, presented another legal technicality for the assumption of his interim sheriff status and his transfer of ballot boxes to Kingston. Flagged by an observant state canvasser, the question as to the validity of Otsego's ballot box delivery was referred to the state legislature. After a loud and contentious debate, the legislature then deferred the decision to the two sitting state senators, Aaron Burr and Rufus King. Burr's interpretation of the law and his persuasive argument as to the illegality of the ballot box delivery convinced the state regulators to disqualify all of Otsego County's votes. Gov. Clinton went on to defeat John Jay by receiving 132 more of the 16,782 votes cast in the 1792 gubernatorial election. Van Rensselaer also lost his bid for lieutenant governor by a slim margin. Had Cooper's 585 Federalist votes been counted, there would have been little doubt as to Jays and Van Rensselaer's victories. [31]

In the aftermath of Clinton's narrow victory, a firestorm of recriminating accusations was hurled from both sides of the political chasm. Federalists were indignant, and rightfully so, over the disqualification of Otsego's votes. Judge Cooper was calling for an armed rebellion against the Anti-Federalists who had hijacked the election from Jay and Van Rensselaer. Throughout the summer of 1792 and into the spring of '93, riots broke out in Albany, Kingston, and New York City while brawls and even pistol fights erupted in the outlying frontier settlements. Scathing editorials filled the newspapers as petitions began circulating demanding the legislature call for another election. Otsego's disenfranchised voters who had cast their ballots in good faith were outraged over having their suffrage denied and their significance marginalized.

Multiple affidavits were filed by Judge Cooper in the courts of common pleas against those who had accused him of mishandling the balloting and strong-arming his Otsego electorate into voting for John Jay. Insults and slanderous allegations were focused on the Republican Clintonians, with some of the worst verbal abuses reserved for the Harpers and their extended family members. Milford's Justice of the Peace John Cully, the brother of Col. Harper's niece's husbands, was targeted and accused of all sorts of immoral offenses. Cooper accused him of, '...*the most scandalous Fornication by taking another without Marriage into his Bed...false swearing...to say nothing of his poorness of circumstances & total want of Respectability...*'. He went on to publicly rebuked the Harpersfield frontiersmen as being '...*weak-minded men...almost constantly intoxicated...and moral reprobates self-placed beyond the pale of decent society by their sexual and alcoholic transgressions...*'.

The Clintonian frontiersmen answered the haughty judge's taunts with thirteen affidavits of their own against him and his Otsego cronies. Alexander and William Harper along with James Moore, John Cully and James and Andrew Cannon, were joined by Joseph Tunnicliff, Joseph Mayall, and James Butterfield in filing charges against Judge Cooper. Associate Judge Hudson and seventy other Clintonians filed an affidavit alleging that Cooper, '...*as first judge of Otsego had been guilty of mal & corrupt conduct and sundry misdemeanors in the execution of his office...*'. The affidavit against Cooper's conduct so enraged the disgruntled Sheriff Richard R. Smith that he responded with a withering assault on Associate Judge William Harper, '...*I despise the drunken fool who made the affidavit...and however dignified his station in this county may be, I am not afraid to contrast my reputation with his. I am seldom seen staggering about; neither am I in possession of those talents for cringing and servile flattery by which he is so eminently distinguished...*'. While both sides accused the other of misconduct, the Federalists displayed a visceral hatred for their opponents with their vicious ad hominem attacks.

Cooper continued his vitriolic attacks by using his judicial influence to call for an Otsego County grand jury to file suits against several of his political enemies, particularly the *'scandalous'* Harpers. Peeved over their recent commissions as commanders of the 1st Otsego regiment, Judge Cooper's grand jury filed an indictment for forgery against Lt. Col. Alexander Harper and Major William McFarland. After being jailed and released on bond, Alexander called upon the judge and publicly treated him to an old frontier form of public mortification. The grabbing and twisting of an unsuspecting rival's nose, known as snouting, was a painful and embarrassing affront for any public official, especially one as proud as William Cooper. In June of '93, a year after the indictment of Harper and McFarland, both were acquitted by a trial jury which prompted the attorney general to drop the frivolous charges of forgery.

Preoccupied with the many lawsuits filed by and against him, Cooper ultimately fared no better in the courts than he did with his Otsego ballot boxes. Gov. Clinton sued him for the slanderous remarks he publicly made against the governor as being an embezzler and traitor, having gone as far as to compare his conduct to that of Benedict Arnold. The court and jury sided with Clinton and demanded Cooper pay him £500 in damages and legal expenses. Shortly after Harper's exoneration of the charge of forgery, Cooper filed another suit against the lieutenant colonel accusing him of murder. This of course provoked Harper into filing his own charges by publicly accusing Cooper of slander and forgery. But by now, the Otsego jurist had grown wary of both Cooper and Harper's ungentlemanly behavior and ruled against both. Cooper was convicted of slandering Harper as a murderer and was forced to award Alexander £200 in damages and court costs. The jurist also convicted Harper of slandering Cooper and ordered him to pay a little under £150 to the judge. Monetarily, the suspected murderer and ruthless snouter fared slightly better than the bruise nosed slandering forger. [32]

With the political turmoil over the 1792 election continuing into '93, anger and frustration overshadowed every aspect of the state's political landscape. The Federalists were beginning to gain momentum while many of the Republicans found themselves being swept from office by the undertow of resentment following Clinton's dubious reelection. Cooper's own political fortunes were on the rise, and his electioneering talent '...*to flatter the toothless and decrepit...*' would again come into play. In 1793, he made a bold if not over-zealous bid to run for New York's western district seat in the U.S. House of Representatives. Again, he managed to persuade most of the Otsego electorate into voting for him and the Federalist candidates. The Federalists won both houses of the New York legislature that year, but unfortunately for the judge, the western district had two Federalists running for the same congressional seat. Cooper's Otsego votes were not enough to push him over the top and he lost to Silas Talbot in a relatively close race. Had he been a more pragmatic man, he might have been satisfied to run for a seat in the state legislature instead of Congress and would have joined his friends in the next legislative session.

Although probably not of his own volition, Col. John Harper's name was put forth as a candidate for one of the western district's two state senate seats in '93. Desperate to draw votes away from the two Federalist candidates, both of whom won by overwhelming margins, the colonel was only able to win a paltry 1% or 117 of the district's 10,500 total votes. He was also unable to garner any more than eighty-nine of his Otsego County's 1,500 votes. The Federalist wave washed over the colonel and the state's Republican party like a tsunami that year. His Harpersfield kinsmen notwithstanding, Col. Harper's fame and popularity had faded significantly since he saved the Schoharie Valley from MacDonell's Tories at the Battle of The Flockey in '77. [33]

Mired in his litany of litigations with the Clintonians while nursing his bruised ego after his congressional defeat, Judge Cooper was hit with another symbolic snouting from the man he had come to loathe. Viewed by Cooper as a fraudulent governor, Clinton was solidly in control of the state's Council of Appointments and was anxious to stymie the power of the man who had compared him to Benedict Arnold. One of Clinton's first orders of business as he began his sixth term was to call for the formation of another Otsego County Militia Regiment. He proceeded to commission officers to the 2nd Militia Regiment with many of the judge's political enemies and Harper family relatives. Lieutenant Colonel David Bates's 2nd Regiment was staffed with three of Cooper's most annoying rivals, 1st Major James Butterfield and 2nd Major Joseph Tunnicliff, the two supporters of that '...*infernal damned rascal Governor Clinton...*', and Paymaster John Cully, the '...*scandalous fornicator...*'. Cully's brother Matthew was commissioned captain of one of the regiment's ten companies, with his brother-in-law James Moore as the company ensign. Col. Harper's nephew James had defied Cooper's insistence that he vote for John Jay during the '92 balloting and had earned a top spot on the judge's list of enemies. Another one of the Cully brothers, Thomas, who had been an ensign in Col. Harper's Tryon County Regiment during the war, was commissioned lieutenant in another one of Otsego regiment's companies.

Clinton continued his retribution on Cooper's dominion by sacking Sheriff Benjamin Gilbert and replacing him with one of Cherry Valley's original Scots-Irish family members, Samuel Dickson. Samuel was the thirteen-year-old boy who had spotted his mother's brilliant red hair hanging from a drying pole the day after the Cherry Valley Massacre. Relieved of his commission, Sheriff Gilbert ran for and won Otsego County's assembly seat in '93, easily beating his opponent Major McFarland. William had been beaten for the same seat the year before by Otsego County's Federalist clerk, Jacob Morris. Continuing to benefit from the patronage of their former brigadier general and governor for a few more years, the frontiersmen who had won the west for the new republic were soon altogether displaced by the country's evolving political landscape. [34]

New Guard

By the mid-1790s, the Harpers had begun to question their allegiance to the state they had sacrificed so much to free from an overbearing and oppressive sovereign. Their new nation's inclination to drift towards a form of governance that to them was reminiscent of the one they had just freed themselves from, was a hard pill for the Scots-Irish frontiersmen to swallow. In January 1795, fifty-six-year-old George Clinton announced he was retiring from public life after thirty years of service to the state. Federalist John Jay easily won the following election for governor and was sworn in in July of '95. The politics of the old border region was turning away from the principles men like the Harpers held so dear to their hearts. Harpersfield, Cherry Valley and the other early frontier settlements of the old border region were being marginalized both politically and geographically. The rise of Federalism and the recently purchased Iroquois lands were inciting men of adventurous spirit to abandon their father's land for the promise beyond the western horizon.

The year following Jay's election, Alexander Harper and William McFarland began making new plans for themselves and their families. In April of '96, Lt. Col. Harper and 1st Maj. McFarland resigned their militia commissions. Their Otsego regiment was reorganized with 2nd Maj. Witter Johnston promoted to commander. Col. Harper's son James and stepson William were promoted to captain and lieutenant of their light infantry company after their Capt. Benjamin Morse was promoted to 1st major on Lt. Col. Johnston staff. Col. Harper's oldest son Archibald, who at fourteen had been drafted by his father during the war to serve as his waiter, was promoted to captain of another company in the Otsego regiment following his uncle's resignation. Harpersfield's Lt. David Hendry was also promoted to captain of his company following the resignation of Capt. John M. Brown due to infirmity. Isacc Patchin, one of Alexander's sugar boilers, became Capt. Hendry's lieutenant while David's good friend Levi Gaylord became the company's ensign. The old guard was slowly giving way to the next generation of frontier military leaders. [35]

As old Tryon/Montgomery County and all the other old frontier counties continued to be partitioned into more and smaller counties, Cooper's Otsego County gradually lost over half of its original real estate. It was reduced in 1795 by the breakaway of western Albany County to form Schoharie County, which then annexed a small portion of eastern Otsego County. In 1797, it was drastically reduced by the formation of Delaware County. The northwestern half of the new county of Delaware claimed all of Otsego's land between the West Branch of the Delaware and the Susquehanna/Charlotte Creek waterways from Harper Patent to the old Indian property line. The new county also annexed the northwestern portion of old Ulster County to include the East Branch of the Delaware and its watershed, except for the upper Beaver Kill and Willowemoc Creek, from its source to the Pennsylvania state line. Delaware County was established by an act of the New York legislature on March 10th, 1797, and organized two-and-a-half months later by the supervisors of the new county's first seven townships. Harpersfield, Kortright, Franklin and Walton were designated on the old Otsego side of the West Branch, while Colchester, Middletown and Stamford were on the old Ulster County side of the river. It appears that by '97, both William Cooper and his Harpersfield Republican adversaries had found something they could both agree upon, the separation of each from the other and the remapping of a boundary line between them.

The formation of Delaware County had its opponents, many of whom belonged to the families of old Ulster County who had settled along the East Branch of the Delaware before the Revolution. Ever since the first party of Dutch settlers came to Paghatakan in 1763, the East Branchers had done their business in Kingston. Many of them still thought of Kingston as their gateway to the outside world. Harpersfield's Joshua H. Brett, now a member of the New York Assembly, was joined by Judge Cooper and another Federalist assemblyman from Orange County named Ebenezer Foote in petitioning the legislature to take up the issue of establishing the new county. After finally agreeing upon acceptable boundary lines, an unusual cabal of Federalists and Republicans succeeded in defeating the opposition to the formation of the new county.

The many descendants of Robert R. Livingston owned most of the new county lands south of the West Branch in the Hardenburgh Patent, while the lands north of the river belonged to the patent proprietors of the old Harper and Bradstreet purchases. Through the first fifty years of Delaware County's existence, the property rights of those who lived on the Hardenburgh side of the river continued to be limited to the provisions in their land/leases. It would take the Anti-Rent War of 1845 and the murder of Undersheriff Steele to finally force the legislature to abolish the archaic system that families like the Livingstons and Van Rensselaers amassed their fortunes and built their empires on. [36]

During the organization of Delaware County, the Harper family's settlement at The Centre found itself gradually being pushed aside by political and commercial interests. Harpersfield Supervisor Roswell Hotchkiss, Col. Harper's son-in-law, met with the other six town supervisors at Gideon Frisbee's house near today's Delhi and came away without gathering any support for making Harpersfield the county seat. Geographically, The Centre was no longer the center of anything other than the Harper family's patent. As western migrants began traveling through the old border region, Harper Patent and The Centre were gradually reduced to just another watering hole along the way. No longer were Harper Patent's homestead lots eagerly sought-after by men looking to escape the overcrowded eastern settlements. The spirit that inspired old John Harper and his wife Abigail to bring their seven children to the edge of Christendom nearly fifty years before, still lingered in the hearts of three of their younger children and many more of their Scots-Irish kinsmen. The western horizon would soon beckon them to another frontier far from the reaches of ensnaring political annoyances, lawsuits, and slanderous accusations from men with untethered ambitions.

After being defeated in 1793 for a seat in the U.S. House of Representatives, William Cooper finally achieved his lifelong obsession for social recognition by being elected to Congress in '94. He went on to be defeated in '96 but was reelected again in '98 and served in Congress, on and off, from 1794 until 1800. Judge Cooper's later years were plagued with financial difficulties and his pugnacious nature that continued to get him into trouble. He was said to have been beaten in the streets of Cooperstown by a man with a walking stick in 1807. His death in December 1809 was said to have been due to a blow to the head received during an altercation with another man he had insulted. The charming little village he left us on the shores of Lake Glimmerglass and his son's historical novels about early life on the New York frontier were his legacy. Men like the Harpers, who James Fenimore Cooper heard tales of from his father in his youth, were undoubtedly some of his composite protagonists in his famous books; *The Pioneers, The Deerslayer, and The Leatherstocking Tales.* Now another frontier to the west was about to need another bard to romanticize the frontiersmen who were about to set off into the Great Northwest Territory. [37]

8
Ohio
1793-1814
'It was with feelings akin to horror that our little party saw our provisions dwindle away'

As the nineteenth century approached, New York's frontier border region was slowly being eclipsed by more attractive territories to the west. Once the extreme edge of white settlement and civilization, Cherry Valley, Harpersfield, Johnston's Settlement, Paghatakan and the Cushetunk were now just stops along the way for pioneer families heading west. The postwar treaty councils at Forts Herkimer and Stanwix had eradicated the old Indian property line of '68 and extinguished Iroquois titles to a substantial portion of their lands in west central New York. America's frontier colonization and the genocidal marginalizing of the Indigenous population was accelerating at a steady pace. The opening of the western lands was stirring the appetites of men who felt entitled to its bounty. For men like the Harpers, it was a time for action as the allure of making a quick profit in the lucrative real estate markets of the developing frontier proved too irresistible to ignore.

Northwest Territory

While Gov. Clinton and Congress were holding their negotiations with New York's Oneida, Tuscarora, Onondaga, Cayuga and Seneca Nations, Congress had its eye on another territory further west. The lands ceded to England by France in 1763, following The Seven Years' War and America's French and Indian War, expanded British Colonial America as far west as the Mississippi River. Twenty years later, at the close of the Revolution, England reluctantly surrendered all their vast colonial lands south of the Great Lakes to America. The immediate concern for Congress was how to incorporate the additional territory into the new republic and allocate its lands for future settlement and statehood. The Northwest Ordinance of 1787 that was renewed by the United States Congress in '89, chartered a government for the new territory and provided for the eventual admission of not less than three nor more than five new states. The ordinance also included a bill of rights for the territory, guaranteeing religious freedom, habeas corpus, trial by jury, and encouraged education and forbade slavery. Over the course of the next seventy years, the states of Ohio, Indiana, Illinois, Michigan, Wisconsin, and the eastern third of Minnesota would all be carved out of the Northwest Territory. The Northwest Ordinance would be used as a template for subsequent western territories and admitting new western states into the union.

The old property line that extended west from New York through north central Pennsylvania's great pine forests to the Allegheny River no longer separated whites from Indians. But the portion of the old property line that continued down the Ohio River from Pittsburgh to Paducah would continue to serve as the southern border of the Great Northwest Territory. The Ohio River boundary line that originally terminated at the mouth of the Tennessee River was extended on another forty miles to the Mississippi and the postwar border with Spain's Louisiana Territory. With the Ohio to the south, the Mississippi on the west, and the Great Lakes to the north, the eastern boundary of the Northwest Territory would run along Pennsylvania's western state line north of the Ohio River. At the close of the Fort Stanwix treaty conference in '84, the Seneca sold a large tract of their southern Allegheny territory to Pennsylvania for $5,000 with another $2,000 eventually going to the Lenape and Wyandots for their portion of the land. Two years later, the Pennsylvania state line was surveyed due north from the Mason Dixon Line to Lake Erie, crossing the Ohio River at the mouth of Little Beaver Creek, thirty miles northwest of Pittsburgh. [1]

The Indian nations of the Northwest Territory, who lived on their lands north of the Ohio River to the Great Lakes, were about to be faced with the same unhappy options their eastern brethren in New York were dealing with. England's abandonment of their Indigenous allies following the Revolution, paved the way for Congress to capitalize on the Indian's vulnerability. Joseph Brant was quoted as saying after reading the details of the 1783 Paris Peace Treaty, '...*England has sold the Indians to Congress*...'. Within months of Gov. Clinton's and Congress' 1784 treaty negotiations at Fort Stanwix, Congress held another council fire in early '85 at Fort McIntosh on the Ohio River, twenty miles below Pittsburgh. Two of the commissioners who had been at the Fort Stanwix conference, Richard Butler and Arthur Lee, were sent to join Gen. George Rogers Clark at Fort McIntosh.

General Clark, 'The Washington of the West' and hero of the Revolution's western border war, was no friend to the western Indian nations. His proposal for a new property line that would push the Indians further north from the Ohio River boundary was reluctantly accepted by the small delegation of Delaware and Wyandot who attended the council fire. But when word of the new treaty line reached the northwest nations, it was roundly rejected and ignored by Brant, Shawnee Chief Blue Jacket, and the Miami's Little Turtle. In response to the Treaty of Fort McIntosh, the Lenape, Miami, Odawa, Chippewa, Potawatomi, Shawnee, Wabash, Wyandot, and the western Iroquois formed the Northwest Confederation of Nations. Congress' aggressive campaign to force the Indians from the Northwest Territory would continue over the next ten years through a series of treaty conferences held along the Ohio River at Fort Finney in '86, Fort Harmer in '89, and finally Detroit in '93. [2]

After Joseph Brant and the Northwest Confederation's rejection of the Fort McIntosh and Fort Finney treaties, violence on the frontier intensified as Kentucky squatters began settling on lands north of the Ohio River. Attempting to quell the unrest and enforce the treaties contested property lines, Gen. Clark led a military campaign against the Indians in the Wabash River region of the Indiana territory. After a botched campaign and humiliating retreat from the Wabash, Clark was replaced on the frontier by Maj. Gen. Arthur St. Clair in 1787. St. Clair was commissioned first territorial governor of the Northwest Territory and given authority to establish a territorial government at Marietta on the confluence of the Muskingum and Ohio Rivers. Calling for another treaty conference at Fort Harmer with Brant's delegation, the governor tried again to resolve the northwest boundary dispute. Brant proposed extending the boundary line north from the Ohio River along the Muskingum and Tuscarawas Rivers to the Cuyahoga, from Marietta to present-day Cleveland. Brant's compromise proposal to cede the eastern third of the present-day state of Ohio to Congress was rejected and the treaty conference ended with another unresolved property line agreement. The failure of the Fort Harmer treaty conference predictably led to another series of military campaigns.

Generals St. Clair and Josiah Harmer led two separate campaigns of Kentucky militiamen into the Indian territory in 1790 and '91, both of which were defeated by Blue Jacket and Little Turtle's Shawnee, Potawatomi, and Miami warriors. Their defeats prompted Washington and Congress to replace St. Clair with yet another general, the hero of Stony Point and celebrated Revolutionary War commander, Maj. Gen. 'Mad' Anthony Wayne. General Wayne initiated an aggressive escalation of force by building more forts and fortifying blockhouses throughout the Ohio and Indiana frontier and by the spring of '92 commanded a force of 5,000 army troops and militiamen. [3]

Detroit Treaty Conference

Endeavoring to avert another ineffective military solution to the Northwest Territory impasse, Washington tried one last attempt to negotiate an acceptable boundary line between the Indians and whites. Massachusetts' Timothy Pickering and Benjamin Lincoln were commissioned along with Virginia's

Beverly Randolph to hold another treaty conference with the western nations in hopes of reaching a peaceful resolution to the boundary dispute. While Gen. Wayne continued to gather and ready his troops for the inevitability that force might be needed to resolve the issue, the three commissioners prepared to head west to meet with the Indians. The Detroit Conference may never actually have been expected to achieve its intended diplomatic goals, being designed instead to simply stall for more time for Gen. Wayne and his troops to prepare for the ultimate solution.

During the first week of May 1793, the three commissioners met at Schenectady and began preparations for their long journey to the northwest frontier and Fort Detroit. At the time, traveling west through New York State any further than the Finger Lakes Region was not yet open to overland travel. It would not be until the late '90s before pioneers in caravans of wagons could make it any further west than the frontier outpost of Canandaigua, seventy-five miles shy of Buffalo Creek and Lake Erie. The only way to get from the Hudson River to the Great Lakes was by way of the ancient waterway route, up the Mohawk River by boat and over the portage to Lake Ontario. The Detroit emissary's small flotilla of river bateaux, loaded with provisions and gifts for the Indians, set out up the Mohawk on the 9th of May for Fort Stanwix. They hoped to reach Detroit by mid-June. After portaging over the old Oneida Carry and rowing down Wood Creek to Oneida Lake, the bateaux crossed over to the lake's western outlet and the river that would carry them down to Fort Oswego and Lake Ontario. Fort Oswego and a half dozen other forts on the American side of the border with Canada were still occupied by British forces. In protest against the confiscation and retention of loyalist properties, England obstinately refused to evacuate the forts after the war. The commissioners, however, were granted passes to continue their journey onto Lake Ontario without incident.

On the 25th, having sailed along Lake Ontario's southern shoreline to the mouth of the Niagara River, the commissioners reached British held Fort Niagara. Across the river at Navy Hall, they found the lieutenant governor of Upper Canada, John Graves Simcoe, to be a most gracious and accommodating host. The governor's charming demeanor and patronizing hospitality proved irresistible, so much so, the commissioners tarried about on the Niagara Peninsula for a month-and-a-half longer than they should have. By design, Simcoe's intent was to delay the commissioner's arrival at Detroit and learn from them as much as he could about America's plans for the Northwest Territory. Besides giving Gen. Wayne more time to prepare his troops, the delay also gave Blue Jacket's Shawnee and Little Turtle's Miami scouts more time to watch the Americans' movements and prepare their own warriors for battle, should it come to that. [4]

While dining and schmoozing with Gov. Simcoe and other officers and dignitaries, the commissioners toured the sights and visited the Great Falls. On one of their excursions, they crossed the Niagara River on a ferry from Fort Erie to the American side and visited a Seneca village on Buffalo Creek. The commissioners and their entourage were welcomed by their Seneca hosts who entertained them with ceremonial festivities and speeches. On a similar occasion they met with Joseph Brant and a small delegation of Iroquois at the governor's Navy Hall. Brant voiced his concerns over Gen. Wayne's activities on the frontier and asked why, if the Americans wanted a peaceful resolution to the boundary dispute, was he amassing such a large force and building more forts. The commissioners tried to reassure Brant that they were there to peacefully negotiate a fair and equitable border agreement that might restore order to the region and avoid bloodshed. The Indians left the meeting knowing full well their assurances of a peaceful resolution would never come to pass.

In mid-July, the three commissioners finally left the Niagara Peninsula and set sail across Lake Erie for the Detroit River. Reaching their destination, they found agreeable lodging on the Canadian side of the river at the Amherstburg home of British Indian Agent, Capt. Matthew Elliott. On their week-long journey across the lake, Benjamin Lincoln wrote in his journal, '*...so that if the savages cannot be civilized and quit their present pursuits, they will, in consequence of their stubbornness, dwindle and molder away...until the whole race shall become extinct...*'. Lincoln's opinion of Native Americans and their culture was typical of most eighteenth-century gentlemen, but a curious one for someone about to negotiate with them. Washington's commissioners may never have held any illusions as to the likelihood of their convincing the Indians to give up any of their lands without a fight. [5]

The Detroit Treaty Conference stumbled along for three weeks between late July and mid-August. After an initial but brief council fire with a small delegation of Wyandots and Miamis at Capt. Elliott's house, the negotiations lapsed into a terse exchange of letters between the commissioners and the Indians in council on the Maumee River, near today's Toledo. The nations of the Northwest Confederation were divided as to whether they should concede some of their lands north of the Ohio or holdfast to the Ohio River boundary line. Brant and most of his followers were in favor of a peaceful resolution and a modest concession of some of their lands north of the Ohio and east of the Muskingum. The Wyandot and Delaware, along with Blue Jacket's Shawnee and Little Turtle's Miamis were adamantly opposed to any concessions and demanded the removal of all white settlers north of the Ohio. Growing increasingly impatient with the slow response to their letters and failed attempts to arrange a meeting on the Maumee River, the commissioners concluded the talks had reached a stalemate. They sailed for Fort Erie and home on the 17th of August, after a month of futile attempts to reach a settlement. Gov. Simcoe and Capt. Elliot had both plotted to impede the commissioner's efforts. The pretense of a treaty resolution merely gave both the Indians and Gen. Wayne more time to prepare for war. [6]

Leading his forces from Fort Washington on the Ohio River, at today's Cincinnati, General Wayne advanced up the Great Miami River while building a supply line of forts along the way. Two months after the commissioners left Amherstburg for home, Gen. Wayne's 2,600 Kentucky volunteers and four hundred regular army troops of the Legion of the United States reached Fort Jefferson in mid-October. Fort Jefferson had fallen into disrepair after St. Clair launched his disastrous campaign there in 1790. Accordingly, Gen. Wayne's troops built another fort five miles north of the old fort and garrisoned Fort Greenville through the winter of 1793/'94. Advancing another thirty miles north in the spring, Wayne's troops built another fort on the site of St. Clair's defeat on the Wabash River, Fort Recovery. Their objective was to continue north towards Lake Erie and the Miami villages on the lower Maumee River before marching on to recapture Fort Detroit from the British. In response to Wayne's advance, Gov. Simcoe ordered a fort to be built near the villages at the Maumee Rapids and sent a company of well-seasoned frontier fighters to defend Fort Miami, and to forestall Wayne's advance. By building a fort on U.S. territory and ordering British Canadian troops to garrison it, the governor violated American sovereignty which threatened to start another war between the United States and Great Britain.

On the morning of August 20th, 1794, in a forest windfall outside Fort Miami, Mad Anthony Wayne's 3,000 troops faced off against Blue Jacket's 1,500 Shawnee and Ottawa warriors and a company of British rangers led by the notorious Capt. William Caldwell. Attempting to deny any British culpability in the affair, Capt. Caldwell disguised his rangers in Indian garb, just as he and Col. Butler's rangers had done during their raids on the Mohawk River settlements and at Wyoming Valley during New York's border war. After an hour-long battle in which many of the Indians and their chiefs were killed, the Americans scored a decisive victory in what became known as the Battle of Fallen Timbers. A year after the battle, a disarrayed Northwest Confederation of Nations met with Gen. Wayne at Fort Greenville and signed a treaty establishing a new Indian property line. The Greenville Treaty Line gave American's frontier settlers access to the lower two-thirds of the present state of Ohio and all the lands east of the Cuyahoga River from Cleveland to the Pennsylvania state line. The summer of 1795 also witnessed the ratification of John Jay's treaty with England that normalized trade between the two former enemies. Furthermore, Jay's Treaty stipulated that the British relinquish control of the American forts on the U.S. side of the Canadian border, from Michilimackinac to Detroit, and Niagara to Oswego and Lake Champlain. Fort Detroit was taken with the stroke of a pen, while the war that Simcoe teased had to wait another twenty years. [7]

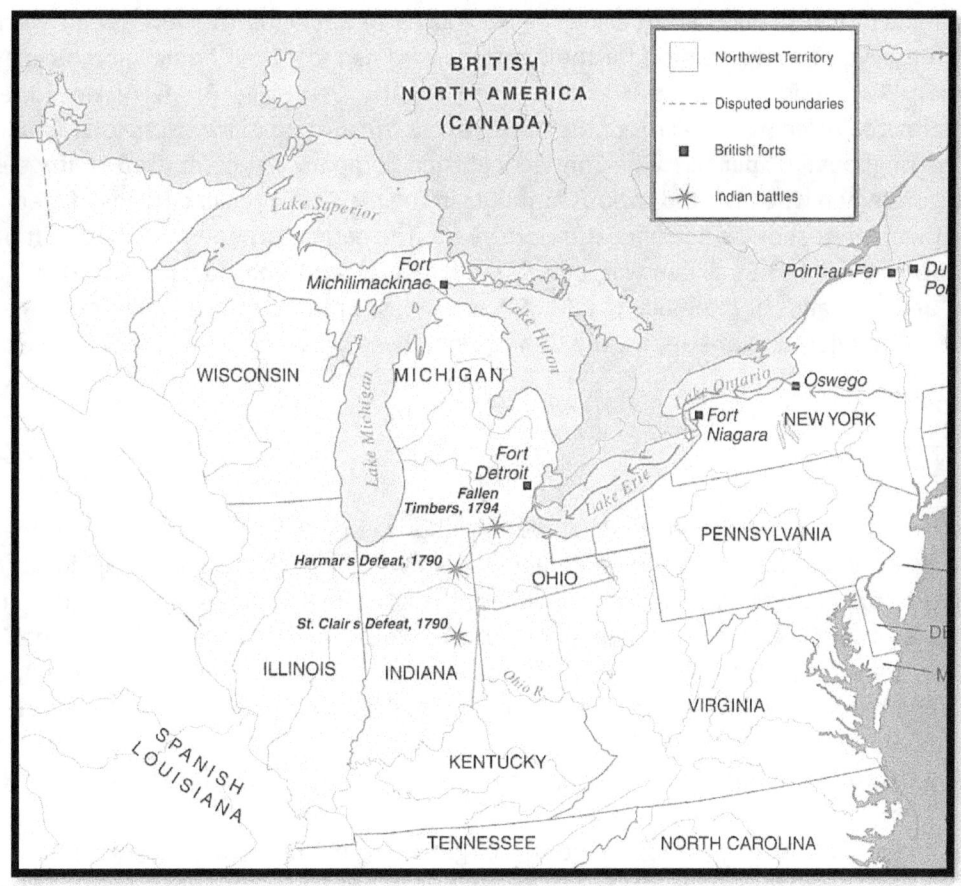

*Green-Greenville Treaty Line; **Purple-The Western Reserve**; Red-Commissioners Path to Detroit*

The Western Reserve

In the mid-1780s, while Gov. Clinton and the State of New York were rushing ahead of Congress to settle their claims with Massachusetts and the Iroquois Nations, Connecticut was grappling with how to deal with their Royal Charter's western lands in the Northwest Territory. In 1786, their legislature agreed to yield to Congress the far western portion of their lands between the 41° and 42° 2' parallels, from Lake Erie's Sandusky Bay to the Mississippi River. Congress, in exchange, assumed Connecticut's war debts. Retaining the eastern 120 miles of their charter lands between the Sandusky and the Pennsylvania State Line, Connecticut authorized a survey of their Western Reserve's 3,500,000 acres. The survey, however, would have to wait another ten years before only the eastern half could be conducted, and another twenty years before the whole extent of the Western Reserve survey was completed. It was not until Gen. Wayne's victory at Fallen Timbers and the Indian's concession of their Ohio lands at the Greenville Treaty Conference of '95, could Connecticut finally run their surveys and capitalize on part of their Western Reserve lands. All the lands east of the portion of the Greenville Treaty Line that ran along the Cuyahoga River from the forty-first latitude to Lake Erie, between today's Akron and Cleveland, were now open for development. In 1796, the process of surveying the Western Reserve into township sections for speculators and investors began. But the lands west of the Cuyahoga would need to wait for another treaty council fire and another Indian property line before that portion of the Western Reserve could be opened to the theodolites and chains.

Connecticut had previously set aside the 500,000-acre Firelands Tract on the far western end of the Western Reserve as compensation for their citizens who had lost their homes and businesses during the Revolution. Two months after the establishment of the Greenville Property Line, they sold the remaining estimated three million acres of the Reserve to a consortium of investors for 1.2 million dollars, the equivalent of about .40¢ per acre. The Connecticut Land Company was comprised of fifty-eight wealthy Connecticut gentlemen who invested various amounts in the project by posting bonds of credit payable in five years with an interest of 6% accruing after two years. The early erroneous estimate that put the total acreage of the Reserve at 3.5 million, was subsequently estimated to be closer to 3,350,000 acres. With the 500,000-acre Firelands and remaining 830,000 acres west of the Cuyahoga still under the domain of the Northwest Confederation of Nations, the Connecticut investors were left with a little over two million acres. [8]

Survey of 1796

The lands east of the Cuyahoga River were authorized by the directors of the Connecticut Land Company to be surveyed into tiers and range lines on a five-mile grid, making townships of twenty-five square miles or 16,000 acres each. When completed, their two million acres would render one hundred and twenty-five townships, some of which were surveyed into smaller sections. One of the Connecticut Land Company's seven directors, Brig. Gen. Moses Cleaveland, was appointed to oversee and lead the survey expedition as soon as preparations could be arranged and the season allowed. In early April 1796, General Superintendent Cleaveland, Principal Surveyor Augustus Porter, and Assistant Surveyor and Mathematician Seth Pease, met in Schenectady and began organizing the first Western Reserve survey expedition.

Albeit late in the season after two months of gathering the necessary equipment and provisions, the 1796 surveying expedition finally got underway on the 26th of May. Gen. Cleaveland and the surveyors were accompanied by a team of forty-five axe men, chain bearers, bateau men and two of the workmen's wives. They also brought along a physician and a chaplain. On the first leg of their journey up the Mohawk River, their flotilla of four large river bateaux were piloted by the bateau men to Fort Stanwix, then portaged across the old Oneida Carry to Wood Creek. Just as the Detroit Commissioners had done three years before, they were heading for the Great Lakes that would take them all the way to the Western Reserve. Upon reaching Oneida Lake, the bateau men alternated between sailing and rowing across the length of the lake to the west end outlet before entering the Oneida and Oswego Rivers that would take them to Lake Ontario. Besides battling the head winds and inclement weather that slowed their daily progress, the expedition had another formidable portage to transverse before reaching the lake. After successfully transporting their boats and cargo around Oswego Falls, locks 2 and 3 on today's Oswego Canal, the expedition finally reached Lake Ontario.

Reaching the lake on the 6th of June, the surveyors found Fort Oswego still occupied by a garrison of British troops although Jay's Treaty had required the evacuation of all British held American forts by the 1st of June. The fort's commander had no intention of complying with the treaty's deadline. Gen. Cleaveland was surprised and dismayed to have to acquiesce to the British commander's authority and wait for him to grant the expedition a pass. Not being particularly interested in delaying their progress or giving the Brits the slightest measure of satisfaction, the American bateaux laid in wait until dark and then quietly rowed past the fort's snoozing sentries. The expedition's curiously late start may have been purposely planned to avoid any trouble passing by Forts Oswego, Niagara, and Erie, all of which should have been evacuated by the time they reached the first of them.

It would take the surveyors another week to row and sail along Lake Ontario's shoreline before arriving at the mouth of the Niagara River. Discovering that Fort Niagara had only been evacuated by the King's 5th Regiment a few days before their arrival, they were not bothered by the last small company of

British troops still lingering in the fort. Passing by the fort and into the river without incident, they rowed a couple of miles up to Queenstown Landing to prepare for their portage around Niagara Falls. The expedition remained another two weeks on the Canadian side of the river, transporting their boats and all their gear by wagon from the lower Queenstown Landing to the upper Chippawa landing, two miles above the falls. Here, their boats were reloaded and readied for the trip up the rest of the Niagara River and into Lake Erie. The expedition was joined on the Niagara portage by a group of their workmen who had been sent overland to Canandaigua while they were still on the Mohawk River at Fort Stanwix. By the late '90s, Canandaigua had become a bustling little frontier village with two hundred households and forty framed houses, a courthouse and jail, and several accommodating taverns for thirsty travelers. The overland party had been instructed to purchase ten horses and ten head of cattle at Canandaigua which they were to bring on to Buffalo Creek along the old Indian trail and catch up with the rest of the expedition on the Niagara River. After their perilous journey through the wilderness and reunion with their comrades, one of the tired drovers later commented '...*we were all wet and cold, but after pushing about the bottle and getting a good fire and supper, we were as merry as grigs...*'.

While the workmen were tending to their portaging duties and marveling at the great Niagara cataract, Superintendent Cleaveland attended a conference with the Seneca and Mohawk leaders on the American side of the river at Buffalo Creek. Red Jacket, Farmer's Brother and the ubiquitous Joseph Brant were there to demand appropriate compensation for their lands east of the Greenville Property Line. Seeking cooperation with an acceptable compensation for the full and legal extermination of the title to their former lands on the Western Reserve, Cleaveland offered a one-time payment of $1,000 along with customary gifts and whiskey. The unassailable Capt. Brant countered with $1,500, plus an annual annuity of $500. Accepting Brant's proposal, Cleaveland assured him he could convince the federal government to pay the annual annuity and left the council fire with a clear deed to their lands. A nominal gift of New York currency, two beef cattle, and a hundred gallons of whiskey were left with the Buffalo Creek Indians. The Connecticut Land Company would interpret the agreement to have only been for the one-time payment of $1,500, while Congress never did pay any of the $500 annuity payments.

A few days after covering the Buffalo Creek council fire on the 24th of June, the surveyors and their fully loaded bateaux began the journey down along Lake Erie's southern shoreline. Coming upon the survey marker that defined the northern point of Pennsylvania's western boundary line they reached the Western Reserve on the 3rd of July and continued another five miles to the mouth of Conneaut Creek. The men who had driven the livestock from Canandaigua to Buffalo Creek and had continued their overland trek down the lake's shorefront, arrived shortly thereafter. The tired voyagers rejoiced in their journey's end and celebrated the twentieth anniversary of their young republic's independence with a day of feasting and toasting to America's future success. Finding a small Indian village at the mouth of the Conneaut, a gesture of good faith and friendship was extended to the Massasagoes tribe of the Lenape Nation. Their chief Paqua reciprocated in kind, extending his hand in friendship, and welcoming the white visitors to his lands. The New England surveyors would have little trouble with the local Indians and their curious young warriors who would often follow and help them as they ran out their tier and range lines.

After a brief rest, five survey parties, each with a surveyor and seven or eight hands, were organized and readied to head out into the unbroken wilds of the Ohio frontier. After identifying the Reserve's easternmost boundary line along the Pennsylvania line, the surveyor's followed it south sixty-six miles to the 41^0 parallel that ran west to the Greenville Treaty Line at the portage between the Cuyahoga and Tuscarawas Rivers. From these two lines the teams could run their tier lines east to west between Pennsylvania and the Cuyahoga, and the range lines from south to north between the 41^0 parallel and Lake Erie. One of the primary objectives of this first survey was the establishment of a township on the east side of the Cuyahoga at the lake. Establishing a major settlement was paramount to the success of any frontier tract. Moses Cleaveland was most interested in plotting out a township on the lake to encourage development of a port city that could serve as the Reserve's center of transportation and commerce. His lakefront township was surveyed into ten-acre lots on a grid surrounding a village square. The village he envisioned would eventually grow into one of the first major metropolises west of the Appalachians, that but for a single vowel, would bear his name.

The Western Reserve survey of 1796 concluded after just three and a half months of field work. Having started late in the season and taken five weeks to reach the Reserve, completing a survey of over 3,000 square miles in that amount of time was simply not possible. The tier and range lines in the southern and eastern portions of the Reserve would need a second survey to complete. By mid-October, with the days growing shorter and winter fast approaching, Gen. Cleaveland and the surveyors decided it was time to return to Connecticut before they became snowed in on the frontier. The men were more than ready to go home. Dwindling provisions, sickness, exhaustion, and relentless attacks from gnats and mosquitoes had conspired to undermine the morale of the workmen, who at one point had threatened to mutiny and go home earlier. To quell their angst, Cleaveland offered each of them the right to purchase, on credit and good terms, a lot in any township of their choice. This seems to have had the desired effect of convincing the workmen to see the survey through to the end.

With the wind to their backs and unburdened by most of their provisions and heavy barrels of whiskey, the survey party boarded their bateaux and left their Conneaut Creek encampment on the 21st of October. The trip home followed the same general course they had taken to get to the Reserve, but only as far as Lake Ontario's Irondequoit Bay, at today's Rochester. Here they left their bateaux at the swampy head of the bay and hiked twenty-five miles south to Canandaigua where they arranged for all their surveying equipment to be stored for the next survey expedition. After a comfortable night's rest in a warm bed beneath a friendly tavern roof, the surveyors and the workmen set off on foot and horseback for their homes and families in Connecticut. They were all back home by the middle of November. Moses Cleaveland, Augustus Porter, and nearly all of the first expedition's workmen would never again return to the Western Reserve. [9]

Survey of 1797

Upon Cleaveland's and Porter's return to Hartford with their partial survey and unfinished maps, the committee members of the Connecticut Land Company were not at all satisfied with the first survey's results. Right away they began planning and arranging funding for a second survey to finish what the first had left undone. With Schenectady again being the port of departure, and the surveyors being better prepared for what lay ahead, the second Western Reserve survey got under way on the 20th of April 1797. They were departing three full weeks ahead of the '96 expedition. Six river bateaux were loaded with all the necessary gear, including tents, blankets, candles, lanterns, cooking utensils, axes, compasses, medicine, flour, sugar, and soap. The daily allotment of rations per man was set at one bowl of porridge with sugar, one bottle of tea and one of rum, five pounds of pork for six men, and one pound of chocolate for the whole party. If the Connecticut surveyors had learned anything on their first expedition, it was that a well-fed crew was a happier one.

While the main body of the expedition was still on the Mohawk, a smaller group of men were again sent out to Canandaigua on horseback with instructions to purchase six more horses, six cows and a bull, and all the pork, whiskey, and cheese they could carry. The trip up the Mohawk and across Oneida Lake to Lake Ontario progressed seamlessly, and within two weeks of leaving Schenectady they had reached Irondequoit Bay. A week was spent shuttling supplies and equipment back to the bateaux from Canandaigua where they had left their surveying equipment the year before. They had arranged to meet Principal Surveyor Augustus Porter at Canandaigua, who with his family was lodging in Nathaniel Sanborn's tavern. Upon their arrival, Porter informed the party that he had quit the Connecticut Land Company and was now under the employment of the Holland Land Company, surveying their lands in western New York.

Porter informed his Assistant Surveyor and Mathematician Seth Pease that he would oversee the second survey expedition from here on.

Launching their flotilla of fully loaded bateaux from Irondequoit Bay, Principal Surveyor Pease's expedition proceeded slowly along Lake Ontario's southern coastal waters for a week before reaching Queenstown Landing on the Niagara River. The party that was sent out from the Mohawk River to Canandaigua to purchase the horses and cattle, rendezvoused with the expedition on the Niagara River, just as the '*merry grigs*' had in '96. The portage around the falls took almost a week, after which another week was spent rowing and sailing down Lake Erie while the drovers herded the livestock down along the shoreline and cliffs above. The second survey expedition reached the Western Reserve and Conneaut Creek on the 26th of May, the same day the first survey party of '96 left Schenectady. With the extra month afforded them, Pease's party was poised to complete the survey the first expedition had failed to finish.

The extra time spent on the Ohio frontier by the second expedition did indeed allow for the completion of the survey, but it also contributed to more suffering and misfortune for the workmen. From the time they left Canandaigua and Irondequoit Bay, fever, dysentery, and ague plagued the men. Very few of them were spared the bilious fever that ravaged their ranks. Half a dozen men would die of the insidious malaise, never returning to their Connecticut families. One man was thrown from his horse and drowned while crossing the Cuyahoga. Three more were lost when their boat capsized near Cattaraugus Creek. The ailing survey teams struggled miserably throughout that hot, humid summer as they broke their way through the brush and bramble. But Pease and his men were determined to finish all the Reserve's tier and range lines between Pennsylvania and the Cuyahoga River. By early October, the men were waking up covered by a light frost that signaled winter was not far off. While the first bateaux loaded with sick and weakened workmen prepared to leave their encampment at the mouth of the Cuyahoga River, a few teams of surveyors started working their way eastward to the Chagrin and Grand Rivers, surveying the last of their tier lines on a general course for home.

Seth Pease

On the evening of the 3rd of October, Seth Pease wrote in his journal, '*...In the afternoon we ran ashore and spoke with some strangers from Harpersfield in New York State, Col. Moss who appeared their principal man rode on ward to Cleveland with two other gentlemen. One whom they called Capt. [Alexander] Harper who was on foot took a passage in our boat to the Chagrin River...*'. After surveying throughout the Chagrin River area in today's Lake County, Pease's party continued running their tier lines through the Grand River ranges before encamping for another night. That night he again wrote in his journal, '*...Rode to the Grand River, Capt. Harper accompanied us on foot, moved upriver and encamped at the Indian Village on the west side...*'. On the night of the sixth, Pease again wrote, '*...The three gentlemen we saw the other day going to Cleveland hailed us. As they contemplate being settlers, we furnished them with a loaf of bread. Capt. Harper went with them, and all bid us goodbye...*'. The youngest of the Harper brothers had come to the Western Reserve to explore the countryside and scout out a suitable location for a new frontier settlement for his family and those who might follow him.

Three weeks after their encounter with the strangers from New York, Pease and his surveyors started their return journey back to civilization and their Connecticut homeland. Leaving a dozen of their comrades behind in shallow graves, the surviving surveyors boarded their bateaux and paddled off into Lake Erie's howling gales. October was threatening to turn into November, and they still had a month-long trip ahead of them. All but one of the surveyors and workmen were back in Connecticut by late-November. Principal Surveyor Pease stayed in Canandaigua until mid-December, working on his map and preparing his Western Reserve report. He finally reached his home and wife Bathsheba in Suffield a few days before

Christmas. By the first of the year, he had submitted his report and survey map to the commissioners of the Connecticut Land Company in Hartford. In late January 1798, the commissioners were finally ready to begin advertising the availability of township and homestead lots in the eastern half of the Western Reserve. [10]

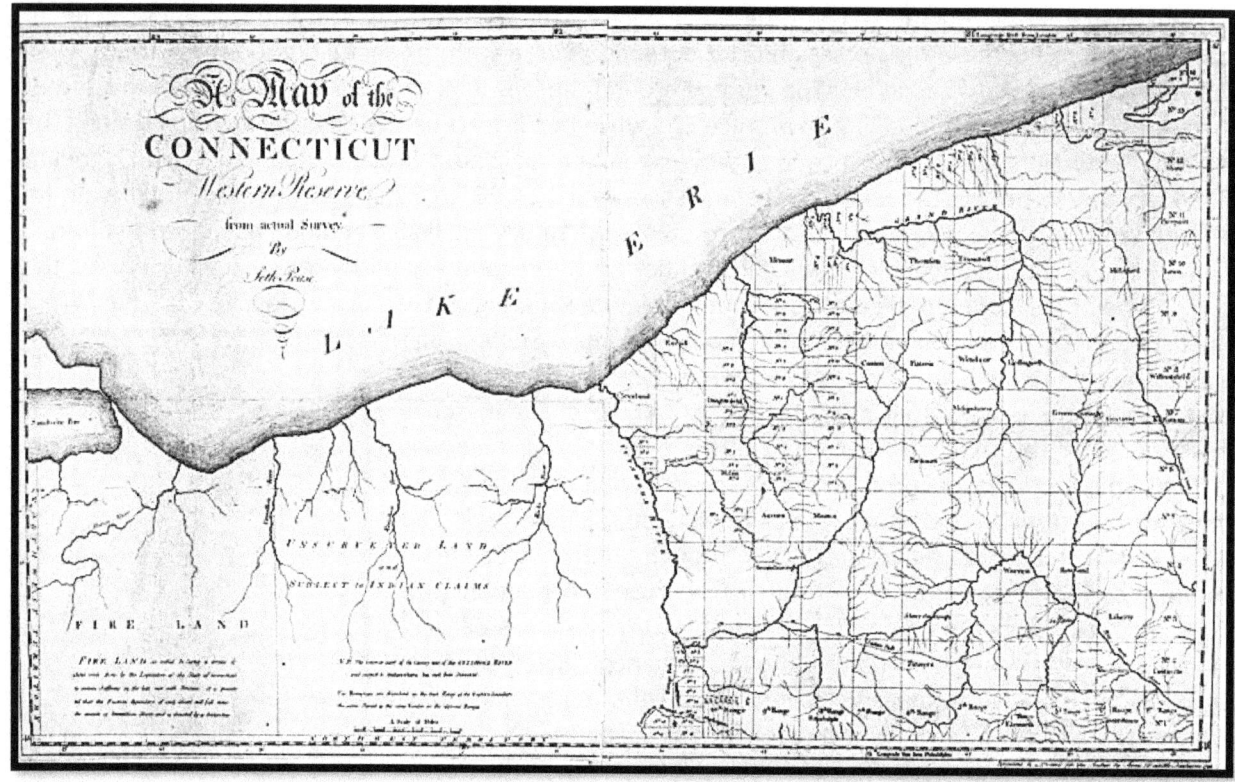

A Map of the Connecticut Western Reserve from Actual Survey by Seth Pease

Harpersfield Expedition

In early 1797, Alexander Harper formed an investment company with several family members and associates with the goal of purchasing as much land in the Western Reserve as they could secure. Three of the Old Harpersfield Land Company's principal investors included the Harper's brother-in-law William McFarland, Alexander's son-in-law Aaron Wheeler and Col. Harper's son-in-law Roswell Hotchkiss. Other longtime associates and friends of the Harpers to have invested in the company included members of the Hendry, Gaylord, Gregory, Patchin, Montgomery, and Bartholomew families. Pooling their resources, the investors entered into contract with two of the Connecticut Land Company's principal shareholders, Oliver Phelps and Gideon Granger. They proposed purchasing, on credit, six township lots in the Western Reserve, totaling 96,000 acres. Three of their township allotments were in the surveyed eastern half of the Reserve, while the other three were purchase options to be exercised once the lands west of the Cuyahoga were surveyed and opened to settlement. [11]

In September of '97, Alexander embarked upon his exploratory journey to the Western Reserve to assess the terrain and select the choicest township lots for the investors of the Old Harpersfield Land Company. Along the way he fell in with Capt. Zeally Moss and two other gentlemen who were heading for the Reserve for the same reason. Referred to in Seth Pease's journal as Col. Moss, Capt. Moss had served in the Virginia Line during the Revolution and in several Northwest Territory campaigns fighting Indians throughout Kentucky, Indiana, and Ohio. Alexander was fortunate to have fallen in with the experienced western frontiersmen who were excellent companions and guides for the New Yorker who had never been further west than Fort Niagara. Upon reaching the Western Reserve, Capt. Moss and the two other gentlemen continued to the Cuyahoga River while Alexander joined the survey party that was heading up the Grand River. According to Pease's journal, Alexander spent a few days with the surveyors, helping them run their chains while evaluating the layout of the land for future settlement. Finding the Grand River area to his liking, he recommended townships ten, eleven and twelve in the fifth range (Trumbull, Harpersfield, Geneva) to the Harpersfield investors. Township eleven in the fifth range was soon to be home to three of the first pioneer families on the Western Reserve. [12]

Having resigned their commissions in the 1st Otsego County Militia Regiment in April 1796, Lt. Col. Harper and Major McFarland began organizing the Old Harpersfield Land Company and planning their departure from Harpersfield. Both had had their fill of New York politics and the defamatory lawsuits with the Otsego Federalists and their nemesis Judge Cooper. The two militia commanders had plenty of loose ends to tie up before they could launch their next adventure and continue the dream of empire old John Harper had instilled in all four of his Scots-Irish sons. It had been eighty years since the Harper family landed on Boston's Long Wharf and over forty since they had settled on New York's border frontier. Col. John Harper was now approaching his mid-sixties and well past the age at which a prudent man would consider taking on another risky and physically challenging adventure. The passing of the torch from the paterfamilias to his son John would now be passed on to the youngest Harper brother Alexander.

In early March 1798, eight months after entering into contract with the Connecticut Land Company, Alexander, William and one other member of the Old Harpersfield Land Company gathered their families and their belongings and set out for the Western Reserve. Seven of Alexander and Elizabeth Bartholomew Harper's eight children joined their parents on their journey to the wilds of the Ohio frontier. They were fortunate to have their three oldest sons with them on the trip west. John-24, James-21, and William-19 were immense help for their fifty-five-year-old father, forty-nine-year-old mother and their four younger siblings, Elizabeth-14, Mary-12, Alexander Jr-10, and Robert-7. The oldest of the Harper children, Margaret, had recently married another investor in the land company, Aaron Wheeler, and while they remained in Harpersfield for the time being, they too would soon follow Margaret's family to the Western Reserve. Alexander's younger sister Miriam and husband William McFarland had no children of their own but had adopted a young boy after the war. In the years following the Revolution, there were no shortages of orphaned children or large families without one or both parents. Benjamin Hartwell was now around seventeen when he headed west with the McFarlands and Harpers. The McFarlands were also granted guardianship of a young lady who had recently been widowed before giving birth to her first child. Twenty-year-old Parthenia Mingus and her four-year-old son William had little choice but to remain with William and Miriam and accompany them on their westward journey. [13]

The Harpers and McFarlands were joined on their journey to the Western Reserve by one other couple and their seven children. Ezra Gregory had moved his family in the final years of the war from Connecticut's war-torn coastal community of Norwalk to New York's lower Dutchess County township of Carmel, in today's Putnam County. During the Revolution, Ezra had served in a Connecticut regiment with Isaac Patchin who may have influenced him to settle on the Harper family's New York patent in the early 1790s. While living in Harpersfield, Ezra and his wife Rebecca Hopkins Gregory became acquainted with the Harpers and once they learned of Alexander's plans to colonize the Western Reserve, invested in the land company and joined his western expedition. In addition to Ezra and Rebecca's three older children, Anna-22, Jonathan-21, and Eli-20, they brought along their four younger children, Eleanor-12, Daniel-9, Elizabeth-4, and Ezra Jr-2. Alexander and William certainly welcomed the extra hands Ezra, and his two older sons brought to the expedition. Said to have been a short, stout man, Ezra Gregory would become a valued and indispensable member of the Western Reserve's early settlements. [14]

Westward

On March 7th, 1798, twenty-three members of the Harper, McFarland, and Gregory families set out on a long journey to the Old Harpersfield Land Company's three frontier townships on the Western Reserve. The first phase of their journey was by ox-drawn sleighs with the men and older children alternating from snowshoes to horseback. Alexander's exploratory trip to the Western Reserve the previous fall had convinced him that an overland passage to the Reserve might be particularly dangerous for a group with so many women and young children. There were still no traversable roads further west than Canandaigua that could accommodate wagon traffic, and nothing between New York's Buffalo Creek and the Reserve but narrow Indian trails. Instead of heading west towards the Reserve, the Harper party pointed their sleds north towards the Mohawk River and the waterway route taken by the commissioners in 1793 and the surveyors in '96 and '97.

Bidding their friends and loved ones farewell, Alexander led his party down Harpersfield's Center Brook to Charlotte Creek and down to the Susquehanna River. Traveling in winter by sleds was a convenient mode of travel, especially when the rivers and streams were frozen over with a thick layer of ice and snow. The first leg of their journey might have been easy-going and even fun for the excited young children. Gliding up the Susquehanna towards Otsego Lake, the expedition could have made it all the way to the mouth of Cherry Valley Creek and the Cully family homesteads by the first night. Alexander's older sister Mary Harper Moore and his two nieces, Abigail and Mary Cully, would have welcomed their relatives with warm food and warmer embraces. The Harpers were saddened, however, to find sixty-four-year-old Mary gravely ill and on her deathbed. The oldest daughter of John and Abigail Harper had known her share of heartache. She had survived the horrible Cherry Valley Massacre, only to have been abducted and carried off to Fort Niagara with her three daughters and held captive for over two years. Mary died on April 10th, a month after her last visit with her younger brother and sister Miriam.

From the Cully's Milford homesteads, the Harper party would have continued up Cherry Valley Creek over a well-traveled road to the frontier village where old John Harper brought his family in 1754. The trail from Cherry Valley to the Mohawk River Valley would have been easy sledding along the old road to Canajoharie. From here it was a straight shot up the Mohawk past Fort Plain and on through German Flatts to old Fort Stanwix and the Oneida Carry. The frozen roads and waterways that made their progress relatively easy up to this point, now posed a significant obstacle to any further advancement toward their goal. Alexander's expedition to the Western Reserve would now have to wait another seven weeks for the ice breakup and spring freshet to open their pathway forward.

While waiting at Rome's Fort Stanwix for the ice to melt, Alexander sold the sleds and ox and began inquiring about for a good bateau man and crew to ferry the expedition down Wood Creek to Lake Oneida and on to Lake Ontario. He also purchased a large stock of provisions to accommodate the next phase of his westward journey. Rome had no shortage of taverns and lodging for the weary passengers who traveled the old Mohawk River waterway route to Lake Ontario. Gould Brother's Tavern, Logan's Hotel, or John Barnard's Tavern may have housed the expedition's families while they waited for the ice breakup. The many boatsmen who lingered about river portages were said to have been a rude and spirited bunch, rendering many taverns a bit too rowdy for the more refined and cultured traveler. The Harper men were no strangers to frontier tavern life and the type of men who frequented them, but their wives may have demanded shelter for themselves and their young children in a more orderly tavern.

While languishing in Rome, two more young men attached themselves to the Harpersfield expedition. Alexander hired a young man name Gleason who, unfortunately, no one bothered recording anything more than just 'J' for a first name. J. Gleason would become Alexander's right-hand man and trusted companion throughout the rest of the trip. Another young twenty-year-old man named Ephraim Clark joined the expedition in Rome. Ephraim would settle briefly with the Harpers after reaching Ohio, but soon after he moved further west to a settlement on the upper Cuyahoga River. Gleason and Clark were welcomed hands for the Harper party, bringing the expedition's total number to twenty-five. [15]

Needing to find an experienced and trust-worthy bateau man to guide them through the next phase of their journey, Alexander hired a man named William Gilchrist for £40 to pilot the expedition from Fort Stanwix to Oswego. With five and a half tons of cargo, two tons of passengers and three and a half tons of provisions and gear, Gilchrist would have determined they needed at least five or six bateaux to carry them to Lake Ontario. The doubled bowed Schenectady Bateau was thirty-five feet long and three to five wide. With its flat bottom and shallow draft, it could maneuver narrow streams, wide rivers, and open waters with efficiency. Each could carry a one-ton load, or about five to seven passengers and 1,000 lbs. of cargo. They were equipped with an eight-foot setting pole, a small mast and sail, a rudder paddle and two sets of oars for rowing during unfavorable winds. It took four men to crew the boat. Two oarsmen managed the sail or rowed when necessary, while a headsman on the bow signaled directions to the steersman on the stern who used an eighteen-foot paddle as a steering rudder. [16]

A Schenectady Bateaux

The ice did not break sufficiently enough for Mr. Gilchrist to feel confident about launching the loaded bateaux into the chilly waters of Wood Creek until the first day of May. After rowing and poling four miles down the narrow creek, the convoy reached the larger Canada Creek that took them down another ten miles to Oneida Lake. It is unfortunate that no one in the Harper party thought to keep a journal of their travels from New York to Ohio. Nevertheless, the journals of Benjamin Lincoln and Seth Pease gave a fairly good idea as to just how long it might have taken Gilchrist's bateaux to reach each landmark along their way. Favorable winds and a little luck had enabled the '97 survey expedition to cross Oneida Lake's thirty miles in just four hours, while Lincoln and the commissioners took about eight hours to cross. The survey party of '96, however, took two full days to reach the western outlet of the lake. These three expeditions were almost entirely made up of men with some experience in frontier travel and bateau navigation. Considering the Harpersfield expedition's limited workforce and additional women and children, it seems likely they would have taken at least two days to navigate the lake, even with favorable winds.

Upon reaching old Fort Brewerton on the west end of Oneida Lake, the weary travelers might have spent a raucous night in Oliver Stevens' rude frontier tavern before continuing the next day down the Oneida River to Three Rivers. With favorable conditions, the bateaux could have continued down Oswego River another twelve miles to Oswego Falls where they would have spent the next night at Daniel Masters' hotel at the upper landing. For half a dollar, after the boat's cargo and passengers were hauled by wagon about a mile down to the lower landing, William Shorter would slide an empty bateau on rollers about sixty yards down a steep track. The unloading, hauling, and reloading of the bateaux would have taken at least a day, if not two. Back on the water, it was clear sailing down the river twelve more miles to Oswego and the open waters of Lake Ontario. A journey by boat down a raging river or across a turbulent lake could turn into a perilous and deadly affair in a heartbeat. [17]

The next phase of the Harper expedition had taken the surveyors about six days to complete the hundred-and-fifty-mile journey along Lake Ontario's southern coastline to Niagara. They had been forced at one point to hold up for several days while the lake and weather halted their progress. On any given day, the lake's clear azure surface could turn into a mountain range of whitecaps and snarling dragons. In an uncharacteristic show of discretion, Alexander opted not to challenge the lake in his river bateaux. He wisely chose instead to charter a much larger and safer schooner to transport his families across the lake's unpredictable waters. As it happened, an English schooner bound for Niagara was in port at Fort Oswego.

Having served as a naval quartermaster in the Royal Navy during the Revolution, 2nd Lt. James Richardson of the Provincial Marine was now working for the Northwest Company running furs and supplies back and forth between Kingston and the Queenstown Landing. Although they were once enemies and unaware that in fewer than fifteen years they would be again, the Harper party happily boarded Lieut. Richardson's *Kingston Packet* and sailed off for the Niagara River. Alexander paid another $80 to secure his party's safe passage to Queenstown Landing, reaching there in just three days. [18]

When the *Kingston Packet* reached the mouth of the Niagara in late May, the schooner would have had to pass beneath the fort where Capt. Harper and his sugar boilers were held captive eighteen years earlier. Curiosity may have gotten the better of Alexander and he may have paid a visit to old Fort Niagara that was now in American custody. Remembering the day when he and his fellow captives were ushered into the fort without having to run the gauntlet, he might have thought of his niece Jane and her husband, Capt. John Powell, whose collusion with Capt. Brant had spared the sugar boilers' lives. At war's end, when Col. John Butler's Rangers were disbanded, the Powells joined the other exiled New York loyalists who settled on the Niagara Peninsula in British-held Upper Canada, today's Ontario Province. In the summer of 1784, John and Jane settled in the Welland County settlement of Bertie. By '98, John had been awarded over 2,000 acres throughout Bertie for his meritorious service to the king during the war. The Powells were now living with their three children, ages 8-12, on one of John's lots on Frenchman's Creek a few miles north of Fort Erie. While paying his respects to the commanding officer at Fort Niagara, Alexander appears to have inquired as to the whereabouts of his niece Jane and the Powells. [19]

While portaging around Niagara Falls from Queenstown Landing to the upper Chippawa Landing, the families of the Harper expedition settled into lodgings on the Canadian side of the river near Fort Erie. Alexander's family would have been welcomed by his niece Jane who would have insisted they stay with her and her family. The expatriated Harper would have been anxious to hear all the news of her mother Mary, sisters Abigail and Mary, and her brothers John and James Moore, all of whom she had not seen for twenty years. The Harpers would have brought along a few letters and cherished mementos from Jane's siblings who had grown up with her in Cherry Valley before their lives were forever torn apart by war. But they also brought along the sad news of Jane's mother Mary's recent death, assuming word of her death had reached them before they left Rome. The otherwise joyous reunion of the Harper cousins was a welcomed and much needed break for the whole entourage, but it might have lasted longer than it should have. The expedition spent nearly a full month on the Niagara Peninsula, while June and the growing season got well underway. With Lake Erie ahead of them and many more miles to go, they needed to hurry on to the Reserve to establish their new homesteads and get a late crop in the ground before winter closed in around them. These lost weeks in Rome and at the Powells would end up costing them dearly.

Fort Erie was an actively garrisoned British fort used primarily as a supply depot and trading post for the western forts and settlements along the Canadian side of the Great Lakes. With British Capt. Powell's help, Alexander arranged passage for his party on a military transport vessel about to deliver supplies to the settlements along Lake Erie's north shore. Due to weight restrictions, only the members of the Harper party and a limited amount of their belongings and provisions were taken aboard the British schooner heading for Long Point Peninsula. Arrangements were made for the party's remaining belongings and a large store of provisions to be delivered to their settlement on another chartered schooner in the fall. While the expedition sailed for John Cartwright's Long Point Landing at Port Rowan, Alexander sent his eldest son John and another one of the expedition's young men down along the southern shore of the lake. They were riding the horses Alexander had purchased at Fort Erie and were driving a few head of cattle and hogs ahead of them.

Another week was wasted at Port Rowan before another schooner could be hired to carry the expedition sixty miles across the lake to the Western Reserve. On the 28th of June, the Harper expedition finally reached the mouth of Cunningham Creek, today's Arcola Creek, just west of present-day Geneva-on-the-Lake. A week shy of four months had passed since the expedition left their homes in the western

Catskills and New York's Harper Patent. The Connecticut Land Company's survey teams of '96 and '97 had both taken a little over a month to travel the same basic waterway route from Rome to the Western Reserve. Few subsequent pioneering expeditions would ever again travel to the Western Reserve using the same long and dangerous waterway route taken by Alexander Harper in the summer of 1798. [20]

Alexander Harper's Field

The New Harpersfield pioneers had little time to relax or celebrate the end of their aquatic odyssey. After disembarking on the shore at Cunningham Creek, the exhausted voyagers spent their first night on the Western Reserve encamped on the beach. At sunrise, Alexander and the women started walking inland along the surveyor's line between the fifth and sixth ranges that serves today as the boundary between Ashtabula and Lake County. Later in the day, having built sleds to drag their gear and provisions on, the rest of the three families caught up with Alexander's group on the plot of land he had chosen for an initial encampment. For the first three weeks on the Reserve, they all lived together under the draping boughs of a gigantic pine tree in a makeshift shelter of poles and slabs of overlapping chestnut bark. Their first sylvan abode was on the northwest corner of township eleven in the fifth range, four miles south of the lake near the present-day hamlet of Unionville. The men's first task was to fell the tall trees used to build their family's log cabins, thereby opening up small clearings in the forest canopy to accommodate their gardens. By the 4th of July, the women had planted their first rows of beans, corn, potatoes, and turnips.

Seth Pease's journal from the year before recorded the first frost as having arrived on the Western Reserve during the first week of October. Should that again be the case, the Harpersfield pioneers had but a ninety-day growing season ahead of them. It was nearing August before the men finally finished building their three log cabins that would shelter their families through their first winter on the frontier. The Harpers and McFarlands stayed close to each other on lot #16 in the far northwest corner of today's Harpersfield Township. The Gregorys built their first cabin two miles due south of the Harpers and McFarlands near the Grand River on lot #80. Ezra Gregory would eventually move further up the river to lots #89, 90 and 74, closer to the center of the township. Within a few years the McFarlands would also relocate to the south side of the Grand River on lot #76 near the Gregorys. But through that first year on the frontier, the families all stayed close to each other. With no more than fifteen other families living on the entire Western Reserve in 1798, the three Harpersfield families had little hope of any support from anyone other than themselves. [21]

In late August, the Harpersfield families suffered the first of two blows that would rock their settlement to its core. The malaise that had infected so many of the Connecticut Land Company's surveyors the year before, seems to have lingered about on the Reserve. Alexander's hired man and companion, J. Gleason, was the first to fall victim to the feverish chills that had killed a half dozen surveyors in '97. There was nothing more than cinchona bark, aka Peruvian bark, sling liquor, and liquid laudanum to treat the sick. A few weeks after Gleason's death, on the morning of September 10th, the man who had led the Harpersfield expedition to the Western Reserve succumbed to the same illness. At fifty-four, Alexander Harper's sudden death devastated his family and the New Harpersfield settlement he founded two months earlier. He had fought alongside his brothers through the early years of the Revolution and survived two-and-a-half years in a British/Canadian prison where smallpox killed so many. It was believed at the time that his death was caused by the unhealthy vapors emanating from the Grand River's swampy wetlands. It would take another hundred years before the cause of malaria would be assigned to the Plasmodium parasite that infected mosquitoes transmitted to humans through their bites. Alexander's remains were placed in a hollowed-out log coffin with a hewn plank top while a grave was dug on the sandy knoll he had chosen as a suitable burial place for the settlement, not knowing he would be its second inhumation. His daughter Elizabeth would later write, '...*Imagination can scarcely conceive the dread solemnity of his burial...all was dread, all was desolate...*'.

While Alexander lay resting in his log coffin, the Harper family's patriarchal responsibilities fell on the shoulders of William McFarland who was affectionately referred to by his nieces and nephews as 'Uncle Mack'. Alexander's three oldest sons, John A., James A., and William A., along with their stalwart mother Elizabeth, were also charged with taking care of their family in Alexander's absence. In reference to her upper-leather German heritage, Elizabeth Bartholomew Harper was said to have '...*possessed native talents of a superior caste, with a large proportion of firmness and decision, blended with a gentleness of heart...*'. Widowed at forty-nine, Elizabeth had little time to mourn for the man she had been married to for twenty-seven turbulent years and with whom had raised eight strong children.

By late September, with the first frost just weeks away, the provisions they had brought with them were already running low and their first harvest promised to be disappointing. The Harpers, McFarlands and Gregorys were all bracing for the long winter ahead of them. To make matters worse, the schooner full of supplies chartered by Alexander before leaving Fort Erie had not arrived by the first snowfall. As the lake began icing over, the realization that their precious manna might not arrive at all sent a tremor of panic through the New Harpersfield settlement. That relief ship would in fact never arrive, having either sank or its skipper had absconded with Alexander's money. This was to be just one more unfortunate turn in a series of mishaps and tragedies that would very nearly terminate the settlement before it even got started.

Being the shallowest of the five Great Lakes, the waters of Lake Erie are considerably warmer during the summer months. In the fall and into winter, as the lake cools down, it warms the air above it and mixes with the colder moist air blowing down from the north to create the lake-effect snowstorms that pound the eastern lakeshore communities from Ohio to New York. The shallow lake also freezes over sooner and stays frozen longer. The New Harpersfield settlement would have been buried in deep, heavy snow as early as Thanksgiving, with the lake and surrounding streams icing over soon after. The ice and snow enveloped the Harpersfield settlement in an impenetrable winter wilderness that cut them off from any outside communication or relief. By January, it was becoming painfully obvious to all that they might not survive the winter without outside help.

With no exposed grasslands or available fodder for their animals, the Harpersfield families were at risk of losing all their livestock. Before the lake's shoreline became too difficult to traverse, the two oldest Harper brothers, John and James, rode the horses back up to Buffalo Creek and ferried them across the Niagara River to the Powells for winter boarding. The few cows and hogs that had not already been consumed had apparently all wandered off into the wilderness. After securing the horse's winter quarterage, James returned to his family on the Reserve, but John would not return to New Harpersfield until the following summer. Being the oldest heir and executor of his deceased father's will, John had legal business to deal with back in New York and with the other shareholders of the Old Harpersfield Land Company. With the oldest Harper sibling away, widow Elizabeth relied on her two sons, James and William, and their sister Elizabeth to help her take care of the younger Harper children. At one of several low points during the winter of 1798/99, Elizabeth was reduced to feeding her four youngest children a single meal of six kernels of corn boiled in a weak broth of forest leeks. Other times there were nothing but boiled leeks. Years later, young Elizabeth would write '...*It was with feelings akin to horror that our little party saw our provisions dwindle away...*'. The two remaining adult Harper brothers had no choice but to seek relief for their starving family by

John A. Harper

embarking upon a dangerous overland journey to try to find someone who might share some of their food with them. [22]

One of the closest frontier settlements the Harpers would have had any knowledge of, was a scattering of homesteads up along the Allegheny River's French Creek and around Presque Isle in Pennsylvania's Erie triangle. In 1798, there were around thirty to thirty-five families living on the upper West Branch of French Creek and around the old Fort La Boeuf portage to Elk Creek and Lake Erie. The Fort La Boeuf portage was first used by the French, and later the British, as a communication and supply line portage between the Great Lakes and their chain of frontier forts and trading posts down along the Allegheny and Ohio Rivers. Elk Creek meanders west from the portage and drains into the lake between Presque Isle and Conneaut, today's city of Erie and the Ohio State line. An Elk Creek family who lived a few miles up the creek near today's village of Girard had harvested a considerable crop of grain and corn during the summer of '98. Desperate for food, twenty-one-year-old James and his nineteen-year-old brother William set out on a fifty-mile trek up along the frozen shoreline of Lake Erie in search of Elk Creek and the family who might save their family from starvation.

James A. was said to have been taller and leaner than his younger brother William A. who possessed a more athletic frame. William also possessed a gleeful and fun-loving spirit, '...*Forward and frolic glee was there, the will to do and the soul to dare...*'. James, on the other hand, was more reticent in nature and occasionally subject to bouts of melancholy. All of Alexander Harper's sons were endowed with their father's indomitable spirit and his Christian name as their middle names. Not knowing if they could find the Elk Creek family or if they could convince them into parting with any of their precious crops, the brothers plowed their way through the waist deep snow in blind pursuit of their family's salvation. They could very well have failed in their mission to save their loved ones and quietly disappeared into the frigid, unforgiving forests.

Remarkably, the two brothers succeeded in finding the Elk Creek family and their patriarch who was graciously amenable to their proposition. As it turned out, William Miles had known their father Alexander and held him in high esteem. At seventeen, William had been captured by Spanish John McDonell at Northumberland's Fort Freeland in the summer of 1779. After being marched off to Fort Niagara with twenty-two other prisoners, he eventually ended up in a Quebec prison alongside Alexander and some of the sugar boilers. Through those darkest of days, Capt. Harper aided the young Pennsylvania militiaman who never forgot his benevolent guardianship. Mr. Miles was sorry to hear of their father's recent death and unhesitatingly agreed to provide his family with as much grain and corn as the two boys could carry on their backs. James and William would make several more trips to Elk Creek before that winter loosened its grip on the New Harpersfield settlement. With packets of grain strapped to their backs, they would drag sleds loaded with corn over the snow and ice along the lake's shoreline. On one of their trips back from Elk Creek, the Harper brothers and one of the Gregory boys met with disaster and very nearly lost all their cargo and their lives.

Returning along the shoreline late one afternoon in early spring, the three hikers alternated their path from the lake's ice to the beach while also crossing over the many streams along their way. It was a precarious time of year to be traveling over thinning ice with heavy loads. As fate would have it, they treaded onto a particular patch of ice before realizing it was much too thin for them and their sleds. After breaking through and plunging into the dark freezing waters of Lake Erie, all three struggled to save themselves. Struggling through the broken ice to shore, all but William gave up trying to retrieve their sleds and packets. Taking charge of the situation, he instructed James and the Gregory boy to gather some kindling and wood to flint start a fire. Plunging back into the icy water, William was somehow able to recover most of their goods before hypothermia numbed his limbs and sapped his strength. Upon rejoining his companions back on shore, he discovered to his dismay they had failed to light a fire and had fallen into the peaceful sleep that eases the unconscious dreamer into their final slumber. Reviving his freezing comrades and finding the strength to start a fire, William huddled together with them around the lifegiving bonfire. After warming themselves back to their senses and drying their frozen clothing, the intrepid trio regained their strength and struggled back to Harpersfield with most of their hard-earned bounty and their harrowing tale of survival. Without Mr. Miles' generosity and the Harper brothers' many trips to Elk Creek, it is highly likely their entire colony would have been lost. [23]

The Harpersfield families had one other benefactor besides William Miles to help them through their first winter on the frontier. Less spoken of by the Harper children and grandchildren who wrote memoirs of their forebears' early days on the Ohio frontier, this other individual may have been equally responsible for their ancestors' survival. An old Oneida warrior named Scanodewan was known to have made himself useful to the Harpersfield families by procuring game and teaching the younger boys the secrets of the western forests. Scanodewan was presumed to have been a friend of Alexander's brother, Col. Harper, and had served under the colonel in his Tryon company of scouts and rangers during the border war. After Alexander died in September, seventy-year-old Scanodewan built a canoe and paddled up Lake Erie to visit the two or three families settled around the mouth of the Cuyahoga River. He was treated kindly by the struggling families on the Cleveland settlement but was told they could do little to help him and his friends back on the Grand River.

Like the early colonial settlements in Massachusetts and Virginia, the earliest homesteaders on the Western Reserve may not have survived their first couple of winters without the help of Native Americans like Scanodewan and other local Indians. On many occasions the Massasagoes Lenape helped the fledgling white settlers who upon occasion reciprocated by helping the Indians through the harsh winter months. For many generations, when hunting for game in the northern extremities was virtually impossible, small bands of Ojibway Indians from the north shores of Lake Superior paddled their birchbark canoes down the lakes to their annual winter quarters on Ohio's Grand River. The Harpersfield pioneers who extended their hospitality by sheltering an Indian on a frigid winter night, were often rewarded in spring with a fresh elk or bear carcass left on their cabin doorsteps. The older generation of Harpers were known for their tolerance and admiration for the Indigenous peoples at a time when most whites held opposing points of view. Those opposing points of view were exhibited in letters and memoirs written by Alexander and Elizabeth's granddaughters many years later. No mention of Scanodewan merited referencing, nor did any other Indian who might have helped save their ancestors from starvation. [24]

Early signs of spring would have given a breath of relief to every member of the Harpersfield colony, especially the mothers who had barely kept their children alive through that first winter of '98/99. By mid-March, squawking skeins of homeward bound Canadian geese were signaling a new and gentler season. The gradually melting snow meant that game would soon be moving about in the forests and the disappearing ice invited bateaux back on the lake for trips to Canada for more provisions. Spring, however, did not bring an immediate end to their need to import grain and corn, as it would be many more months before they could harvest their own crops.

Grinding Corn in a Hand Quern Mill

The older boys continued their trips to Elk Creek while the mothers and daughters ground the grain into flour. The Gregorys had brought along a small hand-operated quern mill which would prove to be an indispensable tool for all the families. It took all day for two women to grind a bushel of grain or corn into a coarse flour or samp using the quern mill. Johnnycakes and hot water cornbread were then fried in oil and served to their hungry children and exhausted husbands. A device was eventually cobbled together using a hollowed-out pestle in an oak stump, and pounding the grain or corn therein with an oak log mortar attached to a bent-over sapling for recoil. It would be several more years before the first gristmills were built on the Reserve, the Gregorys being one of the first families to build one on the Grand River.

Come spring, the Harpers, McFarlands, and Gregorys vowed not to let another winter catch them unprepared. As soon as they could, the young men began working feverishly to chop down more trees to open more of the dense forest canopy for sunlight to nourish their crops and grasslands. The axe and hoe proved every bit as valuable to the frontier newcomers as their rifles and stump mills. [25]

A Stump Mill

Western Expeditions

By the close of the eighteenth century, shareholders in the Old Harpersfield Land Company were ready for the challenges of a new frontier and anxious to get started on their own westward journeys. The Western Reserve offered incredible opportunities for the adventurous risk-taker with the capital and grit to stake their fortunes on an untamed wilderness with no guarantees of success or even survival. During the fall of 1798, while the New Harpersfield settlers were reeling from the loss of their leader and preparing for the winter ahead of them, two kinsmen from New York's Old Harpersfield paid them an unexpected visit. Thomas Montgomery and his young friend Aaron Wright had journeyed to the Western Reserve to visit their relatives and scout out prospective sites for themselves and their families. Robert and Mary White Montgomery's oldest son Thomas and his friend returned to Old Harpersfield and reported their impressions of the Western Reserve to others who were contemplating moving west. They would have also reported the death of Alexander and the dire situation their relatives found themselves in. Alexander and the Harper brothers were first cousins to Robert Montgomery, as their mother Abigail had been sister to Robert's father James Montgomery. The Montgomery and Harper families had been intertwined with each other since arriving together on Boston's Long Wharf in 1718.

Throughout the winter months of '98/99, while their relatives fought desperately to survive on the Ohio frontier, the Montgomerys began organizing and preparing for their own expedition to the Reserve. Having learned firsthand of the Harpers' difficult and time-consuming waterway journey to the Reserve, Thomas and his friend recommended the Montgomery party take a more direct land route to the Reserve. Robert and Mary Montgomery were both near sixty when they and their five other children, ages 10-19, joined son Thomas and his family and headed west to New Harpersfield. Thomas was married to his second cousin, Col. John Harper's daughter Rebecca, with whom he had six young children, ages 3-9. While Aaron Wright and the sixteen-member Montgomery expedition were packing their belongings and provisions into wagons, another family was preparing their own wagons for the road west. Samuel and Sarah Bemus and their six young children, ages 2-12, joined the expedition that was now burdened with thirteen of its party under the age of twelve. Being short of hands, two brothers were eagerly accepted into the party when they volunteered their services and joined the troupe. Nathan and John King were both capable young men who brought more than just brawn to the expedition, as their future exploits would prove. The Montgomerys now had one more member than the Harper expedition had when they left the Mohawk River for the Western Reserve.

It is not exactly clear how the Montgomery overland expedition traversed through west central New York on route to the Western Reserve. But by the spring of 1799, settlers had been traveling through and settling on the Military Tract and Clinton's Twenty Townships for over a decade. The First Great Western Turnpike Corp. had just begun work on the Western Turnpike toll-road from Albany to Skaneateles by '99. Although not yet the main east/west thoroughfare, or U.S. Highway #20 as it was destined to become, portions of the old frontier road that the turnpike followed had already been in use for several years. The old road from Albany ran west to Duanesburg and across Schoharie Creek to Sloansville before continuing through Sharron Springs to Cherry Valley and Springfield at the head of Otsego Lake. While the

Harper expedition bypassed the old road at Cherry Valley and continued to the Mohawk River and their waterway route, the Montgomery expedition chose to follow the frontier road and overland route to the Reserve.

The Montgomery's route would have taken them through Richfield Springs and to the West Branch of the Unadilla River at Bridgewater before continuing through the northern five townships of Clinton's Twenty Townships to Cazenovia, in the survey gore between the two tracts. Depending on the road conditions, the Montgomerys would have either headed northwest from Cazenovia for Manlius along today's route #92 or continued west along route #20 and the Western Turnpike to Skaneateles. Either way, they would have picked up the old Seneca Trail that was used by the survey expedition's overland parties that were sent from the Mohawk River to Canandaigua. By the mid-1790s, the old Seneca Trail had been incorporated into The Great Genesee Road from Rome's Fort Schuyler to Canawaugus/Avon on the Genesee River. From the outlet of Cayuga Lake near Seneca Falls, the Montgomerys would have traveled along U.S. Hwy #20 through Canadesaga/Geneva to Canandaigua and on to Canawaugus. The road from the Genesee to Buffalo Creek and Lake Erie had only just been completed and opened to wagon traffic by 1799. Alexander Harper's decision to take his waterway route to the Reserve the year before, was perhaps influenced by the knowledge that the road from Canawaugus to the lake was not yet passable in '98.

After reaching Lake Erie, the Montgomerys would have been informed that travel by land down the lake's shoreline was still too difficult to attempt in wagons. Having made their way to Buffalo Creek by land, they then opted to charter a few bateaux to ferry them the rest of the way to the Reserve. Upon reaching the Pennsylvania state line and the mouth of Conneaut Creek just beyond, the Montgomerys found the terrain around the creek much more to their liking than the Harper's Grand River settlement. Here they found and took full advantage of the cabins left behind by the surveying parties of '96 and '97. Arriving on the frontier much earlier in the season than the Harpers, the Montgomerys had more time to prepare for their first grueling winter on the frontier. [26]

Another expedition left Old Harpersfield in the spring of '99. The oldest of Alexander and Elizabeth Harpers' sons, John A. Harper, had not returned to his family after taking the horses back to Canada the previous fall. He had gone instead directly back to New York to take care of his deceased father's financial affairs and inform prospective settlers of the conditions on the Western Reserve. While his brothers struggled to keep their family alive, John spent the winter months of '98/99 helping his uncle Joseph and sister Margaret's families prepare for their overland journey to join their loved ones on the Ohio frontier. Major Joseph Harper and his wife Catherine were packing up their belongings and bundling up the three youngest of their eight children, Alexander-4, Montgomery-3, and Joshua-1. Having been severely wounded while fighting alongside his brother Col. Harper on Klock's Field in 1780, Joseph's shattered left shoulder would have left him with just one good arm to guide his ox-drawn wagon. He would have relied heavily on his young nephew John to help him with his family during their long journey to Ohio.

John and his uncle's family were joined by the oldest Harper sibling, twenty-seven-year-old Margaret, the only member of the Harpers who had not been with the family on their trip to the Reserve the year before. Margaret had met a young boy in New Lebanon, New York, during the period her mother Elizabeth was harboring the younger Harper children there during Alexander's incarceration. Aaron Wheeler and Margaret were not yet teenagers when they first met in the final years of the war, but by '99 they had long been married and had four children, ages 1-6. Mr. Wheeler was one of the original shareholders in the Old Harpersfield Land Company. John A. Harper's second expedition set out on the 350-mile overland wagon journey to the Reserve with Aaron and Margaret's four children and fifty-seven-year-old Joseph and wife Catherine's seven children, all of whom were under the age of seven. [27]

With the Harpers and Montgomerys leading the way, more families from Old Harpersfield began feeling confident enough to follow them to New Harpersfield. In early March 1800, Alexander Harper's widow Elizabeth welcomed two of her nephews, Daniel, and his younger brother Abraham, to the Reserve. The Bartholomew brothers had journeyed west the summer before to scout out a large tract of land their father Joseph purchased in Geneva township, adjacent to Harpersfield. The two young men cleared a site and built a log cabin before returning to their Charlotte Creek homesteads to prepare Daniel's wife and four young children, ages 2-7, for a return trip back to the Reserve. Traveling over the late winter snow in ox-drawn sleighs to Canandaigua and on to Buffalo Creek, they continued their sleighride to Geneva over Lake Erie's still frozen surface. All the Bartholomeus eventually settled on their family's 6,000-acre tract of land around Geneva's Cowles Creek, just north of the Harpers. [28]

Later that spring, three more families arrived on the Western Reserve with the intent of joining the Montgomerys in their Conneaut Creek New Salem settlement. The Harper and Montgomery family bonds that were formed in the forests of southeastern Maine and in Massachusetts' Irish Rows, were about to be forged again in the forests of northeastern Ohio. Just as Col. John Harper's daughter Rebecca had married her second cousin Thomas Montgomery, the colonel's son James had married his second cousin Sarah Montgomery, Thomas' sister. James Harper had risen to captain in his uncle Alexander's Otsego County militia regiment and was accordingly referred to as Capt. Harper. Along with their four young children, ages 1-7, Capt. Harper and Sarah led a party of nine adults and thirteen children on yet another overland trip to the western frontier. They were accompanied by another one of Sarah's brothers, James Montgomery and his second wife Polly and their six children, ages 1-8 and a newborn. Polly's brother Daniel Baldwin and two of his close friends, James and Nathaniel Laughlin, also came along on the Harper/Montgomery expedition. Another couple, Seth and Huldah Harrington joined the entourage with their three children, the oldest of which was not yet five. The oldest of the expedition's thirteen children was just eight years old. Upon the party's arrival at New Salem, Robert and Mary Montgomery were grateful to finally have all their children and grandchildren safely together again in one place. [29]

Over the next five years, having heard of the progress made on the Harpersfield, Geneva and New Salem settlements, other settlers primarily from New York and Connecticut began arriving on the Western Reserve. In 1798, when the first Harper expedition arrived on the shore at Cunningham Creek, there were but fifteen or sixteen families living on the entire Reserve, east of the Cuyahoga River. In 1804, a circuit preacher traversed the twenty-eight townships that would eventually become Ashtabula County and recorded ninety-three families with about 450 souls living in the future county. Twenty-seven families were found living in Harpersfield Township, with another thirty in the two adjacent townships of Austinburg and Morgan. Conneaut/New Salem was home to twenty more families with another sixteen families scattered about the county.

In 1805, two of widow Elizabeth Harper's brothers arrived on the Ohio frontier and settled a few miles north of her on their Geneva property. Seventy-five-year-old Tewald (Theobald) and his sixty-one-year-old brother Joseph Bartholomew joined Joseph's sons, Daniel and Abraham, on the Cowles Creek property the two had settled on five years earlier. Joseph and Tewald's brother Benjamin had recently died, leaving his widow Abigail Patchin Bartholomew with four grown children and two minors. A year after Tewald and Joseph arrived on the frontier, Benjamin's twenty-nine-year-old son Isaac brought his mother and five of his younger siblings to Geneva and joined the rest of the Bartholomew families. Isaac also brought along his twice-widowed aunt, Hannah Stevens Skinner, and her twenty-one-year-old adopted blind son Joshua O'Daniel. Elizabeth's younger sister Hannah lost her first husband, William Stevens, during Alexander Harper's sugar boiler debacle in 1780, and her second when Alexander's tavern owner partner, Nathaniel Skinner, died in '95. Elizabeth, Hannah, and their sister-in-law Abigail had gone through most of the war sheltered together with their children in Schoharie's Middle Fort. Together again after seven long years, their reunion must have been a joyous occasion. The Harper and Bartholomew cousins of Harpersfield and Geneva might have gathered throughout the years with their Montgomery cousins in Conneaut for family reunions. On the 28th of June 1888, ninety years to the day after the Harpers landed at Cunningham Creek, descendants of the Harper, Montgomery and Bartholomew families gathered for a reunion near Unionville, Ohio. The family tradition was repeated for many years thereafter. [30]

In 1806, another expedition brought several more families from Old Harpersfield to New Harpersfield. Members of at least a dozen families who had settled on Harper Patent before and shortly after the war traveled to the Reserve in a nine-wagon caravan. The Harper family's friend and wartime comrade, David Hendry, and his wife Selinda and their four young children were joined by Selinda's brothers Joseph, Thelus, and Ebenezer Hotchkiss on the trail to Ohio's frontier. David's good friend Levi Gaylord Jr and family joined the westward procession along with several of their Harper Patent neighbors, including the families of Benjamin Morse, Isaac Patchin, James Morrison, Palmer Wood, and Ezekiel Woodworth. Doctor Joshua Brett's three sons, William, Isaac, and Joshua Jr, joined the '06 expedition that included another one of Col. Harper's children, thirty-year-old Ruth, and her husband Thomas Dunbar. A few families from the nearby Charlotte Creek settlements came to Ohio around this time. The Brakeman, Burget, and Hagedorn families were originally from Schoharie's Palatine German settlements and had fought alongside the Harpers and the Bartholomeus through the desperate years of New York's border war.

Another former and noteworthy resident of New York's Harpersfield came to the Western Reserve two years after Alexander Harper's expedition of 1798. Edward Paine had lived briefly after the war with his brother Ezra on the Harper's patent. Ezra was the Otsego County enumerator who had tallied a portion of Harpersfield District for the 1790 census. Like Alexander, Edward had traveled to the Reserve during the second Connecticut survey expedition of '97 and scouted for a suitable settlement site for himself and his family. Edward and Alexander may have been aware of each other's visit, as they were well known to each other and may in fact have been competing for the choicest tracts of land. Like Alexander, Edward had served as a captain in the Revolution alongside a couple of his brothers and had served in his older brother Lt. Col. Brinton Paine's Dutchess County militia regiment. Following the war and after briefly residing in Harpersfield, Captain Paine was commissioned lieutenant colonel of a regiment in New York's Onondaga County postwar militia, just as Alexander had been in Otsego County. But unlike Lt. Col. Harper, Lt. Col. Paine was later promoted to brigadier general of an Onondaga and Cayuga County militia brigade. In 1800, Gen. Paine and his wife Elizabeth and their eight children came to the Grand River and settled on a 1,000-acre tract of land in the eleventh township of range eight, fifteen miles west of New Harpersfield. Sixty-six other settlers were said to have been influenced by Gen. Paine to join his settlement near the mouth of the Grand River at what would become known as Painesville.

Eventually being designated as the county seat for Geauga and later Lake County, the prosperous little village of Painesville would surpass New Harpersfield in growth and commerce and even outpaced the settlement of Cleveland until the 1830s. The first reliable Ohio census of 1820 recorded 202 Painesville households, 140 Harpersfield households, and 112 households in both Cleveland and New Salem. [31]

New Harpersfield

Alexander Harper paid the ultimate price to be one of the first settlers on the Western Reserve. His untimely death left his sons with a host of overwhelming responsibilities. The Harper brothers were left with having to save their family from starvation and developing their homesteads to ensure they would never face another winter like their first. They also had the task of finishing the Harpersfield survey their father had started. The Connecticut surveyors ran the tier and range lines that delineated the one hundred and twenty-five townships east of the Cuyahoga, but each of the townships still needed to be surveyed into homestead lots. As the Harpers had done thirty years before, back on their 22,000-acre New York patent, Alexander's sons followed their father's plan to similarly divide their 16,000-acre New Harpersfield township into 160, 100-acre homestead lots. The lots were then divvied up amongst the Old Harpersfield Land Company's shareholders. Eight lots in the far northwest corner of the township, #12-16, and #28-32, were reserved for the Harpers and their closest relatives, including the McFarlands and Wheelers. David Hendry, their longtime friend, settled on a couple of these eight lots next to the Harper brothers and their in-laws. David had helped the Harpers survey their New York patent before the war and had been one of their first homesteaders. [32]

In 1800, the whole of the Western Reserve east of the Cuyahoga was designated as one large county and partitioned into nine smaller districts. The northeast corner of the county of Trumbull was designated as the district of Richfield, containing all three of the Old Harpersfield Land Company's townships, Geneva, Harpersfield, and Trumbull. Several of the first appointments to Richfield District's civil offices were filled with the Harpers and their relatives. James A. Harper was chosen to serve as one of the district's three commissioners and the county recorder. John A. was appointed constable while his brother-in-law, Aaron Wheeler, served as one of the first justices of the peace. When Trumbull County was reapportioned in 1811, the district of Richfield was integrated into the northern two-thirds of the new county of Ashtabula. David Hendry was appointed to the position of county treasurer and Esquire Wheeler was made an associate judge of the new county.

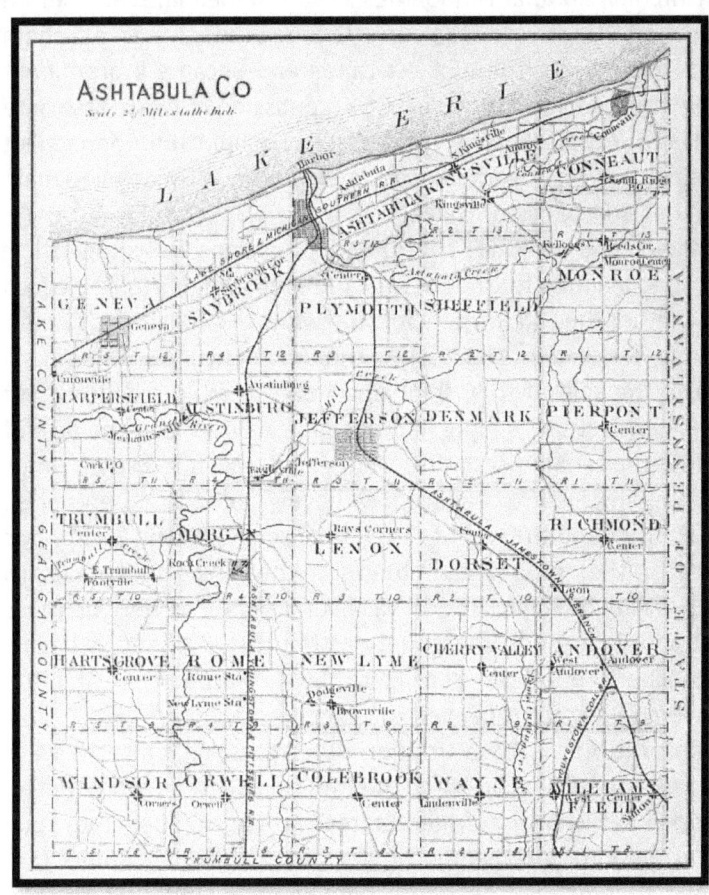

The Twenty-Eight Townships of Ashtabula County

Throughout the next two decades, the Harpers and their relatives would continue to occupy many of Ashtabula County's and Ohio's civil offices. Between 1813 and 1825, both William A. and his younger brother Robert A. Harper were elected to several terms in the Ohio state assembly. Robert was also a prominent lawyer in the local judiciary and served for years as Harpersfield's prosecuting attorney. Brother-in-law Aaron served as a state senator from 1816-1820. In New Salem, where the Montgomerys and Capt. James Harper settled, both James and his cousin James Montgomery filled many of that communities' public offices. [33]

In June of 1805, commissioners from the Connecticut Land Company and representatives from the federal government held a treaty conference with the chieftains of the Wyandot, Ottawa, Potawatomi, Chippawa, Lenape, Munsee, and Shawnee nations at Fort Industry on the Maumee River, at today's Toledo. The Connecticut commissioners agreed to pay $7,000 and another $2,000 per annum for the next six years in exchange for the extinction of Indian titles to all their Western Reserve lands west of the Cuyahoga River. This would include the Fireland's 500,000 acres and the Excess Land's 830,000 acres. The government also agreed to pay a hefty annual annuity to the Indians forever, or at least until they ignored to pay it forever. Anxious to survey their western lands as soon as possible and prepare them for sale, the commissioners hastily arranged for two independent surveys to be conducted on the Firelands and Excess Lands. The Firelands were entrusted to Almon Ruggles, a Connecticut Yankee from Danbury who had been one of the surveyors with Cleaveland and Porter in 1796 and Pease in '97. The Excess Land survey was contracted to Anson Sessions, Abraham Tappan and Abraham's soon-to-be brother-in-law, James A. Harper.

Arriving on the Ohio frontier in 1801, shortly after the Harpers, Abraham Tappan briefly lived at the mouth of the Grand River before settling near the Harper family. An educated and accomplished young man, Abraham joined his friend James Harper's mother Elizabeth, and his sixteen-year-old sister Elizabeth in what was thought to have been the first schoolhouse on the Western Reserve. Abraham and his young tutorial partner soon found out they shared more than just the love of letters and were married in April 1806. The couple settled on a 241-acre homestead lot next to the Harpers, sold to Abraham by his other brother-in-law John Harper. Within days of their wedding, Abraham and Elizabeth's brother James set out for the Cuyahoga and the Excess Lands. James served as Abraham's principal surveyor in charge of a fourteen-man crew employed in running the chains and clearing the path for the tier and range lines. Throughout that spring and summer and well into fall, Abraham and James' crew ran their lines and before the winter shut them down, they completed their 1,300 square-mile survey of the Excess Lands. Abraham Tappan served as the legal recorder of deeds and titles on the Excess Lands and became a prominent member of his Unionville community, serving at various times as sheriff, commissioner, clerk, associate judge and postmaster for the village and Lake County's township of Madison. He built the Connecticut Land Company Office near his impressive classical revival and federal style brick house on Unionville's main street, both of which are now on the National Register of Historic Places. [34]

When Alexander and the Old Harpersfield Land Company contracted for options on six townships on the Western Reserve, three of them had waited in limbo for the Excess Land's Indian titles to be cleared and the surveys run. It is not clear, however, whether the Old Harpersfield investors ever did exercise their options to purchase land in the three western townships. By 1807, when the Connecticut Land Company finally released the Excess Lands for purchase, the sale of townships and homestead lots had not yet proven profitable. The anticipated influx of eastern settlers simply had not materialized, and the lack of land sales put investors and their creditors in an untenable situation. Two years after the Excess Lands were put up for sale the Connecticut Land Company filed for bankruptcy, having failed to raise enough capital to meet their creditors' demands. The Harpers and the rest of the Old Harpersfield Land Company's investors may have thought it prudent to settle for their properties in the three townships on the eastern side of the Cuyahoga. When Ashtabula County was erected in 1811, It was estimated there were no more than two hundred families and about 1,000 people living in the county at that time. Although having doubled in population since the circuit preacher's unofficial census of 1804, Harpersfield and the surrounding townships of Ashtabula County were falling short of their investors' expectations. [35]

During the early years of making a go of it on the Ohio frontier, other pressing concerns were beginning to rattle the nerves of the Western Reserve settlers. In 1805, the free trade agreement between America and Canada was threatened as relations between the United States and England began to sour. The Napoleonic Wars were drawing all of Europe into what would be yet another global conflict that threatened the new world order. England was trying to restrict trade between the United States and France. They began committing the intolerable practice of seizing American ships and conscripting their sailors into their Royal Navy. The high seas and the frontier border region between America and Canada were about to play host to yet another fight between two European peoples, with the Native American population caught in the middle.

War of 1812

By 1810, British Canadian authorities and military commanders were quietly negotiating with the nations of the Great Northwest Territory to form an alliance with them in the war that was sure to come. In November 1811, after sporadic skirmishes between the Indians and settlers throughout the Ohio, Indiana, and Illinois territories, Indiana's territorial governor and Brig. Gen. William Henry Harrison initiated a preemptive strike on the Shawnee stronghold of Prophetstown. The battle at the confluence of the Wabash and Tippecanoe Rivers was indecisive in military advantage but did succeed in destroying the village and killing the brother of the great Shawnee war chief Tecumseh. Outraged by the unprovoked attack and death of his brother, Tecumseh convinced the Northwestern Confederation to declare an open alliance with the British Canadians and ready their warriors for battle.

In April 1812, Ohio Governor Jonathan Meigs ordered Brig. Gen. William Hull to assemble the Army of the Northwest on the Mad River at Dayton. After a month and a half of drilling and preparation, Gen. Hull marched his army north and took control of Fort Detroit. In mid-June, the United States declared war on Great Britain and within two months a panicked Gen. Hull was outfoxed by an inferior British and Indian army and compelled to surrender Fort Detroit back to the British. All 2,200 of his troops were turned over to Maj. Gen. Isaac Brock. The humiliating defeat stunned the Ohio frontier's young men who, '...*On a call of emergency in consequence of a rumor of invasion...*', hastened to form up into militia companies with their fellow neighbors and compatriots. The young men of New Harpersfield began preparing for a war that was about to threaten their homeland, just as an earlier war had threatened their father's frontier homeland. [36]

The third American generation of Harpers and their relatives were uniquely qualified to take advantage and excel in the opportunities military service offered. Their grandfathers had fought against the French grenadiers and their Abenaki warriors in the forests of Maine, while their fathers had fought the Iroquois, Tories, and British Regulars in New York's frontier border war. Alexander and Elizabeth's five sons and two of their sons-in-law were ready to prove their valor alongside their cousins, the Bartholomeus and Montgomerys. After Hull's disastrous Fort Detroit surrender, he was replaced as commander of The Army of the Northwest by Gen. Harrison, the purported hero of Tippecanoe and future president of the United States. Harrison's first order of business was to begin improving the roads throughout Lake Erie's frontier and establishing a supply line of forts and blockhouses along the lake's southern tier. Harrison's 4th Division of Ohio militia, commanded by Maj. Gen. Elijah Wadsworth, was assigned to defend the Ohio frontier from Presque Isle to the Maumee River, from Erie to Toledo. The youngest of the Harper brothers, twenty-one-year-old Robert A. Harper, was commissioned to serve on Gen. Wadsworth's field staff as the asst. principal forage master in charge of securing provisions and supplying the necessary accoutrements for the troops while in the field. It was a heavy responsibility for the young man who rose to the occasion and went on to prove his merit as a capable officer and administrator through the remainder of the war. [37]

The 3rd regiment in Gen. Wadsworth's 4th Division was organized in late August 1812, with Col. James Stewart as the commanding officer. Col. Stewart was soon replaced by Lt. Col. Nathan King, the young man who had come to Conneaut with his brother John and the Montgomerys in the spring of '99. Robert Harper was reassigned to Col. King's staff as the regiment's quartermaster sergeant, with his older brother James A. as quartermaster clerk. Two companies in Col. King's regiment were comprised primarily of Ashtabula County volunteers from Harpersfield and Geneva. The Harper brothers and their Bartholomew cousins filled several of the higher and lower ranks in both companies. Capt. John R. Reed's company was officered by Lieutenant Alexander A. and Corporal William A. Harper. The Harper brothers' sister Elizabeth's surveyor husband, Abraham Tappan, was a private in his brothers-in-law's company. Thomas Dunbar, the husband of Col. John Harper's daughter Ruth, also served as a private in Capt. Reed's company along with the colonel's other daughter Rebecca and husband Thomas Montgomery's son John H. Montgomery. Three sons of the late Benjamin Bartholomew and his wife Abigail, John, Joseph, and Peter, served alongside their Harper cousins just as their father and his brothers had done alongside the Harper brothers during the old New York border war not so long ago.

Col. King's other Ashtabula County company was commanded and filled with the sons of Tewald, Joseph and Benjamin Bartholomew. This second company was led by Tewald's son Capt. Jacob Bartholomew, with brother Joseph's son Daniel as company corporal and Benjamin's teenage son Benjamin Jr as the company's fifer. Benjamin's son Isaac, the son who had brought his widowed mother Abigail and the rest of his family to the Western Reserve in '06, served as a private in the same company.

Three other sons of Joseph Bartholomew, Abraham, John, and Samuel, also served as privates in their cousin Capt. Jacob's company. The Harper brothers' youngest sister Mary's husband Adna Cowles, Ezra Gregory's son Daniel, Robert and Mary Montgomery's son Eli, and the Gaylord brothers Levi Jr and Elihu were also listed as privates on Capt. Bartholomew's company roster. [38]

As soon as they were organized, Captains Reed and Bartholomew's Ashtabula companies were hurriedly deployed and sent west across the Cuyahoga to the Huron River, '...*in consequence of a rumor of invasion*...'. They were immediately put to work clearing the roads and building Gen. Harrison's defensive string of forts and blockhouses. The Harper brothers and their kinsmen may have been involved in several of the skirmishes with the Indians that took place on Sandusky Bay's Marblehead Peninsula through the month of September. In early November they were ordered to march with the rest of the militia to Fort Stevenson on the lower Sandusky River. As was customary, they were discharged in late November and sent home on furlough for the winter months.

In late April 1813, another company in Col. Nathan King's militia regiment was formed and commissioned with Capt. William Morrow, Lieutenant James A. Harper, Sergeant Alexander A. Harper, and Corporal John A. Harper. Throughout the spring and summer of that year, the British finally launched their rumored invasion into northern Ohio. Their objective was to take Fort Stevenson on the Sandusky and Fort Meigs on the Maumee River, near today's Toledo, by siege. The Army of the Northwest and the Ohio militia successfully repelled their siege of both forts and drove the British and Tecumseh's warriors from Ohio's frontier, back into Michigan to Fort Detroit. The families of the Western Reserve would have let out a collective sigh of relief at the news of Forts Stevenson and Meigs' rescue at the hands of their brave sons in the field. With their success came word that Gen. Harrison was beginning to make plans to mobilize a major offensive to retake Fort Detroit and drive the British and Tecumseh further back into Canada. [39]

On September 10th, Gen. Harrison received an incredible dispatch from Commodore Oliver Hazard Perry, '... *We have met the enemy, and they are ours; two ships, two brigs, one schooner and one sloop...*'. Perry and his nine warships had won a stunning victory off the coast of Marblehead Peninsula at Put-In-Bay over British Commander Robert Barclay's Lake Erie squadron of six warships. With their supplies already running low, the loss of the British fleet cut off the supply line to the British forces at Fort Detroit, leaving them no choice but to retreat through Upper Canada and back to the Niagara Peninsula. This was the opening Gen. Harrison had been waiting for and without delay he mobilized his 1,000 mounted dragoons to advance up the western shoreline of Lake Erie to Fort Detroit. At the same time, he arranged to send 2,500 Kentucky riflemen and Ohio militiamen across the lake in Perry's ships to rendezvous with his light horse after they secured Fort Detroit and crossed over into Canada.

With Maj. Gen. Henry Procter's British troops and Tecumseh's warriors in full retreat up the Thames River, Gen. Harrison's combined forces caught up with them on the morning of October 5th at Moraviantown, a small Lenape village forty miles east of Detroit near today's Chatham, Kent County. The ensuing Battle of the Thames was a decisive victory for the Americans and a major setback for the British Canadian army and the Northwest Confederation of Nations. Tecumseh, the great chief and leader of the Confederation was killed in the fierce fighting. With the death of Tecumseh and the British exit from Detroit and Lake Erie, the Indians abandoned their support for their English allies and returned to their villages in the northwest territories. [40]

It is not clear if Col. King's militia regiment or any of the Harper brothers took part in the Battle of the Thames, but three of the Bartholomew brothers were known to have been there that day. After serving in their cousin Jacob's Ashtabula militia company, Abraham, Samuel, and John Bartholomew re-enlisted in the 27th Infantry Regiment of the Army of the Northwest, in Capt. George Sanderson's company of light horse. Sanderson's company was in the field during the battle at Moraviantown and took part in some of the fiercest fighting.

All three of the Bartholomew brothers survived Tecumseh's warclubs, but poor old Samuel would not survive a blow to the back of his head eight years later. While the veteran of the War of 1812 sat quietly eating his breakfast with his two young children in the spring of 1822, his wife Susanna split his skull with an axe in a most unladylike manner. Indicted and tried for murder in the second degree, Susanna Bartholomew was spared the hangman's noose through the clever lawyering of Samuel's cousin, Robert A. Harper. Winning an acquittal for his client on the grounds of insanity, the estranged wife spent the rest of her days in the Ashtabula County Infirmary for the Poor, registered as an insane inmate. [41]

Border War II

After the Battle of the Thames and the death of Tecumseh, the immediate threat to Ohio's frontier families was put to rest, but their kinsmen back east had another brutal year-and-a-half of war ahead of them. New York's border with Upper Canada along the Niagara and St. Lawrence rivers would bear witness to some of the bloodiest battles of the war. The loyalists who settled on Upper Canada's Niagara Peninsula after the Revolution had many old friends and relatives back home in New York. The angst between the two former enemies had softened since the fathers of the current generation fought against each other during New York's border war. Trade and communication between New York and Upper Canada had been steadily increasing prior to Europe's war against Napoleon and England's harassment of American ships at sea. Unlike Ohio, whose western boundaries were not yet fully realized, New York had completed its expansionist conquest of the Iroquois' territory by 1812. Justification for another war with Great Britain was a much harder sell for the New Yorkers than it was for their Ohio countrymen.

As the inevitable war between England and America drew closer, anti-war sentiments were being argued in rural taverns and urban coffeehouses throughout the state. New York's Federalist anglophiles and their sympathizers were passionately arguing for peace, and a return to America's amicable trade agreement with Europe and Canada. Leaders of the Democratic-Republican party, such as Jefferson and President Madison were pushing for war and hoping that a victory over Canada might lead to annexation of all or part of Upper Canada. The War Bill submitted to Congress in June 1812, passed but without the overwhelming support the president would have preferred. Five of New York State's twelve Dem/Rep congressmen voted with all four of the state's Federalist congressmen against the declaration, just three Dem/Rep congressmen voted in favor of war while the other four abstained. In general, enthusiasm for the war amongst the state's citizenry and the sons of the frontiersmen who had driven the English from their soil thirty years before, was tepid at best. The young state of Ohio's single representative to the United States Congress, Jeremiah Morrow, reflected the western frontier's opposing point of view and voted in favor of war. [42]

Lt. Col. Harper and Major McFarland's Otsego County militia regiment had gone through many reorganizational changes since their resignations in '97. In the leadup to the War of 1812, it was one of three Delaware County regiments in Brig. Gen. Erastus Root's 8th Division of the 25th Brigade of New York Militia. With all of Alexander Harper's sons and their sister's husbands mustering into Ashtabula County regiments alongside their cousins, Col. John Harper's last two sons, Archibald and John, left Old Harpersfield to join their siblings and cousins on the Western Reserve. The old colonel had but one stepson and three nephews still serving in a New York State militia regiment. After taking in and adopting seventeen-year-old William Harper when he married his cousin Joseph's widow Isabella McKnight Harper, the boy grew up to become an extraordinarily capable young man with the character and qualities required to rise in military rank. Now forty-five, Lt. Col. William Harper was in command of his late uncle Alexander's former Otsego and now Delaware County militia regiment. William's meteoric rise through the ranks had been propelled at least in part by his family's military reputation and his stepfather's tutelage and influence. [43]

Three other members of the extended Harper family served in high military ranks throughout the quiet years before the buildup to war. The Harper brothers' sister Mary and husband James Moore's two sons, John and James, both followed the tradition of military leadership that was woven into the fabric of their Scots-Irish families. The Moore's daughter Mary's husband Matthew Cully seems to have been cut from the same cloth and possessed the qualities of a man who could lead others into battle. By 1804, both Moore brothers were serving as staff officers in Lt. Col. David Bates' second Otsego County militia regiment, James as 2nd major and John as the regimental adjutant. Three years later Adjutant John Moore was serving in his brother-in-law Lt. Col. Matthew Cully's Otsego County regiment, first as 2nd major and shortly after 1st major. In '09, Col. Cully resigned his commission at the age of sixty-three, whereupon 1st Major Moore was promoted to replace him as the regiment's commanding officer.

By 1811, rumors of war had given way to the reality that it was indeed imminent. New York's military leaders and Council of Appointments rushed to reorganize local militias and reassign officers to lead them. The three regiments in Brig. Gen. Root's 8th Division were reorganized and placed under the command of Delhi's Lt. Col. Putnam Farrington of the 70th Regiment, Walton's Lt. Col. Abraham Howell of the 69th and Harpersfield's Lt. Col. William Harper of the 87th Regiment.

What might seem puzzling and Incongruous with the Harper family's tradition of military prowess, two of their favorite sons resigned their commissions on the eve of war. At the age of forty-four, Lt. Col. John Moore resigned his commission in the Otsego County regiment in late 1811 after just two years in office. A year later his second cousin Lt. Col. William Harper relinquished his commission and command of the 87th Regiment, five months into the war. Whether or not health played any part in either of their decisions to abandon their posts is unclear. Their political convictions may have played a role in their refusal to take up arms against the Canadians. With the Federalists opposition to the war, many of New York's young men were reluctant to take up arms against their Canadian neighbors, some of whom were friends or relatives. Lt. Col. Moore would have had to face off against his sister Jane's husband Capt. John Powell and his nephews. Having spent his formative years with his mother and father Joseph on the Connecticut River, Lt. Col. Harper might have been indoctrinated into his father's New England politics that lent itself to the Federalist anti-war point of view.

As many as 1,500 New York militiamen refused to take part in a Canadian campaign to take Montreal early in the war. In fact, New York's militia laws were such that militiamen were not required to cross a border or leave their state while carrying arms. Any suggestion of cowardice on William Harper or John Moore's part is absurd, as many other reputable men of lower, equal, or higher office resigned their commissions at the onset of the War of 1812. The political opponent of Harpersfield and Cherry Valley's Scots-Irish, Jacob Morris, also gave up his command on the eve of war. Butternuts Creek's outspoken Federalist had served as brigadier general of Otsego County's militia from 1797 to 1806. Morris was called back again in 1810 to help reorganize the militia as major general of the 6th Division. But being a staunch opponent of the war, his commission was superseded a year later.

There was at least one former Harpersfield resident who did not retire from active duty when the war finally did arrive. Freegift Patchin had spent two and a half years in a Canadian prison with Capt. Harper after their sugar boiler fiasco in 1780. Having removed from Harper Patent to the upper Schoharie Valley's Blenheim area following the Revolution, Freegift quickly rose through the ranks of Schoharie's militia and by 1806 was brigadier general of the Schoharie Brigade. The resolute Gen. Patchin led his 28th Brigade through the entire war and finally resigned his commission in 1814 at the age of fifty-six. It was Freegift's daughter Abigail Patchin who had married Benjamin Bartholomew and traveled to the Western Reserve with her son Isaac in 1806. [44]

Legacies

Had Lt. Col. Alexander Harper not grown up in the shadow of his two older and extraordinarily successful brothers, John and William, he might not have felt the need to take the risks he so often did. A charismatic and persuasive leader, people believed in him and were willing to follow him wherever he led them, which in more than one instance got them into more trouble than they bargained for. The deception and murder of Hermanus Dumond, his reckless sugar boiler fiasco, his expedition's late arrival on the Ohio frontier and his untimely death jeopardized his whole family and very nearly led to their demise. Alexander's legal shenanigans and snouting of Judge Cooper exhibited another side of him that suggests he may have had anger management issues as well. All things considered, he might better fit the definition of an anti-hero than hero.

Alexander and Elizabeth's oldest son John A. Harper was the executor of his father's will and intermediary between his estate and the investors in the Old Harpersfield Land Company. It would be five years after the death of Alexander before his will could be probated and proved, being that there was no authority in Ohio to adjudicate legal documents until March 1st, 1803. Alexander's will was Trumbull County's first will to be proved and recorded. His appraised holdings were valued at $3,326, and his debts at $1,584, leaving his estate's distribution at $1,741. Alexander owed the Connecticut Land Company $500, with the five-year mortgage due on October 1st, 1803. The will provided his widow Elizabeth with $580 and all the household items including bedding, kitchen implements, pewterware and a lady's sidesaddle. The remaining $1,170 was divided into six equal shares of $195, going to each of his six youngest children. The two oldest Harper children, John A. and Margaret Harper Wheeler, had settled their affairs with their siblings before their father's will was probated. One might suspect that Alexander's true wealth was more than what was recorded in the Trumbull County probate records.

Alexander's last will and testament provides an insight into the man's intellectual and political interests. Of the forty books listed in his inventory of estate, about a quarter of them were conventional bibles, psalms, and prayer books, while the subject matter of the remaining books reveals him to have been a proponent of the Age of Enlightenment. Thomas Salmon's *Geographical and Astronomical Grammar*; Jacob Giles' *Everyman His Own Lawyer*; John H. Moore's *The Young Gentleman and Lady's Monitor*; three volumes of James Burgh's *Political Disquisitions*, eight volumes of *The Works of Alexander Pope in Verse and Prose*, *Julius Caesar's Commentaries* and a *Latin Dictionary* were a few of the books Alexander thought important enough to bring to Ohio. His books were each appraised anywhere from .50¢ to $2, his farming and carpentry tools at around $30, his blacksmithing equipment $36, and his surveying instruments at $20. Besides his horses and cattle, Alexander's $20 anvil and his $12 compass were two of his most valuable possessions. [45]

Having arrived a year after his brother Alexander's momentous journey to the Western Reserve in 1798, Joseph Harper died just six years later in 1805 at the age of sixty-three. In his last will and testament, he left his wife Catherine and each of his eight children a 100-acre lot, with two more lots going to cover his debts. With what remained he specified it to be used to provide schooling for his grandchildren. [46]

Major William McFarland, aka Uncle Mack, outlived his two Harper wives and all the Harper brothers and sisters. The youngest of the Harper siblings, Miriam Harper McFarland, passed away on the Ohio frontier in 1813 at the age of sixty-four. Upon his death in 1820, William left all his money, property, and earthly belongings to his nephews, nieces, friends, and the Templars Lodge. Earlier, he may have given some of his property or money to the boy and young lady he and Miriam adopted after the war and brought with them to the frontier in '98. The seventeen-year-old boy who helped William on the long trip to Ohio, Benjamin Hartwell, grew up to become a well-respected member of his Ohio community. The McFarlands had obviously seen to the boy's education and military training, as he taught school for years and rose to captain of a militia company. He was an early postmaster for New Harpersfield before being one of the first mail carriers between Erie and Cleveland, a precursor to the legendary pony express riders.

William and Miriam's other young ward, Parthenia Mingus, may have been given a dowery of sorts not long after their arrival on the Western Reserve. After reaching the Ohio frontier, a young bachelor on the Cuyahoga near the Cleveland settlement heard of the arrival of the Harper expedition and of the comely young widow who had accompanied them. Prospects being as they were, the young frontiersman wasted little time before setting out on a quest for the young lady's hand. With two horses, one for himself and the other for the lady he hoped to bring back home with him, James Hamilton journeyed fifty miles east to the Harper settlement with a proposal of matrimony. With few other options, Parthenia accepted the bold young man's proposition, mounted his spare steed, and headed west with him with her young son William on James' saddle. On their way back to the Cuyahoga settlement and James' log cabin, they found an itinerant preacher who performed the solemn act that made them husband and wife. [47]

After their adventures in the War of 1812, Alexander and Elizabeth's five sons all became, to one degree or another, prominent members of their Harpersfield community and torchbearers of their father's and grandfather's legacy. Robert, Alexander, William, and James all remained active in their local militia units, rising through the ranks to high office. The oldest of the Harper brothers, John, concentrated on real estate and invested some of the capital he inherited from his father's estate in a tract of land adjacent to his family's Harpersfield lot on the Lake County side of the line. He and his wife Loraine settled on the lot that now constitutes the western half of the village of Unionville and soon after sold it to his sister Elizabeth and her husband Abraham Tappan. John and Loraine moved on to another lot near today's village of Madison before eventually settling for good near Painesville in the village of Perry.

The youngest of the Harper brothers, Robert A., seems to have been the most active and aggressive entrepreneur of the bunch. He had proven his competence at an early age during the war and remained active in his local postwar militia, rising to major in Ohio's 2nd Brigade of the 4th Division. Having received an exceptional frontier education from his older sister Elizabeth and her husband Abraham, Robert also received training in law from his brother-in-law Judge Aaron Wheeler. He pursued a career as an attorney and prosecutor but invested much of his time and money in his many business ventures. After the War of 1812, he and his brothers formed the Harpersfield Commercial Company with the intent of developing a commercial port on Lake Erie at the mouth of Cunningham Creek. Robert advocated for the abolishment of slavery and was presumed to have been involved in helping escaped slaves make their way to Canada on the Underground Railroad. Ironically, he was also known to have taken and won cases for slaveowners seeking the return of their runaway property.

Robert A. Harper

Robert Harper's many business interests suffered mightily from the volatility of economic cycles that plagued his times. Cunningham Creek's Madison Dock proved to be unsuccessful, leaving him and his brothers heavily in debt and facing multiple litigations that lasted for years. By the age of fifty-nine, his health and finances were failing, and his wits were at an end. He finished his life in the lunatic asylum in Columbus, having suffered a stroke and becoming unmanageable for his children. Robert did, however, leave behind a lasting tribute to the Harper family's Ohio legacy. Having married Polly Hendry, the daughter of his family's old friend David Hendry, Robert built a modest yet elegant home for his wife and family in 1815. After being passed down to daughter Jane and her 1st cousin husband, Alexander J. Harper, Shandy Hall continued to be home to their spinster daughters, Stella and Ann Harper until the 1920s. A mile east of Unionville on South Ridge Road, the Western Reserve Historical Society maintains Shandy Hall as a museum, with all the original furnishings and Robert's law office. [48]

Polly Hendry Harper

As he neared the end of his life's journey, Col. Harper kept himself busy writing letters to old friends and wartime comrades. Ironically, one of the oldest and dearest friends he exchanged letters with had once been his sworn enemy. Having befriended Joseph Brant in his youth while attending Rev. Wheelock's Charity School for Indians, the two combatants had maintained their mutual respect despite having fought against each other through a long and brutal frontier war. Col. Harper's fondness for the Mohawk chief was extended to the many other Indians who were said to have visited him in his Harpersfield home after the war. The congenial colonel was perhaps more comfortable with his Indigenous visitors than he might have been with some of his fellow white guests, as it was said of him, he was prone to fly into a rage when one of his white guests referred to the Indians as savages.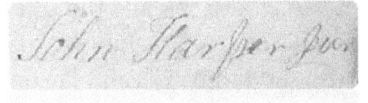

The man who saved Schoharie Valley from McDonell's Tories and led the cavalry charge at the Battle of the Flockey was nearing his eighties when the second war with England approached. The news of Gen. Harrison's battle on the Tippecanoe that ignited the War of 1812 may have only just reached Old Harpersfield by the 20th of November 1811 when seventy-seven-year-old Colonel John Harper gasped his last breath. Lt. Col. William Harper would have been too busy organizing his 87th Regiment to have spent much time with his dying stepfather. Had the old Colonel lived a few months longer he might not have understood why his stepson and nephew John Moore resigned their lieutenant colonel commissions on the verge of war. While his war had been one of uncompromising convictions, this new war would not be as justifiable for all those involved.

The year before his death, Col. Harper had watched with a sense of regret as his oldest son Archibald and younger son John I. Harper, joined their brother James and sisters Rebecca Montgomery and Ruth Dunbar on the Western Reserve. Archibald was the son who had gone to war as a waiter for his father at the age of fourteen and upon turning sixteen had served as a private in his father's Tryon County Regiment. Throughout his final years, the old colonel must have been disappointed to watch most of his children and friends leave Old Harpersfield and move on to greener pastures in Ohio. The ageing soldier's distress at seeing his hard-earned patent abandoned might not have been as irksome as his own infirmities that kept him from joining them on their grand new adventure. The man who had lived such an incredible life of action and risk-taking, might have regretted being left behind. At his bedside vigil, Col. Harper's wife of twenty-five years, Isabella, was joined by one of their two daughters, Polly and husband James Ells. The colonel was said to have died in his oldest daughter Margaret's and husband Roswell Hotchkiss' house in West Harpersfield, not far from The Centre where he and Miriam built their first log cabin in 1771. His last surviving brother, William, might have been at his dying brother's side, reminiscing about more glorious times and the adventures they had both shared during their long life.

Some years after the colonel's death, a maddening event occurred that would obfuscate much of what we could have learned of this man of two worlds. An unusually rare tornado swept through Harpersfield in the mid-1800s, blowing the roof off the house and the top off the chest in which Col. Harper's papers and letters were kept. What information might we have gleaned of this enigmatic adventurist had those irreplaceable letters, documents and memoirs not been scattered to the four corners of the county. [49]

William Harper Esq. was the only Harper brother to have lived long enough to witness the end of his young nation's second war with England. The state assemblyman who had cast his dissenting vote against New York's ratification of the United States Constitution was eighty-seven when he finally died in 1817 at the Milford home of his nephew Col. John Moore. Judge Harper's wife Margaret had died ten years before, leaving him with no surviving children to take care of their aging father in his final years. The judge's two nieces, Abigail and Mary Cully, were living near their brother John's Milford homestead and would have surely been there for their mother Mary's brother in his final days.

Epitaphs

Col. Harper's grave in the Harpersfield Center Rural Cemetery is just across a small stream from where he and wife Miriam built their family's first cabin in 1771. While surprisingly few of his children are there beside him, the mother of most of his children is not there either. Miriam Thompson Harper had died during the war in '78 and was presumably buried near Johnstown and Daniel Claus's sequestered estate where she and the colonel were living at the time. The colonel lay next to his second wife Isabella and his oldest daughter Margaret and husband Roswell Hotchkiss. John and Isabella's daughter Polly and husband James Ells also lay nearby. Isabella's son and the colonel's stepson, Lt. Col. William Harper, rests nearby with his wife Hannah Hotchkiss Harper and their son William. A tall obelisk was eventually erected over Col. Harper's grave by his well-meaning descendants, but the inscription they had carved upon it might not please the man beneath it. '...*Col. Harper was a pioneer settler in the town that now bears his name before the Revolutionary War and the gallant leader of a few patriot spirits in defending the frontier settlers from their* **savage** *foes...*'. [50]

Many of the other original Harper Patent settlers who did not move west, found their final resting place in the Stevens Cemetery a few miles west of Stamford off State Hwy #23 on Peck St. Several of Alexander Harper's sugar boilers were either buried or memorialized in this cemetery. Inscribed on a stone commemorating John Hendry's plight '...*When my brother was murdered, I was standing by, but in Quebec prison I was doomed to die...*'. On another nearby cenotaph memorializing his brother James '...*While British tyranny overspread this land, I was slain by cruel hands...*'. William Stevens, Thomas Hendry and his son James, were said to have been buried where they fell on that cold April morning in 1780. The Thorp brothers, Ezra and Daniel, survived their long imprisonment in Canada and after returning and living out their lives in Harpersfield, both were buried in Stevens Cemetery. The father who had brought his eleven-year-old son Willy along with him on Alexander's expedition, William Lamb Sr, was also buried here. William Stevens, the poor soul who was killed by the Indians as he lay sick in his cabin, was misidentified as James Stevens on a memorial to his memory. The Honorable Dr. Joshua Brett and his wife Anna Dunbar Brett can also be found among their contemporaries in the Stevens Cemetery. [51]

The sandy rise where Alexander Harper and his hired man Gleason were the first to be laid to rest is now the little village of Unionville's Colonel Alexander Harper Memorial Cemetery. Both Alexander and Elizabeth now rest there alongside most of their children and many of their grandchildren. Some of the Bartholomeus who settled near the Harpers on Geneva's Cowles Creek were buried in Geneva's Evergreen Cemetery. Other smaller cemeteries in and around the Harpersfield/Geneva area are filled with other New York expatriates who came to the Western Reserve in the early nineteenth century. In Conneaut, where the Montgomerys settled, Robert and Mary White Montgomery are buried in the Conneaut City Cemetery with at least three of their children. Capt. James Harper and his wife Sarah Montgomery Harper are buried there alongside Sarah's parents, her brother Eli, and sister Anna and husband Aaron Wright. Community cemeteries throughout Ohio, Indiana, Illinois, Michigan, Wisconsin, and beyond are filled with descendants of the early pioneers who paused briefly in the Western Reserve before continuing their relentless westward migration. More than a few of New York and Ohio's earliest pioneers now lie beneath blank headstones that time and the elements have deprived of names and dates. [52]

The four Harper brothers were born in an America much different from the America they left behind. They were all born loyal subjects of the king, but unlike their forebears they died free men. Their grandparents, James and Janet Lewis Harper and William and Mary Aiken Montgomery, had come to colonial America in 1718 with the first significant wave of Scots-Irish immigrants. They found their new countrymen unaccepting of their non-conformist Presbyterianism and settled amongst a population of inhospitable New England puritans. Ostracized by Boston's magistrate and citizenry, they and their kinsmen were forced to settle in the Irish Rows of New England's frontier outposts on the hostile periphery of Christendom. James and Janet's youngest son John Harper fought his way through the 4th Anglo/Abenaki war in the desolate forests of Maine's coastal interior with the Montgomery brothers, John and James. The marriage of John Harper Sr to Abigail Montgomery would yield one of early America's most enterprising and controversial frontier families. From East Boston's Noodle's Island to the Connecticut River's inland port of Middletown, the first generation of American born Harpers came of age before beginning their epic journey from one hostile frontier to the next. They came to New York's Cherry Valley in 1754 when it was one of the furthest and westwardly most white settlements in all British Colonial America.

As patent proprietors, the Harpers were said to have been *'...kind and generous to the poor and ready at any time to do anything in their power to make all around them happy...'*. Their patent, which became New York's Delaware County township of Harpersfield, was barely settled when the Revolution's border war drove them and their homesteaders into the Schoharie Valley forts. There they fought and sacrificed for their country's Independence and to hold on to their hard-earned patented lands. New York's postwar exploitation of the Iroquois lands and the mass migration of white settlers into their western territories foreshadowed another mass migration and genocidal conquest of the lands of the Wyandot and Shawnee nations, west of the Alleghenies on the Ohio frontier. The two younger Harper brothers could not resist the urge to continue their family's westward legacy and their young nation's self-proclaimed Manifest Destiny. The generations of Harpers and their Scots-Irish kinsmen who followed, would carry on their forefather's visions and dreams of empire. [53]

Montgomery Harper came to the Ohio frontier with his parents, Maj. Joseph and Catherine Douglas Harper, in 1799 at the age of three (p.194). Montgomery died in Rock Co., Wisconsin in 1864 at the age of sixty-eight with his second wife Angelina and ten of his fifteen children by his side.

Acknowledgments

There is no way I could have ever authored this book without the encouragement and counsel of my dear friend Sam, Dr. Eric S. Loker, Emeritus Distinguished Professor, Biology Department, University of New Mexico, Albuquerque. The suggestions and editorial corrections he generously contributed to this book improved the quality of it enormously. His friendship and informative conversations have enriched my life immeasurably. Another old friend, David B. Mattern, Retired Professor and Senior Associate Editor of the Papers of James Madison, University of Virginia, Charlottesville, helped with the clarification of some of my phrasing and historical uncertainties. David's book, 'Benjamin Lincoln and the American Revolution', was a hugely helpful tool in the formatting of my book about another less chronicled hero of the Revolution. Without the contributions of these two scholarly gentlemen, the prospective reader would have been subjected to far more awkward glitches and misinterpretations. The brilliant books of Pulitzer Prize winning author, Alan Taylor, were a rich source of information and inspiration for parts of this book and come highly recommended for those interested in early American history. My book's title teases at the title of Taylor's 1995 book, *William Cooper's Town,* an exposé in part on the conflict between the Harpers and the postwar politics of New York's former frontier border region. Ryan DeCaire, Assistant Professor in the Department of Linguistics and Center for Indigenous Studies, University of Toronto, was kind enough to lend his expertise in translating the Mohawk/Oneida names and terms essential to my story. And of course, my thanks go to my precious wife Jean who never failed me when I needed the spelling of a word that totally escaped me.

To the memory of my sister,
JoAnne Miller Lewin,
"<i>To the land vaguely realized westward.</i>"

Sources

Chapter 1: New England

1. Charles K. Bolton, *Scotch Irish Pioneers in Ulster and America*, (Boston: Bacon & Brown, 1910), 320.
- Rebecca Graham, *The Cork Settlement of Merrymeeting Bay*, (www.academia.edu).
2. John Thomson, *Ireland, Thomson's New General Atlas*, (London: Cradock & Joy, 1815), 10.
3. Bolton, *Scotch Irish Pioneers,* 317-323.
4. Edward L. Parker, *History of Londonderry, New Hampshire, Comprising the Towns of Derry and Londonderry*, (Boston: Perkins & Whipple, 1851), 34.
- Bolton, *Scotch Irish Pioneers,* 319, 324-330.
5. Bolton, *Scotch Irish Pioneers,* 141-145.
6. William W. Sumner, *A History of East Boston,* (Boston: J. E. Tilton & Co., 1858), 184,256-257,314-323.
7. Bolton, *Scotch Irish Pioneers,* 204.
- Henry J. Ford, *The Scotch-Irish in America*, (Princeton, NJ: Princeton University, 1915), 140-149.
8. George A. Wheeler, *History of Brunswick, Topsham and Harpswell Maine, Including the Ancient Territory Known as Pejepscot,* (Boston: A. Mudge & Sons, 1878), 29-30, 37, 42-43.
- Bolton, *Scotch Irish Pioneers,* 141-144, 218-222.
9. Wheeler, *History of Brunswick, Topsham and Harpswell*, 49-53.
- William D. Williamson, *The History of the State of Maine,* (Hallowell, ME: Glazier, Masters & Co., 1839), Vol. 1, 515-553, 604-650, Vol. 2, 87-110.
10. Harold L. Prins, *The Crooked Path of Dummer's Treaty, Anglo-Wabenaki Diplomacy and the Quest for Aboriginal Rights, Papers of the Algonquian Conference*, (Winnipeg: University of Manitoba Press, 2002), Vol. 33, 362-369.
- Williamson, *The History of the State of Maine*, Vol. 2, 38-79, 111-151.
11. Williamson, *The History of the State of Maine*, Vol. 2, 106-108.
12. Wheeler, *History of Brunswick, Topsham and Harpswell,* 869-872.
13. Williamson, *History of the State of Maine*, 108-109.
- Wheeler, *History of Brunswick, Topsham and Harpswell*, 875.
14. Bolton, *Scotch Irish Pioneers*, 231-232.
- Williamson, *History of the State of Maine*, Vol. 2, 114-116.
15. Wheeler, *History of Brunswick, Topsham and Harpswell*, 53.
- Williamson, *History of the State of Maine*, Vol. 2, 118.
- Henry B. Wright, *Soldiers of Oakham, Mass. in the Revolution, the War of 1812, and the Civil War,* (New Haven, CT: Tuttle, Morehouse & Taylor Press, 1914), 95-111.
- Parker, *The History of Londonderry*, 34-66.
- Hamilton D. Hurd, *The History of Worcester County, Mass., With Biographical Sketches of Many of the Pioneers and Prominent Men,* (Philadelphia: J. W. Lewis, 1889), Vol. 2, 1425-1426, 1080-1081.
- William J. Montgomery, *A Montgomery Family Genealogy, William and Mary, Robert and Mary*, 2020. https://www.wjmontgomerygenealogy.com
16. Robert E. Cray, *Lovewell's Fight, War, Death and Memory in Borderland New England*, (Amherst, Boston: University of Massachusetts Press, 2014).
- Williamson, *History of the State of Maine*, Vol. 2, 129-132.
17. H. B. Wright, E. D. Harvey, *The Settlement and Story of Oakham, Mass.*, (New Haven, CT:

Earnest L. Hayward, 1947), 910-912.
- *The New York Genealogical and Biographical Record*, (New York: NYGBS, Jan. 1922), Vol. 53, 28-31
18. Wheeler, *History of Brunswick, Topsham and Harpswell*, 875.
- Sumner, *A History of East Boston*, 314-317.
- Jane C. Ford, *Records of the Harper Family*, (A. C. Rogers Co., 1905), 38, 58-59.
19. Bolton, *Scottish Irish Pioneers*, 230-232, 235.
20. *Vital Records of Oakham, Mass. to the End of the Year 1849*, (Worcester, MA: F. P. Rice, 1905), 30,37,77,86.
- H. B. Wright, E. D. Harvey, *The Settlement and Story of Oakham, Mass.*, 761-766, 910-912.
- Hurd, *The History of Worcester County, Mass.*, 1080-1081.
21. Henry R. Stiles, *The History and Genealogy of Ancient Windsor, Connecticut, 1635-1891*, (Hartford, CT: Case, Lockwood, Brainard & Co., 1892), Vol. 2, 753-755.
- Henry R. Stiles, *The History of Ancient Windsor, Connecticut*, (New York: Charles B. Norton, 1859), 292-295.
- Mary A. T. Elliott, *Thompson Genealogy, The Descendants of William and Margaret Thompson, First Settlers of That Part of Windsor Connecticut Now East Windsor and Ellington*, (New Haven, CT: Tuttle, Morehouse & Taylor, 1915), ix-xi, 1-109.
22. Bolton, *Scottish Irish Pioneers*, 236.
- Montgomery, *A Montgomery Family Genealogy*.
- *Vital Records of Hopkinton, Massachusetts to the Year 1850*, (Boston: New England Historical Genealogical Society, 1911), 328.
- *Manual of the First Congregational Church of Hopkinton, Massachusetts, With Historical Sketches, 1724-1881*, (Boston: Alfred Mudge & Sons, 1881), 42, 43.
- *History of Middlesex County, Massachusetts, Containing Carefully Prepared Histories of Every City and Town in the County*, (Boston: Estes & Lauriat, 1880), 485-486.
- William H. Eldridge, *Henry Genealogy, The Descendants of Samuel Henry of Hadley and Amherst Massachusetts, 1734-1790*, (Boston: T. R. Marvin & Son, 1915), 72-76.
23. James Otis, *The Story of Pemaquid*, (New York: T. Y. Crowell & Co., 1902), 117-137.
- Arlita D. Parker, *A History of Pemaquid*, (Boston: MacDonald & Evens, 1925), 191-204.
24. *Vital Records of Hopkinton*, 231, 289.
- Bolton, *Scottish Irish Pioneers*, 175, 333, 335.
- Stiles, *The History and Genealogy of Ancient Windsor*, 365-368.
- Ford, *Records of the Harper Family*, 58-59.
- W. W. Munsell, *History of Delaware County, N.Y*, (New York: W. W. Munsell & Co., 1880), 217-218.
25. J. M. Pelton, *Genealogy of the Pelton Family in America*, (Albany: Joel Munsell's Sons, 1892), 75-78.
26. Ford, *Records of the Harper Family*, 58-59.
27. Hugh Hastings, *The Public Papers of George Clinton, First Governor of New York*, (Albany: State of New York and the University of New York, 1900-1914), Vol. 4, 410-415.
28. Isabel T. Kelsay, *Joseph Brant, 1743-1807, Man of Two Worlds*, (Syracuse, NY: Syracuse University Press, 1984), 71-91.
- William Stone, *The Life of Joseph Brant, Thayendanegea*, (Cooperstown, NY: H. & E. Phinney, 1844), Vol. 2, 493.
- Neal O. Hammon, ed., *My Father Daniel Boone, The Draper Interviews with Nathan Boone*, (Lexington, KT: University of Kentucky Press, 2012), 9-21.
29. *Calander of New York Colonial Manuscripts, Indorsed Land Papers*, (Albany: Weed, Parsons

& Co., 1864), 213,219,223,230,235.
- Hamilton D. Hurd, *History of Otsego County, N. Y. with Illustrations and Biographical Sketches of Some of its Prominent Men and Pioneers*, (Philadelphia: Everts & Farriss, 1878), 12-13.
- William W. Campbell, *Annals of Tryon County, or The Border Warfare of New York During the Revolution*, (New York: J. J. Harper, 1831), 17-21.
- Jeptha R. Simms, *The Frontiersmen of New York*, (Albany: George C. Riggs, 1882), Vol. 1, 194-197.

30. John Sawyer, *History of Cherry Valley, 1740-1898*, (Cherry Valley, NY: Gazette Print, 1898), 1-7.
- Campbell, *Annals of Tryon County*, 21-27.
- Colin D. Campbell, *They Beckoned and We Came, The Settlement of Cherry Valley*, New York Historical Journal, Vol. 79, No. 3, (Cornell, NY: Cornell University Press, 1998), 215-232.
- Parker, *The History of Londonderry*, 194-200.

31. F. A. Gault, *Dear Old Greene County*, (Catskill, NY: 1915), 316-318.
- Rev. H. V. Swinnerton, *Map of Cherry Valley at the Time of the Massacre*, (Draper Manuscripts, State Historical Society of Wisconsin, 1877).

32. Parker, *The History of Londonderry*, 194-200.
- Munsell, *History of Delaware County, N.Y.*, 218.

33. Simms, *The Frontiersmen of New York*, Vol. 1, 200-208.
- Kelsay, *Joseph Brant*, 55-70.
- Fintan O'Toole, *White Savage, William Johnson and the Invention of America*, (Albany: State University of New York Press, 2005), 41-44.
- *Calander of New York Colonial Manuscripts*, 228.

34. Campbell, *Annals of Tryon County*, 24-25.
- Martha J. Lamb, Constance C. Harrison, *History of the City of New York, Its Origin, Rise and Progress*, (New York: A. S. Barnes & Co., 1896), Vol. 1, 34.

35. Simms, *Frontiersmen of New York*, Vol. 1, 217-223.

36. Simms, *Frontiersmen of New York*, Vol. 1, 295-308, (Albany: Court of Appeals, Book A, Page 35).

37. Simms, *Frontiersmen of New York*, Vol. 1, 230-231, 241-245.
- Alan Taylor, *American Colonies, The Settling of North America,* (New York: Penguin Books, 2001), 43

38. Campbell, *Annals of Tryon County*, 24-26.
- Simms, *Frontiersmen of New York*, Vol. 1, 233-236.
- Francis Parkman, *Montcalm and Wolfe, France and England in North America*, (Boston: Little, Brown & Co., 1898), Vol. 2, 8-9.
- Ford, *Records of the Harper Family*, 38, 58.
- Sawyer, *History of Cherry Valley*, 6.

39. Kelsay, *Joseph Brant,* 99-100,108-110.
- *Calander of New York Colonial Manuscripts*, 459.
- The Occom Circle, *Theophilus Chamberlain to Eleazer Wheelock Letter, July, 29, 1765; Kind Brothers Letter, Isaac and Good Peter to Rev. Wheeler, Onaquaga, Nov. 12, 1764 (John Harper Interpreter)*. https://www.library.dartmouth.edu
- Richard Berleth, *Bloody Mohawk, The French and Indian War & American Revolution on New York's Frontier,* (Delmar, NY: Black Dome Press, 2010), 99.

40. *Calander of New York Colonial Manuscripts*, 784, 882, 909.

41. Ford, *Records of the Harper Family*, 38.

- Elliott, *Thompson Genealogy*, 167-171.
- Pelton, *Genealogy of the Pelton Family in America*, 60, 75-78.

42. Ford, *Records of the Harper Family*, 59.
- Cherry Valley Cemetery, https://www.findagrave.com

Chapter 2: Property Lines

1. Alan Taylor, *The Divided Ground*, (New York: Vintage Books, 2006), 40-42.

2. Francis W. Halsey, *The Old New York Frontier*, (New York: Charles Scribner's Sons, 1902), 73-79.
- William J. Campbell, *Negotiating at the Oneida Carry*, (Fort Stanwix National Monument Historic Resource Study, 2017), 35-38.
- Kelsay, *Joseph Brant*, 92-107.

3. Alan Taylor, *The Divided Ground*, 40-45.
- Campbell, *Negotiating at the Oneida Carry,* 45-76.
- Richard Berleth, *Bloody Mohawk*, (Delmar, NY: Black Dome Press, 2010), 150-151.
- James T. Clark, *Sir William Johnson and Pontiac,* Proceedings of the New York State Historical Association, (Cornell, NY: Cornell University Press, 1914), Vol. 13, 85-107.

4. Halsey, *The Old New York Frontier*, 87-115.
- *Calendar of New York Colonial Manuscripts Indorsed Land Papers*, (Albany: Weed, Parsons & Co., 1864), Vol. 22, 417; Vol. 32, 586; Vol. 27, 497; Vol. 38, 669.

5. Halsey, *The Old New York Frontier,* 95-98.
- H. Fletcher Davidson, *Delaware County Fur Trading to Farming*, (Delhi, NY: R. B. Decker Advertising, 1976), 15.

6. John D. Monroe, *Chapters in the History of Delaware County New York*, (Delhi NY: Delaware County Historical Association, 1949), 11-12.
- *Calendar of New York Manuscripts*, Vol. 27, 497, 501, 502.
- Halsey, *The Old New York Frontier,* 106-111.
- Davidson, *Delaware County Fur Trading to Farming,* 46-48, 55-56.

7. A. T. Volwiler, *George Croghan and the Development of Central New York, 1763-1800*, (Cooperstown NY: Fenimore Art Museum, 1923), The Quarterly Journal of the New York State Historical Association, Vol. 4, 21-40.
- *Calendar of New York Manuscripts*, Vol. 23, 447.

8. Monroe, *Chapters in the History of Delaware County*, 12.
- Richard Smith, Francis W. Halsey ed., *A Tour of Four Great Rivers; The Hudson, Mohawk, Susquehanna and Delaware in 1769; Being the Journal of Richard Smith of Burlington, New Jersey*, (New York: Charles Scribner's Sons, 1906), 29-38.
- *Calendar of New York Manuscripts*, Vol. 24, 459; Vol. 23, 441.
- James Sullivan Ph.D., State Historian, *The Papers of Sir William Johnson*, (Albany: The University of the State of New York, Division of Archives and History, 1921), Vol. 12, 346, 542.

9. Davidson, *Delaware County Fur Trading to Farming*, 38-39.
- *Calendar of New York Manuscripts*, Vol. 26, 481.

10. Monroe, *Chapters in the History of Delaware County*, 9-13.
- Davidson, *Delaware County Fur Trading to Farming*, 38-70.
- *Calendar of New York Manuscripts*, Vol. 26, 482, 485, 487-489, 491.

11. Munsell, *History of Delaware County New York*, (New York: W. W. Munsell & Co., 1880), 46.
- Alf Evers, *The Catskills, From Wilderness to Woodstock*, (Garden City, NJ: Doubleday & Company, 1972), 33-39.
- *Calendar of New York Manuscripts*, Vol. 4, 81-84
- Davidson, *Delaware County Fur Trading to Farming*, 11-15.

12. Charles H. Lincoln ed., *A Calander of the Manuscripts of Col. John Bradstreet*, (Worcester, MA: American Antiquarian Society), 151-181.
- *Monroe, Chapters in the History of Delaware County*, 23-26.
- Evers, *The Catskills, From Wilderness to Woodstock*, 112-120.
- E. B. O'Callaghan, ed., *The Documentary History of the State of New York*, (Albany: Weed, Parsons & Co., 1849), Vol. 1, 587-591; Vol. 2, 917-919.

13. Davidson, *Delaware County Fur Trading to Farming*, 56-60.
- *Calendar of New York Manuscripts*, Vol. 41, 702-703.

14. Evers, *The Catskills, From Wilderness to Woodstock*, 101-102.
- *Calendar of New York Manuscripts*, Vol. 11, 699.
- Monroe, *Chapters in the History of Delaware County*, 29-30.

15. George N. MacKenzie, *Colonial Families of the USA, 1607-1775*, (New York, Boston: Grafton Press, 1907), Vol. 4, 138-141.
- Roswell R. Hoes ed., *Baptismal and Marriage Register of the Old Dutch Church of Kingston*, (New York: DeVinne Press, 1891).

16. Munsell, *History of Delaware County New York*, 157-159.

17. Rev. Angus MacDonald, Rev. Archibald MacDonald, *The Clan Donald*, (Inverness, Scotland: Northern Counties Publishing Co., 1904), 308-316, 320-328, 345-359.
- William L. Scott, *The MacDonells of Leek, Collachie and Aberchalder, MacDonells on the Pearl in 1773; A New Perspective*, (The Clan Donald Society of Scotland). www.clandonald.org
- Monroe, *Chapters in the History of Delaware County*, 28-29.

18. George W. Bartholomew Jr, *Records of the Bartholomew Family*, (Austin, TX: The Compiler, 1885), Part 2, 457-463.
- Monroe, *Chapters in the History of Delaware County*, 69.
- Stephen W. Mabie, Mary T. Smith, *Our Heritage*, (San Antonio, TX: San Antonio Genealogical and Historical Society, 2015), Vol. 57, 55-68.

19. Monroe, *Chapters in the History of Delaware County*, 29.

20. Charles D. Griffin, *A History of Stamford*, (Stamford, NY: Stamford Historical Society, 1988), 28-31, 37-42.
- Munsell, *History of Delaware County*, 292.
- Monroe, *Chapters in the History of Delaware County*, 27-28.

21. Munsell, *History of Delaware County*, 282-284.
- Monroe, *Chapters in the History of Delaware County*, 26.
- Halsey, *The Old New York Frontier*, 56-62, 129-135.

22. Smith, *A Tour of Four Great Rivers*, 52-57.
- *Calendar of New York Manuscripts*, Vol. 13, 240-241.
- Davidson, *Delaware County Fur Trading to Farming*, 37.
- Griffin, *A History of Stamford*, 19-20.
- Munsell, *History of Delaware County*, 292, 293, 315-316.
- Jack Harpster, Ken Stalter, *Captive! The Story of David Ogden and the Iroquois*, (Santa Barbara, CA: Praeger, 2010).
- *Dutch Reformed Church Records of Niskayuna and Schoharie*, Book 36, 359. www.ancestry.com

23. Munsell, *History of Delaware County*, 217-220.
- John Barber, Henry Howe, *Historical Collections of the State of New York*, (New York: S. Tuttle, 1846), 128-129.

24. *Revolutionary War Pension and Bounty Land Warrant Application*, M804, 841, W20992.

25. Ford, *Records of the Harper Family*, 15.

- Bartholomew, *Records of the Bartholomew,* Part 2, 462-463.
26. George A. Wheeler & Henry W. Wheeler, *History of Brunswick, Topham and Harpswell, Maine,* (Boston: Alfred Mudger & Sons, 1878), 37-39.
- Charles K. Bolton, *Scotch Irish Pioneers in Ulster and America,* (Boston: Bacon & Brown, 1910), 228-236, 183-187.
- Ford, *Records of the Harper Family,* 58-59.
- Jeptha R. Simms, *The Frontiersman of New York,* (Albany: Geo. C. Riggs, 1883), Vol. 2, 57-63.
- H. B. Wright, E. D. Harvey, *The Settlement and Story of Oakham, Massachusetts,* (New Haven, CT: Ernest L. Hayward, 1947), Vol. 1, 294-295; Vol. 2, 761-766.
27. Davidson, *Delaware County Fur Trading to Farming,* 37.
- *Calendar of New York Manuscripts,* Vol. 12, 231-241.
28. Munsell, *History of Delaware County,* 174.
- *New York State Road Atlas,* (Round Lake, NY: Jimapco, 2015).
- Dorothy Kubik, *West Through the Catskills, The Story of the Susquehanna Turnpike,* (Fleischmanns, NY: Purple Mountain Press, 2001), Delaware County Historical Assoc., 2020.
29. Swiggett, Howard, *War Out of Niagara,* (Port Washington, NY: Ira Friedman, 1963). 67-68.
- Berleth, *Bloody Mohawk,* 183-185.
- Kelsay, *Joseph Brant,* 176-177.
- William W. Campbell, *Annuals of Tryon County or The Border Warfare of New York During the Revolution,* (New York: J & J Harper, 1831), 62.
- Simms, *Frontiersmen of New York,* Vol. 1, 560-570.
30. Nelson Greene, ed., *History of the Mohawk Valley, Gate to the West 1614-1925, Mohawk Valley Revolutionary Forts 1776-1777,* (Chicago: S. J. Clarke Publishing Co., 1925), Vol. 1, 770-785.
- Simms, *Frontiersmen of New York,* Vol. 1, 571-577.
31. Halsey, *The Old New York Frontier,* 168-172.
- *Calendar of Historical Manuscripts Relating to the Revolution,* (Albany: Weed Parson & Co., 1868), Vol. 1, 629-630, 654.
- Hugh Hastings, ed., *Public Papers of George Clinton the First Governor of New York,* (Albany: James B. Lyon, 1899), Vol. 10, 712.
- *Journals of the Provincial Congress, Committee of Safety and Council of Safety of the State of New York,* (Albany: Thurlow Weed, Printer of the State, 1842), Vol. 1, 800.
- William L. Stone, *Life of Joseph Brant (Thayendanegea), Including the Border War of the American Revolution,* (Albany: J. Munsell, 1865), Vol. 1, 177-179.
32. Berleth, *Bloody Mohawk,* 202-203.
- Stone, *Life of Joseph Brant,* Vol. 1, 178-180.
- Munsell, *History of Delaware County,* 222.
- Halsey, *The Old New York Frontier,* 171-172.
- Jay Gould, *History of Delaware County and Border Wars of New York,* (Roxbury, NY: Keeny & Gould, 1856), 74-77.
- F. W. Beers, *Atlas of Delaware County, New York,* (New York: F. W. Beers, A. D. Ellis, G. G. Soule, 1869), Harpersfield Map.
- Simms, *Frontiersmen of New York,* Vol. 2, 55-57.
33. Swiggett, *War Out of Niagara,* 79.
34. Campbell, *Annuals of Tryon County,* 63-64.
- Kelsay, *Joseph Brant,* 193-194.
- Halsey, *The Old New York Frontier,* 173-175.

35. Stone, *Life of Brant*, Vol. 1., 180-186.
- Halsey, *The Old New York Frontier*, 176-184.
- Simms, *The Frontiersman*, Vol. 2, 15-20.
36. Berleth, *Bloody Mohawk*, 217-220.
- Campbell, *Annuals of Tryon County*, 71-76.
- Halsey, *The Old New York Frontier*, 185-187.
- Jeff O'Connor, *Thunder in the Valley*, (Cobleskill, NY: Times-Journal, 2002), Schoharie County Historical Society, 14.
37. Jeptha R. Simms, *History of Schoharie County and Border Wars of New York*, (Albany: Munsell & Tanner Printers, 1845), 265.
- Swiggett, *War Out of Niagara*, 79-97.
- Nelson Greene, *The Story of Old Fort Plain and the Middle Mohawk Valley*, (Fort Plain NY: O'Conner Brothers Publishing, 1915), 48-64.
- Kelsay, *Joseph Brant*, 196-208.
- Berleth, *Bloody Mohawk*, 222-237.
- Campbell, *Annuals of Tryon County*, 76-95.
- William Scudder, *The Journal of Lt. William Scudder an Officer in the Late New York Line 1794*, Reprint as *The Narrative of North American Indian Captives*, (New York: Garland Publishing, 1977), Vol., 18.
- Gavin K. Watt, *Rebellion in the Mohawk Valley, The St. Leger Expedition of 1777*, (Toronto, Oxford: The Dundurn Group, 2002), 136-261.
- Simms, *The Frontiersman*, Vol. 2, 66-116.
- Paul A. Boehlert, *The Battle of Oriskany and General Nicholas Herkimer, Revolution in the Mohawk Valley,* (Charleston, SC: The History Press, 2013).
- Simms, *Frontiersmen of New York,* Vol. 1, 303.

Chapter 3: Border War
1. Jeptha R. Simms, *History of Schoharie County, New York*, (Albany: Munsell & Tanner, 1845), 232-236.
- Jeff O'Conner, Schoharie County Historical Society, *Thunder in the Valley* (Cobleskill, NY: Times-Journal, 2002), 1-9.
2. 1790 Census, Albany County, Schoharie District, www. ancestors.com
- Don Chrysler, *The Blue-Eyed Indians, The Story of Adam Crysler and His Brothers in the Revolutionary* War, (Zephyrhills, FL: Chrysler Books, 1999), Chapter 2.
3. William McLennan, *Spanish John*, (London & New York: Harper & Brothers, 1898), 7, 93-128.
4. O'Conner, *Thunder in the Valley*, 10-20.
- Gavin K. Watt, *Rebellion in the Mohawk Valley*, (Toronto & Oxford: The Dundurn Press, 2002), 58, 64, 110.
5. Simms, *History of Schoharie*, 225.
- O'Conner, *Thunder in the Valley*, 23.
- *Revolutionary War Pension and Bounty-Land Warrant Application*, W.4128, Margaret Harper Wheeler Deposition.
- *Journals of the Provincial Congress, Provincial Convention, Committee of Safety and Council of Safety of the State of New York*, (Albany: Thurlow Weed, 1842), Vol. 1, 1001-1002.
6. O'Conner, *Thunder in the Valley*, 23-25.
- W.W. Munsell, *History of Delaware County, New York*, (New York: W.W. Munsell, 1880), 219.
7. Simms, *History of Schoharie*, 237-238.
- O'Conner, *Thunder in the Valley*, 25-26.

8. Simms, *History of Schoharie,* 239-240.
- O'Conner, *Thunder in the Valley,* 26-28.
- Oliver B. Bunce, *The Romance of the Revolution,* (Philadelphia: Porter & Coates, 1870), 221-222.

9. Jane Cowles Ford & Carrie Harper White, *Records of the Harper Family,* (Cleveland: A.C. Rogers Co.,1905), 40-41.
- Simms, *History of Schoharie,* 241-242.
- O'Conner, *Thunder in the Valley,* 28-29.

10. William E. Roscoe, *History of Schoharie County, New York,* (Syracuse: D. Mason & Co., 1882), 37-43.
- Simms, *History of Schoharie,* 243.
- O'Conner, *Thunder in the Valley,* 30.

11. O'Conner, *Thunder in the Valley,* 30-32.
- Simms, *History of Schoharie,* 243-247.

12. Simms, *History of Schoharie,* 247.

13. O'Conner, *Thunder in the Valley,* 33-34.

14. Revolutionary War Pension Application, W.12234, S.42258.
- National Archives Catalog, *List of Officers and Men of Col. Elisha Sheldon, Col. Stephen Moylan and Major Henry Lee's Legion of Dragoons 1776-1781,* (record group 93: M853: roll 16: target 4: Vol. 11).
- Dean Snow, *Continental and Militia Cavalry Compared,* Journal of the American Revolution, (August 31, 2021).
- Gavin Watt, *Continental Dragoons in the Schoharie Valley,* Journal of the American Revolution, (August 12, 2013).
- Simms, *History of Schoharie,* 248.
- O'Conner, *Thunder in the Valley,* 34.

15. Simms, *History of Schoharie,* 249-251.
- O'Conner, *Thunder in the Valley,* 40

16. John Monroe, *Chapters in the History of Delaware County New York,* (Delhi, NY: Delaware County Historical Association, 1949), 29-31.
- Francis W. Halsey, *The Old New York Frontier: Its Wars with Indians and Tories: Its Missionary Schools, Pioneers and Land Titles, 1614-1800,* (New York: Charles Scribner's Sons, 1902), 201-206.
- *Journals of the Provincial Congress,* Vol. 1, 1051.
- Simms, *History of Schoharie,* 269-271.
- O'Conner, *Thunder in the Valley,* 41.

17. Alf Evers, *The Catskills, From Wilderness to Woodstock,* (Garden City, NY: Doubleday & Co., 1972), 147-150
- *New York in the Revolution as Colony and State,* (Albany: J. B. Lyon Co., 1904), Vol. 1, 199.
- Thomas B. Allen & Todd W. Braisted, *The Loyalist Corps, Americans in the Service of the King,* (Takoma Park, MD: Fox Acres Press, 2011), 52.
- Hugh Hastings, *The Public Papers of George Clinton, First Governor of New York,* (Albany: James B. Lyon, State Printer, 1900), Vol. 1, 750-800.

18. Evers, *The Catskills,* 150-151.

19. Evers, *The Catskills,* 151-154.

20. Evers, *The Catskills,* 154-156.

- Monroe, *Chapters in the History of Delaware County*, 43-48.
21. Halsey, *The Old New York Frontier*, 207-209.
- William W. Campbell, *Annals of Tryon County or The Border Warfare of New York During the Revolution*, (New York: J. & J. Harper,1831), 100-102.
- Simms, *History of Schoharie*, 281.
22. Isabel T. Kelsay, *Joseph Brant 1743-1807, Man of Two Worlds*, (Syracuse: Syracuse University Press, 1984), 216-217.
- Halsey, *The Old New York Frontier*, 207-208.
- Richard Berleth, *Bloody Mohawk, The French and Indian War and American Revolution on New York's Frontier,* (Delmar, NY: Black Dome Press, 2010), 253-256.
- Simms, *History of Schoharie*, 273-281.
- Roscoe, *History of Schoharie*, 153.
23. Monroe, *Chapters in History of Delaware County*, 70.
- Simms, *History of Schoharie*, 285-289.
- Richard B. LaCrosse Jr., *Revolutionary Rangers, Daniel Morgan's Riflemen and their Role on the Northern Frontier 1778-1783*, (Berwyn Heights, MD: Heritage Books, 2019), 19-23.
24. Howard Swiggett, *War Out of Niagara*, (Port Washington, NY: Ira J. Friedman, 1963), 124-134.
- Kelsay, *Joseph Brant,* 218-222.
- Halsey, *The Old New York Frontier*, 216-220.
- Berleth, *Bloody Mohawk*, 258-260.
- Jeanne W. Adler, *Chainbreaker's War, A Seneca Chief Remembers the American Revolution*, (Delmar, NY: Black Dome Press, 2002), 93.
- Thomas Campbell, *Gertrude of Wyoming or The Pennsylvania Cottage*, (New York: D. Appleton & Co., 1858).
25. Berleth, *Bloody Mohawk*, 257.
- Simms, *History of Schoharie,* 282.
- Kelsay, *Joseph Brant*, 223-224.
- Halsey, *The Old New York Frontier*, 211.
26. Hastings, *Public Papers of George Clinton*, Vol. 4, 103-112, 139-141.
- John T. Posey, *General Thomas Posey, Son of the American Revolution*, (Michigan: Michigan University Press, 1993).
- Monroe, *Chapters in History of Delaware County*, 53-60.
- Munsell, *History of Delaware County*, 258.
27. Hastings, *The Public Papers of George Clinton*, Vol. 4, 17-18.
- Munsell, *History of Delaware County*, 135-136.
- Monroe, *Chapters in the History of Delaware County*, 61-62.
- James E. Quinlan, *History of Sullivan County, Embracing an Account of its Geology, Climate, Aborigines, Early Settlement, Organizations; with Biographical Sketches*, (Liberty, NY: G. M. Beebe & W. T. Morgans, 1873) 459-463.
- E. M. Ruttenber & L. H. Clark, *History of Orange County New York*, (Philadelphia: Everts & Peck, 1881) 49.
28. Kelsay, *Joseph Brant*, 225-226.
- Halsey, *The Old New York Frontier*, 223-228.
- Berleth, *Bloody Mohawk*, 261.
- Hastings, *Public Papers of George Clinton*, Vol. 4, 47-50.
29. Swiggett, *War Out of Niagara*, 136-145.
- Halsey, *The Old New York Frontier*, 229-237.

- Monroe, *Chapters in the History of Delaware County*, 71-73.
- Berleth, *Bloody Mohawk*, 261-263.
- Hastings, *Public Papers of George Clinton*, Vol. 4, 222-231.
- LaCrosse, *Revolutionary Rangers*, 30-33.

30. Ford & White, *Records of the Harper Family*, 38.
- Halsey, *The Old New York Frontier*, 341.
- Simms, *Frontiersmen of New York*, Vol. 1, 269.
- Hastings, *Public Papers of George Clinton*, Vol. 4, 712-717.
- Mary A. Elliott, *Thompson Geneology, Descendants of William and Margaret Thomson*, (New Haven, CT: Tuttle, Morehouse & Taylor Co., 1915), 2-8.
- *New York in the Revolution as Colony and State*, Vol. 2, 245-246

31. Kelsay, *Joseph Brant*, 228-230.

32. Hastings, *Public Papers of George Clinton*, Vol., 410-415, 457-459.
- John Sawyer, *History of Cherry Valley from 1740-1898*, (Cherry Valley, NY: Gazette Printers, 1898), 14-36.
- Swiggett, *War Out of Niagara*, 145-168.
- Halsey, *The Old New York Frontier*, 238-247.
- Monroe, *Chapters in the History of Delaware County*, 73.
- Campbell, *Annals of Tryon County*, 96-120.
- Alonzo Chappel, Thomas Phillibrown engraver, *Incident in Cherry Valley-Fate of Jane Wells*, (New York: Martin, Johnson & Co., 1856).

33. Halsey, *The Old New York Frontier*, 240-246, 335.
- Hastings, *Public Papers of George Clinton*, 574-578.
- Swiggett, *War out of Niagara*, 156,157.

34. Hastings, *Public Papers of George Clinton*, 334-340, 345-346, 363, 414.

35. Simms, *The Frontiersmen of New York*, (Albany: G. C. Riggs, 1882), Vol. 2, 306-307.
- Monroe, *Chapters in the History of Delaware County*, 79.
- Jack Harpster & Ken Stalter, *Captive! The Story of David Ogden and the Iroquois*, (Santa Barbara, CA: Praeger, 2010), 103-104.
- William Walton, *The Captivity and Suffering of Benjamin Gilbert and His Family, 1780-83*, (Cleveland: Burrows Brothers Co., 1904), 57, 63, 89, 93, 94, 104.
- James B. Richardson III, *The Destruction of Hanna's Town*, http://journals.psu.edu, Pt. 2, 31-32.
- Simms, *The Frontiersmen of New York*, Vol. 2, 327.
- Cherry Valley Cemetery, http://findagrave.com

36. Collections of the New York Historical Society, Portion of 'A Map of Two Tracts of Land on the Southside of the Mohawk River, Philip Livingston & Frederick Young Patents, 1772', Mohawk Valley Maps & Sketches, https://www.fort-plank.com

Chapter 4: Haudenosaunee

1. Hugh Hastings, *Public Papers of George Clinton, First Governor of New York*, (Albany: James B. Lyon, State Printer, 1900), Vol. 4, 615-618.
- Isabel T. Kelsay, *Joseph Brant 1743-1807, Man of Two Worlds*, (Syracuse, NY: Syracuse University Press,1984), 254.
- Frederick Cook, *Journals of the Military Expedition of Major General John Sullivan Against the Six Nations of Indians in 1779*, (Auburn, NY: Knapp, Peck & Thomson, 1887), 16-18, 192-194.
- Edward G. Lengel, ed., *The Papers of George Washington, Letter from George Washington to Major General John Sullivan, May 31, 1779*, (Charlottesville, NC: University of Virginia Press, 2010), War Series, Vol. 20, 716-719.

- George Washington to Andrew Montour, 10 Oct. 1755, *The Writings of George Washington,* (Washington, DC: Government Printing Office, 1931), Vol. 1, 198.
2. Francis W. Halsey, *The Old New York Frontier: Its Wars with Indians and Tories; Its Missionary Schools, Pioneers and Land Titles, 1614-1800,* (New York: Charles Scribner's Sons, 1902), 263-264.
- Richard Berleth, *Bloody Mohawk, The French and Indian War & American Revolution on New York's Frontier,* (Delmar, NY: Black Dome Press, 2010), 271-273.
- Hastings, *Public Papers of George Clinton*, Vol. 6, 702-704.
- David A. Ranzan, Matthew J. Hollis, ed., *Hero of Fort Schuyler, Selected Revolutionary War Correspondence of Brigadier General Peter Gansevoort, Jr.,* (Jefferson, NC: McFarland and Co., 2014), 116-119.
3. Howard Swiggett, *War Out of Niagara,* (Port Washington, NY: Ira J. Friedman, 1963), 183-187.
4. Cook, *Journals of the Military Expedition of Maj. Gen. John Sullivan*, 315-329.
- Berleth, *Bloody Mohawk*, 275-277.
- William W. Campbell, *Annals of Tryon County; or the Border Warfare of New York During the Revolution,* (New York: J. & J Harper, 1831), 121-124.
5. Bradly J. Crytzer, *Allegany Burning: George Washington, Daniel Brodhead and the Battle of Thompson Island,* (Journal of the American Revolution, May 12, 2015).
6. W. W. Munsell, *History of Delaware County, N. Y. With Illustrations, Biographical Sketches and Portraits of Some Pioneers and Prominent People,* (New York: W. W. Munsell & Co., 1880), 222, 232-233.
7. Halsey, *The Old New York Frontier*, 265-269.
- Kelsay, *Joseph Brant*, 250-254.
- Hastings, *Public Papers of George Clinton*, Vol. 5, 148-150, 162-163, 166.
8. Frederic A. Godcharles, *History of Fort Freeland,* (Williamsport, PA: Lycoming Historical Society, 1922)
- Todd Braisted, ed., *Letter from John McDonel to Col. Butler, Aug. 5th 1779,* (The On-Line Institute for Advanced Loyalist Studies, Library and Archives Canada: MG23, GIII23), Vol. 3, 185-188.
9. Cook, *Journals of the Military Expedition of Major General John Sullivan*, 53, 241.
- Norman B. Leventhal, *Map of General Sullivan's March from Easton to the Seneca and Cayuga Countries, 1779,* (Map and Education Center, Boston Public Library).
10. Swiggett, *War Out of Niagara*, 183-196.
- Simon L. Adler, *Sullivan's Campaign in Western New York, 1779,* (Rochester, NY: Rochester Historical Society, 1898).
11. Hastings, *Public Papers of George Clinton*, Vol., 152-156.
12. Halsey, *The Old New York Frontier*, 255-262.
- Campbell, *Annals of Tryon County*, 123-124.
13. Jack Harpster, Ken Stalter, *Captive! The Story of David Ogden and the Iroquois,* (Santa Barbara, CA: Praeger, 2010), 11-25, 29, 77-79.
- John Barr, *Orderly Book of the 4th New York Regiment, 1778-1780, The 2nd New York Regiment 1780 -1783, John Barr's Diary,* (Albany: Almon W. Lauber, 1932), 795-797.
- Leonard Bleeker, *Order Book of Capt. Leonard Bleeker, Major of Brigade in the Early Part of the Expedition under General James Clinton,* (New York: Joseph Sabin, 1865), 112-130.
- Halsey, *The Old New York Frontier*, 273-275.
14. Hastings, *Public Papers of George Clinton*, 181-183, 188-189, 244-248, 252.
- John Barr, *Orderly Book of the 4th New York Regiment, John Barr's Diary*, 791, 798-800.

- Halsey, *The Old New York Frontier,* 275-277.
15. Crytzer, *Allegany Burning: George Washington, Daniel Brodhead and the Battle of Thompson Island.*
- Cook, *Journals of the Military Expedition of Maj. Gen. John Sullivan,* 306-309.
16. Bleeker, *Order Book of Capt. Leonard Bleeker,* 122-130.
17. Cook, *Journals of the Military Expedition of Maj. Gen. John Sullivan,* 18-27.
- Hastings, *Public Papers of George Clinton,* Vol. 5, 224-228.
- Berleth, *Bloody Mohawk,* 278-279.
18. Bleeker, *Order Book of Capt. Leonard.*
- John Gano, *Biographical Memoirs of the Late Reverend John Gano of Frankfort, Kentucky,* (New York: Southwick & Hardcastle, 1806), 105-111.
19. Harpster & Stalter, *Captive! The Story of David Ogden and the Iroquois,* 78-79.
- Cook, *Journals of the Military Expedition of Maj. Gen. John Sullivan,* 111, 174, 234.
- Benjamin L. Huggins, ed., *Papers of George Washington, Revolutionary War Series, Letter from Maj. Gen. Sullivan to Gen. Washington, Chemung, Sept. 28, 1779,* (Charlottsville, VA: University of Virginia Press, 2013), Vol. 22, August 1- October 22, 1779.
20. Campbell, *Annals of Tryon County,* 128-130.
- Kelsay, *Joseph Brant,* 266-267.
- William L. Stone, *Life of Joseph Brant (Thayendanegea) Including the Border War of the American Revolution,* (Albany: J. Munsell, 1865), Vol. 2, 29-33.
- Swiggett, *War Out of Niagara,* 254-256.
- Cook, *Journals of the Military Expedition of Maj. Gen. John Sullivan,* 30-32, 74-75.
21. Kelsay, *Joseph Brant,* 267.
- Stone, *Life of Joseph Brant (Thayendanegea),* Vol. 2, 460.
- Fon W. Broadman Jr., *Against the Iroquois: The Sullivan Campaign of 1779 in New York State,* (added notation by author).
22. Jeanne W. Adler, ed., *Chainbreaker's War, A Senaca Chief Remembers the American Revolution,* (Delmar, NY: Black Dome Press, 2002), 110.
- Cook, *Journals of the Military Expedition of Maj. Gen. John Sullivan,* 228-242.
- Kelsay, *Joseph Brant,* 267.
- Lengel, *The Papers of George Washington, Letter from John Sullivan to George Washington, Sept. 28, 1779,* (Charlottesville, NC: University of Virginia Press, 2013), Vol. 22, 528-541.
- Campbell, *Annals of Tryon County,* 121-136.
- C.L. Marlatt, *The Periodical Cicada,* U.S. Dept. of Agriculture Bureau of Entomology, (Washington, DC: Government Printing Office, 1907), Issue July 18, 102-104.
- Dehowähda-dih, *The Cicada and George Washington,* https://www.onondaganation.org
23. Berthold Fernow, *Documents Related to the Colonial History of the State of New York,* (Albany: Weed, Parsons & Co., 1887) Vol. 15, 297.
- National Archives Microfilm Publications, *Revolutionary War Rolls 1775-1783.* Harper Regiment, Roll 74, Folder 112, Images 483.
- *New York in the Revolution as Colony and State,* (Albany: J. B. Lyon Co. 1904), Vol. 1, 68, 128.
24. Halsey, *The Old New Frontier,* 288-289.
- Munsell, *History of Delaware County,* 220-222.
- Jeptha R. Simms, *History of Schoharie County and the Border Wars of New York,* (Albany: Munsell & Tanner, 1845), 325-338.
- John D. Monroe, *Chapters in the History of Delaware County New York,* (Delaware County Historical Association, 1949), 79-85.

- Richard B. LaCrosse Jr, *Revolutionary Rangers; Daniel Morgan's Riflemen and their Role on the Northern Frontier*, (Berwyn Heights, MD: Heritage Books, 2019), 98-100.

25. Hastings, *Public Papers of George Clinton*, Vol. 4, 578-638.
- John E. Raitt, *Ruts in the Road,* (Delhi NY: John E. Raitt, 1982), Vol. 1, 71-77.
- Jeptha R. Simms, *The Frontiersmen of New York*, (Albany: Geo. C. Riggs, 1883) Vol. 2, 297-310.
- Stone, *Life of Joseph Brant,* Vol. 2, 493.
- Grace P. Leggett, Myrtle M. Jillson, ed., *The History and Genealogy of the Patchin-Patchen Family*, (Waterbury, CT: The Patchin-en Family Assoc., 1952), 224-241.
- Munsell, *History of Delaware County,* 221.
- Jay Gould, *History of Delaware County and Border Wars of New York*, (Roxbury, NY: Keeny & Gould Publishers, 1856), 104-126.

26. Josiah Priest, *The Deeply Interesting Story of Gen. Freegift Patchin: Stolen when a lad by Brant and his Indians,* (Lansingburgh, NY: W. Harkness, 1840).

Chapter 5: Johnstown

1. Francis W. Halsey, *The Old New York Frontier, Its Wars with Indians and Tories; Its Missionary Schools, Pioneers and Land Titles 1614-1800,* (New York: Charles Scribner's Sons, 1902), 287-290.
- Jeremiah Fogg, *Journal*, (Exeter, NH: The New Letter Press, 1879).

2. Howard Swiggett, *War Out of Niagara*, (Port Washington, N.Y.: Ira J. Friedman, Inc., 1963) 214-216.
- Jeptha R. Simms, *History of Schoharie County, and Border Wars of New York*, (Albany: Munsell & Tanner, 1845), 343-364.
- Halsey, *The Old New York Frontier*, 291-292.
- The Miriam & Ira D. Wallach Division of Art, Prints and Photographs: Print Collection, The New York Public Library. "Colonel John Johnson". The New York Public Library Digital Collection. https://digitalcollection.nypl.org

3. New York Historical Society, *Excerpts from the Papers of Col. William Malcolm*, Sept. 8 – Oct. 14, 1780.

4. Simms, *History of Schoharie*, 381.

5. Simms, *History of Schoharie*, 367-370.

6. Hugh Hastings, *Public Papers of George Clinton, First Governor of New York* (Albany: James B. Lyon, State Printer, 1900), Vol. 6, 77-82.
- William B. Campbell, *Annals of Tryon County, or The Border Warfare of New York During the Revolution*, (New York: J&J Harper Printers, 1831) 163-164.
- Simms, *History of Schoharie*, 373.
- Wayne Lenig, *Fort Plain, Fort Plank, and Fort Rensselaer, The Revolutionary War Forts at Canajoharie*, (Fort Plain, NY: Fort Plain Museum, 2020) 106-111.

7. Simms, *History of Schoharie, 375-384.*

8. Swiggett, *War Out of Niagara*, 220-222.

9. Richard Berleth, *Bloody Mohawk, The French and Indian War & American Revolution on New York's Frontier,* (Delmar, NY: Black Dome Press, 2010) 288-292.
- Isabel T. Kelsay, *Joseph Brant 1743-1807, Man of Two Worlds*, (Syracuse, NY: Syracuse University Press, 1984), 293-294.

10. Simms, *History of Schoharie*, 399-420.
- Michael Aikey, *Ballston Raid of 1780: Military Operation or a Time to Settle Old Scores,* (Journal of the American Revolution, Dec. 6, 2017).

11. Willis T. Hanson, *A History of Schenectady During the Revolution*, (Printed Privately, 1916),

265-266.
- Halsey, *The Old New York Frontier*, 295-300.
- Walter W. Spooner, ed., *The Rensselaer Family Papers*, (American Historical Magazine, Vol. 2, No. 1, Jan. 1907) 195-198.
- Hastings, *Public Papers of George Clinton*, Vol. 6, 318-323, 345-347, 351-355.
- Lenig, *Fort Plain, Fort Plank and Fort Rensselaer*, 111-119.
- Simms, *History of Schoharie*, 421-434.
- Jeptha R. Simms, *The Frontiersmen of New York*, (Albany: George C. Riggs, 1883) Vol. 2, 417-471.
- Kelsay, *Joseph Brant*, 296-299.

12. Hastings, *Public Papers of George Clinton*, Vol. 6, 692-703.
13. Halsey, *The Old New York Frontier*, 312-313.
- Kelsay, *Joseph Brant*, 301-302.
14. Halsey, *The Old New York Frontier*, 313.
- Kelsay, *Joseph Brant*, 302-303.
15. Lenig, *Fort Plain, Fort Plank and Fort Rensselaer*, 121.
16. Simms, *History of Schoharie*, 454-455.
- Kelsay, *Joseph Brant*, 306-308.
17. Halsey, *The Old New York Frontier*, 303
- Lenig, *Fort Plain, Fort Plank and Fort Rensselaer*, 125-127.
18. Berleth, *Bloody Mohawk*, 301-303.
- Lenig, *Fort Plain, Fort Plank and Fort Rensselaer*, 130-133.
- Halsey, *The Old New York Frontier*, 303-305.
- Simms, *History of Schoharie*, 455-462.
19. Nathaniel B. Sylvester, Jonathan W. Hasbrouck, *History of Ulster County, New York, With Illustrations and Biographical Sketches of its Prominent Men and Pioneers*, (Philadelphia: Evert & Peck, 1880), 276-279.
- Halsey, *The Old New York Frontier*, 305. **20** Halsey, *The Old New York Frontier*, 306.
- Lenig, *Fort Plain, Fort Plank and Fort Rensselaer*, 135-136.
- Kelsay, *Joseph Brant*, 323.
21. Swiggett, *War Out of Niagara*, 239-240.
- Lenig, *Fort Plain, Fort Plank and Fort Rensselaer*, 136-138.
- Simms, *History of Schoharie*, 470-477.
- Berleth, *Bloody Mohawk*, 303-304.
22. Lenig, *Fort Plain, Fort Plank and Fort Rensselaer*, 138-140.
- Berleth, *Bloody Mohawk*, 304-305.
23. Hastings, *Public Papers of George Clinton*, Vol. 7, 472-475.
- Berleth, *Bloody Mohawk*, 305-307.
- Lenig, *Fort Plain, Fort Plank and Fort Rensselaer*, 140-144.
- Simms, *History of Schoharie*, 478-480.
- Swiggett, *War Out of Niagara*, 240-246.
- Simms, *The Frontiersmen of New York*, 545-547.
24. Don Chrysler, *The Blue-Eyed Indians, The Story of Adam Chrysler and His Brothers in the Revolutionary War*, (Zephyrhills, FL: Chrysler Books, 1999).
25. Willian E, Roscoe, *History of Schoharie County, New York; 1713-1882 With Illustrations and Biographical Sketches of Some of its Prominent Men and Pioneers*, (Syracuse, NY: D. Mason & Co, 1882), 151-152.
- Charles D. Griffin, *A History of Stamford*, (Stamford, NY: The Stamford Historical Society,

1988), 34-36.
- Simms, *History of Schoharie*, 481-486.
- George H. Warner, *Military Records of Schoharie County Veterans of Four Wars*, (Albany: Weed, Parsons & Co. 1891), 3-71.

26. Lenig, *Fort Plain, Fort Plank and Fort Rensselaer*, 153-155.
- Simms, *History of Schoharie*, 498-515.
- Chrysler, *The Blue-Eyed Indians.*

Chapter 6: Resettlement

1. Francis W. Halsey, *The Old New York Frontier, its Wars with Indians and Tories, its Missionary Schools, Pioneers and Land Titles 1614-1800,* (New York: Charles Scribner's Sons, 1902), 190-192.
- William W. Campbell, *Annals of Tryon County or the Border Warfare of New York during the Revolution*, (New York: J. & J. Harper, 1831), 96-100.
- Henry U. Swinnerton, *The Story of Cherry Valley*, (Cherry Valley, NY: 1908).
- *The Public Papers of George Clinton, the First Governor of New York 1777-1795, 1801-1804,* (Albany & New York: James B. Lyon, 1900), Vol. 4, 338-340, 410-415, 674-675, 786-788.
- Orsamus Turner, *Pioneer History of the Holland Purchase of Western New York*, (Buffalo, NY: Jewett, Thomas & Co., 1850), n276.

2. Simms, *The Frontiersmen of New York*, Vol. 2, 656-664.
- Wayne Lenig, *Fort Plain, Fort Plank and Fort Rensselaer: the Revolutionary War Forts at Canajoharie*, (Fort Plain, NY: The Fort Plain Museum, 2020), 188-191.
- Campbell, *Annals of Tryon County*, 177-189.
- Greene, *History of the Mohawk Valley*, Vol. 2, 1110-1126.

3. Jane C. Ford, *Records of the Harper Family,* (Cleveland: A.C. Rogers Co., 1905), 59.

4. Jeptha R. Simms, *The Frontiersmen of New York*, (Albany: George C. Riggs, 1883), Vol. 1, 317-326.
- *New York County Maps: Interactive History and Complete List,* https://www.mapofus.org

5. Ford, *Records of the Harper Family*, 38.
- Mary Ann T. Elliott, *Thompson Genealogy, Descendants of William and Mary,* (New Haven, CT: Thompson Family Assoc., 1916), 3

6. Ford, *Records of the Harper Family,* 59.

7. Ford, *Records of the Harper Family,* 59.

8. Simms, *The Frontiersmen of New York*, Vol. 1, 335-340.
- Nelson Greene, ed., *History of the Mohawk Valley: Gateway to the West 1614-1925*, (Chicago: S.J. Clarke Pub. Co., 1925), Vol. 1, 431, https://www.schenectadyhistory.org
- *Samson Occom Journal, April 6, 1787*, (visited Esq. Harper at Fort Hunter). https://www.library.dartmouth.edu

9. *Mohawk Valley Maps and Sketches,* https://www.fort-plank.com patent maps.
- *New York State Archives Map Collection*, #AO272-78, Vol. 46, 129.
- Secretary of State of New York, *Calendar of New York Colonial Manuscripts Indorsed Land Papers,* (Albany: Weed, Parsons & Co., 1864), 241-244, 675, 784, 654, 882, 909.
- W. Max Reid, *Ye History of St. Ann's Church in Ye City of Amsterdam New York*, 10.

10. W. J. Montgomery, *A Montgomery Family Genealogy, Robert and Mary Montgomery,* https://www.wjmontgomerygenealogy.com
- William H. Eldridge, *Henry Genealogy, The Descendants of Samuel Henry of Hadley and Amherst Massachusetts, 1734-1790,* (Boston: T.R. Marvin & Son, 1915), 74.

11. W. W. Munsell, *History of Delaware County New York,* (New York: W. W. Munsell & Co.,

1880), 217-225.
- Archive Publications, *Revolutionary War Pension and Bounty-Land Warrant Application Files*, W.21910; W.18702; S.11545; S.23023. https://www.ancestry.com

12. The Cayuga County Independent, *The Obituary of the Late Mrs. Warrick, William Lamb Jr's Daughter Caroline Lamb Warrick,* (Aurelius, NY: Nov. 1902).
- Peggy Dymond Leavy, *Molly Brant, Mohawk Loyalist and Diplomate*, (Toronto: Dundurn Group, 2015).
- Munsell, *History of Delaware County*, 222.
- New York State Comptrollers Office, *New York in the Revolution as Colony and State,* (Albany: J.B. Lyon Co., 1904), 39.

13. George W. Bartholomew, *Records of the Bartholomew Family*, (Salem, MA: The Salem Press, 1885), Pt. 2, 463.
- U.S. Federal Census Collection, *1790 Canajoharie District, Montgomery County, New York*, 108. https://www.ancestry.com

14. Archive Publications, *Revolutionary War Pension Application Files*, S.4293; W.3990. ancestry.com
- Williams Brothers, *History of Ashtabula County Ohio,* (Philadelphia: J. B. Lippincott & Co., 1878), 116-119.

15. Eldridge, *Henry Genealogy,* 55-58.
- Ruth M.G. Wiley, *Gibbs Genealogy*, (Whittier, CA: R.&L. Letter Shop, 1967), 44.
- Munsell, *History of Delaware County*, 230.
- Slyvester Judd, *Thomas Judd and his Descendants*, (Northampton, MA: J.&L. Metcalf, 1856), 21-23.
- William E. Roscoe, *History of Schoharie County, New York,* (Syracuse: Mason & Co.,1882), 142-153.

16. Munsell, History of Delaware County, 223.
- Burgis P. Starr, *History of the Starr Family from the Ancestry of Comfort Starr*, (Hartford, CT: the Case, Lockwood & Brainard Co., 1892), 371-372, 374-386.

17. Munsell, *History of Delaware County,* 217-230.
- *Delaware Gazette,* (Delhi, NY: July 8, 1891), 4
- *Hobart Independent,* (Hobart, NY: August. 9, 1888), 3
- Evangeline MacLaury, *Those Rugged Hills and Green Valleys*, (Harpersfield, NY: 1987), 118-119.
- Archive Publications, *Revolutionary War Pension Appl.*, S.13453.
- David Murray, ed., *Delaware County New York History of the Century Centennial Celebration*, (Delhi, NY: William Clark Pub., 1898), 415-458.

18. Munsell, *History of Delaware County,* 219.
- *Historic USGS Maps of New England and New York*, (Durham, NH: University of New Hampshire Dimond Library Documents Dept. and Data Center, 2001), Hobart, NY Quadrangle, NW Corner, 1904. [overlay by author]

19. John L. Miller, *Pioneer Homesteaders of the Western Catskills*, (Delhi, NY: Delaware County Historical Association, 2021), 163-171.

20. Munsell, *History of Delaware County*, 293.
- Charles D. Griffin, *A History of Stamford*, (Stamford, NY: The Stamford Historical Society, 1988), 19, 31, 37.

21. Munsell, *History of Delaware County*, 150.
- John D. Monroe, *Settlement of the Village of Delhi*, (Delhi, NY: DCHA, Delaware County New York Genealogy and History Site), https://www.dcha-ny.org

- Tim Duerden, *Frisbee House History,* (Delhi, NY: DCHA), https://www.dcha-ny.org
- Pierre DeNio, *The Winding Delaware*, (Equinunk, PA: Equinunk Historical Society, 1999), 235-238.

22. H. Fletcher Davidson, *Delaware County Fur Trading to Farming,* (Delhi, NY: R.B. Decker Advertising, 1976), 61-69.

23. John A. Stevens Jr, ed., *Colonial Records of the New York Chamber of Commerce*, (New York: John F. Trow & Co., 1867), 55-68.
- Thomas McIlworth, *Portrait of William Walton 1731-1796*, (ca. 1760, oil on canvas).

24. Davidson, *Delaware County Fur Trading to Farming,* 44-45.
- Munsell, *History of Delaware County,* 325-326.
- Helen Lane, *The Story of Walton,* (Walton, NY: Walton Historical Society, 1975), 5-8.
- David W. Lupton & Dorothy R. Lupton, *Lancaster Platt Lupton the Legacy of a Fur Trader, the Road to Delhi,* (Bayboro, NC: Buckhorn Press, 1994), Vol. 1, 79-81.

25. Munsell, *History of Delaware County,* 325-326.
- Arthur W. North, *Founders and Founding of Walton,* (Walton NY: Walton Historical Society, 1924), 8-11.
- Arthur W. North, *The First Grandmother,* (Walton, NY: Walton Historical Society, 1926), 21-28.

26. Mary Pine, *Early Settlement of Walton, Delaware Co., NY,* (Walton, NY: Walton Historical Society, 2015), 7-12, 14-17.
- North, *The Founders of Walton*, 11-13.

27. North, *The Founders of Walton*, 38-39.
- The Walton Journal, June-October 1857, *Walton the Early Years,* (Walton, NY: Walton Historical Society, 2009), 19-23.
- E. Alfred Jones, *The Loyalists of New Jersey, Their Memorials, Petitions, Claims, etc. from English Records,* (Boston: Gregg Press, 1972).
- Munsell, *History of Delaware County*, 326.
- Lane, *The Story of Walton*, 14-15.
- Thomas C. Stockton, *The Stockton Family of New Jersey and other Stocktons,* (*Washington, D.C.,* The Carnahan Press, 1911).

28. The Delaware County Clerk's Office, *Book A of the Deeds,* (Delhi NY: Delaware County, New York Genealogy Website), https://www.dcnyhistory.org
- Munsell, *History of Delaware County,* 208, 313-314.
- DeNio, *The Winding Delaware,* 49-52.

29. Harry P. Smith, *History of Broome County, New York*, (Syracuse: D. Mason & Co., 1885), 65-72, 267-275, 324-328.
- Marjory B. Hinman & Maurice R. Hitt Jr, ed., *The Letters and Diaries of William Macclure: Surveyor and Pioneer 1725-1826,* (Binghamton, NY: Broome County Historical Society, 1994).
- Archive Publications, *Revolutionary War, Pension Appl.*, W.4509.
- Munsell, *History of Delaware County*, 206-207.
- DeNio, *The Winding Delaware,* 15-22.
- Rev. Francis A. Dony, *Obituary of Prudence Parks Lakin* (Plymouth, NY: 1833).
- Barbara F. Sivertsen & Barbara L. Covey, *The Legends of Cushetunk, The Nathan Skinner Manuscript and the Early History of Cochecton,* (Westminster, MD: Heritage Books, 2011), 58-60.

30. Munsell, *History of Delaware County*, 205-208.

31. James E. Quinlan & Thomas Antisell, *The History of Sullivan County: Embracing an Account of its Geology, Climate, Aborigines, Early Settlement, Organization and Biographical Sketches*, (Liberty, NY: G.M. Beebe & W.T. Morgan, 1873), 490-512.

32. Archive Publications, *Rev. War. Pension Appl.,* R.10005, W.21684.
- John D. Monroe, *Chapters in the History of Delaware County, New York,* (Delhi NY: Delaware County Historical Association, 1949), 31.
- Munsell, *History of Delaware County,* 133-142.

33. Public Archives, *Memorial Applications of the American Loyalists Claims Commission,* 1776-1835, (Ottawa, Canada).
- Munsell, *History of Delaware County,* 133-142.

34. Jay Gould, *History of Delaware County,* (Roxbury, NY: Keeny & Gould, 1856), 203.
- Munsell, *History of Delaware,* 256-273.
- Mary Pine, *Early Settlement of Walton,* 1-6.
- Roswell, Randall & Hoe, ed., *Baptismal and Marriage Register of the Old Dutch Church of Kingston, Ulster County, New York, 1660-1809,* (Baltimore: Genealogical Publishing Co., 1980), 644.

35. Alf Evers, *The Catskills from Wilderness to Woodstock,* Garden City, NJ: Doubleday & Company, 1972), 139-156.
- Edmund J. Longyear, *The Descendants of Jacob Longyear of Ulster County, New York,* (New Haven, CT: Tuttle, Morehouse & Taylor Co., 1942), 1-10.
- Office of the Secretary of State, *Calendar of Historical Manuscripts Relating to the War of the Revolution,* (Albany: Weed, Parsons & Co., 1868), 113-115, 165.
- Monroe, *Chapters in the History of Delaware County,* 43-48.

36. Quinlan & Antisell, *The History of Sullivan County,* 184-210.

37. DeNio, The Winding Delaware, 15-22.
- Sivertsen & Covey, *The Legends of Cushetunk,* 12-13, 58-60.

38. Munsell, *History of Delaware County,* 206-208.
- Richard C. Adams, *The Delaware Indians, A Brief History,* (Saugerties, NY: Hope Farm Press, 1995), 5.
- Jean Churchill, Another Look at Josiah Parks, (The Parke Society Newsletter, 2010), Vol. 46, No. 3, 41-45.

39. *New York State Wills and Probate,* Vol. 035-039, 1782-1787, 431-432; Vol. 038, 1785-1786, 492-494.

40. Ford, *Records of the Harper Family,* 58.
- *New York in the Revolution as Colony and State,* 68, 112, 229.
- Hamilton D. Hurd, *History of Otsego County, New York with Illustrations and Biographical Sketches of Some of its Prominent Men and Pioneers,* (Philadelphia: Everts & Fariss, 1878), 192-195.

41. *Calendar of New York Colonial Manuscripts Indorsed Land Papers,* 266, 282, 284, 287.
- George W. Schuyler, *Colonial New York, Philip Schuyler and His Family,* (New York: Charles Scribner's Sons, 1885), Vol. 2, 470.
- Hurd, *History of Otsego County,* 298-302.
- Richard Berleth, *Bloody Mohawk, The French and Indian War & American Revolution on New York's Frontier,* (Delmar, NY: Black Dome Press, 2010), 257, 343n44.
- Zoe H. Tunnicliff, *Tunnicliff Genealogy,* (Albany: Private Printing, 1965).
- Mohawk Valley Maps & Sketches, *David Schuyler Patent Map,* https://www.fort-plank.com
- W. T. Bailey, Richfield Springs and Vicinity, (New York & Chicago: A.S. Barnes & Co., 1874), 12-14, 20-21.

42. Hurd, *History of Otsego County,* 257-259.
- Alan Taylor, *William Cooper's Town, Power and Persuasion on the Frontier of the Early American Republic,* (New York: Vintage Books, A Division of Random House, 1995), 65-70.

- L. H. Butterfield, *Judge William Cooper (1754-1809): A Sketch of His Character and Accomplishments*, (Cornell, NY: Cornell University Press, October 1949), New York History, Vol. 30, No. 4, 385-408.
- Samuel Shaw & Isaac Arnold, *A Centennial Offering; Being a Brief History of Cooperstown with a Biographical Sketch of James F. Cooper*, (Cooperstown: Freemans Journal, 1886), 15-18.

43. Taylor, *William Cooper's Town,* 70-73.
- William Cooper, *A Guide in the Wilderness*, (Dublin: Gilbert & Hodges, 1810).
- James F. Cooper III, *The Legends and Traditions of a Northern County*, (New York & London: G.P. Putnam's Sons, Knickerbocker Press, 1921).
- Halsey, *The Old New York Frontier,* 357-364.

44. Simms, *The Frontiersmen of New York*, Vol. 1, 155-158.
- John W. & Martha B. Harper, *The Palatine Migration of 1723 from Schoharie to Tulpehocken*, (Historical Review of Berks County, October 1944).
- U.S. Federal Census Collection, *1790 Canajoharie District, Montgomery County, New York*.
- National Archives Microfilm Publication, *U.S. Revolutionary War Rolls, 1775-1783*, Roll 74, Image 477-525.
- *Oneonta 001, West Oneonta, Otsego County 1868*, (New York: F.W. Beers Atlas, 1868). https://www.historicmapworks.com

45. Dudley M. Campbell, *The History of Oneonta from its Earliest Settlement to Present Time*, (Oneonta, NY: G.W. Fairchild & Co., 1906), 15-30.
- Halsey, *The Old New York Frontier,* 334-335.
- U.S. Federal Census Collection, *1790 Otsego District, Montgomery County, New York*.

46. Hurd, *History of Otsego County*, 167-168.
- Taylor, *William Cooper's Town*, 174.
- Campbell, *Annals of Tryon County*, 188-189.
- *New York in the Revolution as Colony and State,* 68-70, 79-81.
- Dudley M. Campbell, *A Sketch of the History of Oneonta*, (Oneonta, NY: Harold & Democrat Office, 1883), 58-59.
- Edwin F. Bacon, *Otsego County New York Geographical and Historical Review,* (Oneonta: 1902), 35.

47. Munsell, *History of Delaware County*, 282-284.
- Monroe, *Chapters in the History of Delaware County*, 26.
- Leonard A. Morrison, *The History of Windham in New Hampshire, Rockingham County 1719-1883*, (Boston: Cupples, Upham & Co., 1883), 124-125, 607-610.

48. Halsey, *The Old New York Frontier,* 104-105, 366-367.
- Richard Smith, Francis W. Halsey, ed., *A Tour of Four Great Rivers; The Hudson, Mohawk, Susquehanna and Delaware in 1769; Being the Journal of Richard Smith of Burlington, New Jersey*, (New York: Charles Scribner's Sons, 1906), 13.
- *Calendar of New York Colonial Manuscripts Endorsed Land Papers*, 344, 466, 468,487,658, 727, 971.
- John Burke, *A Genealogical and Heraldic Dictionary of the Peerage and Baronetage of the British Empire*, (London: Henry Colburn Pub., 1839), 1026-1027.

49. *Calendar of New York Colonial Manuscripts Endorsed Land Papers*, 14, 658, 727, 971.
- Halsey, *The Old New York Frontier,* 365-367.
- Taylor, *William Cooper's Town*, 160.
- Hurd, *History of Otsego County,* 204-205.
- Joyce Foote, *Morris, New York*, (Sherburne, NY: Mid-York Press, 1986), 94-100.
- Hugh Hastings, *Military Minutes of the Council of Appointments of the State of New York*,

1783-1821, (Albany: J.B. Lyon, 1901), 393, 790, 1148, 1265.

50. Hurd, *History of Otsego County*, 201-219.

- Helen G. Ecob, *Reminiscence of Early Days, Abijah Gilbert 1747-1811, Joseph T. Gilbert 1783-1867*, (Gilbertsville, NY: Helen G. Ecob, 1927), 1-27.

51. *Calendar of New York Colonial Manuscripts Endorsed Land Papers*, 482.

- Luna M. Hammond, *History of Madison County, State of New York*, (Syracuse, NY: Truair, Smith & Co., 1872), 165-168.

52. Simeon De Witt, Surveyor General of the State of New York; *Map of the Headwaters of the Rivers Susquehanna & Delaware, Embracing the Early Patents on the South Side of the Mohawk River*, (Albany: Richard Rease, Lith, 1790).

Chapter 7: Empire

1. Jabez D. Hammond, *The History of Political Parties in the State of New York: from the Ratification of the Federal Constitution to December 1840, Vol. 1*, (Cooperstown, NY: H. & E. Phinney, 1846), 1-29.

- Extract from the Journal of New York, *Ratifying Convention*, 25 July 1788, https://www.founders.archives.gov

2. Franklin B. Hough, ed., *Proceedings of the Commissioners of Indian Affairs, Appointed by Law for the Extermination of Indian Titles in the State of New York*, (Albany: Joel Munsell, 1859), Vol 1, 9-10.

- Alan Taylor, *William Cooper's Town, Power and Persuasion on the Frontier of the Early American Republic*, (New York: Vintage Books, a Division of Random House, 1995), 142-150.

3. Isabel T. Kelsay, *Joseph Brant 1743-1807, Man of Two Worlds*, (Syracuse, NY: Syracuse University Press, 1984), 356-361.

- Alan Taylor, *The Divided Ground: Indians, Settlers, and the Northern Borderland of the American Revolution*, (New York: Vintage Books, 2006), 154-162.
- Hough, *Proceedings of the Commissioners of Indian Affairs*, 10-36.

4. Chad. L. Anderson, *The Storied Landscape of Iroquoia, History, Conquest, and Memory in the Native Northeast*, (Lincoln, NE: University of Nebraska Press, 2020), 98.

- Taylor, *The Divided Ground*, 154-157.
- Hough, *Proceedings of the Commissioners of Indian Affairs*, 41, 44.
- Arthur Pound, *Johnson of the Mohawk, A Biography of Sir William Johnson, Irish Immigrant, Mohawk War Chief, American Soldier, Empire Builder*, (New York: The MacMillan Co., 1930), 20.
- Ryan DeCaire, Assistant Professor in the Department of Linguistics and Center for Indigenous Studies at the University of Toronto. Translation of *Thaonhwentsawá:kon* and correct spellings of Iroquois terms.

5. Hugh Hastings, James A. Holden, ed., *Public Papers of George Clinton, First Governor of New York, 1777-1795, 1801-1804*, (Albany: Oliver A. Quayle, 1904), Vol. 8, 323-381.

- Hough, *Proceedings of the Commissioners of Indian Affairs*, 58-66.

6. Taylor, *The Divided Ground*, 157-162.

- Hough, *Proceedings of the Commissioners*, 63-66.
- Kelsay, *Joseph Brant*, 361-367.
- Jeanne W. Adler, *Chainbreaker's War, A Seneca Chief Remembers the American Revolution*, (Delmar, NY: Black Dome Press, 2002), 140-156.

7. *The 1785 New York Fort Herkimer Treaty with the Oneida*, https://www.academic.edu

- *Key Figures in Oneida History*, https://www.oneidaindiannation.com
- Hough, *Proceedings of the Commissioners*, 67-84.
- Taylor, *The Divided Ground*, 162-166.

8. *Consolidated Laws of New York, Pennsylvania Boundary Line*, Chap. 57, Article 2, Sec. 6,

https://www.nysenate.gov
- Hough, *Proceedings of the Commissioners*, 84-91.

9. Hiram C. Clark, *History of Chenango County, New York, Containing the Divisions of the County and Sketches of the Towns, Indian Tribes and Titles,* (Norwich NY: Thompson & Pratt, 1850), 22-32.
- Henry P. Smith, *History of Broome County, New York, with illustrations and Biographical Sketches of Some of its Prominent Men and Pioneers,* (Syracuse: D. Mason & Co., 1885), 84-93.
- James Smith, *History of Chenango and Madison Counties, New York, with illustrations and Biographical Sketches of Some of its Prominent Men and Pioneers,* (Syracuse: D. Mason & Co., 1880), 66-70, 155-179.
- Taylor, *The Divided Ground,* 162-166.
- Hough, *Proceedings of the Commissioners*, 92-110.

10. *Calendar of New York Colonial Manuscripts Indorsed Land Papers; in the Office of the Secretary of the State of New York,* (Albany: Weed, Parsons & Co., 1864), 684.

11. Simeon De Witt, *A Map of the Military Lands and Twenty Townships in the Western Part of the State of New York, ca. 1790*, Digital Collection of Yale University Beinecke Rare Book and Manuscript Library, (BrSides Folio 2017 98, Orbis Record 13267707, OID 16195021). (Overdraw by Author).

12. *Calendar of New York Colonial Manuscripts*, 712-722, 737, 740, 742, 850, 860, 876.
- Taylor, *The Divided Ground*, 165.
- Simeon De Witt, *1st Sheet of De Witt's State Map of New York*, (New York: C. Tiebout, Sculp., 522).

13. Orsamus Turner, *Pioneer History of the Holland Purchase of Western New York*, (Buffalo, NY: Jewett, Thomas & Co., George H. Derby Co., 1850), 325-337.
- Taylor, *The Divided Ground*, 169-179.
- Hough, *Proceedings of the Commissioners*, 119-127.
- William B. Gay, *Historical Gazetteer of Tioga County, New York, 1785-1888*, (Syracuse: W. B. Gay & Co., 1887), 5-27.
- George S. Conover, ed., Lewis C. Aldrich, *History of Ontario County, New York*, (Syracuse: D. Mason & Co., 1893), 78-80.

14. *Calendar of New York Colonial Manuscripts*, 448-466, 842, 851, 980, 998, 1008.
- Taylor, *The Divided Ground*, 179-185.
- Hammond, *The History of Political Parties*, 57-58.
- Hough, *Proceedings of the Commissioners*, 117-225.
- Leroy W. Kingman, ed., *Our County and its People, A Memorial History of Tioga County, New York*, (Elmira, NY: W. A. Fergusson & Co., 1900), 44-51.
- Smith, *The History of Broome County*, 84-93.
- Clark, *The History of Chenango County*, 22-34.

15. *Calendar of New York Colonial Manuscripts*, 335, 431, 446, 447, 459, 604, 663, 678, 682, 709.
- Edward G. Williams, *The Provosts of the Royal Americans*, (The Western Pennsylvania Historical Magazine, Vol. 56, No. #1, January 1973), 1-38.

16. Jonathan Bayer, *Society at Auction: Coffee-House Culture in Occupied New York*, (Journal of the American Revolution, Nov. 10, 2016), https://www.allthingsliberty.com

17. Shirley A. Houck, ed., *The Evolution of Delaware County, New York, Being a History of its Land*. (Nashville, TN: Express Media Corp., 1995), 38-40.
- *Calendar of New York Colonial Manuscripts*, 772, 784, 785.
- Munsell, *History of Delaware County, New York, with Illustrations, Biographical Sketches and*

Portraits of Some Pioneers and Prominent Residents, (New York: W. W. Munsell & Co., 1880), 170-171.
- Jay Gould, *History of Delaware County and Border Wars of New York*, (Roxbury, NY: Keeny & Gould, 1856), 143-145.
- H. Fletcher Davidson, *Delaware County, Fur Trading to Farming,* (Deposit, NY: R. B. Decker Advertising, 1976), 61-69.

18. James Sullivan, ed., *The Papers of Sir William Johnson*, (Albany: The University of the State of New York, Division of Archives and History, 1921), Vol. 12, 346.
- A. B. McCullogh, *Currency Conversion in British North America, 1760-1900*, (1983), 83-93. https://www.archivaria.ca

19. *The United States Constitution, Article 1, Section 2*.
- William Thorndale, William Dollarhide, *Map Guide to the U. S. Federal Censuses, 1790-1920*, (Baltimore: Genealogical Publishing, 1987), xiii-xiv, 236.
- S.N.D. North, ed., *First Census of the United States, 1790*, New York Department of Commerce and Labor, Bureau of the Census, (Washington, DC: Government Printing Office, 1908), 1-11. https://www.babel.hathitrust.org
- *An Act Providing for the Enumeration of the Inhabitants of the United States,* (Act of Congress Approved March 1, 1790, Session 2, Chapter 3), 101-103. https://www.archives.gov
- Frederick Cook, *Laws of the State of New York Passed at the Session of the Legislature Held in the Years 1789-1796,* (Albany: Weed, Parsons & Co., 1887), Vol. 3, 109-113.
- Andrew Babin, *U. S. Marshals Overcame Hardships and Challenges to Count 3,929,214 People in a Young America,* (US Census Bureau, Resource Library, 2020). https://www.census.gov
- Map by Author

20. Edward F. Bacon, *Otsego County, New York, Geographical and Historical*, (Oneonta, NY: The Oneonta Herald, 1902), 41,72.
- Joyce Foote, *Morris, New York, A Look Back 1773-1923* (Morris, NY: 1970).
- Warren Ryther, *The Morris Manor Farm; A History and a Memoire, 2015*, 4-5. https://ourtownnews
- Oxford Review-Times, May 15, 1931, *Tobias Houk of North Gilford, New York*.
- 1790 Federal Census; *New York, Montgomery County, Otsego District*. https://www.ancestry.com
- D. Hamilton Hurd, *History of Otsego County, New York, With Illustrations and Biographical Sketches of Some of its Prominent Men and Pioneers*, (Philadelphia: Everts & Farris, 1878), 204-205.

21. Munsell, *History of Delaware County,* 224, 229.
- Lucy B. Goodenow, *Brett Genealogy*, (Cambridge, MA: Murrey & Emery, 1915), 133-136.

22. Munsell, *History of Delaware County,* 224.
- Henry D. Paine, ed., *Paine Family Records; A Journal of Genealogy and Biographical Information Respecting the American Families of Payne, Paine, Payn,* (Albany: J. Munsell, 1880), Vol. 2, 120-128, 284.
- Henry P. Johnston, ed., *Record of Service of Connecticut Men in the War of the Revolution*, (Hartford, CT: Adjutant Generals Office, 1889), 398.
- *New York in the Revolution as Colony and State*, (Albany: J. B. Lyon, 1904), Vol. 1, 144-149.

23. John L. Miller, *Pioneer Homesteaders of the Western Catskills*, (Delhi, NY: Delaware County Historical Association, 2021), 163-173.
- Marjory B. Hinman, ed., Maurice R. Hitt, ed., *The Letters and Diaries of William Macclure, Surveyor and Pioneer, 1725-1826,* (Binghamton, NY: Johnson City Publishing, Broome County

Historical Society, 1994), 40.
24. Smith, *History of Chenango and Madison Counties*, 155-167.
- John E. Goodrich, ed., Chauncey L. Knapp, ed., *State of Vermont Rolls of the Soldiers in the Revolutionary War, 1775-1783*, (Rutland, VT: The Tuttle Co., 1904), 822-834.
- 1790 Federal Census; New York, Montgomery County, Harpersfield District.
https://www.ancestry.com
25. *Laws of the State of New York, 1789-1796*, (Albany: Weed, Parsons & Co., 1887), Vol. 3, 206-209.
- *New York County Maps: Interactive History and Complete List.* https://www.mapofus.org
26. Hammond, *The History of Political Parties*, Vol. 1, 1-29, 51-53.
- Franklin B. Hough, *New York Civil List Prepared from the Official Records*, (Albany: Weed, Parsons & Co., 1858).
- Barbara Shupe, ed., Janet Steins, ed., Jyoti Pandit, ed., *New York State Population, 1790-1980: A Compilation of Federal Census Data,* (London, New York: Neal-Schuman Publishing, 1987), v-xxv.
- A New Nation Votes American Election Returns, *1787-1825; New York 1792 Election for Otsego County's One Assembly Seat*, (Albany: Albany Gazette, June 4, 1792).
https://www.elections.lib.tufts.edu
- Taylor, *William Cooper's Town*, 60, 183-187.
27. D. Hamilton Hurd, *History of Otsego County*, 23-26.
- Taylor, *William Cooper's Town,* 162-165.
28. Hugh Hastings, *Military Minutes of the Council of Appointments of the State of New York*, (Albany: J.B. Lyon, State Printer, 1901), Vol. 1, 213.
- Cook, *Laws of the State of New York Passed at the Sessions of the Legislature Held in the Years 1789-1796*, (Albany: Weed, Parsons & Co., 1887), Vol. 3, 440-450.
29. Taylor, *William Cooper's Town,* 165-174.
- Hammond, *The History of Political Parties*, 76-77.
- Lyman H. Butterfield, *Judge William Cooper (1754-1809), A Sketch of his Character and Accomplishments*, (New York History Magazine, October 1949) Vol. 30, No. #4, 397-399.
https://www.jstor.org
30. Taylor, *William Cooper's Town,* 174-176.
- James Fennimore Cooper III, *Legends and Traditions of a Northern County*, (London, New York: G. P. Putnam's Sons, 1921), 143
31. A New Nation Votes; *New York 1792 Election for Governor, New York 1792 Election for Lieutenant Governor,* (New York: The Daily Advertiser, May 30, May 31, 1792).
- Hammond, *The History of Political Parties*, 62-70.
- Taylor, *William Cooper's Town*, 176-180.
- National Archives Founders Online, *The Disputed Election of 1792, Editorial Note*.
https://www.founders.archives.gov
- Laws of the State of New York, *An Act of Regulating Elections*, (New York, Thomas Greenleaf, 1792), Vol. 1, 322-323.
32. Cooper, *Legends and Traditions of a Northern County*, 144-150.
- Taylor, *William Cooper's Town*, 180-187.
- Hammond, *The History of Political Parties*, 70-77.
33. A New Nation Votes, *New York 1793 Election for State Senate Western District, New York 1793 Election for U.S. House of Representatives District #10, (*New York: The Daily Advertiser, June 10, March 1, 1793).
34. Hugh MacDougall, *Sheriffs of Otsego County from 1791 to Present*, (Otsego Office of the

Sheriff), 1-2.
- Hammond, *The History of Political Parties*, 85.
- Taylor, *William Cooper's Town*, 172, 192-195.
- Hastings, *Military Minutes of the Council of Appointments,* 234-235.
- A New Nation Votes, *New York 1792 Election for Assembly Otsego County, New York 1793 Election for Assembly Otsego County. (*Albany: The Albany Gazette, June 4, 1792), (Poughkeepsie, NY: Poughkeepsie Journal, June 12, 1793).

35. Hamond, *The History of Political Parties*, 86-90.
- Hastings, *Military Minutes of the Council of Appointments*, 351-352.

36. John D. Monroe, *Chapters in the History of Delaware County, New York*, (Delhi, NY: Delaware County Historical Association, 1949), 5-6, 40-41.
- *Laws of the State of New York*, *An Act to Erect Part of the Counties of Ulster and Otsego into a Separate County,* (Albany: Weed, Parsons & Co., 1887), Vol. 4, 39-41.
- Henry Christman, *Tin Horns and Calico*, (Cornwallville, NY: Hope Farm Press, 1978).
- New Horizons Genealogy, *New York State Federal and State Census of Electors Map 1800*, https://newhorizonsgenealogicalservices.com

37. Monroe, *Chapters in the History of Delaware County*, 5.
- J. Fenimore Cooper, *Historical Stories of American Pioneer Life,* (Philadelphia: American Book and Bible House, 1897), *Hurry Harry and Deerslayer*, Michal E. Audriolli-illustrator, Edmund Evans-Engraver.
- A New Nation Votes, *New York 1793, 1794, 1796, 1798 Election for U. S. House of Representatives District #10,* (Albany: The Albany Register, March 4, 1793; The Albany Gazette, Feb. 20, 1795; Jan. 20, 1797; June 22, 1798).

Chapter 8: Ohio

1. John W. Ray, *A History of Western Pennsylvania*, (Erie, PA: by Author, 1941), 68.
- National Archives, *Northwest Ordinance,* https://www.archives.gov

2. Isabel T. Kelsay, *Joseph Brant 1743-1807 Man of Two Worlds*, (Syracuse: Syracuse University Press, 1984), 340, 367-368.

3. Arthur St. Clair, *A Narrative of the Manner in Which the Campaign Against the Indians in the Year 1791 was Conducted Under the Command of Maj. Gen. St. Clair,* (Philadelphia: Jane Aitkens, 1812).

4. David B. Mattern, *Benjamin Lincoln and the American Revolution*, (Colombia, SC: University of South Carolina Press, 1995), 197-203.
- Alan Taylor, *The Divided Ground; Indians, Settlers, and the Northern Borderland of the American Revolution,* (New York: Vintage Books, 2006), 277-282.
- Benjamin Lincoln, *Journal of a Treaty Held in 1793 with the Indian Tribes Northwest of the Ohio by Commissioners of the United States,* (Massachusetts Historical Society), 116-122. https://www.babel.hathitrust.org

5. Lincoln, *Journal of a Treaty Held in 1793*, 123-142.

6. Lincoln, *Journal of a Treaty Held in 1793,* 142-172.
- Kelsay, *Joseph Brant,* 489-504.

7. Taylor, *The Divided Ground*, 283-294.
- Kelsay, *Joseph Brant,* 510-519.

8. Harvey Rice, *Pioneers of the Western Reserve*, (Boston: Lee & Shepard, New York: Charles T. Dillingham, 1883), 39-40.
- Harriet T. Upton, *History of the Western Reserve*, (Chicago, New York: Lewis Publishing Co., 1910), Vol. 1, 7-12.
- Claude L. Shepard, *The Connecticut Land Company and Accompanying Papers*, (Cleveland:

Western Reserve Historical Society, 1916), 69-84.
- Moina W. Large, *History of Ashtabula County, Ohio*, (Topeka-Indianapolis: Historical Publishing Co., 1924), Vol. 1, 86-89.
- William W. Williams, *History of Ashtabula County, Ohio*, (Philadelphia: Williams Brothers, 1878), 9-14.

9. Upton, *History of the Western Reserve*, 19-25.
- Charles Whittlesey, *The Early History of Cleveland, Ohio*, (Cleveland: Fairbanks & Benedict Co., 1867), 164-273. https://www.pressbooks.ulib.csuohio.edu
- Charles M. Robinson & Augustus Porter, *Narratives and Journals of Pioneer Surveyors of Western New York and Adjacent Tracts in Pennsylvania and Ohio*, (Buffalo: Buffalo Historical Society, 1904), 302-314.
- Seth Pease, *Journals of Seth Pease to and from New Connecticut, 1796-1798*, (Cleveland: Western Reserve Historical Society, Annual Report, Part 2, 1913-1914), 29-46.
- Peter Porter, *A Brief History of Old Fort Niagara*, (Niagara: 1896), 58-62.
- Pease Map, 1796, https://www.clevelandhistorical.org ID: 2436.

10. Margaret M. Butler, *A Pictorial History of the Western Reserve, 1796-1860*, (Cleveland: World Publishing Co., 1963), 2.
- Pease, *Journals of Seth Pease*, 106-107.
- James H. Kennedy, *A History of the City of Cleveland, its Settlement, Rise and Progress, 1796-1896*, (Cleveland: The Imperial Press, 1896), 28-75.
- Dave DeOreo, *Cleveland Pioneers Persevered Through the Ague*, (Ideastream Public Media, 2020), https://www.ideastream.org
- Upton, *History of the Western Reserve*, 32-36, 47-124.
- Albert J. Granger, *The History of Canandaigua*, (Canandaigua: Ontario Repository and Messenger, 1876), 8-9.
- Whittlesey, *The Early History of Cleveland*, 311-312.

11. William W. Williams, *History of Ashtabula County, Ohio*, (Philadelphia: Williams Brothers, 1878), 25, 169.
- Moina W. Large, *History of Ashtabula County*, Vol. 1, 86-89.

12. Jenny Moss, *Archives Publications, Revolutionary War Pension and Bounty-Land Warrant Application File*, W.24164. https://www.ancestry.com

13. Elizabeth F. Ellet, *Pioneer Woman of the West*, (New York: Charles Scribner, 1856), 258.
- Jane C. Ford, *Records of the Harper Family*, (Cleveland: A. C. Rogers Co. 1905), 59.

14. Grant Gregory, *Ancestors and Descendants of Henry Gregory*, (Rutland, VT: Tuttle Publishing Co., 1938), 106-107.
- Henry P. Johnston, *Record of Service of Connecticut Men in the War of the Revolution, War of 1812, Mexican War*, (Hartford, CT: Adjutant Generals Office, 1880), 81, 458.
- New York Comptrollers Office, *New York in the Revolution as Colony and State,* (Albany: J. B. Lyon Co., 1904), Vol.1, 151.
- Williams, *History of Ashtabula County*, 25, 169.

15. Pomroy Jones, *Annuals and Recollections of Oneida County*, (Rome, NY: Published by Author, Printed by A. J. Rowley, 1851), 372-374.
- Ford, *Records of Harper Family*, 59.
- William B. Doyle, *Centennial History of Summit County, Ohio and Representative Citizens*, (Chicago: Biographical Publishing Co., 1908), 111.

16. Rick Harper, ed, *Descendants of James Harper/ Research Behind Move from New York to Ohio, 1798*. https://www.newmediamarket.com
- Mark L. Peckham, *Early History of Bateaux, Drawing of a Typical Eighteenth-Century*

Bateaux, (Albany: State University of New York Press, 2019), 1-9. https://www.sunypress.edu
- Joseph F. Meany Jr., *Bateaux and Battoe Men: An American Colonial Response to the Problem of Logistics in Mountain Warfare*, 2-4. https://www.museum.dmna.ny.gov

17. Lincoln, *Journal of a Treaty Held in 1793*, 121.
- Pease, *Journal of Seth Pease*, 37, 54.
- Crisfield Johnson, *History of Oswego County New York with Illustrations and Biographical Sketches of Some of the Prominent Men and Pioneers,* (Philadelphia: H.L. Everts & Co., 1877), 44, 48, 51, 226.

18. Harper, Descendants of James Harper/ *Research Behind Move from New York to Ohio, 1798*.
- Walter Lewis, *Dictionary of Canadian Biography, James Richardson (b-1832), Vol. 6 (1821-1835)*. https://www.biographi.ca

19. Ernest Cruikshank, *A Century of Municipal History 1792-1892, County of Welland*, (Welland, OT: Tribune Print, 1892), Part 1, 1792-1841.
- R. Robert Mutrie, ed., *The Niagara Settler Township Papers, Berti Settlers, P-R; Soldiers and Supporters, P; Niagara Settlers Land Records Township of Berti Settlers, P.* https://www.sites.google.com/site/niagarasettlers
- William D. Reid, *The Loyalists in Ontario, The Sons and Daughters of the American Loyalists in Upper Canada,* (Lambertville, NJ: Hunterdon House, Genealogical Publishing Co., 1973), 254.
- Ernest Cruikshank, *The Story of Butler's Rangers and the Settlement of Niagara*, (Welland, OT: Tribune Printing House, 1893).

20. Ron Brown, *The Lake Erie Shore, Ontario's Forgotten South Coast*, (Toronto, OT: Natural Heritage Books, Dundurn Press, 2009), 88-89.
- Williams, *History of Ashtabula County*, 169.
- Large, *History of Ashtabula County,* Vol. 1, 86-89.

21. Ellet, *Pioneer Women of the West*, 254-266.
- Williams, *History of Ashtabula County*, 25, 169.
- Harper, *Descendants of James Harper/ Maps*.

22. Williams, *History of Ashtabula County*, 171.
- Ford*, Records of the Harper Family*, 16, 32.
- Josephine L. Harper, *Guide to the Draper Manuscripts*, (Madison, WI: Wisconsin Historical Society Press, 1983), *Letters Between Rice Harper and Lyman Draper; April 14, 1863, March 3, 1863, March 19, 1863. Malvina P. Sherwood Essay,* Draper Mss., 16 F, 86-102 (microfilm edition, 1949), State Historical Society of Wisconsin.
- Eric S. Loker & Bruce V. Hofkin, *Parasitology A Conceptual Approach, Second Edition*, (Boca Raton, FL: CRS Press, Taylor & Francis Group, 2023), 94, 437.
- Ellet, Pioneer *Women of the West*, 258-279.
- Rice, *Pioneers of the Western Reserve*, 177-181.
- Upton, *History of the Western Reserve*, Vol. 1, 529-530; Vol. 2, 861-862.

23. William Miles, *Revolutionary War Pension Application*, S.22400.
- Samuel P. Bates, Whitman, Russell, Brown and Weakley, *The History of Erie County, Pennsylvania*, (Chicago: Warner & Beers Co., 1884), 66, 229-231, 263, 835-851.
- Ford*, Records of the Harper Family*.
- Draper*, Rice Harper to Lyman Draper Letters*, Draper Mss., 16 F 86-102. Note 22.
- Upton, *History of the Western Reserve*, Vol. 1, 529.

24. Whittlesey, *The Early History of Cleveland*, 345-346.
- Ellet, *Pioneer Women of the West*, 264-265.

25. Whittlesey, *The Early History of Cleveland*, 356-357.
- Ellet, *Pioneer Women of the West*, 259-280.

- Thomas Pennant, *A Tour of Scotland, 1769,* (London: Benjamin White at Horace's Head, 1772), Moses Griffith, Engraver.
- Florence Bass, *Stories of Pioneer Life for Young Readers,* (Boston: D.C. Health & Co., 1900), 108.

26. Williams, *History of Ashtabula County,* 25-26, 145, 156, 161.
- Upton, *History of the Western Reserve,* Vol. 2, 550.
- Bates, *The History of Erie County,* 233-244, 242.
- William J. Montgomery, *A Montgomery Family Genealogy; William and Mary, Robert and Mary,* (Website Recorded and Developed by W. J. Montgomery, 2020). https://www.wjmontgomerygenealogy.com

27. Williams, *History of Ashtabula County,* 25, 169.
- Ellet, *Pioneer Women of the West,* 263-264.
- Large, *History of Ashtabula County,* Vol. 1, Chapter 4.
- Harper, *Descendants of James Harper/ Descendants.*

28. Ohio Tax Records 1800-1850, Ashtabula County, Vol. 71, 1828; *Geneva, 42-51, Harpersfield, 51-67.* https://www.familysearch.org
- George W. Bartholomew, *Record of the Bartholomew Family,* (Austin, TX: G. W. Bartholomew, 1885), 459-470.
- Delaware County, New York, Genealogy and History Site, *Book A of Deeds, Dec. 17, 1798, 3 lots to Hubbard.* https://www.dcnyhistory.org

29. Williams, *History of Ashtabula County,* 26, 156-157.
- Upton, *History of the Western Reserve,* Vol. 2, 550.
- Montgomery, *A Montgomery Family Genealogy, William and Mary, Robert and Mary.*
- https://www.conneautohio.us/conneauthist.htm

30. Ford, *Records of the Harper Family,* 43.
- Upton, *History of the Western Reserve,* Vol. 1, 561.
- Large, *History of Ashtabula County,* Vol. 1, 88-89.
- Williams, *History of Ashtabula County,* 173.
- Bartholomew, *Record of the Bartholomew Family,* 459-493.

31. DAR, *A Record of the Revolutionary War Soldiers Buried in Lake County, Ohio,* (Columbus, OH: Champlin Press, 1902), 42-43.
- Williams, *History of Ashtabula County,* 173.
- Carl T. Engel, *Lake County Heritage, A Magazine of Local History and Culture, Gen. Edward Paine, Pioneer Settler of Lake County,* 1-8. https://www.painesville.com
- Census for Ashtabula County Townships of Harpersfield, Geneva and Salem, 1820. https://www.ancestry.com
- Hugh Hastings, Harry H. Nobles, ed., *Military Minutes of the Council of Appointments of the State of New York, 1783-1821,* (Albany: James B. Lyon State Printer, 1901), 338, 461, 515.
- New York Comptrollers Office, *New York in the Revolution,* Vol. 1, 77, 144, 228, 245, 250.
- Williams, *History of Geauga and Lake County,* 211-212.

32. Harper, *Descendants of James Harper/Maps, Harpersfield, No. 11, 5th Range.*
- Williams, *History of Ashtabula County,* 170.

33. Williams, *History of Ashtabula County,* 28-31.

34. Dan Maxson, *Unionville: The Tiny Town That Time Forgot,* (Local Lore by Max, News-Herald Community Media Lab, 2010-2016). https://www.lakehistorycenter.org
- DAR, *A Record of the Revolutionary War Soldiers,* 45-49.
- Henry Howe, *Historical Collections of Ohio,* (Cincinnati: C. J. Krehbiel & Co., 1907), Vol. 1, 141.

- Williams, *History of Geauga and Lake County*, 22, 24, 144, 231.
- Ellet, *Pioneer Women of the West*, 278.
- Williams, *History of Ashtabula County*, 26, 170.
- Whittlesey, *Early History of Cleveland*, 400-414.

35. Williams, *History of Ashtabula County*, 49.

36. Benson L. Lossing, *The Pictorial Field Book of the War of 1812*, (New York: Harper & Brothers, 1868), 204-207, 251-252.

37. Ohio Adjutant General's Office, *Roster of Ohio Soldiers in the War of 1812*, (Columbus, OH: Edward T. Miller Co., 1916), 4.
- Lossing, *Pictorial Field Book*, 340-343.

38. Ohio Adjutant General's Office, *Roster of Ohio Soldiers*, 81-82, 84, 86.
- Williams, *History of Ashtabula County*, 57.
- Bartholomew, *Record of the Bartholomew Family*, 459-493.

39. Lossing, *Pictorial Field Book*, 473-504.
- Ohio Adjutant General's Office, *Roster of Ohio Soldiers,* 131, 353-354.

40. Edward S. Ellis, *Outdoor Life and Indian Stories*, (Philadelphia: 1912), 112-113.
- Lossing, *Pictorial Field Book*, 544-559.
- John C. Fredrikson, ed., *The War of 1812 in Person: Fifteen Accounts by U. S. Regulars, Volunteers and Militiamen*, (Jefferson, NC: McFarland & Co., 2010), 238-246.

41. Bartholomew, *Record of the Bartholomew Family*, 469, 488-489.
- Access Genealogy, *Roll of Capt. George Sanderson's Company, 27th U.S. Infantry, Served 1813-1814*. https://www.accessgenealogy.com
- Alice Bliss, ed., *The Western Reserve Chronical, April 13, 1822, Samuel Bartholomew Murder- Article 2*, (From the Genealogical Collection of the Geneva Library).

42. *To Reject H.R. 184, To Declare War with Great Britain*. https://www.govtrack.us
- Robert Malcomson, *The A to Z of the War of 1812*, The A to Z Guide Series, No. 55, (Lanham, Toronto, Plymouth, UK: The Scarecrow Press, 2009), 140, 373.

43. Hastings, Nobles, *Military Minutes of the Council of Appointments*, Vol. 1, 231, 351, 480, 733, 742, 782, 819, 827, 918; Vol. 2, 1106, 1079, 1270, 1332, 1361, 1368, 1418.
- Gary M. Gibson, ed., *New York State Military Index as of 4 July 1812*, (War of 1812 Magazine, Issue 28, April 2018). https://www.napoleon-series.org

44. Malcomson, *The A to Z of the War of 1812*, 373-374.
- Hastings, Nobles, *Military Minutes of the Council of Appointments*, Vol. 1, 393, 790, 853; Vol. 2, 1016, 1149, 1265, 1400, 1407, 1500.

45. *Trumbull Probate Records, Vol. 1-3, 1803-1825*, 2-9.

46. Trumbull Probate Records, Vol. 1-3, 1803-1825, 28-30.

47. Ashtabula Probate Records, Vol. A-B, 1811-1833, 212-215.
- Ashtabula Telegraph, *Benjamin Hartwell Obituary*, April 1874.
- Lyman W. Densmore, *The Hartwells of America, A Genealogy of all the Hartwell families of the United States and Canada*, (Saginaw, MI: Hartwell and Lorenzen, 1956), 10, 24.
- Williams Brothers, *The History of Geauga and Lake County, Ohio*, (Philadelphia: Press of J. B. Lippincott & Co., 1878), 20-21.

48. Ford, *Records of the Harper Family*, 27-30, 59.
- Rick Harper, *Robert Harper, b. 1791*, (The Harper Herald, Vol. 1, Issue 12); *John A. Harper, 1774-1841*, (The Harper Herald, Vol. 1, Issue 4).

49. Draper, *Letter from J.F. Harper of North Kortright, N.Y. to Jonas M. Preston, Delhi, N.Y., May 12, 1870. "Balance", Albany, Dec. 10, 1811, Obituary of John Harper*, Draper Mss., 16 F; 3 Q.
- Jeptha R. Simms, *The Frontiersmen of New York: Showing Customs of the Indians,*

Vicissitudes of the Pioneer White Settlers, and Border Strife in Two Wars, (Albany: G. C. Riggs, 1882), Vol. 2, 63.

- Ford, *Records of the Harper Family*, 59.

50. Find A Grave, *Harpersfield Center Cemetery Grave Memorial ID Numbers; Col. John Harper ID 40081350; Isabella McKnight Harper ID 119178127; Col. Wiliam Harper ID 40081210; Hannah Hotchkiss Harper ID 40081283; Roswell Hotchkiss ID 114518982; Margaret Harper Hotchkiss ID 58556031; James Ells ID 58765653; Polly Harper Ells ID 108796369.*
https://www.findagrave.com

51. W. W. Munsell, *History of Delaware County, New York*, (New York: W. W. Munsell & Co., 1880), 221.

- Find A Grave, Harpersfield Rural (Stevens) Cemetery Grave Memorial ID Numbers; *William Lamb Sr. and James Stevens ID 67849705; James Hendry ID 63913230; John Hendry ID 111449652; Thomas Hendry ID 111533964; Ezra Thorp ID 67850579; Daniel Thorp ID 67850880; Joshua Brett ID 67805133.* https://www.findagrave.com

52. Find A Grave, Alexander Harper Memorial Cemetery Grave Memorial ID Numbers; *Alexander Harper ID 9769324; Elizabeth Bartholomew Harper ID 9769455; Joseph Harper ID 108579526; John A. Harper ID 9769503; James A. Harper ID 9769482; William A. Harper ID 136042858; Alexander A. Harper ID 9769444.* *https://www.findagrave.com*

- Find A Grave, Geneva Evergreen Cemetery Grave Memorial ID Numbers; *Abigail Patchin Bartholomew ID 14463336; Jacob Bartholomew ID 105873722; Benjamin Bartholomew ID 105336897; Peter Bartholomew ID 76429403.* *https://www.findagrave.com*

- Find A Grave, Conneaut City Cemetery Grave Memorial ID Numbers; *Robert Montgomery ID 30625962; Mary White Montgomery ID 44293424; Eli Montgomery ID 30626055; James Harper ID 45755668; Sarah Montgomery Harper ID 129673620; Aaron Wright ID 97935151; Anna Montgomery Wright ID 97935264.* *https://www.findagrave.com*

53. Henry R. Stiles, *The History and Genealogies of Ancient Windsor, Connecticut, 1635-1891*, (Hartford, CT: Case, Lockwood & Brainard Co., 1892), Vol. 2, 367.

Illustration Credits and Attributions

Chapter 1
4 Thompson, John, *Ireland, Thompson's New General Atlas*, (London: Cradock & Joy, 1815), 10. Northern Portion of Ireland Map.
7 Bolton, Charles K., *Scotch Irish Pioneers in Ulster and America*, (Boston: Bacon & Brown, 1910), 320. Early Casco Bay Settlements.
11 Vetromile, Eugene, *Indian Good Book*, (New York: E. Dunigan & Brother, 1858), Frontispiece. Strong, Thomas W., lith., *Death of Father Sébastien Râle of the Society of Jesus, 1856*.
12 Almon, John, *Map of the Environs of Boston*, (London: J. Almon, 1775), Library of Congress. https://www.loc.gov/item/gm71005484
19 Swinnerton, Rev. H.V., *Map of Cherry Valley at the Time of the Massacre*, 1877. Lyman Draper Manuscripts, 5 F (microfilm edition 1949), State Historical Society of Wisconsin. (Additions by Author).
21 Halsey, Francis W., *The Old New York Frontier*, (New York: Charles Scribner's Sons, 1901), McIlworth, Thomas, *Sir William Johnson Portrait 1763*, (copy c.1840, after the lost original). World Encyclopedia, Last Modified Dec. 14, 2021. https://www.worldhistory.org/image/14981/sir-william-johnson-portrait
24 Trumbull, John, *Peter Agwirongdougwas, 'Good Peter' (1717-1793), Chief of the Oneida Indians, 1792*, (Courtesy of Yale University Art Galley).

Chapter 2
29 Ellis, Edward S., *The History of Our Country*, (J.H. Woolling Co., 1900), *Pontiac Delivering the Wampum Belt to Sir William Johnson at Fort Oswego as a Sign of Peace and the End of Pontiac's War, 1766*. Classic Image/Alamy Stock Photo, Image ID: EBHBC1.
30 Halsey, Francis W., *The Old New York Frontier*, (New York: Charles Scribner's Sons, 1901), frontispiece, *The Frontier of New York in the Revolution*, (New York: Bormay & Co., Engraver, 1901), Map by Ray A. Billington. FLHC DBA7/Alamy, Image ID: 2PNYBFP.
34 Map by Author.
36 McIlworth, Thomas, *General John Bradstreet 1764*, National Portrait Gallery, Smithsonian Open Access. https://commons.wikimedia.org
42 Photo by Author.

48 Stuart, Gilbert, *Joseph Brant (1742-1807)*, 1786, oil on canvass, Fenimore Art Museum, Cooperstown, NY, Gift of Stephen C. Clark, NO199.1961. Photograph by Richard Walker.

Chapter 3
55 Yvonne, *Spanish John McDonald of Scotus*, Courtesy of the Macdonell-Williamson House, Chute-a-Blondeau, Ontario, Canada.
57 Chapin, John R., *The Illustrated American Advertiser Vol. 5, The Historical Picture Gallery or Scenes and Incidents in American History*, (Boston: D. Bigalow & Co., 1856), 447. *Adventures of Col. Harper*. https://babel.hathitrust.org
58 Simms, Jeptha R., *History of Schoharie County*, (Albany: Munsell & Tanner, 1845*)*, 241. *Col. Harper Confronting the Indians*.
63 Howe, Lt. Gen. William, *First Battalion of Pennsylvania Loyalist Troops*, (Philadelphia: James Humphreys Jr, 1777), *All Intrepid Able-Bodied Heroes*.
69 Peale, James, *Miniature Portrait of Thomas Posey, 1795*, Gift of Addison Cecil Posey to the Society of Cincinnati in the State of Virginia, 1982. Courtesy of the American Revolution Institute. www.americanrevolutioninstitute.org
75 Chappel, Alonzo (Artist), Thomas Phillibrown (Engraver), *Incident in Cherry Valley-Fate of Jane Wells*, (New York: Martin Jones & Co., 1856). https://www.loc.gov/recource/cph.3c11117
77 Cockburn, William, *A Map of Two Tracts of Land on the Southside of the Mohawk River 1772*, Collection of the New York Historical Society of New York, Mohawk Valley Maps & Sketches. Courtesy of Ken D. Johnson, Fort Plank Historian. https://fort-plank.com

Chapter 4
81 Tenney, A., *General John Sullivan 1873*, New Hampshire State House, https://commons.wikimedia.org
82 Hall, Henry B., Engraver, *Major General James Clinton*, Picture Collection New York Public Library Digital Collection, https://commons.wikimedia.org
82 Unknown Artist, *Lt. Col. Daniel Brodhead*, https://commons.wikimedia.org
90 Unknown Artist, *Major John Butler*, National Park Service, https://www.nps.gov
91 Grafton, John, *The American Revolution, A Picture Sourcebook*, (Mineola, NY: Dover

Publishing, 1975), fig. 360. *Burning of an Indian Village.*
93 Boardman, Fon W. Jr, *Against the Iroquois, The Sullivan Campaign of 1779 in New York State,* (New York: H.Z. Walck,1978), Chemung County Historical Society, Elmira, NY, Alchetron Free Social Encyclopedia, (Additions by Author).
https://alchetron.com

Chapter 5
99 Anonymous, Unknown Artist, *Sir John Johnson, 1792.* https://commons.wikimedia.org
103 Simms, Jeptha, *History of Schoharie County,* (Albany: Munsell & Tanner, 1845), 379. *The Onistagrawa and Scene Beneath it. Assault on the Vrooman Family.* Alamy Stock Photo, Image ID: PNGN01.
110 Trumbull, John, *Colonel Louis of the Oneida*, Pencil Sketch, 1785, (Courtesy of the Yale University Art Gallery). *Lt. Col. Louis Cook, Akiatonharonkwen.* https://en.wikipedia.org
112 Willett, William M., *A Narrative of the Military Actions of Colonel Marinus Willett,* (New York: G. & C. & H. Carvill, 1831), frontispiece. *Colonel Marinus Willett.* https://commons.wikimedia.org
118 Martin, David, *Lt. John Ross of the 34th Foot Grenadier Company 1769.* (Courtesy of the Museum of the American Revolution). *Maj. John Ross.* https://commons.wikimedia.org

Chapter 6
122 Gollmann, Julius, *Col. Samuel Campbell (1738-1824), ca.1855,* pastel, Fenimore Art Museum, Cooperstown, NY. Gift of A. Pennington Whitehead. N0002.1991. Photograph by Richard Walker.
Gollmann, Julius, *Jane Cannon Campbell, 1855*, pastel, Fenimore Art Museum, Cooperstown, NY. Gift of A. Pennington Whitehead. N0002.1991. Photograph by Richard Walker.
125 Simms, Jeptha, *History of Schoharie County,* (Albany: Munsell & Tanner, 1845), 134, *Queen Anne's Chapel Parsonage.*
https://schoharie.nygenweb.net
130 *Historical USGS Maps of New England and New York; Hobart, NY Quadrangle, NW Corner,* 1904, (Durham, NH: University of New Hampshire Dimond Library Documents Dept. and Data Center, 2001). (Overlay of Harper Patent Homestead Lots by Author).
133 Lupton, Frances P., *Miniature Portrait of Dr. Platt Townsend*, Copy, (Courtesy of Richard Grossmann and the Walton Historical Society, Walton, NY.)
141 Stuart, Gilbert, *William Cooper, (1754-1809), ca.1794-1797,* oil on canvas, Fenimore Art Museum, Cooperstown, NY, Gift of Dr. Henry S.F. Cooper. No.144.1977. Photo by Richard Walker.
145 Peale, Charles W., *Miniature Portrait of Major Jacob Morris*, Find A Grave Memorial ID: 54599158, Added by Elizabeth Tupper Curtiss Wilson, 9/26/2021, Maintained by your Sister in Christ – Dona (Carr) Mooring.
148 DeWitt, Simeon, *Map of the Headwaters of the Rivers Susquehanna and Delaware: Embracing the Early Patents on the Southside of the Mohawk River 1790.*

Chapter 7
151 Ames, Ezra, Artist, John C. Buttre, Engraver, *U.S. Vice President George Clinton*, Library of Congress, Washington, DC, (neg. no. LC-USZ62-110647), Encyclopedia Britannica.
https://www.britiannica.com
155 DeWitt, Simeon, *A Map of the Military Lands and Twenty Townships in the Western Part of the State of New York 1790*, Digital Collection of Yale University Beinecke Rare Book and Manuscript Library, (BrSides Folio 2017 98 Orbis Record 13267707, OID 16195021), (Overdraw by Author).
159 Hayward, George, Lithograph for D.T. Valintine's *Manuel of the Corporation of the City of New York,* (New York: Macedon & Baker, 1856), *Coffee House Slip & New York Coffee House.*
161 *New York's 1790 Frontier Districts*, (Map by Arthor).
166 New York County Maps: Interactive History and Complete List, *New York Counties, 1791.*
https://www.mapofus.org
173 New Horizons Genealogy, *New York State Federal and State Census of Electors Map 1800.*
https://newhorizonsgenealogicalservices.com

Chapter 8
179 *Northwest Territory Locator Map 1787,* (Commissioner's Path, Western Reserve, Greenville Property Line, Added by Author).
https://commons.wikimedia.org
183 Pease, Seth, *A Map of the Connecticut Western Reserve from Actual Survey by Seth Pease,* (New Haven, CT: Engraved & Printed by Amos Doolittle 1798), JCB Library.
https://jcb.lunaimaging.com

184 Butler, Margaret M., *A Pictorial History of the Western Reserve 1796-1860,* (Cleveland: World Publishing Co., 1963), 2. *Seth Pease.*

187 Peckham, Mark L., *Early History of Bateaux, Drawing of a Typical Eighteenth-Century Bateaux,* (Albany: State University of New York Press, 2019). Courtesy of Mark Peckham, Bateaux Below, and Hudson River Maritime Museum.
https://www.themua.org

190 Descendants of James Harper, Unidentified Family Photos at Shandy Hall, *John A. Harper.*
https://www.newmediamarkets.com

192 Pennant, Thomas, Moses Griffith, Engraver, *A Tour of Scotland 1769,* (London: Benjamin White at Horace's Head, 1772), 328. *Grinding Corn in a Hand Quern Mill.*

193 Bass, Florance, *Stories of Pioneer Life for Young Readers,* (Boston: D.C. Health & Co., 1900), 108. *Stump Mill.*

197 William Brothers, *History of Ashtabula County, Ohio,* (Philadelphia: J.B. Lippincott & Co., 1878), 7. *The Twenty-Eight Townships of Ashtabula County.*

203 Descendents of James Harper, *Signatures of Alexander and Joseph Harper on a February 1771 Indenture Between John Harper Sr and his Heirs.*
https://www.newmediamarkets.com

204 Upton, Harriet T., *History of the Western Reserve,* (Chicago, New York: Lewis Publishing Co., 1910), Vol. 2, 860. *Polly Hendry Harper and Robert A. Harper.*

205 Descendents of James Harper, *Signatures of John and William Harper on a February 1771 Indenture Between John Harper Sr and his Heirs.*
https://www.newmediamarkets.com

207 As found on Multiple Public Family Trees for Montgomery Harper. *Montgomery and Angelina Parshall Harper.* https://www.ancestry.com

Bibliography

A New Nation Votes, American Election Results 1787-1825, www.elections.lib.tufts.edu

Access Genealogy, *Roll of Capt. George Sanderson's Company, 27th U.S. Infantry, Served 1813-1814*. www.accessgenealogy.com

Adams, Richard C., *The Delaware Indians, A Brief History*, (Saugerties, NY: Hope Farm Press, 1995).

Adler, Jeanne W., *Chainbreaker's War, A Seneca Chief Remembers the American Revolution*, (Delmar, NY: Black Dome Press, 2002).

Adler, Simon L., *Sullivan's Campaign in Western New York, 1779*, (Rochester, NY: Rochester Historical Society, 1898).

Aikey, Michael, *Ballston Raid of 1780: Military Operation or a Time to Settle Old Scores*, (Journal of the American Revolution, Dec. 6, 2017).

Allen, Thomas B., & Braisted Todd W., *The Loyalist Corps, Americans in the Service of the King*, (Takoma Park, MD: Fox Acres Press, 2011).

An Act Providing for the Enumeration of the Inhabitants of the United States, Session 2, Chapter 3, March 1, 1790. www.archives.gov

Anderson, Chad L., *The Storied Landscape of Iroquoia, History, Conquest, and Memory in the Native Northeast*, (Lincoln, NE: University of Nebraska Press, 2020).

Ashtabula Probate Records, *Vol. A-B, 1811-1833*. www.ancestry.com

Ashtabula Telegraph, *Benjamin Hartwell Obituary, April 1874*.

Babin, Andrew, *U.S. Marshalls Overcome Hardships and Challenges to Count 3,929,214 People in a Young America*, (US Census Bureau, Resource Library, 2020). www.census.gov

Bacon, Edward F., *Otsego County New York Geographical and Historical Review*, (Oneonta, NY: 1902).

Bailey, W.T., *Richfield Springs and Vicinity*, (New York: A.S. Barnes & Co., 1874).

Barber, John & Howe, Henry, *Historical Collections of the State of New York*, (New York: S. Tuttle, 1846).

Barr, John, *Orderly Book of the 4th New York Regiment, 1778-1780, the 2nd New York Regiment 1780-1783, John Barr's Diary*, (Albany: Almon W. Lauber, 1932).

Bartholomew, George W. Jr, *Records of the Bartholomew Family*, (Austin, TX: The Compiler, 1885).

Bass, Florence, *Stories of Pioneer Life for Young Readers*, (Boston: D.C. Health & Co.,1900).

Bates, Samuel P., *The History of Erie County, Pennsylvania*, (Chicago: Warner & Beers Co., 1884).

Bayer, Jonathan, *Society at Auction: Coffee-House Culture in Occupied New York*, (Journal of the American Revolution, Nov. 10, 2016). www.allthingsliberty.com

Beers, F.W., *Atlas of Delaware County New York*, (New York: F.W. Beers, A.D. Ellis, G.G. Soule, 1869).

Berleth, Richard, *Bloody Mohawk, The French and Indian War & American Revolution on New York's Frontier*, (Delmar NY: Black Dome Press, 2010).

Bleeker, Leonard, *Orderly Book of Capt. Leonard Bleeker, Major of the Brigade in the Early Part of the Expedition Under General James Clinton*, (New York: Joseph Sabin, 1865).

Bliss, Alice, ed., *The Western Reserve Chronical, April 13, 1822, Samuel Bartholomew Murder- Article 2*, (Genealogical Collection of the Geneva Library).

Boelhert, Paul A., *The Battle of Oriskany and General Nicholas Herkimer, Revolution in the Mohawk Valley*, (Charleston, SC: The History Press, 2013

Bolton, Charles K., *Scotch Irish Pioneers in Ulster and America*, (Boston: Bacon & Brown, 1920).

Braisted, Todd, ed., *Letters of John McDonel to Col. Butler, Aug. 5th, 1779*, (The On-Line Institute for Advanced Loyalist Studies, Library and Archives Canada: MG23, GIII23).

Broadman, Fon, W., *Against the Iroquois: The Sullivan Campaign of 1779 in New York*.

Brown, Ron, *The Lake Erie Shore, Ontario's Forgotten South Coast*, (Toronto, OT: Natural Heritage Books, Dundurn Press, 2009).

Bunce, Oliver B., *The Romance of the Revolution*, (Philadelphia: Porter & Coates, 1870).

Burke, John, *A Genealogical and Heraldic Dictionary of the Peerage and Baronetage of the British Empire*, (London: Henry Colburn Pub, 1839).

Butler, Margaret M., *A Pictorial History of the Western Reserve, 1796-1860,* (Cleveland: World Publishing Co., 1963).
Butterfield, L.H., *Judge William Cooper (1754-1809): A Sketch of His Character and Accomplishments,* (Cornell, NY: Cornell University Press,1949).
Calander of Historical Manuscripts Relating to the Revolution, (Albany: Weed Parson & Co., 1868).
Calander of New York Colonial Manuscripts, Indorsed Land Papers, (Albany: Weed, Parsons & Co., 1864).
Campbell, Colin D., *They Beckoned and We Came, The Settlement of Cherry Valley, New York Historical Journal, Vol. 79, No. 3,* (Cornell, NY: Cornell University Press, 1998).
Campbell, Dudley M., *A Sketch of the History of Oneonta,* (Oneonta, NY: Harold & Democrat Office, 1883). *The History of Oneonta from its Earliest Settlement to Present Time,* (Oneonta, NY: G.W. Fairchild & Co., 1906).
Campbell, Thomas, *Gertrude of Wyoming or The Pennsylvania Cottage,* (New York: D. Appleton & Co.,1858).
Campbell, William J., *Negotiating at the Oneida Carry,* (Fort Stanwix National Monument Historic Resource Study, 2017).
Campbell, William W., *Annals of Tryon County, or The Border Warfare of New York During the Revolution,* (New York: J.J. Harper,1831).
Carwitham, John, *A South End View of the Great Town of Boston in New England in America,* (London: Carington Bowles Map & Print Seller, 1730-1760).
Cayuga County Independent, (Aurelius, NY: Nov. 1902).
Cherry Valley Cemetery, www.findagrave.com
Christman, Henry, *Tin Horns and Calico,* (Cornwallville, NY: Hope Farm Press, 1978).
Chrysler, Don, *The Blue-Eyed Indians, The Story of Adam Chrysler and His Brothers in the Revolutionary War,* (Zephyrhills, FL: Chrysler Books, 1999).
Churchill, Jean, *Another Look at Josiah Parks,* (The Parke Society Newsletter, Vol. 46, No.3, 2010).
Clark, Hiram C., *The History of Chenango County, New York, Containing the Divisions of County and Sketches of the Towns, Indian Tribes and Titles,* (Norwich, NY: Thompson & Pratt, 1850).
Clark, James T., *Sir William Johnson and Pontiac,* Proceedings of the New York State Historical Association, (Cornell, NY: Cornell University Press, 1914).
Collections of the New Historical Society, *A Map of Two Tracts of Land on the Southside of the Mohawk River,* (Mohawk Valley Maps & Sketches), www.fort-plank.com
Conover, George S. & Aldrich, Lewis C., ed., *History of Ontario County, New York,* (Syracuse: D. Mason & Co., 1893).
Consolidated Laws of New York, *Pennsylvania Boundary Line, Chap. 57, Article 2, Sec. 6.* www.nyssenate.gov
Cook, Frederick, ed., *Journals of the Military Expedition of Major General John Sullivan Against the Six Nations of Indians in 1779,* (Auburn, NY: Knapp, Peck & Thomson, 1887). *Laws of the State of New York Passed at the Session of the Legislature Held in the Years 1789-1796, Vol. 3; 1797-1800, Vol. 4,* (Albany: Weed, Parsons & Co., 1887).
Cooper, J. Fennimore, *Historical Stories of American Pioneer Life,* (Philadelphia: American Book and Bible House, 1897).
Cooper, James F. III, *The Legends and Traditions of a Northern Country,* (New York: G.P. Putman's Sons, Knickerbocker Press, 1921).
Cooper, William, *A Guide in the Wilderness,* (Dublin: Gilbert & Hodges, 1810).
Cray, Robert E., *Lovewell's Fight, War, Death and Memory in Borderland New England,* (Amherst, Boston: University of Massachusetts Press, 2014).
Cruikshank, Ernest, *A Century of Municipal History 1792-1892, County of Welland,* (Welland, OT: Tribune Print 1892).
Crytzer, Bradly J., *Allegheny Burning: George Washington, Daniel Brodhead and the Battle of Thompson Island,* (Journal of the American Revolution, May 12,2015).
DAR, *A Record of the Revolutionary War Soldiers Buried in Lake County, Ohio,* (Columbus, OH: Champlin Press, 1902).
Davidson, Fletcher H., *Delaware County Fur Trading to Farming,* (Delhi, NY: R.B. Decker Advertising, 1976).

De Witt, Simeon, *1st Sheet of De Witt's State Map of New York,* (New York: C. Tiebout & Sculp). *A Map of the Military Lands and Twenty Townships in the Western Part of the State of New York, ca. 1790.* (Digital Collection of Yale University Beinecke Rare Book and Manuscript Library). *A Map of the Headwaters of the Rivers Susquehanna & Delaware, Embracing the Early Patents on the South Side of the Mohawk River,* (Albany: Richard Rease, Lith, 1790).

DeCaire, Ryan, Assistant Professor in the Department of Linguistics and Center for Indigenous Studies at the University of Toronto, (Translation and Correct Spelling of Iroquois Names and Terms).

Dehowähda-dih, *The Cicada and George Washington.* https://www.onondaganation.org

Delaware County Clerks Office, *Book A of the Deeds,* (Delhi, NY: Delaware County Genealogy Website). www.dcnyhistory.org

Delaware Gazette, (Delhi, NY: July 8, 1891).

Denio, Pierre, *The Winding Delaware,* (Equinunk, PA: Equinuck Historical Society, 1999).

Densmore, Lyman W., *The Hartwells of America, A Genealogy of all the Hartwell Families of the United States and Canada,* (Saginaw, MI: Hartwell & Lorenzen, 1956).

DeOreo, Dave, *Cleveland Pioneers Persevered Through the Ague,* (Ideastream Public Media, 2020). www.ideastream.org

Dony, Francis A., *Obituary of Prudence Parks Lakin,* (Plymouth, NY, 1833).

Doyle, William B., *Centennial History of Summit County, Ohio and Representative Citizens,* (Chicago: Biographical Publishing Co., 1908).

Draper, Lyman, ed., *Letters Between Rice Harper and Lyman Draper; Malvina P. Sherwood Essay; Letter from J.F. Harper of North Kortright, N.Y. to Jonas M. Preston, Delhi, N.Y., May 12, 1870; "Balance", Albany, Dec. 10, 1811, Obituary of John Harper.* (Draper Mss.,16 F, 3 Q, Microfilm Edition, State Historical Society of Wisconsin, 1949).

Duerden, Tim, *Frisbee House History,* (Delhi, NY: DCHA), www.dcha-ny.org

Dutch Reformed Church Records of Niskayuna and Schoharie, Book 36. www.ancestry.com

Ecob, Helen G., *Reminiscence of Early Days, Abijah Gilbert 1747-1811, Joseph T. Gilbert 1783-1867,* (Gilbertsville, NY: Helen G. Ecob, 1927).

Eldridge, William H., *Henry Genealogy, The Descendants of Samuel Henry of Hadley and Amherst Massachusetts, 1734-1790,* (Boston: T.R. Marvin & Son, 1915).

Ellet, Elizabeth F., *Pioneer Women of the West,* (New York: Charles Scribner, 1856).

Elliot, Mary Ann T., *Thompson Genealogy, The Descendants of William and Margaret Thompson, First Settlers of That Part of Windsor Connecticut Now East Windsor and Ellington,* (New Haven, CT: Tuttle, Morehouse & Taylor Press, 1915).

Ellis, Edward S., *Outdoor Life and Indian Stories,* (Philadelphia: 1912).

Engel, Carl T., *Lake County Heritage, A Magazine of Local History and Culture, Gen. Edward Paine, Pioneer Settler of Lake County,* www.painesville.com

Evers, Alf, *The Catskills, Fron Wilderness to Woodstock,* (Garden City, NJ: Doubleday & Co., 1972).

Fernow, Berthold, *Documents Related to the Colonial History of the State of New York,* (Albany: Weed, Parsons & Co., 1887).

Find A Grave, *Harpersfield Center Cemetery; Harpersfield Rural (Stevens) Cemetery; Alexander Harper Memorial Cemetery; Geneva Evergreen Cemetery; Conneaut City Cemetery.* www.ancestry.com

Fogg, Jeremiah, *The Journal of Jeremiah Fogg,* (Exeter, NH: The New Letter Press, 1879).

Foote, Joyce, *Morris, New York,* (Sherburne, NY: Mid-York Press, 1986).

Ford, Henry J., *The Scotch-Irish in America,* (Princeton: Princeton University Press, 1915).

Ford, Jane C., *Records of the Harper Family,* (Cleveland: A.C. Rogers Co., 1905).

Fredrikson, John C., *The War of 1812 in Person, Fifteen Accounts by U.S. Regulars, Volunteers and Militiamen,* (Jefferson, NC: McFarland & Co., 2010).

Frost, Robert, *The Gift Outright, The Poetry of Rober Frost,* (Henry Holt & Co., 1969).

Gano, John, *Biographical Memoirs of the Late Reverend John Gano of Frankford, Kentucky,* (New York: Southwick & Hardcastle, 1806).

Gault, F. A., *Dear Old Greene County,* (Catskill, NY: 1915).

Gay, William B., *Historical Gazetteer of Tioga County, New York, 1785-1888,* (Syracuse: W.B. Gay & Co., 1887).

Gibson, Gary M., ed., *New York State Index as of 4 July 1812*, (War of 1812 Magazine, Issue 28, April 2018). www.napoleon-series.org

Godcharles, Federic A., *History of Fort Freeland*, (Williamsport, PA: Lycoming Historical Society, 1922).

Goodenow, Lucy B., *Brett Genealogy*, (Cambridge, MA: Murrey & Emery, 1915).

Goodrich, John E. & Knapp, Chauncey L., ed., *State of Vermont Roll of Soldiers in the Revolutionary War, 1775-1783*, (Rutland, VT: The Tuttle Co., 1904).

Gould, Jay, *History of Delaware County and Border Wars of New York*, (Roxbury, NY: Keeny & Gould, 1856).

Graham, Rebecca, *The Cork Settlement of Merrymeeting Bay*, (www.academia.edu).

Granger, Albert J., *The History of Canandaigua*, (Canandaigua, NY: Ontario Repository and Mesenger, 1876).

Greene, Nelson, ed., History of the Mohawk Valley, Gate to the West 1614-1925, Mohawk Valley Revolutionary Forts 1776-1777, (Chicago: S.J. Clarke Publishing Co., 1925). *The Story of Old Fort Plain and the Middle Mohawk Valley*, (Fort Plain, NY: O'Conner Brothers Publishing, 1915).

Gregory, Grant, *Ancestors and Descendants of Henry Gregory*, (Rutland, VT: Tuttle Publishing Co., 1938).

Griffin, Charles D., *A History of Stamford*, (Stamford, NY: Stamford Historical Society, 1988).

Halsey, Francis W., *The Old New York Frontier*, (New York: Charles Scribner's Sons, 1902).

Hammon, Neal O., ed., *My Father Daniel Boone, The Draper Interviews with Nathan Boone*, (Lexington, KT: University of Kentucky Press, 2012).

Hammond, Jabez D., *The History of Political Parties in the State of New York: from the Ratification of the Federal Constitution to December 1840, Vol.1*, (Cooperstown, NY: H.&E. Phinney, 1846).

Hammond, Luna M., *History of Madison County, State of New York*, (Syracuse: Truair, Smith & Co., 1872).

Hanson, Willis T., *A History of Schenectady During the Revolution*, (Printed Privately, 1916).

Harper, John W. & Harper, Martha B., *The Palatine Migration of 1723 from Schoharie to Tulpehocken*, (Historical Review of Burks County, PA, 1944).

Harper, Josephine L., *Guide to the Draper Manuscripts*, (Madison, WI: Wisconsin Historical Society Press, 1983).

Harper, Rick, ed., *Dependents of James Harper, Research Behind Move from New York to Ohio*, 1798. www.newmediamarket.com

Harpster, Jack & Stalter, Ken, *Captive! The Story of David Ogden and the Iroquois*, (Santa Barbara, CA: Praeger, 2010).

Hastings, Hugh, ed., *Military Minutes of the Council of Appointments of the State of New York, 1783-1821*, (Albany: J.B. Lyon, 1901). *The Public Papers of George Clinton, First Governor of New York*, (Albany: State of New York and the University of New York, 1900-1914).

Hinman, Marjory B. & Hitt, Maurice R., *The Letters and Diaries of William Macclure: Surveyor and Pioneer 1725-1826*, (Binghamton, NY: Broome County Historical Society, 1994).

Historic USGS Maps of New England and New York, (Durham, NH: University of New Hampshire, Dimond Library Documents Dept. and Data Center, 2001).

History of Middlesex County, Mass., Containing Carefully Prepared Histories of Every City and Town in the County, (Boston: Estes & Lauriat, 1880).

Hobart Independent, (Hobart, NY: Aug. 9, 1888).

Hoes, Roswell R., *Baptismal and Marriage Register of the Old Dutch Church of Kingston*, (New York: DeVinne Press, 1891).

Houck, Shirley A., *The Evolution of Delaware County, New York, Being a History of its Land.* (Nashville, TN: Express Media Corp., 1995).

Hough, Franklin B., ed., *New York Civil List Prepared from the Official Records*, (Albany: Weed, Parsons & Co., 1858). *Proceedings of the Commissioners of Indian Affairs, Appointed by Law for the Extermination of Indian Tittles in the State of New York*, (Albany: Joel Munsell,1859).

Howe, Henry, *Historical Collections of Ohio*, (Cincinnati: C.J. Krehbiel & Co., 1907).

Huggins, Benjamin L., ed., *Papers of George Washington, Revolutionary War Series*, (Charlottesville, VA: University of Virginia Press, 2013).

Hurd, Hamilton D., *History of Otsego County, New York, with Illustrations and Biological Sketches of Some of its Prominent Men and Pioneers*, (Philadelphia: Everts & Farris, 1878). *The History of Worchester County, Mass., With Biographical Sketches of Many of the Pioneers and Prominent Men*, (Philadelphia: J.W. Lewis, 1889).

Johnson, Crisfield, *History of Oswego County, New York*, (Philadelphia: H.L. Everts and Co., 1877).
Johnston, Henry P., ed., *Record of Service of Connecticut Men in the War of the Revolution*, (Hartford CT: Adjutant Generals Office, 1889).
Jones, Alfred E., *The Loyalists of New Jersey, Their Memorials, Petitions, Claims, etc. From English Records*, (Boston: Gregg Press, 1972).
Jones, Pomroy, *Annuals and Recollections of Oneida County*, (Rome, NY: Published by Author, A.J. Rowley Printing, 1851).
Journal of New York, *Ratifying Convention, July 25, 1788.*
Journals of the Provincial Congress, Committee of Safety and Council of Safety of the State of New York, (Albany: Thurlow Weed, Printer of the State, 1842).
Judd, Slyvester, *Thomas Judd and His Descendants*, (Northampton, MA: J.&L. Metcalf, 1856).
Kelsay, Isabel T., *Joseph Brant, 1743-1807, Man of Two Worlds*, (Syracuse: Syracuse University Press, 1984).
Kennedy, James H., *A History of the City of Cleveland, its Settlement, Rise and Progress, 1796-1896*, (Cleveland: The Imperial Press, 1896).
Key Figures in Oneida History. www.oneidaindiannation.com
Kingman, Leroy W., ed., *Our Country and its People, A Memorial History of Tioga County, New York*, (Elmire, NY: W.A. Fergusson & Co., 1900).
Kubik, Dorothy, *West Through the Catskills, The Story of the Susquehanna Turnpike*, (Fleischmanns, NY: Purple Mountain Press, 2001).
LaCrosse, Richard B., *Revolutionary Rangers, Daniel Morgan's Riflemen and their Role on the Northern Frontier, 1778-1783*, (Berwyn Heights, MD: Heritage Books, 2019).
Lamb, Martha J. & Harrison, Constance C., *History of the City of New York, Its Origin, Rise and Progress*, (New York: A.S. Barnes & Co., 1896).
Lane, Helen, *The Story of Walton*, (Walton NY: Walton Historical Society, 1976).
Large, Moina W., *History of Ashtabula County, Ohio*, (Topeka-Indianapolis: Historical Publishing Co., 1924).
Laws of the State of New York, Vol.1, (New York: Thomas Greenleaf, 1792). Vol. 4, (Albany: Weed, Parsons & Co., 1887).
Leavy, Peggy D., *Molley Brant, Mohawk Loyalist and Diplomate*, (Toronto: Dundurn Group, 2015).
Leggett, Grace P., Myrtle, Jillson M., ed., *The History and Genealogy of the Patchin-Patchen Family*, (Waterbury, CT: The Patchin-en Family Association, 1952).
Lengel, Edward G., ed., *The Papers of George Washington*, (Charlottesville, NC: University of Virginia Press, 2010).
Lenig, Wayne, *Fort Plain, Fort Plank and Fort Rensselaer, The Revolutionary War Forts at Canajoharie*, (Fort Plain, NY: Fort Plain Museum, 2020).
Leventhal, Norman B., *Map of General Sullivans March from Easton to the Seneca and Cayuga Countries, 1779*, (Map and Education Center, Boston Public Library).
Lewis, Walter, *Dictionary of Canadian Biography, Vol. 6, James Richardson (b-1832)*. www.biographi.ca
Lincoln, Benjamin, *Journal of a Treaty Held in 1793 with the Indian Tribes Northwest of the Ohio by Commissioners of the United States*, (Boston: Massachusetts Historical Society). www.babel.hathitrust.org
Lincoln, Charles H., *A Calander of the Manuscripts of Col. John Bradstreet*, (Worcester, MA: American Antiquarian Society).
Loker, Eric S., & Hofkin, Bruce V., *Parasitology, A Conceptual Approach, Second Edition*, (Boca Raton, FL: CRS Press, Taylor & Francis Group, 2023).
Longyear, Edmund J., *Descendants of Jacob Longyear of Ulster County, New York*, (New Haven, CT: Tuttle, Morehouse & Taylor Co., 1942).
Lossing, Benson L., *The Pictorial Field Book of the War of 1812*, (New York: Harper & Brothers, 1868).
Lupton, David W. & Lupton, Dorothy R., *Lancaster Platt Lupton the Legacy of a Fur Trader, the Road to Delhi*, (Bayboro, NC: Buckhorn Press, 1994).
Mabie, Stephen W. & Smith, Mary T., *Our Heritage*, (San Antonio, TX: San Antonio Genealogical and Historical Society, 2015).
MacDonald, Angus & MacDonald, Archibald, *The Clan Donald*, (Inverness, Scotland: Northern Counties Publishing Co., 1904).

MacDougall, Hugh, *Sheriffs of Otsego County from 1791 to Present,* Otsego Office of the Sheriff.
MacKenzie, George N., *Colonial Families of the USA, 1607-1775*, (New York, Boston: Grafton Press, 1907).
MacLaury, Evangeline, *Those Rugged Hills and Green Valleys,* (Harpersfield, NY: 1987).
Malcomson, Robert, *The A to Z of the War of 1812, The A to Z Series, No.55*, (Lanham, Toronto, Plymouth, UK: The Scarecrow Press, 2009).
Manual of the First Congregational Church of Hopkinton. Mass., With Historical Sketches, *1724-1881*, (Boston: Alfred Mudge & Sons, 1881).
Marlatt, C.L., *The Periodical Cicada, U.S. Department of Agriculture Bureau of Entomology,* (Washington, DC: Government Printing Office, 1907).
Mattern, David B., *Benjamin Lincoln and the American Revolution,* (Columbia, SC: University of South Carolina Press, 1995).
Maxson, Dan, *Unionville: The Tiny Town That Time Forgot,* (Local Lore by Max, News-Herald Community Media Lab, 2010-2016). www.lakehistorycenter.org
McCullogh, A.B., *Currency Conversion in British North America, 1760-1900*, (1983). www.archivaria.ca
McLennan, William, *Spanish John,* (London: Harper & Brothers, 1898).
Meany, Joseph F., *Bateaux and Battoe Men, An American Colonial Response to the Problem of Logistics in Mountain Warfare.,* www.museum.dmna.ny.gov
Miller, John L., *Pioneer Homesteaders of the Western Catskills*, (Delhi, NY: Delaware County Historical Association, 2021).
Mohawk Valley Maps and Sketches, www.fort-plank.com
Mollo, John & McGregor, Malcolm, *Uniforms of the American Revolution in Color,* (New York: MacMillan Pub. Co., 1975).
Monroe, John D., *Chapters in the History of Delaware County New York*, (Delhi, NY: Delaware County Historical Association, 1949).
Montgomery, William J., *A Montgomery Family Genealogy, William and Mary, Robert and Mary, 2020.* www.wjmontgomerygenealogy.com
Morrison, Leonard A., *The History of Windham in New Hampshire, Rockingham County 1719-1883,* (Boston: Cupples, Upham & Co., 1883).
Munsell, W.W., *History of Delaware County, New York,* (New York: W.W. Munsell & Co., 1880).
Murray, David, ed., *Delaware County New York History of the Century Centennial Celebration,* (Delhi, NY: William Clark Publisher, 1898).
Mutrie, Robert R., ed., *The Niagara Settler Township Papers, Berti Settlers, P-R; Soldiers and Supporters, P; Niagara Settlers Land Records Township of Berti Settlers, P.* www.site.google.com/site/niagarasettlers
National Archives Catalog, *List of Officers and Men of Col. Elisha Sheldon, Col. Stephen Moylan and Major Henry Lee's Legion of Dragoons 1776-1781,* (Record Group 93: M853: Roll 16: Target 4: Vol.11).
National Archives Founders Online, www.founders.archives.gov
National Archives Microfilm Publications, *Revolutionary War Rolls 1775-1783.*
New Horizons Genealogy, *New York State Federal and State Census of Electors Map 1800.* www.newhorizonsgenealogicalservices.com
New York County Maps: *Interactive History and Complete List.* www.mapofus.org
New York Genealogical and Biographical Record, Vol. 53, (New York: NYGBS, Jan. 1922).
New York Historical Society.
New York in the Revolution as Colony and State, (Albany: J.B. Lyon Co., 1904).
New York State Archives Map Collection.
New York State Road Atlas, (Round Lake, NY: Jimapco, 2015).
New York State Wills and Probate. www.ancestry.com
North Arthur W., *The First Grandmother of Walton,* (Walton, NY: Walton Historical Society, 1926). *The Founders and the Founding of Walton New York*, (Walton, NY: Walton Historical Society, 1924).
North S.N.D., ed., *First Census of the United States, 1790,* New York Dept. of Commerce and Labor, Bureau of the Census, (Washington, DC: Government Printing Office, 1908). www.babel.hathitrust.org
O'Callaghan, E.B., ed., *The Documentary History of the State of New York, Vol. 1,* (Albany: Weed, Parsons & Co., 1849).

O'Conner, Jeff, *Thunder in the Valley*, (Cobleskill, NY: Times-Journal, 2002).
O'Toole, Fintan, *White Savage, William Johnson and the Invention of America*, (Albany: State University of New York Press, 2005).
Occom Circle, *Theophilus Chamberlain to Eleazer Wheelock Letter, July 29,1765; Kind Brothers Letter, Isaac and Good Peter to Rev. Wheeler, Onaquaga, Nov. 12, 1764*, (John Harper Interpreter). www.library.dartmouth.edu
Occom, Samson, *Journal, April 6th, 1787*. www.library.dartmouth.edu
Ohio Adjutant General's Office, *Roster of Ohio Soldiers in the War of 1812*, (Columbus, OH: Edward T. Miller Co.,1916).
Ohio Tax Records 1800-1850, *Ashtabula County, Vol. 71*, (Geneva, Harpersfield,1828). www.familysearch.org
Otis, James, *The Story of Pemaquid*, (New York: T.Y. Crowell & Co., 1902).
Oxford Review-Times, May 15, 1931, *Tobias Houk of North Gilford, New York*.
Paine, Henry D., ed., *Paine Family Records, A Journal of Genealogy and Biographical Information Respecting the American Families of Payne, Paine, Payn,* (Albany: J. Munsell, 1880).
Parker, Arlita D., *A History of Pemaquid*, (Boston: MacDonald & Evens, 1925).
Parker, Edward L., *History of Londonderry, New Hampshire, Comprising the Towns of Derry and Londonderry*, (Boston: Perkins & Whipple, 1851).
Parkman, Francis, *Montcalm and Wolfe, France and England in North America*, (Boston: Little, Brown & Co., 1898).
Pease, Seth, *Journals of Seth Pease to and from New Connecticut, 1796-1798*, (Cleveland: Western Reserve Historical Society Annual Report, Part 2, 1913-1914).
Peckham, Mark L., *Early History of Bateaux*, (Albany: State University of New York Press, 2019). www.sunypress.edu
Pelton, J.M., *Genealogy of the Pelton Family in America*, (Albany: Joel Munsell's Sons, 1892).
Pennant, Thomas, *A Tour of Scotland,1769*, (London: Benjamin White at Horace's Head, 1772).
Pine, Mary, *Early Settlement of Walton, Delaware Co., NY,* (Walton, NY: Walton Historical Society, 2015).
Porter, Peter, *A Brief History of Old Fort Niagara*, (Niagara: 1896).
Posey, John T., *General Thomas Posey, Son of the American Revolution*, (Michigan: Michigan University Press, 1993).
Pound, Arthur, *Johnson of the Mohawk, A Biography of Sir William Johnson, Irish Immigrant, Mohawk War Chief, American Soldier, Empire Builder,* (New York: The MacMillian Co., 1930).
Priest, Josiah, *The Deeply Interesting Story of Gen. Freegift Patchin: Stolen when a Lad by Brant and his Indians*, (Lansingburgh, NY: W. Harkness, 1840)
Prins, Harold L., *The Crooked Path of Dummer's Treaty, Anglo-Wabanaki Diplomacy and the Quest for Aboriginal Rights, Papers of the Algonquian Conference,* (Winnipeg: University of Manitoba Press, 2002).
Public Archives, *Memorial Applications of the American Loyalists Claims Commission, 1776-1835,* (Ottawa, Canada).
Quinlan, James E. & Antisell, Thomas, *The History of Sullivan County, New York*, (Liberty, NY: G.M. Beebe & W.T. Morgan, 1873).
Raitt, John E., *Ruts in the Road*, (Delhi, NY: 1982).
Ranzan, David A., Hollis, Matthew J., ed., *Hero of Fort Schuyler, Selected Revolutionary War Correspondence of Brigadier General Peter Gansevoort Jr.*, (Jefferson, NC: McFarland & Co., 2014).
Ray, John W., *A History of Western Pennsylvania*, (Erie, PA: by Author, 1941).
Reid, Max W., *Ye History of St. Ann's Church in Ye City of Amsterdam, New York*.
Reid, William D., *The Loyalists in Ontario, The Sons and Daughters of the American Loyalists in Upper Canada*, (Lambertville, NJ: Hunterdon House, Genealogical Publishing Co., 1973).
Revolutionary War Pension and Bounty Land Warrant Applications. www.ancestry.com
Rice, Harvey, *Pioneers of the Western Reserve*, (Boston: Lee & Shepard, New York: Charles D. Dillingham, 1883).
Richardson, James B., *The Destruction of Hanna's Town*, www.journals.psu.edu
Robinson, Charles M. & Porter, Augustus, *Narratives and Journals of Pioneer Surveyors of Western New York and Adjacent Tracts in Pennsylvania and Ohio,* (Buffalo: Buffalo Historical Society, 1904).

Roscoe, William E., *History of Schoharie County, New York, 1713-1882*, (Syracuse: Mason & Co., 1882).
Roswell, Randell & Hoe, ed., *Baptismal and Marriage Register of the Old Dutch Church of Kingston, Ulster County, New York, 1660-1809*, (Baltimore: Genealogical Publishing Co., 1980).
Ruttenber, E.M. & Clark, L.H., *History of Orange County New York*, (Philadelphia: Everts & Peck, 1881).
Ryther, Warren, *The Morris Manor Farm, A History and a Memoire*, 2015. www.ourtownnews
Sawyer, John, *History of Cherry Valley From 1740-1898*, (Cherry Valley, NY: Gazette Printers, 1898).
Schuyler, George W., *Colonial New York, Philip Schuyler and His Family*, (New York: Charles Scribner's Sons, 1885).
Scott, William L., *The MacDonells of Leek, Collachie and Aberchalder, MacDonells on the Pearl in 1773, a New Perspective*, (The Clan Donald Society of Scotland). www.clandonald.org
Scudder, William, *The Journals of Lt. William Scudder an Officer in the Late New York Line*, Reprint as, *The Narrative of North America Indian Captives*, Vol. 18, (New York: Garland Publishing, 1977).
Shaw, Samuel & Arnold, Isaac, *A Centennial Offering; Being a Brief History of Cooperstown with a Biographical Sketch of James F. Cooper*, (Cooperstown, NY: Freemans Journal, 1886).
Shepard, Claude L., *The Connecticut Land Company and Accompanying Papers*, (Cleveland: Western Reserve Historical Society, 1916).
Shupe, Barbara & Stein, Janet & Pandit, Jyoti, ed., *New York State Population, 1790-1980: A Compilation of Federal Census Data*, (London, New York: Neal-Schuman Publishing, 1987).
Simms, Jeptha R., *History of Schoharie County and Border Wars of New York*, (Albany: Munsell & Tanner Printing, 1845). *The Frontiersmen of New York, Vol. 1, Vol. 2*, (Albany: George C. Riggs, 1882, 1883).
Sivertsen, Barbara F. & Covey, Barbara L., *The Legend of Cushetunk, The Nathan Skinner Manuscript and the Early History of Cochecton*, (Westminster, MD: Heritage Books, 2011).
Smith, Harry P., *History of Broome County New York*, (Syracuse: D. Mason & Co., 1885).
Smith, James, *History of Chenango and Madison Counties, New York*, (Syracuse: D. Mason & Co., 1880).
Smith, Richard & Halsey, Francis W., ed., *A Tour of Four Great Rivers; The Hudson, Mohawk, Susquehanna, and Delaware in 1769; Being the Journal of Richard Smith of Burlington, New Jersey*, (New York: Charles Scribner's Sons, 1906).
Snow, Dean, *Continental and Militia Cavalry Compared*, (Journal of the American Revolution, Aug. 31, 2021).
Spooner, Walter W., ed., *The Rensselaer Papers*, (American Historical Magazine, Jan. 1907).
St. Clair, Arthur, *A Narrative of the Manner in Which the Campaign Against the Indians in the Year 1791 was Conducted Under the Command of Maj. Gen. St. Clair*, (Philadelphia: Jane Atkins, 1812).
Stevens, John A., ed., *Colonial Records of the New York Chamber of Commerce*, (New York: John F. Trow & Co. 1867).
Stiles, Henry R., *The History and Genealogy of Ancient Windsor, Connecticut, 1635-1891, Vol. 2*, (Hartford CT: Case, Lockwood, Brainard & Co., 1892). *The History of Ancient Windsor, Connecticut*, (New York: Charles B. Norton, 1859).
Stockton, Thomas C., *The Stockton Family of New Jersey and other Stocktons*, (Washington, DC: The Carnahan Press, 1911).
Stone, William L., *Life of Joseph Brant (Thayendanegea), Including the Border War of the American Revolution*, (Albany: J. Munsell, 1865). *The Life of Joseph Brant, Thayendanegea*, (Cooperstown, NY: H.& E. Phinney, 1844).
Sullivan, James, ed., *The Papers of Sir William Johnson*, (Albany: The University of the State of New York, Division of Archives and History, 1921).
Sumner, William W., *A History of East Boston*, (Boston: J.E. Tilton & Co., 1858).
Swiggett, Howard, *War Out of Niagara*, (Port Washington, NY: Ira J. Friedman, 1963).
Swinnerton, Henry, *The Story of Cherry Valley*, (Cherry Valley, NY: 1908).
Sylvester, Nathaniel B. & Hasbrouck, Jonathan W., *History of Ulster County New York, With Illustrations and Biographical Sketches of its Prominent Men and Pioneers*, (Philadelphia: Evert & Peck, 1880).
Taylor, Alan, *American Colonies, The Settling of North America*, (New York: Penguin Books, 2001).
The Divided Ground, (New York: Vintage Books, 2006). *William Cooper's Town, Power and Persuasion on the Frontier of the Early American Republic*, (New York: Vintage Books, 1995).
The 1785 New York Fort Herkimer Treaty with the Oneida. www.academic.edu
Thomson, John, *Ireland, Thomson's New General Atlas*, (London: Cradock & Joy, 1815).

Thorndale, William & Dollarhide, William, *Map Guide to the U.S. Federal Censuses, 1790-1920*, (Baltimore: Genealogical Publishing, 1987).
To Reject H.R. 184, *To Declare War with Great Britian*, www.govtrack.us
Trumbull Probate Records, *Vol.1-3, 1803-1825*. www.ancestry.com
Tunnicliff, Zoe H., *Tunnicliff Genealogy*, (Albany: Private Printing, 1965).
Turner, Orsamus, *Pioneer History of the Holland Purchase of Western New York,* (Buffalo: Jewett, Thomas & Co., 1850).
U.S. Federal Census Collection. www.ancestry.com
Upton, Harriet T., *History of the Western Reserve*, (Chicago, New York: Lewis Publishing Co., 1910).
Vital Records of Hopkinton, Mass. to the Year 1850, (Boston: New England Historical Genealogical Society, 1911).
Vital Records of Oakham, Mass. to the End of the Year 1849, (Worcester, MA: F.P. Rice, 1905).
Volwiler, A.T., *George Croghan and the Development of Central New York, 1763-1800*, The Quarterly Journal of the New York State Historical Association, Vol. 4, (Cooperstown, NY: Fenimore Art Museum, 1923),
Wallach, Ira D. & Wallach, Miriam, *Colonel John Johnson*, (Division of Art and Photographs: Print Collection, New York Public Library Digital Collection). www.digitalcollection.nypl.org
Walton Journal, 1857, *Walton the Early Years*, (Walton, NY: Walton Historical Society, 2009).
Walton, William, *The Captivity and Suffering of Benjamin Gilbert and His Family,* (Cleveland: Burrows Brothers Co., 1904).
Warner, Geroge H., *Military Records of Schoharie County Veterans of Four Wars*, (Albany: Weed, Parsons & Co.,1891).
Watt, Gavin K., *Rebellion in the Mohawk Valley, The St. Leger Expedition of 1777*, (Toronto, Oxford: The Dundurn Group, 2002). *Continental Dragoons in the Schoharie Valley*, (Journal of the American Revolution, Aug. 12, 2013).
Wheeler, George A. & Wheeler, Henry W., *History of Brunswick, Topsham and Harpswell Maine, Including the Ancient Territory Known as Pejepscot*, (Boston: A. Mudge & Sons, 1878).
Whittlesey, Charles, *The Early History of Cleveland, Ohio,* (Cleveland: Fairbanks and Benedict Co., 1867). www.pressbooks.ulib.csuohio.edu
Willey, Ruth, *Gibbs Genealogy*, (Whittier, CA: R.&L. Letter Shop,1967).
Williams Brothers, *History of Ashtabula County, Ohio,* (Philadelphia: J.B. Lippincott & Co., 1878).
Williams, Edward G., *The Prévosts of the Royal Americans,* (The Western Pennsylvania Historical Magazine, Vol. 56, No. 1, January 1973).
Williamson, William D., *The History of the State of Maine*, (Hallowell, ME: Glazier, Masters & Co., 1839).
Wright, H.B. & **Harvey E.D.**, *The Settlement and Story of Oakham, Mass.*, (New Haven, CT: Earnest L. Harward, 1947).
Wright, Henry B., *Soldiers of Oakham, Mass. in the Revolution, the War of 1812, and the Civil War*, (New Haven: Tuttle, Morehouse & Taylor Press, 1914).
Writings of George Washington, (Washington, DC: Government Printing Office, 1931).

Index

Ackerly, Benjamin, 137
Adaquatingie, (Oneonta), 143
Adams, John, 161
Adams, Robert, 158,159
Adaquataugie, (Charlotte Creek), 31,32,39,40-44,48,143
Adgate, Matthew, 154
Adiga, (Otego), 143,144
Adirondacks, 117
Adonwentishon, Catherine, 97
Ahwaga, (Owego), 88
Akiatonharankwen, Lt. Col. Louis Cook, 109,110,116,117,157
Aksiaktatye, Capt. Jacob Reed, 153
Albany, 31,36-39,47,50,52,53,56-58,62,66,76,79,95,102,104107,111,113,118,121,123, 140,146,149,161-163,166,167,170,173,193
Albout, 72
Alden, Col. Ichabod, 74,75,79,81,144
Amherstburg, ON, Canada, 177,178
Amherst, Field Mar. Jeffrey, 23,24
Amsterdam, NY, 100,116
Anderson, George, 69
André, Maj. John, 104
Andrustown, NY, 31,67,121
Anglo/Abenaki War, 4th, 7-11,13,14, 43,206
Anglo/Abenaki War, 3rd, 9
Anti-Federalists, 149,162,167,169-171
Army of the Northern Department, 94,95
Army of the Northwest, 199, 200
Arnold, Gen. Benedict, 103-105,109,51-53,78,103-105,109,145,171,172
Ashtabula County, OH, 189,195,197-201,204
Augusta, Dowager Princess of Wales, 145
Aurelius, Marcus, 111
Auriesville, NY, 107
Austin, Jacob, Joel, 137

Babington Patent, 164
Baldwin, Daniel, 195
Balls Town (Ballston Spa), 105-107
Bainbridge, Village of, 44,72,165
Banyar, Goldsborough, 37,159
Barclay, Rev. Henry, 126
Barclay Patent, 126
Barclay, Robert, 200
Barnard, John, 186
Barr, Ens. John, 87
Barrows, John, 38,68,137
Bartholomew, Benjamin & Abigail Patchin, 119,124,128,143,195,199,202
    Daniel & Abraham, 194,195
    Fifer, Benjamin Jr, 199
    Cpl. Daniel, 199
    Hannah, Stevens, Skinner, 96,128,143,195
    Isaac, 195,199,202
    Johan & Dorothy, 39,40,42,143
    Capt. Jacob, 199,200
    John, Joseph, Peter, 199
    Lt. Joseph, 95,128,143,195,199,200
    Samuel, Abraham, John, 200,201
    Susanna, 201,204
    Tewalt, 119,128,143,195,199
    Theophilus, Samuel, Isaac, 128
Bartholomew Settlement, 39,42,43,55,56,128,143
Basset, Pvt. Edward, 60
Bates, Lt. Col. David, 172,202
Battle of Carillon, 23
Battle of Cobleskill, 64-66
Battle of Fallen Timbers, 178,179
Battle of the Flockey, 54-61,75,94,118,119,127,172
Battle of Johnstown, 115-119,135
Battle of Klock's Field, 109,111,118,124,157,194
Battle of Lake George, 20-23,146
Battle of Lake Utsayantha, 118-119
Battle of Long Island, 45,128
Battle at Minisink Ford, 83-85,135
Battle of Monmouth, 65
Battle of Newtown, 89-91,118
Battle of Oriskany, 49-54,76,109,121
Battle of Saratoga, 53,60-64,53
Battle of Stone Arabia, 107-111,113,118,135
Battle of Stony Point, 86
Battle of the Thames, 200,201
Battle of Velletri, 54
Battle of White Plains, 128
Battle of Yorktown, 115
Beacraft, (The Tory), 103
Beard, Abijah, 129
Beaver Dam Patent, 18,20,21,25,42,123
Becker, Johannas, (Stone House), 57,59
Becker, Lodowick, Philip, 128,143
Bedford Crossing, Long Island, NY, 133
Bellinger, Col. Peter, 50,59,61
Bemus, Samuel & Sarah, 193
Bennet, Daniel & Abijah, 41,131
Ben Shanks, Lt., 69,70,115,136,138
Bernhardt, George, 137
Berry, Maria, 41
Bertie, Welland Co. ON, Canada, 188
Binghamton, NY, 87,88
Black Creek, 117
Bloody Morning Scout, 22
Blue Jacket, 176-178
Boone, Daniel, 17
Boston, 3-6, 9-15,45,123,160
Bouck, William, 101-103,114
Bowker, Daniel, Silas, 136
Boyd, Lt. Thomas, 91-93,106
Boyd, Rev. William, 5
Braddock, Maj. Gen. Edward, 21
Bradford, Cornelius & Catherine, 159
Bradstreet, Col. John, 35-38,40,134,135,154
    Samuel, 37

Bradstreet, Purchase, 35-38,133,154,174
Bradt, Arendt, Patent, 41,44
Brant, Capt. Joseph, 22,24,45-50,54,64-72,74-79,83-92,96-99,102-108,113-115,118,120,124,127,131,135,138,144,147,150-153,176,177,181,188
    Molly, 22,127
Breakabeen, 54,56,57,119
Brett, Dr. Joshua & Anna Dunbar, 163-165,168,174,196,206
    William, Isaac, Joshua Jr, 196
Brickman, Capt. Lodowick, 128,143,196
Bristol, Richard & Candice Gibbs, 129
Brock, Maj. Gen. Issac, 199
Brodhead, Lt. Col. Daniel, 82,83,88,92
Brown, Capt. Christian, 65
Brown, David, 41,96,97
    John, Doctor, Solomon, 96
Brown, Col. John, 108-111
Brown, Capt. John M., 168,169,173,169,173
Buckaloon, 88
Buffalo Creek, 181,186,190,194,195
Buffalo Conference, 177,181
Burch, John, 137
Burgh, James, 203
Burgher, Peter & Margaret, 38,137
Burgoyne, Gen., John, 47,49,52,53,61,62,78,99,115
Burlington Company, 141
Burr, Aaron, 141,158,160,170
Butler, Maj., Col. John, 36,45-50, 66-70,74,77,84-92,97,104,113,115,121,129,135,139,144-146,178,188
Butler, Richard, 176
Butler, Capt. Walter, 45-50,66,74-77, 89,104,115-118,121
Butler, Lt. Col. William, 65-69,71-81,83,84,96,131
Butler, Col. Zebulon, 67,139
Butterfield, Capt. James, 169-172
Butternuts Creek, 41,102,162,163,144,146,202

Caesar, Julius, 203
Caldwell, Capt. William, 70,71,74,75,114,115,178
Callicoon, 138
Campbell, Capt., Col. Samuel & Jane Cannon, 21,56,65,76,77,121,122,139,140
    James, 18,76,121,139
    Matthew, 76,121,122
    John, 121,122,139
    Eleanor, 76,121
    Robert, 121
Canadarago Lake, (Schuyler Lake), 140-142,146,162
Canadesaga, (Geneva), 84,85,194
Canandaigua, (Kannandaguah), 91,177,181-183,186,194,195
Canajoharie, 19,20,24,46,50,53, 70,76,82,83,99,102,107,108,110,113,122,141,146, 162,166,186,189
Canawaugus, (Avon), 194
Canniskutty Line, 34, 36, 37,133

Cannon, Benjamin, 135
Cannon, James & Andrew, 139,168,171
Canoe Place, 143
Canowaroghare, (Oneida Castle), 110
Cantine, Col. John, 68,69
Carlton, Maj. Christopher, 105,106
Caroga Creek, 117
Carr, John, 48
Carr, Sergt. Percifer, 71,147,163
Cartwright, John, 188
Casco Bay, ME, 6-13,43
Castle William, 165
Catherine's Town, (Queanettquaga), 90
Catskill, Village of, 44
Caughnawaga, (Fonda, NY), 70,101,107,161
Cayuga, 30,45,70,74,89,90,100,104,150,152,157 175
Cayuga Lake, 90,92,157,194
Cayuga Reservation, 157
Cazenovia, 116,194
Census, 1790 Federal, 161-167
Chagrin River, 183
Chamblee, (Chambly), QC, Canada, 97
Charlotte Creek Patent, 31,32,39,40,38,54,55,131
Charleston, 69,99,103,115,158
Chemung Census District, 161,162,166
Chemung River, 83,84,88-90
Chemung, Village of, 84,89
Chenango Census District, 161,162,166
Chenango County, 157
Chenango River, 88,116,150,154,158,162
Chenango, Town of, 155,157
Cherry Valley, NY, 18-25,48,50,55,56,64,65,71,78-82,85,86,97,99,111-114,117,121-125,139-142,144,162,166-169,172,173,175,186,188,193,194,202,207
Cherry Valley Massacre, 74-77,118,172,186
Chippawa Landing, 181,188
Choconut, 88
Church, Col. Timothy, 165
Cicada, Periodical, 94
Clark, Ephraim, 186,187
Clark, Gen. George Rogers, 176
Clark, Capt. Samuel, 70,136
Clarke, Lt. Gov. George, 18
Claus, Daniel & Nancy Johnson, 73,94,100,125,206
Claverack Manor, 111
Cleaveland, Gen. Moses, 180-182,197
Cleveland, OH, 176-179,183,192,196,203
Clinton, Brig. Gen., Gov. George, 46,69,73,77-83,89,94,101,108,110.118,122,123,144,149-162,165,166-173,175,176,179
Clinton, Gen. Henry, 62
Clinton, Maj. Gen. James, 78-94,122,143,146,156
Clyde, Lt., Col., Sheriff, Samuel, 56,76,110,121,139,141
Cobleskill, NY, 64,65,66,113,114,162
Cochecton, NY, 83
Cockburn, William, 37
Coke-ose, (Cookhouse), 30,36,41,83,84,97,135,165

251

Col. Alexander Harper Memorial Cemetery, 206
Collier, Isaac & Peter, 140,162
Colliersville, NY, 47,87,140,162
Commissioners of Forfeiture, 132
Committee of Safety, 45,46,54,55,62,64
Committee of Sequestration, 32,148
Condawhaw, 90
Conesus Lake, 91
Conewago, 88
Conklin, William, 139
Conley, John, 60
Conneaut, OH, 191,195,199,206
    City Cemetery, 206
    Creek, 181-183,194,195
Connecticut Land Company, 180-182,184,185,189,197,198,203
Connecticut Royal Charter, 123,138,179
Conotocaurious, 78
Cooper, James Fenimore, 23,174
Cooperstown, 82,142,168,169,174
Cooper, William, 141,142,147,158,162-174,185,203
Cooquago, (West Branch of Delaware River), 135
Cornbury, Gov. Edward, 35
Cornelius Ogeanyola, 153
Cornelious Ojistalak, 154
Cornelius Statshete, 153
Cornplanter, 89,104,108,152
Cornwallis, Lord Charles, 103,113,115,118,119
Council of Appointments, NY, 94,150,166-168,170,172,202
Cowles, Adna & Mary Harper, 185,200
Cowley, St. Leger, 41,72,83,88,94,101,131
Cox, Col. Ebenezer, 50,52,76,121
Craig, Andrew, 141,142
Croghan, George, 32,36,37,140,141,158
Croghan Patent, 140,141,169
Crown Point, 21-23,100,122,146
Cruger, John, 132
Crysler, Lt. Adam, 54,56,59,60,67,118-120
    Anna Marie, 118
Cuddebackville, 84
Cully, David & Abigail Moore, 97,140,186,188,205
    Matthew Sr, David, Matthew Jr, John, 140,171,172
    Thomas, Ens.,140,143,146,172
    Lt. Col. Matthew Jr & Mary Moore, 97,140,172,186,188,202,205
Cummings, Capt. John, 91,92
Cunnahunta, (Afton), 73,78,87
Cunningham Creek, (Arcola), 188,189,195,204
Currytown, 113,114,116
Cushetunk, 83,138,139,175
Cuyahoga River, 176,178-185,187,192,195-197,200,203
Cuyler, Henry, 158

Dakayenensere, Isaac, 24,33
Davidson, Patrick, 18,20
Day-Lewis, Daniel, 23
Dickerson City, 134,135,165

Dickerson, Jesse, 134,135
Dickson, William & Elizabeth Campbell 19,20,75,139
    Samuel, 75,172
Dingmans, 48
DeLancey, James, 133
Delaware Company, 138
Delaware County, NY, 31,123,173,174,201,207
Delhi, Village of, 73,132,164,174,202
Dem/Rep Party, 167,168,171,173,201
Denio, Joseph & William, 132
Deposit, Village of, 30,36,41,84,135
Desbrosses, Elias, 132
De Dieskan, Gen. Baron, 22
De Vernejoux, Capt. Jean Louis, 58-60
De Villar, Louis, 146,163
De Witt, Simeon, 146,148,159
Deyo, Johannis, 38
Docksteder, Lt. Johannas, 114,115,138
Dorlach, (Sharon Springs), 113-114
Douglas, James & Elizabeth, 42
    James Jr, 42
Downsville, Village of, 31,37,70,136
Drake, Capt. Joshua, 110
Duanesburg Road, 57,58,193
Dubois, Col. Lewis, 64,82,108
Dumond, Hermanus, 68,69,96,137,203
    Igenas & Catherine Schuyler, 38,137
    Petrus, John, 38,137
Du Mont, Wallerand, 38
Dunbar, Col. David, 14
Dunbar, Thomas & Ruth Harper, 196,199,205
Dunlop, Rev. Samuel, & Elizabeth Gault, 18,19,43,75,121,139,140

East Branch of the Delaware, 135-138,174
Easton, PA, 81,85-88,92,138
East Windsor, CT, 13-17, 25,74,124,164
Edick, Conrad, 135
Edmeston, Capt. William, 146,147
    Lt. Robert, 146,147
Edmeston Patents, 147
Elk Creek, PA, 191,192
Ellerson, David, 66
Elliott, Capt. Matthew, 177,178
Ells, James & Polly Harper, 205,206
Elmira, NY, 92
English, Thomas Dunn, 61
Equinunk Island, 139
Esopus Creek, 38,44,137,138
Esopus/Jericho Turnpike, 44
Esopus War, 2nd, 38
Evans, Charles J., 37,134
Evans Patent, 134
Excess Lands, 197,198

Fanning, Col., Edmund, 62-64,137
Farmers Brother, 181
Farrington, Thomas, 132

Lt. Col. Putnum, 202
Feck, Johannas, 61,101
Federalists, 149,162-165,167,169,170-174,185,201,202
Ferguson, James, 6,13
Ferris, Samuel, 40
Firelands Tract, 180,197
Fish Carrier, 89
Fisher & Norton Patent, 135
Flint, Royal W., 157
Foote, Ebenezer, 174
Forbidden Path, 89,92,97
Fort Alden, 75,76
Fort Ann, 105,107
Fort Brewerton, 187
Fort Clinton, 62,64,138
Fort Dayton, 46,50,52,71,113
Fort Detroit, 113,118,131,177,178,199,200
    Treaty Conference of '93, 176-179
Fort Edward, 22,23,53
Fort Erie, 178,180,188,190
Fort Finney Treaty of '86, 176
Fort Frederick, 21,22
Fort Freeland, 85,191
Fort George, ME, 9,10,13
Fort George, (New York), 105
Fort Greenville, 178
    Property Line of '95, 178-181
Fort Haldimand, 117,118
Fort Harmer Treaty of '89, 176
Fort Herkimer, 46,71,110,113,117,150
    Treaty of '85, 153-156,158,159,175
Fort Hunter, 46,107,108,114,116,122,125,126,144
Fort Industry, 197
Fort Jefferson, 178
Fort Johnson, 19,46,73,100,116,125
Fort La Boeuf Portage, 191
Fort Lackawack, 61,69,70,114
Fort McIntosh Treaty of '85, 176
Fort Meigs, 200
Fort Miami, 178
Fort Michilimackinac, 178
Fort Minisink, 61
Fort Montgomery, 62,64,138
Fort Niagara, 21,45,69,75,77,82,85,91-93,96,97,99,103,104,112,113,115,117,118,120,121,124,131,140,150,177,180,185,186,188,191
Fort Ontario, 29
    Treaty of '66, 29
Fort Oswego, 1,23,47,49,52,55,60,62,104,110,112,115-118,120,124,180,187
Fort Paris, 46,108
Fort Pitt, 82,88,92
Fort Plain, 46,108-112,114,116,121,186
Fort Recovery, 178
Fort Rensselaer,111
Fort Schuyler, 46,47,49-56,61,79,80,92,97,100,102,104,110-113,116,153,154,194

Treaty of '88, 157,158
Fort Stanwix, 29,33,46,150,177,180,181,186,187
    Treaty of '68, 30,31,144
    Treaty of '84, 150-153,157,175,176
Fort Stevenson, 200
Fort Shandaken, 67,68
Fort Sullivan, 88,93,97
Fort Ticonderoga, 23,122
Fort Washington, 178
Fort William Henry, 23
Forty Fort, 67
Franchot, 146
Franklin, Benjamin, 35
    Patent, (Meredith Patent), 35
    William, 35
Fraser, William, 132
French and Indian War, 20,23-25,28-36,54,121,125,138,140,144,146,175
Frenchman's Creek, 188
Frisbee, Gideon, 132,164,174
Frost, Robert, 2
Furlow, Cornelius, 138
Fultonham, 54,59,61,119
Furman, William, 133,136,137

Ganniwissey, (Trout Creek), 134
Gano, Rev. John, 90
Gansevoort, Col. Peter, 49-52,79,82,87,92,97,112,168
Gates, Gen. Horatio, 51-53,58,62,78,79,103
Gathchegwarohare, Village of, 88,91,92,106
Gault, William Sr & Elizabeth Dickson, 19,75
    William Jr & Margaret Harper,
    15,19,20,34,65,74,139,140
    William III,139,140
    John, James, Joseph, Matthew, Alexander, 140
    Miriam Gault Church, 140
Gaylord, Pvt. Elihu, 200
    Jedediah, 128
    Joel & Achsah Gibbs, 129
    Levi Jr, 128,173,196,200
    Levi Sr, 128
Genesee River, 82,88,90-92,97,156,162,194
Geneva, NY, 90
Geneva, OH, 195,197,199,206
Geneva Evergreen Cemetery, 206
Geneva-on-the-Lake, 188
George, (The Ship), 40
German Flatts, 17,19,23,46,49,52,53,70,71,83,99,110,113,140,147,166 150,153,161,186
Gibbs, Deacon Caleb, 128,129
Gilchrist, William, 187
Gilbert, Abijah, 146,162,163
Gilbert, Sheriff Benjamin, 170,172
Gilbertsville, NY, 144
Giles, Jacob, 203
Giles, Capt. John, 9-13

Gleason, J., 186,187,189,206
Good Peter (Gwedethes Akwirondongwas), 24,33,154
Gorham, Nathaniel, 156
Goshen, NY, 84,138
Gosline, Richard, 134
Gould Brother's Tavern, 186
Graham, Lt. John, 70,115
Graham, Col. Morris, 105
Grand River, OH, 183,185,189,192,194,196,198
Granger, Gideon, 184
Grant Families, 40
Grasshopper, (Cornelius Ojistalak),
Great Genesee Road, 194
Great Pumpkin Flood of '86, 134,135
Great Sacandaga Lake, 100
Great Shandaken, 38,63,64,137,138
Great Warrior Path, 85,86
Great Western Turnpike, (NY, Rt. 20), 193
Greene, Gen. Nathaniel, 145
Gregory, Ezra & Rebecca Hopkins, 185,189-191,200
    Pvt. Daniel, 185,200
    Anna, Jonathan, Eli, Eleanor, Elizabeth, Ezra Jr, 185
Gregory, Russell, Timothy, Thomas, 136
Criswold, Edward, 168

Hagedorn, Hendrick, Bartholomew, 128,143,196
Hager, Capt. Jacob, 57,101-105,119
Hale, Capt. Aaron, 119
Hamilton, Alexander, 141
Hamilton, Eden, 129
Hamilton, James & Parthenia Mingus, 203,204
Hamilton, Robert & Agnes Lecky, 9,11,14
Hancock, John, 145
Hancock, NY, Village of, 30,31,36,131,135,138,154
Hand, Brig. Gen. Edward, 81,88
Hannah, William, 162
Hardenburgh, Johannis, 35,36
Hardenburgh, Capt. John A., 63
Hardenburgh Patent, 33,35-38,40,131,132,134,136,137,156,174
Hardenburgh/Bradstreet Controversy, 35-37
Harmer, Gen. Josiah, 176
Harper, Alexander A., 185,199,200,204
Harper, Alexander, Lt., Capt., Lt. Col. & Elizabeth Bartholomew, 15,43,56,68,69,95-99,101,119,127,128,131,137,143,164,168,169,171,173 183-196,198,199,201-204,206
    Harper, Alexander J. & Jane Harper, 204
        Stella & Ann, 204
Harper, Anne & James Miller, 9-13
Harper, Archibald, 25,42,56,74,95,124,173,201,205
Harper Expedition, 184-189,194,196,203
Harper Family Chart, 26,27
Harper, George, 43
Harper, James A., 56,98,124,185,190,191,197-200,204
Harper, James & Janet Lewis, 9-10,12,206
Harper, James, 15,23-25

Harper, Capt. James & Sarah Montgomery, 168,173,195,197,205,206
Harper, Capt., Col. John Jr, & Miriam Thompson, 12-14,15,22-25,33,42,46-48,55-61,66,69,71-74,77,79, 82,83,87,89-95,97,98,100-102,108,112,116-119,122,124,125,129,131,140,143,144,149-163,165,168-173,184,185,192-196,199,201,202,205,206
Harper, John A. & Lorraine Minor, 56,98,124,185,188,190,194,197,198,200,203
Harper, John I. 205
Harper, John Sr & Abigail Montgomery, 9,10,11,17-20,25,33,42,43,94,123,124,126,174,185,193,206,207
Harper, Joseph Sr & Miriam Thompson, 9,13,25,34,186
Harper, Lt., Maj. Joseph & Catherine Douglas, 15,42,56, 94,95,98,101-109,124,125,194,203,207
    Alexander, 194
    Montgomery & Angelina Parshall, 194,207
    Joshua, 194
Harper, Joseph Jr & Isabella McKnight, 74,124,201,202
Harper, Margaret & William Gault Jr, 15,20,42
Harper, Mary & James Moore, 15,20,21,34,42
Harper, Miriam & William McFarland, 15,42,43
Harper/Montgomery Expedition, 195
Harper, Moses, 9,10
Harper Patent, 38,41,44,47,48,55,89,95,123-131,142,160,163-166,173,174,189,202,206,207
Harper Purchase, 33,89,131,133,154,160,174
Harper, Robert A. & Polly Hendry, 185,197,199-201,204
Harper, Sarah & John Montgomery, 10,12,14
Harper, William & Rachel Robinson, 9,13
    George, 13,43
    Jean & Alexander McFarland, 13,43
    Sarah & James Henderson,13
Harper, William A., 98,124,185,190,191,197,199,204
Harper, Esq. William & Margaret Williams, 15-17,24,25,42,55,73,76,98,101,108,111,122,125,126,149,153,154,168,171,184,202,205
Harper, Lt. Col. William & Hannah Hotchkiss, 124,173,201,202,205,206
Harpersfield, NY, (The Centre), 42,44,47,56,61,83,94-99,102,103,111,121,124-129,142,149,156,163,164,166-169,171-175,185,186,193-196,199-202,205-207
    Census District, 161-166,196
Harpersfield, OH, 185,186,189,192-198,203,204
Harpersfield Commercial Company, 204
Harpersfield Center Rural Cemetery, 206
Harpur, Robert, 156
Harpursville, 156
Harrington, Seth & Huldah, 195
Harrisburg, PA, 143
Harrison, Brig. Gen. William Henry, 198-200
Hartwell, Benjamin, 185,203
Hartford, CT, 156,164,182
Hasbrouck, Capt. Elias, 70
Hasbrouck, Col. Jonathan, 62
Hathorn, Col. John, 84,135
Haudenosaunee, 79,87,88,92,154

Hazen, Col. Moses, 136
Helmer, Lt. Hans Adam F., 71,147
Hendricks, Peter & Eva Markle Kittle, 38,137
Hendry, Lt., Capt. David & Selinda Hotchkiss, 56,95,127,128,169,173,196,197,204
    James, 95,127,129,206
    James Jr & Phoebe Gibbs, 129
    Lt. John, 95-97,127,206
    Lt., Maj. Thomas, 56,94-96,127,129,206
    Thomas Jr, 95
Herkimer, Gen. Nickolas, 49-52,55,76,87,109
Herkimer County, 166-168
Hill, Capt. Aaron, 152
Hiokatoo, 84,85
Hobart, NY, Village of, 44,72,83,164
Holland Land Company, 182
Hopkins, Col. Roswell, 164
Hopkinton, MA, 11,12,14,15
Horseheads, NY, 92
Hotchkiss, Joseph & Hannah Atwater, 129
Roswell & Margaret Harper, 129,165,168,174,184,205,206
    Thelus, Ebenezer, Joseph Jr, 129,196
Houk, Tobias, 146,162,163
    Slave Stephen, 162
Howe, Gen. Sir William, 47,62
Howell, Lt. Col. Abraham, 202
Hudson, Ephraim, 168,171
Hull, Brig. Gen. William, 199
Hunter, Gov, 143
Hynpagh, Peter, 38

Indian Property Line of '68, (Fort Stanwix), 30,35-41,72,87,149,150,154,173,175
Irish Rows, 11,13-15,43,195,206
Irondequoit Bay, 182,183
Iroquois Confederation, 18,20,29-31,46
Iroquois Reservations, 155

Jacobite Rebellion, 5
Jay, Chief Justice, Gov. John, 156,169,170-173
Jay's Treaty, 178,180
Jefferson, Thomas, 129,158,161,201
Jefferson, Town of, 129
Jericho, Town of, 155,165
Jerseyfields, 117
Johnson, Sir William, 19-24,29-33,45,46,51,54,73,89,94,121,125,132,145,146,149-151
Johnson, Col., Gen. Sir John, 40,45,49-51,54,55,60,66,97,99-101,104-111,114,115,118
Johnson Hall, 32,33,100,116
Johnston, Rev. William, 41,48,49,72,74,87,95,144
    Hugh, 48,144
    Lt. Col. Witter, 48,49,87,95,144,168,173
Johnston Settlement, 41,46,48,50,73,87,121,144,168,175
Johnston Summit, 48,49,87
Johnstown Raid, 99-101,104,111

Jones, Richard, Benjamin, 135
Judd, Stephen & Statira Gibbs, 129

Kairn, Jacob, 137
Kanadaseago, 90-92,121
Kanawaholla, 90
Kanowalohale, 151,152,154
Karighoudonte, 54
Kawiensinck, 37
Keator's Rift, 108
Kendaia, 90
Kidder, John & Abel, 132
Kingsborough Patent, 32
Kingston, NY, (Wiltwyck), 38,44,55,61-64,76,137,170,174
Kingston Packet, (The Ship), 188
King George II, 36
King George III, 28,34,35,145
King Hendrick's Ford, 110
King, Col. Nathan, 193,199,200
    John, 193,199
King Philip's War, 7
Kingsland Grant, 32
Kings Landing, 86
King's Royal Regiment of New York Loyalists, 34,40,45,104,115
King, Rufus, 170
King William III & Mary II, 4,5,8
King William's War, 7,8
Kirkland, Samuel, 24
Kittle, Frederick, 38,137
    Jeremias, 38
Klock, George, 109
    Col. Jacob, 50,52,76
Knapp, Samuel & John, 129
Knapp, Ebenezer, 146
Kortright, Lawrence, 34,44,132,158,159
Kortright Patent, 34,38,41,55,121,124,131,163-166

Lake Champlain, 20-22,45,47,49,53,80,99,100,105,116,122,178
Lake County, OH, 189,196,198,204
Lake Erie, 156,177,179,181,183,188,190-195,199,200,204
Lake George, 20,100,105,116
Lake Ontario, 47,64,78,82,83,156,161,177,180,182,183,187
Lake Superior, 192
Lake Utsayantha, 36,72,119
Lamb, Col. John, 82
Lamb, William Sr, 96,127,206
    William Jr, 96,127
Laughlin, James, Nathaniel, 195
Laurens, NY, 163
Law, James, 3,6
Lawyer, Johannas, 57,58
Leake, John, 35
Leake Patent, 35,164

Lee, Arthur, 176
Lee, Gen. Charles, 145
Lenape-wihituck, 135
Lincoln, Gen. Benjamin, 99,158,176,177,187
Lindsley, John, 19-21
Lindsley, Matthew & John, 129
Lindsley Patent, 19-21,140
Little Beards Town, 88,91,92
Little Turtle, 176-178
Livingston, Col. John, 52,156,157
    Peter V.B., 132,158
    Philip, 132
    Robert R., 35,37,40,174
    Walter, 156
Livingston Company/Leasers, 156
Livingston, P.V.B. Patent, 132,158-160,164,168
Logan's Hotel, 186
Londonderry, NH, 3-6,11, 18-20
Long Point Peninsula, 188
Long, Capt. Gabriel, 66
Longyear, (Langjahr), Jacobus, 63,64,137
    Christopher, 137
    Jacob Jr, Andries, 64,137,138
Lower Walton Patent, 134
Luddington, Col. 136
Lull, Benjamin, Nathan, Joseph, 146

MacClure, William, 135,165
MacCullum, (The ship), 3,6,7,9,12-14,43,127
MacDonell, Archibald, 39
    Capt. Donald, 51
    Capt. Spanish John, 54-60,74,75,84,85,89,95, 118,124,127,131,143,172,191
Macomb, Alexander, 158
Madison Dock, 204
Madison, James, 158,201
Malcolm, Col. William, 101,108,112,116
Mamakating District, 61,69,84,138
Manckatawangum, 88
Mann, George, 54,55,57-60
Mann, Micheal, 23
Marblehead Peninsula, 200
Marbletown/Hurley, 37,38,62,63,137
Margaretville, Village of, 31
Massachusetts Royal Charter, 123,150,156
    Preemption Line, 156-157,161,162
Massasagoes Lenape, 181,192
Masters, Daniel, 187
Mattice, Henry, 72,73
Maumee River, 178,197,199,200
Maxwell, Brig. Gen. William, 81
Mayall, Joseph, 144,163,171
Mayflower, (The Ship), 163
McComb, Malcolm, 158
McFarland, Alexander & Jane Harper, 43,56
McFarland, James, 9,43

McFarland, Maj. William & Abigail Harper & Miriam Harper, 15,42,43,95,124,125,127,164-168,171,172,173,184,185,189,190,196,201,203
    Eunice, 43
McGregor, Rev. James, 5,11,13
McKean, Capt. Robert, 21,23,74,79,108,114
    Samuel, 114
McKee, Alexander, 35
Mckee, Anne, 83,101
McKenzie, Pvt. John, 71
Mead, Lt. Col. John, 133
Meigs, Capt. Jehiel, 128
Meigs, Gov. Jonathan, 199
Merchants Coffee House, 159,160
Merkle, James, 38,137
Merrymeeting Bay, ME, 6,9,10
Middagh, Pvt. Jacob, 63,64,136,137
    John, Stephen, Martin, 63
Middleburg, NY, 54
Middleton, Dr. Peter, 146,147
Middleton Patent,
Middletown, CT, 15-17, 25,207
Miles, William, 191,192
Milford, NY, 140,162,171,186,205
Military Tract, 155,157,158,193
Miller, John, 9,10,13
Mingus, Parthenia, 185,203,204
    William, 185,204
Minisink, 61,72,74,78,84,85,97,99,138
Misner, Coonradt, 138
Mitchell, Nathan, 139
Mohawk Frontier, 111-115
Monro, Capt. John, 105,106
Montgomery Family,
    Pvt. Eli, 200,206
    Expedition, 193,194
    James & Mary Hendry, 14,126,193
    James & Polly Baldwin, 195,197,207
    Maj. Gen. Richard, 45,78,112,123
    Pvt. John H., 199
    Robert & Mary White, 126,193,195,200,206
    Thomas & Rebecca Harper, 193,195,199,205
    William & Mary Aiken, 9,12,14,206
    John & Sarah Harper, 14,126,207
Montgomery County, NY, 123,125,139,141,149,159,161-163,166-168,173
Montreal, 23,24,45,92,97,101,105,112,131
Moore, James & Mary Harper, 15,20,21,34,65,74-77,79,97,98,121,140,186,188,201,205
    James Jr, 65,74-77,140,169,171,172,188,201,202
    Lt. Col. John, 65,74-77,140,188,201,202,205
Moore, John, 20,76,121
Moore, John H. 203
Moore, Jonathan, 146
Moore, Gov. Sir Henry, 33
Moors Indian Charity School, 17,22,89

Moraviantown, 200
More, John, 40
Morgan, Col. Daniel, 66,68,81
Morrisania, 145,156
Morris, Maj. Jacob, 145-147,156,162-168,172
    Lewis, 145
    Lewis Jr, 146
    Robert, 156
    Staats Long, 144,145
Morris Patent, 145-147
Morris, Village of, 144
Morrison. James, 196
Morrow, Gov. Jeremiah, 201
Morrow, Capt. William, 200
Morse, Capt., Maj. Benjamin, 173,196
Moss, Capt. Zeally, 183-185
Mount Morris, 91
Murphy, Timothy, 66,91,95,106,119,144

Nanisnos, 35
Napoleonic Wars, 198
Navy Hall, 177
New Lebanon, NY, 98,194
New Salem/ Conneaut, 195-197
New Stamford, (Town Plot), 40,41,44,55,96,131
Newtown Limavady, 4,6,14
Niagara Portage, 181,183
    River, 177,181,183,187,190
Nieggen Aoghyatonghsera, (Peggy Brant), 24
Niew Nederlands, 38,40,70
Nine Years' War, 4, 8
Noodle's Island, 6,12-16,123,207
Norridgewock, ME, 9-11
North Benjamin & Margaret Furman, 133,134
    Robert & Gabriel, 133,134,136
Northern Department, 100,101,107,111-113,115,145
Northern Ireland, 3-5,127,145
Northern Trail, (Rt,#10), 117
North Harpersfield, 129
Northumberland, 85,191
Northwest Confederation of Nations, 176,178,180,199,200
Northwest Ordinance of '87, 175
Northwest Territory, 23,174-177,179,184,198

Oakham, MA, 43
Oak Lodge, 141,146,163
O'Daniel, Joshua, 128,195
Ogden, Daniel, 41,48,49,87,88,95,143,162
Ogeyonda, David, 54,58,59
Old Abram, 139
Old English District, 144-147,163,166
Old Harpersfield Land Company, 184-186,190,193,194,196-198,203
Old Seneca Trail, 194
Onaquaga, Village of, 20,24,32,33,36,46-48,64,66,67,70,71,74,75,78,83-85,87,96,97,131,151,152,165

Onaquaga Campaign, 71-74
Oneida Carry (Deowainsta), 31,49,177,180,186
    Lake, 55,79,116,117,158,177,180,186,187
    Oneida/Tuscarora Purchase of '85,135,154-158,162,165,168
    Reservation, 155,157
Oneonta, Village of, 31,36,140,143,162
Oneyanha, (Peter the Quartermaster), 153,154
Onondaga Campaign, 78-80,83,112
    Reservation, 155,157
Ontario Co., 156,162,167,168
Oquaga Creek, 135,165
Oswego, Village of, 40,99,105
Otego, Village of, 41,162
Otsego Census District, 161,162,163,166
    County, NY, 33,71,123,126,139,140,167-173,195,196,201,202
    Election of '92, 166-172
    Lake, 32,41,64,65,67,82-84,87,92,102,114,116,122,141,142,146,162,168,186,193
    Patent, 33,141,158,162,165,166
Otsquago Creek, 102,122
Ouleout Creek (Oweritowit), 34,36,41,48,72,73,159,165
Ousterhout, Hanse, 136
Ousterhout, Jacob, 69
Owego, 30,154,158

Paghatakan, 31,37,38,40,44,62,63,67-69,96,136,137,174,175
Paine, Maj. Brinton, 164,196
    Col., Gen. Edward, 164,196
    Ezra, 164,165,196
Painesville, OH, 196,204
Palatine Dutch,(German), 53,54,65,70,76,87,101,128,196
Paqua, 181
Paris Peace Treaty of '83, 123,144,150,176
Parker, Sgt. Michael, 91-93,106
Parks, Josiah, (Bo'son), 139
Parr, Capt. James, 66,71,72
Patchin, Gen. Freegift, 96,98,127,202
    Isaac & Sally Gibbs, 96,127,129,169,173,185,196
Patrick, Capt. William, 65
Pawling, Col. Albert, 87,115
Pawling, Col. Levi, 63
Pawling, Lt. Col. Moses, 82
Pawpachton, 31,36-38,62,63,67,68,135-137
Pay d'en Haut, 28,29
Pearl, (The Ship), 40,54
Pease, Seth, 180,183-185,187,189,197
Peck, Jedediah, 163,168
Peenpack, 84,138
Pejepscot Patent, 6-8,14
Pelton, John, 16
    Nathan & Ruth Thompson, 16,25
Pemaquid Patent, 14
Penn, William, 138

Pennsylvania Dutch, 143
Pepacton, 37,38,137
   Reservoir, 137
Perry, Cdre. Oliver Hazard, 200
Phelps, Oliver, 156,184
Philadelphia, 134,138,139,146
Phinney, Elihu, 168
Phoenix, James, 137
Pine, Joshua Sr, 133
   Daniel, Capt. John, Joshua Jr, 133
    Philip, 133
    Peter, 133
Pickering, Timothy, 176
Pittsburgh, 82,175
Platner, Jacob, 132
Poconos, 84,85
Pontiac Rebellion, 24, 29,31,36
Poor, Brig. Gen. Enoch, 81,88
Pope, Alexander, 203
Port Jervis, (Mahackamack), 83,84
Port Rowan, 188
Portsmouth Treaty, 8,9
Porter, Augustus, 180,182,183,197
Poscy, Capt. Thomas, 66,68,69
Potawa Trail, 44
Powell, Capt. John & Jane Moore, 77,97,98,188,190,202
Presque Isle, 191,199
Prévost, Maj. Gen. Augustine Sr, 35,132,158,159
   Maj. Augustine, Jr & Susannah Croghan, 32,141,158
   James Marcus, 158
Prévost Patent, 33,158,159
Priest, Josiah, 98
Proclamation Line of '63, 28,37
Procter, Maj. Gen. Henry, 200
Prophetstown, 198
Protector, (The Ship), 163
Put-In-Bay, 200
Putman, Lt. Gerrett, 91,95

Quackenboss, Lt. Isaac, 143
Quackyack, 114
Quebec, 23,45,47,78,80,85,92,99,104,109,112,191
Queen Anne, 35,53
Queen Anne's Chapel Parsonage,122,125,126
Queen Anne's War, 5,6,8,53
Queen Ester's Town, 86
Queenstown Landing, 181,183,188
Quern Mill, 192
Quick, Tom, 139

Rale, Father Sebastian, 9-11
Ramsey, David, 18,29
Red Jacket, 181
Remsen, Capt. Abraham, 133
Republican, (See Dem/Rep)
Randolph, Beverly, 177
Rapalje, John, 37
Rapalie Patent, 133,134

Reed, Capt. John R., 199,200
Rénouard, André, 146,163
Richardson, Lt. James, 188
Richfield District, OH, 197
Richfield Springs, NY, 121,141,194
Robert, (The Ship), 5,6,13
Rock Edy, (Downsville), 136
Rome, Village of, 29,46
Rondout Settlements, 63,69,115
Roose, Lt., Capt. Jacob, 62-64,137
Roose's Rangers, 62-64,137
Root, Brig. Gen. Erastus, 201,202
Roscoe, NY, 136
Rose, Hugh, 41,102,131
Rose, Pvt. Thomas, 60
Rose, William, 70
Ross, Maj. John, 115-118
Ross, Joseph, 139
Rowley, Maj. Aaron, 116
Ruggles, Almon, 197

Sage, Col. Comfort, 164
Salamanca, NY, 88
Salmon, Thomas, 203
Sampson, Ezekial, Isaac, Henry, 135
Sanborn, Nathaniel, 182
Sanderson, Capt. George, 200
Sanders, Thomas, 10
Sandusky Bay, OH, 179,200
Saratoga, 49,51, 53,60-62,64,78,104,115,116,122
Sawyer, Isaac, 41,72,73,83,88,94,101,131
Sayenqueraghta, 89,104
Scanodewan, 192
Schenectady, 46,50,56,61,70,76,81,88,104-106,111-116,118,125,139,140,144,177,180,182,183
Schenectady Bateaux, 187
Schenevus Creek, 41.47,48,87,140
Schoharie, NY, 53,54-60,65,70,83,84,87,95,96,98-108,110,111,115-120,124,127-129,143,173,196,202,207
   Lower Fort, (Old Reformed Dutch Church), 61,106
   Middle Fort, 56,57,59, 61,65,67,68,71-73,81,94,96,98,103-107,124,127,128,143,195
   Upper Fort, 61,101-107,119
Schuyler, Catherine, 38
   David, 38,140
   Peter, 167
   Maj. Gen. Philip, 46,78 ,107,167,169,170
Schuyler Patent, 140,162
Scott, Pvt. Amasa, 60
Scottish Bush, 55
Scrambling, George, Henry, David, 48,143,162
Scranton, PA, 81
Seneca Lake, 90,92,123,156,162
Servos, Cristopher & Clara, 39,40,43,55,65,66,128
   Lt. Daniel, 66
   Lt. Jacob, 66

John, Philip, Christian, 66
Servos, Peter, 39
Sessions, Anson, 197
Seth's Henry, 54,58,83,94,101-103,107,114,119,131
    Brother Joseph, 114
Seymour, Lt., Capt. Thomas, 60
Seven Years' War, 20,139,145,175
Shades of Death, (Swamp), 85
Shandy Hall, 204
Sharon Springs, (New Dorlach), 31,107,116,162,193
Shaver, John, Adam, Jacob, 136,137
Shavertown, 136,137
Shehawken, 30,36,84,135,138,139
Sheldon, Col. Elisha, 58,60
Shinhopple, NY, 136
Shirley, Gen., Gov. William, 21,145
Shorter, William, 187
Shute, Gov. Samuel, 5
Sidney, Village of, 30,32,41,44,49,154,156,165
Simcoe, John Graves, 177,178
Skaneateles, 193,194
Skenesborough, (Whitehall), 100
Skinner, Daniel, 138,139
    Joseph Sr, Joseph Jr, Thomas, Moses, 138
Skinner, Nathaniel, 128,195
Skoi-Yase, 91
Sleeper, John, 143,144,163
Sloansville, 106,193
Sluyter, Albertus, 38,137
Sluyter, Peter & Anne Johnston, 144
Smith, Israel Sr, 165
Smith, Jedediah Sr, 165
    Jedediah Jr, 165
Smith, Joseph, 165
Smith, Col. Josiah, 133
Smith, Martha North, 134
Smith, Lt. Col. Seth, 165
Smith, Sheriff Richard R., 168,170,171
Smith, Lt. Col. William S. & Abigail Adams, 161,162
Society for the Propagation of the Gospel in Foreign Parts, 126
Sodus Bay, NY, 156
South Kortright, NY, 102
Spencer, Col. Oliver, 81
Sprague, Abraham, Abel, 136
Springfield, NY, 31,64,65,67,82,111,114,121,193
Stamford, NY, 119,131,173,206
Starr, Eleazer, 129
Stevens Cemetery, 206
Stevens, Oliver, 187
Stevens, Lt. William, 72,96,128,206
Stewart, Col. James, 199
Stewart, Dr. James, 40
Stewart, Jehiel, William, Luther, 136
Stiles, Stephen & Nancy Johnston, 144
Stillwater, 58,60
St. Clair, Maj. Gen. Arthur, 176,178

St. Johnsville, NY, 109
St. Leger, Gen. Barrymore, 47,49-56,60,99
Stockton, Ens. Charles W. & Elizabeth North, 133,134,136
    Richard, 134
    Capt. Richard W., 134
Stone Arabia, 46,70,109-111,113,118
Stony Point, 69,86,176
Strasburg Patent, (Butler Patent), 129
Stuart, John, 29
Stump Mill, 193
Sugar Boilers, 95-99,124,127,128,131,169,173,188,191,195,202,206
Sullivan/Clinton Campaign, 79-94,96,104,110,112,118,152
Sullivan, Maj. Gen. John, 78-94,97,99,101,105,145
Summit Lake, 32,65,104
Survey of '96, 180-182,194,197
Survey of '97, 182-184,194,196,197
Susquehanna/Catskill Turnpike, 44,128
Susquehanna/Charlott Creek Trail, 119
Susquehanna Company, 138
Syracuse, 157

Talbot, Silas, 172
Tappen, Abraham & Elizabeth Harper, 98,185,190, 197-199,204
Tecumseh, 199-201
Tedle, John & Eunice McFarland, 42,43,125
Templars Lodge, 203
Temple, Robert, 6-12,15,16, 20
    Sir Thomas, 6,12
Tesse, 134
Teunis, 38
Thames River, 200
Thaonhwentsawá:kon, 151,152,154
Thaosagwat, Lt. Han Yost, 91
Thayendanegea, 22
The Noses, 107,108,113
Theghtaghgwesele, (Tall William), 153
The Twelve Thousand, 140
Thomas, Joseph, 139
Thompson, William & Margaret Milne, 13
    Miriam & Joseph Harper, 13
Thompson, James & Janet Scott, 25
    Miriam & John Harper, 25
Thorp, Daniel & Ezra, 96,127,206
Thurston, Increase, 146
Tioga County, 167,168
Tioga Point, 85,88-90,92,93,97,143
Tioga Ten Townships, 158
Tiondadon, 140
Tioughnioga River, 158
Tippecanoe River, 198,199
Toledo, OH, 197,199,200
Topsham and Brunswick, ME, 7,9-13
Townsend, Dr. Platt, 132-134,136,165,168
    Isaac, William, 133

Tremper Kill, 137
Tribes Hill, 100
Trumbull County, OH, 197,203
Tryon County, NY, 45-52,67,68,73,76,81,94,95,107,110-113,116,118,120-123,125,131,135,140,143,161,167, 168,173
    Committee of Safety, 76,121,125
    Committee of Sequestration, 73
Tryon, Gov., Gen. William, 129
Tubbs, Samuel, 142
Tug Hill Plateau, 118
Tulpehocken Creek, 143
Tunnicliff, John, 140,141,146,162,163
    William, Joseph, John Jr, 141,169,171,172
Tusten, Lt. Col. Benjamin, 84
Twenty Townships, 155,157,162,193,194
Tyler, Bezaleel, 139

Ulster County, 47,61,63,67,68,70,80,87,111,115,123,131,136,137,139 149,173
 Unadilla, 20,30,41,71,73,75,78,131,162
    River, (Tianaderha), 30,36,116,147,154,157,162,163,194
    River Patents, 144-146
Underground Railroad, 204
Unionville, OH, 189,195,204,206
Upper Canada, 157,177,188
Upton, Clotworthy, (1st Baron of Templetown), 144-147
Upton Patent, 144-147

Van Alstyne, John, Peter, Martin, 128
Van Cortlandt, Col. William, 51,52,82,112,116
Van Der Mark, Silvester, 138
Van Der Werker, Capt. John, 143,162
Van Rensselaer, Brig. Gen. Robert & Catherine Schuyler, 101,107-111,116
    Lt. Gov. Stephen, 167,169,170
Van Schaick, Col. Goose, 58,79,80,83,93,94,112
Van Waggenen, Johannis & Helena Kittle, 38,137
    Simeon, 38,69,137
Van Volkenburgh, Joachim & Maria, 41,48,87,88,95,119,140
Veeder, Lt. Col. Volkert, 106
Vermont Sufferers, 165
Verplank, Samuel, 132,137
Verplanksburgh, 137
Visscher, Col. Frederick, 50
Vrooman's Flatts or Land, 54,101-103,119
Vrooman, Lt. Ephraim & Christina, 102,103,119
    Isaac, 119
    Col. Peter, 54,57-60,66,95,96105-108,119
    Capt. Wouter, 110

Wabash River, 176,178,198
Wadsworth, Maj. Gen. Elijah, 199
Wadsworth, Brig. Gen. James, 164
Waldo, Col. Samuel, 14

Wallace, Alexander & Hugh, 32,41,132
Wallace Patent, 32,38,131,132
Wallkill, 63,138
Walton Patent, 35,132,133,164
Walton, William, Gerard, Thomas, 132,134
Walton, William III, 132,133
Walton, Village of, 134,165,173,202
Ward, Col. Andrew, 128
Warner, George, 65
Warraghiyagey, 21,151
Warrensbush, 116
Warren, Sir Peter, 21
War of Austrian Succession, 54
War of Spanish Succession, 8,53
War of 1812, 198-204
    War Bill of 1812, 201
Washington, George, 45,47,65,67,68,78,80,86,103,112,115,122,133,161,176
Washington, John, 78
Waterloo, NY, 90
Watkins Glen, NY, 90
Watkins, John W., 157
Wattles, Nathaniel, 44
Wattles, Sluman, 132,159,160
Wayne, Gen. 'Mad' Anthony, 86,176-179
Weisenberg, Chatherine,
Weisenfeld, Col. Frederick, 82
Weiser, Johann Conrad Jr, 143
Wells, Robert & Mary, 75
    Jane, 75
West Branch of the Delaware, 131-135,163-165,173
Westbrook, Col. Thomas, 9,10
West Canada Creek, 70,117,118
West, Pvt. Charles, 60
West Harpersfield, NY, 129,205
Westchester Guides, 133
Western Turnpike, (Rt. #20), 58,116,194
Western Reserve, (see Surveys), 179-185,188,190-206
Westmoreland, PA, 138
West Point, 104,105
Wharton, Thomas, 34
Wheeler, Aaron & Margaret Harper, 124,184,185,194,196,197,203
Wheelock, Rev. Eleazer, 17,22,24,89
Whitaker, Squire, 135
White, Thomas & Henry, 35,132
White House Tavern, 169
Whites Patent, 35,132,164
Widow Cole, 136
Wilcox, Samuel & Sally Gibbs, 128
Willett, Lt., Lt. Col. Marinus, 51-53,79,82.109,112,114,116-118,135,163
William and Mary, (The Ship), 5,6
William's Flatts, 69,70,136
Williams, Capt. John F., 163
Williamite War, 5,6,8
William Kayentaronghquah, 153
Willowemoc, 135,136,173

Wilson, Daniel, Isaac, Daniel Jr, 136
Windsor, Village of, 24,46,72,87,156
Winthrop, Rev. John, 3
Wirt, Lt. David, 60
Woodcocks, 48
Wood, Palmer, 196
Woodside, Rev. James, 6
Woodworth, Ezekiel, 196
Woodstock District, 131
Woolsey, Maj. Melanchthon L., 105-107,116
Wooster, Gen. David, 129
Worchester Settlements, 11,13,14,41,43
Wright, Aaron & Anna Montgomery, 193,206
Wyalusing, 86
Wynner, Christian, 138
Wyoming Valley, 81,83-85,135,138,178
    Massacre, 66,67,75,86,114,118,135

Yaple, William, 38
Yendes, Bartholomew, 132
Yerry, Yan, 50
Yoghroonwago, 88
Yorktown, 69,115
Yost, Lt. Han, (Thaosagwat), 91
Young, David, 139
Young, John, Andrew, 143

www.ingramcontent.com/pod-product-compliance
Lightning Source LLC
Chambersburg PA
CBHW081418230426
43668CB00016B/2277